PERFORMANCE ASSESSMENT

Other books edited by Ronald A. Berk

Criterion-Referenced Measurement: The State of the Art
Educational Evaluation Methodology: The State of the Art
Handbook of Methods for Detecting Test Bias
A Guide to Criterion-Referenced Test Construction

Performance Assessment

METHODS & APPLICATIONS

Edited by Ronald A. Berk

THE JOHNS HOPKINS UNIVERSITY PRESS
Baltimore & London

The Johns Hopkins University Press
701 West 40th Street
Baltimore, Maryland 21211
The Johns Hopkins Press Ltd., London

The paper used in this publication meets the minimum requirements of American
National Standard for Information Sciences—Permanence of Paper for Printed
Library Materials, ANSI Z39.48-1984.

Library of Congress Cataloging-in-Publication Data

Performance assessment.

Bibliography: p.
Includes index.
1. Employees, Rating of.   2. Performance standards.   3. Psychology,
Industrial.   I. Berk, Ronald A.
HF5549.5.R3P475   1986   658.3'125   86-2947
ISBN 0-8018-3142-3 (alk. paper)

In memoriam

Arthur I. Siegel

CONTENTS

PREFACE

Definition of Performance Assessment

More than twenty-five years ago Cronbach (1960, p. 582) identified three principal features of *assessment:* (1) use of a variety of techniques, (2) primary reliance on observations, and (3) the integration of information. In distinguishing it from psychometric measurement, he defined assessment in terms of clinical analysis and prediction of performance. Within this context, he emphasized that the manner in which the data were analyzed for decision making was based more on quasi-artistic synthesis than on statistical combination.

Just how far the state of assessment has progressed should become evident in the chapters of this volume. What Cronbach meant by assessment then is akin to the notion of performance assessment today. The technological advances that have occurred during the intervening years have been evidenced in the shift toward the statistical manipulation of the data and the amalgamation of "psychometric measurement" with "impressionist assessment."

In order to reflect the earlier characteristics of assessment, as well as these more recent developments, the following operational definition is proffered:

Performance assessment is the process of gathering data by systematic observation for making decisions about an individual.

There are five key elements in this definition. First, performance assessment is a *process,* not a test or any single measurement device. Second, the focus of this process is *data gathering,* using a variety of instruments and strategies. Third, the data are collected by means of *systematic observation.* The emphasis is on direct observational techniques rather than on paper-and-pencil tests, especially the garden variety multiple-choice test, although such tests may also be employed in the assessment. Fourth, the data are integrated for the purpose of making specific *decisions.* These decisions should guide the form and substance of the assessment. Finally, the subject of the decision making is the *individual,* usually an employee or a student, not a program or product reflecting a group's activity.

Subsumed under the rubric *performance assessment* are a host of other related terms that are often used synonymously with it. Two of these are performance appraisal and performance test. In this book they are clearly distinguished. A *performance appraisal* is a special type of performance assessment conducted for the expressed purpose of making personnel decisions. A *performance test* is a test in which performance is demonstrated through directly observable behavior as

TABLE 1. Major Determinants of Performance Assessment Methodology

	Subject of Assessment	
	Employee	Student
Measurement purpose	To differentiate among levels of performance (successful vs. unsuccessful)	To differentiate among levels of performance (high achievers vs. low achievers, masters vs. nonmasters)
Decisions	Administrative personnel decisions: Selection Promotion Retention Demotion Transfer Termination Salary increase	Administrative and instructional decisions: Screening Diagnosis Classification/placement Formative Summative
Actions	Counsel to improve motivation Train to improve skills	Prescribe appropriate instructional program or treatment Certify License

opposed to paper-and-pencil written response. Examples include work sample tests, situational tests, in-basket tests, and trainability tests (see Siegel, chapter 4, for details). Stiggins and Anderson (1981) have also reviewed various definitions, descriptions, and types of performance tests (Fitzpatrick & Morrison, 1971; Glaser & Klaus, 1962; Lindquist, 1951; Ryans & Fredericksen, 1951).

The subject of a performance assessment may be an *employee* at any level of an organization or institution or a *student* at any level of the educational structure. Typically the measurement purpose of the assessment is similar: to differentiate among levels of performance. This is illustrated in Table 1. Beyond this similarity, the orientation of the assessment in each application is usually quite different.

Among the major determinants of performance assessment methodology listed in the table, it is the nature of the decision to be made with the results that distinguishes an employee assessment (performance appraisal) from a student assessment. The type of decision (personnel or instructional) ultimately governs how the assessment is planned and executed. What information is gathered and how it is gathered are a function of the intended use(s) of the information. Ergo, the first step in the assessment process is to specify the individual decisions to be made. The next step is to tailor the measurement and data collection strategies so that the essential information is provided for those decisions.

In addition to the decisions rendered according to the assessment results, the specific level of individual performance demonstrated frequently indicates that particular actions need to be taken. When an employee's performance is judged to be unsatisfactory, a decision to demote or retain may be accomplished by a recommendation to train the employee to improve his or her skills in the areas identified as inadequate or deficient. Diagnostic and formative instructional decisions based on a student's level of performance are typically followed by prescriptions designating the appropriate instructional materials or treatment. If criterion levels are attained in professional programs, certificates or licenses may be issued. All of these actions can be viewed as consequences of the decision-making process and, as such, must be considered in conjunction with the decisions in planning the assessment. They can serve to steer the assessment along a proper course so that all parties involved will find the results meaningful.

Purposes of the Book

This book has three major purposes: (1) to evaluate what has been done, (2) to suggest what still needs to be done, and (3) to recommend what should be done in the performance assessment of employees and students. It concentrates on methods, methodological issues, and practical applications.

The first purpose requires a synthesis of the most significant methodological research evidence that has been amassed over the past twenty-five years. This research can be found in such diverse areas as business, industry, education, psychology, and the military. The synthesis consists of a critical review of alternative methods, strategies, and statistics in order to bring into sharp focus the important issues that have been resolved and those that need resolution.

The second purpose concentrates on the conclusions from the research review in order to pinpoint gaps in the research that need to be filled. Certainly sifting through the published and unpublished works on the topic can help identify avenues for further study. However, the difficulties experienced in applying performance assessment methods can also indicate directions for investigation.

The third purpose also builds on the findings of the review. The research results are translated into forms that are meaningful and useful to practitioners. The specific advantages and disadvantages of using different approaches are outlined. Applications of assessment methods are also presented in the context of performance assessment systems. Alternative approaches are proffered, where possible, so that an assessor is not restricted to a single strategy for attacking a technical problem in the assessment process. The recommendations are consistent with the *Standards for Educational and Psychological Testing* (AERA/ APA/NCME Joint Committee, 1985), the *Uniform Guidelines on Employee Selection Procedures* (U.S. Equal Employment Opportunity Commission et al., 1978), the 1978 Civil Service Reform Act, and the major court decisions on employment practices that have accumulated to date (see the review of standards by Nathan and Cascio in the Introduction).

Specifically, the volume is intended to convey the rationale underlying a performance assessment and the procedures essential to its design and execution and to the interpretation and use of the results for decision making. The evaluation of alternative methods or competing strategies is stressed with the prospect that certain "best" methods/strategies may be deduced for particular applications. By furnishing the practitioner with these assessment tools and concrete examples of their use, it is expected that he or she will be able to tailor a performance assessment to the decision requirements of an educational or business/industrial setting. Ultimately this should produce information that is meaningful and useful to both the assessor and the assessee.

The methods and applications chosen for scrutiny in this book have been deemed crucial to the attainment of the aforestated purposes. Admittedly, other important topics germane to performance assessment, such as biodata and production data as well as psychometric theory and statistical methods, were omitted or only partially treated. This was due primarily to the availability of other sources that have previously synthesized the contributions in those areas. Furthermore, it was desirable to obtain a balanced presentation between methods and applications in view of the disproportionate amount of attention assigned to methods in most volumes on performance assessment.

Organization of the Book

The book consists of an introduction and nineteen chapters. The Introduction, "Technical and Legal Standards for Performance Assessment," lays the foundation and justification for all of the chapters. The technical and legal standards germane to the design and execution of a performance assessment have been extracted from the 1985 *Standards* and the 1978 *Guidelines,* mentioned previously. Pertinent court cases were also reviewed. The Introduction provides not only the answer to why the "best" methods should be considered but also a comprehensive set of guidelines for evaluating the components of a performance assessment. The conclusions drawn from the standards by Professors Nathan and Cascio are some of the most important reasons for heeding the recommendations of the authors in the succeeding chapters.

The nineteen chapters are then organized into two parts: "Methods and Methodological Issues" and "Applications." Each part is preceded by introductory remarks about the structure and the contents of the chapters. Part 1 contains nine chapters and part 2 the remaining ten.

Intended Uses of the Book

Consistent with its structure, contents, and orientation, this volume should be used as a textbook or reference for graduate level courses in the fields of industrial/organizational psychology, management, educational measurement, educational administration, and business administration. Such courses might include personnel selection and evaluation, performance appraisal or assessment, educational administration and supervision, and personnel management. It can also be a valuable resource for training programs and workshops in these areas.

The book should also serve as a handbook for anyone who is charged with the tasks of designing, executing, interpreting, or evaluating a performance assessment in government, business, industry, the military, certification and licensing agencies, and educational institutions. Practitioners who will find certain sections of this book relevant to their specializations are industrial/organizational psychologists, professional test developers and evaluators, personnel managers, educational administrators and supervisors, managerial consultants, vocational guidance counselors, and training and development specialists.

In addition, the review of methodological issues in part 1 should provide a stimulus for researchers, especially psychometricians, to investigate further the most important problems and issues that may diminish the effectiveness of a performance assessment and restrict the decisions that can be made based on the results.

References

AERA/APA/NCME Joint Committee. (1985). *Standards for educational and psychological testing.* Washington, DC: American Psychological Association.

Cronbach, L. J. (1960). *Essentials of psychological testing* (2nd ed.). New York: Harper and Row.

Fitzpatrick, R., & Morrison, E. J. (1971). Performance and product evaluation. In R. L. Thorndike (Ed.), *Educational measurement* (2nd ed., pp. 237–270). Washington, DC: American Council on Education.

Glaser, R., & Klaus, D. J. (1962). Proficiency measurement: Assessing human performance. In R. M. Gagné (Ed.), *Psychological principles in system development* (pp. 419–474). New York: Holt, Rinehart and Winston.

Lindquist, E. F. (1951). Preliminary considerations in objective test construction. In E. F. Lindquist (Ed.), *Educational measurement* (pp. 119–158). Washington, DC: American Council on Education.

Ryans, D. G., & Fredericksen, N. (1951). Performance tests of educational achievement. In E. F. Lindquist (Ed.), *Educational measurement* (pp. 455–494). Washington, DC: American Council on Education.

Stiggins, R. J., & Anderson, B. L. (1981, June). *The nature and role of performance assessment.* Portland, OR: Center for Performance Assessment, Northwest Regional Educational Laboratory.

U.S. Equal Employment Opportunity Commission, U.S. Civil Service Commission, U.S. Department of Labor, & U.S. Department of Justice. (1978). Uniform guidelines on employee selection procedures. *Federal Register, 43*(166), 38290–38309.

ACKNOWLEDGMENTS

This book represents the culmination of the support and a tremendous amount of work by several individuals. Beginning with the performance assessment symposium, held in 1982, from which most of the chapters derive, the administrative support of Dean Emeritus Roman J. Verhaalen and Dean Stanley C. Gabor of the School of Continuing Studies of the Johns Hopkins University made it all possible. The fourth Johns Hopkins University National Symposium on Educational Research (NSER), titled "Performance Assessment: The State of the Art," was held in Washington, D.C., in November 1982. James M. McPartland and Richard J. Stiggins were instrumental in the final selection of the topic. Nambury S. Raju, Samuel A. Livingston, Jessie H. Pollack, Richard J. Stiggins, Dean Nafziger, Robert M. Guion, and Marvin D. Dunnette provided valuable suggestions for structuring the symposium and for identifying appropriate speakers and discussants.

The result of this input was a symposium that attracted researchers from universities, private corporations, and R & D laboratories, and practitioners from business, industry, the military, and educational agencies at the federal, state, and local levels. More than 170 distinguished professionals from thirty-five states, Canada, Bermuda, England, Ireland, and the Netherlands attended the symposium.

Performance Assessment: Methods and Applications comprises sixteen chapters that are major revisions of the symposium papers plus an introduction and three additional chapters prepared especially for the volume—"Technical and Legal Standards for Performance Assessment," "Utility Analysis," "A Performance Appraisal System," and "Job Evaluation." For their editorial work on several chapter drafts and their persistence, remarkable patience, and cooperation over the three years since the symposium, I extend my deepest appreciation to the twenty-eight authors. Inasmuch as this book is my fifth with the Johns Hopkins University Press, I acknowledge the outstanding editors involved in this project: Anders Richter and Eric Halpern. My association with the press's editorial staff over the past seven years has proven to be extremely rewarding, and my writing and editing have been influenced greatly by their advice, criticism, and, above all, standards for book publishing. Finally, I express my sincere appreciation to Karen A. Simmons for typing several sections of the book, completing editorial corrections on numerous chapter drafts, and for her assistance in preparing the final version of the manuscript. Her translations of my barely legible manuscripts, notes, and editorial marks into typescript form are noteworthy achievements.

INTRODUCTION. TECHNICAL & LEGAL STANDARDS

Barry R. Nathan & Wayne F. Cascio

Over the past two decades performance assessment has become one of the most complex issues faced by people in organizations. Regardless of whether one is in education, government, health services, business, or industry, the consequences of making the right, or wrong, decision about what to do when it comes to hiring, firing, transferring, promoting, demoting, licensing, or certifying an individual in the organization can be considerable from a productivity standpoint as well as legally. This book presents current methods and applications developed by industrial/organizational psychologists, educators, and physicians that have been found to be the most effective in assessing human performance. This introductory chapter focuses on the technical and legal standards that organizations should follow to assess human performance fairly and effectively.

There are two major functions of this chapter. First, it reviews the technical and legal standards for performance assessment documented in the *Standards for Educational and Psychological Testing* (AERA/APA/NCME Joint Committee, 1985), the *Uniform Guidelines on Employment Selection Procedures* (U.S. Equal Employment Opportunity Commission et al., 1978), and the court cases that have relied on these standards for determining employment discrimination. Second, it relates these standards to the topics addressed by the chapters in part 1 of this book in order to justify the use of rigorous methods in developing and executing performance assessments. The chapter is divided into three sections: technical standards; legal standards, including discussions of both the guidelines and relevant court cases; and finally, summary and conclusions.

Technical Standards

Legally, performance assessment is considered a "test." Scientific standards for tests are contained in *Standards for Educational and Psychological Testing* (1985), jointly prepared by the American Educational Research Association, the American Psychological Association, and the National Council on Measurement in Education. Although the *Standards* applies primarily to constructed performance tasks, questionnaires, and structured behavior samples, it may also be applied usefully in varying degrees to the entire range of assessment techniques. The

1

1985 *Standards* includes a much broader range of material than did the 1974 *Standards,* as the following outline indicates.

The 1985 *Standards* is divided into four sections. Part 1, "Technical Standards for Test Construction and Evaluation," contains five chapters that include standards for validity, reliability, test development, scaling, norming, comparability, equating, and publication.

Part 2, "Professional Standards for Test Use," contains seven chapters that cover standards for clinical testing, educational and psychological testing in the schools, the use of tests in counseling, employment testing (chap. 10), professional and occupational licensure and certification, and program evaluation.

Part 3, "Standards for Particular Applications," contains standards for testing linguistic minorities and people with handicapping conditions. Part 4, "Standards for Administrative Procedures," contains standards regarding test administration, scoring, and reporting, as well as standards for the protection of test takers' rights. All four parts deal with technical issues, but each also addresses how technical issues, professional practice, and professional ethics interface.

The *Standards* also contains a glossary, a bibliography, and an index. The glossary provides definitions of terms as they are used in the *Standards* specifically.

The purpose of this selection of the chapter is not to summarize the 1985 standards, but rather to provide a general overview of the applicability of the standards to the nine methods and methodological issues addressed in this volume. In many instances, the same standards cover multiple methodological issues. This is natural and to be expected, for the issues themselves are not independent of one another. Following the section on job analysis, therefore, will be a section on those standards that apply generally to all performance assessment methods.

JOB ANALYSIS

Job analysis unquestionably is the building block for any performance assessment procedure. It provides the foundation of information from which judgments of job relevance are derived. Not surprisingly, therefore, job analysis receives considerable emphasis throughout the *Standards.*

Chapter 1 of the *Standards* makes clear that "the first task for test developers is to specify adequately the universe of content that a test is intended to represent, given the proposed uses of the test" (p. 10). And in chapter 11 we are told that "job analyses provide the primary basis for defining the content domain" (p. 64). In the context of licensure and certification, for example, where written as well as performance tests are frequently used, emphasis "is limited appropriately to knowledge and skills necessary to protect the public" (p. 64).

How should a job content domain be defined? What rationale should guide the choice of appropriate performance criteria? Chapter 10 of the *Standards* addresses both of these questions.

> *Standard 10.3:* The rationale for criterion relevance should be made explicit. It should include a description of the job in question and of the judgments used to determine relevance. (p. 60)
>
> *Standard 10.4:* Content validation should be based on a thorough and explicit definition of the content domain of interest. For job selection, classification, and promotion, the characterization of the domain should be based on job analysis. (p. 60)

Standard 10.6 emphasizes that job content domains may be described in terms of tasks to be performed or in terms of the knowledge, skills, abilities, or other personal characteristics (KSAOs) necessary to do the work. Regardless of which approach is chosen, ratings of the relative frequency and criticality of the elements should be included as well.

In the context of performance assessment, evidence of criterion-related validity is often difficult to develop. When the job-relatedness of a particular performance assessment procedure is challenged, a demonstration of content validity may be all that is technically feasible. Job analysis information provides the basis for linking job content and the content of the performance assessment procedure.

Finally, judgments about the appropriateness of any performance assessment method in a situation different from that in which the method was developed originally hinge upon the similarity of critical job content factors in the two (or more) situations. These inferences should be based upon job analysis (standard 10.7). A key consideration here is that there are no discernible features of the new situation that would change substantially the original meaning of the performance assessment material.

DEVELOPMENT AND USES OF PERFORMANCE ASSESSMENT METHODS

Once one moves beyond job analysis and into the realm of methods and methodological issues in performance assessment, the following issue is encountered: Is the specific performance assessment method (e.g., an assessment center or performance test) being used as a predictor or as a criterion? What distinguishes these intended uses?

One distinction is on the basis of timing. That is, if performance assessment information is collected prior to a personnel decision, then it is a predictor. If such information is collected after a personnel decision has been made, then it is a criterion. Evidence of validity and reliability must be provided in either case, as stated in standard 1.1:

> Evidence of validity should be presented for the major types of inferences for which the use of a test is recommended. A rationale

should be provided to support the particular mix of evidence presented for the intended uses. (p. 13)

If performance assessment information is used to predict future performance, evidence of criterion-related validity should be developed, if it is technically feasible to do so. If the same information is used to describe current performance, then evidence that the performance assessment information is a representative sample of actual on-the-job performance (i.e., content validity) is most appropriate. If a performance assessment method refers to theoretical constructs about the nature of human behavior, then evidence of construct validity is necessary. For example, if a particular performance dimension is intended as a measure of the construct "dependability," it must be shown first that "dependability" in fact is being measured, and second, that "dependability" is an important part of the content domain of the job in question.

Another general issue relates to the assignment of individuals to categories. In performance assessment this is done routinely, in terms of an overall verbal or numerical rating. The *Standards* points out that the categories chosen should be based on carefully selected criteria. The least stigmatizing labels, consistent with accurate reporting, should always be assigned (standard 16.6).

Five other standards relate to criterion development in general. All are relevant to performance assessment in particular.

Standard 1.7: When criteria are composed of rater judgments, the relevant training, experience, and qualifications of the experts should be described. Any procedure used to obtain a consensus among judges about the appropriate specifications of the universe and the representativeness of the samples for the intended objectives should also be described. (p. 15)

Standard 1.12: All criterion measures should be described accurately, and the rationale for choosing them as relevant criteria should be made explicit. (p. 16)

Standard 1.13: The technical quality of all criteria should be considered carefully. Criteria should be determined independently of predictor test scores. If evidence indicates that a criterion measure is affected to a substantial degree by irrelevant factors, this evidence should be reported. [In performance assessment, such irrelevant factors might include the particular territory a salesperson is assigned to, the population density of the territory, and advertising expenditures devoted to product promotion in that territory.] If special steps are taken to reduce the effects of irrelevant factors, these steps should be described in detail. (p. 16)

Standard 1.14: When criteria are composed of rater judgments, the degree of knowledge that raters have concerning ratee performance should be reported. If possible, the training and experience of the raters should be described. (p. 16)

Standard 1.15: If more than one criterion measure is obtained, but, for purposes of a particular study, a single composite criterion score is used, the rules for criterion combination should be described. (p. 16)

Standard 2.8 relates further to the need for assessment of interrater reliability:

> Where judgmental processes enter into the scoring of a test, evidence on the degree of agreement between independent scorings should be provided. If such evidence has not yet been provided, attention should be drawn to scoring variations as a possible significant source of errors of measurement. (p. 22)

Interrater agreement is particularly important when observational data that involve subtle discriminations are collected.

A final general issue relates to the need to monitor performance assessment instruments for possible revision. Standard 3.18 states:

> A test should be amended or revised when new research data, significant changes in the domain represented, or new conditons of test use and interpretation make the test inappropriate for its intended uses. . . . It is the responsibility of test developers . . . to monitor changing conditions and to amend, revise, or withdraw the test as indicated. (p. 29)

The standards noted in this section are those that have the most direct implications for the development of performance assessment instruments. They are by no means inclusive. Standards that apply more specifically to the eight other methods and methodological issues covered in this volume are described in succeeding sections.

NUMERICAL RATING SCALES

Numerical rating scales are especially useful for quantitative analyses of performance data. Major requirements for these scales, as with others, are that performance dimensions and scale anchors be defined, preferably in terms of observable behaviors. This is difficult to do for some characteristics, such as "loyalty," "initiative," or "reasoning ability." These are psychological traits; their continued use in performance assessment depends on evidence of their construct validity. The *Standards* makes clear that

> the construct of interest for a particular test should be embedded in a conceptual framework, no matter how imperfect that framework may be. The conceptual framework specifies the meaning of the construct, distinguishes it from other constructs, and indicates how measures of the construct should relate to other variables. (pp. 9–10)

In the context of performance assessment, simply asking raters about the reasons for their numerical ratings can suggest hypotheses that enrich the definition of a construct. The combination of this information with evidence from content and criterion-related validity studies can provide considerable insight and understanding of the construct(s) in question.

BEHAVIOR-BASED RATING SCALES

Behavior-based rating scales are subject to the same standards as numerical rating scales. However, several standards relate specifically to this method. Among them:

> *Standard 3.2:* The specifications used in constructing items or selecting observations and in designing the test instrument as a whole should be stated clearly. The definition of a universe or domain that is used for constructing or selecting items should be described. (p. 25)

> *Standard 3.3:* Domain definitions and the test specifications should be sufficiently clear so that knowledgeable experts can judge the relations or items to the domains they represent. (p. 26)

> *Standard 1.6:* When content-related evidence serves as a significant demonstration of validity for a particular test use, a clear demonstration of validity for a particular test use, a clear demonstration of the universe represented, its relevance to the proposed test use and the procedures followed in generating test content to represent that universe should be described. *When the content sampling is intended to reflect criticality rather than representativeness, the rationale for the relative emphasis given to critical factors in the universe should also be described carefully.* (p. 14; italics added)

These standards have special relevance to behavior-based rating scales because the methods used to develop them focus on (1) sampling representative performance dimensions that cover the job content domain(s) in question, and on (2) use of critical incidents as anchors for the rating scales.

PERFORMANCE TESTS

All of the standards identified thus far that relate to the specification of job content domains are relevant to the construction and use of performance tests. However, the *Standards* also notes that

> systematic observations of behavior in a job may be combined with expert judgments to construct a representative or critical sample of the job domain, which can then be administered under standardized conditions in an off-the-job setting. . . . Also, if some aspects of the job are judged relatively unimportant, they may be excluded from the test. (p. 10)

How are performance tests to be validated? The comment to standard 10.5 notes:

> If the test content samples job tasks with considerable fidelity (e.g., actual job samples such as machine operation) or, in the judgment of experts, correctly simulates job task content (e.g., certain assessment center exercises), or samples specific job knowledge required for successful job performance . . . then content-related validity can be offered as the principal form of evidence of validity. If the link between the test content and the job content is not singular and direct, additional evidence is required. (p. 61)

Three other standards deal with the use of performance tests:

> *Standard 3.14:* The sensitivity of test performance to improvement with practice, coaching, or brief instruction should be studied as part of developmental research, especially on performance tests that use an unfamiliar response mode, such as computer-administered tests. A test that is intended to measure improvement from practice, coaching, or instruction should be shown to do so, and a test that is designed to be unaffected by these forms of learning should be shown to be so. (p. 28)

> *Standard 3.22:* The directions presented to a test taker should be detailed enough so that test takers can respond to a task in the manner that the test developer intends. When appropriate, sample material and practice or sample questions should be provided. (p. 29)

> *Standard 2.23:* When structured behavior samples are collected within a standardized testing format, the specific type of behavior expected should be defined clearly. Directions to a test taker that are intended to produce a particular behavior sample (often called a "prompt") should be standardized, just as the directions are standardized for any other test. (p. 30)

With respect to scoring procedures, standard 3.25 notes:

> Where judgments enter into test scoring, the bases for scoring and the procedures for training scorers should be presented by the developer in sufficient detail to permit a level of agreement among scorers comparable to that under which the norms were generated. When appropriate, attention should be drawn to scoring variations as a possible significant source of errors of measurement. (p. 30)

A final standard that is relevant to all performance assessment methods pertains to what has been labeled "informed consent." The comment to standard 16.1 notes:

> Informed consent implies that the test takers . . . are made aware, in language that they can understand, of the reasons for testing, the type of

tests to be used, the intended use and the range of material consequences of the intended use, and what testing information will be
released and to whom. (p. 85)

ASSESSMENT CENTERS

Assessment centers are characterized by the use of multiple performance
assessment procedures. Some of these procedures are performance tests (e.g.,
the in-basket, the leaderless group discussion, the business game), although in
some centers aptitude tests are used along with personality and interest inventories. When the latter are used, standard 3.15 applies:

> For interest or personality measures intended for selection or placement
> purposes, evidence should be presented on the extent to which scores
> are susceptible to an attempt by test takers to present false or unduly
> favorable pictures of themselves. (p. 28)

To the extent that distortion is evident, this will introduce error into any
subsequent analysis of the validity of these procedures.

Standard 5.7 pertains to the marketing of test information. It states: "Promotional material for a test should be accurate. Publishers should avoid using
advertising techniques that a test can accomplish more than is supported by its
research base" (p. 36). To date, fortunately, this has not been a widespread
problem with assessment centers. Professionals in the assessment center community have done a commendable job of policing themselves.

Standard 15.9 is relevant to the retention of assessment center reports:
"When data about a person are retained, both the test protocol and any written
report should also be preserved" (p. 84).

In a broader context, the concern is with the use of assessment center
information. Chapter 6 of the *Standards* states:

> The principal questions to be asked in evaluating test use are whether or
> not the test is appropriate (valid) for its specific role in the larger
> assessment process, and whether or not the test user has accurately
> described the extent to which the score supports any decision made or
> administrative action taken. (p. 14)

A final standard particularly relevant to assessment centers, but in fact
relevant to all attempts to convey performance feedback, is Standard 15.10:

> Those responsible for testing programs should provide appropriate
> interpretations when test score information is released. . . . The in-
> terpretations should describe in simple language what the test covers,
> what scores mean, common misinterpretations of test scores, and how
> scores will be used. (p. 84)

APPRAISAL INTERVIEW

The primary objective of appraisal interviews is not to collect performance-related information, but rather to disseminate it in the form of constructive feedback that will enhance a subordinate's motivation to perform well in the future. Certainly there should be a sound basis for any information that is fed back. Standard 3.16 states: "The score report forms, . . . including computerized reports and materials, should facilitate appropriate interpretations" (p. 28).

Another relevant section of the *Standards* for appraisal interviews is chapter 9, "Test Use in Counseling." Standard 9.1 emphasizes:

> Testing for counseling should have as [one of] its primary goals . . . the reporting of . . . information with appropriate interpretations so that clients from diverse backgrounds can be assisted in making important educational, personal, and career decisions. (p. 56)

Standard 9.6 provides especially useful information:

> Counselors should review the test materials that are provided to the test takers [e.g., performance appraisal forms] to be sure that such materials properly caution the test taker not to rely on the test scores solely when making life-planning [or career-planning] decisions. The counselor should encourage the [ratee] to consider other relevant information on personal and social skills, values, interests, accomplishments, experiences, and on other test scores and observations [e.g., previous performance appraisal data]. (p. 57)

UTILITY ANALYSIS

The *Standards* addresses this issue obliquely by emphasizing that questions of utility are relevant to all testing applications. However, the relative cost assigned to erroneous acceptances and erroneous rejections is a value judgment; depending on that judgment, the subsequent interpretation of the utility of testing may differ. *Value judgments are always involved in selection decisions, if only implicitly.* The question of what value judgments are appropriate in individual applications is not addressed in the *Standards.*

Nevertheless, chapter 10 of the *Standards* emphasizes that the relative frequency of various kinds of decision error, the utility of a correct decision (and the value judgment that that utility determination entails), comparisons of alternative strategies, and the availability of prior information are all relevant considerations: "Competent use of tests [indeed, of all performance assessment methods] in employment settings depends on sound professional judgment to take these considerations into account formally or informally, as is appropriate" (p. 59).

VALIDITY GENERALIZATION AND PREDICTIVE BIAS

Validity generalization. The standards identify two uses for the results of validity generalization studies: (1) to draw scientific conclusions and (2) to use the results of validity evidence obtained from prior studies to support the use of a test in a new situation. However, in conducting studies of validity generalization, the *Standards* emphasizes that the prior studies that are included may vary according to several situational facets. Some of these are

1. differences in the way the predictor construct is measured,
2. the type of job or curriculum involved,
3. the type of criterion measure,
4. the type of test takers, and
5. the time period in which the study was conducted.

In any particular study of validity generalization, any of these facets might vary, and a major objective of the study is to determine whether variation in these facets affects the generalizability of validity evidence. Standard 1.16 notes:

> When adequate local validation evidence is not available, criterion-related evidence of validity for a specified test use may be based on validity generalization from a set of prior studies, provided that the specified test-use situation can be considered to have been drawn from the same population of situations on which validity generalization was conducted. (p. 16)

Present and prior situations can be judged to be similar according to factors such as the characteristics of the people and job functions involved. Relational measures (correlations, regressions, success rates, etc.) should be selected carefully to be appropriate for the inference to be made.

Predictive bias. The primary symptom of bias, according to the *Standards,* appears when different regression slopes, intercepts, or standard errors of estimate are found among different groups. Subsequent selection decisions will be biased when the same interpretation is made of a given score without regard to the group from which a person comes. Under these circumstances, a given predictor score yields different criterion predictions for people in different groups, and a given criterion score yields a different predictor cut score for people in different groups:

> Several proposed ways of evaluating selection bias rest on different definitions of the fairness of a selection procedure. Unlike selection bias, however, fairness is not a technical psychometric term; it is subject to different definitions in different social and political circumstances. At present a consensus of technical experts supports only one approach to selection bias as technically appropriate [the regression model]. This

approach is adopted in the *Standards* with the understanding that it does not resolve a larger issue of fairness. (p. 13)

The standard that applies most directly to investigations of predictive bias is standard 1.20:

> Investigations of criterion-related validity for tests used in selection decisions should include, where feasible, a study of the magnitude of predictive bias due to differential prediction for those groups for which previous research has established a substantial prior probability of differential prediction for the particular kind of test in question. (p. 17)

PERFORMANCE DISTRIBUTION ASSESSMENT

This method of performance assessment incorporates in a systematic fashion several features of methods discussed previously. There are five steps required of the rater: (1) quantitative job analysis, (2) definition of seven levels of outcomes potentially achievable on each job function identified during job analysis, (3) assignment of numerical values to each possible outcome, (4) rating of the expected frequency of occurrence of each outcome level, and (5) rating of the actual frequency of occurrence of each outcome level. Quantitative performance appraisal scores are then derived. The method itself will be described more fully in chapter 9, but for our purposes, the relevant portions of the *Standards* that we have identified for job analysis, numerical rating scales, behavior-based rating scales, and appraisal interviews also apply when performance distribution assessment is used.

Legal Standards

In addition to technical and professional standards, performance assessment is also subject to government regulation and judicial scrutiny. The most important law protecting individuals against any form of employment discrimination is Title VII of the 1964 Equal Employment Opportunity Act. Title VII is enforced by the Equal Employment Opportunity Commission (EEOC), and all charges against an employer brought forth under Title VII must begin with the EEOC or a state or local referral agency.

The EEOC has issued a set of guidelines for Title VII compliance, the most recent being the *Uniform Guidelines on Employee Selection Procedures* (U.S. Equal Employment Opportunity Commission et al., 1978). In addition, the EEOC has also issued the *Adoption of Questions and Answers to Clarify and Provide a Common Interpretation of the Uniform Guidelines on Employee Selection Procedures* (U.S. Equal Employment Opportunity Commission et al., 1979). Unlike statutes, the *Guidelines* is not law, but only a formal statement of the EEOC's policy regarding employee selection procedures. However, while not enforceable as law, in two key Title VII cases that reached the Supreme Court, *Griggs* v. *Duke Power Co.* (1971) and *Albemarle Paper Co.* v. *Moody* (1975) the Court stated that the *Guidelines* is entitled to "great deference." As a result, they have often been treated as if they were, in fact, law.

The *Guidelines* applies to every kind of personnel assessment technique when used to make an employment decision. As spelled out in section 16Q, they cover

> any measure, combination of measures, or procedure used as a basis for any employment decision. Selection procedures include the full range of assessment techniques from traditional paper and pencil tests, performance tests, training programs or probationary periods and physical, educational, and work experience requirements through informal or casual interviews and unscored application forms. (p. 38308)

The purpose of the *Guidelines* is outlined in section 1B:

> These guidelines incorporate a single set of principles which are designed to assist employers, labor organizations, employment agencies, and licensing and certification boards to comply with requirements of Federal law prohibiting employment practices which discriminate on grounds of race, color, religion, sex and national origin. They are designed to provide a framework for determining the proper use of tests and other selection procedures. (p. 38296)

The *Guidelines* provides definitions of discrimination and adverse impact, information on how adverse impact is determined, standards for conducting validity studies, and related validation issues such as the use of alternative selection methods, cooperative validation studies, fairness evidence, and the kinds of documentation of adverse impact and validity evidence the user needs to collect and maintain.

A primary concern of the EEOC, as outlined in the *Guidelines,* is whether an assessment or selection procedure results in adverse impact against members of a protected race, sex, or ethnic group. In general, the EEOC will consider a performance assessment procedure that has no adverse impact as complying with Title VII. However, if adverse impact is found in the use of a performance assessment procedure, it will have to be justified. Usually this would be by a demonstration of validity. It is for this reason that so much of the *Guidelines* is concerned with techniques for validating selection or assessment procedures.

The standards described by the *Guidelines* were written to be consistent with the 1975 *Principles of the Validation and Use of Personnel Selection Procedures* (APA, Division of Industrial and Organizational Psychology, 1975), and recognize three strategies for test validation: criterion-related validity, content validity, and construct validity. As with the discussion of the 1985 *Standards,* the purpose here will not be to summarize the *Guidelines,* instead it will be to present an overview of how the guidelines apply to the methods and methodological issues addressed in this volume. In addition, the important court cases that speak to these issues will be discussed.

Chapter 1 of this book reviews the most crucial step in validating any performance assessment techniques, "job analysis." The *Guidelines* is clear regarding the importance of a job analysis for test validation. "Any validity study should be based upon a review of information about the job for which the selection procedure is to be used" (sec. 14A, p. 38300). For criterion-related validity, this is "to determine measures of work behavior(s) or performance that are relevant to the job or group of jobs in question" to be used as criteria (sec. 14B [2], p. 38300). For content validity, it should include "an analysis of the important work behavior(s) required for successful performance and their relative importance and, if the behavior results in work product(s), an analysis of the work product(s)" (Sec. 14C [2]). For construct validity, "the job analysis should show the work behavior(s) required for successful performance of the job, or the groups of jobs being studied, the critical or important work behavior(s) in the job or group of jobs being studied, and an identification of the construct(s) believed to underlie successful performance of these critical or important work behaviors in the job or jobs in question" (sec. 14D [2], p. 38303). Furthermore, this information is considered essential for documentation of validity evidence where the selection process, that is, any employment decision, has an adverse impact (secs. 15B [3], 15C [3], 15D [4]).

A recurring theme in the court cases that will be reviewed throughout this chapter is the importance of job analyses. The courts will generally expect more than just the job description kept by most employers (Schlei & Grossman, 1983). Instead, a comprehensive analysis of all of the job duties and responsibilities, working conditions, and the knowledge, skills, and abilities necessary to perform the job will be required.

In *Albermarle Paper Co. v. Moody* (1975), one of the reasons the Supreme Court struck down the employer's test was because no job analysis had been conducted to show that the skills and attributes were needed for all of the jobs included in the company's validation study.

In *United States v. City of Chicago* (1977), the Court noted that the city had failed to comply with the federal guidelines or the APA standards by not having conducted a job analysis for the job of patrolman either before the examination or the criterion-related validation study, "indicating that the criteria used in the study were in fact chosen for their availability rather than because they would accurately predict job performance" (p. 431). For this reason, along with other inadequacies in the validation study, the Court struck down the examination.

Likewise in *Kirkland v. New York Department of Correctional Services* (1974), a content validity case, the Court made the following statement:

The cornerstone in the construction of a content valid examination is the job analysis. Without such an analysis to single out the critical knowledge, skills and abilities required by the job, their importance relative to each other, and the level of proficiency demanded as to each attribute, a test constructor is aiming in the dark and can only hope to achieve job relatedness through their importance relative to blind luck. (p. 1373)

Of course simply conducting a job analysis is not sufficient for showing that a performance assessment technique is content valid. For example, in *Easley* v. *Anheuser-Busch, Inc.* (1983), the court ruled that content validity could not be proven where the job analysis did not include a measure of the relative importance of identified work behaviors. In *Thomas* v. *City of Evanston* (1985), the court ruled that a physical agility test was not content valid where those completing the job analysis did not show adequate agreement in their ratings of the physical requirements needed to perform the job of police officer, and where the job analysis did not adequately sample what those requirements should be.

Finally, the courts may require that relevant "source" material documenting how the job analysis was conducted be kept. For example, in *Bigby* v. *City of Chicago* (1984), the court criticized the city of Chicago for failing to keep records of what questions were asked on the job analysis questionnaire, which employees were asked to complete the questionnaire, and how those employees given the questionnaire responded.

NUMERICAL AND BEHAVIOR-BASED RATING SCALES

Methods of measuring performance on the job are given little attention in the *Guidelines*. Since the *Guidelines* was written with an eye towards paper-and-pencil tests, this is not surprising. It is, however, unfortunate. Promotion, discharge, salary, and demotion decisions are all based solely or in part on job performance. Where the *Guidelines* does speak directly to job performance assessment, it is in regard to criterion measurement in criterion-related validity studies. Specifically, section 14B(3), covering the technical standards for criterion measures in criterion-related validity studies, states:

Whatever criteria are used should represent important or critical work behavior(s) or work outcomes. Certain criteria may be used without a full job analysis if the user can show the importance of the criteria to the particular employment context. These criteria include but are not limited to production rate, error rate, tardiness, absenteeism, and length of service. A standardized rating of overall work performance may be used where a study of the job shows that it is an appropriate criterion. (pp. 38300–38301)

Given this very limited discussion of performance assessment, the courts and personnel practitioners have had to look elsewhere in the *Guidelines* for standards of evaluating performance appraisal systems. They have found them by applying the technical standards for content validity studies: "A selection procedure can be supported by a content validity strategy to the extent that it is a representative sample of the content of the job" (sec. 14C [1], p. 38302). The *Guidelines* goes on to state that "in addition, to be content valid, a selection procedure measuring a skill or ability should either closely approximate an observable work behavior, or its product should closely approximate an observable work product" (sec. 14C [4], p. 38302). Where appraisals are based on observed work behavior or work products, proving the content validity of the evaluation system is the logical defense in the face of a discrimination charge.

Unfortunately, the standards applied by the courts when determining content validity have not been consistent. In assessing the content validity of paper-and-pencil tests, for which the *Guidelines* was specifically written, Kleiman and Faley wrote: "The courts have not agreed upon a uniform set of standards. In some instances tests are judged solely on the basis of their face validity; in others, extensive evidence is required. The major factor accounting for these differences appears to be the philosophy and/or sophistication of the judges with respect to the area of personnel testing" (1978, p. 709).

The application of the *Guidelines* to performance appraisal is even more complex, requiring more interpretation than that of paper-and-pencil tests. Judicial decisions in the area of performance appraisal (and for that matter, performance assessment in general) are not based simply on whether a properly or improperly developed performance appraisal system was used. Instead, violations of Title VII or any other discrimination law are typically found where there are numerous deficiencies in the system used and adverse impact has been shown. Conversely, where performance appraisal systems have been upheld, the courts typically have cited both the absence of adverse impact and the presence of a number of safeguards against the possible discriminatory use of the system (Schlei & Grossman, 1983). Kleiman and Durham (1981) reviewed twenty-three cases involving performance appraisal systems used for promotion decisions. In twenty-two of them, the employer lost the case if adverse impact was found and won the case if adverse impact was not found. Whether employers won because their procedures were valid, because of the lack of adverse impact, or because their procedures led to an absence of adverse impact is not known. However, the *Guidelines* does not require validation where there is not adverse impact (secs. 1B and 3A), nor have the courts opposed even extremely subjective criteria when the overall effect of the system has been favorable to the protected group's race or sex (*Anderson v. U.S. Steel Corp.*, 1979).

A number of factors have been considered by the courts when evaluating performance appraisal systems, only some of which relate to the technical standards outlined in the *Guidelines*. The remainder are what could otherwise be considered proper personnel practices that help to safeguard against discrimination in employment decisions. The factors discussed below are taken from Cascio and Bernardin (1981) and Bernardin and Beatty (1984). Similar conclusions have been reached by others reviewing court cases involving performance appraisal systems, in particular, Kleiman and Durham (1981) and Schlei and Grossman (1983).

Standards for performance should be based on a job analysis. As noted earlier, a job analysis is critical for proving content validity. In addition to the cases cited earlier (*Kirkland* v. *N. Y. Department of Correctional Services*, 1974; *United States* v. *City of Chicago*, 1977) in which defendants were criticized for not having conducted a job analysis, the courts have also cited the absence of job analysis–based performance standards as contributing to employers' discriminatory practices. For example, in *Patterson* v. *American Tobacco Company* (1976), the court ruled that a system of "unwritten qualifications" used for promoting personnel to supervisory positions worked to deny black employees the opportunity for promotion. The court found and struck down a similar procedure in *Sledge* v. *J. P. Stevens and Co.* (1976). In both *Rowe* v. *General Motors* (1972) and *Robinson* v. *Union Carbide Corp.* (1976), the court cited "vague and subjective" standards in ruling against the employer. Other rulings against employers where the courts cited the absence of performance standards or written guidelines for raters to make standardized appraisals include *Baxter* v. *Savannah Sugar Refining Corp.* (1972), *Equal Employment Opportunity Commission* v. *Radiator Specialty Co.* (1979), *Meyer* v. *Missouri Highway Commission* (1977), *Parson* v. *Kaiser Aluminum and Chemical Corp.* (1978), and *Mistretta* v. *Sandia Corp.* (1977).

On the other hand, in *Cintron* v. *Adams* (1978) the court noted that the performance appraisal system used for promotion was job related, and it ruled in favor of the employer though no specific reference to a job analysis was made (Kleiman & Burham, 1981). Likewise, in *Crawford* v. *Western Electric Co.* (1980), the court ruled in favor of the employer in part because the use of printed performance review standards in the company's operations manual was seen as reducing rater subjectivity. These standards also should be communicated to employees. Cascio and Bernardin (1981) referred to the following cases in which failure to communicate job requirements, policies, and performance standards were cited by plaintiffs in their claims of wrongful discharge: *Donaldson* v. *Pillsbury Co.* (1977) and *Weahkee* v. *Perry* (1978).

Evaluation should be based on specific job dimensions, not on a global or overall measure. Three cases in particular address this issue. In *Albemarle Paper Co.* v. *Moody* (1975), the Supreme Court noted that the criteria used to validate the company's selection battery, a paired-comparison evaluation procedure in which raters were asked to compare employees in different jobs at different levels of progression in the company, involved "vague and inadequate standards," which could result in bias against blacks. Likewise, in *Watkins* v. *Scott Paper Co.* (1976) the court, in ruling against the employer, cited the use of paired comparisons based on who is "better" as a situation "subject to racial bias." Finally, a procedure was struck down in *Bigby* v. *City of Chicago* (1984), in which raters first made global ratings of all subordinates and then made subscale ratings that had to average to the global values.

Where individual dimensions are evaluated but the employment decisions are based on an overall evaluation, some specified weighting scheme is necessary (*Allen* v. *City of Mobile*, 1978; *Stallings* v. *Container Corporation of America*, 1977; *Watkins* v. *Scott Paper Co.*, 1976; and *Sawyer* v. *Russo*, 1979, a reverse discrimination case).

Ratings should be made on behaviorally based performance dimensions rather than on personality traits. The courts have consistently objected to trait ratings as overly subjective and "susceptible to partiality and to the personal taste, whim, or fancy of the evaluator" (*Wade* v. *Mississippi Cooperative Extension Service*, 1974, p. 142). Examples of such traits include: attitude to detail, interest in job, and all-around ability (*Young* v. *Edgcomb Steel Company*, 1974); attitude, personality, temperament, and habits (*Wade* v. *Mississippi Cooperative Extension Service*, 1974); adaptability, bearing, demeanor, manner, maturity, drive, and social behavior (*Robinson* v. *Union Carbide Corp.*, 1976); leadership ability, general intelligence, general business acumen, and past job performance (*Stallings* v. *Container Corporation of America*, 1977); personal appearance, cooperation, dependability, stability, and leadership (*Williams* v. *Andersons*, 1977); promotability based on aptitude, ability, and work habits (*Gilmore* v. *Kansas City Terminal Railway Co.*, 1975); and cooperation, dependability, and industry (*James* v. *Stockham Valves and Fittings Co.*, 1977).

All three methods for evaluating on-the-job performance reviewed in this book—numerical rating scales (chapter 1), behaviorally based rating scales (chapter 2), and performance distribution assessment (chapter 9)—could be acceptable to the courts since they base performance ratings on work-related behaviors. However, the use of a rating form that includes items important for successful performance does not guarantee that such a form will be used objectively (*Loiseau* v. *Department of Human Resources of the State of Oregon*, 1983). It is possible that in the presence of severe adverse impact a judge would rule against an employer regardless of the type of rating scale used. As noted earlier, Kleiman and Durham (1981) found that the presence of adverse impact was related to a finding of discrimination in twenty-two of the twenty-three cases they reviewed.

An observation made by Bernardin and Beatty is worth repeating: "Unfortunately, there have been no court decisions in which ratings from a rigorously developed, behaviorally based rating scale were assessed for validity after adverse impact had been established" (1984, p. 53).

Documentation should be kept and should be accurate. There are really two considerations in regard to documentation. First, the absence of rating documentation may be held against the company. For example, in *Brito* v. *Zia Co.* (1973), where Hispanic and Native American workers charged the company with discriminatory layoffs, the court ruled against the Zia Company, noting that "no records of performance were maintained, and thus no specific performances were documented to justify the ratings" (Cascio & Bernardin, 1981, p. 217).[1] Similarly in *Loiseau* v. *Department of Human Resources of the State of Oregon* (1983), the defendant could not provide evidence in support of the low performance ratings that were used to deny a promotion to the plaintiff.

Second, an employment decision contrary to performance data will be held against the company. For example, it was considered racial discrimination when no reason could be given for removing an employee's name from a promotion list after fifteen years of excellent ratings and consistent evaluations as promotable (*Marquez* v. *Omaha District Sales Office, Ford Division of the Ford Motor Co.*, 1971). Likewise, it was ruled age discrimination when an employer decided to discharge an employee with fourteen years of satisfactory performance ratings and steady increases in salary.

To summarize, the *Guidelines* provides only limited direction where employment decisions are based on subjective evaluations. Possibly as a result, where subjective criteria for evaluating performance have been used, the presence of adverse impact appears to have been a guiding factor in the decisions rendered by the courts. Still, there are a number of recommendations that follow from the *Guidelines* and have been referred to by the courts in their decisions. These include (1) the presence of a job analysis, (2) performance appraisals based on job behaviors or work outcomes rather than personality traits, (3) decisions based on ratings of individual dimensions of performance rather than on a single evaluation of overall performance, and (4) accurate documentation. These recommendations conform to the first of two strategies Kleiman and Durham (1981) suggest for defending one's performance appraisal system, that is, presenting evidence that the performance appraisal system is valid or job related. Their second strategy, presenting evidence that the appraisal system does not intentionally discriminate, is discussed below in the section on appraisal interviews.

As a final comment in this section, in situations involving white-collar jobs, especially management and professional jobs, but also including white-collar supervisory jobs, the courts have been more accepting of subjective criteria. Schlei and Grossman (1983) cite as examples *Ramirez* v. *Hofheinz*, 1980 (supervisory clerical personnel); *Equal Employment Opportunity Commission* v. *Aetna Insurance Co.*, 1980 (casualty underwriter); *Guy* v. *Peaches Records and Tapes, Inc.*,

---

1. In fact, the validity of the system as a whole was questioned in this case: "The appraisal system was struck down because Zia could provide 'no empirical data demonstrating that the appraisal system was significantly correlated with important elements of work behavior relevant to the jobs for which the appellants were being evaluated'" (Cascio & Bernardin, 1981, p. 217).

1979 (supervisor of cashiers); *Nath* v. *General Electric Co.,* 1977 (design engineers); *Frink* v. *United States Navy,* 1979 (naval architect); and *Milton* v. *Bell Laboratories,* 1977 (patent attorney). Chapter 14 of this book discusses various techniques and applications of managerial performance assessment.

The courts have been even more favorable where academic personnel are involved. While faculty evaluations have not been an issue in case law and are not discussed in the *Guidelines,* the broader issue of tenure has received a great deal of attention. The courts have in general been reluctant to reexamine tenure and promotion decisions despite their subjectivity (*Banerjee* v. *Board of Trustees of Smith College,* 1981; *Hereford* v. *Huntsville Board of Education,* 1978; *Kunda* v. *Muhlenberg College,* 1980; *Zahorik* v. *Cornell University,* 1984). For example, in *Kunda* the court stated:

> It is clear that courts must be vigilant not to intrude into that determination, and should not substitute their judgement for that of the college with respect to the qualifications of faculty members for promotion and tenure. Determinations about such matters as teaching ability, research scholarship, and professional stature are subjective and unless they can be shown to have been used as the mechanism to obscure discrimination, they must be left for evaluation by the professionals, particularly since they often involve inquiry into aspects of arcane scholarship beyond the competence of individual judges. (p. 548)

Likewise, the court in *Hereford* was unwilling to strike down performance evaluations made on factors that had been cited in cases involving blue-collar jobs as being prone to bias. Here the court stated that employment decisions based on factors such as an applicant's knowledge of his or her subject, philosophy on education and on life in general, appearance, references, leadership ability, and aggressiveness were not discriminatory simply because the evaluations were subjective. On the other hand, such a "hands off" policy toward academic tenure decisions has also been criticized in other cases, though not overturned (*Jepsen* v. *Florida Board of Regents,* 1980; *Sweeney* v. *Board of Trustees of Keene State College,* 1978).

PERFORMANCE TESTS

Unlike on-the-job performance appraisal, performance testing is clearly covered in the *Guidelines.* While some performance tests may be validated by showing a relationship to job-related criteria, in most cases performance tests will require a demonstration of content validity (sec. 14C) if their use results in adverse impact. As with performance appraisal systems, performance tests must be based on a job analysis (secs. 14C[2], 14C[3], and 15C[3]). In addition, the *Guidelines* describes the following "standards for demonstrating content validity" (sec. 14C[4]) that apply to performance testing:

To demonstrate the content validity of a selection procedure, a user should show that the behavior(s) demonstrated in the selection procedure are a representative sample of the behavior(s) of the job in question or that the selection procedure provides a representative sample of the work product of the job. In the case of a selection procedure measuring a knowledge, skill, or ability, the knowledge, skill, or ability being measured should be operationally defined. In the case of a selection procedure measuring a knowledge, the knowledge being measured should be operationally defined as that body of learned information which is used in and is a necessary prerequisite for observable aspects of work behavior of the job. In the case of skills or abilities, the skill or ability being measured should be operationally defined in terms of observable aspects of work behavior of the job. For any selection procedure measuring a knowledge, skill, or ability the user should show that (a) the selection procedure measures and is a representative sample of that knowledge, skill, or ability; and (b) that knowledge, skill, or ability is used in and is a necessary prerequisite to performance of critical or important work behavior(s). In addition, to be content valid, a selection procedure measuring a skill or ability should either closely approximate an observable work behavior, or its product should closely approximate an observable work product. If a test purports to sample a work behavior or to provide a sample of work product, the manner and setting of the selection procedure and its level and complexity should closely approximate the work situation. The closer the content and the context of selection procedure are to work samples or work behaviors, the stronger is the basis for showing content validity. As the content of the selection procedure less resembles a work behavior, or the setting and manner of the administration of the selection procedure less resemble the work situation, or the result less resembles a work product, the less likely the selection procedure is to be content valid, and the greater the need for other evidence of validity. (p. 38302)

These standards are reiterated in questions and answers numbers 73 through 80 in *Adoption of Questions and Answers to Clarify and Provide a Common Interpretation of the Uniform Guidelines* (1979). For example, number 78 states that

paper-and-pencil tests which are intended to replicate a work behavior are most likely to be appropriate where work behaviors are performed in paper-and-pencil form (e.g., editing and bookkeeping). Paper-and-pencil tests of effectiveness in interpersonal relations (e.g., sales or supervision), or of physical activities (e.g., automobile repair) or ability to function properly under danger (e.g., firefighters) generally are not close enough approximations of work behaviors to show content validity. (p. 12007)

Number 79 states:

Q. What is required to show the content validity of a test of a job knowledge?

A. There must be a defined, well-recognized body of information, and knowledge of the information must be prerequisite to performance of the required work behaviors. The work behavior(s) to which each knowledge is related should be identified on an item by item basis. The test should fairly sample the information that is actually used by the employee on the job, so that the level of difficulty of the test items should correspond to the level of difficulty of the knowledge as used in the work behavior. (p. 12007)

While a variety of performance tests have been developed, the courts have typically been concerned with three general types: (1) physical ability tests; (2) knowledge tests, that is, tests that require knowing how to do something, for example, how to follow directions, fill out forms, use a particular tool or piece of equipment; and (3) exercises, such as those found in assessment centers.

Performance testing for physical abilities has become a major concern of law enforcement and fire protection officials in the past decade. Traditional minimum height and weight requirements assumed to represent physical ability consistently have been struck down by the courts as not being job related in the presence of severe adverse impact against women, Hispanic Americans, and Asians. The extremity of adverse impact on women in the presence of a height requirement was presented by Arvey (1979). Based on United States population data, a 5 ft. 8 in. height requirement would prevent 95.3 percent of the women, but only 41.3 percent of the men, from being considered for employment.

Judicial decisions in which height or weight requirements have been struck down as inappropriate include one Supreme Court case, *Dothard* v. *Rawlinson* (1977), in which a minimum 5 ft. 2 in. height and 120-pound weight requirement for correctional counselor trainees was struck down, as well as numerous lower court decisions.[2]

Instead of height and weight requirements, a more appropriate strategy is to select on the basis of physical strength and agility. However, since these requirements will in most cases have adverse impact against women, they are required to be job related through a showing either of criterion-related validity or of content validity as shown in their relationship to job demands determined through a job analysis.

2. In the following lower court cases, height or weight requirements were struck down as discriminatory because of their adverse impact in the absence of validity evidence: *Meith* v. *Dothard* (1976); *Officers for Justice* v. *Civil Service Commission* (1975); *Smith* v. *Troyan* (1975); *League of United Latin American Citizens* v. *City of Santa Ana* (1976); *Craig* v. *County of Los Angeles* (1980); *United States* v. *Lee Way Motor Freight, Inc.* (1979); *Davis* v. *County of Los Angeles* (1977); *Horace* v. *City of Pontiac* (1980); *Blake* v. *City of Los Angeles* (1979); *Fox* v. *Washington* (1975); *Meadows* v. *Ford Motor Co.* (1973); and *Laffey* v. *Northwest Airlines, Inc.* (1973), a reverse sex discrimination case in which a shorter height requirement for female flight attendants was discriminatory.

In *Officers for Justice* v. *Civil Service Commission* (1975), the court struck down the use of a physical ability test for female applicants for the job of police officer because of its severe adverse impact but allowed it to be used for male applicants. In *Blake* v. *City of Los Angeles* (1979), the appeals court overturned a lower court ruling that the relationship between the physical abilities test and job requirements without a job analysis could be "obvious" and, therefore, job related. In the presence of severe adverse impact, the appeals court demanded that statistical proof of the job-relatedness be presented. Likewise, in *Harless* v. *Duck* (1980) an appeals court, in reversing a lower court decision, ruled that a physical ability test used to select police officers was not job related. Though physical standards were required for the job, the court found no justification in the job analysis for the tasks involved in the test, such as sit-ups, push-ups, and broad jump, or for the required passing marks.

Finally, the courts have recently indicated that in the face of severe adverse impact against women, not only the content, but the scoring of physical ability tests must bear a relationship to the job analysis if the test is to be considered content valid (*Thomas* v. *City of Evanston*, 1985; *Evans* v. *City of Evanston*, 1985). For example, in *Evans* the court agreed with a female plaintiff that a physical ability test scored on the basis of speed was not job related because it failed to measure other qualities such as foresight, endurance, and pacing that were also necessary to perform the job of firefighter.

In summary, where physical abilities are required, the courts have been generally unwilling to accept surrogate standards for physical abilities, such as height and weight, without evidence or expert testimony of their relationship to job performance. Likewise, physical ability tests that result in adverse impact against females will also be carefully reviewed for their job-relatedness. The courts have relied on standards outlined in the *Guidelines* to guide their decisions.

Performance tests requiring job knowledge have also been challenged in the courts. In *United States* v. *South Carolina* (1978), a case involving teacher evaluation (see chapter 16), the Supreme Court, in refusing to review a lower court decision, upheld the use of the National Teacher's Examination for the purpose of teacher certification and hiring. The exam was upheld as content valid because it measured knowledge relevant for a teacher, even though it did not measure ability to teach. Similarly, in *Bridgeport Guardians* v. *Bridgeport Police Department* (1977), the court upheld the use of a paper-and-pencil knowledge test as content valid, despite its adverse impact against blacks. However, in *Guardians Association of the New York City Police Department* v. *Civil Service Commission* (1980), a paper-and-pencil test for selecting police officers was struck down. The court first identified five criteria for content validity that are required by the *Guidelines:*

> The first two concern the quality of the test's development: (1) the test-makers must have conducted a suitable job analysis, and (2) they must have used reasonable competence in constructing the test itself. The

next three attributes are more in the nature of standards that the test, as produced and used, must be shown to have met. The basic requirement, really the essence of content validation, is (3) that the content of the test must be related to the content of the job. In addition, (4) the content of the test must be representative of the content of the job. Finally, the test must be used with (5) a scoring system that usefully selects from among the applicants those who can better perform the job. (p. 95)

The court dismissed as a "practical impossibility" arguments that the content of an exam must represent *all* knowledge, skills, and abilities required in proportion to their importance on the job. The court concluded that while the first four of these requirements were adequate, though not optimal, and that it might have accepted the exam as content valid, it would rule against the use of the test because the ordering of applicants and the cutoff score were not job related: "A cutoff score unrelated to job performance may well lead to the rejection of applicants who were fully capable of performing the job" (p. 105).

Finally, in *Vanguard Justice Society* v. *Hughes* (1984), the court ruled that a job knowledge test could not be considered valid where items were written and selected for inclusion on the test in a "haphazard" manner. Specifically, the judge stated that the item writers were not trained, no evidence was presented that items were selected on the basis of the job analysis material or were reviewed by incumbents for accuracy, there was no assurance that the knowledge tested would not be acquired in a subsequent training program, and no preliminary item analyses, or item-impact or discrimination analyses were conducted before the test was implemented.

The preceding cases indicate that paper-and-pencil tests of knowledge have been upheld by some courts despite their adverse impact. However, in other cases, the courts have struck down paper-and-pencil tests as not being job related and have advocated an alternative testing procedure—assessment centers.

ASSESSMENT CENTERS

Assessment centers (chapter 5) must be job related if their use results in adverse impact. As with other selection procedures, this is demonstrated by one or more of the three validation strategies described in the *Guidelines:* criterion-related, content, or construct validation. Since assessment centers are multiple assessment techniques, it is possible that all three validation strategies could be employed. For example, a criterion-related strategy might be used for a mental abilities measure, a content validity strategy might be required for a work sample test, such as an in-basket test on a business game, and a construct validation strategy might be used for personality tests or interest inventories, all of which might be included in the assessment center. What strategy is chosen ultimately depends on the exercises included in the assessment center, the availability of job-related performance data, and the "technical feasibility" (usually sample size) of the particular strategy desired. Typically, however, conducting a construct or criterion-related validity study is not technically feasible because the number of persons put through an assessment center and for whom adequate job performance data are available is too small. As a result, the content validity of assessment centers, particularly work sample–like exercises, have received increasing attention (Byham, 1983; Dreher & Sackett, 1981; Norton, 1977, 1981; Sackett & Dreher, 1981).

At issue in assessment centers is whether assessors are evaluating samples of work behaviors, which would make a content validity strategy appropriate, or constructs exemplified in the assessment center exercises, which would be inappropriate for content validity. The ambiguity arises because while the exercises represent samples of joblike situations and assessors are supposed to base their evaluative ratings on observed behaviors, these ratings are typically given on dimensions such as leadership, flexibility, decision making, and risk taking, which are abstract characteristics, constructs inappropriate for a content validity strategy.

Like any assessment procedure relying on content validity, assessment centers fall under section 14C of the *Guidelines* in which the necessity and standards of job analyses used for content validation are discussed. However, number 75 in *Questions and Answers* is particularly relevant to assessment centers:

> *Q*. Can a measure of a trait or construct be validated on the basis of content validity?
> *A*. No. Traits or constructs are by definition underlying characteristics which are intangible and are not directly observable. They are therefore not appropriate for the sampling approach of content validity. Some selection procedures, while labeled as construct measures, may actually be samples of observable work behaviors. Whatever the label, if the operational definitions are in fact based upon observable work behaviors, a selection procedure measuring those behaviors may be appropriately supported by a content validity strategy. (p. 12007)

Following up on this interpretation, Byham (Solotoff, 1983) has argued that to the degree that an exercise measures observable functional behaviors that are similar, in that they all relate to a general category label such as "leadership," then the exercise is measuring leadership behaviors and is therefore content valid and not the trait or construct of "leadership." However, Dreher and Sackett (1981) note that this line of reasoning has not yet been adequately scrutinized by the courts.

The most important employment discrimination case involving assessment centers has been *Firefighters Institute for Racial Equality* v. *City of St. Louis* (*F.I.R.E.* v. *St. Louis*, 1980). In the original case, *United States* v. *City of St. Louis* (1976), the district court upheld the city's use of a paper-and-pencil job knowledge test for promotion to fire captain as content valid, despite a finding of adverse impact. The case was appealed (*F.I.R.E.* v. *St. Louis,* 1977), and the district court's decision was overturned. Based on expert testimony, the court recommended an assessment center as an alternative method for testing the supervisory skills of the applicants. After the new written test and assessment center were developed, F.I.R.E. sought an injunction against its implementation. Although the assessment center as a whole was not found to have adverse impact, the written test, and more important, the combination of both, were found to have an adverse impact.

The district court (*F.I.R.E.* v. *St. Louis,* 1979) again found the tests to be content valid based on the careful linking of the job analysis with test item content, and it ruled in favor of the city. Again the results were appealed (*F.I.R.E.* v. *St. Louis,* 1980), and again the district court decision was reversed. Here the court dismissed the written, multiple-choice part of the exam as not being content valid because the fire captain's job was a "physical, hands-on job." More important, a fire scene simulation assessment exercise, in which candidates responded by writing down their observations and the orders they might give in response to a slide of a fire screen, was also considered a paper-and-pencil test "far removed from the content and context of the candidates' actual work behavior" (p. 360). It was thus not considered valid. Two other exercises included in the assessment center, a role-playing exercise and an interview simulation, were also criticized because of the short amount of time candidates were observed and the limited training the assessors received, though the court was "hesitant" to consider these as invalid, stating, "These latter portions more closely comply with the spirit of the *Guidelines* than does either the multiple choice examination or the Fire Scene Simulation" (p. 362).

In summary, the circuit court took an extremely narrow view of what would be acceptable for content validity, essentially arguing that any test or exercise requiring writing, where writing is not a major component of the job, could not be considered content valid, and "greater evidence of validity is required" (p. 357).[3]

Byham (1983) presents a number of cases in which assessment centers have been adopted by employers as an alternative selection procedure where previous paper-and-pencil selection procedures were ruled discriminatory. However, with the exception of *F.I.R.E.* v. *St. Louis* (1980), in none of these cases has the content validity of the implemented assessment center been reviewed by the courts. For example, in *Friend* v. *Leidinger* (1977), a combination paper-and-pencil test and assessment center was challenged as discriminatory. However, neither the assessment center nor the selection procedure as a whole was found to have adverse impact. Since the burden of proof did not, therefore, shift to the

---

3. A new assessment center examination has been developed by testing specialists representing the St. Louis City Department of Personnel, the Justice Department, and black and white firefighters, which eliminates the major flaws of the previous examinations (Byham, 1983). Candidates' responses regarding what they observe and orders they would give are no longer written, but instead are tape recorded.

defendant (city), the court ruled it was not necessary to prove the job-relatedness of the assessment center by showing it was valid.

A similar situation occurred in *Rivera* v. *City of Wichita Falls* (1982), another police officer case. While the paper-and-pencil test showed adverse impact, no adverse impact was found for any of the other elements of the selection system, including the assessment center and the selection procedure overall. Again, the court ruled that, in the absence of adverse impact in the selection system overall, there was no need to test further for the validity of any of the components of the selection procedure. Thus, in both of these cases, the court looked at the "bottom line" effect of the selection procedures on adverse impact and, finding none, did not pursue the issue of whether the assessment center met the *Guidelines* standard for content validity. [4]

In *Tillery* v. *Pacific Telephone Co.* (1982) (cited in Byham, 1983), an assessment center for sales representatives was challenged. Not only was no adverse impact found, but the judge went on to note that the assessment center used had significantly criterion-related validity.

To summarize, in only one instance, *F.I.R.E.* v. *St. Louis* (1980), has the content validity of an assessment center been reviewed by the courts for compliance with the *Guidelines*. In that case, the appeals court took a very narrow interpretation of the standards acceptable for content validity and ruled against the assessment center used by the city. On the other hand, where paper-and-pencil tests were found to be discriminatory, the courts have been quick to suggest and to approve the use of assessment centers as an alternative selection procedure. (This was the situation in *United States* v. *St. Louis,* 1976, which led to the *F.I.R.E.* v. *St. Louis* decision.) Finally, in a number of cases, the validity of the assessment center was not reviewed by the courts, since the courts found no adverse impact.

APPRAISAL INTERVIEWS

Chapter 6 discusses characteristics of appraisal interviews that can lead to improved employee performance, motivation, and satisfaction. Appraisal interviews can take on additional importance for legal reasons when they serve as

---

4. While it did not involve an assessment center, the "bottom-line" defense of a selection system (i.e., no adverse impact) was recently overruled by the Supreme Court in *Connecticut* v. *Teal* (1982). However in this case, Connecticut had employed a "multiple hurdle" selection strategy for promotion to supervisor, in which passing the initial paper-and-pencil test, which had an adverse impact on blacks, was required before other selection criteria would be considered. The state argued that since there was no adverse impact against blacks by the state in the number of blacks ultimately promoted, the "bottom line" was nondiscriminatory. The Supreme Court, however, ruled that since the test acted as a "pass-fail barrier," the nonvalidated test acted to deprive individuals of employment opportunity, even though there was no adverse impact against blacks as a group. Where assessment centers are used in a compensatory selection strategy, that is, where all individuals take all parts of the selection process as in the cases cited previously, the "bottom-line" defense may still hold.

vehicles for communicating and reviewing employees' performance. That appraisal interviews can help to protect a company from a charge of discrimination has emerged from employment discrimination case law, not from technical standards prescribed in the *Guidelines*. Here the courts have considered whether there was evidence showing (1) that the employer's performance assessment procedure did not discriminate, and (2) that personnel procedures existed to minimize the likelihood of bias. In contrast to the recommendations for validating performance appraisal systems, conducting appraisal interviews can serve as evidence that the employer had no intention of discriminating.

In a number of cases, the courts have commented on whether the appraisal results were reviewed by the employee. In their review and statistical analysis of sixty-six discrimination cases, Feild and Holley (1982) found this issue to be strongly and statistically related to the judicial decision. In an often cited case, *Pouncy* v. *Prudential Insurance Co.* (1980), employees were allowed to review, discuss, and add comments to their evaluations. In other cases such as *Equal Employment Opportunity Commission* v. *E. I. du Pont de Nemours and Co.* (1978), *Thompson* v. *McDonnell Douglas Corp.* (1976), *Crawford* v. *Western Electric Co.* (1980), *Movement for Opportunity and Equality* v. *General Motors Corp.* (1980), *Page* v. *U.S. Industries, Inc.* (1984), and *Rich* v. *Martin-Marietta Corp.* (1975), a formalized system existed in which supervisory ratings were reviewed by second- or third-level supervisors or personnel officials. Employees, after reviewing their ratings, could formally complain or challenge their evaluation to officials within the organizational system. Finally, in *Lewis* v. *National Labor Relations Board* (1985), the court stated that where safeguards for preventing discrimination in promotional decisions existed, the "process did not possess the degree of subjectivity necessitating an inference of discrimination" (p. 1396). In this case, these safeguards included having all appraisals reviewed by more than one supervisor; allowing employees the opportunity to review, comment, and discuss the appraisal with their supervisor; providing employees with a grievance procedure for challenging the appraisal; training supervisors in evaluating employees; and presenting supervisors with written guidelines for completing the rating form.

To summarize, the courts have suggested personnel practices that are not related to the *Guidelines* but that help to ensure fairness. These include the communication of performance standards to employees, a formal system in which supervisory ratings are reviewed by others in the organization, and where employees can review, discuss, and, if necessary, challenge the ratings they received.

UTILITY ANALYSIS

Standards for conducting a utility analysis of performance assessment procedures, discussed in chapter 7, are not addressed in the *Guidelines*. However, section 14B(6) of the *Guidelines* does warn test users that:

reliance upon a selection procedure which is significantly related to a criterion measure, but which is based upon a study involving a large number of subjects and has a low correlation coefficient will be subject to close review if it has a large adverse impact. . . . The appropriateness of a selection procedure is best evaluated in each particular situation and there are no minimum correlation coefficients applicable to all employment situations. In determining whether a selection procedure is appropriate for operational use the following considerations should also be taken into account: The degree of adverse impact of the procedure, the availability of other selection procedures of a greater or substantially equal validity. (p. 38301)

As will be seen in chapter 7, the *Guidelines* is not completely correct in inferring that utility is simply a function of the size of the validity coefficient. Regardless, the *Guidelines* states that validity alone may not be a sufficient defense against a charge of discrimination; the EEOC will also look at the degree of adverse impact resulting from the assessment procedure and will weigh the utility of the procedure against its adverse impact in determining whether the use of the procedure is appropriate.

The most accurate utility analyses show that for a valid test there is a linear relationship between selecting the highest performers on the predictor and its ultimate utility. In other words, a rank-ordering of scores is the most effective way to select applicants with the highest probability of increasing employee productivity. The *Guidelines* is generally less tolerant of this approach; that is, it results in greater adverse impact than would have occurred had a cutoff score been used to predict "acceptable behavior." For example, section 5H reads:

Where cutoff scores are used, they should normally be set so as to be reasonable and consistent with normal expectations of acceptable proficiency within the work force. Where applicants are ranked on the basis of properly validated selection procedures and those applicants scoring below a higher cutoff score than appropriate in light of such expectations have little or no chance of being selected for employment, the higher cutoff score may be appropriate, but the degree of adverse impact should be considered. (p. 38298)

Thus the *Guidelines* implies that an organization should use a cutoff that will maintain present employee proficiency if it results in less adverse impact, rather than ranking applicants or using a higher cutoff that will, on the average, improve future employee proficiency.

Likewise, for performance assessment techniques defended using a content validity strategy, in order to use a ranking procedure, the user must show with a job analysis that "the selection procedure [measures] those aspects of performance which differentiate among levels of job performance" (sec. 14C[9], p. 38303). In others words, a user cannot simply assume that higher scores on a content valid test will result in higher job performance.

None of this is to imply that the *Guidelines* is always wrong regarding the use of cutoffs versus rank ordering. Rather, they require clear evidence that rank ordering is appropriate. Thus answer 47 states that "if a research study shows only that at a given passing score the test satisfactorily screens out probable failures, the study would not justify the use of substantially different passing scores, or ranked lists of those who passed" (*Questions and Answers*, p. 12003). Likewise, in response to a question also regarding the use of ranking, answer 62 states:

> Criterion-related and construct validity strategies are essentially empirical, statistical processes showing a relationship between performance on the selection procedure and performance on the job. To justify ranking under such validity strategies, therefore, the user need show mathematical support for the proposition that persons who receive higher scores on the procedure are likely to perform better on the job. . . .
>
> Any conclusion that a content validated procedure is appropriate for ranking must rest on an inference that higher scores on the procedure are related to better job performance. The more closely and completely the selection procedure approximates the important work behaviors, the easier it is to make such an inference. Evidence that better performance on the procedure is related to greater productivity or to performance of behaviors of greater difficulty may also support such an inference.
>
> Where the content and context of the selection procedure are unlike those of the job, as, for example, in many paper-and-pencil job knowledge tests, it is difficult to infer an association between levels of performance on the procedure and on the job. (*Questions and Answers*, p. 12005)

In one decision the court has made specific reference to the results of a utility analysis. The judges in *Pegues* v. *Mississippi State Employment Service* (1980) accepted expert testimony regarding the utility of the GATB tests, noting that "in addition to the statistical significance the USES tests have practical significance and a high degree of utility" (p. 255). The judge also noted, "It was also demonstrated that a very considerable dollar value is associated with the reported levels of validity. There is no truth to the plaintiff's allegation that the levels of reported validities are so low as to be of no practical value" (p. 254).

Utility was also a major consideration in *Spurlock* v. *United Airlines* (1972). Here the defendant used statistics to show that the number of pretraining flight hours was related to success in a training program, and that the high cost of the training program made the requirement of a minimum amount of previous flight hours a business necessity. The court further stated that where it can be shown that "the job clearly requires a high degree of skill and the economic and human risks involved in hiring an unqualified applicant are great, the employer bears a correspondingly lighter burden to show that his employment criteria are job related" (p. 219).

Finally, despite research evidence of its utility, the courts have consistently rejected the use of rank ordering, even where the court accepted the test as job-related. The rationale typically used by the courts can be found in *In re Birmingham Employment* (1985). The court held that while tests can be valid for groups of individuals, even a valid test does not assess the relative qualifications of two specific individuals with enough accuracy to say that the one with the higher score is better qualified. In *Guardians Association of the New York City Police Department* v. *Civil Service Commission* (1980), discussed earlier, the court struck down the Police Academy entrance exam primarily because of flaws in the use of rank ordering of applicants as the basis for setting passing scores. In *Ensley Branch of the NAACP* v. *Seibels* (1980), *Louisville Black Police Officers Organization* v. *City of Louisville* (1979), and *Allen* v. *City of Mobile* (1978), the courts rejected the use of rank ordering of applicants, but approved the use of the test with a pass-fail cutoff. In the previously mentioned *Pegues* case, in which expert testimony had been accepted regarding a utility analysis, the defendant used cutoff scores rather than rank ordering. In summary, though not entirely prohibited, rank ordering is clearly not favored by the EEOC or the courts unless strong evidence of its job-relatedness can be presented. Utility analysis may be a method of providing that evidence.

VALIDITY GENERALIZATION AND PREDICTIVE BIAS

A recent and important development in the area of test validation has been the introduction of validity generalization procedures (Hunter, Schmidt, & Jackson, 1982; Pearlman, Schmidt, & Hunter, 1980; Schmidt, Gast-Rosenberg, & Hunter, 1980). These statistical procedures combine validation results across large numbers of studies, while simultaneously taking into consideration psychometric factors such as the unreliability of the measures, range restriction in scores, and small sample sizes found in most validation studies. Validity generalization procedures and issues surrounding their use are discussed in chapter 8. One important conclusion reached by researchers is that for a variety of jobs—clerical workers (Pearlman, Schmidt, & Hunter, 1980), mechanical repairmen (Schmidt & Hunter, 1977), computer programmers (Schmidt, Gast-Rosenberg, & Hunter, 1980), first-line supervisors (Schmidt et al., 1979), and machine operator and maintenance workers (Schmidt, Hunter, & Caplan, 1981)—tests exist that are valid across employment situations and geographical locations. Users should not be required to provide additional evidence of validity, only a job analysis showing the similarity between the job in question and those previously tested (Schmidt, Hunter, & Pearlman, 1981).

The validity generalization procedures themselves are not specifically addressed in the *Guidelines*. (With the exception of a few pioneering studies, most of the validity generalization literature has been published since the release of both the *Guidelines* and *Questions and Answers*.) However, the *Guidelines* does

PERFORMANCE DISTRIBUTION ASSESSMENT

Performance distribution assessment (PDA) is not specifically addressed in the *Guidelines*. However, like other subjective rating scales, users should be guided by the standards required for showing content validity. Thus those portions of the *Guidelines* that are relevant to job analysis and to numerical and behavior-based rating scales are also relevant here.

PDA is still relatively new and has not been brought before the courts. However, similar to other subjective evaluation procedures, it will be carefully scrutinized by the courts if its use results in adverse impact. The recommendations based on previous court decisions that apply to numerical and behavior-based rating systems also apply here. In the case of PDA, the recommendations regarding job analysis, use and weighting of specific job dimensions (referred to as "job functions" in PDA), and behaviorally based ratings are all incorporated into the design of the system. However, other recommendations, such as accurate documentation and the personnel practices discussed above in the appraisal interview section that indicate an absence of intent to use the system to discriminate, should also be followed.

Summary and Conclusions

From the review of the new *Standards,* the *Guidelines,* and the court cases relevant to performance assessment, it should be clear that the most important requirement for any assessment procedure, and the thread that unites all of these areas, is the presence of a thorough job analysis (chapter 1). It is the standard by which content validity will be assessed and criteria must be developed or chosen for criterion-related validity. The absence of a job analysis or a poorly conducted one, or the failure to relate assessment techniques to the content of the job analysis is what has most often been cited by the courts as the reason organizations fail to prove the job-relatedness of their assessment procedures.

A job analysis is necessary for showing the job-relatedness of all performance appraisal methods and is the basis for the performance standards fed back to employees. It is necessary for all types of performance testing, from physical ability tests to assessment centers, and it is especially critical where paper-and-pencil job knowledge tests are involved. It is also the basis on which the EEOC and the courts will judge whether a job is sufficiently similar to those in other studies to warrant the use of validity generalization as an adequate defense when a test has adverse impact. Finally, it is a basis for determining whether rank ordering, the approach used in most utility analyses, is an appropriate means of summarizing test results.

Content validity also underlies all of the methods discussed in this book. This is most apparent in the discussion of those methods typically used to evaluate current employees: numerical rating scales (chapter 2), behavior-based rating scales (chapter 3), and performance distribution assessment (chapter 9). It is also required for predictive techniques such as performance tests (chapter 4) and assessment centers (chapter 5), where either there is no criterion against which one can relate scores on the performance assessment instrument or it is technically infeasible (e.g., small sample size) to use any other validation strategy. However, content validity is also required for the criteria against which tests are validated in criterion-related validity studies. Thus those using validity generalization (chapter 8) and utility analyses (chapter 7) procedures that rely primarily on criterion-related strategies cannot ignore issues of content validity. The requirements for content validity are most clearly and comprehensively described in the *Standards*. The *Guidelines* is essentially a review, albeit a fairly complete one, of these standards.

Certainly the most critical shortcoming of the *Guidelines,* especially in comparison to the *Standards,* is in the area of performance judgments. Where the *Standards* specifies requirements for judging the content of the performance domain, providing evidence of rater agreement, selecting behaviors for observation, and designing the evaluation instrument, the *Guidelines* merely warns of the use of subjective assessments. It may be that the absence of clearly defined standards has led the courts, which rely heavily on the *Guidelines* for their own judgments about the fairness and validity of performance appraisal, to an unwillingness to consider performance appraisal systems valid in the face of adverse impact.

Likewise, the appraisal interview is not addressed in the *Guidelines.* On the other hand, the courts have looked very favorably on its use as a means of communicating performance standards and as an opportunity for discussion and review of an employee's evaluation. Here the courts have been less concerned about validity, than about the fairness of the system. Again, it is the *Standards* that gives users some guidance in how and what should be included in the interview.

APPENDIX. SUMMARY OF STANDARDS FOR PERFORMANCE ASSESSMENT OUTLINED IN THE *STANDARDS, GUIDELINES,* AND THE COURTS

Method	Standards	Guidelines
Job analysis (chapter 1)	*Chapters 1, 10, and 11* A job analysis is necessary for defining the content of the job domain for both performance tests and criteria. The job content domain can include	*Section 14A* Any validity should be based on a job analysis. *Section 14B(2)* For criterion-related validity, a job analysis is critical for

Requirements for developing performance tests and assessment centers are, like other performance assessment techniques, more completely explained in the *Standards* than in the *Guidelines*. In particular, technical issues, such as reliability, sampling, scoring procedures, and the effects of practice, are either ignored or mentioned only briefly in the *Guidelines;* in contrast, there are sections of the *Standards* directed toward each technical issue.

The *Guidelines* makes no specific reference to validity generalization, but it does recognize the need to rely on past studies when local validation studies are not feasible. Appropriate sections, in particular section 14B(8)(b), should be reviewed by anyone considering using validity generalization. On the other hand, conditions when validity generalization would be appropriate are discussed in standard 1.16 in the *Standards*.

Utility analysis is not referred to at all in the *Standards* but is indirectly addressed in the *Guidelines*, which states that the EEOC will weigh the size of the validity coefficient (implying utility) against the amount of adverse impact resulting from an assessment procedure. In addition, the *Guidelines* is far more supportive of cutoff scores, which generally have less utility for the test user, than it is of rank-ordering test scores. To date, neither validity generalization nor utility analysis has been a major issue in the courts. However, both have the potential to affect court decisions in the future—validity generalization, because it will relieve many test users from having to conduct expensive validation studies, and utility analysis because it can show empirically the value and, therefore, the "business necessity" of tests with even small validity coefficients.

The Appendix presents a summary of the standards found in the *Standards,* the *Guidelines,* and the court cases that apply to the methods of performance assessment that are discussed in this book. It is intended to serve as a helpful review of the issues and standards discussed in this chapter. Of course, anyone who is considering developing a new assessment procedure or who is concerned about an old one is strongly advised to study the *Standards* and the *Guidelines* in their entirety.

Court Cases	Comments
Albemarle Paper Co. v. Moody (1975) No job analysis was conducted showing that the skills tested were needed in all of the jobs; therefore, the court would not accept the results of the company's validation studies.	All three standards are consistent; job analysis is an essential first step in conducting any kind of validation study, and without one that the courts view as adequate, tests resulting in adverse impact will be struck down.

(continued)

APPENDIX *(cont.)*

Method	Standards	Guidelines
	tasks to be performed or knowledge, skills, abilities or personality characteristics (KSAs) necessary to do the work, and ratings of their frequency and criticality.	determining criteria for job performance. *Section 14C(2)* For content validity, a job analysis is required to determine the important work behaviors or outcomes for successful performance, and their relative importance. *Section 14D(2)* For construct validity, a job analysis is necessary for identifying critical work behaviors and constructs, and how the constructs underlie successful performance of those behaviors. *Sections 15B(3), 15C(3), 15D(4)* A job analysis is essential for documentation of an assessment procedure having adverse impact.
Numerical rating scales (chapter 2) and behavior-based rating scales (chapter 3)	*Standard 1.7* Expertise of those judging the content domain of the criteria and the judgmental procedure should be described. *Standard 1.12* Criteria and rationale for choosing them must be described accurately. *Standard 1.13* Technical quality of all criteria should be considered and irrelevant factors identified.	*Section 14B(3)* Criteria should represent important or critical work behaviors or outcomes. *Section 14C(1)* To be supported by a content validity strategy, selection procedure should be a representative sample of the job domain. *Section 14C(4)* For content validity, the measures of skills or abilities

Court Cases	Comments

United States v. City of Chicago (1977)
No job analysis was conducted to show
that the criterion used in the city's
criterion-related validation study was
job related, thus the job-relatedness of
the test was unacceptable to the court.

*Kirkland v. N.Y. Dept. of Correc.
Serv. (1974)*
In the absence of an adequate job
analysis, content validity of a test could
not be proven.

Easely v. Anheuser-Busch (1983)
The job analysis must also measure
the relative importance of work
behaviors, not just identify work
behaviors.

Thomas v. City of Evanston (1985)
Those completing the job analysis must
agree on the physical requirements of
the job if the requirements are to be
considered content valid.

Bigby v. City of Chicago (1984)
Relevant "source" material
documenting how the job analysis was
conducted must be kept.

U.S. v. City of Chicago (1977)
The city's test was thrown out when
no evidence was presented that the
criteria were based on a job analysis.

Rowe v. General Motors (1972)
"Vague and subjective" performance
standards were not acceptable for
basing promotion decisions.

*Crawford v. Western Electric Co.
(1980)*
Printed performance review standards
were seen as reducing rater
subjectivity.

The *Guidelines* provides little direction
regarding performance appraisal
systems; users must infer standards
for content validity. The *Standards*
gives far more guidance about
requirements for developing
performance appraisal systems. The
courts have been skeptical of
subjective rating systems where
adverse impact has been found.
The following practices are advised:
1. Standards for performance should
be based on a job analysis.

(continued)

APPENDIX (*cont.*)

Method	*Standards*	*Guidelines*
	Standard 1.14 Expertise of raters should be reported.	should approximate observable work behavior.
	Standard 1.15 Basis for combining criteria should be specified.	
	Standard 2.8 Evidence on the degree of agreement among raters should be provided, especially for observational data.	
	Standard 3.2 Specifications for selecting items of observations and the design of the instrument should be determined.	
	Standard 3.3 Relationships between items or scales chosen and the content domain should be clarified.	
	Standard 1.6 For content validity, user should demonstrate how items are to be used, the universe represented, procedures followed in generating content, and if criticality is an issue, what the rationale is for the relative emphasis on critical factors.	
Performance tests (chapter 4)	All standards related to content validity apply. *Chapter 1* Systematic observation of behaviors judged as critical for the job can be administered off the job as a test. Aspects of the job judged unimportant	*Section 14C* Everything regarding content validity applies, in particular are those sections that pertain to job analysis, whether the tested behaviors are a representative sample of job behaviors, and whether the

Court Cases	Comments
Watkins v. Scott Paper Co. (1976) *Albemarle Paper Co. v. Moody (1975)* *Bigby v. City of Chicago (1983)* Evaluations based on global measures are inadequate and subject to bias. *Wade v. Miss. Coop. Exten. Serv. (1974)* Traits are overly subjective. *Brito v. Zia (1973)* *Loiseau v. Dept. Human Resources (1983)* Absence of information to document ratings may be discriminatory.	2. Evaluations should be of specific dimensions, not a global measure. 3. Ratings should be based on behaviorally based dimensions, not on traits. 4. Ratings should be documented.
Dothard v. Rawlinson (1977) Height and weight requirements were struck down by the Supreme Court as not being job related and having severe adverse impact on women. *Harless v. Duck (1980)* A test consisting of physical exercises could not be considered job related just	The *Standards* is more specific and helpful for determining the requirements for a valid performance test than is the *Guidelines*. The courts will examine performance tests very carefully for the relationship between the job analysis and the test content, especially where severe adverse

(continued)

APPENDIX *(cont.)*

Method	*Standards*	*Guidelines*
	should be excluded from the test.	KSAs are operationally defined and representatively sampled.
	Comment to Standard 10.5 If the link between the test content and the job content is not direct, additional evidence is required.	*Section 15C* Everything regarding documentation required for content validity applies.
	Standard 3.14 Sensitivity of the test to improvement with practice, coaching, etc., should be studied.	
	Standard 3.22 Directions should be appropriate for the level of test-taker ability and understanding.	
	Standard 3.23 Where behavior samples are collected, the types of behaviors desired should be clearly defined, and directions to test takers should be standardized.	
	Standard 3.25 The bases for scoring and the training procedures for scoring where judgments are involved should be presented in sufficient detail to permit high levels of agreement.	
	Comment to Standard 16.1 Test takers should be made aware of reasons and intended uses of the test, and who will be privy to the information.	
Assessment centers (chapter 5)	All standards relevant to criterion-related, content, and construct validity apply.	Standards for content validity apply, unless assessment center is validated by a

Court Cases	Comments

because a job analysis showed that physical exertion was necessary for a police officer's job.

Blake v. City of Los Angeles (1979)
Relationship between physical test and job analysis was not sufficient in the presence of severe adverse impact. Court demanded statistical proof.

Guardians Assoc. N.Y. City Police v. Civil Serv. Comm. (1980)
Court outlined requirements for content validity for a job knowledge paper-and-pencil test. It struck down the test because the scoring system was deemed inappropriate for content validity.

U.S. v. South Carolina (1978)
Supreme Court upheld the use of a standardized exam for teachers as content valid for hiring and certification.

Vanguard Justice Soc. v. Hughes (1984)
A job knowledge test cannot be considered content valid if the items are written in a "haphazard" manner.

impact exists. Both physical abilities tests and job knowledge tests can be valid when constructed and used properly.

F.I.R.E. v. St. Louis (1980)
Despite job analysis, written portion of assessment center was not considered

Assessment center exercises will typically require a content validation strategy if adverse impact is shown.

(*continued*)

APPENDIX (*cont.*)

Method	*Standards*	*Guidelines*
	Standard 3.15 For interest and personality measures, evidence should be presented that scores are not susceptible to faking. *Standard 5.7* Promotional material should be accurate. *Standard 15.9* Test protocols and written reports should be retained for test takers. *Standard 15.10* Where assessment center results are fed back, information about the test and test scores should be interpretable by the test taker.	criterion-related or construct validation strategy where sections 14B and 14D, respectively, would apply. *Question and Answer No. 75* Traits and constructs that are operationalized as samples of observable work behaviors can be validated using a content validity strategy.
Appraisal interview (chapter 6)	*Standard 3.16* The score report forms should facilitate appropriate interpretations (i.e., assessment forms should facilitate feedback). *Standard 9.1* The results used in counseling should be reported so that the information can be used by clients to make important decisions. *Standard 9.6* Counselors (supervisors) should caution the test takers (ratees) to consider other relevant information (e.g., previous performance appraisal data).	Not Applicable.

Court Cases	Comments
valid, because most of the job did not involve writing skills. Likewise, a fire scene simulation was struck down because applicants had to write down answers. (The appeals court took a very narrow view of acceptable standards for content validity.) The courts have approved the use of assessment centers as alternative selection strategies to paper-and-pencil tests (Byham, 1983).	As such, the requirements outlined by the *Standards* and the *Guidelines* apply. In only one case has the content validity of an assessment center been reviewed by the court. The court did not find the assessment center to be valid, but a revised version of it is presently in use. Likewise, assessment centers have been the alternative of choice by the courts where traditional tests had resulted in adverse impact.
Friend v. Leidinger (1977) *Rivera v. City of Wichita Falls (1982)* Courts did not rule against the content validity of these assessment centers where they did not result in adverse impact.	
Tillery v. Pacific Telephone Co. (1982) Assessment center was found to have criterion-related validity.	
Pouncy v. Prudential Ins. Co. (1980) *EEOC v. E. I. du Pont (1978)* *Thompson v. McDonnell Douglas (1976)* *Crawford v. Western Electric Co. (1980)* *Movement for Opportunity v. G.M. (1980)* *Rich v. Martin-Marietta (1975)* *Lewis v. N.L.R.B. (1985)* Employees reviewed and could challenge their evaluations.	Appraisal interviews are not discussed in the *Guidelines* and relate only indirectly to the *Standards*. However, the courts have looked extremely favorably on their use as evidence of fairness in ratings.

(*continued*)

APPENDIX (*cont.*)

Method	*Standards*	*Guidelines*
Utility analysis (chapter 7)	Only referred to obliquely, in that value judgments are always involved in selection decisions.	Utility analysis is not specifically addressed. *Section 14B(6)* Implies that the EEOC will weigh the size of the validity coefficient against the amount of adverse impact resulting from a test. *Section 5H* Warns against the use of ranking or cutoff scores that are not closely job related, the choice of which can affect the outcome of a utility analysis. *Section 14C(9)* Rank ordering of scores based on a content validation strategy may be difficult to defend.
Validity generalization and predictive bias (chapter 8)	*Standard 1.16* Validity generalization may be used where local validation evidence is not feasible. Test situation must be similar. *Chapter 1* Predictive bias is based on an analysis of regression slopes, intercepts, and standard errors of estimate among groups. *Standard 1.20* Where past research has	Validity generalization is not specifically addressed. However, sections of the *Guidelines* apply indirectly. *Section 14B(8)(b)* Evidence from other studies may be relied on for information about fairness if a local study is not technically feasible. *Section 8* Cooperative studies are encouraged.

Court Cases	Comments
Pegues v. Miss. State Empl. Serv. (1980) Court accepted the results of a utility analysis that the test demonstrated considerable value to the user. *Spurlock v. United Airlines (1972)* Court noted that where large risks because of hiring an unqualified applicant existed, proof of job-relatedness is less burdensome. Numerous court cases have struck down the use of rank ordering as discriminatory and have advocated cutoff scores instead. *Allen v. City of Mobile (1978) Louisville Black Police Officers Assoc. v. City of Louisville (1979) Ensley Branch of NAACP v. Seibels (1980) Guardians Assoc. NYC Police Dept. v. Civil Serv. Comm. (1980) In re Birmingham Employment (1985)* Rank-ordering applicants is not acceptable unless it can be proven that the test is accurate enough to distinguish between individuals. Pass-fail cutoff scores are acceptable.	Ultimately, utility analyses may prove to be useful by showing the practical value of a selection procedure, but only one case has relied on a true utility analysis. Likewise, they may be useful in gaining greater acceptance of rank ordering, which has not been well received by either the EEOC or the courts because of its greater tendency toward adverse impact.
Pegues v. Miss. State Empl. Serv. (1980) Expert testimony based on validity generalization was accepted by the court in lieu of a local validation study.	This is still a relatively new technique. The EEOC does not seem likely to accept the results of a validity generalization study without clear documentation that the jobs and situations are similar. Except for one case, *Pegues,* where testimony about validity generalization results was accepted by the court, there is little precedent on this issue.

(*continued*)

APPENDIX *(cont.)*

Method	*Standards*	*Guidelines*
	found evidence of differential prediction among groups, predictive bias should be included.	*Section 7* Validation and fairness evidence from other studies can be used where job analyses show the jobs and testing situations are similar.
Performance distribution assessment (chapter 9)	Not specifically addressed. However, the standards discussed for numerical and behavior-based rating scales would also apply to performance distribution assessment.	Not specifically addressed. However, the guidelines for numerical and behavior-based rating scales would also apply to performance distribution assessment.

References

Albemarle Paper Co. v. Moody. (1975). 422 U.S. 405.
Allen v. City of Mobile. (1978). 464 F. Supp. 433.
AERA/APA/NCME Joint Committee. (1985). *Standards for educational and psychological testing*. Washington, DC: American Psychological Association.
Anderson v. U.S. Steel Corp. (1979). 492 F.2d 132.
APA, Division of Industrial and Organizational Psychology. (1975). *Principles for the validation and use of personnel selection procedures*. Washington, DC: American Psychological Association.
Arvey, R. D. (1979). *Fairness in selecting employees*. Reading, MA: Addison-Wesley.
Banerjee v. Board of Trustees of Smith College. (1981). 648 F.2d 61.
Baxter v. Savannah Sugar Refining Corp. (1974). 495 F.2d 437.
Bernardin, H. J., & Beatty, R. W. (1984). *Performance appraisal: Assessing human behavior at work*. Boston, MA: Kent-Wadsworth.
Bernardin, H. J., & Cascio, W. F. (1984). *An annotated bibliography of court cases relevant to employment decisions (1980–1983)*. Boca Raton, FL: Florida Atlantic University.
Bigby v. City of Chicago. (1984). 38 FEP 844.
Blake v. City of Los Angeles. (1979). 595 F.2d 1367.
Bridgeport Guardians v. Bridgeport Police Dept. (1977). 431 F. Supp. 931.
Brito v. Zia Co. (1973). 478 F.2d 1200.
Byham, W. C. (1983). *Review of legal cases and opinions dealing with assessment centers and content validity* (rev. ed.). Pittsburgh, PA: Development Dimensions International.

Court Cases	Comments
Not specifically addressed. However, the court cases discussed for numerical and behavior-based rating scales would also apply to performance distribution assessment.	Comments appropriate to numerical rating scales and the behavior-based rating scales also apply to performance distribution assessment.

Cascio, W. F., & Bernardin, H. J. (1981). Implications of performance appraisal litigation for personnel decisions. *Personnel Psychology, 34,* 211–216.

Cintron v. Adams. (1978). 458 F. Supp. 43.

Connecticut v. Teal. (1982). 457 U.S. 440.

Craig v. County of Los Angeles. (1980). 626 F.2d 659.

Crawford v. Western Electric Co. (1980). 614 F.2d 1300.

Davis v. County of Los Angeles. (1977). 566 F.2d 1334.

Donaldson v. Pillsbury Co. (1977). 554 F.2d 825.

Dothard v. Rawlinson. (1977). 433 U.S. 321.

Dreher, G. F., & Sackett, P. R. (1981). Some problems applying content validity
evidence to assessment center procedures. *Academy of Management Review, 6,*
551–560.

Easley v. Anheuser-Busch, Inc. (1983). 572 F. Supp. 1138.

Ensley Branch of the NAACP v. Seibels. (1980). 449 U.S. 1061.

Equal Employment Opportunity Commission v. Aetna Insurance Co. (1980). 616 F.2d
719.

Equal Employment Opportunity Commission v. E. I. du Pont de Nemours & Co.
(1978). 445 F. Supp. 223.

Equal Employment Opportunity Commission v. Radiator Specialty Co. (1979). 610
F.2d 178.

Evans v. City of Evanston. (1985). 37 FEP 1290.

Feild, H. S., & Holley, W. H. (1982). The relationship of performance appraisal
characteristics to verdicts in selection employment discrimination cases. *Academy of Management Journal, 25,* 392–406.

Firefighters Institute for Racial Equality v. City of St. Louis. (1977). 549 F.2d 506.

Firefighters Institute for Racial Equality v. City of St. Louis. (1979). 19 FEP 1643.
Firefighters Institute for Racial Equality v. City of St. Louis. (1980). 616 F.2d 350.
Fox v. Washington. (1975). 396 F. Supp. 504.
Friend v. Leidinger. (1977). 446 F. Supp. 361.
Frink v. U.S. Navy. (1977). 609 F.2d 501.
Gilmore v. Kansas City Terminal Ry. (1975). 509 F.2d 48.
Griggs v. Duke Power Co. (1971). 401 U.S. 424.
Guardians Assoc. of the New York City Police Dept. v. Civil Service Commission. (1980). 630 F.2d 79.
Guy v. Peaches Records & Tapes, Inc. (1979). 477 F. Supp. 656.
Harless v. Duck. (1980). 619 F.2d 611.
Hereford v. Huntsville Board of Education. (1978). 574 F.2d 268.
Horace v. City of Pontiac. (1980). 624 F.2d 765.
Hunter, J. E., Schmidt, F. L., & Jackson, G. B. (1982). *Meta-analysis: Cumulating research findings across studies.* Beverly Hills, CA: Sage.
In re Birmingham Employment. (1985). 37 FEP 1.
James v. Stockham Valves & Fittings Co. (1977). 559 F.2d 310.
Jepsen v. Florida Board of Regents. (1980). 610 F.2d 1379.
Kirkland v. New York State Department of Correctional Services. (1974). 374 F. Supp. 1361; 520 F.2d 420.
Kleiman, L. S., & Durham, R. L. (1981). Performance appraisal, promotion, and the courts: A critical review. *Personnel Psychology, 34,* 103–121.
Kleiman, L. S., & Faley, F. (1978). Assessing content validity: Standards set by the court. *Personnel Psychology, 31,* 701–713.
Kunda v. Muhlenberg College. (1980). 621 F.2d 532.
Laffey v. Northwest Airlines, Inc. (1973). 366 F. Supp. 763.
League of United Latin American Citizens v. City of Santa Ana. (1976). 410 F. Supp. 873.
Lewis v. National Labor Relations Board. (1985). 36 FEP 1388.
Loiseau v. Department of Human Resources of the State of Oregon. (1983). 567 F. Supp. 711.
Louisville Black Police Officers Org. v. City of Louisville. (1979). 511 F. Supp. 825.
Marquez v. Omaha Dist. Sales Office, Ford Motor Co. (1971). 440 F.2d 1157.
Meadows v. Ford Motor Co. (1973). 62 F.R.D. 98.
Meyer v. Missouri State Highway Commission. (1977). 567 F.2d 804.
Milton v. Bell Laboratories, Inc. (1977). 428 F. Supp. 502.
Meirth v. Dothard. (1976). 418 F. Supp. 1169.
Mistretta v. Sandia Corp. (1977).
Movement for Opportunity & Equality v. General Motors Corp. (1980). 622 F.2d 1235.
Nath v. General Electric Co. (1977). 438 F. Supp. 213.
Norton, S. A. (1977). The empirical and content validity of assessment centers versus traditional methods for predicting managerial success. *Academy of Management Review, 2,* 442–453.
Norton, S. A. (1981). The assessment center process and content validity: A reply to Dreher and Sachett. *Academy of Management Review, 6,* 561–566.
Officers for Justice v. Civil Service Commission. (1975). 395 F. Supp. 378.

Parson v. Kaiser Aluminum & Chemical Corp. (1978). 575 F.2d 1374.

Patterson v. American Tobacco Co. (1976). 535 F.2d 257; cert. denied, 429 U.S. 920, 586 F.2d 300 (1978).

Pearlman, K., Schmidt, F. L., & Hunter, J. E. (1980). Validity generalization results for tests used to predict job proficiency and training success in clerical occupations. *Journal of Applied Psychology, 65*, 373–406.

Pegues v. Mississippi State Employment Service. (1980). 488 F. Supp. 239.

Pouncy v. Prudential Insurance Co. (1980). 499 F Supp. 427.

Ramirez v. Hofheinz. (1980). 619 F.2d 442.

Rich v. Martin-Marietta Corp. (1975). 522 F.2d 333.

Rivera v. City of Wichita Falls. (1982). 665 F.2d 531.

Robinson v. Union Carbide Corp. (1976). 538 F.2d 652.

Rowe v. General Motors Corp. (1972). 457 F.2d 348.

Sackett, P. R., & Dreher, G. F. (1981). Some misconceptions about content-oriented validation: A rejoinder to Norton. *Academy of Management Review, 6*, 567–568.

Sawyer v. Russo. (1979). 19 FEP 44.

Schlei, B. L., & Grossman, P. (1983). *Employment discrimination law* (2nd ed.). Washington, DC: Bureau of National Affairs.

Schmidt, F. L., Gast-Rosenberg, I., & Hunter, J. E. (1980). Validity generalization results for computer programmers. *Journal of Applied Psychology, 65*, 643–661.

Schmidt, F. L., & Hunter, J. E. (1977). Development of a general solution to the problem of validity generalization. *Journal of Applied Psychology, 62*, 529–540.

Schmidt, F. L., Hunter, J. E., & Caplan, J. R. (1981). Validity generalization results for two groups in the petroleum industry. *Journal of Applied Psychology, 66*, 261–273.

Schmidt, F. L., Hunter, J. E., & Pearlman, K. (1981). Task difference as moderators of aptitude test validity in selection: A red herring. *Journal of Applied Psychology, 66*, 156–185.

Schmidt, F. L., Hunter, J. E., Pearlman, K., & Shane, G. S. (1979). Further tests of the Schmidt-Hunter Bayesian validity generalization procedure. *Personnel Psychology, 32*, 257–281.

Sledge v. J. P. Stevens & Co. (1976). 16 FEP 1652.

Smith v. Troyan. (1975). 520 F.2d 492.

Solotoff, L. (1983). Legal brief concerning content validity. A legal overview: The assessment center content validation strategy an appropriate procedure in constructing and administering a selection procedure. In W. C. Byham, *Review of legal cases and opinions dealing with assessment centers and content validity* (Appendix A, pp. 1–5). Pittsburgh, PA: Development Dimensions International.

Spurlock v. United Air Lines, Inc. (1972). 475 F.2d 216.

Stallings v. Container Corp. of America. (1977). 75 F.R.D. 511.

Sweeney v. Board of Trustees of Keene State College. (1978). 569 F.2d 169.

Thomas v. City of Evanston. (1985). 610 F. Supp. 422.

Thompson v. McDonnell Douglas Corp. (1976). 416 F. Supp. 972.

Tillery v. Pacific Telephone Company. (1982). No. 80-0701, Slip on (N.D. Cal.), as summarized in Byham, 1983.

United States v. City of Chicago. (1977). 434, U.S. 875.

United States v. City of St. Louis. (1976). 410 F Supp. 948.

United States v. Lee Way Motor Freight, Inc. (1979). 625 F.2d 918.

United States v. South Carolina. (1978). 434 U.S. 1026.

U.S. Equal Employment Opportunity Commission, U.S. Civil Service Commission, U.S Department of Labor, & U.S. Department of Justice (1978). Uniform guidelines on employment selection procedures. *Federal Register, 43* (166), 38290–38309.

U.S. Equal Employment Opportunity Commission, U.S. Civil Service Commission, U.S. Department of Labor, & U.S Department of Justice (1979). Adoption of questions and answers to clarify and provide a common interpretation of the Uniform Guidelines on Employee Selection Procedures. *Federal Register, 44,* 11996–12009.

Vanguard Justice Society v. Hughes. (1984). 592 F. Supp. 245.

Wade v. Mississippi Coop. Extension Service. (1974). 372 F. Supp. 126.

Watkins v. Scott Paper Co. (1976). 530 F. 2d 1159.

Weahkee v. Perry. (1978). 587 F.2d 1256.

Williams v. Andersons. (1977). 562 F.2d 1081.

Young v. Edgcomb Steel Co. (1974). 499 F.2d 97.

Zahorik v. Cornell University. (1984). 729 F.2d 85.

PART 1

Methods & Methodological Issues

Part 1 reviews the methods used to conduct a performance assessment along with pertinent methodological issues. The topics covered are arranged sequentially according to some of the key steps in the process. A deliberate effort has been made to address the most important components or ingredients of a performance assessment and also the most pressing practical problems and thorny technical issues that one must confront in planning and executing the assessment.

TABLE 1. Major Design Considerations in a Performance Assessment

Question	Task(s)	Subject of Assessment	
		Employee	Student
What is to be measured?	Define the domain of behaviors/skills/ competencies	Job analysis	Domain specifications
Who will conduct the measurement?	Decide who will supply or collect the data	Superiors Subordinates Peers Self Outsiders Committee	Teacher/professor Counselor Psychologist Educational specialist Parents Self
How will the domain be measured?	Develop appropriate instruments	Tests Scales Checklists Questionnaires Inventories	Tests Scales Checklists Questionnaires Inventories
	Determine types of data and strategies for collection	Test data Biodata Personnel data Objective production data Judgmental data Work samples Miniature job training and evaluation Interview Assessment center	Test data Projects and reports Judgmental data Anecdotal records Developmental and medical histories

Table 1 provides a framework for identifying the contributions of chapters 1 through 5 to the design of the assessment. The basic questions that need to be answered are expressed as tasks and then defined for the subject of the assessment—employee or student. The first and, perhaps, most important question of *what* is to be measured is addressed in chapter 1. *Who* will conduct the measurement is dealt with in the first section of chapter 2. *How* the domain will be measured is answered in chapters 2 through 5, which examine numerical rating scales, behavior-based rating scales, performance tests, and assessment centers.

The remaining four chapters focus on the use of the data gathered from those tools. Chapter 6 presents strategies for giving feedback on assessment results to the assessee. The weighting of value judgments in the decision-making process is the subject of chapter 7. Chapter 8 reviews the technical validity considerations needed to determine the adequacy of predictor and criterion measures for personnel decisions, especially selection. Chapter 9 assembles many of the elements of the preceding chapters into a new quantitative performance appraisal system.

For ease of use by practitioners, chapters 1 through 8 have the same quadripartite structure: (1) "Introduction," (2) "Review of Methods," (3) "Advantages and Disadvantages of Alternatives," and (4) "Recommendations." Within this structure, the authors present a lucid, step-by-step outline of the various methods, with illustrative data where appropriate, then evaluate and compare their advantages and disadvantages, and finally make recommendations for the "best" or most promising approach(es). The structure of chapter 9 is slightly different inasmuch as it concentrates on a complete system rather than on an evaluation of one particular component.

1. JOB ANALYSIS

Sidney A. Fine

Introduction

Performance assessment is concerned with the evaluation of worker behaviors, including knowledges, skills, and abilities, that have been determined by job analysis to contribute to the quantity and quality of work performed. Job analysis methods for getting at the knowledges, skills, and abilities (KSAs) and establishing their relevance for particular tasks vary considerably (see McCormick, 1976, 1979). The ways in which they vary include the language they use, the training of the analysts, the rationale for relating work performed to KSAs, the methods for processing the data, and the communicability of the data. Ultimately, these variations affect such fundamental issues as who shall provide the data, the comprehensiveness of the data obtained, the reliability and validity of the data, the linkage between worker characteristics and job requirements, and the practicality or cost of obtaining the data. These are crucial issues. They have become even more important since the government and the courts have been playing a vital role in the determination of the fairness of employment practices. As a result of this government role, scholars have intensified their research of the various methods, comparing them, evaluating them, and seeking ways to improve them. This chapter shall briefly call attention to the findings of research, reiterate and define some of the salient issues in job analysis, recall some relevant history that throws important light on them, and describe the approach of functional job analysis (FJA) to these issues.

Review of Job Analysis Methods

One difference in job analysis methodology that has significantly affected the kinds of items used for performance appraisal has been whether the method focused on what got done (i.e., was work oriented) or whether it focused on what the worker did (i.e., was worker oriented). Worker-oriented methods such as McCormick's position analysis questionnaire (PAQ) (Jeanneret & McCormick, 1969; McCormick, Jeanneret, & Mecham, 1969; Mecham & McCormick, 1969) and Fleishman's (1975) ability requirements scales (ARS) are based on the notion that there is a finite set of dimensions—a taxonomy of aptitudes, abilities, or characteristics—that can be used to describe a job and that accounts for the variability of human performance. My functional job analysis approach (FJA) is

53

TABLE 1.1. Major Methods of Job Analysis

Task-based	Attribute-based	Behavior-based
Functional job analysis Task inventory/compre- hensive occupational data analysis programs Department of Labor task analysis	Functional job analysis Position analysis question- naire job element meth- od Ability requirements scales	Critical incident technique Position analysis questionnaire Functional job analysis

likewise based on the idea of a universal taxonomy of behaviors. The taxonomy proposed is derived from my analysis of work into three ordinal hierarchies of defined worker functions relating to things, data, and people. On the other hand, widely used methods like comprehensive occupational data analysis programs (CODAP) (Christal, 1974) and job element method (Primoff, 1975) are strictly empirical approaches. The former is task oriented, using checklists that can contain over one thousand items, while the latter is oriented toward behaviors that are critical to job success and which are collected from subject matter experts (SMEs).

Ash (1982) has classified seven commonly used methods by the type of information they yield. They are shown in Table 1.1. His task-based and attribute-based categories appear to correspond to the work- and worker-oriented categories. In addition, he has a behavior-based category apparently referring to action descriptions such as "analyzing information or data," which are free of specific content. Ash assigned critical incident technique, PAQ, and functional job analysis to this category.

Recently, Levine, Ash, Hall, and Sistrunk (1981) conducted an opinion survey among ninety-three experienced analysts concerning the effectiveness of seven job analysis methods for eleven organizational purposes and eleven practicality concerns. As they more or less expected, different methods were preferred for different purposes and for different practical circumstances, although FJA, PAQ, and CODAP appeared to be more generally preferred than some of the other methods. Perhaps their chief finding was that the analysts responding to their survey (who, although not a true sample, nevertheless work in a respectable variety of settings) prefer a multimethodological approach. The researchers had hypothesized that analysts would prefer a mix of task-, behavior-, and attribute-based approaches, but this was not the case. Good examples of the application of such a multimethodological approach are the studies conducted by Ash (1982) for condominium managers and by Sistrunk and Smith (1982) for criminal justice organizations. The fact that such studies can now be conducted and supported by government grants attests to the growing interest in and importance of job analy-

FIGURE 1.1. Job analysis in relation to personnel functions

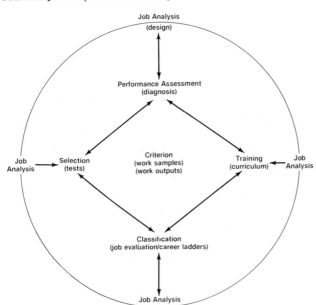

sis. Just ten to fifteen years ago, these studies could not have been carried out. For one thing, the various job analysis methods had not matured. Undoubtedly, this interest and developmental work has been spurred by government interventions such as the *Uniform Guidelines* (U.S. Equal Employment Opportunity Commission et al. 1978). However, there has been a simultaneous awakening of industrial psychologists to the technical importance of job analysis in the whole gamut of personnel operations.

The importance of job analysis is illustrated in Figure 1.1. The circle labeled "job analysis" is all pervasive, circumscribing and influencing a whole array of personnel functions. In the center is the criterion. For the criterion, job analysis suggests using a work sample or actual outputs as a measure of performance. Job analysis can also provide the behaviors that might be used to construct selection tests, the knowledges and abilities that need to be incorporated in training curricula, and the relevant dimensions for assessment and diagnosis of performance. The information on the basis of which job evaluation systems for compensation can be applied and career systems developed also depends on job analysis. All the data developed in these various personnel operations in turn become useful inputs to job design. Thus, as shown in Figure 1.1, job analysis provides the fundamental input for personnel operations.

Some background may shed further light on current issues in job analysis.

RECENT HISTORY

An understanding of the fundamental importance of job analysis was central to the Occupational Research Program of the United States Employment Service (USES), initiated in 1935 and directed by Carroll Shartle (Stead, Shartle, & Assoc., 1940). This program was designed to develop materials to implement the Wagner-Peyser Act, which established USES. It was one of the most comprehensive programs ever undertaken in the field of personnel research.[1]

One of the major tools it developed was the *Dictionary of Occupational Titles* (U.S. Federal Security Agency, 1939). The dictionary was intended as a tool for classifying workers according to their work experience so that they could be matched with employer job orders for placement. The Wagner-Peyser Act required that workers make themselves available for work, and only if a job could not be found could they become eligible for unemployment insurance. Thus, on one level, they were being matched for experience. But it was also recognized that even if a worker did not have specific experience, he or she nevertheless did have potential—namely, the skills and abilities or other attributes—for many of the job orders. Hence it was necessary to evaluate workers' potential as well as their experience, and a job order's worker characteristic requirements as well as the obvious specific content requirements. This need was the justification for the development of the General Aptitude Test Battery (GATB), for training vocational counselors, and for using worker characteristics and physical capacity requirements checklists with the job analysis schedule. The concept prevalent then as now was to match persons to jobs, worker characteristics to job requirements (Dunnette, 1982; Peterson & Bownas, 1982; Stead & Masincup, 1942; Stead, Startle, & Assoc., 1940). However, there was no clear idea of the correspondence between characteristics and requirements. To discover the commonalities in jobs in terms of both job requirements and worker characteristics became the objective of job family research.

Job families were designed to group jobs according to varying degrees of commonality with a critical or base job. The base job was analyzed for the work performed, expressed in the form of verbs such as "machining" or "carpentering," "welding" or "riveting." Quite a few verbs might be used to express the work performed. Other jobs, the descriptions of which contained the same verbs, were related to it; the greater the number of verbs that were the same or similar, the closer the relationship. Similarly matched were the forty-eight characteristics on the worker checklist adapted from the Viteles psychograph (Viteles, 1932), and the twenty-seven physical capacities and twenty-seven working conditions developed by the United States Bureau of Employment Security (1945). A base

---

1. I was on the staff of the Occupational Research Program from 1940 to 1959. From 1950 to 1959, I directed the development of the occupational classification system for the *Dictionary of Occupational Titles.*

TABLE 1.2. Components for the Functional Occupational Classification Project

Task-based	Attribute-based	Behavior-based
Working conditions—6 factors	Aptitudes—11 factors	Worker functions: What workers do
What got done— indefinite	Interests—10 factors	Things—3 levels
Specific vocational preparation—9 levels	Physical demands—7 factors	Data—6 levels
	Reasoning—6 levels	People—6 levels
	Math—5 levels	
	Language—6 levels	

job could have as many as twelve groups of related jobs with increasing commonality. Decreasing commonality was based on fewer and fewer common descriptive verbs and characteristics. Groups were organized as long as it was felt that the commonalities would shorten training for the base job.

These job families were compiled for more than ten years. Significant manpower policy decisions relating to the movement of workers from civilian to military jobs and back again to civilian jobs or to the keeping of workers in jobs that involved critical and scarce abilities were based on the job families.

Several lessons were learned from the development of job families: (1) the value of the verbs in bringing similar jobs together; (2) the extent to which estimated characteristics were the same for the individual jobs brought together by "what workers do" verbs, such as "operating," "setting up," "feeding machines"; and (3) the extent to which certain jobs continued to occur together in these groups in relation to different base jobs. All of these lessons made sense. Operationally, they seemed to point to certain potential generalizations that would make the matching job easier. This phenomenon can be regarded as an early version of validity generalization. Because of the careful attention to language ("descriptors" in the current jargon), the job families created without benefit of statistical analysis are still likely to hold up today. Very recent research indicates that descriptor types are the critical consideration in how job families are composed (Pearlman, 1980; Sistrunk & Smith, 1982), and that the statistical algorithm makes virtually no difference in the composition of job families (Cornelius & Lyness, 1980).

These same job family ingredients, enlarged in scope in 1950, became the basis for the scientific investigation to develop a new classification system for the dictionary and also the basis for functional job analysis. The worker characteristics checklist was expanded to include separate analysis for eleven aptitude factors, twelve temperament factors, ten interest factors, seven physical demand factors, and six working condition factors as well as separate lists of "what got done" and "what workers did" verbs (see Table 1.2). These latter verbs were the worker function verbs arranged in three hierarchies according to things, data, and people

FIGURE 1.2. FJA scales for controlling the language of task statement: Summary chart of worker function scales

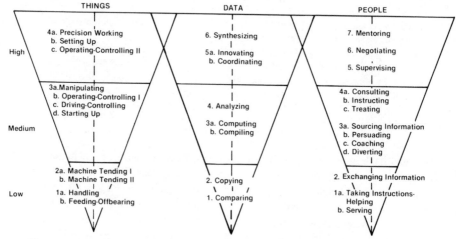

Notes

1. Each hierarchy is independent of the other. It would be incorrect to read the functions across the three hierarchies as related because they appear to be on the same level. The definitive relationship among functions is within each hierarchy, not across hierarchies. Some broad exceptions are outlined in note 2.

2. Data are central since a worker can be assigned even higher data functions even though things and people functions remain at the lowest level of their respective scales. When a things function is at the third level, e.g., precision working, the data function is likely to be at least compiling or computing. When a people function is at the fourth level, e.g., consulting, the data function is likely to be at least analyzing and possibly innovating or coordinating. Similarly for supervising and negotiating. Mentoring in some instances can call for synthesizing.

3. Each function in its hierarchy is defined to include the lower numbered functions. This is more or less the way it was found to occur in reality. It was most clear-cut for things and data and only a rough approximation in the case of people.

4. The functions separated by a comma are separate functions on the same level, separately defined. The empirical evidence did not support a hierarchical distinction.

5. The hyphenated functions, taking instructions–helping, operating-controlling, etc., are single functions.

6. The indented functions in the things hierarchy are machine oriented as opposed to the hand- or hand tool-oriented functions (handling, manipulating, or precision working). They can be considered as parallel hierarchies.

(Figure 1.2). This development emerged from the job family work and purports to be a taxonomy of worker-oriented behaviors (Fine, 1955). These were the verbs that seemed to relate consistently to certain aptitude and interest patterns of groups of jobs, groups that repeatedly showed up in the same form in different job families.

Additional components that provided useful data were "general educational development" (consisting of three separate scales for reasoning, mathematics, and language) and "specific vocational preparation" (a nine-level scale). Four thousand jobs, an 18 percent sample of the approximately 23,000 in the second edition of the dictionary, were rated for their estimated requirements on each of the components for successful performance. The estimations were the product of judgments of trained analysts using a manual that contained task benchmarks for each component rated. The benchmarks had been developed previously for each rating scale in preliminary trial studies that established the efficiency of the procedures and the reliability of the ratings. Recent work indicates that judgmental methods of synthesizing ability and task information appear as useful as the more rigorous quantitative approaches for selection purposes. A quarter of a million data points were generated by a staff of about fifteen trained analysts over a period of three years (Fine & Heinz, 1957). For the first time, in 1953, electromechanical data processing equipment was brought into use for large-scale research. One result was the "Green Monster," otherwise known as *Estimates of Worker Trait Requirements for 4,000 Jobs Defined in the Dictionary of Occupational Titles* (U.S. Department of Labor, 1955). It was an instant best-seller when published in 1955. Five thousand copies disappeared in a matter of weeks, to everyone's surprise and dismay considering the unfinished state of the research. Another printing was required. Evidently there was a real hunger and need for such information and the *Estimates* filled that need. The ultimate product of this research was a functional occupational classification system that was the basis for the third edition of the *Dictionary of Occupational Titles* (U.S. Department of Labor, 1965), the current fourth edition of the dictionary (U.S. Department of Labor, 1977), and the 1973 *Canadian Classification and Dictionary of Occupations.*

This history indicates that the challenge of matching people and jobs today is still conceptualized in the same way it was fifty years ago. For example, Dunnette (1982) states that achieving productivity in work settings is ultimately a problem of "improving the match between worker characteristics and job requirements." Peterson and Bownas (1982) acknowledged that there is another component to the "human resources allocation" problem, namely, "information about task environments." They nevertheless focus on tasks and requirements and describe an optimal grand design for linking a human characteristic taxonomy with a task/job taxonomy in a large-scale predictive validity study. After combing the literature, they list fifty-one human characteristics that are more or less factorially pure. These characteristics cover cognitive abilities (12), psychomotor abilities (18), personality (25), and vocational preferences (6). These factors have been drawn from the work of McCormick with the PAQ, and of Fleishman, Browne, and Howarth, and Holland. A careful examination of each of these instruments will show significant borrowings from the functional occupational classification project.

Functional job analysis is the job analysis method that grew out of the functional occupational classification project. Attention is devoted to this method for three reasons: (1) it derives from the mainstream of the job analysis research carried out at USES since 1936; (2) much of the FJA developmental work of recent years is buried in unpublished research reports; and (3) discussing this method in some detail will perhaps provide a basis for understanding why it has shown up as a preferred method in recent research.

A good place to begin is to answer the question: What data should job analysis focus on? To know what to focus on, particularly as it relates to performance assessment, is to have some idea of what the whole picture of a job is like and what the components of the whole picture might be. This is a crucial consideration in FJA, as can be seen from Figure 1.3.

Figure 1.3 shows the work system as consisting of three interacting components, namely the worker, the work organization, and the work. The worker is defined in terms of experience, education, aptitudes, interests, temperament, and physical capacities. The work organization is defined in terms of purpose, goals, and objectives relating to a specific technology, and of resources, constraints, and physical, social, and environmental conditions. The work is defined in terms of things, data, people functions, performance and training requirements. The interaction of these components is directed at productivity and worker growth and satisfaction. The criteria for performance emerge from the interaction.

Thus, from the point of view of FJA, job analysis for performance assessment must pick up the results of the interaction and all of the relevant inputs to that interaction. The issue is not whether to be work oriented or worker oriented. Job analysis must be both, and it must focus on the environment of the work organization as well. The job analyst must understand and be aware of all three components and capture them in his or her observations. FJA is the only job analysis method that provides for such an approach.[2] It does this in its definition of a task, as shown in Table 1.3, and in the procedure prescribed for writing a task statement.

Thus, the behavior (action) is within the focus of the work and must be reliably translatable to a specific set of functions. The result derives directly from the objective of the work organization. The moderators relate to the capability or potential of the worker to deal with the job content and meet the requirements of the result. Thus the task is a minisystem, an organic part of the overall system. Figure 1.4 shows a sample of such a task.

When a task is written according to the schema just described, certain consequences result. The performance dimensions are directly derivable. They

2. It is no accident that FJA is listed under each of the three categories of Table 1.1, namely, task-based, attribute-based, and behavior-based job analysis.

FIGURE 1.3. A systems approach to manpower planning

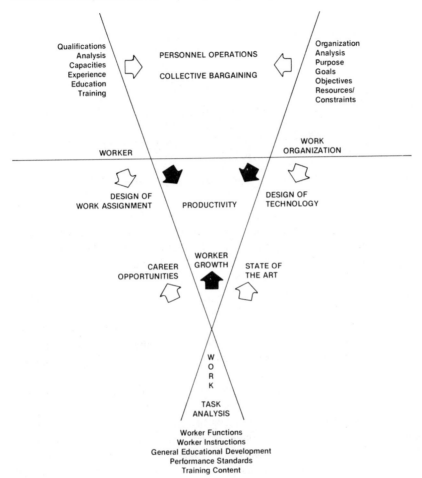

are self-evident and job related, as is the training necessary to achieve those standards. This is expressed in the following paradigm: "To do this task, to these standards, the worker needs this training." These very same data become the material for training curricula. Thus, using the functional performance language of FJA, job requirements and worker qualifications are directly related.

Another important consequence of writing tasks in this manner is that they have permanence, inasmuch as the task captures an integral part of the work flow. So long as the work is performed as described within the system, the task is a permanent unit in the sequence of operations. A given task can be eliminated from a job assignment because of a change of technology or change of work flow, but the

TABLE 1.3. Definition and Schematic of an FJA Task Statement

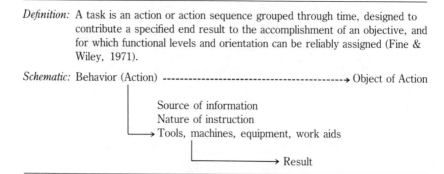

Definition: A task is an action or action sequence grouped through time, designed to contribute a specified end result to the accomplishment of an objective, and for which functional levels and orientation can be reliably assigned (Fine & Wiley, 1971).

Schematic: Behavior (Action) --→ Object of Action

> Source of information
> Nature of instruction
> Tools, machines, equipment, work aids
>
> → Result

task as something done in a process remains viable. Someone or something else must accomplish the result of that task for the work to be done. Thus, once tasks are written, the task statements become part of a permanent inventory that can be put into a computer, printed on lists, and distributed to incumbents to verify, add to, change, or delete. In fact, this last action is the validation procedure of FJA in which incumbents, after reviewing the inventory of tasks, confirm that the inventory covers 95 percent of their job assignment. It is important not to confuse FJA task inventories with checklists that do not provide the kinds of information amenable to job descriptions. FJA task banks now exist for a great many common work activities, such as those involved in police work, corrections, courts, mental health, social welfare, heavy equipment operation, engineering, electronic technology, oil and gas drilling, and merchant shipping. Sadly enough, because of lack of awareness of the existence of these task banks, the same analyses are repeated over and over again. Additional benefits of FJA task banks are that the enormous problem of maintaining job descriptions is minimized and job descriptions are written by simply integrating task statements appropriate to particular job assignments.

How does the map of the work system (Figure 1.3) help with regard to performance assessment? It points to what is well known—the complexity of the criterion. As is perhaps evident from this paradigm, and as Thorndike pointed out long ago (1949, p. 121), although a single criterion, a so-called bottom-line criterion, can be formulated, it is not realistic. Smith has stated, "No single measure can fully express success or failure" (1976, p. 747). Two persons may achieve equivalent total performance with quite different patterns of behavior, thus requiring evaluation on the basis of different measures. Furthermore, statistical analysis of sets of criterion measures rarely yields a single factor. Again the paradigm referred to may suggest why this occurs.

Often, the criterion for performance is a productivity output criterion

FIGURE 1.4. Sample task statement

TO DO THIS TASK

Data	People	Things	Data	People	Things	Reas.	Math.	Lang.	
W.F.—LEVEL			W.F.—ORIENTATION		INSTR.	G.E.D.			TASK NO.
3B	1A	2B	70%	5%	25%	2	3	1	4

GOAL: (To be completed by individual user)	OBJECTIVE: (To be completed by individual user)

TASK: Types/transcribes standard form letter, including specified information from records provided, following S.O.P. (standard operating procedure) for form letter, but adjusting standard form as required for clarity and smoothness, etc., in order to prepare letter for mailing.

TO THESE STANDARDS

PERFORMANCE STANDARDS

Descriptive:
• Types with reasonable speed and accuracy.
• Format of letter is correct.
• Any changes/adjustments are made correctly.

Numerical:
• Completes letter in X period of time.
• No uncorrected typing, mechanical, or adjustment errors per letter.
• Fewer than X omissions of information per X no. letters typed.

THE WORKER NEEDS THIS TRAINING

TRAINING CONTENT

Functional:
• How to type: letters.
• How to transcribe material, correcting mechanical errors.
• How to combine two written sets of data into one.

Specific:
• How to obtain records and find information in them.
• Knowledge of S.O.P. for standard letter format: how/where to include information.
• Knowledge of information required in letter.
• How to use particular typewriter provided.

(Muckler, 1982). Such criteria are eagerly sought. When found, they are typically so riddled with contingencies that they are of limited usefulness. And so one resorts to overall supervisory ratings, which are so general as to be equally limited in their usefulness.

Illustrated in Table 1.4 is a rating scale developed to deal with multiple inputs, in this case, a power dispatcher in an electric utility company. The indicated performance dimensions were ascertained to be relevant for this job by a modified

TABLE 1.4. Performance Dimensions for System Operator in Power Plant: Example of Multidimensional Performance Criterion

Performance Dimensions	Other Performance Aspects
1. Interpersonal interactions	1. Technical job knowledge
2. Analyzing problems and making decisions	2. Leadership/supervisory ability
3. Organizing/coordinating activities	3. Concern for safety
4. Electrical concepts	4. Concern for costs
5. System apparatus and procedures	5. Communication
6. Monitoring/attention to detail	6. Adaptability/versatility
7. Mathematical concepts	7. Quality of work

functional job analysis. Clearly, some of these dimensions relate to knowledge, some to physical, mental, and interpersonal skills, and some to adaptability to environmental conditions and personal health. In addition, there is an overall rating. A fairly jagged profile for most incumbents would probably result,

As noted earlier, performance assessment is undertaken in part to assist people in sharpening their skills. This sharpening of skills is its diagnostic function. To the ordinary observer, the performance of a Perlman or a Horowitz on the concert stage is likely to seem perfect or near perfect. However, a music critic, whose senses and powers of observation are more finely tuned than the ordinary observer's, is likely to differentiate among the skills, commenting not only on technique, but on the knowledge implicit in the interpretation, the relative ability of each performer, the concentration required to master certain difficult passages, and the rapport achieved with the audience. In effect, what the critic is doing is evaluating the performance in terms of functional, specific content, and adaptive skills—the universe of skills that define any performance (Fine, 1967).

The complete performance. Figure 1.5 depicts the whole process of performance. In the center is the unanalyzed, holistic work performance of persons doing their jobs and getting work done. Perhaps they are not doing it well enough and they need help to do it better. How shall this be communicated to them?

The everyday terms "knowledge," "skills," "abilities," "effort," "responsibility," and "working conditions" would appear to be the ones to use for this communication. These terms have come to be used in legislation, such as the Equal Pay Act and Title VII, and have become the everyday language of communicators about job and worker requirements and qualifications. Even when more sophisticated analytic concepts are used, they need to be translated to these terms in order to communicate with the workers, the courts, and the lay public. Instead of forcing a translation, we can use them as components of behavioral analysis and define them operationally so that the vocabularies in each instance are

FIGURE 1.5. A holistic concept of performance skill requirements

distinct from one another. Knowledge, skills, and abilities have a direct bearing on the job content or output of a job. Effort, responsibility, and working conditions relate more to the environmental situation or job context to which the individual worker must adapt.

All of the definitions cannot be provided here, but as Figure 1.5 illustrates, *knowledge* relates to specific "know hows" encompassing the material, product, subject matter, or service, the technology, the organizational procedures, the machines, tools, equipment, or work aids. Knowledges are expressed as nouns. *Skills* relate to "how to" functions in the things, data, people hierarchies of functional job analysis. They are expressed as gerunds, thus serving as both nouns and verbs. *Abilities* relate to the qualities (adjectives or adverbs) or quantities (numbers) that need to be attained by the worker to produce a satisfactory output. These are in effect the work organization's operational criteria for performance assessment as they relate to the work organization's output. *Effort* refers to the concentration (mental), exertion (physical), or stress (emotional) that would seem to be required in the work situation. *Responsibility* refers to the prescription/discretion mix in the instructions and also to involvement with consequences as they may affect money, tangibles, and people. *Working conditions* relate to physical demands and to environmental and social conditions.

Together these six behavioral areas define the three kinds of skill—functional, specific content, and adaptive—that interact to make up a whole performance. Thus FJA can be seen as specifically adapted for performance assessment, both in terms of grasping the totality of performance, diagnosing it, and communicating it to the incumbent.

Data gathering procedure. The data gathering procedure of FJA, which was originally rather complex, is now, after fifteen years of experience, really quite simple. It is useful and interesting to note the similarity between the procedure outlined immediately below and the multimethodological procedure developed by Sistrunk and Smith (1982) for the study of criminal justice occupations.

Step 1: *Preliminaries.* Preparations for FJA can be divided into two parts:
Job analyst preparation. Job analysts prepare for job analysis by reviewing existing materials and data, where available, of the job to be analyzed. They may prepare one or more sample tasks for illustrative purposes.
SME invitation. Subject matter experts (SMEs), including supervisors and experienced workers, are invited to a place where they can be interviewed as a group. The SMEs should represent a range of employment situations. The invitation explains that they come as advisors and experts to the job analyst, and that they will be occupied one to two days.
Step 2: *Group interview.* The agenda for the group interview is roughly as follows:
First hour: *Orientation.* Welcome, introductions, statement of purpose, and brief orientation to the FJA structure of a task. This is done with transparencies of Table 1.3 and Figure 1.4. Illustrations could include similar formulations for the work of the SMEs in the group. The SMEs are told that they will be involved in describing their tasks in a similar manner with the guidance of the job analyst, that each task will be written on a flip chart and hung around the walls for perusal.
Second hour: *List Outputs, knowledges, skills, and abilities.* SMEs are asked to describe their outputs—the work they are expected to get done. This rarely extends beyond a half dozen to a dozen categories of items. These categories of items are written on a flip chart in whatever order they appear to come up. The list of outputs becomes the guide for testing coverage.

It is also useful to have the group separately list (a) the knowledge they draw on, including sources of information; (b) the skills and abilities they use, as they see them without attempting to differentiate them; and (c) the machines, tools, equipment, and work aids they use to get work done. These lists then serve as a reference as the workshop proceeds with task generation.

Third hour: *Initiate task bank.* SMEs select what they consider the number one output and, with a stimulus such as the following, start producing tasks: "What is the first thing that happens to get you started at producing the output you have decided is most important? What is your first initiating task?" The process starts slowly, but by the end of the morning, if not sooner, the group is moving at a productive pace.

Step 3: *Creating the task bank.* The SMEs continue to produce tasks, proceeding systematically through all of the outputs until they are content that 95 percent of their job is covered. The analyst can usually tell when the group is running out of steam, at which point he or she can ask: "What percentage of your job have you covered? 60 percent, 75 percent, 80 percent?" Usually one or two will give a percentage lower than 95 percent. The analyst then responds, "OK. What is not yet covered?" Sometimes this elicits more tasks or some isolated tasks that only one or two people do. These too are recorded. All the SMEs must agree that 95 percent of their job is covered.

Step 4: *Grouping of tasks.* The posted task bank usually reveals that some tasks performed for one output are almost identical to tasks performed for another output. The group may decide to gather such tasks together for the purpose of developing performance standards. They usually come around to this point of view after trying other ways of developing standards such as leaving the tasks grouped by output.

In any case, tasks are grouped for the purpose of zeroing in on critical performance standards by either (a) bringing together charts containing tasks that relate to significant performance standards or (b) listing the numbers of tasks that should be grouped on a separate chart.

Step 5: *Performance dimensions.* Performance dimensions are introduced by the analyst with the stimulus, "How do you know/recognize excellent work/ satisfactory work/ poor work for this group of tasks?" "What do you see or what happens?" The SMEs then proceed to propose performance dimensions with recognizable benchmarks reflecting quantity or quality. They continue this for each group of tasks. The analyst must insist that for every proposed performance dimension, the SMEs point to tasks or aspects of tasks that reflect them.

Figure 1.6 shows the performance dimensions categories independently arrived at by SMEs for ten professional jobs in the Department of Housing and Urban Development. What is especially interesting is how similar performance dimensions show up independently for tasks that are similar in functional content. This commonality is a further indication of the promise that exists for validity generalization through the use of FJA methodology.

Critical Elements[*]	Occupations[**]									
	AO	CP	CPDRep	CCA	DR	EO	FE	NCARep	PS	S
Reviewing/Evaluating/Recording	x									
Analyzing/Evaluating/Reviewing		x								
Reviewing/Monitoring			x							
Reviewing/Analyzing/Recommending				x		x				
Reviewing/Evaluating					x					
Reviewing/Evaluating/Analyzing							x			
Reading/Reviewing/Monitoring								x		
Conceptualization/Review/Writing									x	
Meeting/Conferring/Representing				x			x			
Communicating orally/Providing information				x						
Providing information					x					
Meeting/Conferring/Negotiating/Representing						x				
Contact/Meeting/Discussing								x		
Conferring/Meeting									x	
Working with people face-to-face										x
Gathering data/information				x	x					
Information gathering, research, and data base mgmt.							x			
Resource development/Information gathering								x		
Giving and securing information										x
Writing/Documenting		x					x	x		
Writing			x							
Recording/Documenting/Writing				x						
Writing/Documenting/Completing forms					x					
Writing/Documenting/Information gathering						x				
Writing/Composing										x
Training				x			x	x		
Consulting/Advising/Providing information	x									
Briefing/Negotiating/Consulting		x								
Providing advice/guidance/technical assistance						x				
Providing technical assistance, advice, or guidance							x			
Providing technical assistance/Consulting								x		
Representation										x
Monitoring/Tracking/Following through	x									
Program management/Monitoring		x								
Monitoring						x				
Time management/Self-development	x	x								
Planning/Resource use			x						x	
Time management				x					x	
Time management/Professional development					x		x			
Workload management and professional enhancement						x				
Planning/Self-development								x		
Scheduling/Time management										x

[*]Critical elements grouped together reveal a similarity in the kinds of tasks assigned to the element and in their performance standards. The following elements were unique to their occupations and therefore were not grouped: Observing/Inspecting (Design Representative), Data development (Construction Cost Analyst); Typing, Telephoning, General clerical, Mail handling, Filing, Dictating/Transcribing, Copying/Duplication, Word processing (Secretary); Identifying needs; and Developing/Initiating procedures or actions (Administrative Officer).

[**]The following abbreviations are used for the HUD occupations analyzed: AO: Administrative Officer; CP: Community Planner; CPDRep: Community Planning and Development Representative; CCA: Construction Cost Analyst; DR: Design Representative; EO: Environmental Officer; FE: Field Economist; NCARep: Neighborhood and Consumer Affairs Representative; PS: Policy Specialist; S: Secretary.

Step 6: *Reliability.* The tasks are listed by output on a task inventory and edited for smoothness of expression. Listed separately along with each group of tasks are the performance standards. These lists are submitted by mail to the SMEs for final approval. They are free to change, add, or delete tasks and to confer with supervisors and colleagues.

Step 7: *Validity.* The returned inventories are put in final form and sent to an appropriate sample of SMEs for validation. The individuals in the sample are also free to change, add, etc. They are required to confirm that 95 percent of their assignments are covered within the final task list.

Every time FJA is conducted as described, participants respond with statements like, "This is the first time we have fully understood our own jobs and felt it possible for outsiders to understand them as well." An effective communication has taken place, a creative sharing. The task bank is truly the creation of the incumbents.

FJA rationale for comparison of jobs. Pressure is mounting to compare jobs on the basis of fair and equitable criteria to help overcome what is considered unfair compensation. This comparison process has been referred to as "comparable worth." But how do you compare vastly different jobs? Is this not like comparing apples and pears? In effect, the answer is, They cannot be compared unless dimensions common to all jobs can be established and measurements can be made along these dimensions that are reliable and valid. The identification of these dimensions is the role performed by FJA. All jobs in the entire economy have been classified according to FJA dimensions in the latest edition of the *Dictionary of Occupational Titles.* However, it will take further developmental work to adapt FJA as a method for general comparison and measurement. Its potential for this purpose is outlined briefly below.

The rationale of FJA for comparison of jobs is guided by the concepts expressed in the Equal Pay Act of 1963. This statute provides for the comparison of jobs in terms of the skill, effort, and responsibility required for performance and the similarity of working conditions under which they are performed. The statute recognizes that in comparing the requirements of jobs to establish equality, it is necessary to scrutinize each job as a whole and to look at the job over a full work cycle. The skill, effort, and responsibility elements analyzed are the performance requirements of the job, not characteristics that a worker might happen to have or the excellence with which he or she might perform.

FJA encompasses the dimensions of skill, effort, and responsibility in the following manner. Skill in FJA is defined in terms of physical (things), mental (data), and interpersonal (people) functions and combined with the concept "effort." Each functional level is augmented by the effort level that that particular component requires, namely strength for physical, reasoning and/or math for mental, and language for interpersonal skills.

Responsibility is represented by the worker instructions scale, which delineates the mix of prescription and discretion in any job. As indicated earlier, prescription reflects the specified standards and methods for producing outputs. Discretion relates to the range of judgment allowed where specifications are not available.

Training and education, which are sometimes included in a definition of skill, are treated separately by FJA and are reflected in the specific vocational preparation scale. This is a nine-point scale illustrated with well over a hundred benchmark job descriptions to support the time levels of the scale.

The FJA approach to calculating a job value for job content is based on the proposition that all jobs demand whole-person involvement. Workers in every job are involved to some degree physically, mentally, and interpersonally with three general categories of objects: things, data, and people. All workers are in some degree involved with machines, tools, or equipment (things); information or ideas (data); and clients, customers, or coworkers (people). The degrees of involvement sum to 100 percent. (This is the "orientation" concept defined below.) Tasks can be described in terms of a small number of patterns of behavior (functions) that in turn describe how workers perform in relation to things, data, and people. These functions are listed in the worker function scales, shown in Figure 1.2.

These worker function scales are ordinal scales that proceed from the simple to the complex. The benchmarks in each scale are defined so that each higher level on a scale includes (that is, comprehends) the lower levels but excludes the higher levels (that is, does not include the additional difficulty factors of the higher levels). Relating the data obtained for a particular job task to a particular benchmark on a scale defines that task in terms of the total scale, in other words, in terms of the functions included as well as those excluded.

The things, data, and people hierarchies provide a means of measuring and comparing tasks in terms of (1) level and (2) orientation. *Level* provides a measure of the relative complexity of a task in comparison to other tasks. *Orientation* provides a measure of a worker's relative involvement with things, data, and people. This relative involvement is obtained by focusing on the performance standards for the job and by assigning percentages according to where the emphasis is placed—on things, data, or people. The percentages (orientation weights) are assigned in multiples of 5 percent (see Table 1.5). Thus level and orientation provide a measure of a worker's total mental, physical, and interpersonal involvement in the tasks of a job.

All jobs require workers to use reasoning, math, and language to communicate, understand, and deal with the information involved in their work. These attributes (reasoning, math, and language), like things, data, and people, cut across all jobs and therefore reveal difficulty or complexity. Reasoning, math, and language, which are also ordinal scales, are set forth in Table 1.6.

Similarly, all jobs involve instructions specifying results or outcomes. These instructions contain both prescription (that which is prescribed or specified) and

TABLE 1.5. Orientation Weights

Percentage Assigned*	Value	Weight
60–90	High	3
35–55	Medium	2
5–30	Low	1

*Minimum and maximum percentages that can be assigned are 5% and 90%.

TABLE 1.6. Scales of General Educational Development

Reasoning	Math	Language
6		6
5	5/6	5
4	4	4
3	3	3
2	2	2
1	1	1

Note: For definitions see Appendix A.

TABLE 1.7. Strength Scale

Physical Effort	Weight
Very heavy	5
Heavy	4
Medium	3
Light	2
Sedentary	1

discretion (that which is judgmental). The level of prescription or discretion is scaled from 1 to 8 (see Appendix B).

Two additional scales of difficulty/complexity measure strength (which elaborates on the physical involvement) and specific vocation preparation. These scales are shown in Tables 1.7 and 1.8. Specific vocational preparation (SVP) is a nine-point scale that reflects the training and experience necessary for a particular position in order for the incumbent to reach normal production (RNP).

TABLE 1.8. Scale of Specific Vocational Preparation Time (SVP) to Reach Normal Production (RNP)

Level	Training plus Experience
9	Over 10 years
8	Over 4 years, up to and including 10 years
7	Over 2 years, up to and including 4 years
6	Over 1 year, up to and including 2 years
5	Over 6 mos., up to and including 1 year
4	Over 3 mos., up to and including 6 mos.
3	Over 30 days, up to and including 3 mos.
2	Beyond short demonstration, up to and including 30 days
1	Short demonstration only

TABLE 1.9. Calculation of FJA Job Values for Comparison

Physical Skill/Effort
Things level
+ Strength level
× Orientation =   Subtotal

Mental Skill/Effort
Data level
+ Reasoning level
+ Math
× Orientation =   Subtotal

Interpersonal Skill/Effort
People level
+ Language level
× Orientation =   Subtotal

Responsibility
Worker instructions level =   Subtotal

Specific Vocational Preparation
Reach normal production
(amount of time) =   Subtotal
                           Total

By matching the job information obtained during the job analysis against the benchmarks that define levels on the scales, numerical values are obtained that can be summed and multiplied according to the formulas provided in Table 1.9. The relative difficulty/complexity among different jobs can now be compared since the values relate to common dimensions. These comparisons can be made on the basis of the broad factors (physical skill/effort; mental skill/effort, etc.) or on the basis of total scores. For job evaluation purposes, individual organizations might find it desirable to assign differential weights to each of these factors.

Advantages and Disadvantages of FJA

Some of the advantages of FJA have been described in the foregoing sections and are summarized below.

1. In general, if the initiation of a job analysis is intended to develop data for such personnel purposes as job descriptions and the delineation of knowledge, skill, and ability requirements for recruitment and selection, there is no better method. It generates precisely the information required in an efficient way, say, about two days for a job category.
2. It works well for developing data for achievement and performance tests focused on job content. The task data translate directly to either oral trade questions ("how to" and "know how" knowledges) or skill situations, especially performance, on machines and equipment.
3. FJA is an excellent means for developing performance standards, again with relation to job content. The paradigm "To do this task, to these standards, the worker needs this training" establishes the task relevance of the standards and the degree to which they must be achieved for satisfactory performance. I prefer to use FJA in conjunction with critical incidents, the former to provide insight into the structured aspect of jobs and the latter for their relatively unstructured, more dynamic aspects.
4. FJA is an effective way for establishing curriculum guidelines and course content directed at training workers to meet standards for particular jobs. Considering that the data for training are gathered simultaneously with task data, it is probably the most cost-effective method available. The training data have served me and others as scenarios for films, film strips, and lesson plans.
5. FJA produces permanent task information that, when used in inventories for survey purposes, makes it easy to track changes in the task mix of individual workers as well as changes in technology; for example, functions tend to remain constant although ways of performing them may change (an analytic function inherent in the skills of a craftsman may be performed by a cybernetic piece of equipment tended by a machine operator). The permanence of the task data makes it possible to cut short the costly repetition of job analyses, frequently for the same jobs.
6. FJA does not require any complex statistical analysis to establish validity. The incumbents review the work of the analysts and then attest to the coverage, the wording, and the formulation.
7. The reliability of the meaning (operational consequences) of an FJA task

statement can be easily established by using the ten measures available with which to rate the tasks. More than merely establishing reliability, the measures point to missing, incorrect, or ambiguous information.

8. FJA produces perhaps the most communicable information about productivity. Since each task ends with a result and the results must add up to required outputs, management can track the efficiency and effectiveness with which jobs are designed to achieve management objectives, goals, and purposes.

9. FJA has been used to predict technological change. The hierarchies of things, data, and people functions provide options of how things can be done. Nowadays, practically all work functions can be performed either by workers or machines or varied combinations of the two. Given a particular organizational and economic situation (resources, constraints, geography, logistics), it is possible to design and redesign systems to deliver the products.

10. Because FJA involves a taxonomy of functions that purport to describe all the possible (distinguishable/describable) ways that persons relate to the objects of work (things, data, and people) and these functions occur in ordinal hierarchies from simple to complex, it is possible to compare and relate functions (behaviors) across jobs, regardless of content, and across cultures. These characteristics have considerable usefulness for investigations into "validity generalization" in test development and into "comparable worth" in job evaluation.

The primary disadvantage of FJA is that it takes one week of basic training plus about six months of supervised experience to learn to use it effectively. No special graduate background is required, although courses in industrial and organizational psychology can be helpful. Perhaps the abilities most useful to an FJA analyst are his or her proficiency with the English language and skill in helping people to express themselves.

Additional limitations relate to the scales. They are functional scales and are not intended to be factorially pure, although there is some support for the unidimensionality of the things, data, people scales (Mosel, Fine, & Boling, 1960). The scales, furthermore, are not of uniform ordinality despite the attempt of the definition of functions to achieve this level of measurement. The weakest of the three scales is the people scale. However, these limitations have not hindered the use of the scales for the various purposes listed previously.

Recommendations

Job analysis needs to provide the essential information about worker behavior for performance assessment. This information must be reliable, valid, communicable, and operational if it is to be useful. It must involve a minimum of inference from analytical categories to the knowledge, skills, and abilities of everyday behavior. The problems inherent in this challenge to job analysis have been around from the beginning of its use. The attack upon these problems has not changed very much, as far as the mainstream of psychological research is concerned. The attack has mainly been empirical, factorial, and analytical. Functional job analysis alone has taken a theoretical, holistic, systems approach by drawing upon the common use of language to sort out essential information that is not only reliable and valid, but also produces task banks of permanent usefulness. When applied to performance assessment, FJA generates performance dimensions closely associated with universal performance functions that relate to things, data, and people. Its conceptualization of three kinds of skills—functional, specific content, and adaptive—is singularly effective as far as selection and training are concerned. Its products in the form of task banks and performance tests have proven acceptable to the courts. Several of the theoretical formulations of functional job analysis such as things, data, and people, the three kinds of skills, the worker functions, and their definitions have been widely adapted in career counseling and personnel psychology with, and without, appropriate acknowledgment. This adoption or imitation may be either an acceptance of its soundness or merely an indication of its communicability and convenience. Nevertheless, FJA requires further research so that experience with the method can be fed back to practitioners.

One area of particular interest is that of validity generalization (see Linn & Dunbar, chapter 8). It might be especially useful for two or three job analysis methods to be used to demonstrate the degree of overlap as well as the extent of difference in the functional and specific content KSAs of the jobs involved in a validity generalization study. FJA has already been used by itself in one such study (Caplan et al., 1981) and would be a suitable method along with others such as PAQ, CODAP, and critical incidents for follow-up.

APPENDIX A. SCALES OF GENERAL EDUCATIONAL DEVELOPMENT

Reasoning Development Scale

The reasoning development scale is concerned with knowledge and ability to deal with theory versus practice, abstract versus concrete, and many versus few variables.

LEVEL 1
Has the commonsense understanding to carry out simple one- or two-step instructions in the context of highly standardized situations.

Recognizes unacceptable variations from the standard and takes emergency action to reject inputs or stop operations.

LEVEL 2
Has the commonsense understanding to carry out detailed but uninvolved instructions where the work involves a *few* concrete/specific variables in or from standard/typical situations.

LEVEL 3
Has the commonsense understanding to carry out instructions where the work involves several concrete/specific variables in or from standard/typical situations.

LEVEL 4
Has knowledge of a system of interrelated procedures, such as bookkeeping, internal combustion engines, electric wiring systems, nursing, farm management, ship sailing, or machining.

Applies principles to solve practical everyday problems and deals with a variety of concrete variables in situations where only limited standardization exists.

Interprets a variety of instructions furnished in written, oral, diagrammatic, or schedule form.

LEVEL 5
Has knowledge of a field of study (engineering, literature, history, business administration) having immediate applicability to the affairs of the world.

Defines problems, collects data, establishes facts, and draws valid conclusions in controlled situations.

Interprets an extensive variety of technical material in books, manuals, texts, etc.

Deals with some abstract but mostly concrete variables.

LEVEL 6
Has knowledge of a field of highly abstract study (e.g., mathematics, physics, chemistry, logic, philosophy, art criticism).

Deals with nonverbal symbols in formulas, equations, or graphs.

Understands the most difficult classes of concepts.

Deals with a large number of variables and determines a specific course of action (e.g., research, production) on the basis of need.

Mathematical Development Scale

The mathematical development scale is concerned with knowledge and ability to deal with mathematical problems and operations from counting and simple addition to higher mathematics.

LEVEL 1
Involves counting to simple addition and subtraction; reading, copying, and/or recording of figures.

LEVEL 2
Uses arithmetic to add, subtract, multiply, and divide whole numbers. Reads scales and gauges, e.g., on powered equipment where readings and signals are indicative of conditions and actions to be taken.

LEVEL 3
 Makes arithmetic calculations involving fractions, decimals, and percentages. Mentally acts upon dimensional specifications marked on material or stakes.

LEVEL 4
 Performs arithmetic, algebraic, and geometric procedures in standard practical applications.

LEVEL 5
 Has knowledge of advanced mathematical and statistical techniques such as differential and integral calculus, factor analysis, and probability determination.
 Works with a wide variety of theoretical mathematical concepts.
 Makes original applications of mathematical procedures, as in empirical and differential equations.

Language Development Scale

 The language development scale is concerned with knowledge and ability to speak, read, or write language materials from simple instructions to complex sources of information and ideas.

LEVEL 1
 Cannot read or write but can follow simple oral instructions.
 Signs name and understands ordinary, routine agreements when explained, such as those relevant to leasing a house; employment (hours, wages, etc.); procuring a driver's license.
 Reads lists, addresses, safety warnings.

LEVEL 2
 Reads short sentences; has a simple concrete vocabulary. Reads material on the level of comic books, etc.
 Converses with service personnel (waiters, ushers, cashiers).
 Copies written records precisely without error.
 Can, e.g., keep taxi driver's trip record or service maintenance record.

LEVEL 3
 Comprehends orally expressed trade terminology (jargon) of a specific technical nature.
 Reads material on level of *Reader's Digest* and straight news reporting in popular newspapers.
 Comprehends ordinary newscasting that focuses on events rather than on their analysis.
 Copies written material from one record to another, catching gross errors in grammar.
 Fills in report forms, such as Medicare forms, employment applications, and card form for income tax.

LEVEL 4

Writes routine business correspondence reflecting standard procedures.

Interviews job applicants to determine work best suited for their abilities and experience; contacts employers to interest them in services of agency.

Reads and comprehends technical manuals and written instructions as well as drawings.

Conducts opinion research surveys involving stratified samples of the population.

LEVEL 5

Writes instructions for assembly of prefabricated parts into units.

Writes instructions and specifications concerning proper use of machinery.

Writes copy for advertising. Reports news for the newspapers, radio, or TV.

Prepares and delivers lectures for audiences that seek information about the arts, sciences, and humanities in an informal way.

LEVEL 6

Writes or edits articles for technical and scientific journals or journals of advanced literary criticism (e.g., *Journal of Educational Sociology, Science, Physical Review, Daedalus*).

APPENDIX B. SCALE OF WORKER INSTRUCTIONS

The worker instructions scale defines *responsibility* in terms of the mix of specifications and judgments assigned to the worker. This can range across several levels in a given assignment depending on the activity(ies).

LEVEL 1

Inputs, outputs, tools, equipment, and procedures are all specified. Almost everything the worker needs to know is contained in the assignment. The worker is supposed to turn out a specified amount of work or a standard number of units per hour or day.

LEVEL 2

Inputs, outputs, tools, and equipment are all specified, but the worker has some leeway in the procedures and methods used to get the job done. Almost all the information needed is in the assignment instructions. Production is measured on a daily or weekly basis.

LEVEL 3

Inputs and outputs are specified, but the worker has considerable freedom as to procedures and timing, including the use of tools and/or equipment. The worker may have to refer to several standard sources for information (handbooks, catalogs, wall charts). Time to complete a particular product or service is specified, but this varies up to several hours.

LEVEL 4

Output (product or service) is specified in the assignment, which may be in the form of a memorandum or of a schematic (sketch or blueprint). The worker must work out own way of getting the job done, including selection and use of tools and/or equipment, sequence of operations (tasks), and obtaining important information (handbooks, etc.). Worker may either do the work or set up standards and procedures for others to do it.

LEVEL 5

Same as level 4 above, but in addition, the worker is expected to know and employ theory so that he/she understands the whys and wherefores of the various options that are available for dealing with a problem and can independently select from among them. Worker may have to do some reading in the professional and trade literature in order to gain this understanding.

LEVEL 6

Various possible outputs are described that can meet stated technical or administrative needs. The worker must investigate the various possible outputs and evaluate them in regard to performance characteristics and input demands. This usually requires creative use of theory well beyond referring to standard sources. There is no specification of inputs, methods, sequences, sources, or the like.

LEVEL 7

There is some question as to what the need or problem really is or what directions should be pursued in dealing with it. In order to define the problem, to control and explore the behavior of the variables, and to formulate possible outputs and their performance characteristics, the worker must consult largely unspecified sources of information and devise investigations, surveys, or data analysis studies.

LEVEL 8

Information and direction comes to the worker in terms of needs (tactical, organizational, strategic, financial). Worker must call for staff reports and recommendations concerning methods of dealing with them. He/she coordinates both organizational and technical data in order to make decisions and determinations regarding courses of action (outputs) for major sections (divisions, groups) of his organization.

References

Ash, R. A. (1982). Job elements for task clusters: Arguments for using multimethodological approaches to job analysis and demonstration of their ability. *Public Personnel Management Journal, 11,* 80–90.

Caplan, J. R., Primoff, E. S., Fine, S. A., & Eisner, E. J. (1981). *Analysis of entry-level claims examiner* (Unpublished report). Washington, DC: U.S. Office of Personnel Management.

Christal, R. E. (1974, January). *USAF occupational research project* (Report No. AFHRL-TR-73-75). San Antonio, TX: U.S. Air Force Human Resources Laboratory.

Cornelius, E. T., III, & Lyness, K. S. (1980). A comparison of holistic and decomposed judgment strategies in job analyses by job incumbents. *Journal of Applied Psychology, 65,* 155–163.

Dunnette, M. D. (1982). Critical concepts in the assessment of human capabilities. In M. D. Dunnette & E. A. Fleishman (Eds.), *Human performance and productivity: Human capability assessment* (Vol. 1, pp. 1–12). Hillsdale, NJ: Erlbaum.

Fine, S. A. (1955). A structure of worker functions. *Personnel and Guidance Journal, 34,* 66–73.

Fine, S. A. (1967). Nature of skill: Implication for education and training. In *Proceedings of the seventy-fifth annual convention of the American Psychological Association.* Washington, DC: American Psychological Association.

Fine, S. A., & Heinz, C. A. (1957). Estimates of worker trait requirements. *Personnel and Guidance Journal, 36,* 168–174.

Fine, S. A., & Wiley, W. W. (1971). *An introduction to functional job analysis: A scaling of selected tasks from the social welfare field.* Kalamazoo, MI: W. E. Upjohn Institute for Employment Research.

Fleishman, E. A. (1975). Toward a taxonomy of human performance. *American Psychologist, 30,* 1127–1149.

Jeanneret, P. R., & McCormick, E. J. (1969, June). *The job dimensions of "worker oriented" job variables and their attribute profiles as based on data from the position analysis questionnaire* (Report No. 2). Lafayette, IN: Occupational Research Center, Purdue University.

Levine, E. L., Ash, A. H., Hall, H. L., & Sistrunk, F. (1981). *Evaluation of seven job analysis methods by experienced job analysts* (Law Enforcement Assistance Administration, Grant No. 79-DF-AX-0195). Tampa: Center for Evaluation Research, University of South Florida.

McCormick, E. J. (1976). Job and task analysis. In M. D. Dunnette (Ed.), *Handbook of industrial and organizational psychology* (pp. 651–696). Chicago: Rand McNally.

McCormick, E. J. (1979). *Job analysis: Methods and applications.* New York: AMACOM.

McCormick, E. J., Jeanneret, P. R., & Mecham, R. C. (1969). *A study of job characteristics and job dimensions as based on the position analysis questionnaire* (Report No. 6). Lafayette, IN: Occupational Research Center, Purdue University.

Mecham, R. C., & McCormick, E. J. (1969). *The rated attribute requirements of job elements of the position analysis questionnaire* (Report No. 1). Lafayette, IN: Occupational Research Center, Purdue University.

Mosel, J. N., Fine, S. A., & Boling, J. (1960). The scalability of estimated worker requirements. *Journal of Applied Psychology, 44,* 156–160.

Muckler, F. A. (1982). Evaluating productivity. In M. D. Dunnette & E. A. Fleishman (Eds.), *Human performance and productivity: Human capability assessment* (Vol. 1, pp. 13–48). Hillsdale, NJ: Erlbaum.

Pearlman, K. (1980). Job families: A review and discussion of their implications for personnel selection. *Psychological Bulletin, 87,* 1–28.

Peterson, N. G., & Bownas, D. A. (1982). Skill, task structure, and performance acquisition. In M. D. Dunnette & E. A. Fleishman (Eds.), *Human performance and productivity: Human capability assessment* (Vol. 1, pp. 49–106). Hillsdale, NJ: Erlbaum.

Primoff, E. S. (1975). *How to prepare and conduct job element examinations* (Personnel Research and Development Center Publication No. TS-75-1). Washington, DC: U.S. Government Printing Office.

Sistrunk, F., & Smith, P. L. (1982). *Multimethodological job analysis for criminal justice organizations.* Tampa: Center for Evaluation Research, University of South Florida.

Smith, P. C. (1976). Behaviors, results, and organizational effectiveness: The problem of criteria. In M. D. Dunnette (Ed.), *Handbook of industrial and organizational psychology* (pp. 745–776). Chicago: Rand McNally.

Stead, W. H., & Masincup, W. E. (1942). *The occupational research program of the United States Employment Service.* Chicago: Public Administration Service.

Stead, W. H., Shartle, C. L., & Associates. (1940). *Occupational counseling techniques.* New York: American Book Co.

Thorndike, R. L. (1949). *Personnel selection.* New York: Wiley.

U.S. Bureau of Employment Security. (1945). *Physical demands analysis and physical capacities appraisal.* Washington, DC: U.S. Government Printing Office.

U.S. Department of Labor, Employment Service. (1955). *Estimates of worker trait requirements for 4,000 jobs defined in the dictionary of occupational titles.* Washington, DC: U.S. Government Printing Office.

U.S. Department of Labor, Employment and Training Administration. (1977). *Dictionary of occupational titles* (4th ed.). Washington, DC: U.S. Government Printing Office.

U.S. Department of Labor, Manpower Administration. (1965). *Dictionary of occupational titles* (3rd ed.). Washington, DC: U.S. Government Printing Office.

U.S. Equal Employment Opportunity Commission, U.S. Civil Service Commission, U.S. Department of Labor, & U.S. Department of Justice. (1978). Uniform guidelines on employee selection procedures. *Federal Register, 43*(166), 38290–38309.

U.S. Federal Security Agency. (1939). *Dictionary of occupational titles* (1st ed.). Washington, DC: U.S. Government Printing Office.

Viteles, M. S. (1932). *Industrial psychology.* New York: W .W. Norton.

2. NUMERICAL RATING SCALES

Rick R. Jacobs

Introduction

It is difficult to imagine, in these times of incredible technological advances, modern personnel practices, and advanced management development programs, that one of the most important organizational activities has remained a thorn in the side of supervisors and subordinates alike. The process by which employees are informed regarding their levels of performance, while undergoing cosmetic change, has endured as a rather painful experience for all involved. This chapter examines the various options one should consider in the development of a performance review system. It will cover such diverse issues as what the organization or individual evaluator hopes to accomplish by engaging in performance evaluation and what format is best for conducting performance review. No new empirical findings are given; the chapter synthesizes previously conducted research and experiential findings.

A summary of some major considerations in the development of a performance appraisal system is presented first. The second and most important portion of this work will present several potential formats for the performance evaluation instrument. This section will also offer suggestions on potential scoring schemes that can be used for summarizing performance evaluations. The final portion of the chapter will offer suggestions on implementation of the performance review system. Topics to be covered will include how to introduce and how to evaluate the performance appraisal process.

MAJOR CONSIDERATIONS IN PERFORMANCE APPRAISAL

Before any attention can be paid to the specific details of a performance evaluation system, the forces behind the system must grapple with the most pressing and far-reaching question: What is the purpose of the evaluation? An organization can collect performance information for any number of different reasons. As these reasons are considered, some of the unanswered questions regarding the type of performance evaluation system necessary for the organization begin to be answered. Indeed, one of the more influential papers in the area of performance appraisal (Landy & Farr, 1980) stated explicitly that the "purpose for rating" is of central importance in their model of the entire rating process. Jacobs, Kafry, and Zedeck (1980) have provided a taxonomy of purposes for performance ratings; some of these purposes are examined next.

What is the purpose for rating? One very important purpose for rating is *disciplinary action.* Here performance evaluation is used to identify those employees who have exhibited less than satisfactory performance and to use this information for such activities as demotion, denial of salary increase, or dismissal. Usually such evaluations are carried out and presented to the evaluatee fait accompli. If the purpose of the evaluation includes the use of performance data for disciplinary action, it is crucial that the evaluations be well documented and extensive, covering a variety of events over an extended period of time.

A second purpose for conducting performance appraisals is that of *feedback and employee development.* This focuses on the potential benefits of a well-developed performance evaluation system in relation to those being evaluated. To the degree that performance evaluation offers constructive information on how an employee has been performing and how he or she can improve future performance, the entire process serves to increase the likelihood of positive outcomes, such as salary increases and promotion. Beatty, Schneier, and Beatty (1977) found that specific feedback on behavior during the performance period resulted in improvement in subsequent performance. Landy, Farr, and Jacobs (1982) have highlighted studies across a variety of tasks, documenting a positive effect for performance-related feedback.

Ilgen, Fischer, and Taylor (1979) have delineated the key components of effective feedback. Their findings indicate that feedback must be perceived by the evaluatee as coming from a knowledgeable source, as representing unique performance-related information, and as coming from someone interested in furthering the performance objectives of the evaluatee. The performance evaluator, equipped with an appraisal device designed for the specific job is in a perfect position to meet qualifications for effective feedback. If one of the functions of performance appraisal is feedback with an eye toward performance improvement, then the evaluator must spend time learning the job of the evaluatee and gathering information on performance as it occurs as well as offering suggestions on how performance can be improved. Certain performance appraisal systems offer the evaluator the specificity required for meaningful feedback, while others simply reduce the appraisal process to a series of numbers that offer little information on ways to improve performance.

Another purpose that performance evaluation data often serve is the identification of an individual in line for a *promotion.* Clearly the role of the appraisal is to distinguish the top performers from the average and even above average ones. While it is reasonable to expect a consistency in performance from one position to the next position in the organizational hierarchy, promotions should be based on an analysis of the requisite skills and abilities of the "new position." To the degree that these skills and abilities overlap those of the current position, performance data represent a valuable source of information regarding the evaluatee's suitability for the next job. With this in mind, it is argued that certain types of performance evaluations not only let you sort out individuals with respect to the quality of their performance on various aspects of their jobs, but allow you the opportunity to match the characteristics of the current job to those of the higher position, thereby allowing the organization to promote individuals who are superior on relevant job dimensions.

The fourth purpose a performance appraisal system fulfills within an organization is associated with the *selection* process. Whenever an organization finds itself in a position of personnel shortages, it must attempt to identify, among its applicant pool, the most promising performers. Organizations spend a great deal of time, effort, and money conducting validation studies with the expectation that a selection system will be found that can identify good employees. At the heart of any selection-validation study is a system of performance appraisal. The most important characteristic of the performance appraisal system is its ability to generate scores that can be used in a regression equation. Such a requirement for establishing statistical relationships puts a premium on quantitative information and, depending on the performance appraisal system, may compromise the feedback purpose of an appraisal system that requires a greater qualitative emphasis.

Still another fundamental purpose for performance appraisal data and information involves *training and supervision*. Often the process used to develop an effective performance appraisal system will also result in an explicit statement of how various jobs are performed. When this occurs, the rudimentary elements of a training program are the by-products of the appraisal system. For organizations that look forward (as opposed to backward), one purpose for developing the appraisal system is the simultaneous development of programs for training employees.

The training and supervision portion of appraisal can be viewed independently from either a supervision or training perspective. On the supervision side, the explication of job duties from the appraisal gives the supervisor greater familiarity with the job(s) being appraised. With this knowledge, supervisors can give valuable and specific feedback to each employee. Additionally, when the performance review process continues over an extended period of time, supervisors can identify employees who are improving and those who are not responding to the performance-related feedback. For the employee who does not respond, alternative strategies for making up performance deficiencies can be explored. With respect to the training perspective, not only have the job responsibilities that will make up the major portion of a training program been identified, but by looking at a total group of employees' performance, supervisors can also pinpoint areas of common weakness. When this occurs, it may be cost effective to simply conduct a single training program for all employees rather than relying on individual feedback to each worker performing poorly.

A final purpose for performance appraisal procedures is that of *organizational diagnosis and development.* While this purpose overlaps with the training program designed to correct the poor performance of a group of workers, it has unique benefits. When performance deficiencies are uncovered via performance appraisal and when hiring new employees is an option, the process of performance appraisal can be seen as the stimulus for selecting new workers with specific skills and abilities that can improve the efficiency of the entire organization. With respect to the organizational and development perspective, performance appraisal is taken beyond the scope of performance facilitator specific to individual workers and beyond the realm of a supervisor tool relevant to a specific group of workers into the areas of improving performance across various organizational units and, one hopes, across the entire organization.

It should be evident from the preceding list of purposes for ratings that performance evaluation has many faces. Different purposes often require different information, which in turn requires different methodologies or formats for performance appraisal data collection. It is the intent of this chapter to make recommendations about the various formats currently available for performance evaluation with respect to their appropriateness for the aforestated purposes. Before reviewing the formats, however, a few more considerations in developing a performance appraisal system are examined.

Who should do the rating? Evaluating the performance of an employee is a difficult task. Organizations traditionally place this responsibility on a supervisor. It is reasoned that a supervisor, by virtue of experience, can rise to the occasion and perform the burdensome chore. Additionally, given his or her opportunity to observe, either directly or indirectly, the performance of subordinates, it is felt that the supervisor is the appropriate performance evaluator. Sometimes these reasons are valid. That is, supervisors may be exactly the right people to conduct performance appraisals. However, under many circumstances, asking the supervisor to rate performance is no better than asking anyone else in the organization to evaluate an employee. For example, when a police officer spends twenty eight-hour shifts with a partner over a thirty-day time period and 150 of these hours are spent outside the precinct station and outside the view of the officer's sergeant, the supervisor (i.e., sergeant) is not the appropriate source of performance-based information. Additionally, for certain organizations there may be a need for first-line supervisors to be evaluated on their leadership ability. Asking a supervisor to rate the "follower" on his or her own ability to lead seems misdirected. In the first example, peer evaluations might be useful, while in the second, subordinate ratings might provide the needed information.

These examples point to the variety of sources available for giving performance appraisal information. Supervisors, peers, and subordinates should all be considered as potential performance evaluators. Add to this list the performers themselves and also the possibility of an external auditor, someone from outside the organization. Any one or a combination of these five sources can be chosen. While it is beyond the scope of this chapter to present the advantages and disadvantages of using various sources for performance evaluation, some general information about each source can be offered.

Most appraisals in organizations are conducted by the employee's *immediate supervisor*. While this has a logical basis, since supervisors have the responsibility of employee development and administration of rewards, supervisors are limited in the role of performance evaluation. They may provide information without an understanding of how the job is actually performed or, more frequently, without an opportunity to observe performance.

Peer appraisal appears to be psychometrically superior to other sources of appraisal data. Peer appraisals not only appear to be valid indicators of current performance but are also accurate forecasters of future performance. Their primary liability is their potential for friction among colleagues and coworkers, which has resulted in the rejection of peer appraisal as a tool in many organizations. Since Kane and Lawler (1978) and Lewin and Swany (1976) have provided detailed reviews of the peer appraisal literature, interested readers should consult their work for additional information on the topic.

Subordinate review is an important means for supervisors to gather information about their behavior as it affects those who must respond to it. Such information almost always remains in the minds of the subordinates, never to be shared with the supervisor. This is unfortunate from the standpoint of supervisory development. Little is known about subordinates as a source of performance data. This lack of knowledge includes such things as the psychometric precision of the data and appropriate methods for implementation of a review. Perhaps so few subordinate assessments of supervisors are conducted (and hence the lack of a research literature in the area) because of organizations' inability to develop procedures that counteract the defensiveness on the part of the supervisor acting as ratee and the simultaneous fear of retribution on the part of the subordinate acting as rater.

Self-appraisals can be seen as useful tools because they force an employee to focus his or her attention on performance. Such focus can result in the detection of problems in past performance and identification of appropriate steps for correction, as well as the setting of goals for future performance. From an administrative standpoint, self-ratings may pose a problem because of their potential for leniency bias. While some studies have supported the inflation hypothesis (Beatty, Schneier, & Beatty, 1977; Thornton, 1968), others have shown an opposite effect; that is, supervisory ratings are more positive than self-appraisals (Heneman, 1974; Teel, 1978). Thornton's review of this area (1980) concluded that self-appraisals lead frequently to inflated evaluations, are less reliable than supervisory ratings, and show little convergence with other sources of appraisal data.

Finally, evaluations conducted by *auditors* external to the unit of the performer may be valuable. One procedure suggested by Latham and Wexley (1981) has the external or field auditor observe performance and write a report that is forwarded to the ratee's supervisor. The supervisor reviews and modifies this report and uses the data for performance appraisal feedback or for administrative purposes such as promotion. Questions surrounding the "Hawthorne effect" as it applies to this procedure and issues of inefficient use of manpower and additional costs relative to incremental gains in information cast a serious doubt over the usefulness of external audits for many organizations.

Are objective performance measures recorded by the organization? One very important point to keep in mind in deciding on a performance appraisal system is the amount of information about performance that is readily available as a result of regular record keeping. Many organizations routinely collect data about employees that answer meaningful performance-based questions. For example, some performance evaluation forms ask supervisors to rate subordinates on "dependability." Close examination of the underlying behaviors of interest uncovers the fact that the organization is interested in knowing about employees' absence and tardiness. If the organization uses a time clock or records attendance information in some other way, more precise data are available via records than can be obtained from ratings. Smith (1976) provided a meaningful distinction between *hard criteria* such as absence, tardiness, turnover, accident rate, productivity, sales, and salary progression and *soft criteria* such as impression-based ratings from supervisors and others.

The scrutinization of each potential hard criterion for errors of omission and commission is of critical importance for the purpose of deciding how to develop and how to implement a performance appraisal system. The emergence of soft criteria is largely a response to alleged deficiency and contamination of hard criteria. That is, supervisors and employees alike claim that many of the measures collected by organizations are not useful as performance indicators because either they include information that the performer cannot control or they fail to take into account crucial information. Sales records are often cited as a problematic criterion because they carry so much "excess baggage," such as geographic location or availability of credit for certain customers. Similarly, rate of advancement may be an erroneous indicator of performance when informal quota systems are introduced in the promotion picture.

What is clear from these examples is the need to take a hard look at hard criteria. Once an evaluation of the relative worth of the hard criteria has been made, the organization is in a position to begin considering what additional performance-based information is needed. If some hard criteria survive the evaluation, the organization should consider what supplemental impressionistic data are needed and how they are to be collected. If no hard criteria appear to be valuable, then a total performance appraisal system based on soft criteria must be developed.

How many measures of performance do we need? The question of how many measures are enough must also be considered when an organization begins developing its performance appraisal system. A few related questions that emerge are (1) Should we ask for ratings of overall performance? (2) If we collect ratings on subscales or dimensions of performance, how many dimensions should we measure? (3) After collecting these dimension ratings, how can we combine them into a single score?

For certain uses of performance data, such as selection, promotion, and salary administration, it is useful (if not necessary) to have a single value associated with performance. This value indicates that an organization that intends to use performance evaluation data for administrative purposes must provide a positive or constructive answer to either question 1 or 3, or to both. If an organization is interested in the potential facilitating effects of evaluations on future performance, providing information on several dimensions is necessary. Therefore an organization must consider multiple performance indicators. A final resolution is also important: If there are multiple indicators, how many is enough? How many is too many? Kafry, Jacobs, and Zedeck (1979) have suggested that with respect to performance ratings, collecting more than nine dimensions from raters results in information of questionable utility. From the above descriptions, organizations should consider collecting multiple indicators of performance as well as single summary measures. Any performance appraisal system should possess the flexibility of providing the organization with various types of measures to respond to various needs of the organization.

Review of Rating Scale Formats

Just as an organization must decide how performance evaluation data will be used, who will do the ratings, and how many measures will be collected, an organization must make a decision regarding the format that will be used for collecting performance evaluations. Like the purposes performance data can serve, the variations in performance evaluation formats are numerous. The intent of this section is to explore five different formats for performance evaluation devices. For the first two formats, the system can simply be put in place with very little adaptation to the specific organization or jobs. The remaining three formats require the organization to consider, in depth, the jobs of the employees being evaluated.[1] What will be assumed in the discussion that follows is that the organization has conducted an exhaustive analysis of the jobs being considered, that these analyses have indicated general areas of job responsibility, and furthermore, that specific activities, incidents, or behaviors associated with each general area have been identified and listed. What is being described here is a detailed job analysis. The interested reader is referred to chapter 1 for a complete description

---

1. There are actually four other formats that could be considered. Graphic rating scales, checklists, and mixed standard scales are reviewed in this chapter; behavior-based rating scales are examined by Borman in chapter 3.

of the procedures one would follow to complete such an analysis. For the purposes of this review, the knowledge gained from the job analysis will be the starting point, and the first question is, How shall I arrange this information in such a way as to elicit from my raters reliable and accurate measures of employee performance?

RANKING

One very popular method of assessing employees is to engage in the direct comparison of all workers serving in a single unit or under a single supervisor. This procedure simply asks the rater to rank order, from the top performer to the bottom performer, all of the employees under consideration. The rater is usually given a general criterion statement and directions of the following form:

> Consider the overall performance of your work force and place the name of the highest performer in the space next to the number 1. From the remaining employees place the name of the second highest performer in the space next to the number 2. Continue this procedure until all performers appear on the list.

There are two major problems with the procedure of ranking employees. First, since the finished product is a ranking, only ordinal information is available. That is, the hierarchy of performers (i.e., 1 is better than 2 who is better than 3, etc.) is known, but the magnitude is not. For instance, it is clear that the person appearing on the list as number 3 is a better performer than persons 4, 5, and 6, but there is no measure of how much better. More important, there is no referencing framework to locate the position of these values relative to acceptable or unacceptable levels of performance. While performer 1 may truly be the best performer, performer 1 and all his colleagues may, in reality, be very poor performers. Conversely, the lowest ranking employee may be exhibiting exemplary performance. This situation makes it difficult (perhaps impossible) to make normative comparisons across groups.

A second major problem with ranking stems from its almost exclusive reliance on an assessment of the worker's overall performance. The use of a single, global criterion serves to minimize the utility of the ratings for anything beyond basic administrative purposes. While it is possible to rank all employees on perhaps many different job-related criteria, the number of employees frequently being ranked is so large as to preclude such actions, owing to the tedium involved in the process of repeatedly ranking the same employees.

PAIR COMPARISON

A second form of the employee comparison method is the pair-comparison technique. The task of the rater is simply to decide which of two ratees is the better performer. Once again the rater is asked to consider a global criterion and also to make relative judgments about performance.

The form used in the pair-comparison method has been described by Guilford (1954). It can be summarized briefly. All ratees (n) are arranged in all possible pairs. The total number of pairs is equal to $n(n - 1)/2$. In the case where the number of ratees equals 12, ($n = 12$), the total number of pairs is 66. Pairs should be arranged with the following objective in mind. First, every employee should appear about equally on the left and on the right side of the pairing to control for position bias. Next, as you go down the list of pairings, an employee's name should alternate from one side to the other. Finally, no employee should appear in two successive pairs, and every attempt should be made to place the same names as far apart as space will permit.

Procedures for scoring pair-comparison evaluations are quite involved and complex. Since a description of these procedures is beyond the scope of this chapter, the reader should consult Guilford (1954) for the details of requisite analyses.

Pair comparisons and rankings share the same characteristics related to the use of a single criterion and of relative comparisons, and they thus have some of the same weaknesses. The disadvantages of rankings can apply to the pair-comparison method, with the exception that interval scales can be generated from the pair-comparison format. On the more positive end, both techniques have the advantage of asking raters to engage in tasks they readily understand and have often completed, at least on an informal basis. Additionally, pair comparisons as well as rankings are portable formats; that is, the form developed and used for one job title can be used for any other job title.

GRAPHIC RATING SCALE

Graphic rating scales are the first of four performance evaluation formats most capable of delivering useful performance-related information. The assumption in the development of these scales and the three types that follow is that they are based on a rather exhaustive job analysis. Graphic rating scales are designed to elicit performance ratings on employees on relevant dimensions of their jobs. They accomplish this goal by requiring raters to indicate each employee's standing on a numerically or verbally anchored scale (or on both). In reality, graphic rating scales can take many forms and can be classified easily according to (1) whether the job dimension is defined and (2) whether the scale contains numbers only or a combination of numerical and verbal anchors. An example of the latter is shown in Figure 2.1.

To develop graphic rating scales within an organization, the seven to nine most important dimensions of job performance must be identified from the job analysis. Next, if possible, these dimensions must be defined. Once these steps

FIGURE 2.1. Example of a graphic rating scale with numerical and verbal anchors

INSTRUCTIONS: Circle the number corresponding to the value associated with your evaluation of the manager on the dimension defined below.

LONG-RANGE PLANNING: Forecasts with respect to manpower planning and costs; anticipates future problems and new trends; reviews with his people to constantly update them and uncover new information.

1	2	3	4	5
Unsatisfactory	Fair	Good	Very Good	Exceptional

have been completed, the organization must make a decision regarding the type of response scale desired. The relevant questions include how many response categories are required and whether to include numbers, verbal anchors, or both. A generally accepted rule of thumb is to provide between four and nine scale points; fewer points do not allow enough discrimination, while more than nine results in relatively unimportant differentiation. When deciding on the number of scale points, the organization should also decide on whether they wish to permit central responses, an uncertain or undecided option on an odd-numbered scale (defined as falling at the midpoint of the scale). Reliability is also a factor in determining number of points as well as in providing anchors for each position on the scale. If the "uncertain" option is not desirable, then the organization should use an even number of scale points.

After deciding on the number of scale points, the appraisal system developer must determine whether the response scale will have verbal anchors. Verbal anchors communicate definitions to raters. This is important since it allows raters to develop a better understanding of what each position on the scale means. Whenever possible, verbal anchors should accompany the numerical scale. These anchors can be generated by members of the organization and checked for their ordinal properties; examples of verbal anchors can be found in a paper by Bass, Cascio, and O'Connor (1974).

While the most complete type of graphic rating scale—one with definitions and verbal anchors—requires considerable time and effort to develop, it can serve as a prototype, in many cases, for graphic rating scales for related jobs. That is, the scale may be applicable to other jobs, and the investment in the development can be shared by other jobs. While some experts on rating scales consider this an advantage, others view it as an outgrowth of an underlying deficiency, in that the scales are not specific enough to elicit useful performance-related data. These points will be examined further in the summary section of the chapter.

CHECKLIST

The checklist consists of a series of statements about on-the-job performance. These statements are taken directly from the job analysis and placed on a list with a response blank following each. An example is shown in Figure 2.2. The task of the rater is to check those items that best describe the employee being rated. Each statement appearing on the list has received a numerical value indicative of the level of performance described. The values are most often determined independently, prior to the administrative use of the scales, by a group similar to the prospective raters following a psychometric scaling procedure.

With the responses from the performance raters and the statement values from the scaling procedure, the ratee receives a score based on the sum of the values of the statements checked. Several different scoring schemes are possible. First, ratees can receive a total score based on the values of the statements checked. Next, it may be possible to sort the statements into dimensions of performance (i.e., subscales). Dimension scores can then be generated. Finally, total and subscale scores can be obtained by simply counting the number of checks appearing on the form and for each dimension. This scoring method assumes that all the statements are either positive or negative, but it is insensitive to the degree of positive or negative performance reflected in the statement. This method, called a unit weight system, is simple and often yields scores similar to those obtained with differential scale values.

Forced-choice format. Another variant of the checklist is known as the forced-choice format. In this format, the rater is asked to select from a group of statements a subset that best describes the ratee. By arranging all the statements into groups and "forcing" the rater to select at least some statements, scale developers can control the tendency of some raters to check either very few statements or only extremely favorable ones. The introduction of the forced-choice format was an attempt to control the social desirability of ratings, which can result in elevated or lenient scores.

Although the checklist is a potentially useful format for ratings in many organizational settings because of its focus on job-related statements and its practicability for the rater (simply checking whether the statement describes the ratee), it does have drawbacks. Most important, the result of the checklist, the summated rating, requires an interval between the act of rating and the generation of scores. This puts the checklist in the class of being a *derived rating*. That is, the score is derived from the ratings rather than being a direct result of the ratings. As a derived rating, it suffers from the potential problem of "surprising" the rater. The score the rater has given a ratee may not match the rater's perception of the ratee's performance. With such unanticipated data, a rater often has a difficult time giving feedback to the ratee. A second problem with the checklist pertains to developing the subscales. Like many other techniques, the

FIGURE 2.2. Example of a checklist

INSTRUCTIONS: Below you will find a list of behavioral items. Read each item and decide whether the item describes the person being evaluated. If you feel the item does describe the person, place a check mark in the space provided. If the item is not descriptive of the person, leave the space next to the item blank.

1. Regularly sets vague and unrealistic program goals   _____
2. Is concerned only with the immediate problems of the day and sees very little beyond the day to day   _____
3. Develops work schedules that allow for completion of projects provided no major problems are encountered   _____
4. Is aware of needs and trends in his area of responsibility and plans accordingly   _____
5. Follows up on projects to ensure intermediate goals are achieved   _____
6. Looks for new markets and studies potential declines in current markets   _____
7. Anticipates and plans for replacement of key personnel in the event of corporate relocation   _____

Note: Additional items from other dimensions would be added to this list and the order of presentation of items would be random. Scores are derived based on the number of items checked for a given scale and the scale values of the items checked. A major difference between this scale and the behaviorally anchored scale is that the latter allows the rater to assign a rating directly, while the checklist requires an administrative procedure to calculate the rating.

checklist provides useful information, but only with the price tag of additional costs during the development phase.

MIXED STANDARD SCALE

In 1972 Blanz and Ghiselli introduced the mixed standard scale format for generating performance ratings. It consists of a series of performance dimensions represented by three behaviors or statements per dimension. These statements can be taken directly from the job analysis, but they must be judged (usually by a group of supervisors) to reflect different levels of performance on the dimension. One of the items represents good performance, the second reflects average performance, and the third represents poor performance. The items (numbering three times the number of dimensions) are then randomly arranged to form a single list. An example is given in Figure 2.3.

Raters are instructed to read each statement and then are asked to decide whether the ratee's performance exceeds the statement, falls below the state-

FIGURE 2.3. Example of a mixed standard scale

INSTRUCTIONS: Listed below are a number of descriptions of behavior relevant to the job of manager. Your task is to examine each example carefully and
then to determine the answer to the following question: Is the manager being
rated better than the statement, worse than the statement, or does the
statement describe the manager?

If you believe that the person you are rating is better than the statement, put a
"+" in the space following the statement. If you believe that the person is worse
than the statement, put a "−" in the space provided. Finally, if you believe the
statement describes the person being rated, place a "0" in the space.

Be sure that you write either a "+", a "−", or a "0" after each statement listed
below.

1. Regularly sets vague and unrealistic program goals   _____
2. Is concerned only with the immediate problems of the day and
   sees very little beyond the day to day   _____
3. Develops work schedules that allow for completion of projects
   provided no major problems are encountered   _____

Note: The list continues in the same way as the one described for the checklist (see Figure
2.2).

ment, or whether the statement describes the ratee accurately. If the rater feels
the ratee's performance exceeds the statement, the rater places a plus sign in the
space adjacent to the statement. A rating of "minus" for a statement means that
the rater believes the statement exceeds the performance of the ratee. Finally, if
the rater assigns a zero to the statement, he or she is indicating that the statement
describes the ratee's performance accurately.

Scoring rules for the mixed standard scale result in a range of scores from 1
(obtained by receiving all minuses) to 7 (obtained by receiving all pluses). The
scoring procedures outlined by Blanz and Ghiselli not only allow for the calculation
of ratee scores but also highlight logical errors in evaluations. A logical error
occurs when a ratee receives a positive evaluation on the good performance
statement and a negative evaluation on the average or poor performance statement for a given scale. When a single rater has this tendency over a group of
ratees or on many scales for a single ratee, it may indicate that the rater is not
capable of performing the ratings. On the other hand, when several ratees commit
this logical error on the same scale, it probably indicates a problem with the
statements defining the scale.

Mixed standard scales were introduced to minimize the amount of overlap
among performance ratings on a given individual. The scales were designed to

minimize "halo" error or the tendency for ratings of an individual across a series of performance dimensions to appear identical while performance levels on these dimensions vary. The success of mixed standard scales in achieving this goal is questionable (Finley et al., 1977; Saal & Landy, 1977). Additionally, mixed standard scales are subject to the same problems as checklists, inasmuch as they yield derived rather than direct performance evaluation scores. However, the mixed standard procedure is relatively untested and further information is needed with respect to its application in a variety of organizational settings.

Advantages and Disadvantages of Alternative Formats

Several factors must be considered when evaluating the various formats for potential organizational use. Foremost among these factors is the potential raters' response. Without cooperation from the population of raters, even the most sophisticated and well-developed format is doomed to failure. Additionally, the organization must concern itself with the psychometric precision of the ratings, since the product of the rating process, the value attached to performance, is used for many critical decisions. Finally, one must examine to what extent the performance evaluation system can add to an understanding of performance in terms of influences on performance and how performance can be improved. Here the concern is with the issue of information availability.

RATER ACCEPTANCE

Rater acceptance is influenced by a host of variables, including ease of rating and understanding of the product. With respect to both of these, ranking rates highly. It is easy to perform and the final product, a list, is easy to interpret. On the other end of the continuum are mixed standard scales. Raters often find the scales hard to complete and, more important, do not like the fact that when the ratings are completed, the derived score may not match the rater's a priori evaluation of the ratee. Pair comparisons and checklists also share the problem of derived scores.

Another very basic consideration that influences rater acceptance is the number of ratees that must be rated by a single rater. As was pointed out previously, pair comparisons become unwieldy when the number of ratees exceeds twenty (requiring 190 comparisons). In contrast, ranking is relatively unaffected by the addition of three or four more ratees. Graphic rating scales are reasonable to complete for up to about twenty ratees, even when there are seven to nine scales. Checklists and mixed standard scales begin to tax raters unduly where more than eight ratees are involved.

It should be clear from this discussion that rater acceptance requires trade-offs. Facilitating the actual act of providing the ratings is critical. If the rating process is rather involved (e.g., mixed standard scales), raters may be reluctant to use it. If the involved process best matches the overall needs of the organization, then the organization must provide adequate time and training to overcome the potential resistance on the part of the rater. Similarly, the organization must understand the raters' position on direct versus derived ratings. In some organizations, raters will accept derived ratings, while in other settings such ratings are viewed as liabilities.

PSYCHOMETRIC PRECISION

Much of the early research on behaviorally anchored rating scales was spent comparing them to older procedures such as checklists and graphic scales. Criteria that were used in these studies included traditional rating errors such as halo, leniency, and central tendency, as well as the psychometric properties of reliability and validity. What is rather impressive is the lack of superiority of any single format. It appears that format variations do not lead to differences in the psychometric precision of the evaluation device. Indeed, it is difficult to state specifically the advantages and disadvantages of the various formats.

One conclusion that can be drawn is that rankings and pair comparisons do not allow raters the luxury of evaluating all ratees in a similar way. If an organization has had this problem in the past, one of those two methods can be seen as advantageous compared to the other rating formats. However, one should keep in mind that rankings or pair comparisons merely require the rater to differentiate; there is no guarantee that the differentiation achieved is related to actual performance. That is, there is no definitive evidence documenting the validity of rankings or pair comparisons.

INFORMATION AVAILABILITY

Performance appraisals are conducted to meet administrative needs in most, if not all, organizations. If this were the only purpose for the evaluations, then almost any system would suffice, provided it met some minimal documentation requirements and it resulted in a defined metric. However, performance appraisal is a process, one that develops over time and one that should develop the skills of its participants. If these broader objectives are to be met, then the appraisal system to be preferred is the one that offers the greatest amount of performance relevant information. In this context, rankings and pair comparisons are clearly deficient. They offer information with respect to who performs better and worse than the ratee, but they fail to point out the specific areas in which the ratee needs improvement. Additionally, neither of these methods examine specific behaviors with respect to the ratee.

Ratees need to know how they have performed in specific terms so that they can better integrate the evaluation itself and can better plan for future performance efforts. With respect to these considerations, rating formats that are specific and behavioral can enhance the outcome of performance appraisals. Behavior-based rating scales have a distinct advantage here (for details, see Borman, chapter 3). This type of scale is followed by checklists and mixed standard scales. While the responsibilities of the raters are greater for these formats because of the need for documentation, the payoff becomes apparent in the information they provide.

Recommendations

The preceding sections have suggested a complex series of decisions needed to answer what some people believe is a simple question: How well are my employees doing? When an organization approaches this question for its work force, it is crucial that the organization first consider the many potential methods for gathering performance-related data and the many uses such data can serve.

Perhaps more important than sorting out the different formats by purpose, this chapter should offer the reader some specific guidelines to implement an appraisal system. The following steps are recommended with this goal in mind.

1. Carefully conduct an evaluation of the job for which the evaluations are to be done. This requires a well-documented job analysis. As the organization completes more and more analyses, it may become clear that some jobs share very similar responsibilities. When this is uncovered, families of jobs with similiar responsibilities can be formed and a single set of responsibilities and task statements can be used.
2. Develop specific performance scales for the job being evaluated. This step includes defining the dimensions of performance and listing the statements of behavior indicative of performance within each dimension.
3. Inform raters and ratees of the dimensions that will be evaluated and the purposes the data will serve.
4. Select a performance appraisal format that is acceptable to the organization. There is little evidence suggesting the superiority of any single format (graphic, checklist, mixed standard, or behavior based) based on job analytic information. Therefore the organization should select the format judged to be most appropriate. The selection might be based on a polling of raters with respect to their preference. While the scales are superficially different, provided the organization puts a good faith effort in completely describing the job, any arguments over formats are simply much ado about nothing.
5. Ensure that the raters are capable of rating. Offer training in the use of the device used to gather performance data. Equally important, set aside time for the evaluations. Expect nothing from a performance evaluation system sandwiched in an already busy schedule.

6. Periodically assess the successes and failures of the system. If the system was designed to increase feedback and, subsequently, to improve performance, check whether performance is improving. If the system was primarily intended to establish criteria for selection, determine the effectiveness of the selection system. If gathering data for promotion was an objective, assess the caliber of recent promotees. Additionally, do not overlook raters and ratees using the system. What are their impressions? How can the system be improved from their perspectives?

7. Allow the performance evaluation system to evolve. Performance evaluation yields a product—the ratings. However, performance evaluation is also a process, one that endures along with the organization.

References

Bass, B. M., Cascio, W. F., & O'Connor, E. J. (1974). Magnitude estimations of expressions of frequency and amount. *Journal of Applied Psychology, 59,* 313–320.

Beatty, R. W., Schneier, C. E., & Beatty, J. R. (1977). An empirical investigation of perceptions of ratee behavior frequency and ratee behavior change using behavioral expectation scales. *Personnel Psychology, 30,* 647–658.

Blanz, R., & Ghiselli, E. E. (1972). The mixed standard scale: A new rating system. *Personnel Psychology, 25,* 185–200.

Finley, D. M., Osburn, H. G., Dubin, J. A., & Jeanneret, P. R. (1977). Behaviorally based rating scales: Effects of specific anchors and disguised scale continua. *Personnel Psychology, 30,* 658–669.

Guilford, J. P. (1954). *Psychometric methods* (2nd ed.). New York: McGraw-Hill.

Heneman, H. G., III. (1974). Comparisons of self and superior ratings of managerial performance. *Journal of Applied Psychology, 58,* 638–642.

Ilgen, D. R., Fisher, C. D., & Taylor, M. S. (1979). Motivational consequences of individual feedback on behavior in organizations. *Journal of Applied Psychology, 64,* 349–371.

Jacobs, R. R., Kafry, D., & Zedeck, S. (1980). Expectations of behaviorally anchored rating scales. *Personnel Psychology, 33,* 595–640.

Kafry, D., Jacobs, R. R., & Zedeck, S. (1979). Discriminability in multidimensional performance evaluations. *Applied Psychological Measurement, 3,* 187–192.

Kane, J. S., & Lawler, E. E., III. (1978). Methods of peer assessment. *Psychological Bulletin, 85,* 555–586.

Landy, F. J., & Farr, J. L. (1980). Performance rating. *Psychological Bulletin, 87,* 72–107.

Landy, F. J., Farr, J. L., & Jacobs, R. R. (1982). Utility concepts in performance measurement. *Organizational Behavior and Human Performance, 30,* 15–40.

Latham, G. P., & Wexley, K. N. (1977). Behavioral observation scales for performance appraisal purposes. *Personnel Psychology, 30,* 255–268.

Latham, G. P., & Wexley, K. N. (1981). *Increasing productivity through performance appraisal.* Menlo Park, CA: Addison-Wesley.

Lewin, A. Y., & Swany, A. (1976). Peer nominations: A model, literature critique, and a paradigm for research. *Personnel Psychology, 29,* 423–447.

McCormick, E. J. (1976). Job and task analysis. In M. D. Dunnette (Ed.), *Handbook of industrial and organizational psychology* (pp. 651–696). Chicago: Rand McNally.

Saal, F. E., & Landy, F. J. (1977). The mixed standard rating scale: An evaluation. *Organizational Behavior and Human Performance, 18,* 19–35.

Smith, P. C. (1976). Behaviors, results, and organizational effectiveness. In M. D. Dunnette (Ed.), *Handbook of industrial and organizational psychology* (pp. 745–775). Chicago: Rand McNally.

Teel, K. A. (1978). Self-appraisal revisited. *Personnel Journal, 57,* 364–367.

Thornton, G. C., III. (1968). The relationship between supervisory and self-appraisals of executive performance. *Personnel Psychology, 21,* 441–455.

Thornton, G. C., III. (1980). Psychometric properties of self-appraisals of job performance. *Personnel Psychology, 33,* 236–271.

3. BEHAVIOR-BASED RATING SCALES

Walter C. Borman

Introduction

This chapter focuses on behavioral approaches to rating the job performance of persons in work organizations. Several such methods have been developed, and these strategies will be reviewed and critically evaluated.

Fairly and accurately evaluating job performance in industrial, educational, and government organizations is a critical element in maintaining and enhancing organizational effectiveness. Recognizing and rewarding top performers and identifying poorer performers for appropriate training or other personnel actions are fundamental to effective management of organizations.

Ideally, totally objective performance measures should be used to index individuals' job performance. Objective performance measurement is possible to some degree in certain jobs. For example, piecework in factory jobs can be evaluated somewhat objectively according to quality of product and quantity of output per unit time. However, for the vast majority of jobs, there exist no objective criteria of success, or existing objective indices are woefully inadequate for providing a comprehensive assessment of job performance.

Consider as an example sales jobs. Effectiveness of a salesperson might be assessed according to his or her total sales for some length of time compared to the average sales for the same period, but this does not take into account unequal opportunity to make sales. Some sales territories may provide better opportunities than others for making large sales, and this inequity creates difficulties in comparing effectiveness levels of different salespeople.

Also, there are additional important performance factors in most sales jobs. Two examples are developing a client base for long-term success and providing good follow-up service to maintain customer satisfaction. Thus sales per unit time is often a deficient performance criterion in that it fails to take into account important aspects of the job.

In a similar vein, for a clerical job, consider using number of times late o absent over some period and the number of words or pages typed per unit tim under some specified set of circumstances as indices of performance effective ness on the job. Although these measures may provide some indication of effec tiveness in certain aspects of the job, there is probably differential opportunity t "score well" on these indices. For example, differences in typewriters, differei tial distraction from coworkers, and clarity of different input handwriting can t factors in determining typing output, and this creates potential bias in the words pages per unit time criterion.

100

Again, the central problem is in criterion deficiency. These measures simply do not present anywhere near a complete picture of a person's job performance. Being well organized in filing, creating attractive data tables, getting along with clients (if these are part of the job), and other components of performance effectiveness are not addressed by these two measures.

Likewise, close scrutiny of other so-called objective performance indices reveals serious inadequacies of measurement (Dunnette, 1966; Ghiselli & Brown, 1955; Guion, 1965). Because of these inadequacies, performance appraisal ratings have often been utilized to obtain estimates of individual employees' job performance levels. Related to criterion deficiency, a distinct but seldom mentioned advantage of ratings as job performance measures is that if the performance requirements of a job can be articulated at all, they can be defined on a rating form to guide the rater. This is not to say performance ratings are the answer to performance measurement problems. They unfortunately possess their own set of problems. However, comprehensively defining important job performance requirements *is definitely possible* utilizing a performance rating form. Of course, how best to present those performance requirements on a rating format is at issue.

One type of rating form that gets considerable use is a simple numerical rating scale. Examples of this kind of scale appear in Figure 3.1 (see also Jacobs, chapter 2). The performance dimensions, definitions of the dimensions, and the exact format may vary, but the main feature of the scale is that numbers "anchor" the different levels of performance on the scale.

An obvious problem with numerical rating scales is that the rater has trouble discerning what is meant by different numerical levels on the scale. Raters may have different ideas about the meaning of a "4" on a seven-point scale or a "3.5" on a four-point scale. A "4" to one rater might mean the same performance level as a "5" or a "6" to other raters. Numerical rating scales, then, suffer from a lack of specificity in the meaning of different performance levels.

Likewise, several of the rating formats described by Jacobs in chapter 2 have this problem. The ranking and pair-comparison methods differentiate between employees, but the levels of performance for each ratee remain unspecified, and the trait and graphic rating scales are typically anchored with numbers of adjectives such as "excellent," "adequate," or "poor."

One way to address this lack of specificity is to use behavior-oriented rating scales. The rest of this chapter reviews and evaluates several behavioral approaches to assessing job performance in organizations.

Review of Behavior-based Rating Methods

BEHAVIORALLY ANCHORED RATING SCALES (BARS)

The behavioral expectations scale concept was introduced more than twenty years ago by Smith and Kendall (1963). These scales are now known more gener-

FIGURE 3.1. Numerical rating scales

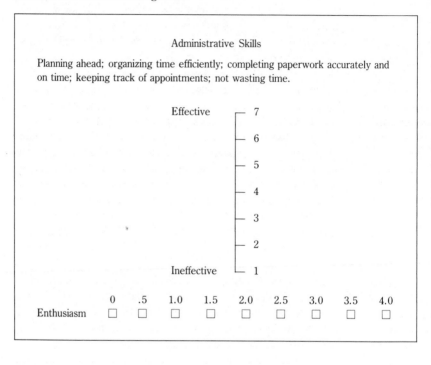

ically as behaviorally anchored rating scales (BARS). Smith and Kendall reasoned that different effectiveness levels on job performance rating scales might be "anchored" using behavioral examples of incumbent performance. Accordingly, they developed performance rating dimensions with scaled behavioral examples anchoring the different effectiveness levels on the dimensions. One such rating dimension appears in Figure 3.2.

Where do these anchors come from and how are the scales developed? A common approach to BARS development is outlined below:

1. Individuals knowledgeable about the target job contribute behavioral examples of job incumbent performance; these individuals are asked to provide examples reflecting all different levels of effectiveness and all different parts of the job.

2. The many examples (often 200 to 300 or more) are clustered by content, and categories of performance (e.g., administration and paperwork, working effectively with coworkers) are named and defined.

3. Each member of another group knowledgeable about the job ("retranslation" group) sorts each behavioral example into the category he or she believes it

FIGURE 3.2. Behaviorally anchored performance category

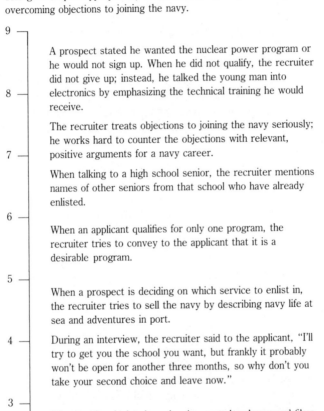

Salesmanship Skills

Skillfully persuading prospects to join the navy; using navy benefits and opportunities effectively to sell the navy; closing skills; adapting selling techniques appropriately to different prospects; effectively overcoming objections to joining the navy.

9 —

A prospect stated he wanted the nuclear power program or he would not sign up. When he did not qualify, the recruiter did not give up; instead, he talked the young man into

8 — electronics by emphasizing the technical training he would receive.

The recruiter treats objections to joining the navy seriously; he works hard to counter the objections with relevant,

7 — positive arguments for a navy career.

When talking to a high school senior, the recruiter mentions names of other seniors from that school who have already enlisted.

6 —

When an applicant qualifies for only one program, the recruiter tries to convey to the applicant that it is a desirable program.

5 —

When a prospect is deciding on which service to enlist in, the recruiter tries to sell the navy by describing navy life at sea and adventures in port.

4 — During an interview, the recruiter said to the applicant, "I'll try to get you the school you want, but frankly it probably won't be open for another three months, so why don't you take your second choice and leave now."

3 —

The recruiter insisted on showing more brochures and films even though the applicant told him he wanted to sign up right now.

2 —

When a prospect states an objection to being in the navy, the recruiter ends the conversation because he thinks the prospect must not be interested.

1 —

best fits and rates the effectiveness level of each example; means, standard deviations, and category frequencies are calculated for each example.

4. The investigator decides which behavioral examples are to be included as anchors on each category, using the criteria of low standard deviations for the effectiveness ratings (i.e., good agreement between retranslation raters) and high agreement between these raters on the sorting task.

5. The final scales are prepared using the behavioral examples that meet the criteria set forth in step 4.

As Smith and Kendall (1963) explained, the rater's task in using BARS to evaluate a ratee is to record a number of behavioral examples of that ratee's performance related to the content of the category and then to compare the effectiveness of those actual examples with the effectiveness reflected in the scaled behavioral examples. To clarify, suppose a rater reviews a navy recruiter's performance over the last six months and generates the following three performance examples related to the category "salesmanship skills" (see Figure 3.2 for the category):

1. Joe wanted an applicant to enlist in a six-year nuclear program, but he was quick to list a number of alternatives when the applicant expressed misgivings about committing himself for so long.

2. When Joe learned that the applicant had hitchhiked to the office, he told him that joining the navy was a good way to earn money to buy a car. The applicant became convinced and enlisted.

3. An applicant failed to qualify for the program he strongly desired. Joe was unable to convince the applicant to join in another program, but he did persuade him to see the senior classifier for more information on other programs.

Now the rater compares the first example to the scaled performance examples and decides its effectiveness level is about the same as the example at the 5+ level. Our rater goes through the same comparison process with the other two examples and decides they fit at about the 5.5 and 6 levels, respectively. Such performance information would probably lead this rater to evaluate Joe at the 6 level on this category.

The important features of the rating process just described are (1) that the rater is essentially forced to think of behavioral performance specimens related to an employee's effectiveness (rather than impressions or vague remembrances of his or her performance), and (2) that the behavioral anchors provide definite benchmarks against which to compare observed ratee performance.

BEHAVIOR SUMMARY SCALES (BSS)

BARS provides a conceptual breakthrough in performance rating scale development. However, several researchers have experienced difficulties with

BARS in the field (e.g., Borman, 1979), and in reaction to these difficulties, the behavior summary scale (BSS) format was developed.

First, what about the problems with BARS? Reconsider for a moment the process a rater must go through to arrive at a rating on BARS. The process Smith and Kendall recommended was just described. In the slightly different approach suggested by Dunnette (1966), a rater is instructed to think carefully of the ratee's typical performance related to a BARS category, and then to compare the level of that performance to the level of performance represented by the behavioral anchors. The rater rates a person by judging where the observed performance "fits in" with respect to the scaled behavioral examples.

Unfortunately, these comparison and fitting steps are difficult for most raters because often they have a hard time discerning any behavioral similarity between a ratee's performance and the highly specific behavioral examples used to anchor the scale. Consider, for example, the difficulty a rater might have in relating a ratee's job performance to the following behavioral anchor, which represents somewhat ineffective performance as a first-line supervisor:

When a manager requested that this supervisor instruct one of her clerks to provide another unit with some data on an exception basis, the supervisor agreed to this, but explained that there would be a week's delay owing to the clerk's heavy workload.

Obviously, few, if any ratees will have exhibited exactly this behavior, even if they are performing at the somewhat ineffective level that the behavioral anchor is intended to represent. In effect, the rater must infer that the above behavior is the kind of action that the ratee *could be expected* to take. This, of course, was the rationale offered by Smith and Kendall when they phrased their behavioral anchors according to an expectation wording (e.g., This supervisor *can be expected* to confront an employee when he or she is late for work). However, although the expectation format eases the logical problem related to asking a rater to match observed ratee behavior with infrequently occurring scaled examples, the rater still must make an awkward judgment about where observed ratee behavior fits on a scale consisting of behavioral examples that the ratee has normally not exhibited.

One means of easing this difficulty is to anchor performance rating scales with more general or abstract behavioral benchmarks. These general statements of performance at different levels of effectiveness add perspective to the depiction of performance and, if properly developed, they may be preferable to specific behavior examples. In particular, the writing of general behavioral descriptions might be formalized by content analyzing and then abstracting behavioral examples that have been successfully retranslated into each performance level and category.

To develop these general behavioral statements, the highly specific incidents representing a given level of performance effectiveness on a particular perfor-

FIGURE 3.3. A behavior summary scale to rate navy recruiter performance

---

Establishing and Maintaining Good Relationships in the Community

Contacting and working effectively with high school counselors, newspaper editors, radio and TV personnel, and others capable of helping recruiters to enlist prospects; building a good reputation for the navy by developing positive relationships with persons in the community; establishing and maintaining good relationships with parents and family of prospects; presenting a good navy image in the community.

9 or 10
Extremely Effective Performance

Is exceptionally adept at cultivating and maintaining excellent relationships with school counselors, teachers, principals, police, news media persons, local business persons, and other persons who are important for getting referrals and free advertising.

Is innovative in informing the public about the navy; actively promotes the navy and makes friends for the navy while doing it; always distributes the most current navy information.

Volunteers off-duty time to work on community projects, celebrations, parades, etc.

6, 7, or 8
Effective Performance

Spends productive time with individuals such as police, city government, or school officials; may lunch with them, distribute calendars, appointment books, buttons, etc., to them, and/or invite them for cocktails.

Arranges for interested persons such navy activities as trips to the Naval Academy; keeps relevant persons informed of navy activities.

Encourages principals, counselors, and other persons important to a prospect to call if they have any questions about the navy.

3, 4, or 5
Marginal Performance

Contacts school officials only sporadically; keeps them waiting for information they want; relationships with counselors, teachers, etc., and persons important to an applicant or recruit are distant and underdeveloped.

Is not alert to opportunities to promote the navy; rarely volunteers off-duty time to promote the navy and is unenthusiastic when approached to do something for the community; rarely accepts speaking invitations.

Is, at times, discourteous to persons in the community; for example, sends form letters to persons who assisted him or other navy recruiters; is not always alert to the family's desire for more information about the navy and the program in which their son or daughter enlisted.

FIGURE 3.3.   (*continued*)

1 or 2
Ineffective Performance

Does not contact high school counselors; does not accept speaking engagements; drives around in car instead of getting out and meeting people.	Alienates persons in community or persons important to an applicant or recruit by ignoring them, not answering their questions, responding rudely, demanding information, encouraging high school students to drop out of school; sometimes does not appear at recruiting presentations for which he or she is scheduled.	Presents negative image of the navy by doing things like driving while intoxicated or speeding and honking impatiently at other drivers; may express dislike for the navy or recruiting.

mance category can be examined for the underlying thread of common behavioral components. Benchmarks may then be written to represent the wider range of scaled, work-related behavior that is representative of and common to the several specific incidents scaled at each level. Using several incidents to form these somewhat broader anchors has the added advantage of making fuller use of all the behavioral incidents that were gathered instead of forcing the researcher to choose just one to represent each scale point.

A brief description of a BSS development effort may clarify the method (Borman, Hough, & Dunnette, 1976). Thirty-seven navy recruiters and their supervisors attended a two-day workshop to generate behavioral examples of recruiter performance. The workshop yielded over eight hundred examples. One hundred and thirty-five additional behavioral examples were gleaned from stories navy recruits provided about their recent interaction with recruiters.

Researchers, with the help of persons intimately familiar with the recruiter job, content analyzed the more than nine hundred behavioral examples and decided tentatively that nine categories adequately described the navy recruiter performance domain. Six hundred and fifteen nonredundant examples from the larger pool were then retranslated by sixteen to thirty-nine navy recruiters and their supervisors according to the procedures outlined by Smith and Kendall described above. Retranslation left 352 performance examples reliably sorted and scaled.

It was concluded that these 352 performance examples formed a representative pool of examples reflecting navy recruiter performance requirements. The goal now was to have the performance scales represent as completely as possible the content of all of these reliably retranslated examples.

This goal was accomplished as follows. First, for each performance category, all the examples were grouped into four levels according to their mean retranslation rating. The levels used were "very high" (7–9), "high" (5–6.99), "low" (2.25–4.99), and "very low" (1–2.249). Then three behaviorally oriented statements were written describing the content of examples at each level for each category. For example, for one category, three statements were written for the "very high" level reflecting the content of the seven performance examples reliably retranslated into that category and level. In this manner, three behaviorally oriented summary statements were generated for each performance level within each performance category.

Examples of these behavioral statements appear in Figure 3.3 where one performance category of a behavior summary scale is shown. Notice that these statements are more general than behavioral examples, and that they attempt to reflect a variety of ways to perform at each performance level. Behavior summary scales have now been developed for several jobs, including among others electric power plant operator, clerical positions, stockbroker, sales manager, correctional officer, and U.S. Army enlisted jobs.

BEHAVIOR OBSERVATION SCALES (BOS)

The behavior observation scale (BOS) approach to obtaining job performance ratings takes a different tack than does BARS or BSS (Latham, Fay, & Saari, 1979). With the BOS approach, observable behavioral statements are presented to the rater and he or she is asked to rate employees on a five-point scale, from almost never (does this) to almost always (does this). Two examples for evaluating foremen are provided.

1. Explains job requirements to new employees in a clear manner (e.g., talks slowly, shows them how to do it).

    Almost Never   0 1 2 3 4   Almost Always
2. Tells workers that if they have any questions or problems to feel free to come to talk to him or her.

    Almost Never   0 1 2 3 4   Almost Always

Many such statements typically emerge from a behavioral job analysis, and they can be presented in a format similar to the preceding one and utilized in rating employee performance. Just as the BARS procedures should result in an exhaustive set of performance categories reflecting all important job performance requirements, the BOS method should provide a comprehensive list of behavioral statements, likewise representing all important performance requirements (Latham & Wexley, 1981). Also, just as the BSS format allows representation of all behavioral information from the performance examples successfully retranslated, the BOS procedure retains all behavioral statements generated.

It is possible with BOS to form categories of performance reflecting different aspects of the job. One approach is to have researchers group the BOS items into categories according to their content and then name and define each category. Retranslation of the category system can then proceed, with a sample of job incumbents and/or their supervisors sorting examples into the categories and using an agreement index to assess the interjudge consensus in the sorting task. Categories with low agreement indices can be studied to reevaluate the items in them or to assess the adequacy of category definitions. To obtain a score for a ratee on a category, ratings on the category's items are simply added, and the total rating is divided by the number of items. High scores indicate effective performance in the category.

Another way to obtain categories is to obtain ratings of job incumbents on each item, intercorrelate items, and then factor analyze the resulting correlation matrix. Items should group together with other items measuring the same category. Performance categories can be developed and ratings can be obtained for each of these categories by averaging ratings on each item belonging to the category.

From a conceptual point of view, the most important feature of this rating approach is that the rater must focus on reasonably specific ratee behaviors when making a rating on an item. Consider the item "Describes to subordinates details of the job change." The judgment of how frequently a ratee does this is relatively straightforward, with few complex inferences required of the rater. This approach has advantages because people often have problems integrating interpersonal information to make complex judgments about behavior (see, e.g., Borman, 1983; Cooper, 1981; Feldman, 1980). The BOS strategy for obtaining performance ratings has been criticized (Bernardin & Kane, 1980; Murphy, Martin, & Garcia, 1982), and the pros and cons of the strategy will be discussed in the next section, but BOS does provide another behavior-based alternative to numerical rating scales.

BEHAVIORAL ASSESSMENT APPROACHES

Although not typically thought of as a method to measure work performance, the behavioral assessment strategy for evaluating behavior has potentially useful application to performance measurement. Cone (1980) recently observed that certain behavioral assessment practices and procedures may be profitably applied in the measurement of job performance. He noted that measurement in behavioral assessment shares many of the problems (and possibilities) of measurement of work performance in organizations.

Komaki and her colleagues (Komaki, 1981; Komaki, Blood, & Holder, 1980; Komaki, Collins, & Thoene, 1980) have actually adapted behavioral assessment tactics to address problems of measuring work performance, and a brief review of this work will demonstrate how behavioral assessment principles might be utilized to provide improvements in performance measurement.

In her work with the marine corps, Komaki studied preventive maintenance jobs and, as part of that work, developed a behavioral performance assessment system. The system was designed with four principles in mind. First, it was to be sensitive to worker efforts, measuring parts of the job that are under the direct control of workers. Second, the system was intended to be objective, with well-defined behavioral indicators identified to help observers make extremely reliable judgments of performance. Third, the behavioral measures were to be made on site at the workplace rather than in a laboratory or simulated work setting. And fourth, measurement was to take place frequently, not just at one time or on an annual basis.

As an example, two performance dimensions were identified for first echelon preventive maintenance personnel: (1) detecting deficiencies and (2) follow through. A trial behavioral checklist was then developed to help observers evaluate performance related to these dimensions. These observers were trained in behavior observation and practiced using the checklist to make ratings of individuals in this job. During the trial measurement period, Komaki assessed interrater agreement with the various items and studied problems that emerged with the checklist. She then made revisions in the instrument. The final checklist is shown in Figure 3.4.

The most important feature of the checklist is the activity and indicator criteria column, which lays out for the observer exactly what is to be assessed in behavioral terms. Interrater agreement on this instrument exceeded 90 percent for all items and, in weekly measurements, continued at that level over a year-long period.

Thus behavioral assessment applied to performance measurement provides a high fidelity, objective evaluation of skills necessary for certain parts of the job. One might question the proportion of the relevant job performance domain that can be addressed using such methods, but for those jobs and dimensions adequately covered, the system certainly avoids difficulties with complex judgment process steps. More will be said about this in the next section.

Advantages and Disadvantages of Behavioral Rating Methods

A seldom noted but distinct advantage of the BARS, BSS, and BOS strategies for developing rating scales is that the performance domain for a target job is exhausted, revealing all important performance requirements of the job. In fact, consider for a moment what behavior scaling workshops are designed to yield. Participants generate performance specimens directly from their personal experience viewing job-relevant behavior. They are not asked to be armchair psychol-

FIGURE 3.4. Behavioral checklist

VEHICLE #: ___H2863_____   UNIT: __Juliet_____

PM PERSONNEL SIGNATURE: __PFC Smith_____   DATE: __18 Feb. '81__

Note √ if satisfactory; X if item needs to be repaired, adjusted, serviced, cleaned, lubed or replaced; or C/C if can't check.

√, X or C/C	COMMENTS	ITEM GROUP 1-ENGINE COMPARTMENT	ACTIVITY AND INDICATOR (criteria)
✓	_____	1. Radiator/Hoses	A. Check radiator for tightness. B. Check hoses for any cracks or leaks. C. Ensure cap present. D. Ensure chain is attached at both ends.
✓	_____	2. Oil level	A. Check engine oil level (between low & full marks). B. Ensure oil fill cap present & not loose fitting. C. Ensure oil fill cap chain is attached at both ends.
X	lower belt missing	3. Belts	A. Check for proper tension (only 1/2″ play, goat not "sloppy"). B. Check for fraying or cracking.
✓	_____	4. Generator/Alter-nator	A. Ensure generator/alternator secured to vehicle. B. Shake each cable connection for tightness.
✓	_____	5. Oil filter/Oil cooler	A. Check seal around filter for leaks.
X	_____	6. Starter/Carbure-tor	A. Ensure engine starts. B. Check all(hoses) (one type jeep carburetor has loose hose) for attachment & tightness.
✓	_____	7. Linkages (all)	A. Check drive shaft for free play (up & down or in excess of 1″) or loose U-bolts. B. Ensure all linkages lubed (not dry): winch, high & low transfer, gas, brake & clutch pedals, hand brake. C. Check for any rust.

ogists responsible for developing performance dimensions or to accomplish other relatively abstract tasks. Participants simply provide "stories" about effective and ineffective job performance, a task they can perform very naturally and well. Provided that the participant groups are instructed to write these stories about all different aspects of the job, the sampling of job content is excellent.

In other words, these approaches focus on precisely the performance criteria of interest—what behaviors on the job differentiate between effective and ineffective performers? Again, the most important point here is that performance examples appear to offer extremely relevant raw material for developing performance dimensions.

One might argue that dimensions from fine-grained task analyses should be most job relevant, provided that the task list exhausts all important job tasks and activities. Grouping tasks according to content or performing factor analyses of task time spent or importance ratings of tasks can certainly yield dimensions that are job relevant. However, when both task and behavioral analyses are conducted on the same job, the behavioral analysis dimensions contain a certain evaluative component not evident in the task dimensions (Borman & Dunnette, 1978; Hollenbeck & Borman, 1976).

For example, a hard work/extra effort dimension has emerged from behavioral analyses, and yet this dimension cannot possibly surface from task analysis results (try to conceive of a task that would be classified into such a dimension). Essentially, tasks and task dimensions are good at measuring *what* people do on jobs, and behavioral performance dimensions are good at measuring *how effectively* people perform on those tasks.

A recent paper examined the relative advantages and disadvantages of different job analysis strategies as perceived by job analysis experts (Levine, Ash, & Bennett, 1980), Levine and his colleagues asked these experts to assess the utility for personnel selection of four job analysis methods (see also Fine, chapter 1). Four jobs were studied, each job employing each of the methods—task analysis, behavioral analysis (i.e., BARS), the position analysis questionnaire method (PAQ), and the job elements approach.[1] Specialists in personnel selection evaluated the information provided by each method. Behavioral analysis results were seen as best for (1) providing "adequate information for performance measures," (2) yielding "an effective picture of general job performance requirements," and (3) providing "a comprehensive picture of performance requirements." Thus, again, for purposes of defining job performance requirements, behavioral criterion development strategies appear most useful.

Of course, the advantages of behavioral analysis for developing dimensions reveal nothing about how these methods actually operate in practice. That is, do the ratings of employees that are generated using behaviorally oriented formats yield higher quality and more accurate performance information?

A number of studies have shown that behavioral expectation scales or BARS

---

1. The position analysis questionnaire method (PAQ) has persons knowledgeable about a job rate the importance of a number of job elements and human attributes for performance on the job. With the job elements method, defined job elements are rated on a scale related to their presence and importance for a job. For further details on these job analysis methods, see chapter 1.

procedures generate ratings with less psychometric error (e.g., leniency, halo, restriction of range) than do other kinds of rating scales (e.g., numerically anchored scales). Studies by Campbell, Dunnette, Arvey, and Hellervik (1973), Groner (1974), Keaveny and McGann (1975), and Borman and Dunnette (1975) are favorable to behavior scale ratings, although in some cases only minor improvements in rating quality are evident for behavior scales over other types of rating scales. Other studies indicate no psychometric superiority for behavior-based scales over other rating formats (Bernardin, 1977; Bernardin, Alvares, & Cranny, 1976; Borman & Vallon, 1974; Burnaska & Hollmann, 1974; DeCotiis, 1977; Zedeck, Kafry, & Jacobs, 1976). A couple of examples can convey the nature of this format comparison research.

In one study, Borman and Dunnette (1975) administered to navy officer supervisors behaviorally anchored scales, scales with the same dimensions but no anchors, and unanchored rating scales with trait dimensions. Officer raters evaluated their subordinate junior officers, and the behavior scales yielded ratings with the lowest means (presumably less leniency), the least halo, and the greatest variation across ratees (least restriction of range). However, the results were not strikingly favorable to the behavior-based scales, and Borman and Dunnette concluded that 5 percent or less of the variance in leniency, halo, and restriction of range could be accounted for by format differences.

Bernardin, Alvares, and Cranny (1976) compared ratings by college students of instructors made on summated scales[2] to ratings made on behavioral expectations scales. Ratings on the behavior-based scales actually resulted in greater leniency and less interrater agreement. In a follow-up study, Bernardin (1977) demonstrated that when more rigor was applied to the development of the behavior scales, the behavioral format performed as well psychometrically as the carefully constructed summated scales. This result suggests that the care taken to develop the rating form may be a more critical factor than the specific kind of format employed.

In sum, behavioral approaches to measuring work performance appear to have several advantages. The most clear-cut advantage relates to the conceptual clarity with which the performance domain is defined using BARS, BBS, or BOS methods. The performance space for a job can be exhaustively sampled with these scale development procedures, and the dimension system derived from the procedures is an elegant behavior-based depiction of the job's performance requirement.

An important spin-off of this advantage is that raters using the dimensions in a

---

2. Summated scales consist of a series of statements related to effective job performance on a dimension, for example, "This person appears well organized and well prepared for the interview." The rater evaluating a ratee responds on a scale from definitely agree (e.g., 5) to definitely disagree (e.g., 1). A dimension score is obtained by summing the ratings on all statements targeted toward that dimension (see chapter 2 for details).

for-research-only mode or in an administrative performance appraisal application are likely to accept the dimension system as representing a fair and accurate portrayal of what is required on the job. This is of course an important prerequisite for getting raters to generate accurate ratings.

A second but less definite advantage is the psychometric error reduction evident with behavior scales compared to other kinds of scales. Several studies have demonstrated slight psychometric superiority for behavior-based scales, although other studies admittedly show no differences in psychometric error. Rating format was found to have no consistent effect on rating accuracy (Borman, 1979), but only one study addressed this directly.

A disadvantage is the relatively high cost of developing behavior-based formats. Considerable effort on the part of the researcher and organization members is necessary to prepare these formats, especially the behavioral assessment scoring systems.

There are also some specific advantages and disadvantages to each of these behavior-based rating methods.

BARS

The most appealing feature of BARS is the specific behavioral anchors that provide concrete benchmarks to guide raters in making their evaluations. This feature is the fundamental breakthrough made by Smith and Kendall, and the BSS and BOS formats we discussed are essentially adaptations of the Smith and Kendall innovation.

As mentioned earlier in the chapter, raters have experienced some difficulty matching observed ratee performance and the often very specific, low–base rate behaviors serving as anchors on the scales. The BSS format was devised primarily in reaction to this problem (Borman, 1979). This rating scale has some advantages, conceptually at least.

BSS

Regarding raters' use of the scales, the most important potential advantage of behavior summary scales is that the behavioral construct underlying each aspect of job performance is made more evident to the rater; in effect, the rater is relieved of the necessity of inferring the dimensionality from a series of highly specific incidents. The inferential step is accomplished in scale development where the behavioral essence from several specific incidents is distilled in each behavior summary statement.

Also important, this approach should increase the probability that raters can match observed ratee behavior directly with scaled behavior. That is, by increasing the scope of behavior representing various performance levels on a scale, chances are greater that one of the anchors will accurately describe a ratee's performance in that job facet. The process of directly matching observed and scaled behavior should be easier for raters than the inferential process necessary with BARS.

This argument makes good conceptual sense, but in the one format comparison study pitting BARS against a BSS format, there were no consistent differences between these format types with respect to psychometric error or accuracy (Borman, 1979). Thus the seeming conceptual advantage of BSS may not make any difference in the actual use of the scale.

BOS

Latham and Wexley (1981) provided a list of advantages of BOS, including the following: (a) Behavior observation scales are developed from a systematic job analysis; (b) the content of the explicit behavioral items provides an excellent listing of the job's performance requirements in concrete behavioral terms; and (c) item analysis and factor analytic procedures can be more readily applied to BOS ratings than to BARS or BSS data. To these should be added that BOS items appear to cut down on the complexity of inferences necessary to make a rating. Research has shown that raters have trouble making complicated evaluative inferences (e.g., Borman, 1983; Cooper, 1981; Feldman, 1981), and so a system that relieves raters of some of this burden probably has an advantage.

The apparent advantage of a relatively direct rating on a straightforward behavioral statement may be illusory, however. Murphy, Martin, and Garcia (1982) have shown that BOS might measure traitlike judgments rather than tapping simple observations. They found that BOS ratings correlated consistently higher with judgmental graphic scale evaluations when ratings were made on both formats one day after the raters viewed ratees in a film than when raters used both formats immediately after viewing the film. The inference is that BOS used as a rating scale under a delayed rating condition (as, presumably, they would be used in practice) yield traitlike evaluations similar to those generated from graphic rating scales.

Another criticism of BOS has been voiced. Bernardin and Kane (1982) pointed out that the frequency metric of BOS ("almost never" to "almost always") reflects different levels of effectiveness on different behavioral items. The example they use is that a "3" on the 0–4 scale (e.g., 90 percent of the time) may be extremely effective with the police detective job item "obtains arrest warrants within three months in homicide cases," but very ineffective for the item "is vindicated by the Internal Review Board for using lethal force." This may be an extreme case, and Latham and Wexley (1981) do mention that the frequency percentages can be changed for different organizations and jobs, but the point here is that even within job and organization the relative effectiveness values of each frequency range should probably be scaled to reflect these possible differences.

To the best of my knowledge, no empirical comparisons have been made between BOS and other rating formats. However, the summated format is very similar to BOS, and several format comparison studies have included summated scales. Campbell, Dunnette, Arvey, and Hellervik (1973) found more psychometric error in summated scales than in BARS, but no item analyses were performed on the summated scale items (as is recommended in BOS development). Bernardin (1977) and Borman (1979) found no substantial differences between summated scales and BARS in psychometric errors or accuracy. Thus BOS formats are not likely to be clearly superior when used in practice, although they seem to perform as well as other relatively sophisticated scales (Latham, Saari, & Fay, 1980).

BEHAVIORAL ASSESSMENT

Behavioral assessment ratings and behavior counts typically require very little inference on the part of the rater/observer. This is a distinct advantage because it has been shown that raters experience significant cognitive limitations related to complex interpersonal perceptions and judgments (e.g., Feldman, 1981; Ross, 1977).

In Cone's discussion of the relevance of behavioral assessment to performance measurement, he described issues that point up both the positive and negative features of using behavioral assessment principles in measuring performance (Cone, 1980; Foster & Cone, 1980). One critical issue is validity of measurement, which refers both to accuracy of the observations with respect to what the researcher is intending to measure and to ecological validity, or how well the measurement system "covers" the constructs of interest. Regarding the first type of validity, as with research in performance ratings, it has often been more convenient not to study validity or accuracy, but rather some other characteristics of the ratings, such as interobserver reliability. One of the important findings of the reliability research is that agreement in ratings, using even carefully developed behavior coding systems, typically starts out high, but "observer drift" (e.g., Kent & Foster, 1977) reduces the interobserver agreement as raters forget details of the coding system or develop idiosyncratic interpretations of the system.

Problems with ecological validity have to do with selecting the proper behaviors to assess, that is, behaviors that are relevant to the construct of interest. Major difficulties akin to personnel psychology's criterion problem of deficiency are likely to occur if the target construct is complex. In addition, there is the issue of which behavioral property to measure (Foster & Cone, 1980). For example, frequency, latency, and duration may be important, as well as qualitative aspects of the behavior. Unfortunately, the familiar fidelity-bandwidth problem is at work here. Very narrow (and in many cases trivial) behavior categories can be measured very precisely and unambiguously, whereas more complex (and often more important) categories are more difficult to measure.

Thus a limitation of behavioral analysis approaches to performance measurement is the difficulty of adequately measuring all elements in the performance domain, especially for complex jobs. Consider, for example, trying to develop a behavioral measurement system to tap successfully all important performance constructs on a management job. Some parts of such a job may be amenable to the method (e.g., interpersonal effectiveness at meetings with subordinates might be indexed by noting head-nodding behavior in support of subordinates' statements and proportion of time subordinates have the floor), but the coverage of other important performance areas may well be more problematic (e.g., decision making).

Nonetheless, for certain elements of the criterion space, it is likely that highly faithful pictures of individuals' performance may be obtained. In particular, lower-level technical jobs and the parts of jobs involving technical skills appear to offer the best possibilities for fruitful application of behavioral assessment methods.

Recommendations

Although distinct conceptual differences are evident between BARS, BSS, and BOS in terms of (1) format development steps, (2) the resulting formats themselves, and (3) the operations raters must employ to make ratings on the formats, actual differences between ratings on these formats in relation to psychometric error and accuracy are likely to be minimal. True, only one study has actually compared different behavior-based formats on these dependent variables (Borman, 1979), but that study showed no consistent differences in the psychometric properties assessed or in accuracy between a BARS format and a BSS format. Moreover, the finding that no substantial differences exist in the quality of ratings (e.g., psychometric properties, interrater agreement) between behavior-based and other carefully developed rating formats suggests that comparisons between BARS, BSS, BOS, and other behavior rating scales are not likely to yield meaningful differences in rating quality. Landy and Farr (1980) called for a moratorium on format-related research, and unless the rating form in question is very different from those presented here, I concur with that position.

It should not be concluded, however, that performance rating scales can be developed carelessly. Consensus in the performance appraisal literature is that small variations in rating format are probably not important as long as the scales are developed carefully. Thus care in the preparation of performance rating scales is probably critical for generating high quality, relatively accurate, and error-free performance evaluations (Bernardin, 1977; Dunnette & Borman, 1979; Landy &

Farr, 1980; Jacobs, Kafry, & Zedeck, 1980). With this qualification regarding proper development, these behavior-based formats are recommended.

This chapter is about rating scales, and therefore the discussion has been limited to that topic, but a closing point should be made to provide perspective on the rating format considerations. Other factors must be addressed in developing performance assessment systems. Rater orientation and training on the assessment system, strategies to introduce and to "sell" the system to users, and consideration of who should perform the assessment (e.g., supervisors, peers, self) are examples of such factors. Also, as Jacobs stated so well in chapter 2, the purpose of assessment (e.g., for promotion, in test validation research) should be carefully considered before developing a performance assessment system. However, this review suggests that these behavior-based rating scales are top candidates for consideration as performance assessment measures.

References

Bernardin, H. J. (1977). Behavioral expectation scales versus summated scales: A fairer comparison. *Journal of Applied Psychology, 62,* 422–428.

Bernardin, H. J., Alvares, K. M., & Cranny, C. J. (1976). A recomparison of behavioral expectation scales to summated scales. *Journal of Applied Psychology, 61,* 564–570.

Bernardin, H. J., Kane, J. (1980). A second look at behavioral observation scales. *Personnel Psychology, 33,* 809–814.

Bernardin, H. J., & Walter, C. S. (1977). Effects of rater training and diary-keeping on psychometric error in ratings. *Journal of Applied Psychology, 62,* 64–69.

Borman, W. C. (1979). Format and training effects on rating accuracy and rater errors. *Journal of Applied Psychology, 64,* 410–421.

Borman, W. C. (1983). Implications of personality theory and research for the rating of work performance in organizations. In F. J. Landy, S. Zedeck, & J. Cleveland (Eds.), *Performance measurement and theory* (pp. 127–165). Hillsdale, NJ: Erlbaum.

Borman, W. C., & Dunnette, M. D. (1975). Behavior-based versus trait-oriented performance ratings: An empirical study. *Journal of Applied Psychology, 60,* 561–565.

Borman, W. C., & Dunnette, M. D. (1978). *Results of the Merrill Lynch office management study.* Minneapolis, MN: Personnel Decisions Research Institute.

Borman, W. C., Hough, L. M., & Dunnette, M. D. (1976). *Development of behaviorally based rating scales for evaluating the performance of U.S. Navy recruiters* (Technical Report TR-76-31). San Diego, CA: U.S. Navy Personnel Research and Development Center.

Borman, W. C., & Vallon, W. R. (1974). A view of what can happen when behavioral expectation scales are developed in one setting and used in another. *Journal of Applied Psychology, 59,* 197–201.

Burnaska, R. F., & Hollmann, T. D. (1974). An empirical comparison of the relative effects of rater response biases on three rating scale formats. *Journal of Applied Psychology, 59*, 307–312.

Campbell, J. P., Dunnette, M. D., Arvey, R. D., & Hellervik, L. V. (1973). The development and evaluation of behaviorally based rating scales. *Journal of Applied Psychology, 57*, 15–22.

Cone, J. D. (1980, April). *The overlapping worlds of behavioral assessment and performance appraisal.* Paper presented at the first annual Scientist-Practitioner Conference in Industrial/Organizational Psychology, Old Dominion University, Virginia Beach.

Cooper, W. H. (1981). Ubiquitous halo. *Psychological Bulletin, 90*, 218–244.

DeCotiis, T. A. (1977). An analysis of the external validity and applied relevance of three rating formats. *Organizational Behavior and Human Performance, 19*, 247–266.

Dunnette, M. D. (1966). *Personnel selection and placement.* Belmont, CA: Brooks-Cole.

Dunnette, M. D., & Borman, W. C. (1979). Personnel selection and classification systems. *Annual Review of Psychology, 30*, 477–525.

Feldman, J. (1981). Beyond attribution theory: Cognitive processes in performance appraisal. *Journal of Applied Psychology, 66*, 127–148.

Foster, S. L., & Cone, J. D. (1980). Current issues in direct observation. *Behavioral Assessment, 2*, 313–338.

Ghiselli, E. E., & Brown, C. W. (1955). *Personnel and industrial psychology* (2nd ed.). New York: McGraw-Hill.

Groner, D. M. (1974). *Reliability and susceptibility to bias of behavioral and graphic rating scales.* Unpublished doctoral dissertation, University of Minnesota.

Guion, R. M. (1965). *Personnel testing.* New York: McGraw-Hill.

Hollenbeck, G. P., & Borman, W. C. (1976, September). *Two analyses in search of a job—the implications of different job analysis approaches.* Paper presented at the annual meeting of the American Psychological Association, Washington, DC.

Jacobs, R., Kafry, D., & Zedeck, S. (1980). Expectations of behaviorally anchored rating scales. *Personnel Psychology, 33*, 595–640.

Kent, R. N., & Foster, S. L. (1977). Direct observational procedures: Methodological issues in applied settings. In A. Ciminero, K. S. Calhoun, & H. E. Adams (Eds.), *Handbook of behavioral assessment.* New York: Wiley.

Keaveny, T. J., & McGann, A. F. (1975). A comparison of behavioral expectation scales. *Journal of Applied Psychology, 60*, 695–703.

Komaki, J. (1981, August). *Behavioral measurement: Toward solving the criterion problem.* Paper presented at the annual meeting of the American Psychological Association, Los Angeles.

Komaki, J., Blood, M. R., & Holder, D. (1980). Fostering friendliness in a fast food franchise. *Journal of Organizational Behavior Management, 2*, 151–163.

Komaki, J., Collins, R. L., & Thoene, T. J. F. (1980). Behavioral measurement in business, industry, and government. *Behavioral Assessment, 2*, 103–123.

Landy, F. J., & Farr, J. (1980). Performance rating. *Psychological Bulletin, 87*, 72–107.

Latham, G. P., Fay, C. H., & Saari, L. M. (1979). The development of behavioral observation scales for appraising the performance of foremen. *Personnel Psychology, 32,* 299–311.

Latham, G. P., Saari, L. M., & Fay, C. H. (1980). BOS, BES, and boloney: Raising Kane with Bernardin. *Personnel Psychology, 33,* 815–821.

Latham, G. P., & Wexley, K. N. (1981). *Increasing productivity through performance appraisal.* Reading, MA: Addison-Wesley.

Levine, E. L., Ash, R. A., & Bennett, N. (1980). Exploratory comparative study of four job analysis methods. *Journal of Applied Psychology, 65,* 524–535.

Murphy, K. R., Martin, C., & Garcia, M. (1982). Do behavioral observation scales measure observation? *Journal of Applied Psychology, 67,* 562–567.

Ross, L. (1977). The intuitive psychologist and his shortcomings: Distortion in the attribution process. In L. Berkowitz (Ed.), *Advances in experimental social psychology* (Vol. 10, pp. 173–220). New York: Academic Press.

Smith, P., & Kendall, L. M. (1963). Retranslation of expectations: An approach to the construction of unambiguous anchors for rating scales. *Journal of Applied Psychology, 47,* 149–155.

Zedeck, S., Kafry, D., & Jacobs, R. (1976). Format and scoring variations in behavioral expectation evaluations. *Organizational Behavior and Human Performance, 17,* 171–184.

4. PERFORMANCE TESTS

Arthur I. Siegel

Introduction

The testing field has been the subject of considerable criticism, especially in the popular press, because of concerns with culture fairness, Equal Employment Opportunity Commission issues involving preemployment tests that are not clearly and directly job related, and differential validity problems. Answers to some of the questions raised by these issues can be derived from statistical analyses, experimental research, and improvements in item content. However, on the general level, the public is not interested in complex analytical studies that "prove" a point either one way or another. Moreover, regardless of validity coefficients that are of "acceptable" magnitude, written test items that depend on spatial relationships, analogies, vocabulary, and the like are frequently resisted by job applicants. Applicants often believe that they can learn and perform on the job although they have performed poorly on paper-and-pencil selection instruments. While there may or may not be merit to such contentions, the applicant with this point of view cannot help but think that he or she has been treated unfairly as the result of a paper-and-pencil testing program that was instrumental in the rejection.

Review of Work Sample and Miniature Job Training and Evaluation Tests

WORK SAMPLE TESTS

Definition. Work sample or performance testing involves a test situation in which the person being tested performs one or more practical tasks drawn from or based on the job itself. The test requires the examinee to demonstrate mastery of task performance and, by implication, possession of the requisite skills required for actual performance on the job. The quality of the examinee's performance is observed and scored while he or she works and the scoring is based on the quality of the product that the examinee produces. A work sample test may require the examinee to perform one of the tasks in the everyday routine, or it may involve a specially designed task that requires the demonstration of a skill essential to the job. Work sample tests are useful for purposes such as (1) assigning personnel to jobs so as to achieve their best utilization, (2) determining whether or not a person can actually perform a job for which he or she was trained, (3) determining who is

121

best prepared to handle special tasks, (4) determining who is best qualified for advancement, (5) assessing the results of training, and (6) identifying strengths and weaknesses in training programs.

Because work sample tests depend on demonstration of the ability to perform a job, they meet the objections of those who claim that they can do a good job but not "talk" a good job. The stress of the approach on doing a job answers the criticisms of those who claim to possess the ability to perform the real job but not the ability to respond to multiple-choice questions about job performance.

Moreover, properly constructed, administered, and scored work sample tests can be objective. Every person who takes the test(s) performs the same task(s) under the same conditions and is scored in exactly the same way no matter who does the scoring.

Background. The work sample approach to assessment is not new. Adkins (1947) presented a description of the method almost forty years ago. Since then, there have been few methodological advances. Most work sample tests have relied on some sort of standardized scoring checklist that is employed to score the performance of an examinee as he or she performs in a standardized task situation.

Asher and Sciarrino (1974) reviewed available realistic work sample tests through 1973. However, because they were interested only in situations in which there was a point-to-point correspondence between predictor and criterion space, their search was limited to those work sample tests created for specific criterion tasks. They identified thirty motor (tests involving the manipulation of things) and thirty verbal (language- or people-oriented) work sample tests. Asher and Sciarrino compared the reported predictive validity of the motor and the verbal work sample tests with the predictive validity of other types of psychometric instruments, as reported by Ghiselli (1966). Ghiselli published the proportion of validity coefficients that resulted when various types of tests were tried for specific jobs. The results of the Asher and Sciarrino comparison are presented in Table 4.1. These data indicate that, aside from biographical predictors, the motor work samples were consistently superior to the other types of predictors in terms of a job proficiency criterion. Biographical predictors contain much the same point-to-point connection between predictor and criterion space as work sample tests. The verbal work sample tests were consistently in the top half of the list in Table 4.1. Intelligence tests, motor work samples, and biographical instruments were consistently superior to verbal work sample tests. It is possible that paper-and-pencil tests of intelligence, which generally measure language and quantitative factors, may be at least equivalent to verbal work sample tests in the verbal area and add additional valid variance in the quantitative area.

When motor and verbal work sample tests were compared on their ability to predict training, Asher and Sciarrino found that while the motor work sample tests were the better predictor of job proficiency, the verbal work sample tests were

TABLE 4.1. Comparison of Validity Coefficients of Work Sample and Other Psychometric Instruments with Job Proficiency as the Criterion

	Proportion of Validity Coefficients		
Instrument	.50 or Higher	.40 or Higher	.30 or Higher
Motor work sample	43	70	78
Verbal work sample	21	41	60
Biographical	55	74	97
Intelligence	28	51	60
Mechanical aptitude	17	48	60
Finger dexterity	13	24	42
Personality	12	22	39
Spatial relations	3	9	16

the better predictor of training. Such results may have been anticipated because success in most training programs depends to a considerable degree on verbal skills.

Other investigations into the validity of the work sample approach have also been completed. Gordon and Kleiman (1976) indicated the superiority of work sample predictors over aptitude tests for predicting success in police training, and Foley (1977) supported their use for Air Force maintenance performance evaluation. Similarly, a laboratory investigation into the concurrent and the predictive validity of work sample tests and paper-and-pencil measures indicated advantages for work samples for personnel selection (Mount, Muchinsky, & Hanser, 1977). Morse code operator training, ground controlled aerial intercept (Briggs & Johnston, 1966), and police selection are among other jobs to which the technique has been applied.

Variants of work sample testing. While the work sample test approach has been more or less generally applied to procedurally oriented jobs, there is no need to restrict the approach to this kind of work. The *situational test* in which an effort is made to reproduce a context-rich situation was described by Weislogel (1954) as "a standard work sample test" that possesses items or situations that are similar to those the applicant will encounter during his or her day-to-day work. He described two field tests that measure leadership and infantry combat performance and a conference test to evaluate the nonintellectual aspects of officer leadership. Havron, Frey, and McGrath (1952) developed an elaborate situational test to measure rifle squad performance. The situation involved a six-hour, daylight scenario that included four basic combat tasks. Although this was a group situational test, evaluation of individual squad leaders was also included.

Perhaps the most elaborate situational test is found at the U.S. Army's National Training Center at Fort Irwin (Edwards, 1979). Here, battalion-size units are exercised over a multiday period on an enormous field range in situations that attempt to include almost all aspects of actual combat. An opposing force is included and there is considerable effort to portray battle realistically. Under both day and night conditions, air attack, artillery fire, tank activity, and the like serve to lend authenticity to the test.

The situational test does not seem to differ from the more rudimentary work sample test in the measures it uses. Ratings, counts, time measures, and checklists are usually employed to derive a "score." The unique contribution of the situational test seems to arise from its setting and administration rather than from its measures. Weislogel and Schwartz (1955) suggested that the scoring of situational tests should be limited to observations of the occurrence or nonoccurrence of specified behaviors. In this regard, they supported the use of critical incidents because the technique meets two additional requirements of situational tests: (1) the test must provide a measure of typical performance, and (2) the measures must be capable of evaluation according to a behavioral definition of job success.

The *in-basket test* (Frederiksen, Saunders, & Ward, 1957) is another variant of the work sample test. The in-basket approach represents an application of the work sample approach and point-to-point correspondence between predictor and criterion space at a higher level. It is often an ingredient of the "assessment center" approach (Bray & Grant, 1966). In the in-basket approach, the examinee is asked to play an administrative role and to take action on various letters, reports, and memoranda, which are in the in-basket. The applicant is asked to take such written action as he or she feels is required. Scoring is performed objectively according to weights assigned to various categories of responses (see Byham & Thornton, chapter 5, for details).

In summary, work sample testing and its variants possess a history of employment and, if properly constructed, seem to represent a useful evaluation approach. According to Robertson and Mindel (1980), they are well accepted by applicants. However, unless a work sample test simulates all the factors in the work situation, scores derived from it may evaluate (1) an incomplete or limited number of skills or characteristics, and (2) behavior that may not be needed or that may be inhibited under the stress of a real job. In this regard, Fiske (1951) believed that situational tests fall between aptitude tests and measures of on-the-job performance, possessing some of the worst features of both. Fiske's reservations about situational tests may equally apply to all types of work sample tests.

Internal aspects of work sample tests. There are also a number of studies that have investigated various internal aspects of the work sample approach. In work sample test scoring, judgments are usually made by the test administrator regarding the manner in which an examinee performs the components of a task. One of the problems with this type of judgment is that the perceptions of the test administrator may vary from time-to-time and may represent an uncontrolled variable in work sample testing. Of course, one way in which this type of variation may be partially controlled is to keep the items to be judged gross enough and objective enough so that misperception is minimized. If a definite frame of reference is written into each element scored, and if the observations required are kept gross, then the danger of perceptual variability in examiners may be minimized.

However, intraexaminer reliability remains a conceptual issue in work sample testing. The ideal method for determining intraexaminer consistency involves a situation in which the examinee's performance is held constant over two separate occasions and the examiner's perceptions are allowed to vary. However, it is not possible for anyone to perform the same job in exactly the same manner on two separate occasions. One method for holding the stimulus situation constant is to take a motion picture or videotape of the examinee performing the work sample task. The picture or tape may then be shown on two separate occasions and, on each occasion, the examiner can score the performance shown in the picture. The result is that the "performance" is constant over the two time intervals and any variation shown can be attributed to examiner unreliability. Two assumptions are that the picture situation is perceived by the examiner in the same manner as the actual work sample test situation and that the examiner scores the pictorial representation in the same manner as he or she scores the work sample test. Further assumptions are those made within any test-retest reliability check.

Siegel (1954b) constructed a drill point–grinding work sample test and made a movie of an examinee performing on the test. Five examiners viewed the motion picture on two separate occasions (with a one-month interval) and scored, during each viewing, the performance employing a standardized checklist. The list contained fourteen items, for example: Did the examinee use a coolant while grinding the drill? Did the examinee tap the grinding wheel or check it for cracks prior to its use? The examiners were all experienced on the task and possessed prior experience in work sample test administration. Siegel calculated the percentage consistency of each examiner across the two viewings. An examiner was judged consistent if an item was scored in exactly the same way on the two occasions. The grand mean for intraexaminer consistency was 83%, with a range from 64 to 100%. This 83% agreement would usually be interpreted as adequate. However, in view of the wide range shown, Siegel recommended that intraexaminer consistency be determined prior to assigning examiners to test administrative duties. If all examiners show low consistency, then either the examiner training has been poor or the objectivity of the test tasks is questionable. Naturally, only those examiners yielding high agreement indices are worthy of consideration as test administrators.

Another conceptual problem associated with work sample tests rests on the often employed analytic method of scoring both the examinee's work process and the quality of the product produced. For example, a performance checklist for welders (Siegel, 1954a) consisted of items relating to the way in which the welder performs (e.g., adjusts oxyacetylene regulators to 4–5 pounds, preheats base metal), adherence of the final product to prescribed standards (e.g., bead width 3–5 times base metal thickness), and to the safety precautions the welder follows (e.g., uses goggles when welding, does not open acetylene cylinder valve more than 1.5 turns). The examinee's final score was based on a compounding of the individual item scores.

The problem, as originally pointed out by Thorndike (1949), is that there may be aspects of a job that are lost in the analytic approach, so that scoring the elements does not give an entirely adequate evaluation. Specifically, the scores obtained by this elementalistic, analytic approach may not correlate with judgments of the overall quality of the final product. However, if analytic scores correlate highly with overall expert judgment, then the analytic method may be preferable. This scoring logic follows because (1) more objectivity may be introduced by the analytic scoring, (2) inter- and intraexaminer consistency may be increased, (3) less background and experience in the test task may be required by the examiner, and (4) the results convey how well, along with why, an examinee performed at a certain level.

Siegel developed a set of work sample tests (welding, plastic repair, fabric repair, and structural maintenance) for aviation structural mechanics, administered them, and employed the analytic scoring approach. The tests were administered to structural mechanics at one location. The examiners were highly experienced structural mechanics and the examinees were unknown by the examiners prior to the testing situation.

The end products produced by the examinees were then taken to another, distant location where a group of five expert aviation structural mechanics were asked to rank them from best to worst. Siegel calculated the correlations among the rankings of the five experts who ranked the final products and the correlation between the rankings and the scores derived by the analytic scoring approach. He found, for three of the four work sample tests, no statistically significant relationship between the experts' rankings and the scores produced by the analytic and synthetic approach.

MINIATURE JOB TRAINING AND EVALUATION TESTS

Definition. Work sample tests are useful for assessing the proficiency of job-experienced persons or persons who have already been trained. They are of little value for assessing applicants who will receive job training before assignment to a job. Here it is acknowledged that the applicant need not possess the ability to perform the job. The question to be answered is whether or not the applicant possesses the ability to succeed in the training program and ultimately on the job. The miniature job training and evaluation approach possesses advantages in these situations.

In the miniature job training and evaluation approach, the applicant is trained on a sample of (limited aspects of) the tasks on which ultimate mastery is expected. Immediately after the training session, the applicant is tested to determine how well he or she can perform the tasks included in the training. If the applicant is able to demonstrate the ability to perform the sample of tasks included in the miniature training/testing, the ability to be able to learn and ultimately perform all of the tasks of the job is inferred.

Because the task sample is directly drawn from a job analysis, the content of an appropriately constructed miniature training and evaluation battery is job relevant. The approach also possesses the advantages of the work sample approach described previously.

Background. The miniature job training and evaluation approach to testing possesses considerable background. Robertson and Downs (1979) called the approach "trainability tests" and pointed out that it was used in the 1960s in the United Kingdom. The purpose of these early tests was to select older workers who wished retraining in order to change their occupational field. For example, an agricultural worker may wish to become a welder. Unfortunately, this early work was reported in journals that are somewhat obscure, at least to persons outside of the United Kingdom. Robertson and Downs summarized much of the work, presenting sixteen separate studies in which the approach was employed and in which some type of follow-up criterion data were available. The jobs studied were largely technical in nature (e.g., carpentry, welding, brick laying, lathe turning, electronic assembly) with one professional occupation (dentistry) included. In most cases, the criterion was training success, although data from longer term follow-ups were reported to be under consideration. Trainability test score correlations with ratings by course instructors after the students were somewhat advanced in their course work ranged from .09 to .81 with a median of .48. The correlations between trainability scores and specific error scores on checklists administered some time into the formal posttest training period ranged from 0 to .72. The median correlation between trainability test score and the error score was .37. Robertson and Downs concluded that trainability tests can be usefully applied in the area of semiskilled manual tasks, particularly because written tests are poor at predicting trainability in these areas. Robertson and Mindel (1980) confirmed this conclusion.

The miniature job training and evaluation work in the United States has been carried out largely by Siegel along with various coworkers. They view the approach as something more than a training add-on to a work sample test. Rather, they place equal emphasis on both the design and administration of the training and the evaluation processes.

Siegel and Bergman (1972, 1975) developed a battery of miniature job training and evaluation situations for the machinist mate rating (occupation) in the navy. They were interested in personnel who scored poorly on the written tests usually administered to entry-level navy personnel. Siegel and Bergman drew their battery directly from the behaviors listed in standard navy job analytic sources in conjunction with an advisory panel composed of five master chief machinist mates and one warrant officer. The behaviors so identified were (1) ability to identify and use hand tools common to job, (2) ability to perform maintenance and to read meters and gauges accurately when under some degree of distraction or when attention sharing is involved, (3) ability to make simple repairs in pressure lines, (4) ability to perform simple troubleshooting and systems analysis in pressure systems, (5) ability to operate equipment common to job, and (6) ability to assemble and disassemble common high-frequency items. Miniature job training and evaluation situations were developed to reflect each of these situations. The training and tests were administered to fifty white and forty-nine black recruits who failed to score above the cutting point for the machinist mate rate on the usual written selection/classification tests. Very low correlations were found between the miniature training and evaluation test scores and among the miniature training and evaluation test scores and the written tests. A set of "hands-on" performance tests was constructed and administered to the members of the sample after they were on their fleet assignments for nine and for eighteen months. For the first follow-up (Siegel, Bergman, & Lambert, 1973), multiple correlations between the test scores and the performance test criterion scores ranged from .22 to .46. These were higher than the parallel multiple correlation coefficients for the written predictors in five out of six cases. For the second follow-up (Siegel & Leahy, 1974), these correlation coefficients attenuated considerably. Siegel and Bergman (1975) concluded that it is quite possible that miniature training and evaluation situations are adequate for predicting success on initial job entry but that continued success and development hinges on verbal and conceptual factors as measured by the written navy tests. Alternatively, it is possible that the job performance test criterion did not reflect the job requirements for a person with eighteen months' experience as well as the requirements for a person closer to job entry.

In another study into the miniature training and evaluation approach (Siegel & Wiesen, 1977), a set of miniature training and evaluation situations was developed that was generic for six navy occupations. The situations were based on job analytic information and were designed to predict success for postal clerks, storekeepers, yeomen, signalmen, machinist mates, and hospital corpsmen. The study combined the miniature job training and evaluation approach with an assessment center context and overall recommendation procedure. On the basis of the miniature training and evaluation situations, each assessor made a prediction of on-the-job success for each individual assessee relative to the assigned job field. Each assessor also rated each examinee on three factors—learning ability, psychophysical and motor ability, and social-motivational ability. Multiple correlations were calculated between the scores on the miniature training and evaluation situations and the various ratings of the assessment center personnel. This is the familiar "policy capturing" approach (e.g., Dawes, 1971; Madden, 1964; Stephenson & Ward, 1971) in which the attempt was to establish whether or not test scores captured the policy of experts relative to a decision (in this case, job success and the three ability factors). The multiple correlation coefficients between the test scores and the assessors' predictions of on-the-job success were .68 (general rates), .81 (machinist mate), and .65 (whole sample). Relative to the three individual ability factors, the multiple correlations were learning, .84; psychophysical-motor, .75; and social-motivational, .63. When Siegel and Wiesen calculated the multiple correlation between scores on the written predictors employed by the navy and the individual ability factors, the correlation coefficients were .12, .41, and .23, respectively.

Cory (1982) followed up the 1977 Siegel and Wiesen sample after the members were on their job assignments for nine and for eighteen months. Cory employed a rating technique to obtain job proficiency ratings. He found that the miniature training and evaluation scores had substantial predictive relationships for job performance criteria and that the miniature training and evaluation scores added .12 and .31 to the validity coefficients of the maximally predictive batteries of operational variables. By maximally predictive batteries, Cory meant the best combination of the usual written military selection and classification tests.

Cohen and Penner (1976) criticized some of the prior work of Siegel and his various colleagues because a few of the regression equations were based on small sample sizes. This criticism was answered in the work of Siegel (1981, 1983). In this work, a battery of ten miniature training and evaluation situations was constructed and administered to 1,034 navy recruits (broken into seaman, fireman, and airman subsamples) who were judged to be ineligible for assignment to a navy school on the basis of their scores on the usual written military selection and classification tests. Two types of job performance ratings were obtained after the members of the sample were on their assignments for nine and for eighteen months. The ratings involved (1) a set of judgments on individual performance items, and (2) an overall proficiency judgment. Siegel found that, in the case of the individual performance item criterion, the miniature training and evaluation tests were again superior to the usual written military selection and classification tests for the seaman and fireman groups. For the airman group, the predictive validity coefficients were about equal. In the case of the overall job proficiency criterion, the predictive validity of the miniature training and evaluation scores was consistently superior to the usual written test scores.

Another view of the value of the miniature training and evaluation approach can be gained by determining how much predictive variance is added by the miniature training and evaluation exercises over that available from written tests. Siegel (1981) calculated hierarchical multiple correlation coefficients according to the following logic: first, those written military selection and classification tests showing statistically significant zero order correlation coefficients with the individual performance item criterion were added one at a time to the predictive equation; next, the miniature training and evaluation exercises that evidenced

TABLE 4.2. Percentage of Contribution to Total Predictive
Variance (PC) and Multiple Correlation (R)

Follow-up	Written Tests Only		Written Tests Plus Miniature Training and Evaluation Battery	
	PC	R	PC	R
9 Months	40	.20	60	.32
18 Months	35	.24	65	.41

statistically significant zero order relationships with the criterion were added. The
percentage of predictable variance added by the miniature training and evaluation
approach over that provided by the statistically significant written predictors was
then calculated. Siegel's results are presented in Table 4.2. The results were
consistent across follow-ups. There was a consistent indication of considerable
advantage to the use of the miniature training and evaluation battery in conjunction
with the written tests.

Interexaminer reliability. There is little reason to suspect that the interexaminer reliability for miniature training and evaluation tests should be different
than for any work sample test. However, a number of interexaminer reliability
studies have been conducted when miniature job training and evaluation tests
were administered. In all of the studies described below, the examiners were fully
trained in the test administration and experienced on the tasks included in the
tests.

In Siegel and Bergman's work (1972, 1975), the examinee group consisted of
an equal proportion of black persons and of white persons. For three of the tests,
one black and one white test administrator simultaneously and independently
scored each examinee. The separate scores, so determined, were compared.
The correlations between the two examiners for the three miniature training and
evaluation tests investigated were .75, .97, and .98. Additionally, the means and
standard deviations of the two examiners were similar.

In the 1977 Siegel and Wiesen work, five evaluative situations were investigated. In each situation, four examiners separately scored the work of from five to
nineteen examinees. The intraclass correlation coefficient was employed to estimate the amount of agreement, by test, between the scores reported by the
independent examiners. The interexaminer reliability coefficients (intraclass correlations) for the five tests were .95, .99, .72, .93, and .92.

Summarizing these interexaminer reliability data indicates (1) a range of .72

to .99, (2) a median of .94, and (3) an interquartile range of .92. Such reliability coefficients appear quite adequate. However, variability in the interexaminer reliability seems present across test situations and the reliability evidently needs to be determined on an individual test basis. In general, with proper examiner training and associated procedures, acceptable levels of interexaminer reliability can be attained in the miniature job training and evaluation context.

Differential validity. One of the purported advantages of the miniature job training and evaluation approach is its "culture fairness." This feature is assumed to be at least in part an artifact of minimizing literacy requirements and the type of training employed in the training situation. Ash and Krocker (1975) have previously cautioned against the use of tests that have a higher reading level than that required by the job. Such tests may be inherently biased against certain classes of people who, for reasons associated with their culture or socioeconomic class, have less formal education, or less successful formal education, than other classes. For a motivated person, formal education, which yields a facility with written English, may have little to do with job success in many jobs.

In the 1975 Siegel and Bergman study, the miniature training and evaluation scores of twenty-nine black and twenty-five white criterion sample subjects were compared using t-tests to determine statistically significant differences. No significant differences were found.

Additionally, the correlations between the composite miniature job training and evaluation scores and scores on a composite job performance criterion were calculated. Differential validity is judged adequate when the correlation coefficients for two groups differ significantly from zero and from each other. The correlation coefficients did not differ from one another to a statistically significant extent. Accordingly, at least for the circumstance involved, there is a suggestion that the miniature training and evaluation situations cannot be held to possess differential validity on the basis of Boehm's (1972) criteria.

Similarly, work samples have been found to be nonracially linked when scored through the checklist method and to possess considerably less adverse impact than a well-constructed written test in metal trades skills (Schmidt, Greenthal, Hunter, Berner, & Seaton, 1977).

Advantages and Disadvantages of Work Sample and Miniature Training and Evaluation Tests

ADVANTAGES

The advantages of the performance testing approaches described in the preceding sections appear to be that they (1) possess high face validity, that is, an obvious direct relationship between predictor and criterion; (2) minimize verbal skill requirements; (3) are accepted as "fair" by test takers; (4) probably possess little, if any, differential validity; (5) can be anticipated to possess validity coefficients equal to, if not greater than, those shown by the customary paper-and-pencil tests; and (6) can be shown to possess adequate interexaminer consistency when properly constructed and administered by trained examiners.

DISADVANTAGES

The major disadvantages of performance tests are that they (1) involve scoring problems especially in regard to the establishment of examiner objectivity and inter- and intraexaminer reliability; (2) may be more costly than paper-and-pencil tests to administer because of the high ratio of required examiners to examinees, the examiner training requirements, and the administrative time involved; (3) seem to be most valid for proficiency prediction during the first year of job assignment but to lack durability for long-term prediction; and (4) may be more useful for testing motor skills than for testing decision-making or judgmental ability.

Recommendations

To develop either work sample or miniature job training and evaluation tests, a systematic procedure is mandatory. Too often, an ad hoc or makeshift approach is employed. Such a haphazard approach can lead easily to a faulty test battery. The recommended steps for developing a miniature training and evaluation battery are listed as follows:

1. Decide on the job(s) for which the battery is to be applied.
2. Analyze the job by the task method.
3. Select the tasks that will form the basis for the tests using job analytic information.
4. Develop standardized test situations and scoring forms.
5. Develop standardized training situations.
6. Develop examiner and examinee instructions.
7. Develop an administrator's manual.
8. Select and train the administrators.
9. Administer the training and evaluation situations to a pretest sample.
10. Revise the various forms and materials as necessary.
11. Retest and again revise all materials, if necessary.
12. Check examiner reliability; retrain examiners as necessary.
13. Validate the tests employing subjects who are similar to those to whom the tests will ultimately be given.
14. Implement and continually monitor the program.

Generally, the same sequence applies to work sample test development. However, because the miniature training and evaluation approach demands both a training and a test situation while work samples are based only on a test situation, step 5 and part of step 9 may be eliminated for work sample test development. The discussion that follows is based on miniature job training and evaluation situation development. Those aspects that are specific to the miniature job training and evaluation approach and, accordingly, not applicable to work sample battery development should become evident.

JOB DECISION, JOB ANALYSIS, AND TASK SELECTION

The decision about the job(s) to which the battery can be applied will depend on the needs and circumstances involved. In general, work sample tests will be less applicable than miniature training and evaluation tests to hiring situations in which some type of training and evaluation test is to be administered before placement. The work sample approach will be preferred in situations in which (1) information about training needs is sought, (2) objective information is sought as a basis for compensation, and (3) objective information is sought about promotion, demotion, transfer, and discharge recommendations.

Once a decision has been reached about the job(s), some form of job analysis is required. The ultimate goal of the battery is to assess those aspects of the job that are most significant. The task-oriented method of job analysis is suggested. In the task-oriented method, each job task is analyzed in terms of such characteristics as frequency of job performance, importance of task, consequences of inadequate performance, time between training and requirement to perform task, and difficulty. Gael (1983) presented the details of the task-oriented method of job analysis (see also chapter 1). The task method of job analysis is believed to be preferred for current purposes to the trait approach, which analyzes a job in terms of its ability requirements, for example, decision making, motor coordination, arithmetic ability, word knowledge. Tasks are selected that are most significant to the job in question. This process will generally mean task selection in terms of one of the job analytic types of information (e.g., the most frequently performed tasks, the most important tasks, the most difficult tasks) or several of these considered in combination (e.g., frequency × importance, frequency × difficulty, frequency × difficulty × importance). Use of combinations is preferred to the use of single characteristics.

DEVELOPMENT OF TEST SITUATIONS AND SCORING FORMS

Once the tasks that are to form the basis for the training and evaluation situations have been selected, both the training situations and the evaluation situations must be developed. It is often more convenient to work backwards.

FIGURE 4.1. Procedural analysis for chemical mixing task

TASK ANALYSIS — CHEMICAL MIXING

PROCEDURE	CARE & USE OF TOOLS	SAFETY PRECAUTIONS
Draw appropriate chemicals.	Dichromate, acid.	Never leave uncapped.
		Restow immediately after use.
		Never pour acid in drain.
Weigh out 3 ounces dichromate.	Scale — Weights on right, chemicals on left.	
	Check for "trueness" prior to use. Center counterweights. Evenly distribute chemicals over pan.	
	Paper—Use clean paper on both pans.	Discard paper immediately after use.
Wash equipment.	Rinse all equipment prior to use.	Use only cold water.
Add dichromate to small quantity of water.	34 ounce graduate.	
Stir while adding.	Stirring rod.	
Completely dissolve dichromate.	Tank.	
Add water to make 1 quart.	Quart container.	
Measure 12 ounces acid.		Add acid at side of dichromate solution.
Add acid to dichromate solution.		Stir rapidly when adding acid.
Fill quart container.		Add acid to dichromate, not reverse.
Labels (Name of solution, who mixed, date mixed).	Labels.	
Wipe down pans and work area.	Sponge.	
Replace weights and materials.	Weights placed in proper places.	
Wash tank, graduate, etc.		

That is, the evaluation situation is first defined and developed; then the training for the evaluation is developed.

The test situation is the end result of a systematic set of steps and, in the case of a procedurally oriented task situation, proceeds from some type of analysis of the procedural sequence. Here the steps in the procedure are listed along with safety precautions and the associated care and use of tools and materials. An example of how such an analysis might appear is shown in Figure 4.1, which was based on a chemical mixing task for photographers. This analysis is then directly converted to checklist form as displayed in Figure 4.2.

In some cases, not only the procedures but also the quality of the final product may be of interest. In such a case, the task-analytic form is expanded to include consideration of the final product. This is given in Figure 4.3, which is based on a welding analysis, and the final scoring checklist is shown in Figure 4.4.

FIGURE 4.2. Scoring checklist for chemical mixing task

PERFORMANCE EXAMINATION
CHEMICAL MIXING
SCORING CHECK LIST

NAME

DATE

Time Started

A. PROCEDURE

   1. Draws correct chemicals 1

   2. Weighs out exactly 3 ounces of potassium dichromate 1

   3. Slowly adds dichromate to small quantity of water 1

   4. Stirs while adding chemical 1

   5. When all of chemical completely dissolved, adds water to make one quart 1

   6. Measures out **exactly** 12 ounces sulfuric acid 1

   7. Stirs rapidly when adding acid 1

   8. Fills quart container with solution 1

   9. Correctly labels (Name of solution, who mixed, date mixed) 1

  10. Time finished_____. Time spent at mixing_____. Finished mixing in 8 minutes or less 1

  11. Wipes scale pans and work area with damp cloth before securing 1

B. CARE AND USE OF TOOLS

  12. Checks scale for "trueness" prior to use 1

  13. Centers counterweights 1

  14. Weights placed on right side of scale, chemicals on left 1

  15. Wipes pans prior to use 1

  16. Uses clean paper on **both** scale pans 1

  17. Evenly distributes chemicals over pan 1

  18. Rinses all equipment prior to use 1

C. SAFETY PRECAUTIONS

  19. Never leaves acid bottle uncapped 1

  20. Restows acid immediately after use 1

  21. Does not pour acid in drain 1

  22. Discards paper immediately after use 1

  23. Uses only cold water in mixture 1

  24. Adds acid at side of dichromate solution 1

  25. Stirs rapidly when adding acid 1

  26. Adds acid to dichromate solution (not reverse) 1

Total Score_____

Of course if only the final product is to be scored, then the analysis need only be performed in terms of the final product quality aspects to be scored.

It is sometimes possible to base the test situation on a paper-and-pencil approach that simulates a real-life situation. But note that the paper-and-pencil approach merely asks the examinee to place a checkmark or similar entry in a

FIGURE 4.3. Procedural analysis for welding task

| TASK ANALYSIS — ALUMINUM BUTT WELD | | | |
PROCEDURE	CARE & USE OF TOOLS	SAFETY PRECAUTIONS	PRECISION OF FINAL PRODUCT
Select rods.	Rods — proper size for given metal thickness.		Start uniform with rest of weld.
Examine metal for dirt or grease. Clean metal and rods.	Metal—restricts cleaning to area of weld.		End uniform with rest of weld.
Set metal on jigs. Mix flux.	Flux — paste-like consistency. Free flowing.		Uniform penetration.
Flux base metal and rods.			
Adjust oxyacetylene regulators for 3-8 pounds.	Oxyacetylene bottle — 3-8 pounds.	Need fire extinguisher in area. Open oxyacetylene cylinders no more than 1½ turns.	Bead width 3 to 5 times metal thickness.
Light torch. Adjust to slightly carborizing flame.	Friction lighter. Torch—proper size tip. Goggles.	Don't use match. Hold torch on bench — don't aim in air.	Bead height 25 to 50% of metal thickness.
Pre-heat base metal.	Metal.		
Tack metal.			
Weld from center to end. Reverse metal and weld from center to other end using "see-saw" motion of torch and rod. Concentrate flame on base metal.		Loose clothing may be dangerous.	No irregularity in bead.
Dip and wash.	Water. Wirebrush.		

space on a recording form. It is not based on item reading comprehension in the usual sense. An example of one test item based on this paper-and-pencil approach is shown in Figure 4.5. In this test, each item shows typical work situations and some tools that might be used to perform the task. The task of the examinee is to check or to mark the best tool for completing the specific task depicted.

TRAINING SITUATION DEVELOPMENT

Systematic development of the training situation is equal in importance to the systematic development of the test situation and scoring form. The training must be standardized and the learning required should not depend on language ability. Generally, the training will include (1) *telling* the examinee(s) what the task is and how to do it; (2) *showing* all aspects of what is to be done including, but not limited to, the use of tools, how to make any required measurements, how to follow safety procedures, how to check the work, and the like; (3) *encouraging questions*

FIGURE 4.4. Scoring checklist for welding task

AM PERFORMANCE EXAMINATION

WELDING

SCORING CHECK LIST

Time Started_____

TOOLS AND MATERIALS

  1. Holds torch at 45° angle to work except for start or finish 1
  2. Always concentrates flame on base metal, not on rod 1
  3. Uses proper flux consistency (free flowing flux) 1
  4. Selects proper size rod for given metal thickness 1
  5. Selects proper size welding tip for given metal thickness 1
  6. Restricts cleaning of base metal to width of weld 1

PROCEDURE

  7. Examines metal for dirt or grease. Cleans both metal and rods 1
  8. Sets metal on jigs. Mixes flux. Fluxes both base metal and rods 1
  9. Adjusts oxygen acetylene regulators to 3-8 pounds (no credit if pressure on oxygen does not equal pressure on acetylene) 1
10. Lights torch and adjusts to slightly carborizing flame (feather should be no more than 1½ times inner cone) 1
11. Pre-heats base metal 1
12. Tacks metal from center to each end, or from center to each end alternately; tacks 1¼ to 1½ inches apart 1
13. Welds from center to one end 1
14. Reverses metal and welds from center to other end 1
15. Uses correct torch and rod motions while welding 1
16. Dips and washes making sure that all flux is removed 1
17. Time finished_____. Finished in 17 minutes or less 1

SAFETY

18. Shirt neck and sleeves buttoned 1
19. Makes sure fire extinguisher in area before igniting torch 1
20. Makes sure that gas bottles are in an upright position 1
21. Uses friction lighter to ignite torch and holds lighter on bench when igniting torch ... 1
22. Does not open acetylene cylinder valve more than 1½ turns 1
23. Uses goggles when welding 1

MEASUREMENT OF THE FINAL PRODUCT

24. Start of weld uniform with rest of weld 3
25. End of weld uniform with rest of weld 3
26. Uniform penetration for entire first 3 inches 3
27. Uniform penetration for entire last 3 inches 3
28. Bead width 3-5 times metal thickness for entire first 3 inches 3
29. Bead width 3-5 times metal thickness for entire last 3 inches 3
30. Bead height 25-50% of thickness for entire first 3 inches 3
31. Bead height 25-50% of thickness for entire last 3 inches 3
32. No bead irregularity in entire first 3 inches 3
33. No bead irregularity in entire last 3 inches 3

Total Score_____

and *questioning* each examinee to assure his grasp of knowledge; (4) *providing practice and feedback* concerning what is correct and incorrect and making constructive suggestions; and (5) *providing personal attention* where problems exist. The full training plan for each situation includes the text of spoken materials,

FIGURE 4.5. Example of paper-and-pencil performance test item

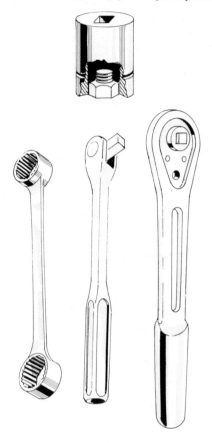

needed training materials, any time limits, and special points to be made during the instructional period. A portion of a training plan developed to support a motor-starting miniature training and evaluation situation is reproduced below.

Lesson 4. Training Procedure for Equipment Operation

To the Instructor: Keep this sheet in front of you at all times during this training session. Do and say *exactly* what is said on these pages.

Procedure

1. Stand next to the motor.
2. Say: "I have in front of me a small motor with a pump attached to it. There are several steps I must perform in order to start up this motor."
3. Say: "My first step is to remove any oily rags or trash lying on or near the motor. You can all see that there is a rag next to the motor.

I will remove it. If I didn't remove the rag, there is a chance that a spark from the motor would ignite the rag and cause a fire."

4. Remove rag.
5. Say: "The second step is to check the fuel level using a long dipstick. Remember to use the long dipstick when you check the fuel level."
6. Hold up long dipstick.
7. Say: "This is the fuel tank."
8. Point to fuel tank.
9. Say: "I will unscrew the fuel tank lid, clean off the dipstick, and put the dipstick in until it touches the bottom of the fuel tank."
10. Unscrew top of fuel tank, clean the dipstick, and put long dipstick in until it touches bottom. Pull dipstick out of fuel tank and hold it up to the class.
11. Etc.

EXAMINER AND EXAMINEE INSTRUCTIONS

Formal examiner and examinee instructions are prepared for each test task. The examinee instructions are administered from a tape. They include a statement of the task, required test materials and test situation organization, general directions, and scoring directions. The examinee directions include statements about what is to be done, time limits, and how the scoring will be performed.

ADMINISTRATOR'S MANUAL AND ADMINISTRATOR TRAINING

A detailed training and test administration manual is then prepared. This manual serves as an information source during the administration of the battery and as a "text" during the examiner training. The administrator's manual includes all information necessary for administering both the training and the test situations, for example, discussion of the logic of the total program, organizational structure of the program, detailed directions for administering and scoring each situation, procedures for assuring standardization, how to handle special problems, test security, and various forms (if any) to be completed for record keeping purposes.

Formal training of the administrators is provided. This includes detailed explanations of all procedures plus practice in administration of the training and the testing situation(s). The practice sessions are observed and criticized by the test situation developer(s).

PRETEST AND REVISION

Once all of the materials have been prepared, they are pretested under conditions that are as similar as possible to the anticipated conditions of use.

Problems with procedures and methods are noted and appropriate revisions are incorporated into the various materials. Then the materials are tried again. The test and revision cycle should continue until all problem areas are eliminated.

EXAMINER RELIABILITY AND VALIDATION

Now is the time for estimating intra- and interexaminer reliability. If adequate reliabilities are not attained, additional training along with new reliability analyses are indicated. Test validation proceeds according to standard predictive and concurrent validity data-gathering procedures (validation is a special topic that is beyond the scope of this chapter).

IMPLEMENT AND CONTINUALLY MONITOR

The situations are now ready for implementation. However, continual "quality control" checks are required to assure that the program is not off track. During the monitoring, checks are performed to assure that (1) administrator performance effectiveness and reliability are maintained, (2) all aspects of the administration are performed in a professional manner, (3) administrators do not know the examiners before the assessment, and (4) administrators and examinees are assigned in a random manner.

References

Adkins, D. (1947). *Construction and analysis of achievement tests.* Washington, DC: U.S. Government Printing Office.

Ash, P., & Krocker, L. F. (1975). Personnel selection, classification, and placement. *Annual Review of Psychology, 26,* 481–508.

Asher, J. J., & Sciarrino, J. A. (1974). Realistic work sample tests: A review. *Personnel Psychology, 27,* 519–533.

Boehm, V. (1972). Negro-white differences in validity of employment and training selection procedures: Summary of research evidence. *Journal of Applied Psychology, 56,* 33–39.

Bray, D. W., & Grant, J. L. (1966). The assessment center in the measurement of potential for business management. *Psychological Monographs, 17* (Whole No. 625).

Briggs, G. E., & Johnston, W. A. (1966). Influence of a change in system criteria on team performance. *Journal of Applied Psychology, 50,* 467–472.

Cohen, S. L., & Penner, L. A. (1976). The rigors of predictive validation: Some comments on "a job learning approach to performance prediction." *Personnel Psychology, 29,* 595–560.

Cory, C. H. (1982). *The assignment of general detail personnel in the navy: Fleet follow-*

up of personnel appraised in a technical classification assessment under pilot study. San Diego, CA: U.S. Navy Personnel Research and Development Center.

Dawes, R. M. (1971). A case study of graduate admissions: Application of three principles of human decision making. *American Psychologist, 26,* 180–188.

Edwards, R. I. (1979). *National training center development plan.* Fort Monroe, VA: U.S. Army Training and Doctrine Command.

Fiske, D. W. (1951). Values, theory, and the criterion problem. *Personnel Psychology, 4,* 93–98.

Foley, J. P. (1977). *Performance measurement of maintenance.* Dayton, OH: Advanced Systems Division, Wright Patterson Air Force Base.

Fredericksen, N., Saunders, D. R., & Ward, B. (1957). The in-basket test. *Psychological Monographs, 9* (Whole No. 438).

Gael, S. (1983). *Job analysis: A guide to assessing work activities.* San Francisco, CA: Jossey-Bass.

Ghiselli, F. E. (1966). *The validity of occupational aptitude tests.* New York: Wiley.

Gordon, M. E., & Kleiman, L. S. (1976). The prediction of trainability using a work sample test and an aptitude test: A direct comparison. *Personnel Psychology, 29,* 243–253.

Havron, M. D., Frey, R. J., & McGrath, J. E. (1952). *The effectiveness of small military units* (PRS Rep. No. 980). Washington, DC: Personnel Research Section, Department of the Army.

Madden, J. M. (1964). *A policy capturing model for analyzing individual and group judgment for job evaluation.* Lackland, TX: Aerospace Division, 6570th Personnel Research Laboratory.

Mount, M. K., Muchinsky, P. M., & Hanser, L. M. (1977). The predictive validity of a work sample: A laboratory study. *Personnel Psychology, 30,* 637–645.

Robertson, I. T., & Downs, S. (1979). Learning and the prediction of performance: Development of trainability testing in the United Kingdom. *Journal of Applied Psychology, 64,* 42–50.

Robertson, I. T., & Kandola, R. S. (1982). Work sample tests: Validity, adverse impact, and application reaction. *Journal of Occupational Psychology, 55,* 171–183.

Robertson, I. T., & Mindel, R. M. (1980). A study of trainability testing. *Journal of Occupational Psychology, 53,* 131–138.

Schmidt, F. L., Greenthal, A. L., Hunter, J. E., Berner, J. G., & Seaton, F. W. (1977). Job sample vs. paper and pencil trades and technical tests: Adverse impact and examinee attitudes. *Personnel Psychology, 30,* 187–197.

Siegel, A. I. (1954a). The checklist as a criterion of proficiency. *Journal of Applied Psychology, 38,* 93–96.

Siegel, A. I. (1954b). Retest reliability by a movie technique of test administrators' judgments of performance in process. *Journal of Applied Psychology, 38,* 390–392.

Siegel, A. I. (1981). *Trainability testing for navy selection and classification.* Wayne, PA: Applied Psychological Services.

Siegel, A. I. (1983). The miniature job training and evaluation approach: Additional findings. *Personnel Psychology, 36,* 41–56.

Siegel, A. I., & Bergman, B. B. (1972). *Nonverbal and culture fair performance prediction procedures: I. Background, test development, and initial results.* Wayne, PA: Applied Psychological Services.

Siegel, A. I., & Bergman, B. B. (1975). A job learning approach to performance prediction. *Personnel Psychology, 28,* 325–339.

Siegel, A. I., Bergman, B. B., & Lambert, J. (1973). *Nonverbal and culture fair performance prediction procedures: II. Initial validation.* Wayne, PA: Applied Psychological Services.

Siegel, A. I., & Jensen, J. (1955). The development of a job sample trouble-shooting performance examination. *Journal of Applied Psychology, 39,* 343–347.

Siegel, A. I., & Leahy, W. R. (1974). *Nonverbal and culture fair performance prediction procedures: III. Cross validation.* Wayne, PA: Applied Psychological Services.

Siegel, A. I., & Wiesen, J. J. (1977). *Experimental procedures for the classification of naval personnel.* San Diego, CA: U.S. Navy Personnel Research and Development Center.

Stephenson, R. W., & Ward, J. H. (1971). Computer assisted decisions to help a policy group assign weights to criterion ratings. *Personnel Psychology, 24,* 447–461.

Thorndike, R. L. (1949). *Personnel selection: Test and measurement techniques.* New York: Wiley.

Weislogel, R. L. (1954). Development of situational tests for military personnel. *Personnel Psychology, 7,* 492–497.

Weislogel, R. L., & Schwartz, P. A. (1955). Some practical and theoretical problems in situational testing. *Educational and Psychological Measurement, 15,* 39–46.

5. ASSESSMENT CENTERS

William C. Byham & George C. Thornton III

Introduction

A variety of methods have been developed to describe, to evaluate, and to predict management effectiveness. Social science researchers and management practitioners have devised numerous objective and subjective means to obtain information about management behavior. This chapter is devoted to one of these methods—the assessment center—and a comparison of its role to other approaches in selection, promotion, training, and development. The chapter will deal primarily with assessment of supervisors and managers, but nonmanagement applications of assessment centers will be discussed where appropriate.

An assessment center is a comprehensive, standardized procedure in which multiple assessment techniques such as situational exercises and job simulations (i.e., business games, discussion groups, reports, and presentations) are used to evaluate individual employees for various purposes. A number of trained management evaluators, who are not in a direct supervisory capacity over the participants, conduct the assessment and make recommendations regarding the management potential and developmental needs of the participants. The results of the assessment are communicated to higher management and can be used for personnel decisions such as promotions, transfers, and career planning. When the results are communicated to the participants, they form the basis for self-insight and development planning.

PROBLEMS OF MANAGEMENT ASSESSMENT

Why has the evaluation of management behavior been so difficult? There are several reasons, most of which center on difficulties in defining the job of manager precisely. In addition to the obvious differences of requirements for supervisors, middle managers, and executives, there are also subtle but real differences within levels. Some management positions are mainly administrative, with a heavy load of paper work; other positions require a large amount of personal contact to coordinate the work of subordinates; still others involve extensive negotiation with persons outside the organization. No one job description deals effectively with the complexity of all sets of requirements. Management jobs are difficult to analyze because of the long-term cycle of activities (e.g., budgets and performance appraisals are usually prepared only once a year). Furthermore, a manager seldom does the same thing repeatedly in the same way, which further complicates the observation and measurement of jobs. Often we do not know what types of organizational and environmental demands will be placed on the manager nor do we know the relevance of the evaluative information we have about an individual to those job demands. However, job analyses and judgment research for assessment centers have contributed to basic understanding of managerial jobs.

Judgments of competence to perform in a future management position are usually based on one of five sources of information: (1) evaluation of job success and potential by current supervisors, (2) results from traditional paper-and-pencil tests, (3) clinical evaluations by psychologists and related professionals, (4) background interviews, or (5) observations in job simulations in an assessment center. Each of these approaches has strengths that can be utilized in a coordinated program for the prediction of management potential; each also has weaknesses. For example, equating performance effectiveness on a lower-level job with effectiveness at a higher-level position where the demands and abilities are different is a tenuous assumption. Such assumptions lead to the situation where a person "rises to the level of his or her incompetence," as popularized in *The Peter Principle* (Peter, 1970).

Judgments by supervisors regarding a person's potential success may be biased in many ways, including lack of knowledge of higher-level job demands and lack of opportunity to observe the person in situations relevant to the higher-level job (Adams & Fyffe, 1969). Problems with the clinical interview center mostly on lack of knowledge of job demands and the maximum potential validity inherent in the procedures. It is difficult for an outsider to know the job requirements and situational pressures in an organization. Abstract diagnoses of adjustment usually do not serve well in the prediction of managerial behavior.

The use of traditional paper-and-pencil tests has proved valid in a number of excellent research studies (Campbell et al., 1970) and will remain a valuable predictor of success. However, the general public's increasing resistance to such tests (because of their sometimes low face validity and intrusion on personal privacy) and the growing demands for evidence of validity and fairness (U.S. Equal Employment Opportunity Commission et al., 1978) have led to a search for alternative methods of assessment (Byham & Bobin, 1972). It will be argued here that the assessment center approach, using simulations of actual managerial behavior, has features that avoid the problems involved in other approaches, although it should be emphasized that an organization could benefit at times from using any one of the five approaches listed earlier.

Review of Assessment Center Characteristics

DESCRIPTION OF AN ASSESSMENT CENTER

An assessment center is a procedure (not a location) that uses multiple assessment techniques to evaluate employees for a variety of manpower purposes and decisions. The approach has been applied most frequently to individuals being considered for selection, promotion, placement, or special training and development in management. The original industrial centers developed by American Telephone and Telegraph (AT&T) involved line personnel being considered for promotion to first-level supervision. Since then, the technique has been applied to the identification of individuals for many positions (e.g., middle managers, top executives, salespeople, and management trainees) (Thornton & Byham, 1982).

Individuals are usually assessed in a group. Group assessment affords opportunities to observe peer interactions and aids the efficiency of observation. Anywhere from one to twelve people might be observed in a program. For illustrative purposes, we will describe a common arrangement of six assessees, three assessors, and one program administrator.

Staff members of the assessment center may consist entirely of trained management personnel, all professional psychologists, or a combination of both. The low ratio of assessees to assessors (typically two to one) is important to the assessment center process because it allows close contact and observation of the participants and makes multiple evaluations possible. Management personnel who serve as assessors are usually two or more levels above the participants in the organization hierarchy, are trained for the task of assessment, and are not in a direct supervisory capacity over the participants.

Industrial assessment centers employ a number of assessment techniques to ensure complete coverage of management abilities. Management games, leaderless group discussions, role-playing exercises, and other simulation techniques are used most frequently, but a few organizations also use a background interview or tests. The job simulations allow the participants to engage in joblike managerial situations and to display job-relevant behaviors: administrative decision making, discussions in small groups, and one-to-one interactions with employees.

The tasks of observing complex social behavior, integrating the information, and making predictions is difficult; therefore most assessment center programs include extensive training for the management assessors. Their ability to make accurate predictions has been borne out in the literature reviewed by Thornton and Byham (1982) and is supported by findings from other multiple assessment procedures summarized by Cronbach (1970) and Taft (1955, 1959). The process of integrating the assessment information and making predictions in an assessment center is quite systematic. Assessors report behavioral observations and dimension ratings for each exercise and then make independent ratings of overall dimension performance. The assessors then reach consensus on dimension ratings and finally make predictions of management success. The process of integrating the assessment information and making predictions in an assessment center has been analyzed in depth by Thornton and Byham (1982).

Although most assessment centers are designed to predict management capabilities, they are also used for the development of participants. Participation in the exercises may be a learning experience per se and may provide personal insights into managerial competence. Feedback of results in the form of oral and written reports to the participant and immediate supervisor may clarify developmental needs. In some cases, time is spent following the assessment period for management development and self-analysis activities, such as viewing oneself in videotapes of exercises or reviewing decisions made in the "in-basket exercise," an exercise developed to simulate the administrative tasks of a manager's job.

THE ASSESSMENT CENTER PROCESS

Managerial assessment centers emerged from a rich tradition of multiple assessment programs developed in the 1940s and 1950s. Multiple assessment procedures can be distinguished from other personality measurement procedures, such as tests and clinical interviews, in several ways: multiple assessment techniques including job simulation exercises, multiple assessors, subjective and objective data gathering, behavioral orientation, judgmental methods of combining the information gathered, concern for the whole person, and prediction of adequacy of performance on a criterion.

Management assessment centers are designed to avoid the disadvantages of two extreme approaches to measurement. At the one extreme, some paper-and-pencil tests require only very limited (and often trivial) behaviors and measure narrowly defined traits. At the other extreme, some personality assessment programs have been concerned with such characteristics as "general adjustment" or "effectiveness."

In contrast, the assessment center process has made a significant modification in these approaches and now emphasizes, first, the observation of an individual's competencies on several separate behaviorally defined dimensions related to job behavior and, second, a prediction of overall job success. In the next section, this sequence is described in more detail.

The assessment center approach also assumes that people possess relatively enduring characteristics that influence their behavior in various settings, but it largely avoids the controversy over traits and whether behavior is determined by person or situation variables (Mischel, 1968, 1973) by emphasizing behavioral observation in work sample and job simulation measurement techniques (see also Siegel, chapter 4). It focuses on job-related skills, abilities, and other characteristics (e.g., problem-analysis skills, ability to plan and organize work, resistance to stress as it affects ability to make decisions under pressure, and interpersonal approaches to the leadership of individuals and groups).

Judgment models. Thornton and Byham (1982) have shown that the assessment center process can be depicted in three stages. Stage 1 covers the observations and ratings in exercises. Stage 2 includes the reporting of exercise information and the derivation of dimension ratings in the staff discussion. Stage 3

FIGURE 5.1. Assessment model for an individual assessee (3 assessors, 5 dimensions, 4 exercises)

Exercises (Primary Observer) Dimensions	Stage I: Dimension Rating by Exercise Assessor A B C	Stage II: Dimension Ratings Considering the Data Preliminary Assessors A B C	Final	Stage III: Overall Assessment Ratings Preliminary Assessors A B C	Final
Analysis Exercise (Assessor A)					
Decision Making	5				
Oral Communication	4	DM: 5 3 1	2		
Written Communication	4				
Leadership Group Discussion (Assessor B)		OC: 3 3 3	3		
Decision Making	3				
Oral Communication	3				
Leadership	4			2 3 2	2
Interview Simulation (Assessor A)		L: 2 4 4	2		
Decision Making	3				
Oral Communication	3	Del: 2 2 2	2		
Leadership	2				
Use of Delegation	2				
In-basket (Assessor C)		WC: 5 2 5	5		
Decision Making	1				
Oral Communication	2				
Leadership	5				
Use of Delegation	2				
Written Communication	5				

Source: Thornton and Byham (1982). Reprinted by permission.

encompasses the integration of dimension ratings to form a final overall assessment rating.

Figure 5.1 (taken from Thornton & Byham, 1982) presents a model of the assessment process for one individual who is observed in a program consisting of three assessors, five performance dimensions, and four assessment exercises. Stage 1 takes place during and immediately after each exercise when observations and dimension ratings are made independently by an assessor. In the hypothetical example, assessor A observed the analysis exercise and rated the person 5 on decision making, 4 on oral communication, and 4 on written communication, based on a rating scale from 1 (low) to 5 (high). Assessor A also observed and rated performance in the interview simulation; in this exercise, two additional dimensions were rated—leadership and use of delegation. Assessor B was the primary observer of this person in the leaderless group discussion, although the other two assessors were present, watching other discussants. Assessor C rated the individual's in-basket performance on all five dimensions.

Figure 5.1 shows that the assessee's written communication was observed twice—in the in-basket and the analysis exercise—but all other dimensions were

FIGURE 5.2. Judgment model for individual assessors at various stages of the assessment center process

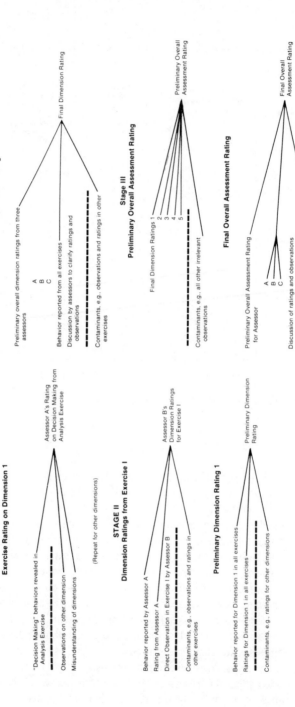

148

Source: Thornton and Byham (1982). Reprinted by permission.

assessed three or more times. It is desirable to have several "readings" on each dimension because assessors are not asked to evaluate dimensions irrelevant to an exercise. For example, written communication cannot be observed in a group discussion.

Stages 2 and 3 take place in the staff discussion when all information is integrated by the assessors. Dimension ratings are derived in stage 2. Assessors report observations and ratings from the exercises. Then each assessor independently records his or her preliminary dimension ratings. Usually these ratings are displayed on newsprint, a "flip chart," or chalkboard for easy examination. In the example, there was clear agreement on oral communication (all 3s) and use of delegation (all 2s). Assessor B rated the person lower than others on written communication, and A rated low on leadership. The assessors disagreed widely on decision making, possibly because of lack of clarity of the dimension.

During the ensuing discussion, the assessment team, guided by a program administrator, arrives at the final dimension ratings. These ratings are consensus judgments, not averages. Many times the team can easily arrive at the final dimension ratings (e.g., 3 for oral communication and 2 for use of delegation). At other times, lengthy discussion is necessary. Considering written communication, the staff would try to understand why assessor B gave a 2. In this instance, discussion led to the higher rating. In contrast, subsequent discussion led the other assessors to concur with assessor A's lower rating for leadership even though initially both scored the assessee above average. The final dimension rating on decision making ended up being unlike any one of the preliminary ratings.

In stage 3, the staff arrives at the overall assessment rating. This might be defined "probability of success if hired," "promotability," or "likelihood of attaining middle management." At this stage, preliminary ratings are made independently, posted for examination, and finally consolidated in a consensus discussion. An overall assessment rating is appropriate for selection and promotion programs, but when assessment is done for diagnostic purposes, stage 3 may be omitted.

Figure 5.2 (also taken from Thornton & Byham, 1982) presents the assessment process from the assessors' points of view. This model depicts the contributions to assessment ratings at each stage, including relevant factors shown above the dotted lines and irrelevant "contaminants" below the line. For example, assessor A's ratings of decision making from the analysis exercise is partly a function of relevant "decision-making" behaviors shown in the exercise plus observations relevant to other dimensions that the assessor might misclassify as decision making to the extent the contaminants are present. The assessee's true level of decision making may be different from the exercise rating given by A.

At stage 2, the primary observers report to the other assessors the behavioral observations and ratings for each exercise. Assessor B listens to the report and makes a rating on the dimension based on the behavior that assessor A reported from the first exercise. This rating would be a function of A's input, possible direct observations B may have made of relevant behavior in the exercise—a situation that only occurs when several assessors observe an exercise, as in a group exercise, or when the result of an exercise can be given to assessors as in-basket responses or as a written analysis—and contaminants.

Preliminary dimension ratings are formulated by each assessor after hearing all exercise reports. Assessors are trained to weight more heavily the exercises that give "stronger" readings on a dimension (e.g., the in-basket is a good measure of delegation skills) and that parallel job activities more closely. An artificially high rating on a dimension may occur if an assessor considers irrelevant behavior; for example, high verbal fluency may be credited for leadership. Once the preliminary dimension ratings are posted, they form the basis for the final dimension ratings. Contaminants can still enter at this stage; for example, an assessor may report some new observation picked up in informal interactions outside of the assessment center. The likelihood of these extraneous inputs having an influence on the ratings is minimized by careful monitoring by the program administrator and other assessors.

It is not until final, summary dimension ratings are derived by consensus that stage 3 can begin. In stage 3, each assessor examines the final dimension ratings and records an independent overall assessment rating. Assessors are encouraged to consider all dimension ratings and to integrate the information in the manner that best reflects job demands. No mechanical or statistical formulas are used. A contaminant at this stage might be some personal information known by one assessor: for example, the fact that a candidate for promotion was recently divorced and is considering a move to another city. The final overall assessment rating is determined by consensus. The recommendation to hire or not hire an applicant should be based on the three assessor ratings, but subjective judgments can play a contaminating role if the administrator does not guide the group. In reality, once the dimension ratings are agreed upon, assessors usually closely agree on the overall assessment rating and there is little chance that extraneous information will bias a decision.

Dimensions in assessment centers. Managerial assessment centers have gone beyond the task and trait approaches to identify behavioral dimensions of managerial work. A *dimension* is a cluster of behaviors that are specific, observable, and verifiable and that can be reliably and logically classified together.

Even though the label *dimension* may appear to be very similar to the label *task* or *trait*, dimensions are quite different. In contrast to a task, which states what is accomplished on the job, a dimension is defined in terms of the specific behaviors the person carries out to accomplish the task. For example, a common management function is planning. The dimension "planning" is often used in assessment center programs and is defined by behavior examples such as "Made a list of meetings with agenda items for his return to the job," "Gave the subordinate a sequence of tasks to complete with target dates to ensure timely comple-

FIGURE 5.3. Job-related behaviors obtained from a job analysis

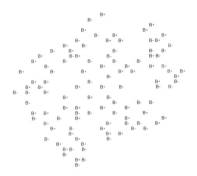

Source: Thornton and Byham (1982). Reprinted by permission.

tion of the projects," and "Anticipated and stated several potential problems that might arise if the recommendation were adopted and gave suggestions for dealing with each problem."

Other common dimensions that look like tasks but are similarly defined with specific behavioral examples are delegation, management control, and decision making.

The use of behavior to define dimensions also distinguishes them from traits. Usually traits are thought to be underlying personality constructs that determine behavioral consistency across situations. They are assumed to be "causal" variables that define a person's stable and enduring nature at work, at home, or during leisure time. Although some dimension labels may at first appear to be traits, they are behaviorally defined and observed and do not require judgments about underlying personality constructs. For example, "sensitivity" subsumes such behaviors as "Asked the person how she would feel if the plan were implemented," "Stated that he thought he understood how the customer felt because a similar thing happened to him," and "Repeated and rephrased what the subordinate suggested to clarify understanding between them."

The following, highly simplified description of how a job analyst goes about defining dimensions may help to clarify the concept. Figure 5.3 shows the behaviors that might be obtained in a job analysis for a specific job or job level. Each letter B indicates a specific behavior. The pluses and minuses indicate whether the obtained behavior was related to job success or lack of success. It is the job of the analyst to find commonalities among the behaviors and to label these commonalities. In other words, as illustrated in Figure 5.4, the job analyst draws circles around the behaviors that form logical homogenous clusters. Then the job analyst labels the constellation of behaviors. The analyst can label one constellation number 1, the next number 2, and the next number 3, and so on; or the

FIGURE 5.4. Categorization of behaviors into "dimensions"

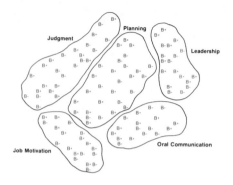

Source: Thornton and Byham (1982). Reprinted by permission.

analyst can use descriptive terms. For example, the analyst might group all the behaviors that have to do with leadership activities and label the constellation "leadership." Or the analyst might combine the behaviors that have to do with planning and label them "planning."

Illustrative dimensions. To illustrate the types of dimensions assessed in assessment center programs, Table 5.1 (taken from Thornton & Byham, 1982) provides three very different lists. The list for the early identification program is relatively short and consists of dimensions that do not presuppose any specific type of prior experience. This list is appropriate for identifying individuals who will benefit from accelerated training programs. By contrast, the list for promotion purposes is much longer and more diverse. It includes personal dimensions, interpersonal dimensions, administrative dimensions, and communication dimensions. These dimensions provide a more detailed assessment that is appropriate for judging whether a person is likely to be an effective manager. A still different list from a diagnostic development planning program for experienced first- and second-level managers is shown on the right side of Table 5.1. Decision making is divided into more refined dimensions: analysis, judgment, and decisiveness. Delegation and management control are added. There are no "personal" dimensions, which are hard to develop. The list has been restricted to dimensions that can be developed in training programs and on-the-job coaching.

Job analysis for assessment centers. For purposes of assessment centers, job analysis has two specific objectives. First, the job analysis is designed to identify clusters of job activities that constitute important aspects of the manager's job. These clusters consist of the kinds of things managers actually do during their work day and should include all of the important tasks, responsibilities, and

TABLE 5.1. Illustrative Assessment Center Dimensions

Early Identification	Promotion	Developmental Planning
Communications skills	Oral communications	Oral communications
		Oral presentation
	Written communications	Written communications
Energy	Energy	
Job motivation (obtained from an interview)	Job motivation (obtained from an interview)	
Career ambition (obtained from an interview)	Career ambition (obtained from an interview)	
Initiative	Initiative	Initiative
	Creativity (obtained from an interview)	
Sensitivity	Sensitivity	Sensitivity
Leadership	Leadership	Individual leadership
		Group leadership
		Behavioral flexibility
		Negotiation
	Tolerance for stress	
Planning and organizing	Planning and organizing	Planning and organizing
	Delegation	Delegation
	Management control	Management control
Decision making	Decision making	Analysis
		Judgment
		Decisiveness

Source: Thornton and Byham (1982). Reprinted by permission.

interpersonal relationships of the job. An example of one set of activities might be the one-to-one supervisory relationships in which a manager advises, directs, or counsels a subordinate. Another set of activities might be the group planning meetings attended by manager and peers. It is important to identify these clusters of activities so that simulation exercises that accurately reflect the target job can be devised. The only way we can ensure that the evaluation tasks are job related is to know what the job entails.

A corollary of this first objective is to determine the relative importance of each of the several job areas and the frequency of each activity. How frequently a manager makes oral presentations outside the company is part of an indication of the importance of that activity to the job and the weight it should get in assessment. Those activities that are most important and that occupy a large portion of a manager's time should be assessed more thoroughly. As a rough guide, the proportion of time in certain assessment activities should match the proportion of time in the manager's work life. If situational exercises are designed to cover a representative sample of job activities, major strides toward content validity will have been taken.

The second objective of job analysis for assessment purposes is to determine the dimensions required to carry out the job activities effectively. The process of identifying these characteristics is one of inference based on careful study of the job activities and critical incidents of success and failure on the job (see Fine, chapter 1).

ASSESSMENT CENTER EXERCISES AND DIMENSION RATINGS

Assessment center exercises mirror the majority of day-to-day activities of individuals performing in the target-level job. But as with the selection of dimensions, other factors must be considered in the selection of specific assessment center exercises. One must consider the ability of the exercise to bring out the target dimensions defined as important, the reliability of the exercise, and the overlap of various possible exercises. Obviously, since the goal is to cover all of the target dimensions for the job, exercises that cover several dimensions and dimensions not covered in other exercises are more appropriate. Exercise selection decisions are based on the capacity of the exercises to bring out reliable judgments of behavior efficiently. Some exercises take an hour to produce the same one or two observations that can be obtained in fifteen minutes in another exercise.

Evaluation of individual assessment techniques. In evaluating the contribution of any assessment technique, it is helpful to note these relationships: (1) the reliability of observers' judgments, (2) the correlation of the technique with overall assessment ratings, (3) the correlation of the technique with subsequent criteria of managerial success (e.g., progress in the company or performance ratings), and (4) the unique contribution of the technique over and above other techniques. The last requirement should be strongly emphasized. We do not want to use an elaborate or costly assessment technique if a simple or less expensive one is just as effective. To decide, then, whether a specific component of an assessment center is of value, we need to know if it adds something to prediction or understanding beyond what is obtained from other measurement techniques.

Validation of exercise ratings against the overall assessment rating (requirement 2 above) assumes that the summary index is a relevant, worthy criterion. The overall assessment rating (OAR) is certainly a readily available synthesis of the multiple observations by multiple assessors in multiple exercises. To use the OAR as a "criterion" may be questionable, but the OAR is highly predictive of several criteria of managerial success. Furthermore, in many situations, no better evaluation of managerial behavior exists. Correlations of assessment components with the OAR give insight into the assessors' judgment processes and can lead to revisions in exercises, dimensions, and assessor training.

Examining the validity of individual assessment techniques may not adequately reflect the complex nature of multiple assessments. The synthesis of the assessment data by several assessors during the staff discussion builds on complex interactions of observations that take place over several days. Nevertheless, knowledge of the contribution of each technique is of practical and theoretical value.

Things to consider in assessment center exercise categories. Nine categories of assessment center exercises have been defined. These categories represent the majority of all exercises used in assessment centers. But this arrangement necessitates that the categories are broad. For example, there are numerous kinds of analysis exercises that fall under the general definition of *analysis exercises*. They range from very simple analysis situations, such as those confronted by a foreman, which may take fifteen minutes, to a very complicated analysis, which may require four to five hours of work by a participant. Thus the reader should be cognizant that in the discussion of the merits of exercises, there are considerable individual differences among exercises within a category.

When reviewing an exercise for possible inclusion in an assessment center, an organization should consider the following characteristics:

1. The appropriateness of the exercise for the target job. Does the exercise represent a frequent and important job activity?
2. The ability of the exercise to stimulate behavior relative to important job-related dimensions defined in a job analysis. The more dimensions on which behavior is stimulated, the better the exercise. Involved here is the notion of probability of observation. Some assessment center exercises are designed to stimulate observation of certain dimensions and always do bring out those dimensions. An example would be an exercise in which an individual is asked to write something, and his or her written communication is being evaluated. However, other assessment center exercises do not guarantee an observation of a dimension to which they are targeted. For example, a group exercise may be designed to stimulate behaviors around the dimension "persuasiveness." However, the dynamics of a particular group in a particular assessment center may be such that an individual never has to use any persuasive behaviors because every single idea he or she presents is automatically accepted by the group. Thus the dimension is not observable in that particular situation even though in the majority of groups it is observable. Obviously, the more sure an assessor is of actually observing a dimension in an exercise, the more preferable the exercise.
3. The efficiency of the exercises. Efficiency deals with a combination of factors, including length of the exercise, number of dimensions on which behav-

ior is stimulated by a particular exercise, and the expense of the exercise material. Exercises requiring only paper and pencil for instructions and response are much cheaper than exercises requiring role players. Similarly, exercises that require two role players are more expensive than those requiring only one.

4. The validity of the exercise as a whole. If one is considering using construct validity evidence, then the validity of the exercise in other similar selection situations becomes critically important. Even if one does not try to establish construct validity, knowing the validity of the exercise in other assessment situations is still important; they lend credibility to exercise selection decisions.

It is useful to know frequency of use of various assessment center techniques in operating managerial assessment centers. The list shown in Table 5.2 was developed from a review of approximately five hundred centers with which we have been associated.

As one reviews the research on assessment center techniques, it is interesting to note the lack of correlation between the frequency with which an assessment center exercise is used in practice and the available research evidence. A great deal is known about paper-and-pencil tests, but they are infrequently used as part of assessment centers. Relatively little is known about in-basket tests or interview simulation, yet they are very frequently used as part of assessment centers. One explanation for these differences is that the knowledge about the pros and cons of a specific technique (for example, specific tests) may well have led to decisions not to use them; that is, if the tests are proven to be ineffective predictors of future performance, then their use would not be justified.

Another contributing factor is the increasing pressure from the federal government to demonstrate the content validity of selection instruments. Content validity evidence is more easily obtained for certain kinds of exercises than others. Again, paper-and-pencil tests are usually (but not always) more difficult to content validate.

To the extent that the choice of exercises is in direct response to the frequency of job activities, certain exercises automatically arise more frequently than others. A good example is the interview simulation exercise, which is becoming much more popular in assessment centers. In our observations of assessment centers established in the last two years, almost 100 percent use interview simulations. This use is in direct response to the fact that almost all supervisory/managerial jobs have a very strong one-to-one component. On the other hand, other exercises seem to be declining in popularity in response to job content studies. A good example of this trend involves some of the group exercises, particularly for supervisory-level jobs, where group activities are found to be important less frequently.

Finally, and perhaps most important, is the growing movement in assess-

TABLE 5.2. Use of Assessment Exercise Categories

Exercise	Time in Use (%)
In-basket	95
Assigned-role leaderless group discussion	85
Interview simulation	75
Nonassigned-role leaderless group discussion	45
Scheduling (primarily for supervisory positions)	40
Analysis (primarily for higher-level positions)	35
Management games	10
Background interview (part of the assessment center as opposed to being part of a promotion system)	5
Paper-and-pencil tests	
Intellectual	2
Reading	1
Mathematics/arithmetic	1
Personality	1
Projective tests	1

ment centers to be more behavioral and less clinical. Paper-and-pencil tests and inputs from projective instruments can be combined with inputs from assessment center exercises as long as the exercises are being evaluated on a clinical level (e.g., the OSS Assessment Centers and even the early AT&T Management Progress Study). Increasingly, assessment centers have turned to a highly behavioral orientation, where assessors observe behavior in the exercises, categorize the behavior by dimensions, and share their ratings of the dimensions along with their recorded observations of behavior. All decisions are based on behavioral evidence. In this kind of situation, nonbehavioral input "signs" (e.g., from tests or a clinical interview) do not readily fit in and thus have been dropped very frequently.

Advantages and Disadvantages of Alternatives

SELECTION

To demonstrate the effectiveness of a selection technique, it is appropriate to have evidence of predictive validity (APA/AERA/NCME Joint Committee, 1974). One type of evidence can be obtained by correlating predictor scores, obtained prior to hiring, with criterion measures, obtained sometime after hiring, for a representative sample of the applicant population. The criterion data should be free from contamination and should give reliable and relevant measures of significant aspects of on-the-job performance. Evidence should show that the proposed selection device adds something different from other currently used or more economical techniques. At a minimum, the predictor should correlate significantly with the criterion and, preferably, should have practical significance in improving levels of work performance. The selection device should not predict differentially for racial or sex subpopulations.

Three studies in the assessment center literature approximate this type of study. Bray and Campbell (1968) reported on seventy-eight sales personnel who were assessed soon after hiring. No relationship was found between overall assessment performance ratings by the staff at a training school or by supervisors on the job, but there were significant correlations against predictions by a staff of trained observers based on field observations of sales behavior. Although criteria were uncontaminated by assessment results, it is not known whether the assessees were representative of the applicant group. Furthermore, the motivation of applicants in an actual selection situation may differ from that of a group already hired.

The Sears assessment program for college recruits has been evaluated for reliability and validity by Kohls (1970). Marquardt (1976) demonstrated that assessment center ratings were predictive against a wide variety of performance ratings gathered at the end of the probationary training period, including ratings on behavioral scales and final ranking by a coordinator assigned to oversee the trainee's first year in an assigned store. One concern about this criterion is its relationship with subsequent job performance. As Marquardt warns, follow-up studies of on-the-job performance are needed, although it must be recognized that the training period is critical and failure here will preclude later success.

Moses and Wall (1975) reported on the external selection program of management recruits at AT&T. The OAR from a one-day program correlated .60 with job performance ratings prepared by special interviewers following a field review of performance one year after assessment.

EARLY IDENTIFICATION OF POTENTIAL

Within any organization, it is essential to be able to identify individuals with the potential for growth and advancement. These individuals must be encouraged to remain with the organization in order to retain the high-level talent necessary for effective operation in the future. They must be given special training and development opportunities to prepare them for higher job responsibilities. No organization has the resources to prepare everyone at a particular job level for higher assignments. It is not usually that funds for training and development are in short supply, but that there is only a limited number of "developmental assignments" that provide early opportunity for decision making and responsibility. An organization must identify potential early in the developmental process if these assignments are to be effectively distributed and not squandered through chance assignment of personnel. Similarly, formal training and development should be provided to those individuals with a high potential for advancement.

As an organization becomes more complex, more and more preparation for higher job assignments is required prior to advancement. Thus an earlier decision on "potential for advancement" is required in order to provide effective training development experiences. A secondary, but also important, consideration is the need to provide special encouragement to individuals with high potential in order to give them the motivation to stay with the organization. Highly motivated "high potential" individuals may seek jobs outside of the organization unless they receive some kind of tangible indication that their chances for advancement are higher than the average. Actually providing special assignments and training opportunities is an effective way of acknowledging potential without a formal promise of promotion. Providing these kinds of encouragement requires a more accurate method of identification of early management potential than is typically available in organizations. Consequently, many organizations have turned to the assessment center method.

The problem of early identification of potential among minorities and women is particularly difficult for many organizations. These persons have not experienced progress comparable to that of white males. Equal employment demands and affirmative action programs have stimulated the advancement of minorities and women. In order to achieve parity of assignments throughout job levels, organizations have been forced to promote minorities and women in greater numbers than previously. Many times an organization finds itself in a situation where its affirmative action plan calls for advancement of five minority employees to second-level supervisory positions when there are not even five represented in first-level supervisory positions. The only obvious solution is to "fast track" representatives of minorities and women into the first-level position so that they can be more quickly prepared to achieve the second-level position. To do this, some form of early identification is necessary, and such programs have been initiated by a number of organizations in this country.

AT&T has devised two programs for early identification of potential that use the assessment center to predict the advancement potential of minorities and women. In one case, a miniature assessment center is used to assess supervisory potential; the other is an assessment program designed to predict engineering potential. The rationale of both programs is that special attention should be paid to the development of new nonmanagement employees who have the general administrative skills to handle a more advanced job. Once individuals with these general skills are identified, the organization can then provide them with opportunities for the acquisition of the information and knowledge needed to carry out the higher-level jobs successfully. The training can focus on the areas of weakness for each individual. This tailor-made development program increases effectiveness of training efforts.

The Early Identification Assessment program (EIA) at AT&T (Moses,

1973b) was designed to assess early potential for management among short-service employees. The EIA is patterned very closely after other management assessment programs at AT&T—most of the same assessment techniques and judgmental predictions are involved. The main difference is that the EIA is only one day long, in comparison with the two days for more common AT&T assessment programs. In one day of assessment, a leaderless group discussion, an in-basket test, a personal interview, a written exercise, and a general mental ability test are administered to six candidates. Four staff members rate the participants on eight management dimensions, such as leadership, forcefulness, and energy, and give an overall rating of their potential to assume supervisory management assignments. Feedback is given to the participants by a separate staff of experienced counselors who work with the individuals and the departments to outline developmental opportunities. Moses (1973b) described a study to evaluate the effectiveness of the judgments of the EIA by using the assessment judgments from the more extensive two-day assessments provided by the Personnel Assessment Program (PAP).

According to Moses (1973a), the one-day engineering assessment process is the first of its kind because of the unique qualities assessed and the special simulation exercises that were developed. Thorough job analyses of the AT&T engineers revealed that the following qualities were important: calculating skills, ability to interpret information, problem-solving skills, and economic judgment. The assessment techniques developed include individual and group problem-solving situations. In one simulation, the individual has three hours to review material on a high-priority engineering project and to prepare forms and make estimates of work that needs to be accomplished. Assessors are concerned with the way the participant attends to detail, goes about solving the problem, and presents findings. Other assessment techniques were devised to evaluate special job-related skills.

The engineering program was evaluated by comparing assessment ratings with criterion ratings for groups of currently employed engineers in two companies. From among 275 engineers rated with a set of behaviorally anchored rating scales, 59 were identified who were high or low performers. Moses reported: "Of those that the assessment staff saw as having good potential, 75% were also seen as above average engineers on the job, while only 39% of the assessment low-rated engineers were good performers" (1972, p. 119). Moses concluded that the early results are encouraging and the program was helpful in identifying this type of managerial potential among engineers.

Other early identification programs have been instituted at the Federal Aviation Administration (Alexander, Buck, & McCarthy, 1975), the Bureau of Printing and Engraving (Hall, 1976; Hall & Baker, 1975), and Bendix (Alexander, 1975). No predictive validity evidence has been reported for these programs, but the organizations that use the assessment center activities believe that they aid in the identification of worthy candidates beyond the information available from existing job records.

A technique for aiding promotion decisions should be validated in a way similar to that used in validating a selection technique. A decision to promote is essentially a decision to select from within an organization those most likely to succeed on a higher-level job. Many of the same research considerations apply. Promotion decisions for an unrestricted sample of employees on a lower-level job should be compared with subsequent measures of success on a higher-level job; the criteria should be uncontaminated and relevant; and the proposed prediction technique should contribute something different from that contributed by traditional techniques (e.g., supervisory evaluations of potential or test information).

Most literature on assessment centers is related to promotion decisions and has been summarized by Thornton and Byham (1982). Validity evidence has been reported for promotion to first-level supervision and middle-level management; no validity studies for higher-level executives have been conducted.

There has been no more thorough body of predictive validity research generated to support the accuracy of an industrial psychology practice than the evidence on assessment centers. While criticisms have been raised about other aspects of assessment centers, even the critics agree that the process accurately identifies persons who, if promoted, are most likely to experience success as managers. We can recommend the use of assessment centers for promotion purposes with few reservations.

TRAINING AND DEVELOPMENT

Assessment centers are used for various developmental purposes: (1) identification of training needs, (2) development of self-insights and stimulation of self-improvement, and (3) as a training experience. Relevant to the first purpose, we need evidence that the assessment procedure possesses sufficient validity to measure a set of separate, differentiated aspects of managerial ability. The evidence suggests that assessment centers measure three or four broad characteristics, namely, administrative skills, interpersonal ability, decision-making skills, and activity level—that is, overall assessee impact in a job. Reliable ratings on more specific dimensions have also been found in a number of studies.

No evidence has been published that assessment centers develop self-insights or lead to management development, although learning and training principles would suggest that these programs should lead to management development.

COMPARISONS WITH OTHER METHODS

Although there are some mixed results in the studies cited by Thornton and Byham (1982), it appears that data generated in assessment centers can yield more accurate predictions of managerial success than paper-and-pencil tests alone. In most cases, the overall assessment rating is more accurate than the typical ability or personality test scores. Situational exercises and dimension ratings by assessors are more valid than single test scores. In some research, multiple correlations of test scores exceed the correlation for the overall assessment rating, but lack of cross-validation and the potential shrinkage in multiple regression analyses (especially with the small sample sizes that typify assessment center research) render the reliability of these findings suspect. The literature reviewed suggests that the validity coefficients of the overall assessment rating are more stable over time and over samples. Slivinski, McCloskey, and Bourgeois (1979) have shown that well-designed studies may reveal more nearly equal effectiveness among the various methods and lead to the notion of a need for a selection or promotion "system" that integrates multiple sources of applicant information (Byham, 1979).

ASSESSMENT CENTERS AND THE COURTS

In today's world, personnel administration and personnel practices must face the close scrutiny of administrative, quasi-legal, and judiciary systems. Personnel decision making in general and decisions about selection, promotion, and assignment to training programs in particular must meet various standards and guidelines of equal employment opportunity compliance agencies. Suits brought by individual parties and the Equal Employment Opportunity Commission have been heard in various levels of state and federal courts. Both statutory (civil rights acts) and constitutional issues have been raised. The United States Supreme Court has rendered several decisions regarding the use of tests and other evaluation techniques in personnel decisions (see Nathan & Cascio, Introduction). Abstracts of these cases are readily accessible in several excellent sources (Byham, 1982; Horstman, 1977; Psychological Corporation, 1978; U.S. Office of Personnel Management, 1979).

The results of these cases are clear in many regards. The organization must show that it followed the *Uniform Guidelines on Employee Selection Procedures* in the development, validation, and use of decision-making procedures (Task Force on Assessment Center Standards, 1980). The organization must be able to provide documented evidence that substantiates the validity and fairness of the procedures being used. Such evidence must demonstrate the use of professionally sound practices, including adequate job analyses, criterion measures, samples of subjects, statistical analyses, and conditions for gathering research data. On the positive side, the courts have affirmed repeatedly that properly validated tests can aid in the effective utilization of human resources, and organizations have the right to use those tests. Numerous examples of acceptable testing programs have been observed. Many testing programs have been scrutinized and found acceptable by compliance agencies; furthermore, they constitute an integral part of many affirmative action programs.

There can be little question that the federal government has become a powerful force in matters of testing in industry. Symposia at recent conventions of the American Psychological Association, the Academy of Management, the American Society of Personnel Administration, and other personnel administration associations have explored the government's impact on personnel practices and the profession of industrial psychology.

The use of the assessment center methodology is covered by the testing guidelines and has been the subject of administrative and judicial review. How have assessment centers fared? According to Byham (1982), quite well. The evidence that is available indicates that assessment centers will be defensible to compliance agencies and the courts. Several lines of thinking lead to this conclusion. The research evidence clearly supports the predictive and concurrent validity and the fairness of assessment centers. Assessment centers can be validated using straightforward, easy-to-understand job analysis procedures. No industrial assessment center application has ever been found illegal, and there are very few court cases (Byham, 1982). In EEOC and court cases involving alleged discrimination from the use of tests and other promotion practices, the assessment center has been accepted as an alternative method of screening. In addition, the EEOC itself has used an assessment center as one part of a reorganization program in the agency.

Recommendations

The complex assessment procedures carried out in assessment centers have been analyzed in terms of several basic principles. Although not all assessment centers conform to the models we have described or use the same steps listed in this chapter, there is enough similarity to warrant certain generalizations. These principles apply to all assessment centers, and it is our contention that when these principles are applied systematically, they lead to accurate assessment and prediction of managerial performance.

1. Assessment should be based on clearly defined dimensions of managerial behavior.
2. Multiple assessment techniques should be used.
3. A variety of types of job sampling techniques should be used.
4. The assessors should know what it takes to succeed. They should be thoroughly familiar with the job and the organization and, if possible, have experience in the job.

5. The assessors should be thoroughly trained in assessment center procedures.
6. Behavioral data should be observed, recorded, and communicated among the assessor team members.
7. Group discussion processes should be used to integrate observations, rate dimensions, and make predictions.
8. The assessment process should be partitioned into stages that delay the formation of general impressions, evaluations, overall ratings, or final predictions.
9. Assessees should be evaluated against a clearly understood external norm group—not against each other.
10. Prediction of managerial success must be judgmental.

Assessment centers started slowly in American industry (Cohen, Moses, & Byham, 1974). During the early industrial application period from 1956 to 1970, only a few large organizations used the method extensively, but each undertook systematic research programs to evaluate the assessment center process. Several studies were reported during this period by each of the following organizations: AT&T, IBM, Sears, SOHIO, and GE. During the general application period starting in the late 1960s, numerous other industrial and governmental organizations adopted the procedure and continued the research efforts. Although other organizations have conducted less extensive research efforts, it is our view that the criticism that practice outruns research evidence in industrial psychology is incorrect for assessment centers—this technique probably has more research support than any other technique in industrial psychology.

We recognize that not all questions have been answered. For example, we need to know more about how the utility of the assessment center method compares to other methodologies and its role in management development. We also recognize that not all assessment center research has been perfect, even though researchers went to great lengths to design and implement adequate studies in the difficult context of organizational practice.

Assessment center methodology is not a panacea and it is not appropriate for all performance assessment situations; but the evidence indicates that it should be a component of most supervisory or managerial selection or evaluation programs. The question is *not* which methodology is best at predicting supervisory and managerial success. The appropriate question is what combination of methodologies produce the best results? The assessment center method would almost always be on any such list of methods.

References

Adams, S., & Fyffe, D. (1969). *The corporate promotables.* Houston, TX: Gulf Publishing.

Alexander, H. S., Buck, J. A., & McCarthy, R. J. (1975). Usefulness of the assessment center process for selection to upward mobility programs. *Human Resource Management, 14,* 10–13.

Alexander, S. J. (1975). Bendix Corporation establishes early identification program. *Assessment and Development, 2,* 10.

APA/AERA/NCME Joint Committee. (1974). *Standards for educational and psychological tests* (rev. ed.). Washington, DC: American Psychological Association.

Bray, D. W., & Campbell, R. J. (1968). Selection of salesmen by means of an assessment center. *Journal of Applied Psychology, 52,* 36–41.

Byham, W. C. (1979, June). *Applying assessment center technology to a personnel system.* Paper presented at the meeting of the Seventh International Congress on the Assessment Center Method, New Orleans.

Byham, W. C. (1982). *Review of legal cases and options dealing with assessment centers and content validity* (Monograph 4). Pittsburgh: Development Dimensions International.

Byham, W. C., & Bobin, D. (Eds.). (1972). *Alternatives to paper-and-pencil testing.* Pittsburgh: University of Pittsburgh.

Campbell, J. P., Dunnette, M. D., Lawler, E. E., III, & Weick, K. E. (1970). *Managerial behavior, performance, and effectiveness.* New York: McGraw-Hill.

Cohen, B. M., Moses, J. L., & Byham, W. C. (1974). *The validity of assessment centers: A literature review* (Monograph 2). Pittsburgh: Development Dimensions International.

Cronbach, L. J. (1970). *Essentials of psychological testing.* New York: Harper and Row.

Edwards, A. L., & Abbott, R. D. (1973). Measurement of personality traits: Theory and techniques. In P. Mussen & M. Rosenzweig (Eds.), *Annual review of psychology* (pp. 241–278). Palo Alto, CA. Annual Reviews.

Fiske, D. S., & Pearson, P. J. (1970). Theory and techniques of personality measurement. In P. J. Mussen & M. R. Rosenzweig (Eds.), *Annual review of psychology* (pp. 49–86). Palo Alto, CA. Annual Reviews.

Hall, H. L. (1976, July). *An evaluation of the upward mobility assessment center for the Bureau of Engraving and Printing* (TM 76-6). Washington, DC: U.S. Civil Service Commission.

Hall, H. L., & Baker, D. R. (1975, August). *An overview of the upward mobility assessment center for the Bureau of Engraving and Printing* (TM 76-6). Washington, DC: U.S. Civil Service Commission.

Horstman, D. S. (1977, September). *1975–76 court case compendium: Legal standards for personnel practices.* Washington, DC: U.S. Civil Service Commission.

Kohls, J. W. (1970, October). *Evaluation of the assessment center approach to the selection of college recruits in the eastern territory.* Chicago: Sears Roebuck and Co.

Marquardt, L. D. (1976, July). *Follow-up evaluation of the second look approach to the selection of management trainees.* Chicago: Sears Roebuck and Co.

McCormick, E. J., Cunningham, J. W., & Thornton, G. C., III. (1967). The prediction of job requirements by a structured job analysis procedure. *Personnel Psychology, 20,* 431–440.

McCormick, E. J., Jeanneret, P. R., & Mecham, R. C. (1972). A study of job characteristics and job dimensions as based on the position analysis questionnaire (PAQ). *Journal of Applied Psychology, 56,* 347–368.

Mischel, W. (1968). *Personality and assessment.* New York: Wiley.

Mischel, W. (1973). Toward a cognitive social learning reconceptualization of personality. *Psychological Review, 80,* 252–283.

Moses, J. L. (1972). Assessment center performance and management progress. *Studies in Personnel Psychology, 4,* 7–12.

Moses, J. L. (1973a). Assessment center for the early identification of supervisory and technical potential. In W. C. Byham & D. Bobin (Eds.), *Alternatives to paper-and-pencil testing.* Pittsburgh: University of Pittsburgh.

Moses, J. L. (1973b). The development of an assessment center for the early identification of supervisory potential. *Personnel Psychology, 26,* 569–580.

Moses, J. L., & Wall, S. (1975). Pre-hire assessment: A validity study of a new approach for hiring college graduates. *Assessment and Development, 2,* 11.

Peter, L. F. (1970). *The Peter principle.* New York: William Morrow.

Psychological Corporation. (1978, April). *Summaries of court decisions on employment testing 1968–1977.* New York: Author.

Schwab, D. P., Heneman, H. H., III, & DeCotiis, T. A. (1975). Behaviorally anchored rating scales: A review of the literature. *Personnel Psychology, 38,* 549–562.

Slivinski, L. W., McCloskey, J. L., & Bourgeois, R. P. (1979, June). *Comparison of different methods of assessment.* Paper presented at the Seventh International Congress on the Assessment Center Method, New Orleans.

Smith, P. C., & Kendall, L. M. (1963). Retranslation of expectations. An approach to the construction of unambiguous anchors for rating scales. *Journal of Applied Psychology, 47,* 149–155.

Taft, R. (1955). The ability to judge people. *Psychological Bulletin, 52,* 1–23.

Taft, R. (1959). Multiple methods of personality assessment. *Psychological Bulletin, 56,* 333–352.

Task Force on Assessment Center Standards. (1980). Standards and ethical considerations for assessment center operations. *Personnel Administrator, 25,* 35–38.

Thornton, G. C., III. (1976). *Job analysis procedure for Kodak Colorado Division, SSW/CDP Programs.* Unpublished manuscript.

Thornton, G. C., III, & Byham, W. C. (1982). *Assessment centers and managerial performance.* New York: Academic Press.

U.S. Equal Employment Opportunity Commission, U.S. Civil Service Commission, U.S. Department of Labor, & U.S. Department of Justice. (1978). Uniform guidelines on employee selection procedures. *Federal Register, 43*(166), 38290–38309.

U.S. Office of Personnel Management. (1979, September). *Equal Employment Opportunity court cases* (OIPP 152-46). Washington, DC: Office of Intergovernmental Personnel Programs.

6. APPRAISAL INTERVIEW

Kenneth N. Wexley

Introduction

In some organizations, employees are never told how they have been assessed by their managers. Consequently, many of them never really know how they stand with their bosses. As one engineer commented, "The only time I know that my manager thinks I'm doing a good job is when my wife, who does our banking, tells me that I've gotten a raise" (Wexley & Yukl, 1984, p. 368). Fortunately, most organizations today conduct what is variously referred to as a performance appraisal interview (PAI), performance review, work planning and review, performance audit, and feedback interview—all of which generally have the same meaning. A survey conducted by the Bureau of National Affairs revealed that in 91 percent of the 139 organizations studied, appraisal results were fed back to employees (Feild & Holley, 1975). Typically, this interview occurs between an employee and his or her manager either once or twice a year. It has two main objectives (Goodale, 1982):

1. Administrative: to communicate and support administrative decisions such as salary increases, promotions, transfers, and layoffs
2. Employee Development: to enable each employee to get feedback as to how well he or she is doing in the opinion of the manager, and to give the manager and employee an opportunity to discuss how the employee can improve performance. (Wexley & Yukl, 1984, p. 369)

It is important, at the outset of this chapter, to distinguish between the PAI and the day-to-day coaching that occurs between a manager and an employee. Unlike performance appraisal interviews, which are formal and scheduled, coaching occurs on an informal and frequent basis. When coaching an employee, the manager explains why things are done the way they are, suggests ways the employee can improve, and shows approval and disapproval regarding the employee's day-to-day job performance (Wexley & Yukl, 1984). Although coaching is not our primary topic of concern, it is nonetheless an important process. After all, if performance assessment is to bring about a behavior improvement or sustain a high level of output, it must be conducted more frequently than once or twice a year. For example, giving golfers feedback from thirty to forty-five minutes once a year is not going to improve their performance. Similarly, telling employees once a year to "keep up the good work" or "try harder in your selling"

167

is going to have little impact on their behavior. What an employee needs to start doing, stop doing, or continue doing must be communicated on an ongoing basis if we hope to increase productivity through performance appraisals (Latham & Wexley, 1981). Moreover, if a manager provides coaching on an ongoing basis, the PAI becomes a review of issues that have already been discussed by the manager and employee in the past. This improves the quality of the PAI since employees are less defensive in response to negative feedback and more apt to be open in discussing their performance-related problems (Beer, 1981).

This chapter provides (1) alternative approaches to conducting PAIs, (2) a critical evaluation of the advantages and disadvantages of each of these approaches, and (3) several suggestions for conducting effective feedback interviews with one's employees. In my opinion, the PAI requires more skill on the part of a manager than any of the other kinds of interviews one is called upon to perform (e.g., selection, disciplinary, exit). The difficulties that managers experience in conducting effective PAIs can be traced to the healthiness of their interpersonal relationships with their employees, their skills in handling a feedback session, and the quality of the performance appraisal system being used to assess employees' job performance (Beer, 1981). In addition, managers and employees often want the PAI to serve conflicting objectives. Employees desire to maintain a positive image with their bosses so as to maximize their pay increases, promotions, and favorable work assignments. Managers, on the other hand, want their employees to be receptive to negative feedback about themselves so as to improve their job performance and promotability, and they want employees to be trusting enough to supply unfavorable information about themselves during the interview. The conflict is over the exchange of information (Beer, 1981; Porter, Lawler, & Hackman, 1975). Given these kinds of difficulties, it is not surprising that many managers are reluctant to conduct PAIs. In fact, here are some of their typical comments:

"I'll do anything to avoid giving my people their yearly performance feedback."
"I hated to criticize Jones and then have to argue about it with him."
"These rating forms are ridiculous."
"I'm just not comfortable trying to be a judge and a helper at the same time."
"I wanted Wilson to talk about her weaknesses, but all she wanted to know about was her pay raise."

Despite these potential difficulties, the PAI can be a valuable employee development tool for managers, if conducted properly. This chapter focuses on the developmental rather than the administrative purposes of the PAI. Specifically, five topics will be discussed: (1) the characteristics of effective interviews, (2) alternative approaches that can be used, (3) guidelines for choosing the correct approach, (4) pointers on making the interview effective, and (5) recommendations for maintaining the new feedback system.

CHARACTERISTICS OF EFFECTIVE INTERVIEWS

Wexley (1979) and other reviewers such as Burke, Weitzell, and Weir (1978) have summarized some of the major research findings on performance appraisal feedback that suggest six general characteristics of effective interviews: participation, support, goal setting, discussing problems, limited criticism, and role splitting.

Participation. If the interview's objective is to motivate employees to change their behavior or improve their performance, the session must be one in which employees get an opportunity to participate actively. Studies have clearly shown that the more the employee participates in the appraisal, the more the employee is satisfied with the appraisal process and the manager who conducted it, and the more likely performance improvement goals will be accepted and met (Latham & Yukl, 1975; Nemeroff & Wexley, 1977; Wexley, Singh, & Yukl, 1973). What do we mean by "participation?" It refers to the employee's sense of significance (i.e., that one's thoughts are welcomed and those topics that one feels require attention are addressed) and contribution (i.e., that one can make suggestions that one feels affect the boss) during the interview (Greller, 1978). Participation is not merely how much the employee talks. Apparently, what one talks about is more important than how much time one spends talking. Essentially, the manager's role should be to collect data from the employee (e.g., self-assessments, performance problems being encountered, suggestions for improvements) and to seriously consider them.

Support. Employee acceptance of the appraisal and satisfaction with the manager increase to the extent that the manager is helpful and supportive (Kay, Meyer, & French, 1965; Nemeroff & Wexley, 1977). In general, the more the manager uses positive motivational techniques (e.g., praising the employee for what he or she has done well, ending the interview on a positive note, trying to be friendly, treating the employee as an equal and with respect), the more open and trusting the employee will be in supplying valid information that the manager needs to know.

Goal setting. Both laboratory and field research has repeatedly shown that the setting of specific goals dramatically improves employee performance (Latham & Locke, 1979). In fact, specific goals can result in up to twice as much improvement in employee performance than does a discussion of general goals (Latham & Yukl, 1975). Telling employees to "do your best," to "try harder," or to "increase sales volume" has little, if any, impact on their productivity. However, telling them to "increase your sales volume by 5 percent by June 1," to "make sure there is enough staff working on weekends to handle customers," and to "stop gossiping about the personal lives of prospective clients" is much better. Goals can be either results oriented (e.g., increase sales volume) or behavior oriented (e.g., stop gossiping). Although both kinds of goals are useful, behavioral goals are much more specific and therefore helpful in letting an employee know exactly what he or she has to do differently to obtain certain results.

Discussing problems. The PAI should focus on discussing and solving problems that are interfering with the employee's current job performance (Maier, 1958; Meyer & Kay, 1964). These problems might include inadequate raw materials, outmoded equipment, poor maintenance, and inadequate training. The difficulties could even involve certain poor supervisory practices on the part of managers. In fact, managers should be encouraged to ask their employees, "Is there anything I can do differently to help solve these problems?"

Limited criticism. Too much criticism by managers during the PAI tends to result in defensive reactions by employees, which lead, in turn, to little performance improvement (Kay, Meyer, & French, 1965). The employees' defensiveness can be explained by their desire to "look good" in their bosses' eyes. Defensiveness can take various forms, such as blaming others for their inadequacies, minimizing the importance of the appraisal process, demeaning the manager or the appraisal forms, and insincerely agreeing to change their ways (Beer, 1981). It is important to minimize criticism because it threatens employees' self-esteem. Whether or not an employee feels criticized depends upon his or her perceptions of the negative feedback given by the manager (Ilgen, Fisher, & Taylor, 1979). A manager can minimize threats to employees' self-esteem by providing specific, behaviorally oriented negative feedback. The more the manager focuses on the personality and mannerisms of their employees (e.g., "Joe, I've rated you below average in dependability" and "Mary, you're terribly awkward with customers") rather than on observed behaviors ("Joe, you're often late for meetings" and "Mary, you rarely smile when talking with customers"), the less employees will be motivated to improve their performance (Cascio, 1982).

Role splitting. As mentioned previously, the PAI has two main objectives from the manager's viewpoint: administrative (evaluative) and employee development. Although these two objectives are important, both cannot usually be accomplished during the same session, inasmuch as the manager is being asked to play the conflicting roles of judge and helper (McGregor, 1957). To alleviate this conflict, it is best to have two separate sessions: one that deals with evaluative and administrative ends, and a second that is directed at employee development. These sessions should be separated in time as much as possible.

Now that the general characteristics of effective PAIs have been discussed, let us turn our attention to four alternative approaches that have some applicability in organizations. These approaches vary in the degree of participation that employees are given during the interview.

Review of Alternative Interview Approaches

Several years ago, Maier (1958) proposed three approaches to conducting performance appraisal interviews: tell and sell, tell and listen, and problem solving (see Table 6.1). More recently, a mixed model approach has been suggested by several writers (e.g., Beer, 1981; Goodale, 1982) that combines several features of Maier's approaches.

TELL AND SELL

The primary objective of the tell-and-sell approach is to communicate the employee's appraisal to him or her as accurately as possible and to persuade the employee to follow the plan that is outlined for his or her improvement. From the viewpoint of the manager, it is an efficient approach, providing it works. It takes less time to present an evaluation than to discuss one; if the employee accepts the manager's feedback, a fairly complete interview can be conducted in fifteen to thirty minutes. Its success depends, to a large extent, on the manager's ability to persuade the employee to change in the recommended manner.

TABLE 6.1. Three Types of Appraisal Interviews

METHOD	TELL-AND-SELL	TELL-AND-LISTEN	PROBLEM-SOLVING
Role of Interviewer	Judge	Judge	Helper
Objective	To communicate evaluation and get employee to change	To communicate evaluation and encourage discussion	To stimulate growth and development in employee
Assumptions	Employee desires to correct weaknesses if he/she knows them. Any person can improve if he/she so chooses. A superior is qualified to evaluate a subordinate.	People will change if defensive feelings are removed.	Growth can occur without correcting faults. Discussion of job problems leads to improved performance.

(continued)

TABLE 6.1.   (*Continued*)

METHOD	TELL-AND-SELL	TELL-AND-LISTEN	PROBLEM-SOLVING
Role of Interviewer	Judge	Judge	Helper
Reactions	Defensive behavior suppressed; attempts to cover hostility.	Defensive behavior expressed; employee feels accepted.	Problem-solving behavior.
Skills	Salesmanship; patience.	Listening and reflecting feelings; summarizing.	Listening and reflecting feelings; reflecting ideas; using exploratory questions; summarizing.
Attitude	People profit from criticism and appreciate help.	One can respect the feelings of others if one understands them.	Discussion develops new ideas and mutual interests.
Motivation increased	Use of positive or negative incentives or both (extrinsic in that motivation is not related to task content).	Resistance to change reduced.	Increased freedom. Increased responsibility (intrinsic motivation in that interest is inherent in the task).
Gains	Success most probable when employee respects interviewer.	Develops favorable attitude to superior, which increases probability of success.	Almost assured of improvement in some respect.
Risks	Loss of loyalty; inhibition of independent judgment.	Need for change may not be developed.	Employee may lack ideas; change may be other than what superior had in mind.
Values	Perpetuates existing practices and values.	Permits interviewer to change views in the light of employee's responses. Some upward communication.	Both learn since experience and views pooled; change is facilitated.

Source: Maier (1958, p. 22).

The manager's ability to persuade in turn hinges on the manager's relationship with the subordinate and the manager's power to control the kinds of incentives that motivate each employee. The approach assumes that the manager knows best about how the employee should do his or her job.

TELL AND LISTEN

The main purpose of the tell-and-listen approach is to communicate the manager's evaluation to the employee and then let the employee respond to it. During the first part of the interview, the manager presents without interruption the employee's strengths and weaknesses. The second part of the interview is devoted to exploring thoroughly the employee's feelings about the evaluation. As with the tell-and-sell approach, the manager's role is that of a judge. However, with this approach the manager encourages the employee to disagree and express personal feelings so as to drain off emotions aroused by the evaluation. The manager tries to understand the employee's attitudes and feelings, makes use of pauses to encourage the employee to speak, and periodically summarizes the employee's feelings.

PROBLEM SOLVING

The main objective of the problem-solving approach is employee development. Unlike the previous approaches, it has no provisions for communicating the appraisal. Moreover, it takes the manager out of the role of judge and makes him or her a helper. Here the manager must limit his or her influence to stimulating the employee's thinking rather than supplying solutions. The manager must be willing to accept for consideration all ideas on job improvement that the employee talks about. If the employee's ideas seem impractical, the manager uses questions in order to determine more specifically what the employee has in mind. The manager and employee together generate solutions to problems and come to agreement on steps to be taken by each of them (i.e., mutual goal setting).

MIXED MODEL

The mixed-model approach combines Maier's problem-solving and telling approaches. According to Beer (1981), it starts with an open-ended discussion and exploration of problems that is led by the employee and followed by the manager. Next there is a problem-solving discussion that the employee continues to lead, but in this discussion the manager begins to take a somewhat stronger role. Then the manager and employee agree on performance problems and a plan for alleviating them. Finally, the manager ends the interview by giving his or her views and final evaluation if the employee has not dealt with important issues or if agreement has not been reached.

Which one of these four approaches is best to use? One answer to this question is, "None of them—each has its own unique advantages and disadvantages." Depending upon particular factors in the organization, a manager might decide to choose one PAI approach rather than another. In the following section, some of the factors influencing the correct choice of approach will be discussed.

Advantages and Disadvantages of Alternative Approaches

CHOOSING THE CORRECT APPROACH

The choice of a PAI approach by a manager will affect employee satisfaction with the appraisal interview and the manager, which in turn affects employee performance. Thus the objective for the manager is to carefully select the PAI approach that will maximize each individual employee's satisfaction, motivation, and performance. To attain this objective, the manager needs to take into consideration a number of forces in the situation. These forces include the various characteristics of the employee, the manager, their dyadic relationship, and the organization. Let us consider these forces impinging on the manager's choice of the PAI approach.

EMPLOYEE CHARACTERISTICS

The ultimate success of the PAI will be dependent on a good match between the chosen approach and employee expectations and level of performance. "Expectations" refer to what each employee considers to be appropriate appraisal feedback behavior on the part of the manager. In other words, some employees expect to be treated in a direct manner during the PAI while others expect to have more say. Years ago, Maier (1958) suggested that his tell-and-sell method has its greatest potential with young and new employees. These people are inexperienced and insecure and desire advice and assurance from an authority figure. To some extent, this desire is also applicable to an employee who is on a new assignment. Research by Hillery and Wexley (1974) suggests that Maier was correct; they found that employees in a training situation preferred nonparticipative appraisal interviews to participative ones. These employees wanted to be evaluated by the manager and were noticeably disappointed when they were asked to participate in their own evaluation. In fact, they appeared to be dissatisfied and frustrated with the participative (i.e., problem-solving) approach in this training setting. Other research involving older and more experienced employees has indicated that they prefer more participative approaches (Greller & Herold, 1975; Wexley, Singh, & Yukl, 1973). Thus it appears that employees who are young, inexperienced, and dependent on their manager for guidance expect to receive a more directive approach. In contrast, employees who are older, more experienced, and accustomed to assessing their own performance expect to receive a more participative approach.

The approach chosen by a manager should also depend upon each employee's level of performance (Cummings & Schwab, 1973). For the excellent performer, the focus of the appraisal interview should be on recognition of competence together with either enlargement of present responsibilities or promotion. For this type of individual, the PAI should emphasize participation. That is, a problem-solving method would be optimal. For the satisfactory employee whose performance is good but not outstanding, the focus should be on maintaining this level of performance (i.e., guarding against deterioration) and, one hopes, generating a little performance improvement. This PAI type of employee requires both the participation and direction that are characteristic of the the mixed-model approach. For the problem employee, the PAI needs to communicate clearly what aspects of performance are unacceptable and what specifically must be changed. If the employee is very weak, the feedback session would also include warnings of possible termination unless performance improves (Carroll & Schneier, 1982). This type of employee obviously requires "telling" (i.e., assigned goal setting) and, thus, a directive PAI approach.

MANAGER CHARACTERISTICS

The manager's general supervisory style is an important factor in determining the choice of approach. A manager who is normally quite directive in dealing with employees will tend to feel most comfortable using a tell-and-sell or tell-and-listen approach. However, those managers who are usually participative in their day-to-day interactions with employees will usually choose to use either a problem-solving or mixed-model approach. It is unlikely that a manager will feel comfortable changing his or her usual style (Carroll & Schneier, 1982). Further, it is equally unlikely for employees even to expect their managers to shift away from their normal supervisory style during the PAI.

MANAGER-EMPLOYEE RELATIONSHIP

Another factor influencing a manager's feedback approach is the level of confidence in the employee. The more confidence or regard the manager has for the individual's competence, the more the manager will allow the employee to participate in setting goals (Carroll, Cintron, & Tosi, 1971) and the less closely the manager will supervise the person (Lowin & Craig, 1968). Thus managers who have favorable opinions about their employees can be expected to use either the problem-solving or mixed-model approaches.

ORGANIZATIONAL CHARACTERISTICS

Organizations differ with respect to several organizational processes, including leadership, communication, decision making, goal setting, and control processes. Likert (1967) devised a continuum or scale with four categories (systems 1–4) to classify an organization in terms of these characteristic differences. Table 6.2 summarizes the attributes of the two extreme types, systems 1 and 4, for each organizational process. Inspection of this table reveals that system 4 organizations have supportive relationships, group decision making, and high performance goals. Managers in this type of organizational environment are expected to be considerate and supportive, to keep their employees informed, to provide recognition for good performance, and to consult with their employees before making decisions that affect them (Wexley & Yukl, 1984). Application of traditional or classical organizing principles (e. g., downward communication, autocratic decision making) results in a system 1 or 2 organization. Managers who find themselves in systems 3 and 4 organizational environments will tend to adopt the more participative PAI approaches, while managers in systems 1 and 2 environments will be more likely to use directive approaches. One important result of this conformity will be the performance appraisal system itself imposed on the manager by the organization; specifically, the type of system will influence such things as the forms used, the organization's commitment to providing feedback to employees, the type of training managers are given in conducting PAIs, and the extent to which managers are rewarded for developing their people. In a system 4 organization, for example, managers are expected to develop their employees. The performance appraisal forms that are provided by the human resources or personnel department allow managers to get a reliable reading of each individual's performance. The forms also stimulate a dialogue regarding strengths, weaknesses, and improvement plans.

SUMMARY

Before choosing the correct PAI approach, a manager needs to take into consideration a number of forces in the situation. These forces can be conveniently categorized as emanating from the employee, the manager, the quality of their relationship, and the organizational environment. Directive interviews are most appropriate with employees who are young, inexperienced, dependent, and having work-related problems. They are appropriate for those managers who normally interact with their employees in a directive manner and who do not have much confidence in their employees' ability. Participative interviews certainly should be the more prevalent approach. After all, most employees can be characterized as older, experienced, independent, and doing satisfactory work. These individuals have high self-esteem and a desire to participate in their own performance assessment. Most managers, one hopes, have come to have high regard

TABLE 6.2. Characteristics of Processes in Systems 1 and 4 Organizations

Process	System 1 Organization	System 4 Organization
1. Leadership	Includes no perceived confidence and trust. Subordinates do not feel free to discuss job problems with their superiors, who in turn do not solicit their ideas and opinions.	Includes perceived confidence and trust between superiors and subordinates in all matters. Subordinates feel free to discuss job problems with their superiors, who in turn solicit their ideas and opinions.
2. Motivation	Taps only physical, security, and economic motives through the use of fear and sanctions. Unfavorable attitudes toward the organization prevail among employees.	Taps a full range of motives through participatory methods. Attitudes are favorable toward the organization and its goals.
3. Communication	Information flows downward and tends to be distorted, inaccurate, and viewed with suspicion by subordinates.	Information flows freely throughout the organization—upward, downward, and laterally. The information is accurate and undistorted.
4. Interaction	Closed and restricted; subordinates have little effect on departmental goals, methods, and activities.	Open and extensive; both superiors and subordinates are able to affect departmental goals, methods, and activities.
5. Decision	Occurs only at the top of the organization; it is relatively centralized.	Occurs at all levels through group processes; it is relatively decentralized.
6. Goal-setting	Located at the top of the organization; discourages group participation.	Encourages group participation in setting high, realistic objectives.
7. Control	Centralized and emphasizes fixing of blame for mistakes.	Dispersed throughout the organization and emphasizes self-control and problem solving.
8. Performed goals	Low and passively sought by managers who make no commitment to developing the human resources of the organization.	High and actively sought by superiors, who recognize the necessity for making a full commitment to developing, through training, the human resources of the organization.

Source: Adapted from Gibson, Ivancevich, and Donnelly (1976, p. 277).

for their employees' ability and do not perceive them as mere children. We know that organizations in our country are slowly shifting from system 1 toward system 4 environments, thereby reinforcing those managers who use participative approaches in dealing with many of their employees.

Despite the fact that I endorse a contingency approach to PAI (i.e., there is no one best way for all situations), there are, nonetheless, certain pointers for maximizing the effectiveness of all interviews. These pointers are presented in the next section.

Recommendations

MAKING THE INTERVIEW EFFECTIVE

As a manager, there are certain things that you should do before, during, and after the PAI to maximize its effectiveness in motivating an employee to improve.

Before the interview. As a manager, you should prepare in advance for each PAI. This means that you should carefully assess the employee's job performance, be prepared to support your assessment by having examples of your observations of employee behavior, and have specific recommendations on how the individual might change for the better. You should also notify the employee well in advance when the PAI will be held and ask the individual to complete the performance appraisal form himself or herself (i.e., self-rating) prior to the session. In addition, the employee should be asked to think about work and career goals for the forthcoming year (Goodale, 1982). Recent research has shown that the more time employees spend preparing for the interview, the more likely they are to be satisfied with the appraisal process, motivated to improve, and actually improve their performance (Burke, Weitzel, & Weir, 1978).

We have seen that the PAI requires more skill from the manager than do the other types of interviews. It is unfortunate that so few organizations give their managers any formal training in how to conduct PAI sessions. Such training should not be left to trial and error. Instead, managers should be trained using a combination of feedback and goal setting to increase their feedback skills, as successfully demonstrated by Nemeroff and Cosentino (1979). Specifically, a manager's employees should each be asked to complete an anonymous questionnaire that taps their perceptions of their manager's behaviors during their most recent PAI. These questionnaire results should then be reported to the manager by a trainer, who also encourages the manager to set specific goals to increase effective behavior prior to the next round of appraisal interview sessions (e.g., "I will clearly and concisely state the purpose of the interview"; "I will help my employee establish priorities for the coming period"; "I will ask my employee to discuss his/her personal goals in order to help with his/her career development"). An alternative training strategy is to use behavior modeling, where managers are shown a list of key behaviors (commonly referred to as "learning points"), observe these behaviors acted out either on videotape or through live demonstration, and then try out these new behaviors during role-play situations (Goldstein & Sorcher, 1972; Wexley & Latham, 1981).

During the interview. A few tasks that managers should perform during the interview session have already been mentioned: encourage participation (in all but the tell-and-sell approach), establish specific goals, discuss work-related problems, minimize criticisms, split roles, and use day-to-day feedback. But there are additional techniques that often prove effective.

Appraisals can be based on traits (initiative, creativity, loyalty), cost-related outcomes (sales volume and units of production), or behaviors (stresses the importance of safety to employees, consults employees for their ideas on ways of making their jobs better). Traits such as initiative, creativity, and loyalty are rather ambiguous from the standpoint of actual performance. Telling an employee to be more creative or to show more initiative may be good advice, but it does not tell the individual what to do to follow this advice (Latham & Wexley, 1981). Furthermore, when employees are given feedback in terms of what they *are* (traits) and not what they *do,* they usually become more defensive when criticized by their managers ("I resent you're saying that I'm not creative or loyal!").

Although senior management, stockholders, and consumers are generally concerned with cost-related outcomes, such outcomes are frequently poor indicators by themselves of an employee's job effectiveness. First, cost-related outcomes are often deficient in that they do not include important factors for which an employee should be held accountable (e.g., being a good member of a work team and maintaining sound customer relations for future sales). This weakness is a major criticism of management-by-objectives (MBO) programs where goals are set in cost-related terms. Employees often complain that there is an overemphasis on quantitative goals and that they do not receive enough credit for aspects of the job that are not easily quantifiable. Second, cost-related outcomes are difficult to obtain on many jobs, especially for high-level managerial positions. Third, even when such outcomes are obtainable, they are only applicable to the work group as a whole, inasmuch as no single employee has control over the amount of output. Finally, cost-related outcomes are often influenced by factors over which the employee has no control (a recessed economy, defective machinery and tools, poor raw materials). Finally, and most important, cost-related outcomes by themselves do not inform employees what they need to do to maintain or to increase productivity. This is not to suggest that outcomes should be ignored; however, they should be downplayed for developmental purposes. Instead, observable job behaviors that are critical to job success or failure should be emphasized.

Behavioral measures can account for far more complexity, can be related more directly to what the employee actually does, and can better minimize irrelevant factors not under the control of the employee than cost-related outcomes. For these reasons, Latham and Wexley, in *Increasing Productivity through Performance Appraisal* (1981), strongly advocated behaviorally based appraisal measures for employee development purposes. In particular, we recommend using behavioral observation scales (BOS), a performance appraisal approach based on critical incidents (see Borman, chapter 3). A BOS instrument asks managers simply to indicate how frequently they have observed an employee engage in certain critically effective and ineffective behaviors. Employees, too, complete the BOS prior to their PAI with their managers. Behavioral observations on the part of the manager and employee become the topic of discussion during the interview rather than the employee's personality or output.

In order to minimize bias in ratings and thereby maximize their legality and the confidence that managers and employees have in them, all raters should be trained to reduce errors of judgment that occur when one person evaluates another. Few organizations incorporate training programs for managers that reduce rating errors. The organizations assume that by using a carefully developed appraisal instrument, rater errors will not occur. This assumption is unfounded.

Latham, Wexley, and Pursell (1975) have developed a workshop for managers consisting of videotapes of individuals being evaluated. More specifically, trainees are asked to give a rating on a nine-point scale according to how they thought the manager in the videotape rated the individual. They are also asked to rate the person themselves. Group discussions follow concerning why each of the twenty or so trainees assigned the ratings they did. In this way, the trainees are given an opportunity to observe other managers making rating errors, to participate actively in discovering the degree to which they themselves make some of these errors, and to practice job-related tasks to reduce those errors (Latham & Wexley, 1981). This training approach has been shown to reduce successfully such rating errors as halo, contrast, first impression, and similar-to-me. Additional approaches for training raters are reviewed by Spool (1978).

Writers such as Johnson (1979), Goodale (1982), Feinberg (1965), and Beer (1981) have provided helpful suggestions for improving a manager's PAI style, especially during the problem-solving and mixed-model interviews. Listed below are some of their prescriptions.

1. Start the interview by getting your employee talking. This can be accomplished by asking open-ended questions such as "How do you feel things are going on your job?" and "What goals do you feel you've accomplished since we met last?"

2. To avoid defensive reactions, you should avoid making general statements ("You're always late getting your reports to me"), attributing motives to behavior ("You're not committed to our team"), or comparing one employee to another ("You're not nearly as innovative as Sam").

3. Allow the employee to do most of the talking by remaining silent, especially

during the early part of the interview. Stimulate conversation by periodically "reflecting" an employee's feelings. For example:

    E: The most miserable part of my job is having to attend those boring meetings each month.

    M: You really despise them.

    E: That's for sure!

4. Your feelings can be conveyed nonverbally as well as verbally (Fugita, Wexley, & Malone, 1975). You might say that you are satisfied with an employee's work, but your facial expressions, gestures, posture, and lack of eye contact communicate something quite different. It is therefore important to be aware of one's nonverbal behaviors.

5. Negative feedback should be tactfully given by being specific about behaviors of the employee that you have observed. Keep your comments at the behavioral level. Minimize attacks on the employee's self-esteem, which will likely be perceived as criticism. BOS can be a great help to the manager.

6. Encourage the employee to suggest performance goals that you can then modify and expand. By letting the employee lead the way, as opposed to you assigning goals unilaterally, you can also reduce defensiveness.

7. Avoid what has come to be known as the "sandwich approach." Here the manager provides negative feedback between heavy doses of positive feedback. The manager begins the interview on a positive note, but the employee barely listens for fear of what is coming next.

8. Avoid providing your employees with a "vanishing performance appraisal." Here managers report having given their employees individual feedback, but the employees report that no such session had been held. To combat this problem, do not conduct your interviews on an airplane or in the company dining room. Make your PAI visible by meeting either in your office or in your employee's office.

9. Be sure to distinguish between your assessment of the employee's performance on his or her current job and his or her potential for promotion. These are different issues that are often incorrectly intertwined.

10. Schedule a follow-up meeting with the employee to ensure that progress is being made toward the goals you have both established.

After the interview. Between the termination of the PAI and the time of the follow-up meeting, it is important that you have the opportunity to observe your employee's job behaviors. This will allow you to assess whether the goals that were established during the interview are, in fact, attainable. It could be that the goals are too difficult for the individual's current level of expertise. It may be that the goals are not really compatible with the organization's current policies. Perhaps the goals are too easy or the individual has already forgotten them (Goodale, 1982). In any case, your job is to coach the employee toward goal attainments.

Once a new PAI system has been implemented in an organization, it should survive. However, this is not always the case! In the last section of this chapter, some of the ways of assuring that the new PAI system has "staying power" will be discussed.

MAINTAINING A NEW PAI SYSTEM

Based upon a review of what occurred in twelve organizations using different human resource systems to enhance productivity, Hinrichs (1978) identified several factors associated with the staying power as well as those factors associated with the discontinuance of programs. Latham and Wexley (1981) have applied Hinrich's factors to the maintenance of new performance appraisal systems. Let us discuss how these same factors can be used to maintain a new PAI system that has recently been implemented in an organization. The new system is one that encourages managers to use different approaches depending upon the situation. The factors that will contribute to its success are outlined below.

1. The PAI system is more likely to survive if it is behavioral in nature. Managers quickly come to realize that increased productivity can be best brought about by giving their employees feedback on how frequently they exhibit behaviors critical to performing their jobs successfully.

2. There must be a significant level of senior management support for taking managers' time to provide appraisal feedback. Active senior management support ensures that middle- and lower-level managers will be committed to the new system.

3. The new system must be implemented throughout a significant portion of the organization so as to become a way of life for employees. In other words, it must be implemented initially on several key fronts rather than in merely one segment of the organization, especially in those segments of the organization where it will be a "winner." Then the system should spread easily to the remaining parts of the organization.

4. The implementation of the new PAI system should be reviewed quarterly by the vice presidents of operations and human resources. They should assess whether the new system is improving employee behavior and thereby increasing productivity. If not, they should determine why.

5. There must be one group of people at company headquarters who are responsible for implementing the system and maintaining it to ensure that it runs smoothly across the entire organization.

6. Each unit of the organization must be "seeded" with knowledgeable people who have the responsibility of making the new system work in their unit. These individuals serve as advocates of the system, answer managers' questions regarding implementation, and report back to company headquarters periodically.

7. The most lasting PAI system is one that trains managers to make accurate

performance ratings and to provide feedback to employees on their assessments using the appropriate interviewing approach.

8. Because managers are busy people and PAIs are time consuming, managers need to be rewarded for developing their employees via recognition, salary increases, and promotions.

CONCLUDING REMARKS

The PAI might be difficult to conduct effectively, but it is certainly not impossible. The main objective of this chapter has been to suggest ways that managers can improve their skills in providing feedback to their employees. There is no one best way. Instead, a manager must take into consideration characteristics of self, employee, their relationship, and the organizational context. Once the new system has been designed, it must be implemented and monitored strategically in order to survive the test of time.

References

Beer, M. (1981). Performance appraisal: Dilemmas and possibilities. *Organizational Dynamics, 9*, 24–36.

Burke, R. J., Weitzel, W., & Weir, T. (1978). Characteristics of effective employee performance review and development interviews: Replication and extension. *Personnel Psychology, 31*, 903–919.

Carroll, S. J., Jr., Cintron, D., & Tosi, H. L. (1971). Factors related to how superiors set goals and review performance for their subordinates. *American Psychological Association Proceedings, 79*, 497–498.

Carroll, S. J., & Schneier, C. E. (1982). *Performance appraisal and review systems.* Glenview, IL: Scott, Foresman.

Cascio, W. F. (1982). *Applied psychology in personnel management.* Reston, VA: Reston Publishing Co.

Cummings, L. L., & Schwab, D. P. (1973). *Performance in organizations: Determinants and appraisal.* Glenview, IL: Scott, Foresman.

Feild, H. S., & Holley, W. H. (1975). Performance appraisal—An analysis of statewide practices. *Public Personnel Management, 7*, 145–150.

Feinberg, M. R. (1965). *Effective psychology for managers.* Englewood Cliffs, NJ: Prentice-Hall.

Fugita, S. S., Wexley, K. N., & Malone, M. P. (1975). An applicant's nonverbal behavior and student-evaluators' judgments in a structured interview setting. *Psychological Reports, 36*, 391–394.

Gibson, J. L., Ivancevich, J. M., and Donnelly, J. H., Jr. (1976). *Organizations: Structure, processes, behavior.* Dallas: Business Publications.

Goldstein, A. P., & Sorcher, M. (1974). *Changing supervisor behavior.* New York: Pergamon.

Goodale, J. G. (1982). *The fine art of interviewing.* Englewood Cliffs, NJ: Prentice-Hall.

Greller, M. M. (1978). The nature of subordinate participation in the appraisal interview. *Academy of Management Journal, 21,* 646–658.

Greller, M. M., & Herold, D. M. (1975). Sources of feedback: A preliminary investigation. *Organizational Behavior and Human Performance, 13,* 244–246.

Hillery, J. M., & Wexley, K. N. (1974). Participation in appraisal interviews conducted in a training situation. *Journal of Applied Psychology, 59,* 168–171.

Hinrichs, J. R. (1978). *Practical management of productivity.* New York: Van Nostrand.

Ilgen, D. R., Fisher, C. D., & Taylor, M. S. (1979). Consequences of individual feedback on behavior in organizations. *Journal of Applied Psychology, 4,* 349–371.

Johnson, R. G. (1979). *The appraisal interview guide.* New York: AMACOM.

Kay, E., Meyer, H. H., & French, J. P. R., Jr. (1965). Effects of threat in a performance appraisal interview. *Journal of Applied Psychology, 49,* 311–317.

Latham, G. P., & Locke, E. A. (1979). Goal setting: A motivational technique that works. *Organizational Dynamics, 7,* 68–80.

Latham, G. P., & Wexley, K. N. (1981). *Increasing productivity through performance appraisal.* Reading, MA: Addison-Wesley.

Latham, G. P., Wexley, K. N., & Pursell, E. D. (1975). Training managers to minimize rating errors in the observation of behavior. *Journal of Applied Psychology, 60,* 550–555.

Latham, G. P., & Yukl, G. A. (1975). A review of research on the application of goal setting in organizations. *Academy of Management Journal, 18,* 824–845.

Likert, R. (1967). *The human organization.* New York: McGraw-Hill.

Lowin, A., & Craig, J. (1968). The influence of level of performance on managerial style: An experimental object lesson in the ambiguity of correlational data. *Organizational Behavior and Human Performance, 3,* 440–458.

Maier, N. R. F. (1958). *The appraisal interview: Objectives, methods, and skills.* New York: Wiley.

McGregor, D. (1957). An uneasy look at performance appraisal. *Harvard Business Review, 35,* 89–94.

Meyer, H. H., & Kay, E. A. (1964). *Comparison of a work planning program with the annual performance appraisal approach* (Behavioral Research Report No. ESR17). General Electric Company.

Nemeroff, W. F., & Cosentino, J. (1979). Utilizing feedback and goal setting to increase performance appraisal interviewer skills of managers. *Academy of Management Journal, 22,* 566–576.

Nemeroff, W. F., & Wexley, K. N. (1979). An exploration of the relationships between the performance feedback interview characteristics and interview outcomes as perceived by managers and subordinates. *Journal of Occupational Psychology, 52,* 25–34.

Porter, L. W., Lawler, E. E., III, & Hackman, J. R. (1975). *Behavior in organizations.* New York: McGraw-Hill.

Spool, M. (1978). Training programs for observers of behavior: A review. *Personnel Psychology, 31,* 853–888.

Wexley, K. N. (1979). Performance appraisal and feedback. In S. Kerr (Ed.), *Organizational behavior* (pp. 241–259). Columbus, OH: Grid.

Wexley, K. N., & Latham, G. P. (1981). *Developing and training human resources in organizations*. Glenview, IL: Scott, Foresman.

Wexley, K. N., Singh, J. P., & Yukl, G. A. (1973). Subordinate personality as a moderator of the effects of participation in three types of appraisal interviews. *Journal of Applied Psychology, 58,* 54–59.

Wexley, K. N., & Yukl, G. A. (1984). *Organizational behavior and personnel psychology* (rev. ed.). Homewood, IL: Irwin.

7. UTILITY ANALYSIS

Nambury S. Raju & Michael J. Burke

Introduction

The financial impact of human resource services such as personnel selection, evaluation, and training programs is of particular interest in many organizations. Contributing to this interest are economic issues and the recent methodological advances in utility analysis (Boudreau, 1983a, 1983b; Boudreau & Rynes, 1985; Cascio, 1982; Landy, Farr, & Jacobs, 1982; Schmidt & Hunter, 1983; Schmidt et al., 1979; Schmidt, Hunter, & Pearlman, 1982).

Prior to these advances, Hunter and Schmidt (1982) maintained that Brogden's (1949) and Cronbach and Gleser's (1965) decision-theoretic utility equations had not been applied because of (1) the belief that data did not fit the assumptions of these equations, (2) the previous difficulty in estimating the standard deviation of job performance in dollars for these equations, and (3) the belief that it was impossible to generalize research findings from one situation to another. Recent empirical and theoretical developments have provided the potential for overcoming problems related to points 1 and 2. In addition, the advances made in validity generalization/meta-analysis have overcome any difficulties concerning point 3 (Hunter, Schmidt, & Jackson, 1982).

This chapter is divided into four sections. The first section reviews the various utility models, including the recent work of Boudreau (1983a). Empirical research with the utility models is summarized in the next section. The third section addresses the advantages and disadvantages of alternative estimation procedures, and the last section concludes with some recommendations for future research in utility analysis.

Review of Utility Analysis Models

THE BROGDEN AND CRONBACH-GLESER UTILITY MODELS

Much of the current research on the financial impact of human resource services is based on the pioneering work of Brogden (1949) and Cronbach and Gleser (1965). They used the linear regression approach to show the relationship

We would like to express our appreciation to Frank L. Schmidt and Jack E. Edwards for reviewing an earlier version of this chapter.

between predictor (X) and job performance measured in dollars (Y), which can be written as

$$Y' = r(SD_y/SD_x)(X - \bar{X}) + \bar{Y}, \tag{1}$$

where SD_y and SD_x are the standard deviations of Y and X, $\bar{Y}$ and $\bar{X}$ are the means of Y and X, and r represents the correlation between predictor score and job performance. (It should be noted that these statistical terms are parameters of the applicant population under consideration, and the notation used here to represent the parameters is consistent with that employed in the utility analysis literature.) When the predictor scores are expressed as Z-scores (Z), equation 1 can be rewritten as

$$Y' = r SD_y Z + \bar{Y}. \tag{2}$$

This equation shows the expected dollar value (Y') of a selected applicant whose predictor score is Z. This value depends on the applicant's predictor score, the mean and standard deviation of the dollar values of the entire applicant population, and the correlation between the predictor scores and job performance measured in dollars. If a subgroup of applicants is hired, N_s (number selected), based on the predictor score, the expected average utility (or dollar value) to the organization can be expressed as

$$\bar{Y} = r SD_y \bar{Z}_s + \bar{Y}, \tag{3}$$

where the subscript s refers to the selected applicants. Similarly, if a subgroup of applicants is selected at random, their average expected utility would be simply $\bar{Y}$, since $\bar{Z} = 0$ for such a sample. Therefore, the increase in average utility, that is, the difference between the average utility with predictor-based selection and random selection, can be written as

$$\Delta \bar{U} = r SD_y \bar{Z}_s, \tag{4}$$

which is equation 3 minus $\bar{Y}$. The total increase in utility for N_s applicants is given by

$$\Delta U = N_s r SD_y \bar{Z}_s. \tag{5}$$

This equation for total utility (Brogden, 1949) was expanded by Cronbach and Gleser (1965) to incorporate the cost of gathering information on the predictor (or testing) for all applicants. The expanded equation can be written as

$$\Delta U = N_s r SD_y \bar{Z}_s - NC, \tag{6}$$

where N is the total number of applicants and C is the average cost of testing an applicant. The significant work of Cronbach and Gleser also addressed the questions of utility for classification, placement, and sequential selection. A discussion of these selection strategies is beyond the scope of our review.

If it is assumed that the predictor scores are normally distributed and that the top scoring N_s applicants are hired, the total utility resulting from such a selection program can be expressed as

$$\Delta U = N_s r\, SD_y\ \phi/p - NC, \tag{7}$$

where $p = N_s/N$, and ϕ is the ordinate corresponding to p. Equations 6 and 7 show the increase in total utility of predictor-based selection over random selection. Personnel psychologists are generally more interested in the difference in the total utility of two predictor-based selection programs than in the difference between a predictor-based selection and random selection. For example, an organization may want to replace an existing selection program with another (better) selection program. When this happens, personnel psychologists' interest is in the increase in the total utility of the new selection program over that of the old selection program rather than over random selection. The difference in total utility between two nonrandom selection programs can be written as

$$\Delta U = N_s\, SD_y\ (r_1\bar{Z}_1 - r_2\bar{Z}_2) - N(C_1 - C_2), \tag{8}$$

where subscripts 1 and 2 refer to the two selection programs under consideration. The values for $\bar{Z}_1$ and $\bar{Z}_2$ are generally not equal unless the two predictors have identical distributions. When both predictors are normally distributed, the total gain in utility can be expressed as

$$\Delta U = N_s\, SD_y\ \phi/p(r_1 - r_2) - N(C_1 - C_2). \tag{9}$$

Equations 8 and 9 as well as equations 6 and 7 express the difference in utility of two selection programs for one year. However, for most jobs in most organizations, the newly hired person is likely to remain on the job for more than a year. If the tenure (T) of an average selectee is greater than one year, equations 6, 7, 8, and 9 underestimate the gain in total utility of one selection program over another; conversely, when T is less than 1, the total utility will be overestimated. Therefore, to reflect accurately the effect of tenure on the total gain in utility, equations 8 and 9 should be rewritten as

$$\Delta U = TN_s\, SD_y\ (r_1\bar{Z}_1 - r_2\bar{Z}_2) - N(C_1 - C_2) \tag{10}$$

and

$$\Delta U = TN_s\, SD_y\,\phi/p(r_1 - r_2) - N(C_1 - C_2). \tag{11}$$

Assumptions. As implicitly indicated, the Brogden-Cronbach-Gleser (BCG) model (equations 6 and 10) assumes that there is a linear relationship between the predictor and job performance measured in dollars. Recently, Hunter and Schmidt reviewed some of the available empirical evidence (Hawk, 1970; Sevier, 1957; Tupes, 1964) concerning linearity and homoscedasticity and concluded:

> These findings, taken in toto, indicate that the linear homoscedastic model generally fits the data in the area well. The linearity assumption,

the only truly critical assumption, is particularly well suited. (1982, p. 245)

Equations 7 and 11 also assume that predictor scores are normally distributed. This assumption of normality, according to Hunter and Schmidt, is not needed in utility analysis research and it was used by Brogden and by Cronbach and Gleser mostly for derivational convenience. The statements of Hunter and Schmidt concerning the assumptions underlying the utility formulations are encouraging and should lead to a wider acceptance of the utility equations in the personnel selection area.

Estimation of parameters. Of the three important parameters in equation 6, $\bar{Z}_s$ can be estimated by simply averaging the $\bar{Z}$-scores of hired (selected) applicants. For the second parameter, r, it has been suggested that the correlation (validity) coefficient between the predictor and job performance expressed as a rating be used as an estimate of r, the correlation between the predictor score and job performance expressed in dollars. The accuracy of this estimate depends upon the degree to which job performance measured in dollars is linearly related to job performance expressed as a rating; the greater the correlation between the two measures of job performance, the more accurate the proposed estimate of r. According to Schmidt, Hunter, McKenzie, and Muldrow (1979), the proposed estimate of r would probably underestimate the true value and therefore would lead to an underestimate of total gain in utility. An underestimate of utility (provided it is not a severe underestimate) is probably more preferable than an overestimate in the present setup. Finally, the proposed estimate of r is well understood by personnel psychologists and is generally easy to obtain.

The third important parameter, SD_y, is the most difficult to estimate in practice. Strictly speaking, the dollar value of each applicant is needed to estimate the standard deviation. It is impossible to gather such data, especially when some applicants are rejected, and therefore their dollar value to the organization can never be computed. Even when current employees are considered, complex cost-accounting procedures generally are believed to be needed to estimate the dollar value of each incumbent. This belief may have discouraged many practitioners from using the utility formulations proposed by Brogden and by Cronbach and Gleser. Until recently, only a handful of studies applied the Brogden and Cronbach-Gleser procedures for assessing the utility of personnel selection programs.

Recently, Schmidt and his colleagues (1979) proposed a practical alternative for estimating the SD_y parameter. This new procedure avoids the complex, often time-consuming cost-accounting procedures. This procedure estimates the dollar value to the organization of the goods and services produced by the average employee and those produced by an employee at the eighty-fifth percentile. Assuming that the dollar value of employees is normally distributed, Schmidt et al.

suggest that the difference between the values associated with the fiftieth and eighty-fifth percentiles be used as an estimate of SD_y. Their procedure also calls for estimating the dollar value of an employee at the fifteenth percentile, which is then used to obtain a second estimate of SD_y. The two estimates of SD_y are averaged to obtain the final estimate of SD_y. In their 1979 study with computer programmers, Schmidt, Hunter, McKenzie, and Muldrow obtained the dollar value of the average employee from supervisors who were supplied the following instructions.

> Based on your experience with agency programmers, we would like for you to estimate the yearly value to your agency of the products and services produced by the average GS 9-11 computer programmer. Consider the quality and quantity of output typical of the average pro-grammer and the value of this output. In placing an overall dollar value on this output, it may help to consider what the cost would be of having an outside firm provide these products and services. (1979, p. 621)

Similar instructions were also used for gathering dollar value data for employees at the eighty-fifth and fifteenth percentiles.

This SD_y estimation procedure assumes that the dollar value of incumbent employees is normally distributed. This assumption appears to have been well received by personnel psychologists, judging from the many empirical studies that have appeared in the professional journals since 1979. Some of the empirical studies that have evaluated the normality assumption as well as studies that have applied this SD_y estimation procedure are discussed in more detail later. But it should be noted at this point that in the 1979 Schmidt work, r is corrected for measurement error in the criterion; the reasons for such correction are detailed in the article.

Another recent development in estimating SD_y is the Cascio-Ramos estimate of performance in dollars (CREPID) (see Cascio, 1982). Essentially, CREPID proportionately distributes the annual salary for a job to each principal job activity based on a weight for each employee's job performance on each activity. These ratings are then translated into dollar values for each person's performance rela-tive to each principal activity. The sum of the dollar values for each employee's performance on each principal activity equals the value of the employee's job performance to the organization. The standard deviation of these sums is as-sumed to be equal to SD_y. Empirical research related to the CREPID SD_y estima-tion procedure is discussed below.

UTILITY MODELS BASED ON A DICHOTOMIZED CRITERION

The BCG model and its modifications and extensions assume that variable Y (job performance expressed in dollars) is continuous. A few researchers (Alf &

Dorfman, 1967; Gross & Su, 1975; Peterson, 1976; Sands, 1973) have proposed decision-theoretic procedures for evaluating the utility of selection procedures based on a dichotomized criterion, that is, when all individuals in the "unsuccessful" group are assigned the same low value on the criterion and all those in the "successful" group are assigned the same high value on the criterion. For instance, Sands (1973) has proposed the rather complex CAPER (cost of attaining personnel requirements) procedure for determining the selection test cutoff score that will minimize the total cost of obtaining a prespecified number of "successful" employees. Problems with the CAPER procedure have been thoroughly delineated by Hunter and Schmidt (1982).

EXTENSIONS AND NEW DEVELOPMENTS

The publication of the 1979 Schmidt article also appears to have generated renewed interest in the psychometric and statistical aspects of utility analysis. This interest has already resulted in several important extensions of the BCG model. These extensions are briefly reviewed below.

Utility analysis of intervention programs. The success of an organization depends not only on hiring the right people but also on correctly placing these people and properly managing them. As to the management of employees, training for such things as technical and nontechnical skills, performance appraisals and feedback, and management by objectives plays a significant role in maintaining the well-being of an organization. The BCG paradigm of Brogden, Cronbach, and Gleser is not directly applicable to these intervention programs. In order to apply the BCG paradigm to these organizational interventions, some modifications to it recently have been proposed by Schmidt, Hunter, and Pearlman (1982) and by Landy, Farr, and Jacobs (1982).

The total gain in utility due to an intervention program can be rewritten as

$$\Delta U = TN_I \, d_I \, SD_y - N_I \, C, \tag{12}$$

where the various terms are as previously defined except for SD_y and d_I. The subscript I refers to the specific intervention/training program under consideration. The SD_y is the standard deviation of job performance in dollars of the untrained group, and d_I is the difference in job performance between the average trained and untrained employee expressed in standard deviation units of the untrained (control) group. Both Schmidt and his colleagues (1982) and Landy and his associates (1982) have provided formulas for converting statistics such as r, t, and F to d_I when the outcomes of interventions are expressed in terms of these statistics. These extensions of utility analysis are significant since they now make it possible to assess the financial contribution of many personnel strategies, in addition to personnel selection.

Boudreau's extensions of the BCG paradigm. In reviewing past utility model research for selection, Boudreau (1983a) identified three economic concepts (variable costs, taxes, and discounting) that he felt were left unaccounted for in the BCG paradigm. The omission of these factors, according to Boudreau, can upwardly bias the existing estimates of utility. Previous utility studies dealt exclusively with the "value of sales" (Cascio & Silbey, 1979) or the "value of products and services" (Schmidt et al., 1979) and therefore misrepresented the financial benefit to the organization. According to Boudreau,

> First, when variable costs rise (or fall) with productivity (e.g., incentive or commission-based pay, benefits, variable raw material costs, variable production overhead), then a portion (V) of the gain in product sales value will go to pay such costs (or will be reflected in additional cost savings). Second, when the organization faces tax liabilities, a portion (TAX) of the organization's profit (sales value less variable costs) will go to pay taxes rather than accruing to the organization. Third, where costs and benefits accrue over time, the value of future costs and benefits must be discounted to reflect the opportunity costs of returns foregone because costs incurred earlier and benefits received later cannot be invested for as many periods. (1983b, p. 397)

Boudreau's formula for total gain in utility can be expressed as

$$\Delta U = N_s \left(\sum_{i=1}^{T} \frac{1}{(1 + i)^t} SD_{y_t} (1 + V_t)(1 - TAX_t) r_t \bar{Z} \right) - NC(1 - TAX),$$

(13)

where i is the discount rate, V is the proportion of sales value represented by variable costs, TAX is the organization's applicable tax rate; and t is the time period in which a productivity increase occurs. The other terms in this equation are as previously defined. Equation 13 can easily be expanded to reflect the total gain in utility of one selection program over another. For example, assuming that TAX, V, SD_y, and r remain constant over the total time period, the equation for the difference in utility between two selection programs can be written as

$$\Delta U = N_s SD_y (1 + V)(1 - TAX)(r_1 \bar{Z}_1 - r_2 \bar{Z}_2) \left(\sum_{t=1}^{T} \frac{1}{(1 + i)^t} \right)$$
$$- N(C_1 - C_2)(1 - TAX).$$

(14)

(It should be noted that Boudreau uses the symbol SD_{sv} instead of SD_y to emphasize the sales value of productivity.) In applying these formulas, practitioners need estimates of i, V, and TAX in addition to the parameter estimates required for equations 10, 11, and 12. According to Boudreau (1983a), the appropriate discount rate (i) should be the rate applied to uninflated benefits and costs given the organization's evaluation of overall risk and return requirements. Similarly, V represents the ratio of cost of sales to sales value, and T is the organization's applicable overall tax rate, not the rate based on the utility associated with a particular selection program. Boudreau (1983a) provides several examples for different values of i, V, and TAX.

It should be emphasized that Boudreau's formulation deals with contribution to profit, whereas the BCG formulation concentrates on the increase in output as sold. Therefore Boudreau's selection utility is generally smaller than the BCG utility. Both utilities are useful in practice, each for a different purpose.

Boudreau (1983b) and Boudreau and Rynes (1985) have extended Boudreau's initial work by incorporating (1) the flow of employees in and out of the work force and (2) the effects of recruitment activities. These extensions are based on equations 13 and 14. Furthermore, equations 13 and 14 can also be used with intervention programs if one replaces $r\bar{Z}$ with d_I or $r_i\bar{Z}_i$ with d_{I_i}.

Empirical research on the utility of job performance. As noted above, since the publication of the 1979 Schmidt article, there has been an increase in empirical research related to assessing the economic utility of personnel programs. However, empirical research related to improving the cost-effectiveness of personnel decisions can be traced to the early work of applied psychologists. For instance, Hugo Munsterberg in his classic book *Psychology and Industrial Efficiency* (1913) advocated the study of individual difference data to improve the economic well-being of such various organizations as the shipping industry and telephone services. Hull (1928) also stressed the importance of the study of individual difference data with respect to worker output. That is, Hull was interested in the ratio of the work output of the least efficient to the most efficient worker in a variety of occupations. In essence, this ratio provided an indication of the range of job performance. For an organization with a variety of jobs, the study of such performance ratios had important implications. Most notable, jobs where the range of performance was relatively large (as indicated by a large ratio) were the most likely to benefit from personnel programs. A number of researchers have reported these ratios for work under nonpiecework compensation systems (Lawshe, 1948; Rothe, 1946, 1947, 1970; Rothe & Nye, 1958, 1961; Stead & Shartle, 1940; Tiffin, 1947), piecerate compensation systems (Rothe, 1951, 1978; Rothe & Nye, 1959), and uncertain compensation systems (Evans, 1940; Hull, 1928; Lawshe, 1948; McCormick & Tiffin, 1974; Stead & Shartle, 1940; Wechsler, 1952).

Recently, Schmidt and Hunter (1983) addressed the problem of expressing individual differences in performance output in terms of percentage increase in output. That is, they were interested in comparing the standard deviation of output as a percentage of mean output (SD_p) for a job with their predicted upper and lower bound values for SD_p. The data for their study were gathered from the above studies that reported performance ratios as well as from studies that reported the mean and standard deviation of actual employee production or output. The latter included work produced under nonpiecework compensation systems (Barnes, 1958; Klemmer & Lockhead, 1962), piecerate compensation systems (Barnes, 1937, 1958; Viteles, 1932) and uncertain compensation systems (Wechsler, 1952). Schmidt and Hunter's findings indicated that whenever employee output was self-paced and there was no piecework or other incentive system, the standard deviation of employee output could be estimated as 20 percent of mean output.

The practical implication of Schmidt and Hunter's 1983 findings is that a personnel researcher can now express for some blue-collar skilled and semiskilled jobs the utility of personnel programs in terms of percentage increase in employee output. For example, one may be interested in expressing the utility of a personnel selection procedure in terms of percentage increase in work-force output. If the standard deviation of output, SD_p, is substituted for SD_y in equation 4, selection utility is expressed in terms of percentage increases in output:

$$\Delta\%\bar{U} = r\,SD_p\,\phi/p, \tag{15}$$

where $\Delta\%\bar{U}$ is the mean percentage change in utility per selectee. Now if one assumes a value of 20 for SD_p (the conservative figure for SD_p noted by Schmidt & Hunter, 1983), a p of .35, and an r of .45, then $\Delta\%\bar{U}$ equals 9.5. Thus one would expect approximately a 9.5 percent increase in employee output as a result of implementing the new selection procedure.

Hunter and Schmidt (1983) have noted that the performance output ratio and the standard deviation of output computed as a percentage of mean output may not be similar for higher-level jobs. The reasoning is that higher-level jobs may allow more for costly errors, which would increase the standard deviation disproportionately relative to salary. Although this factor may lessen the expression of utility gains for some jobs in terms of percentage increase in employee output, other recent developments in utility analysis, as noted above, have increased the potential applicability of decision-theoretic utility equations for most jobs in the economy.

Empirical research related to dichotomized or multichotomized criteria. An example of an application of a modified version of the CAPER procedure was provided by Daum (1983). Daum used the modified procedure to evaluate the economic impact of a new interviewing selection program for entry-level managers as compared to the organization's previous unstandardized hiring practices. It was estimated that the organization would realize approximately $6,997,187 in cost savings from the new interviewing program. This figure is likely to underestimate the incremental gains from selecting more highly qualified individuals.

Other researchers (Lee & Booth, 1974; Schmidt & Hoffmann, 1973) have employed different procedures for evaluating the cost utility of personnel programs where the criterion was dichotomized or multichotomized. Lee and Booth evaluated the economic utility of a weighted application blank in predicting turnover for clerical employees. Their tenure criterion was trichotomized into short-term (terminated within six months), intermediate-term (terminated within seven to fifteen months), and long-term (terminated after sixteen months). The cost of terminating was considered to be the total cost of hiring, training, and orienting a new clerk. The correlation of the weighted application blank with the tenure criterion was .56. Based on an optimal selection ratio of .17, the total dollar savings over a twenty-five-month period from the use of the weighted application blank for hiring 224 employees were expected to be approximately $250,000. Schmidt and Hoffmann (1973) also emphasized the cost-effectiveness of a weighted application blank for predicting turnover among nurse's aides in a large hospital. The total utility of hiring 380 nurse's aides was approximately $161,243 over a two-year period.

Together these two studies point to the substantial economic gains to be accrued from sound personnel selection procedures such as weighted application blanks. In addition, Cascio and McEvoy (1984) illustrated the potential economic gains that could result from reducing controllable turnover costs with realistic job previews and job enrichment. A caution, however, is in order when estimating the utility of a weighted application blank over a period of time. One should periodically check the validity coefficients of weighted application blanks, since the validity coefficients are likely to decline with changing labor market conditions and personnel policies (Brown, 1978) and, consequently, to affect estimated utility gains.

Empirical research related to Brogdon-Cronbach-Gleser equations and the estimation of SD_y. The previous utility studies have focused primarily on dichotomized or multichotomized criterion measures. The Brogden (1949) and Cronbach and Gleser (1965) equations, however, are useful for estimating the incremental gain in utility where job performance (criterion), expressed in dollars, is assumed to be continuous. As previously discussed, an important development in increasing the potential applicability of the BCG equations was the practical procedure Schmidt, Hunter, McKenzie, and Muldrow (1979) proposed for estimating the standard deviation of job performance in dollars (SD_y), which has previously been the most difficult component to estimate. Using their SD_y estimation procedure with a sample of 147 supervisors, Schmidt and his colleagues estimated the average SD_y for computer programmers to be $10,413. Employing this value for SD_y as well as different combinations of the selection ratios and the validity of the previous selection procedure, they demonstrated the substantial economic impact of a valid test (i.e., a programmer aptitude test) on computer programmer productivity in the federal government and national economy.

Cascio and Silbey (1979) employed this SD_y estimation procedure to evaluate the utility of the assessment center as a selection device. The estimated value of the first year standard deviation for second-level sales managers was $9,500. This value, as well as the validity and cost of the assessment center, the validity of the ordinary selection procedure, the selection ratio, and the number of assessment centers was varied. The greatest impact on assessment center utility was exerted by the magnitude of the criterion standard deviation, the selection ratio, and the difference in validity between the assessment center and the previously used selection procedure. This study was instrumental in demonstrating that even personnel selection procedures with relatively low validity and high costs can produce substantial economic gains.

Schmidt, Mack, and Hunter (1984) also applied this SD_y estimation procedure to the job of U.S. Park Service ranger to examine how personnel selection was affected by differences between three selection strategies: (1) top-down selection, (2) minimum required test score equal to the mean, and (3) minimum required test score at one standard deviation below the mean. The average SD_y obtained for the job of park ranger was $4,450.74. Top-down selection produced an increase in average productivity of about 13 percent. When the minimum required test score was equal to the mean, estimated economic gain was only 45 percent of that for top-down selection. When the test cutoff score was set at one standard deviation below the mean, the estimated dollar gain was 16 percent of the top-down result. Schmidt, Mack, and Hunter's 1984 study demonstrated the substantial economic implications of different selection strategies.

Partial support for the normality of SD_y estimates was provided by Schmidt and his colleagues (1979). Their results indicated that mean estimated SD_y between computer programmers at the eighty-fifth and fiftieth percentiles was approximately equal to the difference between the fiftieth and fifteenth percentiles. Likewise, Bobko, Karren, and Parkington's 1983 utility study involving seventeen supervisors and insurance counselors supported the normality assumption for the 1979 Schmidt procedure. Bobko and his associates also found that supervisors' estimates of SD_y adequately reflected actual variation in an objective measure of job performance. Another interesting finding was the large within-column variation for the various percentile estimates. Bobko, Karren, and Parkington noted that judges in their study were using different scales when giving the percentile estimates since the estimates differed drastically within percentile points.

In order to reduce the variability of judges' (supervisors') percentile estimates, Burke and Frederick (1984) evaluated two modified procedures for obtaining estimates of SD_y. The modified procedures consisted of feeding back to managers the mean estimated value for the fiftieth percentile (for the job of district sales manager) and asking the managers to once again make other percentile judgments. Feedback sessions were conducted in group discussions (procedure A) and individually (procedure B). The results indicated that the modified procedures offer alternative means of obtaining SD_y estimates in utility analysis.

Burke and Frederick (1985) have recently compared the per selectee and total utility estimates for an assessment center used to select sales managers, when the two modified procedures (A and B), the 1979 Schmidt procedure, and 40 percent and 70 percent of mean salary (the range hypothesized by Hunter and Schmidt 1982 to contain SD_y) were used for estimating SD_y in Boudreau's utility formula (see equation 14). Based on four percentile estimates (15th, 50th, 85th, and 97th), the total utility estimates as a percentage of the 1979 Schmidt procedure varied from 21 percent to 125 percent. However, the resulting estimated dollar gains from the use of the assessment center to select sales managers were substantial in all cases. The authors discussed some problems in estimating certain economic concepts such as i, the discount rate. However, their study pointed to the value of an interdisciplinary approach for evaluating the economic utility of personnel programs.

Weekley, Frank, O'Connor, and Peters (1985) compared SD_y estimates based on the 40 percent rule, the CREPID procedure, and the 1979 Schmidt procedure. Their results indicated that the SD_y estimates based on 40 percent of the mean salary and the CREPID procedure were relatively consistent; however, the results for the Schmidt procedure were markedly different. As a percentage of the Schmidt procedure, the CREPID procedure was .55 whereas the value for the 40 percent rule was .61. It is not surprising that these latter differences were obtained when one considers that for a rational estimation procedure (i.e., the Schmidt procedure), the judges are often using, in addition to salary considerations, other dimensions. Essentially, the payoff function is defined differently for alternative SD_y estimation procedures, and the resulting differences in SD_y estimates can be expected.

Eaton, Wing, and Mitchell (1985) compared the results for two newly developed SD_y estimation procedures with a rational SD_y estimation procedure and salary percentage strategies. Their newly developed SD_y estimation procedures considered the changes in the numbers and performance levels of system units that lead to increased aggregate performance for the job of U.S. Army tank commander. Eaton and associates concluded that the new strategies appear to provide more acceptable values of SD_y for complex, expensive systems where dollar values of performance are less easily estimated.

Advantages and Disadvantages of Alternative Procedures

As noted previously, although there is one primary decision-theoretic utility model, there are a number of alternative procedures for estimating SD_y. Since most research to date has been directed toward examining the properties of rational SD_y estimates, this discussion will focus primarily on the advantages and disadvantages of the rational procedures.

Rothe (1941) and Schmidt and colleagues (1979) have discussed problems with the cost-accounting approach to obtaining SD_y estimates. Potential problems related to the more widely used SD_y estimation procedures have been noted by Karren and Bobko (1983) and Burke and Frederick (1984). One potential problem is the inability or unwillingness of supervisors to provide SD_y estimates. Related to this point is that some supervisors make inconsistent judgments. For example, the estimate of the value of the employee at the eighty-fifth percentile is less than the estimated value for the fiftieth percentile. This problem has been noted in studies by Bobko, Karren, and Parkington (1983) and Karren and Bobko (1983). Some minimal form of training may be necessary in assisting supervisors to provide these estimates. In addition, Karren and Bobko (1983) have argued that demand characteristics of the SD_y estimation methods probably restrict all percentile point estimates to the positive domain. This does not necessarily appear to be the case in recent research.

Another potential problem is that the normality assumption upon which the use of SD_y estimates is based does not necessarily hold (Karren & Bobko, 1983; Schmidt, Mack, & Hunter, 1984). It has been difficult for most researchers to determine why the non-normality in SD_y estimates occurs. For instance, is the non-normality due to a skewed true performance distribution or to the judges' comparison of the job incumbent with the applicant population in making SD_y estimates? Although answers to this question may not be provided easily, Schmidt and his team (1979) have indicated that non-normality would be expected to have only minor effects on the accuracy of estimates of the utility of personnel selection procedures. An overriding issue, however, is that there is very little research indicating how close the SD_y estimates are to the actual SD_y values. Without some comparative research in this latter area, it will be difficult for personnel administrators to justify the incorporation of personnel program utility estimates into annual budgetary forecasts.

The potential problems with rationally based SD_y estimates should not preclude their use. In a relative perspective, they provide the practitioner with a means of determining SD_y and thus of evaluating the possible economic benefits to be gained from various personnel programs. Consequently, rationally based SD_y estimates may aid practitioners in making relative decisions concerning which personnel programs to implement in order to have the greatest effect on the organization.

Boudreau (1984) has indicated that it may not always be necessary to obtain exact or approximate SD_y estimates in order for human resource professionals to make decisions regarding alternative personnel programs. Instead of estimating the level of expected utility for each alternative program, he suggests focusing on the identification of break-even values that are critical to making decisions. Although break-even analysis offers a useful means for simplifying some decisions, it is important that continued efforts be directed toward accurately evaluating the utility of human resource programs.

Recommendations

In summary, the preceding review has indicated that useful procedures are currently available for estimating the economic utility of various personnel programs. At the present state of development it is difficult to recommend one procedure over another, even though the BCG model with the 1979 Schmidt procedure for estimating SD_y appears to be popular with researchers at the present time. As research in this area continues, it is quite possible that different procedures may prove optimal for different situations.

There is still a great need for both empirical and theoretical research in this area. For example, the recent theoretical work of Boudreau (1983a, 1983b) and Boudreau and Rynes (1985) needs to be tested empirically; to date, there is very little information on the practical problems associated with estimating the variable costs, discount rate, and tax rate.

The potential problems in arriving at SD_y estimates point to the need for continued research in this area as well as research concerning alternative means of estimating SD_y. In particular, further research aimed at comparing CREPID and cost-accounting based SD_y estimates with rationally based SD_y estimates appears worthwhile. Furthermore, research related to the convergence of rationally based SD_y estimates for different jobs would be fruitful. It would also be of interest to determine which dimensions, as well as the importance of the dimensions, judges use in making rational SD_y estimates. This area of research would have important implications for training judges and possibly would provide useful information for coaching judges in what factors to consider in making their estimates.

Another important area where research is needed to increase the applicability of decision-theoretic utility equations is cumulative research across studies to calculate estimates of effect sizes for various organizational interventions. To date, researchers have relied on hypothetical values of the validity of organizational interventions (other than personnel selection procedures) to derive utility estimates. For instance, Landy, Farr, and Jacobs (1982) have presented a hypothetical example, using Schmidt, Hunter, and Pearlman's 1982 equations, of the utility of a performance evaluation and feedback system. Once cumulative research has been conducted on personnel selection procedures and on other organizational interventions (e.g., training programs, incentive programs) to obtain estimates of their true validity, and once methods have been developed for obtaining accurate estimates of SD_y, the personnel decision maker will be provided with refined means for assessing the relative effectiveness of alternative approaches to increasing work-force productivity and, consequently, to increasing the efficiency of personnel decisions.

References

Alf, E. F., & Dorfman, D. D. (1967). The classification of individuals into two criterion groups on the basis of a discontinuous payoff function. *Psychometrika, 32,* 115–123.

Barnes, R. M. (1937). *Time and motion study.* New York: Wiley.

Barnes, R. M. (1958). *Time and motion study* (2nd ed.). New York: Wiley.

Bobko, P., Karren, R., & Parkington, J. J. (1983). Estimation of standard deviations in utility analysis: An empirical test. *Journal of Applied Psychology, 68,* 170–176.

Brogden, H. E. (1949). When testing pays off. *Personnel Psychology, 2,* 171–183.

Boudreau, J. W. (1983a). Economic considerations in estimating the utility of human resource productivity improvement programs. *Personnel Psychology, 36,* 551–576.

Boudreau, J. W. (1983b). Effects of employee flows on utility analysis of human resource productivity improvement programs. *Journal of Applied Psychology, 68,* 396–407.

Boudreau, J. W. (1984). Decision theory contributions to HRM research and practice. *Industrial Relations, 23,* 198–217.

Boudreau, J. W., & Rynes, S. L. (1985). The role of recruitment in staffing utility analysis. *Journal of Applied Psychology, 70,* 354–366.

Brown, S. H. (1978). Long-term validity of a personal history item scoring procedure. *Journal of Applied Psychology, 63,* 673–676.

Burke, M. J., & Frederick, J. T. (1984). Two modified procedures for estimating standard deviations in utility analyses. *Journal of Applied Psychology, 69,* 482–489.

Burke, M. J., & Frederick, J. T. (1985). *A comparison of utility estimates for alternative SD_y estimation procedure.* Unpublished manuscript.

Cascio, W. F. (1982). *Costing human resources: The financial impact of behavior in organizations.* Boston, MA: Kent.

Cascio, W. F., & McEvoy, G. M. (1984, August). *Extension of utility analysis research to turnover reduction strategies.* Paper presented at the annual meeting of the American Psychological Association, Toronto.

Cascio, W. F., & Silbey, V. (1979). Utility of the assessment center as a selection device. *Journal of Applied Psychology, 64,* 107–118.

Cronbach, L. J., & Gleser, G. C. (1965). *Psychological tests and personnel decisions* (2nd ed.). Urbana: University of Illinois Press.

Daum, J. W. (1983, August). *Two measures of R.O.I. on intervention—Fact or fantasy?* Paper presented at the annual meeting of the American Psychological Association, Anaheim, CA.

Eaton, N. K., Wing, H., & Mitchell, K. J. (1985). Alternative methods of estimating the dollar value of performance. *Personnel Psychology, 38,* 27–40.

Evans, D. W. (1940). Individual productivity differences. *Monthly Labor Review, 50,* 338–341.

Glass, G. V., McGaw, B., & Smith, M. L. (1981). *Meta-analysis in social research.* Beverly Hills, CA: Sage.

Gross, A. L., & Su, W. (1975). Defining a fair or unbiased selection model: A question of utilities. *Journal of Applied Psychology, 60,* 345–351.

Hawk, J. (1970). Linearity of criterion-GATB aptitude relationships. *Measurement and Evaluation in Guidance, 2,* 249–251.

Hull, C. L. (1928). *Applied testing.* New York: Psychological Corporation.

Hunter, J. E., & Schmidt, F. L. (1982). Fitting people to jobs: The impact of personnel selection on national productivity. In M. D. Dunnette & E. A. Fleishman (Eds.), *Human performance and productivity: Human capacity assessment* (Vol. 1, pp. 232–284). Hillsdale, NJ: Erlbaum.

Hunter, J. E., & Schmidt, F. L. (1983). Quantifying the effects of psychological interventions on employee job performance and work-force productivity. *American Psychologist, 38,* 473–478.

Hunter, J. E., Schmidt, F. L., & Jackson, G. B. (1982). *Meta-analysis: Cumulating research findings across studies.* Beverly Hills, CA: Sage.

Karren, R., & Bobko, P. (1983). *Conducting utility analysis: Some methodological concerns.* Paper presented at the annual meeting of the Academy of Management, Boston.

Klemmer, E. T., & Lockhead, G. R. (1962). Productivity and errors in two keying tasks: A field study. *Journal of Applied Psychology, 46,* 401–408.

Landy, F. J., Farr, J. L., & Jacobs, R. R. (1982). Utility concepts in performance measurement. *Organizational Behavior and Human Performance, 30,* 15–40.

Lawshe, C. H. (1948). *Principles of personnel tests.* New York: McGraw-Hill.

Lee, R., & Booth, J. M. (1974). A utility analysis of a weighted application blank designed to predict turnover for clerical employees. *Journal of Applied Psychology, 59,* 516–518.

McCormick, E. J., & Tiffin, J. (1974). *Industrial psychology.* Englewood Cliffs, NJ: Prentice-Hall.

Munsterberg, H. (1913). *Psychology and industrial efficiency.* New York: Houghton Mifflin.

Petersen, N. S. (1976). An expected utility model for "optimal selection." *Journal of Educational Statistics, 2,* 333–358.

Rothe, H. F. (1941). Output rates among chocolate dippers. *Journal of Applied Psychology, 25,* 94–97.

Rothe, H. F. (1946). Output rates among butter wrappers: II. Frequency distributions and a hypothesis regarding the "restriction of output." *Journal of Applied Psychology, 30,* 320–327.

Rothe, H. F. (1947). Output rates among machine operators: I. Distributions and their reliability. *Journal of Applied Psychology, 31,* 484–489.

Rothe, H. F. (1970). Output rates among welders: Productivity and consistency following removal of a financial incentive system. *Journal of Applied Psychology, 54,* 549–551.

Rothe, H. F. (1978). Output rates among industrial employees. *Journal of Applied Psychology, 63,* 40–46.

Rothe, H. F., & Nye, C. T. (1958). Output rates among coil winders. *Journal of Applied Psychology, 42,* 182–186.

Rothe, H. F., & Nye, C. T. (1959). Output rates among machine operators: II. Consistency related to methods of pay. *Journal of Applied Psychology, 43*, 417–420.

Rothe, H. F., & Nye, C. T. (1961). Output rates among machine operators: III. A nonincentive situation in two levels of business activity. *Journal of Applied Psychology, 45*, 50–54.

Sands, W. A. (1973). A method for evaluating alternative recruiting-selection strategies: The CAPER model. *Journal of Applied Psychology, 57*, 222–227.

Schmidt, F. L., & Hoffmann, B. (1973). Empirical comparison of three methods of assessing utility of a selection device. *Journal of Industrial and Organizational Psychology, 1*, 13–22.

Schmidt, F. L., & Hunter, J. E. (1983). Individual differences in productivity: An empirical test of estimates derived from studies of selection procedure utility. *Journal of Applied Psychology, 68*, 407–414.

Schmidt, F. L., Hunter, J. E., McKenzie, R. C., & Muldrow, T. W. (1979). The impact of valid selection procedures on work-force productivity. *Journal of Applied Psychology, 64*, 609–626.

Schmidt, F. L., Hunter, J. E., & Pearlman, K. (1982). Assessing the economic impact of personnel programs on workforce productivity. *Personnel Psychology, 35*, 333–347.

Schmidt, F. L., Mack, M. J., & Hunter, J. E. (1984). Selection utility in the occupation of U.S. Park Ranger for three models of test use. *Journal of Applied Psychology, 69*, 490–497.

Sevier, F. A. C. (1957). Testing the assumptions underlying multiple regression. *Journal of Experimental Education, 25*, 323–330.

Stead, W. H., & Shartle, C. L. (1940). *Occupational counseling techniques.* New York: American Book.

Tiffin, J. (1947). *Industrial psychology* (2nd ed.). New York: Prentice-Hall.

Tupes, E. C. (1964). A note on "validity and nonlinear heteroscedastic models." *Personnel Psychology, 17*, 59–61.

Viteles, M. S. (1932). *Industrial psychology.* New York: Norton.

Wechsler, D. (1952). *Range of human capacities* (2nd ed.). Baltimore, MD: Williams and Wilkins.

Weekley, J. A., Frank, B., O'Connor, E. J., & Peters, L. H. (1985). A comparison of three methods of estimating the standard deviation of performance in dollars. *Journal of Applied Psychology, 70*, 127–136.

8. VALIDITY GENERALIZATION & PREDICTIVE BIAS

Robert L. Linn & Stephen B. Dunbar

Introduction

In a 1981 article in the *American Psychologist*, Schmidt and Hunter concluded that "professionally developed cognitive ability tests are valid predictors of performance on the job and in training for all jobs . . . in all settings." They also concluded that "cognitive ability tests are equally valid for minority and majority applicants and are fair to minority applicants in that they do not underestimate the expected job performance of minority groups" (1981, p. 1128). In these two brief but forceful statements, Schmidt and Hunter summarize their position on the two related topics of validity generalization and differential validity that will be considered in this chapter.

Schmidt and Hunter's conclusions are worthy of careful consideration on several counts. First, and most important, their conclusions are based upon an impressive accumulation and analysis of research findings, much of which has been done by Schmidt and Hunter and their colleagues. (With regard to validity generalization, see, for example, Hunter, 1980a, 1980b; Pearlman, Schmidt, & Hunter, 1980; Schmidt & Hunter, 1977; Schmidt, Hunter, & Pearlman, 1981a; and Schmidt et al., 1979. With regard to differential validity, see, for example, Hunter & Schmidt, 1978; Hunter, Schmidt, & Hunter, 1979; Linn, 1978; Schmidt, Berner, & Hunter, 1973; and Schmidt, Pearlman, & Hunter, 1980.) Second, their conclusions stand in sharp contrast, especially on the issue of validity generalization, with the widely held belief that validities are situation specific and possibly group specific. This belief is based upon the observation that observed validity coefficients vary greatly from one situation to another and from one group to another (e.g., Albright, Glennon, & Smith, 1963; Ghiselli, 1966; Guion, 1965; Katzell & Dyer, 1977). Third, and closely related to the second reason, their conclusions seem to conflict with the *Uniform Guidelines on Employee Selection Procedures* (U.S. Equal Employment Opportunity Commission et al., 1978).

There can be little doubt that the work on validity generalization by Schmidt and Hunter and more recently by several other authors (Callender & Osburn,

We thank Nambury Raju, Frank Schmidt, and John Callender for useful comments on an earlier draft of this paper.

1980, 1981; Callender et al., 1982; Hedges, 1982: Linn, Harnisch, & Dunbar, 1981a, 1981b; Linn & Hastings, in press; Pearlman, 1982; Raju, 1981a, 1981b) is, as Tenopyr observed, "one of the more noteworthy contributions to the field of personnel psychology" (1981, p. 1122). Tenopyr went on to note, however, that the "work is just making its impact on the thinking in the discipline" and that it "probably will have little impact on events in the real world for some time." Tenopyr's reasons for the latter conclusion were based largely on the notion that validity generalization runs counter to the idea of validity specificity that is "entrenched in personnel psychology" and reflected in the *Guidelines* (Tenopyr, 1981, pp. 1122–1223). There is also a big gap between concluding that validities are more generalizable than once thought and the apparent implication that there is no such thing as situational specificity or group differences in validity (Novick, 1982). Finally, methodological issues that remain controversial may influence judgments that are rendered on the issues (e.g., Callender & Osburn, 1980; Hedges, 1982; Linn, 1983a, 1983b, 1984; Raju, 1981a).

SITUATIONAL SPECIFICITY

Before getting into the details of the methodological issues and substantive findings of the work on validity generalization and differential validity, it seems desirable to consider briefly the contrasting positions that have been brought into question. Situational specificity is undoubtedly an idea that was derived from the great variability in validity coefficients that is familiar to any personnel psychologist or specialist in educational measurement. This variability was well documented by Ghiselli and led him to observe that "for a specific type of test applied to a particular type of job the validity coefficient given in one report may be high and positive and in another it may even be negative" (1966, p. 28). Ghiselli recognized that some variability was to be expected as the result of sampling error, but he also realized that sampling error alone is an insufficient explanation. Hence he concluded that "much of the variation results from differences in the nature of and the requirements for nominally the same job in different organizations, and in the same organization from one time period to another" (1966, p. 28).

Others have stated similar conclusions. Albright, Glennon, and Smith, for example, argued that "if years of personnel research have proven anything it is that jobs that seem the same from one place to another often differ in subtle but important ways. Not surprisingly, it follows that what constitutes job success is also likely to vary from place to place" (1963, p. 18). Yet another example is Guion's statement that

the first and most pervasive generalization to be made is that jobs
within . . . various organizational groupings, as well as the organizational
climates in which they may be found, will demonstrate extensive
variability. A test or procedure that may be found highly predictive in one

situation may, therefore, prove to be of no value at all in another apparently similar one. (1965, p. 415)

The commonly held view represented by these quotations that validities are situationally specific is also reflected in the earlier version of the *Standards for Educational and Psychological Tests* (APA/AERA/NCME Joint Committee, 1974) and in the 1978 *Guidelines* as elaborated in the published questions and answers concerning the *Guidelines* (U.S. Equal Employment Opportunity Commission et al., 1979). Consider, for example, standard E 5.2.1., which states that "validity coefficients are specific to the situations in which they are obtained" (APA/AERA/NCME Joint Committee, 1974, p. 36). Clearly, here as elsewhere, the concept of situational specificity is taken as if it were doctrine.

It is not completely fair to say that established guidelines have ruled out the possibility that test validity may be generalizable to some extent. The *Guidelines*, for example, does not preclude the use of evidence of validity from studies conducted elsewhere in lieu of a local validity study. It does, however, require that three conditions be met as described in section 7B. These requirements are

> 1. *Validity evidence.* Evidence from the available studies meeting the standards of section 14B below clearly demonstrates that the selection procedure is valid.
> 2. *Job similarity.* The incumbents in the user's job and the incumbents in the job or group of jobs on which the validity study was conducted perform substantially the same major work behaviors, as shown by appropriate job analyses both on the job or groups of jobs on which the validity study was performed and on the job for which the selection procedure is to be used.
> 3. *Fairness evidence.* The studies include a study of test fairness for each race, sex, and ethnic group which constitutes a significant factor in the borrowing user's relevant labor market for the job or jobs in question. (p. 28299)

The first of these three requirements is seemingly straightforward, but the requirements of section 14B are rather ambiguous. The second and third requirements are more demanding. Depending on the stringency with which the job analysis and investigation of fairness requirements are enforced, the use of validity generalization arguments in support of test use in a particular setting may or may not be acceptable. Schmidt, Hunter, and Caplan have claimed that all three requirements can usually be met, the second one because "psychological researchers *always* examine major work behaviors when conducting validity studies" (1981, p. 7) and the third one by review of the literature, which will show that tests are fair. It remains to be seen whether these arguments will be sufficiently persuasive in general.

The idea of validity generalization is given more credence by the *Principles for the Validation and Use of Personnel Selection Procedures* (APA, 1980) than is found in either the 1974 *Standards* or the 1978 *Guidelines*. The *Principles* points out that

> current research is showing that the differential effects of numerous variables may not be as great as heretofore assumed. To these findings is being added theoretical formulations, buttressed by empirical data, which propose that much of the difference in observed outcomes of validation research is due to statistical artifacts. (p. 16)

This argument is further strengthened by research results reviewed below that have appeared since the publication of the *Principles*.

The recently published revision of the *Standards for Educational and Psychological Testing* (AERA/APA/NCME Joint Committee, 1985) also acknowledges the potential utility of validity generalization. The endorsement of the approach to establishing validity is qualified, however. Standard 1.16 states that

> when adequate local validation evidence is not available, criterion-related evidence of validity for a specified test use may be based on validity generalization from a set of prior studies, provided that the specified test-use situation can be considered to have been drawn from the same population of situations on which validity generalization was conducted. (1985, p. 16)

DIFFERENTIAL VALIDITY AND DIFFERENTIAL PREDICTION

In the last fifteen years, a substantial number of studies of differential validity and of differential prediction have been conducted in a variety of employment and educational settings (cf. Hunter, Schmidt, & Hunter, 1979; Linn, 1982b). By now it seems quite clear that the evidence runs strongly counter to early expectations that tests would generally have lower validities for blacks and Hispanics than for whites and would tend to underpredict the actual criterion performance of minority group members. Differential validity is the exception rather than the rule, and a prediction based upon an equation for the total group or one based upon whites is more likely to yield predicted criterion scores for blacks or Hispanics that are higher than actual criterion scores than ones that are lower (Linn, 1982a).

Regardless of the findings, differential validity and differential prediction remain controversial topics. The reasons for this are rather obvious. The results get translated into statements regarding test bias and test fairness, which are emotion-laden topics. Concerns about adverse impact and differing views regarding affirmative action cloud the picture. Differences in social values come in conflict. Neither the empirical findings nor the models of fair test use in selection (cf. Cole, 1981; Petersen & Novick, 1976) can be expected to resolve these conflicts. Nonetheless, the empirical results are important, in part, as Tenopyr suggested, as "a defense against challenges" (1981, p. 1121). The results "also provide part of the necessary background for making policy decisions regarding test use, although they obviously do not provide a sufficient basis for such judgments" (Linn, 1982b, p. 286).

The 1974 *Standards* called for an investigation of the possibility that a test may be unfair whenever technically feasible (APA/AERA/NCME Joint Committee, 1974, pp. 43–44); however, they are ambiguous with regard to what is meant by fairness. The *Guidelines* is generally consistent with the *Standards*. It states that

> Where a selection procedure results in an adverse impact on a race, sex or ethnic group identified in accordance with the classifications set forth in section 4 above and that group is a significant factor in the relevant labor market, the user generally should investigate the possible existence of unfairness for that group if it is technically feasible to do so. (p. 38301)

The requirement is further qualified by reference to the need for sufficiently large samples and to the problems caused by the availability of only restricted ranges of scores. Allowance is also made for the possibility of relying on evidence from other studies showing that "the selection procedure predicts fairly for the group in question and for the same or similar jobs" (p. 38301). Ambiguity with regard to what constitutes fair selection remains despite the stated definition of unfairness: "A condition in which members of one race, sex, or ethnic group characteristically obtain lower scores on a selection procedure than members of another group, and the differences are not reflected in differences in measures of job performance" (p. 38308).

This appears to be a rather clear statement of unfairness in terms of differential prediction. That the above definition is not intended to imply a particular definition of fairness can be seen most clearly in the following section from the 1979 questions and answers regarding the *Guidelines*:

> Differential prediction is a central concept for one definition of test unfairness. Differential prediction occurs when the use of the same set of scores systematically overpredicts or underpredicts job performance for members of one group as compared to members of another group.
>
> Other definitions of test unfairness which do not relate to differential prediction may, however, also be appropriately applied to employment decisions. Thus these Guidelines are not intended to choose between fairness models as long as the model selected is appropriate to the manner in which the selection procedure is used. (U.S. Equal Employment Opportunity Commission et al., 1979, p. 12006)

What is considered an appropriate manner is left undefined.

The *Principles for Validation* (APA, 1980) also leaves open the question of what constitutes a fair selection procedure, noting that there are "many definitions" and that the principles "do not at this stage of the professional debate advocate any one model" (p. 3). But the principles suggest that differential validity

is uncommon and caution that "no variable should be assumed to moderate validities in the absence of explicit evidence for such an effect" (p. 9). Section B.3.c
goes on to suggest that replication or very large samples are needed to "give full
credence to unusual findings" (p. 9) such as moderator effects.

The accumulation of results suggesting that prediction equations rarely underestimate the performance of minorities on criterion measures was recognized
in the development of the 1985 *Standards*. Consequently, standard 1.20 calls for
investigations of

> the magnitude of predictive bias due to differential prediction for those
> groups for which previous research has established a substantial prior
> probability of differential prediction for the particular kind of test in
> question. (AERA/APA/NCME Joint Committee, 1985, p. 17)

Although the terms "biased" and "fair" are often used as modifiers for tests,
and it may be that types of unfairness may be inherent in the features of some
tests, it is widely recognized that bias and fairness depend on the use and interpretation of a test (cf. Cronbach, 1976; Petersen & Novick, 1976). Just as it is
inadequate to say simply that a test is valid, it is inadequate to say that a test is fair.
In both instances, the statement depends on the use and interpretation of the
scores. Indeed, bias and unfairness are most usefully conceived of as types of
invalidity (Shepard, 1982).

Despite these ambiguities, studies of differential prediction represent the
standard approach to obtaining empirical evidence with regard to questions of
fairness. It is the approach that is considered in this chapter. Since several recent
reviews of the differential validity and differential prediction literature are available (cf. Breland, 1978; Hunter, Schmidt, & Hunter, 1979; Linn, 1982a), the
results of the studies will be reviewed only briefly here. More attention will be
given to some methodological issues in the conduct and interpretation of studies of
validity generalization.

Review of Validity Generalization

BASIC IDEAS

Ghiselli's review of the results of hundreds of validity studies had as a goal the
identification of trends and generalizations about validity from which "inferences
could be made about the validity of specific tests for specific jobs, which possibly
would be more generally applicable than the results of any one investigation"
(1966, p. 7). This goal is in keeping with the goal of current validity generalization
research, and more generally with the purposes of what has come to be known as
meta-analysis (Glass, 1977). Ghiselli's work was an integrative review in the
sense that this term is used by Jackson (1980); that is, it relied on quantitative
techniques to analyze and interpret the summary statistics produced by the di-

verse studies, rather than relying on the more common, but less adequate, narrative review of results. For as Glass has aptly observed, the results of numerous studies "can no more be grasped in our traditional narrative discursive review than one can grasp the sense of 500 test scores without the aid of techniques for organizing, depicting and interpreting data" (1977, p. 4).

By current standards, Ghiselli's analytical techniques, which involved the creation of frequency distributions of validity coefficients and the calculation of statistics describing the distributions, were rudimentary. They did not involve the more powerful explanatory analyses that are characteristic of current validity generalization research. Nonetheless, his work and the similar presentations of distributions of validity coefficients by test publishers (e.g., American College Testing Program, 1973; Schrader, 1971) represent a step in that direction.

Artifacts, such as sampling error, unreliability, and range restriction, that affect the magnitude of observed validity coefficients have long been recognized. There is a big difference between recognizing that artifacts affect the magnitudes and variability of observed validities and quantitatively estimating and taking these effects into account. Therein lies the major step forward by Schmidt and Hunter (1977) in validity generalization research. Since that initial work, improvements in the methodology have been made and huge amounts of empirical results have been subjected to analysis. Methodological refinements and debates are currently in progress, as are studies of robustness and analyses of additional data sets. But the fundamental conceptual approach provided by Schmidt and Hunter remains intact.

Two parameters are of primary interest in validity generalization research. These are the mean "true validity" and the variance or standard deviation of the "true validities." Estimates of so-called true validities differ from simple observed validities owing to adjustments for certain artifacts, usually for restriction of range, and unreliability of the criterion measure, and sometimes for unreliability of the test. Estimates of variability of true validities differ from those of variability of the observed validities owing adjustments for differences between studies in the above artifacts as well as adjustments for variability due to sampling error. The estimate of the mean and standard deviation of the true validities are used, along with distributional assumptions, to create credibility intervals for the true validity.

In all, Schmidt and Hunter have identified eight possible sources of variability in observed validities across studies. These are listed as follows:

1. Sampling error
2. Differences across studies in the degree of range restriction
3. Differences across studies in reliability of criterion measures
4. Differences across studies in reliability of the tests
5. Differences in amount and kind of criterion contamination or other deficiencies

6.   Computational, typographical, and data recording errors
7.   Differences in the factor structure of tests
8.   True situational variability

Only the last of these sources should be reflected in the variability of the true validities. Since adjustments in variability are usually made only for the first three, or sometimes four, of the seven artifactual sources of variation listed above, Schmidt and Hunter have argued that their adjustments are, if anything, conservative, that is, that they are apt to overestimate the variability of the true validities. Acceptance of this conclusion obviously depends on the adequacy of the analytical model and of the adjustments that are made for attenuation, range restriction, and sampling error, topics that are addressed next.

ANALYTICAL PROCEDURES

All of the models that have been proposed for use in validity generalization research employ Bayesian concepts. That is, a distribution of true (population) validities, ρ, is hypothesized and the goal is to estimate parameters of this distribution. Of course, the true validities are not observable. Instead of observing ρ_i, $i = 1, 2 \ldots, m$, for the m studies, a sample correlation, r_i, is observed for each study. The sample value for any given study may differ from the true validity owing to the various artifacts listed above. Ignoring, for the moment, all the artifacts but the first, that is, sampling error, a simple model of validity generalization may be considered. Although it is desirable to take other artifacts into account, this "bare-bones" model illustrates the general approach and also reveals an area of controversy over model assumptions.

Bare-bones procedures. The bare-bones model starts with a noncontroversial equation that states that the observed sample validity, r_i, for study i is equal to the population correlation, ρ_i, plus a deviation due to sampling error. Ignoring the subscript, the sample correlation is given by

$$r = \rho + e, \tag{1}$$

where e is a random variable. Assuming that ρ and e are uncorrelated, then the variance of ρ is simply the difference between the variance of r and the variance of e, that is,

$$\sigma_\rho^2 = \sigma_r^2 - \sigma_e^2. \tag{2}$$

The latter two variances are readily estimated by standard formulas given by Pearlman, Schmidt, and Hunter (1980, p. 403). The estimated residual variance of the observed validities is then simply

$$\hat{\sigma}_{\text{res}}^2 = s_r^2 - s_e^2, \tag{3}$$

where s_r^2 is the sample size weighted estimate of the variance of the observed validities, and s_e^2 is the sample size weighted average of the estimated sampling error variance of the individual validity coefficients.

The quantity estimated in equation 3 is properly described as a characteristic of the distribution of *observed* validities. To obtain an estimate of the variance of the distribution of *true* validities, ρ, used in practice, Pearlman, Schmidt, and Hunter (1980) proposed that the estimate in equation 3 be divided by the product of the squared means of the correction factors because of two artifacts: unreliability of the criterion and range restriction. For present purposes this refinement need not concern us.

Even the overly simplified model estimate given in equation 3 will often produce estimated variances that are much smaller than the variance of the observed validities. This is so because sample sizes for validity studies are often small, much smaller than is desirable. According to Schmidt, Hunter, and Pearlman, "except when study sample sizes are very large, most of the variance in the observed correlations that is due to artifacts is due to only one artifact—simple sampling error" (1982, p. 844).

As already stated, equation 2 and therefore the estimate given in equation 3 depend on the assumption that ρ and e are uncorrelated. Hedges (1982) has questioned the reasonableness of this assumption. He noted that the asymptotic variance of e is dependent on ρ, and hence ρ and e cannot be independent. Furthermore, he has shown ρ and e must, in general, be correlated since the expected value of e is a function of ρ. In particular,

$$E(e) = \frac{-\rho(1 - \rho^2)}{2n} .$$
(4)

Consequently, the estimate of the variance of the true validity described above is really an estimate of the variance of ρ plus twice the covariance between ρ and e.

Hedges also suggested that the covariance between ρ and e "is likely to be negative and may be large in comparison to the σ_e^2" (1982, p. 7). In order to illustrate the possible effect of ignoring the covariance term, Hedges derived an expression for the covariance term for the special case where ρ takes on one of two possible values with equal probability. Using this expression, he calculated the degree to which the estimate of the variance of the true validities in equation 2 may be deflated by ignoring the covariance term. For extreme cases, ones that would never be encountered in practice, the underestimation is quite dramatic. For example, if half the studies had true validities of +.6 while the other half had true validities of −.6, the value of the variance of the true validities would be underestimated by 56 percent of the variance of e.

While Hedges's results are of theoretical interest, it is unlikely that the missing covariance term causes any serious difficulty in practice. For example, if a slight generalization of Hedges's formula is used for an extreme but possibly more realistic situation, the amount of underestimation of the variance of the true validities is negligible. Suppose that the true validity is .5 in 90 percent of the studies, but that the measure is completely invalid in the remaining 10 percent of the studies (true validity equals zero). Ignoring the covariance term would deflate the estimated variance of the true validities by only 2 percent. If a large number of studies all had a sample size of fifty in this situation, one could expect to obtain a standard deviation for the true validities of .1489 when the correct value is .15. Compared to other issues considered shortly, the absence of the covariance term from equation 2 is probably of no practical concern. Some of the other issues raised by Hedges, however, are more important.

The general model. A variety of estimation procedures have been presented in the literature, but they are all based on the same general model. Thus, before discussing the individual procedures, it is desirable to consider the general model. The model shown in equation 1 is inadequate because it ignores measurement error and the effects of selection. Even if there were no sampling error, the observed correlations would be attenuated owing (a) to less than perfect reliability of the criterion measure(s), (b) to less than perfect reliability of the test(s), and (c) to the effects of selection (i.e., range restriction). Hence the complete model is

$$r = a \cdot b \cdot c \cdot \rho + e, \tag{5}$$

where:

a = the square root of the reliability of Y, the criterion measure,
b = the square root of the reliability of X, the test, and
c = the multiplicative constant for adjusting a correlation for explicit selection on the test.

Means and variances of r and e may be estimated as discussed above. Means and variances of a, b, and c may also be estimated. Often this is done by assuming distributions of reliabilities and of degrees of selection, since these results are not normally available for the individual studies. From the above estimates, an estimate of the mean and variance of the true population validities is obtained. It is in the accomplishment of this last step that the various procedures differ. The differences in procedure depend upon assumptions that are made regarding the dependence of the terms a, b, c, and ρ.

The simplest approach is to assume that all four of the terms are independent. This assumption cannot be correct since the correction factor, c, depends on ρ. The fact that this assumption is not satisfied does not necessarily cause serious distortion in the final estimates that are derived based upon this assumption. This question will be considered in the context of the various procedures described below and again in the discussion of the results of empirical and Monte Carlo studies.

Original noninteractive procedure. The first validity generalization procedure was developed by Schmidt and Hunter (1977) and applied to four sets of validity study results found in Ghiselli (1966). The procedure, and the revision of it discussed in the next section, is called "noninteractive" because it ignores the interaction between the magnitude of the unreliability and the severity of range restriction. A criterion measure that had a reliability of .64, for example, would attenuate an unrestricted correlation of .6 by .12, whereas the same reliability would attenuate a restricted correlation of .4 by .08 (see Schmidt & Hunter, 1981, for a discussion of this effect).

The procedure used originally by Schmidt and Hunter (1977) also relies on the assumption that the multiplicative terms in equation 5 are independent, as described previously. In implementing the procedure, adjustments were made for sampling error, for differences in criterion unreliability, and for differences in range restriction. Fisher's Z-transformation of the correlations was used. As originally presented, the procedure contained an error in one of the equations, which was subsequently corrected by the Schmidt team (Schmidt et al., 1979). Consequently, the procedure as originally presented is no longer recommended for use. It should be noted, however, that the correction of the error in the procedure did not produce changes in the results large enough to alter the original conclusions. Nor does the error in any way detract from the importance of the conceptualization of the problem of validity generalization presented in Schmidt and Hunter's 1977 landmark paper.

Revised noninteractive procedure. The revised noninteractive procedure incorporates an additional adjustment for between-study differences in test reliability. As originally presented and used by Schmidt and his colleagues (1979), the noninteractive procedure included a conversion of validities using Fisher's Z-transformation. More recently (e.g., Pearlman, Schmidt, & Hunter, 1980; Schmidt, Gast-Rosenberg, & Hunter, 1980), the noninteractive procedure has been used without Fisher's Z-transformation because the transformation has been found to alter the numerical results only slightly (Schmidt & Hunter, 1981). The procedure without the transformation is slightly more conservative in that it tends to produce slightly smaller adjustments for artifacts than when Fisher's Z-transformation is used (Callender & Osburn, 1980; Pearlman, 1982; Schmidt & Hunter, 1981).

Because the noninteractive procedure without Fisher's Z-transformation has been used more recently and tends to yield slightly more conservative results, it is the one that will be considered in greatest detail. Since detailed step-by-step calculation procedures can be found in work by Pearlman (1982, Appendix C) and by Pearlman, Schmidt, and Hunter (1980), they will not be presented here. The conceptual approach will be described briefly, however.

Three distributions of validities are involved in the procedure: (1) the distribution of observed validities; (2) the residual distribution of validities after adjustments have been made for variability in validities for up to four artifacts (sampling error, range restriction, and measurement error in the criterion measures and tests); and (3) the distribution of the true (population) validities. The second distribution is of interest only as an intermediate step in obtaining estimates of the variability of the distribution of unobserved true validities.

The sample size weighted mean and variance of the distribution of observed validities are computed in the usual way. Estimates of the variance due to each of the artifacts (up to four) for which adjustments are to be made are computed. These will be denoted as follows:

s_1^2 = estimated variance due to sampling error,
s_2^2 = estimated variance due to between-study differences in criterion reliability,
s_3^2 = estimated variance due to between-study differences in test reliability, and
s_4^2 = estimated variance due to between-study differences in range restriction.

The four variance estimates are summed to produce a predicted variance in observed validities, that is:

$$s_{\text{pred}}^2 = s_1^2 + s_2^2 + s_3^2 + s_4^2. \tag{6}$$

The predicted variance is then subtracted from the estimated total variance to obtain the estimated residual variance,

$$s_{\text{res}}^2 = s_{\text{total}}^2 - s_{\text{pred}}^2. \tag{7}$$

The residual distribution mean is simply the mean of the distribution of observed validities, $\bar{r}$. Finally, the mean and standard deviation of the residual distribution are multiplied by a constant, k, to adjust for average criterion unreliability and average range restriction, and the resulting estimates are used to compute a credibility interval assuming that the true validities are normally distributed. The constant, k, is the reciprocal of the product of the mean adjustment for range restriction and the mean adjustment for criterion reliability.

Interactive procedure. Although the effects of ignoring the interaction described above were thought to be trivial (Schmidt, Hunter, & Pearlman, 1981a), criticisms led to the development of an alternative, interactive procedure that was first used by Schmidt, Gast-Rosenberg, and Hunter (1980). Rather than adjusting for range restriction and measurement error sequentially, as is done in the noninteractive procedure, a simultaneous adjustment is made for these effects. Thus the predicted variance is

$$s_{\text{pred}}^2 = s_1^2 + s_{234}^2, \tag{8}$$

where s_{234}^2 is the estimated variance due to the combination of differences in criterion and test reliability and to differences in range restriction. Otherwise, the interactive procedure is the same as the revised noninteractive procedure.

Computation of s_{234}^2 is based upon the assumption that the reliabilities of the test(s), reliabilities of the criterion measure(s), and the range restriction effects are mutually uncorrelated. As before, it is also assumed that the true validities are uncorrelated with the adjustment factors.

Independent-multiplicative procedure. Callender and Osburn (1980) developed a procedure that is closely related to Schmidt and Hunter's interactive procedure. As the name implies, the Callender and Osburn procedure is again based on the assumption that ρ, a, b, and c are mutually independent. With this assumption, they derived an expression for the multiplicative term, ρ_{ac}, which in turn is used to estimate the variance of the distribution of true validities.

Using bars to denote means and s^2 with obvious subscripts to denote variances, the equations for the estimated variance of the true validities used in the revised noninteractive procedure, the interactive procedure, and the independent-multiplicative procedure may be readily compared. As shown by Hunter, Schmidt, and Jackson (1983), the three equations may be written as follows:

revised noninteractive

$$s_\rho^2 = \frac{s_r^2 - s_e^2 - \bar{\rho}(s_a^2 + \bar{a}^2 s_b^2 + \bar{a}^2 \bar{b}^2 s_c^2)}{\bar{a}^2 \bar{c}^2} , \tag{9}$$

interactive

$$s_\rho^2 = \frac{s_r^2 - s_e^2 - \bar{\rho}^2 s_{abc}^2}{\bar{a}^2 \bar{c}^2} , \tag{10}$$

and independent-multiplicative

$$s_\rho^2 = \frac{s_r^2 - s_c^2 - \bar{\rho}^2 (\bar{c}^2 s_a^2 + \bar{a}^2 s_c^2 + s_a^2 s_c^2)}{(\bar{a}^2 + s_a^2)(\bar{c}^2 + s_c^2)} . \tag{11}$$

No terms for b occur in the independent-multiplicative equation because Callender and Osburn did not include adjustments for differences in reliability of the test(s). Schmidt, Hunter, and Pearlman (1982) present an analog to equation 11 when this additional artifact is incorporated in the procedure, however. Equations 9 and 10 may also be made directly comparable to 11 by dropping the adjustment for b. To do this, set the mean of b to 1, the variance of b to 0, and delete the b from the subscripts of the multiplicative variance term in equation 10.

Examples comparing the use of the three equations above with actual and simulated validity study results will be presented shortly. Before getting into this presentation, however, four other procedures are described briefly.

Dependent procedure. Callender and Osburn (1980) presented an alternative procedure, referred to as the dependent-multiplicative equation. This equation is of theoretical interest, but is not apt to have much applicability until (a) empirical data on restriction and criterion attenuation are available more frequently for individual studies, and (b) problems involved in estimating covariance terms are overcome (Callender, Osburn, & Greener, 1979). Since ρ is unknown and information about the degree of range restriction and reliability of the criterion measure for individual studies is generally unavailable, the needed covariance term is not directly estimable. A modified dependent procedure that does not include ρ, but does include the covariance between a and c and between a^2 and c^2, has been proposed and evaluated with Monte Carlo techniques (Callender et al., 1982). Results indicate that the modified dependent procedure performs appreciably better than independent procedures when the correlation between a and c is .30 or higher.

Asymptotic distribution procedure. Hedges (1982) has criticized the above estimation procedures on two counts. First, he noted that the procedures treat the variance components as additive when in fact they are not necessarily additive. Second, he pointed out that the usual estimate of the variance of the true validities is not consistent. Having identified these two potential problems, Hedges derived an alternative procedure based upon the asymptotic distribution of correlations that have been simultaneously adjusted for measurement error and range restriction. Equations are presented for three special cases: (1) where reliabilities are available in the unrestricted population, (2) where they are available in the restricted population, and (3) where one reliability is available in one population and the second in the other population.

The procedure developed by Hedges is mathematically elegant and has the potential advantage of not requiring assumptions that have been questioned in other techniques. On the other hand, they are more demanding in that they require estimates of reliability and of the degree of range restriction for each individual study. Such information, though clearly desirable, is generally absent for individual studies, a fact that led Schmidt and Hunter to hypothesize distributions of these artifacts and rely on the use of procedures that depend only on marginal distributions rather than joint distributions of statistics. In addition, it is unclear as to what size samples are apt to be required for the asymptotic approximations to yield better estimates than the alternative techniques. For these reasons, and because comparative results are currently unavailable, it seems premature to attempt an evaluation of the practical importance of Hedges's alternative procedure. The procedure appears promising, however, and worthy of study in simulations and of possible application where the essential information is available.

Taylor series approximations. Raju (1981a) has developed two alternative equations for estimating the variance of ρ based on approximations from the Taylor series expansion. His first procedure rests on the assumption that ρ, a^2, b^2, and the ratio of standard deviations of X in the restricted to the unrestricted populations are pairwise independent. The second procedure makes a parallel assumption substituting a and b for their squared counterparts above. Each procedure involves the evaluation of four partial derivatives that are used along with variances of r, e, a or a^2, b or b^2, and u (where u is the ratio of the restricted to the unrestricted standard deviations of X) to compute an estimate of the variance of ρ.

The correlational procedures developed by Raju were proposed as possible ways of improving the accuracy of the procedures presently in use, which Raju and Burke (1983) have suggested are slightly inaccurate. Raju has also proposed a method based on covariances rather than correlations. While parallel to the preceding approach, the covariance procedure has the potential advantage that corrections for unreliability are unnecessary. This simplification is due to the well-known result of classical test theory that the covariance between observed scores is equal to the covariance between corresponding true scores. However, the covariance method is applicable only where all studies have the same units of measurement, which is not typical of most situations.

Recently, Raju and Burke (1983) have compared Raju's (1981a) procedures to three other procedures in a series of Monte Carlo simulation studies. Some of their results are discussed below. Empirical comparisons with other procedures are currently unavailable.

Empirical range restriction. One final variation was dubbed "empirical range restriction" by Linn, Harnisch, and Dunbar (1981b). This variation could be applied with either the noninteractive (equation 9) or the independent-multiplicative procedure (equation 11). It differs only in the way in which adjustments are made for range restriction. Because selection rarely takes place solely on the basis of scores on a test, the standard correction for range restriction tends to be too small (for a discussion of the reasons for this tendency and for indications of the degree to which adjustments are apt to be too small, see Linn, 1968, 1983a; Linn, Harnisch, & Dunbar, 1981a).

To adjust for range restriction Linn and his associates (1981b) used the empirical relationship between the magnitude of the observed validities and the magnitude of the study standard deviations on the test. The variance in the predicted validities from the quadratic regression of the standard deviations was used as an estimate of the variance c. For the data set where this variation was applied, the variance estimated to be due to differences in range restriction was noticeably larger than the estimate obtained using the usual correction factor. Similar results for multiple correlations have also been obtained by Linn and Hastings (in press).

COMPARATIVE RESULTS

Several studies have reported results of analyses using two or more procedures. Schmidt, Gast-Rosenberg, and Hunter (1980) reported results comparing the revised noninteractive and the interactive procedures; Pearlman (1982) compared these two procedures along with the noninteractive procedure with Fisher's Z-transformation, the independent-multiplicative procedure, and a barebone's procedure; and Linn, Harnisch, and Dunbar (1981b) reported results comparing the noninteractive, the independent-multiplicative, a bare-bones procedure, and their empirical range restriction variation. Callender and Osburn (1980) and Callender and his associates (1982) have also reported comparative results based on simulated validity study statistics.

All of the evidence leads to the conclusion that for practical purposes the differences between the noninteractive, the interactive, and the independent-multiplicative procedures are quite small. For example, Pearlman (1982), who has reported the most comprehensive set of comparisons of these three procedures with actual validity data, found that the percentage of variance accounted for by artifacts differed by an average of only 5.1 percent across a total of fifty-six distributions of validities, by these three procedures. Looked at another way, the average estimated standard deviation of the true validities across the fifty-six distributions was .12 for the noninteractive procedure, and .13 for both of the other two procedures. In only two of the fifty-six distributions was the difference in estimated standard deviations of true validities larger than .03 for the three procedures. Stem-and-leaf plots of the 90 percent credibility values for fifty-six job families are shown in Figure 8.1 for the noninteractive, the interactive, and the independent-multiplicative procedures. The distributions are obviously quite similar and all consistently show 90 percent credibility values clearly greater than zero.

Though the differences are small, there is a clear tendency for the noninteractive procedure to produce the smallest estimate of the standard deviation of the true validities.

Other comparisons of empirical results and comparisons of simulated results show similarly small differences between these three procedures. Indeed, even the bare-bones procedure, which surely overestimates the variability of the true validities, generally yields results that support the same global conclusion regarding validity generalization. Moreover, the simulation results reported by Callender and Osburn (1980) suggest that all three procedures tend to overestimate the standard deviation of the true validities, thereby creating a slight bias that works against a conclusion that validities are generalizable. However, Raju and Burke (1983) found that the interactive and multiplicative procedures overestimate the variance of ρ more than the other three procedures they studied. (The noninteractive procedure with Fisher's Z-transformation, which is no longer recommended for use, produces results that are slightly in the opposite direction.)

FIGURE 8.1. Stem-and-leaf plots of 90% credibility values for true validity derived from three validity generalization procedures

90% CV	Noninteractive	Freq.		Interactive	Freq.		Independent-multiplicative	Freq.
.9		0	.9		0	.9		0
.8	0	1	.8	0	1	.8	0	1
.7	059	3	.7	059	3	.7	059	3
.6	06	2	.6	6	1	.6	6	1
.5	5577	4	.5	33455	5	.5	01222	5
.4	112455789	9	.4	2344555	7	.4	1224555	7
.3	2335678	7	.3	034579	6	.3	034479	6
.2	0234666899	10	.2	012366889999	12	.2	12366888999	11
.1	00123345789	11	.1	1111245678	10	.1	001222556689	12
.0	45678	5	.0	3456788	7	.0	466789	6
-.0	25	2	-.0	37	2	-.0	33	2
-.1	4	1	-.1	5	1	-.1	49	2
-.2	0	1	-.2	0	1	-.2		0

Raju and Burke (1983) have recently reported results of a Monte Carlo study comparing (1) the revised noninteractive procedure applied to correlations (Schmidt et al., 1979), (2) the interactive procedure (Schmidt, Hunter, & Pearlman, 1981b), (3) the independent-multiplicative procedure (Callender & Osburn, 1980), (4) Raju's procedure one (1981a), and (5) Raju's procedure two (1981a). Three cases were analyzed: case 1 had a constant true validity and varied degrees of range restriction and reliabilities of criterion and predictor measures; case 2 had variation in true validities but constant values of range restriction and criterion and predictor reliabilities; and case 3 varied true validities, degrees of range restriction, and predictor and criterion reliabilities. Infinite sample sizes were assumed for all validities so sampling variance was not involved in the estimates. All five procedures yielded generally similar estimates of the mean and variance of the true validities, but overall Raju's procedure one was slightly better than the others.

Results of nine trials with one hundred validities each for Raju and Burke's case 3 are summarized in Figure 8.2. Differences between the estimated mean validities and the actual mean validity of .5 are plotted on the vertical axis for the five procedures. Differences between estimated variances of true validities and the actual variance for each trial are plotted on the horizontal axis. Mean differences have been multiplied by 10^4 and differences in variances by 10^3. The largest overestimate of the mean true validity was only .0135, observed for one trial for both the noninteractive and interactive procedures. All procedures overestimated the mean true validity on every trial, but the amount of overestimation was never large for any procedure. The amount of overestimation of the mean true validity was smallest for Raju's procedure one, averaging only .0041. Occasional underestimates of the variance of the true validities were obtained by two procedures, but generally the variance was slightly overestimated. The noninteractive procedure yielded the smallest discrepancies in variance estimates on the average, followed very closely by Raju's procedure one. There is little prac-

FIGURE 8.2. Deviations of estimated means and variance of true validities from actual values for five methods and nine trials (Monte Carlo results from Raju & Burke, 1983)

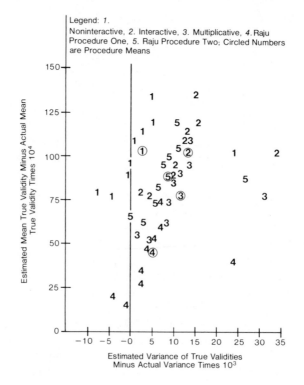

tical basis for choosing among the five procedures from the results summarized in Figure 8.2, but Raju's procedure one can be seen to be the best of the five by a tiny amount.

Callender and his associates (1982) used Monte Carlo techniques to investigate the accuracy of the independent-multiplicative and a modified dependent procedure that takes only the correlation of the range restriction and criterion unreliability artifacts into account. Both procedures were found to provide reasonably accurate estimates. As might be expected, the modified dependent procedure was somewhat more accurate than the independent model when the restriction and unreliability artifacts were correlated .30 or higher. It would be desirable if estimates of these two artifacts were routinely available for individual studies. If available, the modified dependent model would be preferred, especially if there is evidence that the two artifacts are substantially correlated across studies.

RESULTS

Schmidt and Hunter (1981) summarized the validity generalization results produced by the analysis in a variety of studies of 152 distributions of validity coefficients. Two generalizations are clearly supported by the results of those and other more recent studies (Callender & Osburn, 1983; Pearlman, 1982). First, much of the observed variability of validity coefficients in all the studies is attributable to sampling error and to differences in measurement error and range restriction using any of the analytical procedures. According to Schmidt and Hunter, "the first four artifacts . . . accounted for an average of 72% of the observed variance of validity coefficients" in the analyses of 152 distributions of validities that they reviewed (1981, p. 1132). Sampling variability accounts for most of the explained variation (typically about 85 percent according to Schmidt and Hunter) while differences in range restriction and in test and criterion reliability contribute smaller amounts. In addition, some variability may be attributable to other artifacts not accounted for in the analysis (e.g., typographical and computational errors).

The second generalization that is supported by the results is that validities are positive. Using a one-tailed 90 percent credibility interval, that is, the tenth percentile in the estimated distribution of true validities, usually produces a positive value for the distributions that have so far been analyzed. As stated by Schmidt and Hunter, "one finds that in 84% of the 152 test-job combinations, even the validity value at the 10th percentile is positive and substantial enough in magnitude to have practical value in improving the work force productivity" (1981, p. 1133). It might be noted that the above conclusions involve an implicit equating of the terms "work-force productivity" and "criterion measures."

Pearlman (1982) conducted a series of analyses of validity coefficients from 500 independent validity studies involving sixty-one U.S. Navy occupations involving approximately 1.8 million individuals. He compared the validity generalization results for several different job-clustering procedures (molecular work content groupings, worker-oriented job content groupings, attribute requirement groupings, and broad content structure groupings) with random groupings of jobs and ungrouped analyses. To the extent that the groupings are important for purposes of validity generalization, the variance of validities should be more homogeneous within groups and the between-group differences in mean validities should be greater for systematic groupings than for random groupings. The findings were consistent with this expectation, but the differences between systematic groupings and random groupings were surprisingly small. A comparison of the prior standard deviations, that is, the standard deviations of the estimated true validities, obtained by fifteen systematic groupings of jobs with the corresponding random groupings of jobs for six different tests, is provided in Figure 8.3. As can be seen, the difference in the distributions of prior standard deviations is not

FIGURE 8.3. Stem-and-leaf plots of average within-group prior standard deviations of observed validities for systematic and random job groupings (based on Pearlman, 1982)

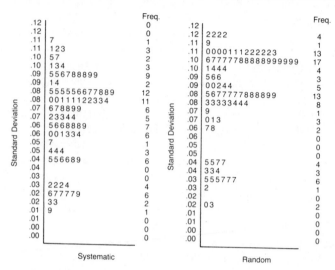

great. These and other results led Pearlman to conclude "that the validity of typical employment tests is not situationally specific and that validity generalization is pervasive" (1982, p. 154).

Results reported by Hunter from an analysis of results of 515 validation studies conducted over a period of forty-five years by the U.S. Employment Service led to the conclusion "that validity changes only with very large changes in job content" (1980b, p. 52). For example, the estimated true validities of cognitive ability tests for jobs classified into five levels of complexity ranging from simple manual labor to highly technical jobs were .56, .58, .51, .40, and .23. The estimated average true validities for psychomotor ability for the same five categories of jobs were .30, .21, .32, .43, and .48. Thus, while there is some systematic difference as a function of job complexity, both types of tests show a potentially useful degree of validity within each category.

There would seem to be little basis for debate of the conclusions that a good deal of the observed variability in distributions of validity coefficients is attributable to artifacts and that true validities of ability tests that are widely used for employee selection and student admissions are almost always positive. There is room for debate, however, regarding other aspects of validity generalization research and the conclusions based upon it. At issue are questions about (1) the accuracy of the adjustments and whether or not they lead to overstatements or understatements of the degree of validity generalization; (2) whether situational specificity exists and, if so, whether it is sufficiently frequent and sizeable to require attention; (3) whether job specificity should remain a concern; (4) whether there are biases in the data bases caused by a tendency to exclude studies with null or negative results; and (5) whether correlation coefficients provide an adequate basis for the interpretations that are made. These five issues are considered briefly below.

ACCURACY OF ADJUSTMENTS

Several questions regarding the accuracy of the adjustments have already been raised. Assumptions about the independence of the true validities and the artifacts have already been discussed (see Hedges, 1982). Agreement between results for the noninteractive and interactive results provides some reassurance but does not fully address questions of effects of dependence. Hedges (1982) has shown that dependence can cause serious problems under extreme conditions. It is implausible, however, that such extremes exist in the real world, and for more plausible conditions, the violations alter the results only slightly, not enough to alter major conclusions. It should also be noted that Callender, Osburn, and Greener (1979) found their dependent procedure "to be less accurate and less stable than the Callender-Osburn independent procedure" (Pearlman, 1982, p. 35) when both procedures were used with simulated results, the only conditions under which the dependent procedure can presently be applied. Thus it would seem that dependence is unlikely to seriously distort results or alter conclusions. Nonetheless, additional analyses with simulated data using the procedures recently developed by Hedges (1982) as a benchmark seem highly desirable.

Assumptions underlying adjustments for attenuation and, more important, for range restriction may also be questioned. Lower-bound reliability estimates can lead to overcorrections, and certain violations of the assumptions of linearity and homoscedasticity required for corrections for range restriction can also lead to overcorrections (Dunbar, 1982; Greener & Osburn, 1979; Novick & Thayer, 1969). There are several reasons to believe that these potential problems are not serious, however. In fact, it is likely that the adjustments for range restriction are, if anything, too conservative.

To begin with, measurement error and range restriction adjustments are usually small compared to adjustments for sampling error, accounting for only about 15 percent of the total adjustment on the average (Schmidt & Hunter, 1981). In addition, the distributions of criterion reliabilities and of selection ratios that have typically been used (see, for example, Pearlman, Schmidt, & Hunter, 1980) are reasonably conservative. Violations of range restriction assumptions are more likely to lead to adjustments that are too small than to ones that are too large (Dunbar, 1982). Finally, the range restriction adjustment model ignores the fact that selection is usually based on more than a single test. Consequently the adjustments can be expected to be too small, sometimes markedly so (Linn, 1968, 1983a; Linn, Harnisch, & Dunbar, 1981a). All in all, violations of assumptions, while worthy of continued study, are not apt to lead to overstatements of validity generalization.

One can conclude that roughly three-fourths of the variability in observed validity coefficients is attributable to artifacts, without concluding that situational specificity is nonexistent or unimportant. If, for example, a distribution of true validities has a mean of .30 and a standard deviation of .18, the 90 percent credibility value is .06, a positive but small value. Taken seriously, these results would imply that in 10 percent of the situations the validity of the test is less than or equal to .06. Justification of test use with a validity of .06 or less may be problematic, whereas in situations where the validity was at or above the mean of the true validity distribution, .30, the test may have considerable utility. Hence one might reasonably conclude that there is good evidence that validities are generalizable across situations in the sense that they are nonzero, yet still conclude that the use of the test is justifiable in terms of the magnitude of the validity in one situation but not another. Unfortunately, there is no way of knowing which situation has one of the atypically low validities. Furthermore, the validity generalization results may be a better way of estimating the validity for a particular situation than a local validation with a small sample.

The previous numerical example is taken from estimates reported from one of the job-test combinations investigated by Schmidt, Hunter, and Caplan (1981). The numbers apply to jobs classified as "maintenance" and to general intelligence tests. The results for this job-test combination are neither the best, in the sense of the highest mean validity and smallest standard deviation, nor the worst that can be found in the literature. For thirty-two individual job-test combinations studied by Pearlman, Schmidt, and Hunter (1980) using proficiency criteria in clerical occupations, for example, estimated mean validities ranged from a low of .15 to a high of .60, and estimated standard deviations of true validities ranged from 0 to .43.

In summarizing the evidence with regard to situational specificity, Schmidt and Hunter concluded that "these findings show that cognitive test validities can *typically* be generalized with confidence across settings and organizations, and there is no factual basis for requiring a validity study in *each* situation" (1981, p. 1133; italics added). We concur with this conclusion but add emphasis to the words *typically* and *each*. These qualifications convey a rather different message and imply greater caution than the earlier quote from the same paper that "cognitive ability tests are valid predictors . . . in all settings" (p. 1128). The latter statement seems to imply that there is no cause for concern about exceptions, whereas the former at least recognizes the possibility of exceptions.

Recent evidence reported by Osburn and colleagues (1983) raises questions about the statistical power of validity generalization procedures for testing the hypothesis that there is no situational specificity (i.e., that the variance of the true validities is zero). Based on their Monte Carlo investigations, the Osburn team concluded "that the power of validity generalization studies to distinguish between populations of studies with zero true validity variance and studies with low to moderate true validity variance is inadequate by commonly accepted standards unless truly massive amounts of data are available, i.e., many studies having unusually large sample sizes" (1983, p. 120). As they acknowledged, however, it is not necessary that the true validity variance equal zero for validity generalization results to be useful. Yet if this conclusion is strictly interpreted, the possibility of some degree of situational specificity or exceptions to the general rule cannot be ruled out based upon the evidence currently available.

Recognizing that there may be exceptions engenders caution. It does not preclude the possibility of generalizing from other studies rather than relying on a local validation, but it does demand that the test user be prepared to defend the use against a claim that the results would be different in that particular situation (Cronbach, 1980).

This position is clearly articulated in comments made by Cronbach in a panel discussion at a 1979 conference on construct validity (U.S. Office of Personnel Management & Educational Testing Service, 1980). He was discussing a court case in which the validity of a test for the selection of firemen was in question.

> The plaintiffs objected to its use in Richmond, Virginia, saying, "you can't use that test here because there was no local validation": The test was validated on firemen in 45 other communities around the country. The judge's remarks were to the effect that to require local validation in every city, village, and hamlet would be ludicrous. The duties of a fireman, he said, don't vary that much. It appears to be a reasonable decision, but it illustrates the form other arguments can take. A plaintiff facing that issue would be intelligent to argue, "But look what firemen do in Richmond: their tasks are different." If plaintiffs can't make that stick, then the IPMA test will almost certainly stand up against the challenge. But if this happened to be a place where, say, oil well fires are common, it would be plausible that the site falls outside the class of sites studied, happens outside the construct for which the validity has been established. (p. 131)

This illustration makes the point elaborated elsewhere by Cronbach (1980) that there is much more to validation than a validity coefficient or, for that matter, a credibility interval from a validity generalization study. Persuasive arguments in terms of the particulars of the situation are required. It remains important to look for the exceptions, to probe for weak spots in the argument, and to evaluate plausible rival hypotheses. Certainly, the findings of validity generalization research strengthen the position of those who defend the use of tests, but they do not guarantee validity once and for all and for all situations as one might be led to believe by some of the more grandiose claims that have been made.

The arguments with regard to the question of job specificity parallel those regarding situational specificity. Schmidt, Hunter, and Pearlman (1981b) demonstrated that there is a considerable degree of generalizability of validities across rather diverse jobs (e.g., clerks, cooks, dental assistants, and machinists were among the thirty-five army jobs in their second study). The results led Schmidt and his two colleagues (1981b) to characterize the idea that task differences in jobs moderate validity of aptitude tests as a "red herring" and led Schmidt and Hunter to conclude that "cognitive ability tests are valid predictors . . . for all jobs" (1981, p. 1128).

In evaluating the "red herring" conclusion, it is important to keep in mind their definition of a moderator effect. They used the term "moderator effect" to mean that an aptitude test has "substantial validity for one grouping of tasks (job) [but is] 'invalid' (i.e., [has] near-zero validity for another grouping of tasks (job)" (Schmidt, Hunter, & Pearlman, 1981b, p. 166). Using this stringent definition of a moderator effect, they were able to reject the idea. On the other hand, there are, as they concede, reliable differences in validities from job to job (see also Hunter, 1980; Schmidt & Hunter, 1981, p. 1133). It would seem that the issue of job specificity is not unlike the question of whether a glass is half empty or half full. There is generalizability, but there are also differences.

A possible objection to validity generalization research is that there is a reporting bias in the validity study results that are available for analysis. The argument in favor of a bias is that investigators are more apt to report significant results than nonsignificant ones. Hence a disproportionate number of low or negative validity coefficients might be excluded from the analyses. This possible objection was recognized by Schmidt and Hunter in their 1977 publication, but they argued at some length that the effect is of little or no consequence. More recent and extensive arguments against the claim of bias due to missing studies are provided by Schmidt, Hunter, and Pearlman (1981a). There they note the similarity of results for studies where "data sets [are] known to be complete" (p. 11) and for those relying on possibly incomplete data sets.

Further evidence against the notion that biased data bases invalidate conclusions is provided by Callender and Osburn (1981) using Rosenthal's "file drawer" procedure (1979). The idea of the file drawer procedure is to calculate the number of missing studies (in file drawers) with null results that would be needed to bring the overall significance level for all studies, reported and unreported, down to the .05 level. Callender and Osburn (1981) included calculation of the number of required file drawer studies for their petroleum industry validity generalization analyses. Their calculations indicated that the number of file drawer studies would have to outnumber available studies by as much as fifty-three to one and no less than nineteen to one for the eight test-criterion combinations in their analyses.

CORRELATION COEFFICIENTS

Tongue-in-cheek calls for the formation of a society against correlation coefficients have been engendered by the well-known limitations of this widely used statistic. A strong case can be made that standard errors of estimate, regression equations, and expectancy tables provide far better summaries of the results of validity studies than do correlation coefficients. The dependence of a correlation on the heterogeneity of the sample is one of its several weaknesses. This weakness leads to the need to use range restriction adjustments, and the adequacy of the adjustments has been questioned, especially in situations of extreme selection where they are most needed (see, for example, Lord & Novick, 1968, pp. 141ff.).

Procedures for analyzing regressions rather than correlations for large numbers of samples are available (e.g., Novick et al., 1972; Rubin, 1980). Where applicable, these techniques have considerable appeal. In many applied settings, however, there are, as Schmidt, Hunter, and Pearlman have stated, "problems standing in the way of cumulating regression slopes (or intercepts) across studies" (1981a, p. 21). The same could be said for Raju's covariance procedure (1981a). The fundamental difficulty is that criterion measures used in different studies are seldom on a common metric. Where results are cumulated across different tests, the metric also differs across tests. Consequently, the standard deviations are not comparable, and therefore neither are covariances or raw score intercepts and slopes. To make comparisons, the standard deviations must be equated in some way, which is, of course, what is done by a correlation coefficient.

There are situations, most notably in educational admissions, where a single test, or a common group of tests, is used and where the criterion measures may reasonably be considered to be comparable (e.g., a five-point grading scale). In such situations, analysis of regression equations and standard errors of estimate is to be preferred, and it is in this setting where such analyses have been performed (Braun & Jones, 1981; Novick et al., 1972; Rubin, 1980).

Though less common, there are also situations where regression equations would better serve the purposes of validity generalization analyses than correlations. For example, if a common criterion measure is used for a given job classification but the data are collected at many sites and validity study results are analyzed by site, then the analysis of regression coefficients would be superior to the analysis of correlation coefficients. A lack of differences in correlations across sites does not preclude the possibility of systematic site-to-site differences in either slopes or intercepts; it is the latter coefficients that are critical for making generalizations about the predictive meaning of test scores across sites. Obtaining the necessary data for regression-based generalizability studies of a given job across sites requires either large organizations, such as the military, or cooperative studies involving a number of smaller organizations. Such efforts should be encouraged.

Review of Differential Prediction and Questions of Bias

The topic of this section, while no less important than that of validity generalization, will be considered in much less detail. A number of reviews of differential validity and differential prediction and discussions of models of fair selection are available (e.g., Cole, 1981; Hunter & Schmidt, 1978; Hunter, Schmidt, & Hunter, 1979; Linn, 1978, 1982b; Petersen & Novick, 1976; Ruch, 1972; Schmidt, Pearlman, & Hunter, 1980). No attempt will be made to repeat that discussion here. We will, however, consider briefly the basis for the claim made by Schmidt and Hunter (1981) that was quoted at the beginning of this chapter and also highlight a few critical considerations for the interpretation of the research on this topic.

Whether or not one is willing to accept the unqualified statement that "cognitive ability tests are equally valid for minority and majority applicants" (Schmidt & Hunter, 1981, p. 1128), it is clear that the once widely held expectation that tests would typically show less validity for minority than for majority group members has not been borne out by empirical evidence. Since differences in validity that are found in the literature occur at levels that are no higher than can be explained by simple sampling variability and other statistical artifacts such as differences in range restriction, there seems to be no solid foundation to argue that important differences in predictive validity are common. Although the true validities are unlikely to be precisely equal all the time, "the evidence is very strong . . . that the magnitude of the difference is small" (Linn, 1978, p. 510).

For purposes of evaluating questions of bias, it is clear that comparisons of correlation coefficients are simply inadequate for the problem. Hence it hardly seems worthwhile to debate the question of whether differential validity is nonexistent, of small magnitude, or possibly even large in some circumstances. This is so because comparisons of validity alone reveal nothing about possible differences in the predictive meaning of test scores or about the direction of any differences that may be found. It is possible, for example, for the validity to be .2 for one group and .5 for another, yet for members of the group with the lower validity to be better off, in the sense that they have higher predicted scores if a combined group equation or the equation for the other group is used rather than their group-specific regression equation. An adequate evaluation of the question of possible predictive bias demands that regression equations and standard errors of estimate or expectancy tables be compared.

When regression equations are compared, "the bulk of the evidence shows either that there are no differences in predictions based on minority and majority group data, or that predictions based on majority group data give some advantage to minority group members" (Linn, 1982b, p. 286). There is, in other words, rather strong and consistent support for Schmidt and Hunter's conclusion that "cognitive ability tests . . . are fair to minority group applicants in the sense that they do not underestimate the expected job performance of minority groups" (1981, p. 1128). Although these statements are reasonable summaries of the existing empirical results, the implications of the findings and the explanation of these findings is much more problematic (Linn, 1984). Differential prediction is also apparently more common for gender, at least in academic settings (Linn, 1973) and for military training criteria (Linn, 1984).

ARTIFACTS

There are several possible artifacts that need to be considered in interpreting the results of studies of predictive bias. The results are all dependent upon the acceptance of the assumption that the criterion measures are themselves unbiased. This is a potentially weak link in the chain, for if the criterion measure that is used in a study is biased, it provides little comfort to know that a test has the same predictive meaning for different groups. However, contrary to expectations, results based on subjective criteria, such as ratings, that are presumably susceptible to bias generally agree with those for more objective criteria that are less apt to be susceptible to bias.

Most validity studies suffer from the limitation that results are available only for persons who are selected and for whom criterion data are obtained. Yet the results must be used in considering total groups of future applicants. This is a general problem in validation work and one that leads to the need for range restriction corrections in correlations. The problem also has potential implications for interpretations of the results of studies of predictive bias.

As shown by Linn (1983a, 1983b), selection effects can lead to the common finding of overprediction for minority groups even if just the opposite would be true for the unselected population. Such a result can occur if selection takes place, at least in part, on variables not included in the regression equations. The effect can also be exacerbated by different degrees of, and bases for, selection in the two groups, conditions that are likely to be encountered in practice.

PRACTICAL IMPLICATIONS

Tenopyr has argued that studies of predictive bias and discussions of models of fair test use are apt to have no impact in the real world. She notes that

> the study of fairness will undoubtedly be incorporated into validity
> studies whenever feasible, but its purpose will be defense against
> challenges; it will not be used with an eye toward using tests differently
> for different groups. Very simply, employers cannot afford to use
> different tests for subgroups, nor can they interpret tests differently for
> different groups. (1981, pp. 1121–1122)

Tenopyr's conclusion may apply in many situations. There are situations, for example, the use of tests with persons with particular handicaps, in which different tests are used for subgroups. The assignment of bonus points to members of particular groups, for example, veterans or minorities, has been upheld in the courts. Nonetheless, Tenopyr's practical view is important in putting the literature on predictive bias into perspective. So too is the recognition "that whether or not tests are biased, their role is only a small part of the complex social policy issues facing legislators, the courts, and the citizenry" (Cole, 1981, p. 1075).

Advantages and Disadvantages of Analytical Procedures

Table 8.1 presents a summary of the analytical procedures that have been developed for use in validity generalization studies. The key assumptions are listed along with summary comments on the advantages and disadvantages of each procedure. Although several of the procedures depend upon questionable assumptions such as the independence of multiplicative terms, the available evidence suggests that violations of these assumptions may have negligible effects. Other procedures, such as Callender and Osburn's dependent procedure (1980) and Hedges's asymptotic procedure (1982), have theoretical appeal but make demands for statistics from individual studies that are typically unavailable.

Raju and Burke's comparative results for five procedures (1983), which were summarized in Figure 8.2, suggest that Raju's procedure one (1981a) has some advantages. However, the general similarity of the results and the small magni-

TABLE 8.1. Summary of Analytical Procedures Used in Validity Generalization

Procedure	Assumptions	Comments
Bare-bones	Population validities and sampling error are uncorrelated	Adjustments for sampling variability only. Assumption questioned by Hedges (1982).
Original noninteractive (Schmidt & Hunter, 1977)	Independence of multiplicative terms	Uses Fisher's Z-adjustment for sampling error, criterion unreliability, and range restriction. No longer recommended for use by authors.
Revised noninteractive (Pearlman, Schmidt, &	Independence of multiplicative terms	With or without Fisher's Z-adjustments for

(*continued*)

TABLE 8.1. (*Continued*)

Procedure	Assumptions	Comments
Hunter, 1980; Schmidt et al., 1979)		sampling error, unreliability of tests, criteria, and range restriction. Criticized for ignoring interactions, but interaction effects found to be negligible.
Interactive (Schmidt, Gast-Rosenberg, & Hunter, 1980)	Test reliabilities, criterion reliabilities, and range restriction effects mutually uncorrelated	Simultaneous adjustment for range restriction and measurement error. Slightly more accurate estimates of percentage of variance accounted for by artifacts and slightly more conservative estimates of true validity variation than noninteractive.
Independent-multiplicative (Callender & Osburn, 1980)	Independence of multiplicative terms	Adjustments for sampling error, criterion unreliability, and range restriction
Dependent (Callender & Osburn, 1980)	Removes assumption of independence of multiplicative terms	Requires estimation of covariance of often unknown quantities and is currently of theoretical interest
Asymptotic distribution (Hedges, 1982)	Asymptotic results applicable to available samples	Requires individual study estimates of reliability and degree of range restriction. Empirical results unavailable.
Taylor series approximation (Raju, 1981a)	Pairwise independence of criterion reliabilities, test reliabilities, and ratios of SDs in restricted and unrestricted populations	Several variations involving analysis of correlations or covariances proposed. Monte Carlo results show some advantage for procedure one.
Empirical range restriction (Linn, Harnisch, & Dunbar, 1981b; Linn & Hastings, in press)	Uses empirical relation of SDs and Rs across studies to estimate range restriction effects, otherwise like noninteractive procedure	Avoids assumptions of range restriction corrections, lacks theoretical base

tude of the bias for all five procedures are reassuring. The slight overestimation of the variance in the true validities implies that the degree of validity generalization is, if anything, apt to be somewhat understated. Hence all five of the procedures compared by Raju and Burke appear viable.

Recommendations

The work on validity generalization and differential prediction has brought into question some long-standing beliefs of personnel psychology. Predictive validities of cognitive tests have been shown to be much more generalizable across situations, tasks, and groups than once believed. The work of Schmidt and Hunter and their colleagues has broken new ground and set a new standard for integrative work in personnel psychology. Still there is a danger of overgeneralizing conclusions and carrying the implications of this work too far. Generalizations are important to any scientific area, but so too are the exceptions. As Cronbach has noted, "No matter how much research accumulates, there is room for divergent interpretations" (1980, p. 102). He goes on to make the important point that "the job of validation is not to support an interpretation, but to find out what might be wrong with it" (p. 103). Our task is not only to seek generalizations, but to find and attempt to understand exceptions.

There is undoubtedly room for further refinement of the analytical procedures used in validity generalization. More comparisons of the procedures using Monte Carlo techniques as well as existing data sets would be useful. It must be recognized, however, that meta-analyses are necessarily dependent upon the quality of the information provided by the individual studies that are analyzed. Study-specific information on criterion reliability, range restriction, or regression equations is rarely available. Routine collection and reporting of such information would greatly enhance the potential yield of studies of validity generalization.

References

Albright, L. E., Glennon, J. K., & Smith, W. J. (1963). *The use of psychological tests in industry.* Cleveland, OH: Howard Allen.
American College Testing Program. (1973). *Assessing students on the way to college: Technical report for the ACT assessment program* (Vol. 1). Iowa City: American College Testing Program.
AERA/APA/NCME Joint Committee. (1985). *Standards for educational and psychological testing.* Washington, DC: American Psychological Association.
APA/AERA/NCME Joint Committee. (1974). *Standards for educational and psychological tests* (rev. ed.). Washington, DC: American Psychological Association.

APA, Division of Industrial and Organizational Psychology. (1980). *Principles for validation and use of personnel selection procedures* (2nd ed.). Berkeley, CA: Author.

Braun, H. T., & Jones, D. H. (1981). *The Graduate Management Admission Test prediction bias study* (GMAC Research Report 81-4). Princeton, NJ: Educational Testing Service.

Breland, H. M. (1978). *Population validity and college entrance measures* (College Board Research and Development Report RDR 78-79, No. 2; Research Bulletin RB78-19). Princeton, NJ: Educational Testing Service.

Callender, J. C., & Osburn, H. G. (1980). Development and test of a new model for validity generalization. *Journal of Applied Psychology, 65,* 543–558.

Callender, J. C., & Osburn, H. G. (1981). Testing the constancy of validity with computer-generated sampling distributions of the multiplicative model variance estimate: Results for petroleum industry validation research. *Journal of Applied Psychology, 66,* 274–281.

Callender, J. C., & Osburn, H. G. (1982). Another view of progress in validity generalization: Reply to Schmidt, Hunter, and Pearlman. *Journal of Applied Psychology, 67,* 846–852.

Callender, J. C., Osburn, H. G., & Greener, J. M. (1979, September). *Small sample tests of two validity generalization models.* Paper presented at the annual meeting of the American Psychological Association, New York.

Callender, J. C., Osburn, H. G., Greener, J. M., & Ashworth, S. (1982). The multiplicative validity generalization model: Accuracy of estimates as a function of sample size, mean variance and shape of the distribution of true validities. *Journal of Applied Psychology, 67,* 859–967.

Cole, N. S. (1981). Bias in testing. *American Psychologist, 36,* 1067–1077.

Cronbach, L. J. (1976). Equity in selection—Where psychometrics and political philosophy meet. *Journal of Educational Measurement, 13,* 31–41.

Cronbach, L. J. (1980). Validity on parole: How can we go straight? In W. B. Schrader (Ed.), *New directions for testing and measurement. No. 5, Measuring achievement: Progress over a decade* (pp. 99–108). San Francisco, CA: Jossey-Bass.

Dunbar, S. B. (1982). Corrections for sample selection bias. Unpublished doctoral dissertation, University of Illinois at Champaign-Urbana.

Ghiselli, E. E. (1966). *The validity of occupational aptitude tests.* New York: Wiley.

Glass, G. V. (1977). Integrating findings: The meta-analysis of research. *Review of Research in Education, 5,* 351–379.

Greener, J. M., & Osburn, H. G. (1979). An empirical study of the accuracy of corrections for restriction in range due to explicit selection. *Applied Psychological Measurement, 3,* 31–41.

Guion, R. M. (1965). *Personnel testing.* New York: McGraw-Hill.

Hedges, L. V. (1982). *Methodological problems in validity generalization.* Unpublished manuscript, University of Chicago.

Hunter, J. E. (1980a). Construct validity and validity generalization. In *Proceedings of a conference on construct validity in psychological measurement* (pp. 119–129). Princeton, NJ: U.S. Office of Personnel Management and Educational Testing Service.

Hunter, J. E. (1980b). *Test validation for twelve thousand jobs: An application of job* classification and validity generalization analysis to the General Aptitude Test Battery (GATB). Washington, DC: U.S. Employment Service, U.S. Department of Labor.

Hunter, J. E., & Schmidt, F. L. (1978). Differential and single group validity of employment tests by race: A critical analysis of three recent studies. Journal of Applied Psychology, 63, 1–11.

Hunter, J. E., Schmidt, F. L., & Hunter, R. (1979). Differential validity of employment tests by race: A comprehensive review and analysis. Psychological Bulletin, 86, 721–735.

Hunter, J. E., Schmidt, F. L., & Jackson, G. B. (1983). Advanced meta-analysis: Quantitative methods for cumulating research findings across studies. San Francisco, CA: Sage.

Jackson, G. B. (1980). Methods of integrative reviews. Review of Educational Research, 50, 438–460.

Katzell, R. A., & Dyer, F. J. (1977). Differential validity revived. Journal of Applied Psychology, 62, 137–145.

Linn, R. L. (1968). Range restriction problems in the use of self-selected groups for test validation. Psychological Bulletin, 69, 69–73.

Linn, R. L. (1973). Fair test use in selection. Review of Educational Research, 43, 139–164.

Linn, R. L. (1978). Single group validity, differential validity, and differential prediction. Journal of Applied Psychology, 63, 507–512.

Linn, R. L. (1982a). Ability testing: Individual differences, prediction, and differential predictions. In A. K. Wigdor & W. R. Garner (Eds.), Ability testing: Uses, consequences, and controversies (pp. 335–388). Washington, DC: National Academy Press.

Linn, R. L. (1982b). Admissions testing on trial. American Psychologist, 37, 279–291.

Linn, R. L. (1983a). The Pearson selection formulas: Implications for studies of predictive bias and estimates of educational effects in selected samples. Journal of Educational Measurement, 20, 1–15.

Linn, R. L. (1983b). Predictive bias as an artifact of selection procedures. In H. Wainer & S. Messick (Eds.), Advances in psychometric theory: A Festschrift for Frederic M. Lord (pp. 27–40). Hillsdale, NJ: Erlbaum.

Linn, R. L. (1984). Selection bias: Multiple meanings. Journal of Educational Measurement, 21, 33–47.

Linn, R. L., Harnisch, D. L., & Dunbar, S. B. (1981a). "Corrections" for range restriction: An empirical investigation of conditions leading to conservative corrections. Journal of Applied Psychology, 66, 655–663.

Linn, R. L., Harnisch, D. L., & Dunbar, S. B. (1981b). Validity generalization and situational specificity: An analysis of the prediction of first-year grades in law school. Applied Psychological Measurement, 5, 281–289.

Linn, R. L., & Hastings, C. N. (in press). A meta-analysis of the validity of predictors of performance in law school. Journal of Educational Measurement.

Lord, F. M., & Novick, M. R. (1968). Statistical theories of mental test scores. Reading, MA: Addison-Wesley.

Novick, M. R. (1982). Educational testing: Inferences in relevant subpopulations. *Educational Researcher, 11,* 4–10.

Novick, M. R., Jackson, P. H., Thayer, D. T., & Cole, N. S. (1972). Estimating multiple regression in groups: A cross validation study. *British Journal of Mathematical and Statistical Psychology, 25,* 33–50.

Novick, M. R., & Thayer, D. T. (1969). *An investigation of the accuracy of the Pearson selection formulas* (Research Memorandum RM 69-72). Princeton, NJ: Educational Testing Service.

Osburn, H. G., Callender, J. C., Greener, J. M., & Ashworth, S. (1983). Statistical power of tests of the situational specificity hypothesis in validity generalization studies: A cautionary note. *Journal of Applied Psychology, 68,* 115–122.

Pearlman, K. (1982). *The Bayesian approach to validity generalization: A systematic examination of the robustness or procedures and conclusions.* Unpublished doctoral dissertation, George Washington University.

Pearlman, K., Schmidt, F. L., & Hunter, J. E. (1980). Validity generalization results for tests used to predict job proficiency and training success in clerical occupations. *Journal of Applied Psychology, 65,* 373–406.

Petersen, N. S., & Novick, M. R. (1976). An evaluation of some models for culture-fair selection. *Journal of Educational Measurement, 13,* 3–29.

Raju, N. S. (1981a). *New procedures and a new model for studying validity generalization.* Unpublished manuscript, Illinois Institute of Technology.

Raju, N. S. (1981b). *A note on two procedures for validity generalization.* Unpublished manuscript, Illinois Institute of Technology.

Raju, N. S., & Burke, M. S. (1983). Two new procedures for studying validity generalization. *Journal of Applied Psychology, 68,* 382–395.

Rubin, D. B. (1980). Using empirical Bayes techniques in the law school validity studies. *Journal of the American Statistical Association, 75,* 801–816.

Ruch, W. W. (1972, September). *A re-analysis of published differential validity studies.* Paper presented at the annual meeting of the American Psychological Association, Honolulu.

Rosenthal, R. (1979). The "file drawer problem" and tolerance for null results. *Psychological Bulletin, 86,* 638–641.

Schmidt, F. L., Berner, J. G., & Hunter, J. E. (1973). Racial differences in validity of employment tests: Reality or illusion? *Journal of Applied Psychology, 53,* 5–9.

Schmidt, F. L., Gast-Rosenberg, I., & Hunter, J. E. (1980). Test of a new model of validity generalization: Results for computer programmers. *Journal of Applied Psychology, 65,* 643–661.

Schmidt, F. L., & Hunter, J. E. (1977). Development of a general solution to the problem of validity generalization. *Journal of Applied Psychology, 62,* 529–540.

Schmidt, F. L., & Hunter, J. E. (1981). Employment testing: Old theories and new research findings. *American Psychologist, 36,* 1128–1137.

Schmidt, F. L., Hunter, J. E., & Caplan, J. K. (1981). Validity generalization results for two job groups in the petroleum industry. *Journal of Applied Psychology, 66,* 261–273.

Schmidt, F., Hunter, J., & Pearlman, K. (1981a). *Analysis of criticisms of validity generalization research and selection programs based on cumulative validity generalization findings.* Unpublished manuscript.

Schmidt, F. L., Hunter, J. E., & Pearlman, K. (1981b). Task differences as moderators of aptitude test validity in selection: A red herring. *Journal of Applied Psychology, 66,* 166–185.

Schmidt, F. L., Hunter, J. E., & Pearlman, K. (1982). Progress in validity generalization: Comments on Callender and Osburn and further developments. *Journal of Applied Psychology, 67,* 835–845.

Schmidt, F. L., Hunter, J. E., Pearlman, K., & Shane, G. S. (1979). Further tests of the Schmidt-Hunter Bayesian validity generalization procedure. *Personnel Psychology, 32,* 257–281.

Schmidt, F. L., Pearlman, K., & Hunter, J. E. (1980). The validity and fairness of employment and educational tests for Hispanic Americans: A review and analysis. *Personnel Psychology, 33,* 705–724.

Schrader, W. B. (1971). The predictive validity of College Board Admissions Tests. In W. H. Angoff (Ed.), *The College Board Admissions Testing Program: A technical report on research and development activities relating to the Scholastic Aptitude Test and Achievement Tests.* New York: College Entrance Examination Board.

Shepard, L. A. (1982). Definitions of bias. In R. A. Berk (Ed.), *Handbook of methods for detecting test bias* (pp. 9–30). Baltimore, MD: Johns Hopkins University Press.

Tenopyr, M. L. (1981). The realities of employment testing. *American Psychologist, 36,* 1120–1127.

U.S. Equal Employment Opportunity Commission, U.S. Civil Service Commission, U.S. Department of Labor, & U.S. Department of Justice. (1978). Uniform guidelines on employee selection procedures. *Federal Register, 43*(166), 38290–38309.

U.S. Equal Employment Opportunity Commission, U.S. Civil Service Commission, U.S. Department of Labor, & U.S. Department of Justice. (1979). Adoption of questions and answers to clarify and provide a common interpretation of the Uniform Guidelines on Employee Selection Procedures. *Federal Register, 44,* 11996–12009.

U.S. Office of Personnel Management and Educational Testing Service (1980). *Proceedings of a conference on construct validity in psychological measurement.* Princeton, NJ: Author.

9. PERFORMANCE DISTRIBUTION ASSESSMENT

Jeffrey S. Kane

Introduction

The search for a breakthrough on the problem of appraising job performance has been underway ever since the deficiencies of graphic rating scales were first recognized about sixty years ago. This effort has focused on finding alternative ways to structure the rating task and has been so thorough that it has exhausted just about all of the possible ways of gathering data through ratings. The net result, as recent reviews have suggested, is that none of these alternative rating configurations has emerged as clearly superior to the others. One is forced to conclude that the long-sought breakthrough lies, not in some as yet untried configuration of the same standard set of components that has been relied upon until now, but rather in a more fundamental reconceptualization of the measurement problem. Any such rethinking of the problem has to begin with the most elementary question: What is this phenomenon called performance that has successfully defied adequate measurement for so long?

WHAT IS PERFORMANCE?

Performance is not a characteristic of a person, like a trait or an ability, but is instead a phenomenon unto itself. However, nowhere in the appraisal literature is an attempt made to define this phenomenon. This failure to explicitly define the independent existence of performance has played a major role in retarding advances in the appraisal field. Unless there is a clear conception of *what* is to be measured, it is impossible to design procedures to *do* the measurement effectively. Performance on a job as a whole is the net result of the performances on the job's component functions. Thus, if performance on each of a job's component functions can be measured, the combination of such measures will yield a measure of performance on the job as a whole. This still does not define performance, but it narrows the focus of interest to performance on job functions. The following definition of performance on a job function is proposed:

Performance on a job function is the record of outcomes achieved in carrying out the job function during a specified period.

This definition can be narrowed still further by recognizing the distinction between two basic types of job functions:

Iterated job functions *are those that are carried out on two or more occasions during an appraisal period.*
Noniterated job functions *are those that are carried out only once during an appraisal period.*

Most functions in most jobs are of the iterated type, and it is functions of this type that also present the greatest difficulties from a measurement standpoint. Accordingly, attention will be limited to the measurement of performance on such iterated functions. Such performance can be defined as follows:

Performance on an iterated job function is the record of outcomes achieved over the multiple instances of carrying out the function during a specified period.

FIGURE 9.1. Example of performance distribution

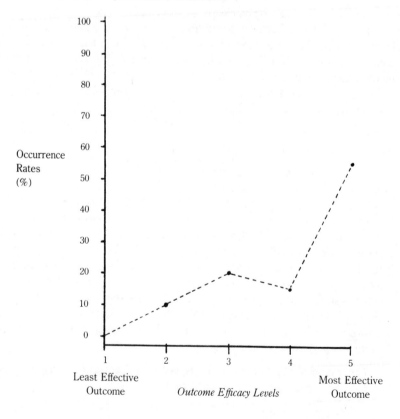

In order to move from the definition of a performance to its measurement, it is necessary to pass through the intermediate step of devising a way to represent performance in quantifiable terms. This representation is called a *performance distribution*.

Quantifiable representation of performance. A performance distribution is a specification of the rates at which a performer achieved all of the potential outcome levels that could be achieved in carrying out a job function during a specified period. The *rate* at which a performer achieved a specified outcome level is the percentage of all the times he or she carried out the particular job function on which he or she achieved the specified outcome level. This information may be specified in either tabular or graphic form. Figure 9.1 illustrates the graph of a hypothetical performance distribution.

A performance distribution comprehensively portrays the record of outcomes achieved in the course of executing an iterated job function during a specified period. In addition, it can be quantified in exactly the same way as any other distribution: numbers called *efficacy values* can be assigned to the outcome categories, and these numbers can then be multiplied by the occurrence rates for their respective outcome categories. The sum of these products is the mean of the distribution, which can then be used as the basis for computing the standard deviation and other higher moments around the mean. The question that arises, however, is, Which of these parameters of performance distributions reflect meaningful information about the performance that is portrayed? How this question is answered constitutes the central basis for distinguishing the alternative measurement models that can be applied to the appraisal of performance.

Review of Alternative Measurement Models

The designation of one or a subset of the parameters of a performance distribution as a source of meaningful information about performance is not an arbitrary or haphazard judgment. It is the logically required consequence of a well-defined theoretical view of the sources of error and nonerror variance in performance. In this section, the measurement model that has conventionally been applied to performance appraisal will be described in an attempt to convey its theoretical rationale for ascribing meaningfulness to only a single parameter of performance distributions. This description will be followed by the presentation of a new measurement model that is proposed as a more realistic framework on which to base the appraisal of performance.

PHYSICAL MEASUREMENT MODEL

All existing approaches to performance appraisal are based on the physical measurement model. Borrowed directly from the physical sciences, it assumes that a person's record of performance is a function of the product of the person's fixed ability to perform and fixed level of motivation. Each instance of executing an iterated job function is viewed as an observation on the direct manifestation of that fixed capability–fixed motivation product. One of the most firmly established principles of measurement in the physical sciences is that the average of multiple observations of a fixed-state phenomenon's status will be the best estimate of the true value of the phenomenon's status (measurement error being assumed to be random). In applying this model to the appraisal of iterated job function performance, it is accordingly assumed that the true value of such performance is reflected by the average outcome level achieved over multiple instances of carrying out the function. Furthermore, it is assumed that all variations around the average outcome level are due to random measurement error. Thus, according to this model, the average of a performance distribution is the only parameter on which nonerror differences between distributions can occur. The following postulates summarize this model as it applies to the measurement of iterated job function performance:

1. Both ability and effort are fixed and stable within individuals.
2. The outcomes that a performer achieves are determined by the multiplicative combination of the performer's fixed ability and fixed effort.
3. Being completely determined by fixed characteristics, performance itself is a fixed-state phenomenon.
4. Like any other fixed-state phenomenon, performance has a fixed true value that is best estimated by the mean of multiple observations on its status, which are the separate outcomes achieved in the case of performance.
5. Variation around the mean of a distribution of outcomes is normally distributed and solely reflects random measurement error.
6. Extraneous constraints on the achievement of outcomes either are nonexistent or remain constant over all trials, and in either case are not a source of variation in performance distributions.

DISTRIBUTIONAL MEASUREMENT MODEL

The application of the physical measurement model to performance appraisal runs into conflict with two widely recognized realities. First, motivational levels are generally considered to vary even over very short periods of time and not to be fixed like abilities. Second, the outcomes achieved from trial to trial are subject to the restrictive influence of variable extraneous constraints beyond the performer's control. (They are also subject to extraneous facilitative influences beyond the performer's control, but these will be ignored for present purposes.)

Variation in the effort that a person exerts in performing any iterated job function will be manifested as variation around the mean of the person's performance distribution on the function. The particular pattern of variation exhibited by a person will be idiosyncratic, meaning that it will differ between individuals as the result of the unique nature and extent of each person's encounters with motivationally relevant events and the person's responsiveness to them. Individuals are assumed to have control over the extent to which they allow their motivational variation to affect their performance distributions.

Variation in the extraneous constraints on the achievement of outcomes on a job function will also be reflected as variation around the mean of a person's performance distribution on the function. This pattern of variation will also be idiosyncratic, being determined by the particular pattern of such constraints that a person encounters during a given appraisal period. However, individuals are assumed to have *no* control over the extent to which this source of variation affects their performance distributions.

It is clearly legitimate for an organization to hold its members accountable for all those facets of performance that are subject to control by the individual. Since motivational variations are subject to individual control, it follows that it is legitimate to hold individual members accountable for the effects of such motivational variations on their performance distributions. (Whether or not such accountability should actually be imposed in the case of any particular job function is determined by whether or not the distributional parameters affected by motivational variation—standard deviation, skewness, etc.—reflect characteristics of performance that the organization values in the particular job function.) However, it is also clear that the effects of motivational variations on performance distributions must be isolated from the effects of variations due to fluctuating extraneous constraints. The latter variation, by definition, is due to factors beyond the performer's control.

Thus it can be concluded that the appropriate measurement model on which to base the assessment of performance is one that designates both central tendency and the variation-based parameters of a performance distribution as sources of potentially meaningful information about performance. The conventional physical measurement model does not meet these specifications; hence the need to propose a new model for measuring performance. In the context of the measurement of performance on iterated job functions, this model consists of the following postulates:

1. The outcomes that a performer achieves are determined by the multiplicative combination of the performer's fixed abilities and variable motivational levels, as restricted by variable extraneous constraints.
2. The mean of a performance distribution reflects the effect of the performer's fixed ability level in multiplicative combination with his or her average moti-

vational level, as restricted by the average level of extraneous constraints encountered.

3. The variation-based parameters of a performance distribution reflect the effects of variations in the performer's motivational level plus variations in the extraneous constraints encountered.

4. Variation around the mean of a performance distribution is distributed idio- syncratically, not normally.

5. Variation within a performance distribution derives from two sources: a portion attributable to fluctuations in the performer's motivational level and a portion attributable to variable extraneous constraints. No portion of the variation is considered to derive from random measurement error.

Up to this point, we have focused on the definition of performance, the representation of performance in quantifiable terms, and the parameters along which it can meaningfully vary. All of these considerations are prerequisites for addressing the question of how performance should be measured, to which we now turn.

Measurement of Performance on Iterated Job Functions

Measurement is defined as the assignment of a *number* to an instance of a *specified category of objects or events* to express the status of the given instance on some *attribute* by which all instances of the specified object or event category can be characterized. The italicized parts of this definition refer to the essential elements that must be specified in order for a measurement activity to occur. Stated more explicitly, and in the order in which they will be addressed, these three elements are as follows: (1) the category of objects or events from which selected instances are to be measured; (2) the attribute on which the statuses of instances of the specified object/event category are to be expressed; and (3) the level at which the set of numbers to be used for expressing statuses on the attribute will be scaled.

Just as any spatial area delineated by boundaries can be referred to as a domain, in an analogous manner the area of conceptual activity delineated by these definitional elements will be referred to as the *measurement domain.*

In the preceding definition of measurement, reference was made to "the assignment of a number." This phrase implies that a human agent must play a role in the causation or execution of this assignment process. This role can range from the minimal one of simply causing an assignment process to be activated and determining that the requisite assignment of numbers has actually been carried out to the maximal one of personally carrying out the assignment process. The nature and extent of this role are defined by a *measurement procedure.* A measure- ment procedure specifies the judgments and actions that must be carried out in the number assignment process and allocates responsibility for them between the human and instrument components of the process. A measurement procedure consists, therefore, of a measuring instrument (embodying the judgments and actions allocated to the instrument component), a human role specification, and the rules for the conduct of the human role.

Measurement procedures can vary along two dimensions. The first of these is *instrumentation dominance,* which can range from a minimum condition in which the only instrument is a piece of paper on which the human measurer writes down the number he or she has assigned to each instance, to a maximum condition of complete instrument control over all actions between the decision to measure and the reception of the assigned numbers by humans. *Rule specificity,* the second dimension, is bounded at the minimum end of its range by rules for conducting the broadest, most complex discrete units of activity into which the measurement process can be decomposed. At this minimum level of specificity, the rules specify the contingencies to take into account in making assignment decisions but not the procedures for doing so. The maximum state of rule specificity occurs at the point where the rules dictate the timing and sequence of the most narrowly defined, least complex units of activity into which the measurement process can be decomposed. At this maximum level of specificity, the rules specify both the contingent conditions to consider and the procedures for taking them into account.

The discussion of measurement up to this point has revealed the necessity of addressing two distinct classes of problems whenever measurement is attempted: the definition of the measurement domain and the design of the measurement procedure. By further revealing the specific issues that must be addressed within each of these problem classes, the foregoing analysis has provided a framework for systematically considering the key conceptual dimensions of the design of systems to measure performance. Imposing this analytical framework upon performance appraisal can be expected to uncover sources of deficiencies in conventional methods, and approaches to remedying them, that were not apparent from the perspectives that have previously guided attempts to analyze the problems of performance measurement. With this expectation, we will now proceed to analyze the problems of measurement domain definition and measurement procedure specification as they relate to the measurement of iterated job function performance.

MEASUREMENT DOMAIN DEFINITION

Designating the object/event category. The object/event category designated to be measured varies principally along a generality-specificity dimension. The less specificity with which the object/event category is described, the more difficult it becomes to define the rules for number assignment precisely. For example, if an appraisal system designates overall job performance as the object/event category to be measured, it implicitly requires that consideration be given to all of the functions encompassed by a job and to the levels achieved on all of the distinct parameters of the performance distribution for each relevant criterion (i.e., quality, quantity, timeliness, cost effectiveness, interpersonal effectiveness, need for supervision) for each of the functions. Imagine the difficulty in trying to specify all of the possible combinations that would qualify for each possible standing on overall job performance. So great is the difficulty, in fact, that the attempt to specify all of the possible combinations is virtually never made. Instead, the rater is left entirely to his or her own devices to come up with a rating.

The problem is reduced, but still present, if the object/event category is designated to be overall performance on a job function. Although performances of multiple job functions would not have to be combined, the relevant criteria and the parameters of the performance distributions on each criterion that should be considered, as well as the rules for combining statuses on the parameters and on the criteria, would still have to be specified. The complexity of such requirements has apparently discouraged any attempts to satisfy them, since existing appraisal methods that require raters to appraise overall job function performance do not specify the criteria and the performance distribution parameters on the criteria that raters should consider or should exclude from consideration.

It is clear, therefore, that when a *judgment about* performance is requested from a rater, the object/event category should be designated in terms of a single performance distribution parameter on a single criterion for a single job function. This parameter-criterion–job function combination is the "thing" that each of the measurements that an appraisal system comprises should measure. Any broader designation of the object/event category results either in rules for number assignment that are too complicated for raters to follow or in the abdication of control over the number assignment process to the whim of the rater. Note, however, that when the rater is simply asked to *describe* the performance distribution in a form that permits the subsequent computation of the distributional parameter indexes, the specification of the object/event category does not need to include the parameter. It only needs to designate the criterion–job function combination. Note also that these remarks only apply to the specification of those object/event categories that are the focus of *direct* measurement. Direct measurement refers to the initial set of numbers assigned to express the statuses (or to provide the data for computing the statuses) of instances of an object/event category on an attribute (i.e., the ratings elicited from a rater). These numbers (or the indices computed from them) subsequently may be mechanically combined in various ways to produce numbers that reflect statuses on higher-order object/event categories (e.g., overall job function performance, overall job performance) and on higher-order measurement attributes (see below). Such measurements produced by the combination of measurements on constituent object/event categories (or on lower-order measurement attributes) will be termed *derived* measurements.

Specifying the attribute on which statuses are to be expressed. There are three attributes on which the parameters of performance distributions can be measured:

1. *Parametric magnitude* is the value of a distributional parameter (e.g., mean, standard deviation, or negative range incidence) computed using the efficacy values of the outcome categories over which a distribution extends and the occurrence rates of these categories. The efficacy values attached to the outcome categories are numbers that represent the degree of favorability or utility of the categories over which the outcomes of the job function can conceivably vary. The scale formed by these numbers (which shall be called an *efficacy scale*) may have ordinal, interval, or ratio properties. The parametric magnitude values will be referred to in abbreviated form as *PM scores*.

2. *Effectiveness* is the extent to which an attained PM score approaches a value defined as the ideal or peak value. This peak value may be defined in reference to the maximally desirable value of a distributional parameter that is mathematically or logically possible on the particular scale of efficacy values being used; in this case *absolute* effectiveness is measured. Alternatively, it may be defined in reference to the maximally desirable value that is feasible to achieve under prevailing circumstances; in this case *relativistic* effectiveness is measured. The extent to which a PM score approaches its absolute or relativistic peak value can be measured on any type of scale: ordinal, interval, ratio, or the new type to be proposed shortly.

3. *Satisfactoriness* is the degree to which the level of effectiveness that a job incumbent exhibits is satisfactory to the organization.

The important point that should be recognized in this postulation of the three measurable attributes of the parameters of performance distributions is the *hierarchical dependence* between the attributes. The most directly measurable attribute of performance is the parametric magnitude of each parameter of a performance distribution. Since the performer's attained magnitude and the peak value of a distributional parameter must be measured before the effectiveness achieved on the parameter can be measured, it is appropriate to characterize the measurement of effectiveness as being hierarchically dependent upon the measurement of parametric magnitude. Similarly, since the attained level of effectiveness on a parameter must be measured before assigning a satisfactoriness score to the performance, the measurement of satisfactoriness is hierarchically dependent on the measurement of effectiveness.

The hierarchical dependence among the attributes on which performance can be measured does not alter the fact that the "bottom line" for practically all work organizations is the satisfactoriness of performance. Appraisal methods in conventional use generally reflect this focus of organizational concern (or they do not remain in conventional use for long). The hierarchical dependence among the attributes reveals, however, that satisfactoriness levels do not have to be directly measured, but instead can be derived from measurements of either of the lower-order attributes on which satisfactoriness is dependent. In fact, satisfactoriness measurements can even be derived from a procedure that generates as its initial output the unprocessed observations from which PM scores are computed. The feasibility of employing derived approaches to producing satisfactoriness scores raises the possibility that such approaches might hold some advantages over the direct approach used by most conventional appraisal methods. Consideration of this possibility, however, will be postponed until the section addressing the design of the measurement procedure.

Selecting the type of scale to use in expressing statuses. Stevens (1951) postulated four basic types of measurement scales, which can be distinguished from each other by the degree of precision with which they describe statuses on attributes. In ascending order of the degree of precision they offer, these four basic scale types are as follows: nominal, ordinal, interval, and ratio scales. Since degree of precision is the principal characteristic that distinguishes these scale types, the issue to be decided in choosing among them is the degree of precision needed by the measurement task to be accomplished. Performance appraisal requires more precision than nominal scales offer and at least enough precision to be able to order performances on one or more of the measurement attributes. Most of the uses of appraisal also require a system that indicates the distance separating the effectiveness of different performances. In the use of appraisal as a basis for standards-based reward allocation, as well as for certain selection and placement decisions, it will also be necessary to know the actual level or magnitude of effectiveness that each performance represents. But this raises an interesting problem, apparently unforeseen by Stevens.

The ratio scale, which is the most precise type of scale proposed by Stevens, is distinguished by the fact that it provides a known zero point in addition to employing constant units of measurement. However, such scales are not required to have an upper limit—theoretically, they can extend to infinity. As a consequence, the points on a ratio scale do not necessarily convey any information about an entity's standing within the maximum limits of the attribute being measured. However, if an upper limit is imposed on a ratio scale, or if an upper limit is intrinsic to the attribute on which the entity is being measured (e.g., speed), the points on the scale can provide this additional meaning. In fact, the distance of each point from the lower limit can be divided by the distance between the upper and lower limits, yielding a scale of percentages. Scales that have both a known zero point and an upper limit will be called *hermeneutic* (meaning interpretive) scales to distinguish them from ratio scales. This name is intended to focus attention on the unique characteristic of these scales—each point on such a scale can be interpreted as a proportion of the maximum level that could be attained on the attribute.

Examples of scales that either have imposed or intrinsic zero points and upper limits include (1) the miles per second scale of speed (0 to 186,000 miles per second, since the speed of light is an absolute upper limit) and (2) the atmospheric saturation scale, which, although conventionally expressed as relative humidity percentage, exists in parallel form as a scale of parts per million of water particles adjusted for atmospheric temperature and ranges from zero to the ppm maximum for each temperature level. More generally, whenever an index is found that is expressed in percentage terms, the scale on which it occurs will be a hermeneutic one (e.g., unemployment rate, batting average, and disease fatality rate).

Hermeneutic scales are uniquely capable of providing the measurements of the level of performance between the zero point and some upper limit that certain important personnel decisions require. Moreover, by providing the highest level of measurement precision, this type of scale can satisfy the precision requirements of all less demanding personnel decisions. It therefore appears to furnish a metric on which a broad spectrum of personnel decisions can be based. Given the potential utility of this new scale type, it seems appropriate to elaborate its most important characteristics.

One aspect of hermeneutic scales that needs further elaboration concerns the alternative approaches to establishing the limits of such scales and their respective advantages. The alternative approaches to establishing the scale limits are the same as those available for defining the upper limit in the case of effectiveness—absolute and relativistic. The absolute approach requires the determination, on theoretical, mathematical, or logical grounds, of the zero point and the upper limit that instances of the object/event category could assume on the measurement attribute. The absolute zero point and the absolute upper limit have very different meanings in relation to parametric magnitude, as compared to their use in relation to effectiveness and satisfactoriness.

For parametric magnitude, the absolute zero point for each parameter refers to the state of the performance distribution at which the value of the statistical index measuring the parameter is zero. In contrast, for effectiveness and satisfactoriness, the absolute zero point for each parameter coincides with that state of the performance distribution where the value of the statistical index measuring the parameter is as distantly removed from the most favorable value of the index as is mathematically possible.

The absolute upper limit of the parametric magnitude of a distributional parameter refers to the state of the performance distribution where the value of the statistical index measuring the parameter is at its maximum, given the set of scale values defined for the efficacy levels in the given case. For effectiveness and satisfactoriness, the absolute upper limit for each parameter refers to that state of the performance distribution where the value of the statistical index measuring the parameter is at the most favorable level that is theoretically, mathematically, or logically possible. Table 9.1 reveals how these differences in meanings are specifically manifested in the definitions of the absolute zero point and the absolute

TABLE 9.1. Definitions of Absolute Zero Points and Absolute Upper Limits

Parameter	Absolute Zero Point	Absolute Upper Limit
1. Central Tendency		
PM Score	A mean, median, or mode (whichever is being used as the central tendency index) with a value of zero	100% occurrence rate of the level with the most extremely positive scale value
Effectiveness	100% occurrence rate of the efficacy level with the most extremely negative scale value	Same as for PM score
Satisfactoriness	Same as for effectiveness	Same as for PM score
2. Standard Deviation		
PM Score	100% occurrence rate for any one efficacy level (which yields a zero standard deviation)	50% occurrence rates for both the extreme highest and lowest efficacy levels
Effectiveness	50% occurrence rates for the extreme highest and lowest efficacy levels (which yields the highest conceivable standard deviation representing the lowest conceivable degree of consistency)	100% occurrence rate for any one efficacy level
Satisfactoriness	Same as for effectiveness	Same as for effectiveness
3. Negative Range Incidence		
PM Score	Zero occurrence rates for all negatively valued efficacy levels	100% occurrence rate for the efficacy level with the most strongly negative scale value
Effectiveness	100% occurrence rate for the efficacy level with the most strongly negative scale value	Zero occurrence rates for all negatively valued efficacy levels
Satisfactoriness	Same as for effectiveness	Same as for effectiveness

upper limit on each attribute for each of the three basic distributional parameters.

The problem with using absolute zero points and absolute upper limits for the measurement of performance is that they can represent performances that differ markedly in their feasibility of attainment depending on the particular job function involved, the particular position in which the job function occurs, the particular job under consideration, and the particular period during which the performance occurs. For example, in most jobs the incumbents would never be allowed even to approach the absolute zero point in effectiveness on any of their job functions; they would undoubtedly be relieved of responsibility for any such functions long before such a point was reached. Thus use of the absolute zero point of effectiveness amounts to giving people credit for avoiding a range of performance that they would never be allowed to exhibit. Similarly, absolute upper limits of effectiveness usually refer to levels of performance that in many cases cannot be achieved owing to extraneous constraints beyond the performer's control. The effect of using such unattainable upper limits is to penalize performers for failing to achieve portions of the range of performance that were, in fact, impossible to achieve, which is unfair. Another reason why absolute upper limits are inappropriate has to do with the fact that the parameters of performance distributions are interdependent. For example, the maximum possible range of standard deviation varies inversely as a function of the distance of the mean from the scale midpoint. The use of absolute upper limits in measuring effectiveness on the standard deviation (i.e., consistency) parameter would ignore such interdependence and would, in effect, redundantly assign credit or blame for portions of the performance on this parameter that were entirely due to the level achieved on the mean parameter. The effects of both of these types of extraneous constraints should be removed from consideration in the appraisal of performance.

The way to exclude the effects of extraneous constraints is to employ a *relativistic* basis for establishing the zero point and the upper limit. Relativizing these scale points consists of moving the zero point upward and the upper limit downward in order to account for limitations in the allowability or feasibility of attaining the absolute limiting values of each parameter. This approach should be applied only to effectiveness scales in the context of performance appraisal; it should not be applied to parametric magnitude scales because scores on such scales (i.e., PM scores) are never generated for the purpose of being directly interpreted as indices of performance. Their only function is to serve as input into the transformation process that first yields effectiveness scores and then satisfactoriness scores. Relativizing these scores would only serve to eliminate their intrinsic mathematical meaning, which would make it very difficult to link appraisal results back to the raw ratings of performance level occurrence rates in order to verify the accuracy of ratings. Thus PM scores should never be generated on relativistic hermeneutic scales. PM scores that are to serve as the basis for relativistic hermeneutic effectiveness scores should only be generated on ratio or absolute hermeneutic scales.

Satisfactoriness scores should not be relativized, but for a different reason. Satisfactoriness scales consist of intervals defined in terms of ranges of effectiveness levels that represent specified degrees of adequacy according to the organization's value scheme. This is not a relativistic judgment. Any considerations of relativity in the limits of performance must be accounted for in the generation of effectiveness scores.

The 0 percent lower limit of relativistic hermeneutic scales of effectiveness designates the level (of a parametric magnitude, or of a combination of such magnitudes expressing overall performance on a criterion–job function combination, or of the average of such combinations expressing overall job function performance, or of the overall average expressing overall job performance) that is as far removed from the perfect level as would have been *allowed* to occur. The upper limit of 100 percent on such scales designates the most nearly perfect level (of parametric magnitude, criterion-specific performance, job function performance, or overall job performance) that a fully qualified performer could possibly have achieved under the circumstances that prevailed during the performance period. The range over which the effectiveness of performance is assessed is thereby restricted to those levels of performance that were possible for a fully qualified performer to have achieved. All variation in the levels of distributional parameters that is attributable to extraneous factors beyond the control of performers is thereby eliminated from consideration on such scales—a major advantage over any other scale type.

The use of relativistic upper and lower limits has the effect of rescaling the absolute effectiveness level achieved on each job function onto a new, relativistic, effectiveness scale with limits that have a common meaning across all job functions, jobs, organizational subdivisions, and even organizations. On this new scale, each percentage level denotes the percentage of best *possible* performance that the performer achieved. Thus the device of relativistic limits in conjunction with hermeneutic scaling allows the creation of scales that permit the effectiveness of all performers to be expressed in terms of a common range of identically defined intervals. The significance of this capability emerges fully as we turn next to an examination of how it allows appraisal to resolve a dilemma that is as old as the concept of appraisal itself.

Performance appraisal has historically been plagued by what I call the *standardization-particularization dilemma*. This dilemma derives from the recognition, on the one hand, that measurements of job performance will be more accurate if they take into account the distinctive content and context of the work encountered in each particular position. On the other hand, up to now the preservation of comparability between appraisal scores has required the use of standardized scales that do not discriminate between particular positions.

Existing approaches to performance measurement, for the most part, employ standardization rather than particularization as their approach to constructing rating scales. The reason for this choice seems to be that particularization is incongruent with the statistical basis for score comparability claimed (and valued over all else) by most extant approaches. The Thurstone or Likert scaling techniques employed in most appraisal methods generate scale values statistically, which requires the generation of scaling data on fairly large samples (e.g., twenty or more). Consequently, such methods do not allow scales to be particularized for groups of positions for which fewer than twenty qualified respondents can be identified. Any factors that differentiate the content or context of the work of groups of less than twenty positions or of individual positions must consequently be ignored by such models.

The one notable exception to the choice of standardization over particularization occurs in the case of MBO (management by objectives) and its offshoots (e.g., work planning and progress review). These methods generally develop scales for each individual position, using highly particularized efficacy level descriptions as standards for each satisfactoriness interval. The only drawback to this approach, and unfortunately it's a devastating one, is that it has no provision for ensuring that the efficacy level descriptions used as the standards for any given level of satisfactoriness represent comparable levels of effectiveness between job functions, positions, jobs at the same organizational level, supervisors, and so on. Fundamental precepts of equity dictate that the requirements for classifying performance in a given satisfactoriness category be comparably stringent (i.e., equally near to the absolute or, preferably, the relativistic upper limit), at the least, among positions with the same job title and, more generally, among jobs with pay range midpoints equal to the same proportion of their respective job market averages. In MBO-type appraisal systems, each rater is essentially left to decide on his or her own, for each job function, position, and job, the degree of stringency to impose in setting the level of effectiveness required for each satisfactoriness category and how to define those levels in terms of outcomes and their occurrence rates. Given the complete absence of control over this idiosyncratic method of standard setting, there is no possibility of achieving the comparability in stringency that equity requires, nor even of assessing the extent to which this requirement has been missed.

The ability to measure effectiveness on relativistic hermeneutic scales allows the performance appraisal process to escape the horns of the standardization-particularization dilemma. On the one hand, this type of scale imposes no restrictions on the extent to which the descriptions and scale values of the efficacy levels for each job function can be particularized to account for the effects of any differentiating factor, such as work assignment differences between positions, work group differences, and distinctions between geographic locations and appraisal periods. Similarly, the relativistic upper and lower limits of the performance distribution that could be achieved over each job function's efficacy levels can be particularized to account for any or all of these same factors. On the other hand, no matter how particularized the efficacy level descriptions, efficacy scale values, and relativistic limits of effectiveness get, relativistic hermeneutic effectiveness scales place all scores on a common 0–100 scale of percentages, where each level has identical meaning across all distributional parameters, criteria, job functions, jobs, or aggregations of jobs. That is, any given percentage score means that the attained performance reached a point equal to the given percentage of the maximum level feasible. This interpretation applies to effectiveness scores on all distributional parameters and to the average effectiveness scores over all the distributional parameters, over all job function criteria, over all job functions, and over any higher aggregate (i.e., the average effectiveness scores over any group of jobs). Thus measuring the effectiveness of performance on a relativistic hermeneutic scale provides the capability of achieving any extreme of particularization without any sacrifice of the comparability normally achieved through scale standardization.

There are two general types of particularizing conditions that should be accounted for when relativistic hermeneutic effectiveness scales are applied within the framework of the distributional measurement model to appraise performance. The first is the *endogenous* type, which consists of characteristics intrinsic to a scaling methodology that cause aberrations in the relativistic limits, in the efficacy level descriptions, and in the efficacy scale values. The prime example of this type of particularizing condition is the restrictive effect of a distribution's mean on the range of the distribution's standard deviation and negative range incidence. The restrictive effect of a distribution's mean should always be reflected in the relativistic limits used in measuring these latter two parameters. More generally, conditions of this type should always be accounted for.

The other type of particularizing condition is the *exogenous* type, which stems from differentiating conditions originating from sources outside of the measurement system. These conditions include distinctions between job functions, positions, jobs, supervisors, appraisal periods, work groups, work locations, and so forth, which can cause a relativistic limit, an efficacy level description, or an efficacy scale value to be applicable to one position and not to another. The guideline to follow in accounting for conditions of this type is that the relativistic limits, efficacy level descriptions, and efficacy scale values should be particularized to the point where the resulting scale only applies to a set of positions that do not differ with regard to any conditions likely to affect the scale's applicability. Within this guideline, scales should be constructed to apply to as many positions as possible, which will reduce the burden on administrators and raters by minimizing the number of narrowly applicable scales that have to be developed, used, and scored.

It was asserted earlier that scale type should be selected on the basis of the closeness of the match between the level of precision offered by each of the scale-type alternatives and the highest level needed by any of the purposes for which the performance measurements are intended to be used. This assertion remains valid for choices among Stevens's four basic scale types. However, the proposal of the two types of hermeneutic scales (absolute and relativistic) requires that the need for the additional features uniquely offered by hermeneutic scales also be considered in selecting a scale type. Briefly summarized, these additional potentially useful features are as follows:

1. Expression of the (absolute or relativistic) magnitude, in addition to the order, interval, and ratio, of statuses on the attribute on which performance is measured.
2. Exclusion of the impact of extraneous influences on performance from consideration in the determination of statuses on the measurement attribute (for the case of relativistic hermeneutic scales only).
3. Scoring in a universally applicable metric (percentage of maximum feasible performance), which ensures that each score level will denote an achievement of identical relative magnitude across all job functions, jobs, work groups, and all higher level aggregates (relativistic version only).
4. Allowance of maximum particularization of scale limits, efficacy level descriptions, and efficacy scale values without loss of the ability to directly compare scores across job functions, positions, jobs, etc. (relativistic version only).

These features, particularly as they are found occurring simultaneously in the relativistic version of these scales, will frequently be valued even in situations where the highest level of precision with which statuses need to be expressed is considerably below that offered by hermeneutic scales. In such situations the cost of the excess amount of precision must be weighed against the benefits that accrue to the other features of hermeneutic scales in order to arrive at an optimal choice. The relative ease of creating a hermeneutically scaled measurement system, which the latter part of this chapter will make apparent, should shift the balance to the choice of this scale type in a substantial number of cases where less precise types were formerly considered adequate.

MEASUREMENT PROCEDURE SPECIFICATION

The instrumentation dominance dimension. Measurement is a human contrivance, imposed upon objects and events that exist (in most cases) in a state of utter indifference as to whether or not they are measured. Since it is, in this sense, a human activity, measurement cannot occur unless humans play at least a minimal role in its conduct. The extent of the role that humans play in a measurement procedure, relative to the extent of the role that inanimate measurement instruments play, represents the status of the measurement procedure on what is called the *instrumentation dominance* dimension.

One of the most well-learned lessons from mankind's attempts at measurement over the millennia can be stated as the following principle: freedom from error of measurement varies inversely with the relative extent of the human role in the measurement procedure. That is, the greatest freedom from error results from the least human involvement in the measurement process. The most accurate measurements occur in the physical sciences, where the human role can be reduced to the minimal one of selecting the sample to be measured, activating the measurement procedure, and reading the measurement results. This is the nature of the human role, for example, in the use of electronic instruments for the measurement of electromagnetic and nuclear (i.e., radiation) phenomena. To the extent that the human role increases beyond this minimum and assumes measurement functions that are instrumented in the ideal case, the fallibility of the measurement procedure increases.

The human role in the measurement procedures employed by performance appraisal methods in conventional use dominates the role played by the instrumentation. The extent of the human role in these measurement procedures can be revealed by conducting a flowchart-like analysis of the process that underlies any method of appraisal. Such an analysis would delineate the nature and sequence of the steps that would have to be programmed into a computer that was to be used to carry out the entire process. Given the machine logic basis for the analysis, it will be called a *cybernetic* analysis. The purpose of such an analysis is not only to reveal the steps that a procedure currently assigns to humans, but also to reveal steps that do not require exclusively human capabilities for their conduct and that could therefore be assigned to the instrument component.

The cybernetic analysis of the appraisal process to be presented shortly does not purport to describe how the human mind would carry out any of the steps of the appraisal process. However, it does reveal what steps have to be carried out in some way by human cognitive processes when those steps are assigned to humans.

In presenting this cybernetic analysis, it will be assumed that the "appraiser" machine has been assigned to observe and appraise the performance of a specified set of performers. The job functions and distributional parameters on which each performer is to be appraised are assumed to have been administratively specified, as are the efficacy scale values for each function, the length of the appraisal period, the nature and measurement level of the scales to be used in assessing performance, and all scoring rules. Finally, all job functions on which all performers are to be appraised are assumed to be of the iterated type. With these stipulations in mind, the cybernetic analysis of the appraisal process can now be presented. It consists of the following ten steps:

1. Start off the new appraisal period with a clean slate, setting the values of pointers j and $k = 1$ for each of the N performers for whom the appraiser has appraisal responsibility; set $i = 1$.
2. For performer P_i, observe a performance relevant event, $E_{i,j}$.
3. Determine if event $E_{i,j}$ required the performance of function $F_{i,k}$; if so, continue to next step; if not, set $k = k + 1$; if $k > K_i$ (the number of functions on which performer i is to be appraised), designate $E_{i,j}$ as not performance relevant and repeat step 2; otherwise, repeat step 3 with the new value of k.
4. Continue with the following two steps:
   a. Decide on the criteria $C_{k,m}$ for function $F_{i,k}$ to which event $E_{i,j}$ was

relevant; decide on the efficacy level exhibited on each such criterion during event $E_{i,j}$ and increment by one the count of times performer P_i attained the particular efficacy level on each criterion for function $F_{i,k}$.

b. Decide on the maximum feasible efficacy level on each relevant criterion for function $F_{i,k}$ during event $E_{i,j}$ and increment by one the count of times the particular efficacy level was determined to be the maximum feasible one on each such criterion for function $F_{i,k}$.

5. Set $i = i + 1$; if $i > N$, reset i to 1; decide if there's sufficient time remaining in the appraisal period to observe another performance relevant event; if there is, set $j = k = 1$ and return to step 2; if there is not, set $i = k = 1$ and continue to next step.

6. At rating time for performer P_i, two procedures are necessary:
a. Recall the frequencies or relative frequencies with which performer P_i attained each efficacy level on each criterion relevant to function $F_{i,k}$; convert these frequencies to percentages of the total observations on each of function $F_{i,k}$'s criteria if they aren't already stored this way; designate these percentages as $R_{ach,e}$.

b. Recall the frequencies or relative frequencies with which the efficacy level on each criterion relevant to function $F_{i,k}$ were determined to be the maximum levels feasible to attain: convert these to percentages if they aren't already stored this way; designate these percentages as $R_{max,e}$.

7. Compute the mean, standard deviation, or any other relevant parameters of the attained distribution (i.e., the $R_{ach,e}$ percentages) on each criterion relevant to function $F_{i,k}$. Compute the corresponding parameters for the maximum feasible distribution (i.e., the $R_{max,e}$ percentages) for each of function $F_{i,k}$'s relevant criteria.

8. Convert the attained PM (parametric magnitude) score on each relevant parameter of the distribution for each of function $F_{i,k}$'s relevant criterion to an absolute or relativistic effectiveness score at the level of measurement specified in the measurement domain definition.

9. Perform the following two calculations:
a. Compute the weighted or unweighted average of the effectiveness scores on all the relevant parameters of the distribution for each of function $F_{i,k}$'s relevant criteria to produce the overall effectiveness score on each criterion; then compute the weighted or unweighted average of the relevant criteria for each function to produce the overall score on the function.

b. Increment the function pointer k by one; if $k > K_i$, set $K = 1$ and continue to the next step; otherwise repeat steps 6a–9a for this next function.

10. Decide on the overall satisfactoriness of performer P_i's performance across all of his or her job functions in one of the following ways:
a. Determine the satisfactoriness level at which the effectiveness score on each of P_i's functions falls and then combine the satisfactoriness levels on

all of his or her job functions according to some combinatorial rule (e.g., conjunctive, disjunctive, compensatory) to produce the overall satisfactoriness score for the performer.

b. Compute the weighted or unweighted average effectiveness score over all of P_i's job functions and determine the satisfactoriness level at which the resulting average falls.

c. Set $i = i + 1$; if $i > N$, then stop; if not, go to step 6a and repeat steps 6–10 for the next performer.

Most methods of appraising job performance in conventional use define the human role in their measurement procedures as encompassing at least seven to nine steps of the measurement process. Some require all ten steps to be carried out by the human component. The specific steps that some of the more popular appraisal methods assign to the human role when they are used to assess job performance are shown below:

Adjective rating scales: Steps 1–9
Graphic rating scales: Steps 1–9
Behaviorally anchored rating scales: Steps 1–9
Mixed standard scales: Steps 1–9
Forced choice: Steps 1–7
Behavioral observation scales: Steps 1–6
MBO: Steps 1–10
Forced distribution: Steps 1–10

All of these methods implicitly allow raters to consider distributional parameters other than the mean in the process of generating measurements, but the extent to which these considerations influence the measurement cannot be determined because the reported measurements are focused on overall job or job function performance.

To the extent that appraisal procedures can be devised that minimize the number of steps in the measurement process assigned to the human role by shifting some to the instrument component, the fallibility of the measurement process can be reduced. This tactic is consistent with well-established precedent in the physical sciences. It would seem that the first six steps constitute the irreducible minimum number of steps that have to be assigned to the human role in the measurement process of performance appraisal. Only one method has been proposed that achieves this minimization of the human role, but this method (behavioral observation scales) is plagued by so many other problems that its use cannot be recommended (see Bernardin & Kane, 1980; Kane & Bernardin, 1982). A new method to be proposed later in this chapter—performance distribution assessment—achieves human role minimization while avoiding the problems afflicting the BOS method.

Rule specificity dimension. One of the goals of a measurement procedure is to maximally restrict the extent to which tacit, subjective processes of human judgment are relied upon as the source of any computational products leading to a measurement score. Progress toward this goal is achieved on the instrumentation dominance dimension by minimizing the number of measurement steps that are assigned to the human role. Once the human role in the measurement procedure has been minimized, the only way to further curtail the influence of human subjectivity is to maximize the degree of rule specificity.

The rules for the conduct of the human role in the measurement procedure are focused on the measurement steps that are assigned to the human role. The rules address both the actions to be taken at each step and the contingencies under which any such actions can be varied. A set of measurement rules that is very low in specificity would refer only to larger, complex units of activity and might simply require some general contingencies to be "taken into account." As an example, consider the rules for carrying out step 9 of the measurement process, which in the case of weighted averages involves the application of relative weights to criteria for use in forming an overall job function performance score. If it has been administratively stipulated that raters are to generate these weights themselves, the rules might simply require that each criterion be assigned a number from 1 to 10 to reflect how much influence the rater thinks the criterion should have in the computation of overall average performance on the function.

In contrast, a highly specific set of rules would not allow human discretion to roam so freely. It would break the measurement step down into very small, elementary units of activity and would describe the action to take in executing each of them. It would also specify exactly how to take all the contingent conditions into account. To return to the preceding example, a highly specific set of rules might designate the factors to consider in deciding on the importance of any criterion. The rules might then specify that the criteria relevant to each function first be rated on a 1–10 scale on each importance factor and that the sum of the ratings assigned to each criterion be computed. The rules might specify further that each criterion's importance rating sum be reduced or increased by a particular number of units for each of a specified set of conditions that were present. In this way, even though the rater carries out this step, his or her actions have been explicitly proceduralized to the point where the likelihood of unintentionally inconsistent judging between criteria is greatly reduced. In addition, the possibility of detecting deliberate misrepresentation is greatly improved, which should serve to suppress its incidence.

These strategies call for the "dehumanization" of performance appraisal. The element of human discretion should be removed from the measurement process of appraisal to the maximum degree possible through rules for the conduct of the human role that serve to make human actions as completely procedural as possible. Performance appraisal is not the place to offer raters the opportunity to derive intrinsic fulfillment through the exercise of their creativity.

Recommendations

The conclusions reached from the foregoing effort at rethinking the problem of measuring performance can be expressed in the form of the following recommendations:

1. Performance must be defined as a measurable phenomenon existing separately from the person who produced the performance.

2. Performance on any job function is defined as the record of outcomes (i.e., efficacy levels) achieved in carrying out the job function during a specified period.

3. Most jobs comprise iterated job functions, which pose the greatest challenge to performance measurement.

4. Performance on an iterated job function is represented in a quantifiable manner by a performance distribution.

5. The distributional measurement model, which allows all parameters of performance distributions to be considered as potential bases on which to appraise performance, is the most appropriate model on which to base the measurement of performance on iterated job functions.

6. The initial score product of a performance appraisal should be measurements of the magnitudes of the performance distribution parameters judged or stipulated to be salient. These measurements are the fundamental building blocks from which measurements of all higher-order attributes of performance can be constructed.

7. The level of performance in object/event categories defined at all levels of aggregation higher than distributional parameter-criterion combinations (e.g., criteria, job functions, overall job) should be measured by means of derived measurements, which are generated by combining lower-order measurements (e.g., effectiveness on three different distributional parameters) into a higher-order measurement (e.g., effectiveness on a criterion relevant to a job function).

8. Performance can be measured on three attributes: parametric magnitude, effectiveness, and satisfactoriness. These three attributes stand in a hierarchically dependent relationship such that the measurement of effectiveness requires the prior measurement of parametric magnitude, and the measurement of satisfactoriness requires the prior measurement of effectiveness. Effectiveness and satisfactoriness measurements do not have to be generated directly but instead can be generated from parametric magnitude measurements. Parametric magnitude measurements can be derived from the occurrence rates and scale values of each job function's efficacy levels.

9. The newly proposed hermeneutic scale, defined with relativistic limits, has several advantages over any other type of scale and should be considered for

use in explicitly generating effectiveness measurements in all appraisal applications.

10. Where relativistic hermeneutic scales of effectiveness are to be used, the content of the anchors for each efficacy scale should be particularized to the point where it is highly relevant to all the positions to which the scale will be applied, even if this necessitates substantially reducing the subset of positions to which the scale is applicable.

11. The human role in any measurement procedure should be reduced to an absolute minimum relative to the role of instrumentation. In the case of performance appraisal, this role consists of steps 1–6 of the generalized measurement process.

12. The human role in the measurement procedure of appraisal should be further restricted by the imposition of highly specific rules for its conduct. These rules should proceduralize as many of the elementary actions in each step of the measurement process as possible.

These recommendations provide a new perspective on performance and its measurement. An appraisal method that incorporated these twelve points in its design would look quite different from any method in conventional use. More important, there is a distinct possibility that it would depart at least as far from conventional methods in the quality of the measurements it produced. Accordingly, the final portion of this chapter is devoted to the presentation of a new appraisal method designed to make the preceding recommendations operational. This new method is intended to be directly implementable in order to meet the needs of the full spectrum of appraisal applications.

Performance Distribution Assessment

Performance distribution assessment (PDA) is designed to conform to all of the recommendations derived from the foregoing reconceptualization of performance measurement. It assumes that the job functions on which performance is to be measured are iterated. Although PDA can be used to measure performance on noniterated job functions, other methods would be preferable for such functions since there is only one distributional parameter to measure for that type of function (viz., the efficacy level achieved on each criterion). The PDA method consists of five basic tasks that the rater is required to carry out, whenever possible (and desirable) with the participation of the ratees. The other component of the method is its scoring procedure.

RESPONSE TASKS REQUIRED OF THE RATER

The five tasks that PDA requires the rater to carry out are outlined below.

Task 1. At the outset of the appraisal period the rater, potentially in conjunction with the ratees, determines (a) the job functions on which the ratee is to be appraised, (b) the criteria relevant to the valuation of performance on each job function, (c) the distributional parameters reflecting valued characteristics of performance on each job function criterion, (d) the relative weights to assign to the parameters designated relevant to each criterion and to those criteria designated as relevant to each job function for use in producing a composite overall job function performance score, and (e) the relative weights assigned to job functions for use in producing a composite overall job performance score. The basis for judging the relative importance of distributional parameters, criteria, and job functions is to be specified in detail. Relative weights should be determined by a ratio scaling procedure (e.g., find the least important parameter, criterion, or function, assign it a value of 1.0, and assign a number to each other parameter, criterion, or function expressing how many times more important it is). All of these weights may, alternatively, be determined for positions or jobs through a scaling process conducted in the course of the system's development, which would eliminate the necessity of this step.

Task 2. Also at the outset of the appraisal period but after the appraisal-relevant criterion–job function combinations have been selected for the ratee's position, the rater (potentially with ratee participation) would describe the following three outcome levels that are potentially achievable on each job function criterion:

Most effective outcome on the criterion that any fully qualified performer could possibly achieve on at least one occasion of performing the function during a typical appraisal period

Least effective outcome on the criterion that would be tolerated on at least one occasion when the function is carried out during an appraisal period without having to remove the performer from further responsibility for the function

Intermediate outcome, which is the outcome on the criterion that falls halfway between the most effective and least effective outcomes in its value to the organization

By directly defining the three outcome levels, two others are indirectly defined, yielding a total of five as follows:

Level 1: Least effective outcome

Level 2: Outcomes falling halfway between the least effective and intermediate outcomes

Level 3: Intermediate outcomes

Level 4: Outcomes falling halfway between the intermediate and most effective outcomes

Level 5: Most effective outcome

The level 2 and 4 outcomes are said to be indirectly defined because they are defined in terms of the two outcomes bordering them in each case rather than directly in terms of the events to which they refer.

Task 3. After defining the three outcome levels for each job function criterion but still at the outset of the appraisal period, the rater (again, potentially with ratee participation) assigns a value to each job function criterion's least effective outcome according to the following instructions:

> Let +*100* points stand for the overall value of what the organization gains each time that the most effective outcome on this criterion is produced. Knowing this, how many *minus* points would you assign to represent the overall value of the damage or loss caused by each instance of producing the least effective outcome on this criterion?

Given the range bisection approach used in defining all outcome levels between the most effective and least effective outcomes, the assignment of this single utility value allows the derivation of values reflecting the relative utilities of all the other outcome levels. At this point the process of establishing the outcome (i.e., efficacy) level descriptions and scale values is complete. Note, however, that in many cases it will be preferable to specifically scale the utility value of the least effective outcome as part of the system development process. This alternative approach is applicable where outcome level descriptions can be assumed to be applicable across appraisal periods.

Task 4. This task can be carried out on a purely predictive basis at the outset of the appraisal period for the purpose of objective setting or frame-of-reference establishment. Whether or not this task is carried out on a predictive basis at the outset of the period, it should always be carried out at the end of the period even if this only serves to update the predicted values in light of events that occurred during the period. The task consists of answering the following questions in reference to the three directly defined outcome levels for each job function criterion:

> Level 1: On what percentage of all the times that the ratee carried out this job function was this *the best* that any fully qualified incumbent could have done? _____%
>
> Level 3: a. On what percentage of all the times that the ratee carried out this job function was it feasible for a fully qualified incumbent to have done *better* than this? _____%
>
> b. On what percentage of all the times that the ratee carried out this job function was this *the best* that any fully qualified incumbent could have done? _____%
>
> Level 5: On what percentage of all the times that the ratee carried out this job

function was it feasible for a fully qualified incumbent to have done *this well or better?* _____%

The words referencing the past tense within each question should be replaced by appropriate future tense equivalents (e.g., "Do you expect there to be . . ."/"will be") when doing this task on a predictive basis at the outset of the appraisal period.

The purpose of this fourth task is to elicit the data necessary to generate the maximum feasible distribution (i.e., the most nearly perfect distribution of performance that was feasible during the appraisal period). This distribution completely determines the relativistic upper limit for the mean parameter, and partly determines (along with the mean of the performance distribution that was actually achieved) the relativistic upper limit for all other distributional parameters. To understand how the maximum feasible distribution is derived from the percentage responses elicited by this task, consider the following example. Column 1 illustrates the percentage responses that a rater may provide and column 2 shows the distribution derived from these responses:

	1 (Responses to questions directed at the three directly defined outcome efficacy levels)	2 (Maximum feasible rates)
Level 1 (least effective outcome):	0%	.00 = level 1 .10 = level 2
Level 3 (intermediate outcome):	a: 75% b: 15%	.15 = level 3 .15 = level 4
Level 5 (most effective outcome):	60%	.60 = level 5

The rates in column 2 are derived in the following manner from the percentages in column 1:

Column 2, level 1 = column 1, level 1 response (%), expressed as a decimal proportion

Column 2, level 2 = column 1, 1.00 minus the sum of the rates (column 2) for all other levels

Column 2, level 3 = column 1, level 3b response (%), expressed as a decimal proportion

Column 2, level 4 = column 1, level 3a response (%) minus the column 1, level 5 response (%), expressed as a decimal proportion

Column 2, level 5 = column 1, level 5 response (%), expressed as a decimal proportion

All of these computations would, of course, be performed by a computerized scoring program, not by the rater.

Task 5. Finally, the rater's best estimates of the rates at which the ratee achieved each of the five outcome levels are elicited. This can be done in at least two different ways, each of which is more appropriate to one of the two possible media through which this information might be elicited. If the ratings are being elicited through an interactive computer-based medium, the best format would be as follows:

> Out of the total number of times that the ratee carried out this function, on what percentage of these times did the ratee actually produce outcomes
>> Level 1: at this level or worse? _____%
>> Level 3: a: worse than this level? _____%
>>   b: about equal to this level? _____%
>> Level 5: at this level or better? _____%

If the medium through which the ratings are being elicited is a paper rating form, the best format would be as follows:

> Describe how the ratee actually performed on this job function during the appraisal period by dividing up 100 percent among the following outcome levels. The percentage you assign to each outcome level should reflect your best estimate of how often the ratee achieved the level. Make sure that the percentages you assign to the five levels add up to 100 percent.

Level 1 (least effective outcome):	(description)	_____%
Level 2:	Outcomes falling between the least effective and intermediate outcomes	_____%
Level 3 (intermediate outcome):	(description)	_____%
Level 4:	Outcomes falling between the intermediate and most effective outcomes	_____%
Level 5 (most effective outcome):	(description)	_____%

MAKE SURE THE SUM OF THE PERCENTAGES YOU ASSIGN = 100%

After the completion of this fifth task, the rater's role in the measurement process comes to an end. The remainder of the process is carried out through a mechanical scoring procedure.

THE PDA SCORING PROCEDURE

The procedures for converting all ratings to distributional form, for computing the outcome level utility weights, and for computing the relativistic effectiveness scores on each of the three distributional parameters of primary interest, on each job function criterion, on the job function as a whole, and on overall job performance are described next. These procedures should be accomplished by a computerized scoring program.

Conversion of ratings to distributional form. The procedure for converting the ratings of maximum feasible performance on each job function criterion to distributional form has already been described. These maximum possible rates will be symbolized as $RMAX_n$, where n refers to outcome efficacy levels 1–5. The procedure for accomplishing this conversion for the *actual* performance ratings elicited through the format recommended for use with a computerized interactive rating medium is very similar. Column 1 below shows the percentage responses elicited from the rater. Column 2 shows the results of converting these responses to distributional form.

	1 (Responses to questions directed at the three directly defined outcome efficacy levels)	2 (Actual occurrence rates)
Level 1 (least effective outcome):	0%	.00 = level 1 .10 = level 2
Level 3 (intermediate outcome):	a: 10% b: 20%	.20 = level 3 .30 = level 4
Level 5 (most effective outcome):	40%	.40 = level 5

The rates in column 2 are derived in the following manner from the percentages in column 1:

Column 2, level 1 = column 1, level 1 response (%), expressed as a decimal proportion

Column 2, level 2 = column 1, level 3a response (%) minus column 1, level 1 response (%), expressed as a decimal proportion

Column 2, level 3 = column 1, level 3b response (%), expressed as a decimal proportion

Column 2, level 4 = 1.00 minus the sum of the rates (column 2) for levels 1, 2, 3, and 5

Column 2, level 5 = column 1, level 5 response (%), expressed as a decimal proportion

These rates should be computed in the following order: levels 1, 2, 3, 5, 4.

The only conversion necessary when the actual performance ratings are elicited through the format recommended with the use of a paper form rating medium is simply to express the percentages obtained for the five levels of each function as decimal proportions.

Regardless of the format from which the actual occurrence rates are derived, these rates will be symbolized as $RACH_n$, where n refers to outcome efficacy levels 1–5.

Computation of outcome level utility weights. In describing how the outcome level utility weights are determined, the number of minus points assigned to the least effective outcome of each job function in task 3 will be symbolized as U and will always be expressed as a negative number. Using the latter quantity, the utility weights for each outcome level are computed according to the following formulas:

$$\text{Level 1 (least effective outcome)} = U \tag{1}$$
$$\text{Level 2} \qquad\qquad = U + [(100 - U)/4] \tag{2}$$
$$\text{Level 3 (intermediate outcome)} = (100 + U)/2 \tag{3}$$
$$\text{Level 4} \qquad\qquad = U + 3[(100 - U)/4] \tag{4}$$
$$\text{Level 5 (most effective outcome)} = 100 \tag{5}$$

These weights will be symbolized as V_n, where n refers to outcome efficacy levels 1–5.

Computation of effectiveness of mean performance. The relativistic effectiveness of mean performance (E_M) on each job function is computed according to the following formula:

$$E_M = \frac{\displaystyle\sum_{n=1}^{5} RACH_n V_n}{\displaystyle\sum_{n=1}^{5} RMAX_n V_n}. \tag{6}$$

The resulting proportion constitutes a relativistic hermeneutic measurement of mean effectiveness since the mean utility level actually achieved is expressed as a proportion of the range between the zero point of utility and the maximum possible utility level. This approach assumes that the point where the utility of outcomes equals zero is also the point of zero effectiveness on the mean parameter. This seems like a reasonable convention to adopt since few organizations would tolerate performances that averaged out at levels that resulted in net losses. It is usually better to have people stop performing than to have them continue to produce losses.

It is conceivable, however, that a person may produce a mean performance on a job function that falls in the negative range of the utility scale. The effectiveness of such a mean performance should be hermeneutically measured by substituting the utility scale value for the function's least effective outcome for the denominator in equation 6, and multiplying the quotient by -1.0. The result will be a negative percentage reflecting the proximity of the mean performance to the *worst conceivable* level of mean performance on the job function.

Computation of effectiveness of consistency. It is first necessary to define the most consistent and least consistent distributions that could occur with means equal to that of the distribution actually achieved. The procedure for defining the *most consistent distribution* consists of first assigning the highest occurrence rates allowed by the maximum feasible distribution to the two outcome efficacy levels bordering the actually achieved mean. The occurrence rates should be distributed between these two outcome levels in such a way that the sum of the products of the occurrence rates and utility weights for the two levels equals the mean. If the rates that are assigned to these two levels do not add up to 100 percent, attempt to reach 100 percent by adding occurrence rates to the levels next furthest away from the mean, and redistribute the originally assigned occurrence rates as necessary to ensure that the sum of the products equals the mean. This iterative process continues, working outward from the mean until occurrence rates totaling 100 percent have been assigned. At that point the most consistent distribution has been defined.

The *least consistent distribution* is defined in the same iterative manner just described, except in this case the process starts with the highest and lowest outcome levels (levels 1 and 5). The process works successively inward toward the mean until occurrence rates totaling 100 percent have been assigned while maintaining the sum of the products (of occurrence rates and utility scale values) at a level equal to the actually achieved mean. The relativistic hermeneutic effectiveness score for the consistency (D) of performance can now be computed according to the following equation:

$$E_D = \frac{S_L - S_{Ach}}{S_L - S_M}, \tag{7}$$

where

S_L = the standard deviation of the least consistent distribution possible,
S_{Ach} = the standard deviation of the distribution actually achieved, and
S_M = the standard deviation of the most consistent distribution possible.

Again, the resulting proportion constitutes a relativistic hermeneutic measurement.

Computation of effectiveness of negative range avoidance. The lowest level of negative range avoidance (i.e., the highest negative range incidence) possible, given the mean actually achieved and the maximum feasible distribution, is the level found in the least consistent performance distribution feasible defined previously. Similarly, the highest level of negative range avoidance is that found in the most consistent distribution feasible. It will be assumed here that the range of outcome levels to be avoided encompasses those levels with negative utility weights. Accordingly, multiply each negative utility weight by the occurrence rate for the respective outcome level in the least consistent distribution feasible, sum the products, and represent the result as N_L. Repeat this procedure using the occurrence rates of the most consistent distribution feasible and the actually achieved distribution, and represent the results as N_M and N_{Ach}, respectively. Then compute the effectiveness score on the negative range avoidance parameter (E_N) according to the following equation:

$$E_N = \frac{N_L - N_{Ach}}{N_L - N_M} , \tag{8}$$

where

N_L = the worst negative range score possible,
N_{Ach} = the actual negative range score achieved, and
N_M = the best negative range score possible.

Computation of effectiveness of overall job function criterion performance. This effectiveness score is computed as a weighted linear combination of the effectiveness scores for the relevant parameters of the distribution achieved for each job function criterion. The equation for this score is as follows (a nonrelevant parameter would receive a weight of zero):

$$E_{F,C} = \frac{(W_{M,F,C} E_{M,F,C} + W_{D,F,C} E_{D,F,C} + W_{N,F,C} E_{N,F,C})}{(W_{M,F,C} + W_{D,F,C} + W_{N,F,C})} \tag{9}$$

where

$W_{X,F,C}$ = the weight assigned to the parameter X on criterion C of function F

$X = M$ = mean

$\quad\quad D$ = consistency (deviation)

$\quad\quad N$ = negative range avoidance

Computation of effectiveness of overall job function performance. The effectiveness of overall job function performance is computed as a weighted linear combination of the effectiveness measurements of the job function criterion performances according to the following equation:

$$E_F = \frac{\sum\limits_{C=1}^{M} B_C E_{F,C}}{\sum\limits_{C=1}^{M} B_C}, \tag{10}$$

where B_C is the weight assigned to job function criterion C.

Computation of effectiveness of overall job performance. The effectiveness of overall job performance is computed as a weighted linear combination of the effectiveness measurements of performance on the job functions, according to the following equation:

$$E_J = \frac{\sum\limits_{F=1}^{K} B_F E_F}{\sum\limits_{F=1}^{K} B_F}, \tag{11}$$

where B_F is the weight assigned to job function F.

Each of the scores produced by the foregoing procedures is a relativistic hermeneutic effectiveness score expressed on a common 0–100 percent scale. Any given percentage score denotes the same level of achievement relative to the maximum level feasible in all positions and jobs throughout an organization. Consequently, the jobs in an organization should be grouped according to the similarity in the degree of stringency judged to be appropriate in evaluating the satisfactoriness of performance in them. Each satisfactoriness level (e.g., outstanding, superior, fully satisfactory, marginal) can then be defined in terms of the same range of effectiveness for all the jobs in each of the resulting groups of jobs. These

FIGURE 9.2. Example of PDA scoring

| | Outcome Levels | | | | |
| | Least Effective | | | Most Effective | |
	1	2	3	4	5
Utility weights	−150	−87.5	−25	37.5	100
Maximum feasible distribution	.00	.10	.15	.15	.60
Actual distribution	.00	.10	.20	.30	.40
Least consistent distribution feasible	.067	.066	.267	.00	.60
Most consistent distribution feasible	.00	.10	.15	.625	.125

Scores

Raw mean of actual distribution	= 37.5
Raw mean of maximum feasible distribution	= 53.125
Absolute effectiveness of mean of actual distribution	= 37.5%
Absolute effectiveness of mean of maximum feasible distribution	= 53.125%
Relativistic effectiveness of mean of actual distribution	= 71%
Relativistic effectiveness of consistency of actual distribution	$= E_D = \dfrac{82.3 - 62.5}{82.3 - 51.35} = 64\%$
Relativistic effectiveness of negative range avoidance of actual distribution	$= E_N = \dfrac{-22.5 - (-13.75)}{-22.5 - (-12.5)} = 88\%$
Overall average job function performance (assuming equal weights for all three parameters)	= 74%

standards (i.e., ranges of effectiveness scores) for each satisfactoriness level that needs to be distinguished for personnel decision-making purposes should be administratively established for each job group. The scoring procedure should then use the standards to mechanistically assign satisfactoriness scores to performances.

Figure 9.2 presents an example of the scoring procedure carried out for hypothetical maximum feasible and achieved performance distributions. This example illustrates well some of the noteworthy aspects of the PDA method. First, the relativistic value of the mean performance score is 71 percent compared to its absolute value of 37.5 percent. The use of relativistic limits has a marked impact. Second, note the disparity between the scores on the three main distributional parameters (i.e., mean, consistency, and negative range avoidance). Clearly, quite different aspects of performance are being measured by those three scores. The hypothetical performer in this case was fairly ineffective at performing this function at a consistent level and yet was quite effective at avoiding the production of negatively valued outcomes. If the latter parameter were more highly valued than the other two, this particular distribution would have ended up with an overall score that would have been much higher than the relativistic effectiveness of the mean alone.

PDA FORMAT CONSIDERATIONS

This presentation has raised the possibility of two alternative media for the elicitation of the requisite input from raters in the use of the PDA method: conventional paper forms and computerized interactive input. The paper form medium is much less preferable than the computerized medium, but it will be the only one accessible to many users until the computer revolution has completed its displacement of paper-based administrative systems. For this reason, it is appropriate to offer some items of advice on the basis of early trials with paper form approaches to implementing PDA.

1. The PDA method requires considerable form space. The only approach that has proven viable in tryouts of the method is one that uses rating booklets with $11'' \times 17''$ fold-out pages. One fold-out page to the right of the booklet seam plus the $8 \frac{1}{2}'' \times 11''$ surface to the left side of the seam should be allocated to each job function. The job function's efficacy levels should be arranged from lowest to highest horizontally across the folded-out right-hand page for the function. In columns under each efficacy level should be spaces for the entries required for the purpose of describing the maximum feasible and actual distributions. The left-hand page for each function presents the function's definition, summary instructions, and the questions to be answered in the spaces available on the right side.

2. Due to the expense of the booklets and the difficulty they present for subsequent entry of this data into computer files, it is best to require raters to enter their answers on separate answer sheets.

3. The question wording recommended previously is the result of many hours of trial and error, discussions with people extensively experienced in questionnaire wording, and feedback from users. While it may not be perfect and better wording may eventually be found, consider any alternative wording extremely carefully before choosing it over the wording that has been recommended here.

The PDA approach can only reach its full potential when it has been implemented in an interactive computerized medium. In this medium the rater would only be asked to make occurrence rate estimates in reference to the three directly defined efficacy levels. Once the maximum feasible rates have been input, these would be used to ensure that no errors were made in the entry of the actual occurrence rates. Work is well underway to achieve a completely computerized operationalization of the method for microcomputers utilizing the MS-DOS operating system.

PDA offers the appraisal function several features that have not been offered by any other method. This section will summarize these features.

1. PDA, as the first method employing relativistic hermeneutic scaling, produces measures of the effectiveness of performance on a relativized 0–100 percent scale, any given level of which remains constant in its meaning regardless of the job, division, organizational level, or even the organization in which it occurs. Thus an overall performance score of 80 percent means exactly the same thing in reference to the performance of a corporate vice president as it does in reference to the performance of his or her secretary: namely, that each person achieved 80 percent of the maximally desirable record of outcomes that was feasible to achieve in the job functions he or she was expected to perform. The achievement of a universal effectiveness metric has implications beyond the capability to compare performances of the incumbents of different jobs. For example, this universal metric permits performance scores to be aggregated across work groups, divisions, and entire organizations. Such collective performance scores might well be the best indices of that elusive phenomenon called productivity.

2. PDA meets the specifications for the maximum degree of instrumentation dominance feasible in an appraisal method. Moreover, all steps in the measurement process that involve computations have, with one possible exception, been removed from the human role. The one exception is the requirement to report the actual and maximum feasible occurrence rates of the outcome levels for each job function criterion directly rather than to report them in terms of raw frequencies that could then be converted to occurrence rates. However, there is some evidence (e.g., Estes, 1975) that people may store frequency information, particularly with regard to unit-sum sets (i.e., sets in which the proportions of occurrence of the elements have to total 1.0), directly in terms of occurrence rates. Thus people may be able to report relative occurrence rates more accurately than they can raw frequencies.

3. PDA is the first appraisal method capable of explicitly and quantifiably excluding from consideration those portions of the range of performance that circumstances beyond the performer's control made impossible to achieve. A performer is thereby only held accountable for achieving what was possible to achieve under the circumstances that prevailed during the appraisal period. This feature represents a major new capability that can greatly enhance the perceived and actual fairness and equity of appraisals.

4. PDA can be varied along the particularization-standardization dimension to suit situational demands and organizational needs without any restrictive effect on the ability to make universal score comparisons. If positions differ appreciably

in the conditions under which they are performed, the scales can be particularized to account fully for these differences. To whatever extent such differences do *not* exist, corresponding advantage can be taken of this fact by standardizing portions of the first four rating tasks, thereby reducing the time and effort required of raters.

5. PDA is the first method capable of yielding an assessment of the consistency of performance and of the performer's success in avoiding negatively valued outcomes. These parameters are critically important with regard to many of the major functions of some of the key jobs in our society, such as those involving public health and safety. It is also worth noting here that assessments on these additional parameters can be generated without requiring any additional rater input beyond that required to assess mean performance.

6. PDA has several characteristics that should serve to reduce rating errors of both the motivated and nonmotivated type. These characteristics are as follows:

a. The relationship between the data elicited from the rater and the scores generated on the basis of such data is effectively concealed. This concealment of a rating method's "order of merit" is a well-established approach to suppressing deliberate distortion.

b. The effects of differences in rater stringency in setting the relativistic upper limit are controlled to at least some degree by the counterbalancing effect of the two processes involved in setting the upper limit. Specifically, descriptions of the most effective outcome that are shifted toward the high extreme can be offset by maximum feasible occurrence rates that are shifted downward for the higher outcome levels. Similarly, excessively lenient outcome level descriptions can be offset by an upward shift in the maximum feasible occurrence rates for the higher outcome levels. It just might be that this two-part process allows natural cognitive compensatory processes to operate better than any single step process (e.g., instructing the rater to write the standard for the fully satisfactory performance level).

c. Specifying the distribution of maximum feasible occurrence rates imposes precise limits on the actual occurrence rate percentages that can be validly reported. The computerized scoring system can detect any violation of the limits in the actual occurrence rates that are reported and earmark the offending form for rerating. Deliberate efforts to inflate ratings seem likely to violate these limits. This unique capability to detect such violations should act as an effective deterrent to efforts of this sort.

7. PDA can be efficiently scored with an easily developed computer program. One such program can be used to score all the PDA appraisals in an organization. Efficacy level descriptions can be changed and job functions can be added or deleted from the appraisal for a job without making any changes to the central core of the program.

8. PDA provides several different points at which the ratee's participation

can be elicited. The nature and extent of participation at each of these points can also be varied. As a result the method can be considered to possess an unusually wide range of possibilities for varying ratee participation. This should facilitate efforts to tailor applications of the method to the level of participation congruent with an organization's policies, traditions, and culture.

Conclusion

This rethinking of the problem of appraising job performance led to a set of principles and specifications that were used as the basis for designing a new appraisal method called performance distribution assessment (PDA). PDA differs quite radically from any method that has been previously proposed. However, these differences are grounded in an explicit conceptual framework instead of being offered merely for the sake of novelty. In fact, it appears to be the first appraisal method that has been derived from a comprehensive model of performance and its measurement. The important implication of the method's having its origins in an explicit model is that future efforts to evaluate the method empirically will also reveal the strengths and weaknesses of the underlying model. Thus, regardless of how effective PDA proves to be, its use will at the very least increase our understanding of performance measurement.

References

Bernardin, H. J., & Kane, J. S. (1980). A closer look at behavioral observation scales. *Personnel Psychology, 33,* 809–814.

Estes, W. K. (1975). The cognitive side of probability learning. *Psychological Review, 83,* 37–64.

Kane, J. S., & Bernardin, H. J. (1982). Behavioral observation scales and the evaluation of performance appraisal effectiveness. *Personnel Psychology, 35,* 635–642.

Stevens, S. S. (1951). Mathematics, measurement, and psychophysics. In S. S. Stevens (Ed.), *Handbook of experimental psychology* (pp. 1–49). New York: Wiley.

PART 2

Applications

Where part 1 describes what methods should be used, part 2 examines which methods have been used and how they have been used in a variety of performance assessment applications. The ten chapters in part 2 provide a survey of the most important and exemplary performance assessment projects that have been conducted in different educational and professional settings. Chapters 10 through 16 deal with personnel applications in business, industry, education, medicine, and law. Here the subject of the assessment is the employee or manager. The remaining three chapters concentrate on the assessment of students in relation to specific educational decisions. The applications surveyed include student evaluation, writing skills, and listening and speaking skills.

Similar to part 1, the chapter structure of part 2 has been standardized. A trinary structure is employed: (1) "Introduction," (2) "Survey of Applications," and (3) "Future Directions and Needs." This provides a framework for reviewing the applications and studies using performance assessment methods in each area. In addition, it facilitates the identification of specific directions for future applications and the needs that should be addressed.

10. A PERFORMANCE APPRAISAL SYSTEM

H. John Bernardin

Introduction

The purpose of this chapter is to present a model for appraisal system development. This approach is certainly not simple. Many of the assumptions of traditional appraisal systems are questioned in this model. Among the most serious obstacles to performance appraisal (PA) effectiveness are the following assumptions, which are basic to many PA systems.

1. The supervisor is not only the best source of information on an employee's performance but is a sufficient source of information as well.
2. Appraisals must be kept as simple as possible so that they do not interfere with the most important duties of the manager/supervisor.
3. Appraisals should be done every six months or once a year.
4. The rater can accurately recall each employee's performance over a long period of time.
5. Appraisals should always be done on individual performance rather than on work units or groups.
6. An overall or average level of performance is sufficient information about an employee's performance.
7. All raters are motivated to rate accurately.
8. Raters can accurately judge the potential of ratees for other positions.
9. The use of a behaviorally based appraisal format will ensure rating validity.

The proposed developmental model assumes only that those who will be most affected by the implementation of a new personnel system should contribute the most to its development. After introducing the diagnostic system of appraisal development, we will describe the procedures to be followed with this model. An example of the use of this model with a large organization will also be presented.

A DIAGNOSTIC MODEL OF APPRAISAL SYSTEM DEVELOPMENT

The purpose(s) for appraisal should not be selected arbitrarily. Rather, the decision should be based on a thorough diagnosis of factors that have been shown to have an impact on appraisal effectiveness. Such a diagnosis is necessary for many other characteristics of the appraisal system as well. In any major organizational change process, the two most important elements of a successful implementation are the technical soundness of the proposed change and the extent to which those who will be affected by the change are supportive of it. A great deal of research in organizational development underscores the importance of involving affected group members in the change process (Likert, 1966). To that end, in Bernardin's diagnostic model of appraisal intervention (1979), a task force of organizational members is assembled. Comprising representatives from groups affected by changes in the installation of an appraisal system, the task force should consider the step-by-step process of developing, implementing, and administering a performance appraisal system. Table 10.1 presents an outline of the diagnostic model. It is recommended that the "cooperation" of those most cynical about the change process be enlisted.

The second step in the basic outline for the diagnostic model is to identify all organizational variables that may affect the validity or fairness of the PA system. Two sources of information are available for this purpose. Questionnaire data can be collected from a sample of the affected work forces, and input can be gathered from the task force. Both of these sources have proven to be valuable for determining all appraisal-relevant parameters that may have an impact on PA system effectiveness (Carlyle & Bernardin, 1980; Taylor, 1984). At this time, quantitative job analysis data can be collected and appraisal-relevant issues can be raised with regard to the job analysis (see Bernardin & Beatty, 1984, chap. 2).

The next step in the basic outline for the diagnostic model is to determine the number and types of PA systems that appear to be feasible for the organization. Data and task-force discussions may indicate that only one type of PA system is appropriate across all positions. However, research in appraisal clearly documents that optimal appraisal-relevant parameters, such as frequency of appraisal, source of appraisal (e.g., peers, supervisors, subordinates), and format for appraisals differ as a function of the job and the circumstances surrounding the job. It is naive to assume that one appraisal system will apply with equal validity across a great variety of jobs and circumstances surrounding those jobs.

The next step in the diagnostic process is to recommend a PA system or systems to the task force for discussion. On the basis of this discussion, prototype systems should be developed, and demonstration projects that involve training outlines for all raters, managers, operators, and administrators involved in systems implementation should be conducted.[1] If possible, the demonstration projects should incorporate an experimental research design to enable the program administrators and the task force to assess the results of manipulated appraisal-relevant parameters. The results of the demonstration projects should also reveal

---

1. There is a great need for demonstration projects before full-scale implementation of the system. This belief is fortified by the experience of the federal government regarding the use of PA data for merit-pay allocation, which has resulted in the U.S. General Accounting Office criticizing the Office of Personnel Management for its failure to set up demonstration projects with regard to performance appraisal and merit pay.

TABLE 10.1. A Diagnostic Model of Appraisal System Development

1. Assemble a task force on appraisal.
2. Identify all organizational variables that may have an impact on appraisal effectiveness by surveying a sample of the work force and by discussion with the task force.
3. Determine the number and types of appraisal systems that appear to be feasible by examining the survey results and job analysis data and by discussion with the task force.
4. Recommend PA system(s) to the task force for discussion.
5. Develop prototype system(s) and propose demonstration projects.
6. Conduct demonstration project(s).
7. Analyze the results of the demonstration project(s) and propose changes to the prototype(s) on the basis of the results.
8. Implement PA system(s).
9. Evaluate the effectiveness of PA system(s).

any changes that may be necessary in the proposed system. The following section presents an example of the use of the diagnostic model for appraisal development.

Assessment of Appraisal-Relevant Parameters

As already stated, one of the primary sources of information regarding appraisal-relevant parameters should be the attitudes of those who will be affected by the appraisal system. A task force can first serve as advisors and critics in the development of a questionnaire to assess these attitudes. Such a procedure was followed in a large-scale project involving a federal agency (Bernardin, 1979) in which a questionnaire was developed to survey a sample of employees about their attitudes toward every major aspect of performance appraisal. This approach is essentially a needs assessment that will provide data for decisions regarding all appraisal-relevant parameters. Table 10.2 presents a listing of these parameters. Next, several questions were written for each of the parameters and subsequently critiqued by the task force. The result was a 212-item questionnaire covering all of the parameters. After a final critique by the task force and the preparation of the final scale, the questionnaire was administered to a sample of the employees who would ultimately be affected by the new appraisal system.

Differences were found in responses to the questionnaire across job families, divisions, and ranks. Among the most significant findings were the following:

1. *Source of appraisal.* Respondents preferred the source of appraisal to be their immediate supervisors and, to a lesser extent, the people for whom they provided service. The majority of respondents favored more than one rater,

TABLE 10.2. Relevant Parameters of a Performance Appraisal System

1. Type(s) of rater (peer, supervisor, external, subordinate, self)
2. What to measure, what to exclude (observability, importance, predictability)
3. Purpose(s) for appraisal (e.g., test validation, feedback, merit pay)
4. Confidentiality of results
5. Frequency of appraisal (e.g., once per year or more often)
6. Timing for appraisal
7. Frequency and type of feedback (e.g., absolute versus relative)
8. Group and/or individual appraisal (level of aggregation)
9. Relationship to other human resource components—establishing a data base
10. Time required for appraisal (practicality)
11. Mode of processing data (e.g., computer compatibility)
12. Rater motivation and ability to rate accurately (cognitive processes)
13. Performance constraints (opportunity bias)
14. Task characteristics
15. Organizational climate (e.g., trust in the appraisal process)

and some divisions felt peers and subordinates were potentially valid sources of information. Both subordinates and supervisors felt subordinates were a valid source of information for appraising supervisors.

2. *Frequency of appraisal.* The majority of respondents preferred two or more appraisals per year and some ranks preferred several per year. Scientists preferred appraisals commensurate with the completion of major projects.

3. *Object of appraisal.* The majority of respondents preferred individual to group appraisal, although one group generally preferred group performance.

4. *Format for appraisal.* Respondents favored measurements of activities or tasks performed and quality of performance over quantitative measures. This was true from the perspective of both raters and ratees. Some positions, however, identified uncontaminated, countable results that could be used.

5. *Format and frequency of feedback.* Respondents preferred more frequent feedback given on an informal, on-the-job basis rather than just after an appraisal period. Few respondents felt formal appraisals were the most useful means for feedback.

6. *Appraisal use.* The majority of respondents thought appraisals should be related to decisions regarding pay, promotions, separations, and training. However, there was a good deal of variability in these responses as well.

7. *Evaluation of present system.* There was moderate but variable satisfaction with the present system(s), but a fairly strong belief that the present system(s) could not be used as criteria for important personnel decisions.

8. *Extraneous factors affecting performance.* Although there were position differences here, employees generally did not feel extraneous factors, such as inadequate equipment or supplies, poor performance by others, or environ-

mental constraints, significantly affected their individual levels of performance. Inadequate rewards for good performance and poorly defined task assignments were cited as more of a problem than extraneous factors. However, there were reliable indications of extraneous factors for certain jobs.

9. *Trust in appraisal.* Across divisions and ranks, there was a high level of trust expressed for ratings if they were made by immediate supervisors or people for whom employees provided service. However, there was also considerable variability on this dimension as a function of organizational assignment.

10. *Supervisory attitudes toward appraisal.* Supervisors expressed less confidence in the accuracy of their ratings than did those who were rated. Additionally, supervisors felt that they had insufficient time to do appraisals and that their own supervisors did not look at appraisals as a critical element of their jobs.

11. *Confidentiality of appraisals.* The vast majority of respondents felt that appraisal scores should be held in the strictest of confidence, known only to employees and their supervisor.

12. *Standard-setting process.* The majority of respondents, both supervisory and nonsupervisory, indicated they would like to participate in setting standards with supervisors. However, incumbents of some job families expressed pessimism regarding the applicability of a goal-oriented, standard-setting process for their jobs.

13. *Training needs.* Fairly large differences were found across job families and divisions in terms of the need for training on performance counseling, goal setting, rating documentation, and trust in the appraisal process.

The results of the survey were reported to the task force, and several suggestions were made for clarification and reanalysis. The task force examined many significant differences detected in responses to the questionnaire to determine if they corresponded with intuitions about appraisal from their various perspectives. On the basis of the differences found in the analysis and the discussion with the task force, four different systems of appraisal were proposed as optimal for particular clusters of job families and within certain divisions of the agency. These systems differed on several characteristics, the most important of which were the following:

1. *Measurement.* Some clusters preferred countable results as a basis for personnel decisions, while other clusters preferred a task- or behavior-based appraisal format.

2. *Format.* Some clusters responded favorably to a combined task-based, results-oriented format of appraisal.

3. *Timing and frequency of appraisal.* One cluster felt the most valid ratings would result when ratings were made upon the completion of particular projects and when multiple raters were used.

4. *Source.* Two clusters felt that a peer review panel would provide the most valid source of information on their work and that immediate supervisors could not be trusted to rate fairly (a project-oriented, peer review panel was thus recommended).

On the basis of the results of the survey, prototype appraisal systems were proposed for consideration by the task force, the department of personnel, and

FIGURE 10.1. Flowchart for the development of performance measures (PMs)

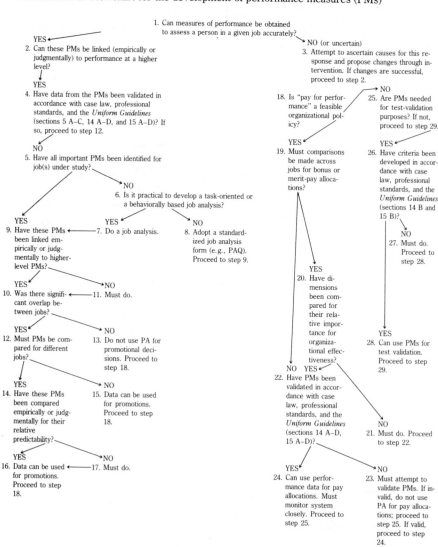

any other interested parties. It was then proposed that a demonstration project be conducted for a sufficient length of time to provide reliable information regarding the effectiveness of the appraisal systems for agencywide application. Results of the demonstration project would then be used as the basis for changes in the prototype system(s) before agency installation.

The main purpose of the appraisal survey, discussion with the task force, and the demonstration project was to provide sufficient information to select the optimal appraisal systems for different jobs within the agency.

Figure 10.1 takes the reader through the various questions and answers pertinent to the development of an appraisal system. It begins with the fundamental issue of whether accurate measures can be made of outcomes, tasks performed, or behaviors exhibited. The selection of the purpose for appraisal should be based on the information compiled from the survey results and the discussion with the task force. The flowchart allows for the possibility that the appraisal will be used for more than one purpose. It is obvious from the chart that appraisal data deemed acceptable for one type of personnel decision are not necessarily acceptable for any other type of decision. For example, a different weighting scheme for importance may be necessary when the purpose of appraisal is to provide data for promotions rather than for merit-pay or probationary decisions (see steps 14, 20, and 31).

The flowchart also provides the opportunity for some form of job analysis as a basis for identifying important tasks, behaviors, or functions (steps 6, 22, and 32). Practical issues really dictate the selection of the format for the job analysis.

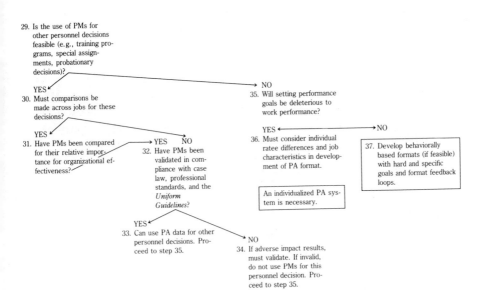

Research does seem to indicate that a task-oriented or behaviorally based job analysis procedure will result in more useful information for appraisal purposes (Levine et al., 1981). However, these methods are quite cumbersome compared with standardized formats. For very large organizations with a great variety of jobs, a behaviorally based or task-oriented job analysis may not be practical.

The first question in Figure 10.1 is probably the most difficult one to answer. However, it is a question of potential as much as reality, since it asks whether performance *can* be measured accurately for a given job with any level or type of measurement. The diagnostic questionnaire discussed above can address this sort of question, and results should reveal potential for success or failure within the different organizational contexts of the responses. For example, in Bernardin's diagnostic study (1979), substantial differences were found in responses to a question on potential for accuracy as a function of the type of job, the unit and division of assignment, the source of appraisal, and the style of supervision. Because over 50 percent of the responses to this question were negative, it was decided to do further probing before recommending any substantial investment in appraisal development or implementation. Research shows that diagnostic information regarding the future use of appraisal is highly predictive of actual ratings made over six months later (Bernardin, Orban, & Carlyle, 1981). Thus causes for a high percentage of pessimistic responses should be explored through other questionnaire responses and discussions with the task force. This information may indicate a need for some type of organizational intervention (e.g., job redesign or attitude change) before appraisal data are even considered as input for important personnel decisions, such as those regarding promotions, merit pay, or reductions in force.

The answer to the first question in Figure 10.1 is also related to several other appraisal parameters that can affect accuracy in measurement. The sections to follow will examine the most important of these parameters. One such consideration is the level of analysis available for appraisal. The key questions here are whether the work performance of individual ratees can be separated from that of colleagues on critical work elements and whether such data collection would be disruptive to organizational effectiveness. There is no absolute basis for excluding group-level appraisal data for use in personnel decision making. Although this level of analysis would pose unique problems for some purposes of appraisal, research on group dynamics has shown that group cohesiveness can lead to higher productivity and greater satisfaction. Thus the use of group-performance data to make merit-pay decisions when individual performance cannot be easily distinguished may ultimately facilitate higher rates of productivity and job satisfaction. So whether group or individual data are most appropriate under certain organizational conditions, the flowchart in Figure 10.1 may still be followed.

The extent to which accurate and fair measurements can be made of outcomes, tasks performed, or behaviors exhibited can be at least tentatively determined through questionnaire responses, discussions with the task force, and perhaps empirical evidence. Before proceeding through the various steps of Figure 10.1, the system developer, working with the task force, should attempt to answer the question at step 1 by going through the steps outlined in Figure 10.1 that address the issues of measurement accuracy. As illustrated in the study described previously, the other important appraisal parameters related to the issue of measurement accuracy can also be examined through questionnaire responses and discussions with the task force. In fact, the purposes to be served by PA data should be based on judgments from these sources (providing there is no legal or regulatory mandate in this regard). With the task force serving as the guide for practical considerations, the parameters should be examined in the context of all feasible purposes for the PA data. As an example, let us assume that the PA data are to be used for decisions regarding promotions. To that end, the task force should address the following questions:

1. Which elements of performance can be measured most accurately and which predict performance in higher-level positions?
2. What level of data specificity is required for maximum predictability (accuracy) and fair comparability across positions?
3. What sources for appraisal will ensure maximum predictability (accuracy) across all of the pertinent content domains?
4. What rating method would maximize the most important psychometric criteria for this purpose (e.g., discriminability, reliability, or validity)?
5. How should performance elements be weighted for this purpose?
6. Should a standardized or individualized rating format be used for this purpose?
7. How frequently must appraisals be made for this purpose in order to maximize accuracy?
8. What measurement model is the most appropriate for the job(s) in question?
9. What is the level of organizational trust in the use of PA data for this purpose?
10. What control procedures are needed, given this level of trust and this purpose for appraisal?

These questions address essentially the what, how, who, when, and by whom of appraisal. An investigation of these questions through questionnaire responses and task-force discussions should provide some hypotheses as to whether the PA data (of any form or from any source) could be useful for each possible purpose that could be served by the data. Demonstration projects can then be conducted to test each hypothesis.

As noted, these questions should be addressed in the context of each possible purpose to be served by appraisal data. Although the ten questions are certainly not exhaustive, they are considered to be the most important for appraisal accuracy. These questions will be examined in more detail in the sections that follow.

BASIC DATA FOR PERFORMANCE MEASUREMENT

Because of the plethora of rating errors reported in research on performance measurement, countable, nonjudgmental data should be used whenever possible. Of course, that ominous phrase "whenever possible" is in need of clarification. Figure 10.2 shows the steps to be followed in the consideration of the use of countable, nonjudgmental data as the basis for performance measurement. Up to this point, there has been no consideration of the purpose(s) for the appraisal. Rather, the concern has been with fair and accurate measures.

Unfortunately, research and experience indicate predominantly discouraging answers to several of the questions in Figure 10.2 (e.g., questions 1, 2, 9, 13, and 17). Also, even if uncontaminated, countable, nonjudgmental data exist for certain jobs, the probability is low that the collection and use of such data will not disrupt organizational functioning and that the data will represent a high percentage of the

FIGURE 10.2. Flowchart for the identification of basic data for performance measurement

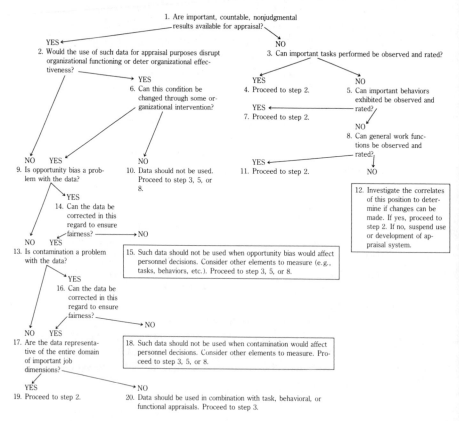

performance domain. Thus there is an inevitable need in most jobs for judgmental data (e.g., a rating), either to augment or to replace countable results.

Guion (1965) has grouped countable measures into two major categories: production data and personnel data. Production data include direct measures, such as the number of items produced, sales volume, or commissions earned. Personnel data include such variables as absenteeism, turnover, tardiness, and accident rates. It should be pointed out, however, that some human judgment is obviously involved in the selection of the variables to be measured and the collection and recording of such data (e.g., what constitutes tardiness or an excused absence?). The first question in Figure 10.2 (i.e., whether important, countable, nonjudgmental data are available) is undoubtedly answered in the negative for the majority of jobs today.[2]

The extent to which the data are important can be determined through the job analysis. It should be clarified that availability means that knowledge of such results is retrievable from records and that there are no restrictions on the use or collection of such data (e.g., union contracts). A positive response to this question should also reflect some degree of verifiability for the data. In other words, are there assurances that such data are indeed accurate?

Assuming important, countable, nonjudgmental results are available and can be determined to be useful, the next question in Figure 10.2 concerns the ramifications of the use of such data in terms of organizational functioning and effectiveness. Odiorne gives the following illustration of this important issue:

> Take the case of the firm that [decided] to initiate [an MBO] program. The managers and staff participated enthusiastically. In addition to . . . objectives for the control of financial, sales, and manufacturing figures, they also added a number of highly innovative and invaluable programs dealing with improved public relations, employee relations, and product and customer service. At the end of the year, the results were reviewed by the top management officials. When the rewards and citations for achievement were issued, it became very clear that only those goals which had measurable outcomes were being recognized. Among those which had been left unrecognized was a complete turnaround of the community's attitude from hostile to friendly and supportive. A general decline in employee hostility was another salutary but unrecognized outcome.
>
> Furthermore, everyone knew that the manager who had come off best in the MBO results sweepstakes had actually done the company considerable damage by the way in which he had obtained the splendid numerical results in his plant. For one thing, he had badly injured labor relations by breaking faith with union officers during the year. Each of

2. Several surveys have indicated that MBO is a common approach to performance appraisal in the U.S. However, many respondents probably misconstrued their own WP & R programs as MBO. As discussed, a most important distinction between MBO and WP & R is that MBO requires "hard," countable results (Bernardin & Beatty, 1984).

these labor leaders made known his intent to "get even" with the company for betrayals at the hands of his manager. A second negative accomplishment which did not appear on the numerical results table worshipped so ardently by top management was the destruction of the careers of two promising young men who had been in his baleful area of influence. Both had been forced from the company for no other offense than that they were sufficiently competent to threaten the manager's own progress. Still another devastating result which did not appear on any account book was his practice with regard to maintenance of the equipment under his control. By cutting necessary repairs during the year, he had shown impressive "savings." Needless to say, the costs in downtime and poor quality in following years exceeded by far what he had "saved." (1974, pp. 123–124)

This illustration needs little elaboration and probably conjures up other examples of dysfunction caused by such results-oriented measurement (e.g., when Wilt Chamberlain set a National Basketball Association record for scoring average, did the Philadelphia Warriors win the title?).[3] If only countable end results are recognized and the means for their attainment are ignored, the use of such data can have far-reaching implications in terms of overall organizational effectiveness. Such a procedure can also lead to a failure to recognize effort and motivation and may impede creativity (see McGraw, 1978). Another potential problem emerges whenever the countable results are linked to rewards for individuals and the attainment of the results was very much a team effort (Kane & Bernardin, in press). Such a policy may ultimately be disruptive to group cohesiveness and future success. As in Odiorne's illustration, concentration of effort on those behaviors most directly linked to the measured results will be accompanied by a corresponding decrease in behaviors that cannot be readily measured in terms of results. As another example, if police officers were appraised on the basis of the number of arrests they made that led to convictions, the number of arrests would probably increase while such behaviors as assisting disabled motorists or informing citizens of crime prevention strategies would probably decrease; also, the mere collection of the number of arrests might be disruptive in that it could lead to fellow officers' disputing claims to arrests.

An estimate of the extent to which the collection and use of countable results will be detrimental to organizational functioning can also be obtained through questionnaire responses and discussion with a task force. Some indication of whether conditions could be made more conducive to the use of such data can also be ascertained through these sources.

If it can be determined that the organizational functioning will not be de-

3. When Wilt Chamberlain set the NBA scoring average in 1962–63, he had a scoring average of 50.4 points per game (and 25.7 rebounds per game). His team finished with a record of 49 and 31, but they did not win the championship. However, in 1966–67, his team did win the championship, and his per game average was 24.1 points and 24.2 rebounds.

leteriously affected by the collection or use of this type of data, the next question in Figure 10.2 is whether such data are affected by opportunity bias. As defined by Brogden and Taylor (1950), *opportunity bias* reflects the extent to which performance is beyond the control of the employee. For example, data consisting of sales volume in a given period of time without a consideration of territorial assignment would probably be affected by opportunity bias (i.e., a superior salesperson assigned to a poor neighborhood might very well sell less than an inferior salesperson selling in a more affluent area). Methods for correcting data for opportunity bias are available (Bernardin & Beatty, 1984). Opportunity bias is a problem whenever comparisons must be made across individuals whose performance is affected by it (e.g., Nicholson, 1958).

Assuming opportunity bias is a problem that can be corrected, the next question in Figure 10.2 with regard to the use of countable results is the extent to which the data are affected by contamination. As defined by Brogden and Taylor (1950), *contamination* is the inclusion of elements in measurement that are not related to job success (i.e., there are items on the appraisal form that are not related to job success). In a more implicit treatment of this source of error, Guion stated that "output measures are all too frequently contaminated by influences not related to the individual's capacity or willingness to produce" (1965, p. 91). Examples of common implicit contaminants are racial and sex biases, which may affect the actual recording of the data or the type of supervision given to the employees, which in turn affects their productivity. Other examples of such contaminants are job tenure and the use of "inside" information that facilitates higher productivity. Like opportunity bias, implicit contamination can be statistically corrected. However, unlike the sources of opportunity bias, the sources of contamination are sometimes impossible to identify, as in many of the examples of racial and sex biases. Fortunately (or unfortunately), contamination for countable results is easier to correct than contamination affecting ratings of performance.

The next question in Figure 10.2 concerns the extent to which data from the countable results represent the entire domain of important job dimensions (e.g., how many points were scored by the people Wilt Chamberlain was supposed to be guarding?). This question is related to the issue of deficiency, which was discussed in the passage from Odiorne (1974) cited earlier. Criterion deficiency is essentially the result of inadequate sampling of the content domain. With regard to the police example, there are other aspects of a police officer's job besides arresting suspects. If these other aspects are not represented by some countable result, the data that are available are deficient. There are very few jobs in which countable results could adequately represent the entire domain of job performance.[4]

---

4. Athletics is probably one exception. Wilt Chamberlain's performance during a season could also be assessed for assists, turnovers, defense, blocked shots, successful picks, and so on—data that might capture the entire domain of job performance. Ratings are unnecessary for any element of Jack Nicklaus's job. The proof is really in the putting.

Once again, data from the appraisal questionnaire and discussions with the task force should provide answers to the questions presented in Figure 10.2. Before an appraisal system that relies heavily on countable results is installed within an organization, these important questions should be resolved.

Primarily because the vast majority of cases involving countable, nonjudgmental results suffer from criterion deficiency and are potentially disruptive to organizational functioning, hybrid methods of performance appraisal have been recommended by numerous writers (e.g., Beatty, 1977; Bishop, 1974; Brady, 1973; Levinson, 1976; Porter, Lawler, & Hackman, 1975; Schneier & Beatty, 1979). To date, no empirical studies support the application of these approaches to personnel decisions.

LEVEL OF SPECIFICITY OF RATING CONTENT AND SOURCES OF APPRAISAL

The level of specificity selected for appraisal depends primarily on the extent to which the various levels can be measured fairly and accurately. Related to this question, of course, is whether raters are in a position either to observe or to obtain information from a representative sample of tasks or functions performed or behaviors exhibited. Here again, questionnaire responses should reveal future raters' perceptions of how observable levels of performance are and how accurate such observations can be.

Assuming that a representative sample of tasks or functions performed or behaviors exhibited can be observed, the same questions presented in Figure 10.2 for countable results can now be applied for the various levels of data specificity. Thus questions regarding the disruptive effects of such data collection and the extent of opportunity bias, contamination, and criterion deficiency in the use of each level of specificity should be addressed. The relative levels of these sources of errors should indicate the best level of specificity available for the organization. Kane (chapter 9) has presented measurability criteria that would be very helpful here as well.

Consideration of the various levels of specificity available for appraisal should also be made in the context of a consideration of the various rating sources available. Barrett (1966) concluded that for certain purposes, less frequently used raters may enhance the validity of ratings. In their review of research on peer assessment, Kane and Lawler (1978) found that all forms of peer assessment have potential for validity and that the peer-nomination method appears to have the highest reliability and validity (see also Brief, 1980; Kane & Lawler, 1979). Bernardin (1984) found strong support for the use of subordinates in managerial evaluation. It is more likely than not that no one organizational position can adequately assess a person's effectiveness. Thus, in terms of the critical question of accuracy in measurement, the selection of the source or sources for rating should at least give consideration to the possible options (e.g., immediate supervisor, other supervisors, self, peers, subordinates, external reviewers, or trained appraisers).

It should be emphasized that the research does not document the superiority of one source of appraisal over any other (e.g., Borman, 1974; Klimoski & London, 1974), despite the predominance of the immediate supervisor as the sole source for appraisal (e.g., Bernardin & Villanova, 1986; Lacho, Stearns, & Villere, 1979).[5] Responses from the questionnaire and discussion with the task force should lead to some hypotheses regarding the best sources for appraisal. As already stated, questionnaire responses in Bernardin's 1979 study clearly indicated differences in perceptions as to the best sources for appraisal as a function of different jobs and different organizational levels. Therefore recommendations for the sources of appraisal should be made at the same time and in conjunction with the selection of one or more levels of data specificity.

With respect to all of the administrative purposes for appraisal, only an overall rating of effectiveness is absolutely necessary. If a majority of respondents to the questionnaire and members of the task force feel accurate measurements can be made of overall job performance, this time- and money-saving approach to appraisal could be tried. A unidimensional forced-choice or personnel-comparison method might be appropriate for this purpose. However, although there is some empirical support for these unidimensional methods, considerable legal difficulty could be encountered if there was evidence of adverse impact.

If the purpose of PA is to provide data for promotions or selection, an empirical or judgmental relationship between the performance elements at one job level and those at another level should be established (Bernardin, Bownas, & Riegelhaupt, 1982). Given evidence of an empirical relationship between overall performance at one job level and performance at a higher level, and no evidence of adverse impact, the use of a global PA would probably be justified. However, the availability of such data is unlikely. A better approach would be to have persons familiar with the two jobs in question determine the content-domain overlap at a fairly specific level of performance elements. For example, through a job analysis, a determination can be made about the extent to which high performance on critical tasks or behaviors at job A is thought to be related to levels of knowledge, skills, abilities, or performance on critical tasks or behaviors at job B.

This approach should result in potentially greater predictive validity than an appraisal that assesses only global performance on such general functions as supervision, management, or technical skills. With more specific performance elements, less interpretation is required of the rater. Thus the greater the speci-

---

5. Bernardin (1984) reported that many companies are using subordinate ratings to appraise managerial performance (e.g., IBM, RCA, Ford). In the federal study discussed throughout this chapter, Bernardin (1979) found a high level of interest expressed in this source of evaluation.

ficity of the performance elements rated, the more valid will be the judgmental overlap that is established between two jobs, and, ultimately, the greater the predictability of the resultant ratings. In addition, if data must be aggregated for some purpose, elements can be aggregated from specific to more general, but not in the opposite direction.

If PA data are to be used to improve performance by creating a better understanding of what the job entails (Figure 10.1, step 36), then the greater the specificity of the performance elements, the more likely the PA format is to accomplish that purpose. Research does indicate that the greater the understanding of the job, the higher the level of performance (Bernardin, 1979; Schneier & Beatty, 1978).

Just to complicate matters a little more, when PA data are used for more than one purpose, it is conceivable that more than one level of specificity could be adopted across performance elements. For example, if data related to supervisory performance were found to be important for promotional considerations, while data related to technical performance were most important for feedback purposes, then the level of specificity for rating could differ even on a single rating format. This poses a problem for comparing scores, which will be discussed later.

Although the research does not strongly support the notion, the position taken here is that the greater the specificity of observable performance elements, the greater the accuracy in the appraisal. Thus, ignoring the practical issues at this point, I recommend more specific, task-oriented or behaviorally based performance elements on which to rate, regardless of the purpose of appraisal, providing such data can be scored for relative effectiveness across jobs (i.e., at this level of specificity, certain task performances or behavior can be judged to be more effective than others). While more general performance functions are adequate for the purposes of personnel decisions, such as those relating to merit pay and retention, and test validation, the potential validity of such data is more questionable than that derived from a more specific rating format. Thus, if some method can be used for deriving task-oriented or behaviorally based information, then a high level of specificity should be adopted for rating.

Once the basic data that can be most fairly and accurately measured are identified, one can return to step 2 in Figure 10.2 in order to begin a demonstration of the appropriate purposes for appraisal. The weighting system applied to the performance elements is closely allied to the various appraisal purposes. This appraisal parameter in the context of Figure 10.2 is examined next.

WEIGHTING PERFORMANCE ELEMENTS

The weighting of performance elements is necessary when the purpose of appraisal is to provide data for personnel decisions (see steps 9, 20, and 31 in Figure 10.2). The type of personnel decision is also very important in determining the weighting scheme to be adopted. In the large-scale federal project discussed earlier (Bernardin, 1979), a standardized job analysis questionnaire was used to derive data for the weighting scheme.

Kane (chapter 9) has proposed a very useful method for deriving dimension weights. This method is most appropriate for obtaining summary judgments for use in decisions regarding pay raises and retention and for use in test validation. The first step in the process is to select one level of specificity for use in deriving weights. Kane recommended focusing the weighting process at the highest level of specificity that occurs among the elements that serve as the performance dimensions for a given job. All dimensions that are more broadly defined should then be broken down into their constituent elements at the level of the most specific element(s). The process of deriving weights for the resulting set of elements (all of which now represent a common level of specificity) involves the following steps: (1) the element thought to have the least influence on overall success in the job as a whole is identified; (2) this element is then assigned a weight of 1.0 (more than one element can be assigned a weight of 1.0); (3) for the remaining elements, determine how many times more the more influential elements are than the least influential element(s); the resulting number constitutes the weight for each of the remaining elements; and (4) the weights for any of the original dimensions that had to be decomposed into their constituent elements for the purpose of generating the weight elements are computed by simply adding the weights of their constituent elements.

A similar procedure could be adopted in the use of appraisal data for promotional purposes. For this purpose, however, the focus of the first step of the weighting process would be on the higher-level job (i.e., what components of the lower-level job are least influential on the overall success of the upper-level job?). This procedure would also allow different jobs with different components to be compared for the purpose of predicting success at a higher-level job (Bernardin, Bownas, & Riegelhaupt, 1982). For example, suppose there are a hundred people eligible for promotion from a given grade level, but that they perform 300 unique tasks or duties. These tasks or duties are first rated for their importance for success at a higher-level job by ten or more subject matter experts familiar with the higher-level job. One or more weighting schemes (e.g., Kane's method, chapter 9) could be derived, with the number of schemes dependent on the number and diversity of target jobs at the predicted level (e.g., across different duty stations). After the weights for the various task statements have been derived, they are maintained confidentially by the personnel department. Next, when a rater is asked to rate an individual's past performance, the administrator selects the most "predictive" task items (plus some nonpredictive items) and requests that qualified raters evaluate eligible employees on these items. Each candidate's performance is then evaluated on each of the tasks (e.g., inadequate = 0; adequate = 1; outstanding = 2). Next, a rating is derived for each ratee by multiplying the subject matter experts' weights by the ratings of the raters.

The advantage to this approach is that the raters' idiosyncratic use of the rating scale is minimized by virtue of the importance of the weights assigned by subject matter experts. These importance weights are, of course, unknown to individual raters. The result is a "predictive" rating with potentially greater validity than the rating of a standardized format that has no importance weights assigned to statements (see, e.g., the discussions by Bernardin & Kane, 1980, and Kane & Bernardin, 1982, regarding summated rating scales with no importance weighting schemes). A more thorough treatment of this procedure is provided by Bernardin, Bownas, and Riegelhaupt (1982).

This problem of weighting performance elements is really one of job grouping and is directly related to the level of specificity adopted for rating performance. As noted earlier, the greater the amount of specificity in the rating format, the greater the accuracy in rating (all other things being equal). In general, the greater the amount of task or behavioral specificity on the rating form, the greater the difficulty in grouping jobs for weighting purposes. The next section will deal with the related issue of choice of a standardized or individualized format for rating.

At the outset of this section, it was stated that a weighting scheme is necessary when PA data are to be used for personnel decisions. In addition, a weighting scheme is necessary for MBO types of appraisal systems when multiple goals are set and the attainment of those goals actually conflict. Barton (1981) introduced a formal method of multiple-criteria decision making (MCDM) that can be used in the formulation of goal-conflict decisions in the context of MBO or work planning and review (WP & R) systems. With this approach, values indicating the relative importance of each goal can be derived in order to assess the relative effects and trade-offs involved in terms of overall organizational effectiveness. The method is also adaptable for linking MBO outcomes to personnel decisions.

RATING FORMAT: STANDARDIZED OR INDIVIDUALIZED?

The choice of an individualized or standardized format for appraisal is also dependent on the purpose of the appraisal. If the purpose is simply to provide feedback on a person's performance in order to foster improvement, a format tailored to each person's position description, with hard and specific goals set according to the important job elements, is usually the optimal strategy. One problem with this general recommendation for short-term performance targets is that, by definition, these targets must be static. This can pose difficulties, particularly at high managerial levels where task elements are necessarily complex and static statements of performance goals may not be appropriate (Kane & Bernardin, in press).

Levinson has stated that the "higher a man rises in an organization and the more varied and subtle his work, the more difficult it is to pin down objectives that represent more than a fraction of his effort" (1970, p. 126). Consider also Mintzberg's findings (1973) that about 50 percent of a manager's activities lasted nine minutes or less, about 10 percent of a manager's activities lasted an hour, over 75 percent of a manager's contacts were ad hoc (not preplanned), and managers preferred to concentrate their efforts on the nonroutine. With the establishment of short-term goals in a WP & R or MBO format, those nonroutine areas not formalized on the work plan may receive little or no weight in the subsequent review and may perhaps focus a worker's concentration on areas less related to overall organizational effectiveness and more oriented to concrete, short-term accomplishment. Thus it is possible that a "by-the-numbers" orientation would seriously impede creativity in management.[6]

Related to this issue, McGraw (1978) has speculated that when motivation or arousal is high for performing a task or achieving a goal, the individual may be so totally preoccupied with achieving the targeted outcome that incidental learning and exploration of different means of achieving results, such as discovering heuristics or making creative integrations, are inhibited. When tasks require such processes for overall success, the results orientation of the goal-setting process can actually impede success. This speculation also applies to the use of money incentives for certain levels of performance.

Although a standardized format does give ratees an impression of where they stand relative to other ratees with the same or similar jobs, there is little evidence that such feedback improves performance. In fact, there are no published studies that indicate that numerical feedback per se is superior to nonnumerical, behaviorally based feedback in improving performance. It is likely that more personalized appraisal formats will result in greater performance improvement than standardized formats. The use of a goal-oriented, hybrid PA method or a WP & R process would be best for this purpose under most circumstances (Schneier & Beatty, 1979).

If the purpose of appraisal is to provide data for personnel decisions, a standardized format is preferable. MBO and WP & R, for example, provide no basis for the comparison of individuals, because no attempt is made to standardize the objectives that have been set or the measurement of attainment of those objectives (Kane & Bernardin, in press). Thus either common performance elements or weighting schemes that can compare different elements are necessary whenever individuals must be compared for personnel decisions.

Some type of rating format is necessary for WP & R to assess the extent to which standards have been achieved. Such a format must reveal numbers that can be compared across ratees when the data are to be used for important personnel decisions. This does not necessitate a standardized format (it would be possible to weight different standards or tasks across jobs), but it makes such a format more

---

6. Wachtel discussed such problems as they apply to the academic community. He stated that the use of quantitative measures of "output, along with the emphasis on sheer numbers (of articles, of dollars in grants, or whatever) has long been prevalent in academic circles" (1980, p. 403). This preoccupation with productivity has led to a "short, sweet, and plentiful" philosophy of research that is probably deleterious to scientific progress.

attractive since the alternative would be quite cumbersome (see the discussion on the level of specificity). In general, whenever there are fifteen or more occupants of the same job class and over 75 percent of their critical work elements are common, a standardized rating format should be adopted if the data are to be used for personnel decisions. (See Jacobs, chapter 2, and Borman, chapter 3, for a discussion of the various advantages and disadvantages of the different standardized formats, e.g., BARS, mixed-standard scales, summated scales, and forced-choice sales.) Once again, data from an appraisal questionnaire should be helpful in the selection of the format.

FREQUENCY OF APPRAISAL

Thus far, four key topics have been addressed: (1) the basic data to be used for appraisal, (2) the level of specificity as well as the appraisal source, (3) the weighting scheme to be used for the performance elements, and (4) the choice of an individualized versus a standardized rating format. Emphasis has been given to a questionnaire on appraisal as a major source of information on which to base decisions regarding the installation of a PA system. Such data can also be used to select the frequency with which appraisals should be made. Traditionally, formal appraisals are done once or twice a year (Bernardin & Villanova, 1986). Research clearly documents the difficulties besetting a rater who is asked to retrieve from memory six or more months of performance exhibited by several ratees. As discussed earlier, a majority of future raters and ratees in Bernardin's 1979 survey expressed dissatisfaction with the use of appraisal data collected only once or twice a year for any important personnel decision. A common recommendation was to do appraisals upon the completion of projects or upon the achievement of important milestones in large-scale projects.

Kane and Lawler (1979) discussed the sparsity of research on the frequency of appraisal. They cited Jacque's time span of discretion (1961) as a concept that could be applied to decisions regarding the frequency of appraisals. The *time span of discretion* (TSD) is defined as the length of time between the point at which a job incumbent is given a task and the point at which below-standard performance could occur. Thus Kane and Lawler hypothesized that the interval between appraisals should consist of at least one TSD. The number of TSDs needed for each appraisal period would also be determined by the need for formal feedback, the effects of the number of TSDs on reliability, and, of course, practical issues. Levine and West (1971) showed that the intervals needed for appraisals in order to discriminate between employees differ according to the difficulty of the jobs. Van Maanen (1976) found that new employees required more frequent appraisals than employees with longer tenure.

The research indicates that greater accuracy can result when the effects of the highly fallible human memory can be limited. Thus more frequent appraisals than the traditional six-month or annual appraisal would probably result in greater accuracy. The use of diary keeping to assist in the rating process can also enhance the accuracy of appraisals (Bernardin & Walter, 1977). Responses to Bernardin's 1979 appraisal questionnaire indicated that both future ratees and raters agreed with these conclusions. Thus a more systematic study should be conducted of the extent to which frequency of appraisal may affect accuracy under certain organizational conditions. Once again, questionnaire data and discussion with a task force should provide insight into this relationship.

A MEASUREMENT MODEL

Related to the issue of frequency of appraisal is the descriptiveness of the data provided in appraisal. The vast majority of appraisal methods ask for only a rating of "typical" ratee performance. Thus, with few exceptions (e.g., Bernardin & Smith, 1981; Kane & Lawler, 1979), no consideration is given to what Thorndike (1949) called *intrinsic unreliability,* which reflects the distribution of a ratee's performance throughout the appraisal period. Once again, through questionnaire responses and discussion with a task force, a determination should be made as to whether variability in individual performance is related to organizational effectiveness. Some research does indicate that ratings of a ratee's stability of performance are not very reliable when they must cover a long period of time (Rambo, Chomiak, & Price, 1983). Thus, if the questionnaire data indicate that intrinsic unreliability is an important factor in organizational effectiveness, a case can be made for more frequent appraisals.

In addition, arguments can be made for rating methods that consider other characteristics of the performance measurement model beyond the "typical" level. Kane has proposed a measurement method that places emphasis on the distribution of ratees' performance (see Kane, chapter 9). Particularly noteworthy in Kane's model is the measurement of *negative-range avoidance,* which is defined as the extent to which the ratee does not exhibit extremely negative types of behavior. For certain jobs, it is critical to avoid even scattered instances of extremely poor performance (e.g., those involving public health or safety). The BARS method discussed by Bernardin and Smith (1981) also considers other characteristics of performance measurement in addition to the average.

TRUST IN THE APPRAISAL PROCESS AND CONTROL PROCEDURES

In the previous pages, the essential mechanics of the PA process (i.e., the who, why, when, what, how, and by whom of appraisal) have been covered. However, little attention has been devoted to one organizational parameter that has been shown to have a powerful impact on the effectiveness of an appraisal system. The final major area of consideration is the extent of organizational trust in the process of appraisal. Very much related to perceived accuracy and fairness in appraisal, the extent of trust in any appraisal process or future appraisal process should also be assessed in the context of the first question in Figure 10.1. If low levels of trust are expressed by future raters and ratees, there is a need to consider control procedures to offset the ramifications of the low trust. The use of a demonstration project, as proposed in the diagnostic model in Table 10.1, would be useful in testing such control procedures.

Bernardin's 1979 study found large differences across units and divisions with regard to perceived trust in the appraisal process. This diagnostic information was helpful in developing training programs and control procedures in preparation for the implementation of the PA system. The study used the "trust in the appraisal process survey" (TAPS) to measure perceived trust in the appraisal process. Data from the TAPS were used to pinpoint trouble spots within the organization. The data indicated a need for greater rater training and data-control mechanisms for particular divisions within the organization. In addition, the TAPS identified particular individuals who seemed in greater need of training in the appraisal process. High TAPS scores might also be used to justify the selection of a forced-choice rating format, which would make it more difficult to deliberately distort ratings to the benefit or detriment of the ratees. As an alternative or in addition to the use of a forced-choice format, formalized management-control procedures would also be important in an organization with low levels of trust in the appraisal process. Other elements of the organizational climate related to the implementation and use of PA, in addition to those "tapped" on the TAPS, should be assessed.

A considerable amount of experience within both the public and the private sectors indicates that without adequate control procedures, an appraisal system linked to personnel decisions can prove disastrous, regardless of the specificity established in the process of setting performance standards. For example, the first "experimental" run of appraisals for the purpose of deciding merit pay under the Civil Service Reform Act resulted in a recommendation that over 90 percent of qualified federal employees receive merit pay. Of course, one interpretation of this result is that managers were working harder because of the incentive of merit pay and thus were deserving of it, but the extremely high percentage of recommended employees leads one to question the credibility of the system. Thus control procedures should be installed for an appraisal system, particularly in situations of low organizational trust. Survey data and discussion with the task force, and perhaps the results of a demonstration project as well, should be used in the development of the control mechanism(s).

One method of controlling the effects of low trust in the appraisal system is to establish a multistep process for decision making. In this approach, a common nomenclature for assessing the contributions of individual employees is created by establishing a panel of subject matter experts who can objectively assess the individual contributions of organizational members. In addition, the burden of final evaluation is removed from the immediate supervisor, who is the person most susceptible to rating inflation because he or she may have to interact with the

TABLE 10.3. A Structural Model of Appraisal Using a Multistep Decision-making Process

Group or Department	Functions
Department of personnel	Maintains data file; monitors entire systems; performs administrative duties.
Review panel or group of subject matter experts	Assesses appraisal validity and documentation; assesses raters on PA responsibilities; provides feed-back to raters; develops weighting scheme for performance elements.
Supervisors of raters	Make personnel decisions regarding ratees; assess potential (if necessary); provide feedback to raters; recommend career development.
Raters	May assist in setting performance standards; do performance counseling; submit formal appraisals to supervisor; recommend career development; describe performance.
Ratees	May assist in setting performance standards; submit reports of accomplishments, activities, and tasks performed, self-ratings, career goals, and geographical references.

appraised individual on a daily basis (see Bernardin & Buckley, 1981); as a result, the immediate supervisor's efforts may be directed toward a strict description of performance and career development. It is left to a higher-level manager or supervisor to evaluate that description and to make any major personnel decisions. This control model is not unlike the typical university promotion and tenure system, in which several hurdles must be negotiated before a final decision is made.

Table 10.3 presents a structural model of appraisal that describes the responsibilities at each step in the multistep decision-making process. In this model, the first decision regarding merit pay is made at an organizational level above the ratee's immediate supervisor. Such an approach has been shown to inhibit rating inflation more than the typical PA procedure, in which the immediate supervisor provides the critical evaluation.

Also supportive of this multistep process is case law in the area of appraisal, which clearly favors multilevel organizational decision making in personnel matters (Cascio & Bernardin, 1981; Nathan & Cascio, Introduction). The courts have not looked favorably at unilateral personnel judgments.

One important feature of the model presented in Table 10.3 is the consideration of performance appraisal as an important aspect of the immediate supervisor's job. Thus the extent to which the supervisor has been timely with well-documented appraisals would weigh heavily in an appraisal of his or her own performance.

Another important feature of the model is that the initial burden of responsibility for personnel action (e.g., deciding merit pay) rests with the appraised individual rather than with his or her supervisor. This process would entail a compilation of documented justification for the personnel action. Here again, the situation is similar to the typical university procedure, which calls for the submission of a detailed report on job activity from each faculty. The contents of the activity report and other sources of information provide for an objective assessment of all evidence in the iterative process of decision making.

The self-report method could be used as the first step in an integrated promotional system tied to performance. For example, each employee who wished to be considered for promotion or reassignment could do self-ratings of the extent to which tasks were important for the jobs she or he has occupied and the extent to which she or he was effective on each. As discussed in the section on weighting, these tasks would have predictability weighting, based on subject matter expert ratings, for various jobs. Employees could also indicate geographical preferences for employment at this point in the process. Once a position became available, the hiring official (e.g., a personnel officer or the supervisor) could examine the task list completed by the employee and weight the importance of each task for the position to be filled. Next, a computer program could identify the most qualified employees available both in terms of geographical preference and the compatibility of the self-reports with the task statements judged by the hiring official(s) to be most important for the open positions. Of course, the list of "most qualified" would be only a first step in the selection process, which would ultimately involve performance ratings for each of the most qualified group by supervisors, peers, or others on the same "predictive" task statements. The major advantage of this approach is that employees themselves serve as the initial screeners, and supervisors are thus spared at least one round of needless ratings.

A review panel could be established to oversee personnel decisions both within and across organizational levels and decisions. The panel would receive descriptive data on appraisals and recommendations for personnel action from immediate and second-level managers. The panel would then be responsible for feedback to managers regarding their appraisal and personnel decision making. The extent to which adequate documentation and justification are provided for a personnel decision and the extent to which appraisals are submitted on schedule would be scrutinized at this level. In addition, the review panel could serve as an appeals panel for formal appeals of the personnel action. Case law in this area documents the importance of a formal appeals process available to personnel (Cascio & Bernardin, 1981). The panel could also serve as an independent validation source for appraisals made at lower managerial levels.

The system of feedback on the appraisal process for individual raters that this structural model provides should prove most beneficial in inhibiting rating errors, particularly inflation. The documentation requirements and the formal process for assessing the documentation should provide sufficient control to enhance rating validity and fairness and should do much to counter the effects of low trust in the appraisal process.

Future Directions and Needs

Several assumptions of traditional performance appraisal have been questioned and a model has been proposed for the development and implementation of a PA system. The selection of the purposes to be served by the PA data should be carefully considered. The system must be technically sound and must be acceptable and supported by members of the organization. In fact, the involvement of those affected by the new system should be given every consideration in the design of the PA system. To that end, I have discussed (and illustrated) the use of organizational surveys to gauge employee trust and needs for a PA system and have included a flowchart of decisions to be made in the development and implementation of the appraisal system.[7]

Some readers may have the impression that organizational members have nothing better to do than to appraise their fellow employees. For example, on the basis of assumptions about PA and given certain circumstances, the following recommendations were offered: (1) the maintenance of anecdotal files, (2) more frequent appraisals, (3) multiple sources for appraisal, (4) task-oriented or behaviorally based scales, (5) the establishment of formal appeals panels, (6) rater training, and (7) a complicated weighting scheme for rating. Such recommendations are a far cry from the suggestions of numerous writers on appraisal to "keep it simple." First of all, the procedures recommended will undoubtedly add to the time required for appraisal. However, they are no more burdensome than other managerial responsibilities required for the administration of organization resources (e.g., financial, material, temporal, and informational resources). Only when the appraisal process is taken more seriously (with all relevant parameters taken into account) will appraisal prove to be a cost-effective human resource device. Thus, while the commitment of time and effort on the part of members of the organization will probably be greater than previous commitments with regard

---

7. The survey should be developed in accordance with the possible purposes to be served by the data and as a means of increasing the effectiveness of the data depending on the prescribed purpose. For example, if criteria must be provided for the purpose of test validation, the extent and type of contamination (e.g., predictor-correlated and nonpredictor-correlated) can be estimated for each possible criterion. This will enable the researcher to predict levels (or ceilings) on validity depending on the criterion used in the analysis and to propose adjustments in the data to control for contamination. Survey questions can also tap the extent to which various possible criteria are distorted or deficient.

to PA, without such a commitment, no type of PA measurement system will work to maximum efficiency.

Three other points should be made in this regard. First, the development of the PA system described previously fits in very well with other personnel functions and should raise their relative effectiveness at the same time (e.g., selection and promotion systems, job analysis, and training programs). Second, more sophisticated PA systems will require the greatest time and energy at the outset of their implementation. Once raters become comfortable with the system, the required effort should be reduced; raters should acquire skills in PA that make the task easier, but it will take patience and practice. Third, once participants become involved in effective systems, they generally perceive the extra effort as well worth their while, providing they are given sufficient time to conduct their appraisals. In terms of the third point, it should be made clear to appraisers that PA is an important element of their jobs and that they themselves will be assessed on the extent to which they have effectively carried out this function (Bernardin, 1984). Perhaps this single factor, holding raters accountable for their ratings, just as they are held accountable for the administration of other expensive organizational resources, will do more to improve the effectiveness of a PA system than any other technique or intervention that could be recommended.

References

Barrett, R. S. (1966). *Performance rating.* Chicago: Science Research Associates.

Barton, R. F. (1981). An MCDM approach for resolving goal conflict in MBO. *Academy of Management Review, 6,* 231–241.

Beatty, R. W. (1977, August). *Integrating behaviorally based and effectiveness-based appraisal systems.* Paper presented at the annual meeting of the American Psychological Association, San Francisco.

Bernardin, H. J. (1979, November). *A study to identify feasible appraisal systems for employees of the U.S. Geological Survey* (Final technical report to the U.S. Geological Survey; available from author).

Bernardin, H. J. (1984). *Innovative approaches to performance appraisal.* Paper presented for the Southern California Personnel Testing Council. Newport, CA. (Unpublished: available from author).

Bernardin, H. J., & Beatty, R. W. (1984). *Performance appraisal: Assessing human behavior at work.* Boston: Kent-Wadsworth.

Bernardin, H. J., Bownas, D., & Riegelhaupt, B. (1982). *Development of a selection/placement system for the Defense Communication Agency* (Final report to the Defense Communication Agency; available from author).

Bernardin, H. J., & Buckley, M. R. (1981). A consideration of strategies in rater training. *Academy of Management Review, 6,* 205–212.

Bernardin, H. J., & Kane, J. S. (1980). A closer look at behavioral observation scales. *Personnel Psychology, 33,* 809–814.

Bernardin, H. J., Orban, J. A., & Carlyle, J. J. (1981). Performance ratings as a function of trust in appraisal, purpose for appraisal, and rater individual differences. *Proceedings of the Academy of Management, 41,* 311–315.

Bernardin, H. J., & Smith, P. C. (1981). A clarification of some issues regarding the development and use of behaviorally anchored rating scales. *Journal of Applied Psychology, 66,* 458–463.

Bernardin, H. J., & Villanova, P. (1986). Performance appraisal. In E. Locke (Ed.), *The generalizability of laboratory experiments: An inductive survey.* Lexington, MA: Lexington Books.

Bernardin, H. J., & Walter, C. S. (1977). The effects of rater training and diary keeping on psychometric error in ratings. *Journal of Applied Psychology, 62,* 64–69.

Bishop, R. C. (1974). The relationship between objective criteria and subjective judgments in performance appraisal. *Academy of Management Journal, 17,* 558–563.

Borman, W. C. (1974). The rating of individuals in organizations: An alternative approach. *Organizational Behavior and Human Performance, 12,* 105–124.

Brady, R. H. (1973). MBO goes to work in the public sector. *Harvard Business Review, 51,* 65–74.

Brief, P. (1980). Peer assessment revisited: A brief comment on Kane and Lawler. *Psychological Bulletin, 88,* 78–79.

Brogden, H. E., & Taylor, E. K. (1950). The theory and classification of criterion bias. *Educational and Psychological Measurement, 10,* 159–186.

Carlyle, J. J., & Bernardin, H. J. (1980, August). *A methodology for developing performance appraisal systems in large organizations.* Paper presented at the annual meeting of the Academy of Management, Detroit.

Cascio, W. F., & Bernardin, H. J. (1981). Implications of performance appraisal litigation for personnel decisions. *Personnel Psychology, 34,* 211–226.

Guion, R. M. (1965). *Personnel testing.* New York: McGraw-Hill.

Jacques, E. (1961). *Equitable payment.* New York: Wiley.

Kane, J. S., & Bernardin, H. J. (1982). Behavioral observation scales and the evaluation of performance appraisal effectiveness. *Personnel Psychology, 35,* 635–642.

Kane, J. S., & Bernardin, H. J. (in press). MBO: The procrustean management model. In J. Orban (Ed.), *Managerial psychology.* Chicago: London House.

Kane, J. S., & Lawler, E. E. (1978). Methods of peer assessment. *Psychological Bulletin, 85,* 555–586.

Kane, J. S., & Lawler, E. E. (1979). Performance appraisal effectiveness: Its assessment and determinants. In B. Staw (Ed.), *Research in organizational behavior* (Vol. 1). Greenwich, CT: JAI Press.

Klimoski, R. J., & London, M. (1974). Role of the rater in performance appraisal. *Journal of Applied Psychology, 59,* 445–451.

Lacho, K. J., Stearns, G. K., & Villere, M. F. (1979). A study of employee appraisal systems of major cities in the United States. *Public Personnel Management, 8,* 111–125.

Levine, E. L., Ash, R. A., Hall, H. L., & Sistrunk, F. (1981). *Evaluation of seven job analysis methods by experienced job analysts* (Law Enforcement Assistance Administration, Grant No. 79-DF-AX-0195). Tampa: Center for Evaluation Research, University of South Florida.

Levine, E. L., & West, J. (1971). Relationship between task difficulty and the criterion: Should we measure early or late? *Journal of Applied Psychology, 55,* 512–520.

Levinson, H. (1970). Management by whole objectives? *Harvard Business Review, 48,* 125–134.

Levinson, H. (1976). Appraisal of *what* performance? *Harvard Business Review, 54,* 30.

Likert, R. (1966). *The human organization.* New York: McGraw-Hill.

McGraw, K. O. (1978). The detrimental effects of reward on performance: A literature review and prediction model. In M. R. Leeper & D. Greene (Eds.), *The hidden costs of reward.* Hillsdale, NJ: Erlbaum.

Mintzberg, H. (1973). *The nature of managerial work.* New York: Harper and Row.

Nicholson, J. R. (1958). *A study of the relationship between response consistency on a personality test and success as a life insurance agent.* Unpublished manuscript. Bowling Green State University.

Odiorne, G. S. (1974). *Management and the activity trap.* New York: Harper and Row.

Porter, L. W., Lawler, E. E., & Hackman, J. R. (1975). *Behavior in organizations.* New York: McGraw-Hill.

Rambo, W. W., Chomiak, A. M., & Price, J. M. (1983). Consistency of performance under stable conditions of work. *Journal of Applied Psychology, 68,* 78–87.

Schneier, C. E., & Beatty, R. W. (1978). The influence of role prescriptions on the performance appraisal process. *Academy of Management Journal, 21,* 129–135.

Schneier, C. E., & Beatty, R. W. (1979). Combining BARS and MBO: Using an appraisal system to diagnose performance problems. *Personnel Administrator, 24,* 51–62.

Taylor, K. (1984). *Performance appraisal system development: The consideration of attitudes toward appraisal, job objectivity, and supervisory style.* Unpublished doctoral dissertation, Virginia Polytechnic Institute and State University, Blacksburg, VA.

Thorndike, R. L. (1949). *Personnel selection: Test and measurement techniques.* New York: Wiley.

Van Maanen, J. (1976). Breaking in: Socialization to work. In R. Dubin (Ed.), *Handbook of work, organization, and society.* Chicago: Rand McNally.

Wachtel, P. L. (1980). Investigation and its discontents: Some constraints on progress in psychological research. *American Psychologist, 35,* 399–408.

11. JOB EVALUATION

Richard W. Beatty & James R. Beatty

Introduction

Historically the allocation of pay has remained a secret, but today's organizations have been asked to detail their compensation policies to employees (Beatty & Beatty, 1984). Unfortunately, research on compensation practices has not been conducted, or perhaps permitted, thus compounding the problems faced by organizations when asked to explain how to attract and maintain a work force (Beatty & Beatty, 1982).

When compensation practices are researched, it is typically from three perspectives: internal equity, external equity, and individual equity. Internal equity concerns the value of one job as compared to another within an organization; external equity concerns the value of a job with respect to similar jobs in other organizations; and individual equity concerns the compensation of an individual employee for the output for his or her work contributions (e.g., merit pay). The focus of this chapter is primarily internal equity: reviewing and critiquing current practices/methods, recognizing the advantages and disadvantages of alternative methods, and reviewing research with respect to the validity of job evaluation.

Schwab (1980) noted that although job evaluation has been practiced for some time, it has not been widely reported in personnel/human resources research. Consultants have performed job evaluations for organizations while keeping methodologies confidential, protecting "trade secrets." This practice has led to considerable confusion in the compensation area. This review discusses the major methods and presents an overview of methods and problems.

Job evaluations develop an internal hierarchy of job worth (i.e., job structure) relative to other jobs within the firm by "evaluating" the job's content, not the incumbent. The worth hierarchy is then usually compared with external labor market prices to assess correspondence between the internal valuing and the labor market value. Traditionally, wages were expected to mirror labor-market prices. Much of the current controversy over job evaluation is therefore moot, when in fact, the determination of the financial worth of jobs as practiced in most internal evaluation methodologies is dictated by the labor market.[1] Consequently,

---

1. Some methods of job evaluation, most notably the Hay system, would deny this practice. However, despite the method, once a job has an internal value, some attempt is made to link it or its class to the labor market. The Hay system is purported to measure "relative job difficulty and importance" and to be independent of the market.

traditional job evaluation methodologies are generally market-based, not based upon an independent, internal system of values developed by an organization, its compensation committee, or society at large.

Job evaluation primarily served as a surrogate for pricing jobs when labor-market prices were not available. When adequate labor-market data existed, the market was used to assign prices; therefore, much of the "mystery" of job evaluation could be relatively easily explained. Certainly organizations have been concerned about external equity, but the concept of internal equity only became a reality when little data existed for external equity comparisons. Thus internal equity (and methods of its determination through job evaluation) might not exist were it not for an inadequacy of labor-market data. Consequently, the current comparable worth/internal equity issue might not exist, at least in its present form, if job evaluation systems had not been developed. In any case, the original purpose was to determine an equitable price for a job (external equity) by assigning an internal value to the job in comparision to the price paid for other jobs within the organization (internal equity).

Before pursuing the job-evaluation research further, the term *compensation* must be clarified. Compensation in its present context is intended to mean direct wage payments and does not include indirect payments such as fringe benefits. Although the debate over indirect compensation has now been confronted by the legal system, it is beyond the scope of job evaluation, except that a job's direct compensation often affects its benefits (i.e., percentage contributions to retirement funds).

JOB ANALYSIS IN JOB EVALUATION

Typically, job-evaluation programs follow the flow-diagram shown in Figure 11.1. Most job-evaluation systems begin with some form of job analysis or field audit of the position to ensure that job content has been adequately captured. Job-evaluation data collection often differs from traditional job analysis, in that job-evaluation systems collect information on "compensable factors," which have been determined by their relevancy to the labor market. Thus traditional job analysis is not usually used for job evaluation in many organizations. That is, one job analysis is conducted for job descriptions, performance appraisals, and selection criteria, while another is conducted for job evaluation in which only information relative to determining a job's value is sought.

Although there are many methods of job analysis, only a few will be discussed here (see also Fine, chapter 1). It should be noted that such discussions are often conducted with reference to the federal government's *Uniform Guidelines on Employee Selection Procedures* (U.S. Equal Employment Opportunity Commission et al., 1978). It would be short-sighted not to recognize these guidelines in an area fraught with controversy and litigation potential (see Nathan & Cascio, Introduction).

FIGURE 11.1. Job evaluation and related processes

Obviously, for any job evaluation system to work, job content must be exhaustively examined; yet job content is frequently overlooked or not assessed effectively in the development of job evaluation instruments. The following excerpt from a recent court case illustrates how this can occur:

> The analyst did not verify the description by making an on-sight inspection of an employee who actually performed. . . . The former procedure was flawed insofar as it created the possibility of inconsistent descriptions, over- or under-inflation of job duties or requirements.
> (*Greenspan v. Automobile Club of Michigan,* 1980)

The judge's opinion raises questions concerning the procedures used in capturing and understanding content for job-evaluation purposes through on-the-job observations (i.e., with job incumbents) or questionnaires (see Figure 11.2). The major issue in job content identification is to ensure that the compensable factor information collected is related to the tasks, personal characteristics, behaviors, and risks required on the job.

The key point is to seek specific information about the job. The information sought has been described by McCormick (1976). It concerns the nature of the work to be performed (work activities, procedures, accountability/responsibility) and information about the worker's personal characteristics (behaviors and movements, tools used, temperament). The purpose of the job evaluation should dictate the method(s) chosen to collect data. Obviously, those selecting the items should at least consider commonly cited compensable factors, such as skill, effort, responsibility, and working conditions (see Equal Pay Act, 1963).

Terminology. Although Sidney Fine has presented a discussion of job analysis in chapter 1, a number of related terms need to be defined here to understand the job evaluation process better. Brief descriptions of five terms are presented below:

1. *Job analysis:* the collection of job-related information for each job for organizational decision-making purposes. The process of job analysis may be looked at as what is to be done (physical and mental responses), how it is to be done (tools, equipment, methods, judgments, calculations, etc.), and why it is to be done (overall purpose and how tasks relate to one another).
2. *Job specifications:* the abilities, skills, background, or characteristics that are presumed to be required to perform the job successfully. These might in-

FIGURE 11.2. Job evaluation

GENERAL DATA

1.	Department Unit Name
2.	Name
3.	Position Title

I.   ORGANIZATION RELATIONSHIPS

1. Employees supervised and titles

   A) _____

   B) _____

   C) _____

   D) _____

   E) _____

   F) _____

   G) _____

   H) _____

   I) _____

   J) _____

7. Organization of department (sketch an
organization chart for
the incumbent's part of
the organization):

| 5. | Total number supervised |
| 6. | Supervision received |

II.   DUTIES OF THE POSITION

8.   A) _____

    B) _____

---

clude such items as hand-eye coordination, typing, years of experience, and stress tolerance for high levels of noise.

3.   *Job description:* a written document that indicates the nature of the job (what, how, why, etc.) by reporting the job's task-related behaviors.

4.   *Job class:* a grouping of jobs based on their functional or task similarities.

5.   *Job evaluation:* the determination of the worth of jobs in dollars. It is often based on the data represented in a job description, although some job evaluation plans require data to be collected beyond traditional job descriptions. Job

FIGURE 11.3. Processes and uses of job content information based on job analysis

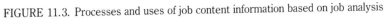
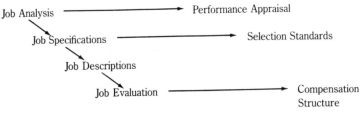

Job Analysis ────────────────▶ Performance Appraisal

Job Specifications ────────────────▶ Selection Standards

Job Descriptions

Job Evaluation ────────────────▶ Compensation
                                                                Structure

evaluation is thus the determination of the worth of a job (or a class of jobs) relative to other jobs within the organization.

The sequence of the development of job-related information is shown in Figure 11.3.

Certainly job evaluation practice has provided numerous approaches to gathering job information, some of which are explored in detail here because many discussions of job evaluation do not provide insight into the critical steps. Job analysts may interview incumbents, observe incumbents, examine the work environment and equipment used, study previous job descriptions and other job information, use a structured (quantitative) job analysis questionnaire, or employ some combination of these procedures as is advocated by Ash (1982). Figure 11.4 summarizes two qualitative and two quantitative approaches to job analysis. As noted before, a much more detailed description of job analysis procedures is found in chapter 1.

Generally the evaluation techniques outlined in Figure 11.4 specify the behaviors or activities that encompass a particular job. Once this information is gathered, education, training, and experience levels or other requirements can be examined. Together with the information about actual worker activities, these data make up the job description, which may be useful in the job evaluation process along with field audits and interviews with incumbents. The frequency of use of the four methods in public personnel positions is summarized in Table 11.1, which clearly indicates that in public jurisdictions the job element and functional job analysis techniques are most commonly used (Levine, Bennett, & Ash, 1979).

Task analysis, the position analysis questionnaire, and numerous quantitative job analysis methodologies all provide useful approaches to job analysis, although questions have been raised as to the reliability of these techniques (Milkovich, 1980; Schwab, 1980). There are also difficulties in deciding what levels of job analysis should be pursued (e.g., task, position, job, occupation, or family level). These are difficult and still unresolved issues (Pearlman, 1980). There is also the possibility that the sex of the job analyst may interfere with the accurate assessment of job content (Schwab, 1980).

A joint publication by the American Society for Personnel Administration and

FIGURE 11.4. Summary of commonly used job analysis techniques

Qualitative

Functional Job Analysis (U.S. Department of Labor, 1973). Questionnaires and interviews with job knowledge experts are used to analyze jobs into component tasks. Job analysts assign ratings to tasks on a number of scales that reflect the abilities, personal traits, and physical demands required of a worker in performing tasks. Tasks are grouped into similar functions.

Critical Incidents (Flanagan, 1954). Job knowledge experts delineate important job dimensions and describe incidents of job behavior illustrative of poor, average, and exceptional performance on that dimension.

Quantitative

Job Elements (Primoff, 1957). In group sessions, job knowledge experts generate skills, knowledges, abilities, and other worker characteristics (the job elements) required to perform the job in question. Experts assign ratings to the elements on a set of scales designed to assess each element's relative importance for selection. Analysis of the ratings yields the most important elements.

Position Analysis Questionnaire (McCormick, Jeanneret, & Mecham, 1972). Job knowledge experts complete a structured, commercially available questionnaire. The responses are analyzed by computer into a number of job dimensions (e.g., processing information) based on previous research with the PAQ.

the American Compensation Association, *Elements of Sound Base Pay Administration* (1981), advocates that whatever the method, descriptions should capture the nature (principal duties) and the level of skill and responsibility of the work performed, the types and amounts of mental and physical effort required, and the general physical conditions under which the work is performed. *Elements of Base Pay Administration* summarizes job description requirements for job evaluation as follows:

1. A *job identification* section including job title, department or location, company, date of completion and an area for approval.
2. A *general summary* or job purpose statement.
3. A list of *principal duties* and *responsibilities* of the incumbent(s). It is not necessary to list every conceivable task. Rather, major responsibility areas should be highlighted. In addition, some indication of priority of duties or percent of time spent on each can be most helpful . . . including some or all of the following information, either in the description itself or in some other document:
   a. The minimum levels of *knowledge, skill and abilities* required to perform the work adequately.
   b. Relevant *scope data,* such as budget, sales or profit responsibility, number of people supervised, etc.

TABLE 11.1. Use of Four Methods of Job Analysis

(N = 106)

Method	Using for job analysis study (%)	Mean no. job analysis studies	Using for exam plans (%)	Mean no. exam plans	Using for validation (%)	Mean no. validation studies
Critical incidents	24.5	2.6 (26)	10.4	2.5 (11)	12.3	2.0 (13)
Job elements	57.5	15.7 (61)	54.7	17.5 (58)	22.6	8.8 (24)
PAQ	8.5	10.7 (9)	6.6	4.9 (7)	3.8	2.3 (4)
Functional language	59.4	20.1 (63)	49.1	12.2 (52)	17.9	10.6 (19)

Source: American Compensation Association Survey (1976, p. 1)
Coverage: 275 larger U.S. corporations employing nearly 3 million employees in 35 different business fields, including manufacturing, finance, food, insurance, transportation, utilities, and health care.

    c. The nature and extent of *supervision* received and given.
    d. The physical and mental *effort* required.
    e. The *physical working conditions* under which the work is performed.
    f. A disclaimer clause, stating that the job description is not necessarily all inclusive in terms of work detail. (1981, p. 7; italics added)

Although the preceding discussion demonstrates a few of the problems with job analysis methods, effective job evaluation requires that every effort is made to obtain accurate job content information. A summary of the major approaches and their advantages and disadvantages to job analysis is provided in Table 11.2 (see also Fine, chapter 1).

Survey of Job Evaluation Approaches

There are many influences on an organization's allocation of pay, including the importance of pay to the organization and the organization's pay philosophy (e.g., training employees and developing stills versus hiring skilled employees), the financial consequences of employee withdrawal (e.g., turnover, absenteeism, and tardiness) due to dissatisfaction with pay, government regulations regarding pay

TABLE 11.2. Comparison of Methods for Collecting Job Analysis Data

Method	Definition
Questionnaire	Obtains occupational information from mailed survey. Employees are asked to describe their job in their own words. They complete form independently.
Checklist	Lists task statements. Employees are asked to check tasks performed in their work. Usually relies on interview or class standard to develop it.
Individual interview	Recording of information from supervisors and employees, usually on-site and using a standardized form.
Observation interview	Same as interview except data are gathered on-site while employee performs various activities being discussed.
Group interview	Group of employees representative of job under study record work activity data on standard form.
Diary	Employee records work activities while actually performing them.

Source: Beatty et al. (1981, p. 118).

systems, and the motivational aspects of pay for employees. These considerations are outlined in Table 11.3.

There are numerous methods that can be used to determine "job worth" and the internal wage structure. The objective is to provide equal pay for jobs of equal worth or importance and differential pay for jobs not of equal worth. Thus the rationale is that jobs are not all equally valuable to an organization and therefore should not be compensated at the same level. For example, some jobs are in high demand and others are in low demand; some have high status and others low; some call for large amounts of responsibility and others little; some are boring and others interesting; some are risky and others safe; some demand a high degree of specialized training or education and others do not.

The market data approach to job evaluation dates back as far as the 1880s, when Frederick W. Taylor designed a formal, systematic way of assigning pay to

Advantages	Disadvantages
Information can be obtained from a large sample. Works well with reasonably verbal employees. Preferable to observation with jobs that require a minimum of overt activity.	Can be a massive organizing job. Possible exaggeration of work done. Responses may be difficult to interpret. Responses may be incomplete.
Depends on recognition rather than recall. Information can be obtained from large sample. Critical tasks, frequency of performance, and time to perform can be identified fairly reliably.	Information about sequences of tasks is not obtained. Varying interpretation of tasks. Employees can lose interest and become bored, and hence unreliable.
Has been found to get more detailed and accurate information than other methods. It is the most reliable.	Slow and time-consuming. Impractical with a large and widely spread out work force.
Takes little time away from the job. Excellent when nature of job makes the activity overt.	Slow in obtaining data. Possible interference with operational activities. Cost is greater than most other methods.
Very economical in terms of work-hour costs. If done in brainstorming format, can generate large amount of data about job.	Dependent on employee's recall of work activity.
Not as dependent on recall. Precise information of time spent on activities and sequences.	May get a nonrepresentative sample of job. Relies on verbal and written information.

jobs for a steel company. Later, Congress attempted to establish a pay system for federal white-collar employees (Federal Classification Act, 1923). This act supported formal compensation systems that used methods for analyzing relative job value. It is believed that the first "point factor" evaluation plan was designed either by Merrill R. Lott in the 1930s or by Edward N. Hay, Eugene I. Benge, and Samuel L. H. Burke in the early 1940s. Four job evaluation systems were noted by the War Manpower Commission as early as 1943, including ranking, grading or classification, factor comparison, and point methods. Usually the first two are characterized as "qualitative" and the latter two as "quantitative" methods. There are also a number of unconventional methods, such as "timespan of discretion" (Jacques, 1964), "decision-banding" (Paterson, 1972a, 1972b), and "direct consensus" (Livy, 1975). In practice, there is an almost limitless variety of evaluation methods emphasizing job content because organizations tailor systems to

TABLE 11.3. Model of the Wage and Salary Determination Process

Organizational and Environmental Constraints	Organizational Techniques	Outcomes
Labor market availability	Job analysis	Job pricing/wage structure
Labor market prices	Job evaluation	Internal equity
Legal requirements (e.g., minimum wage, equal pay, etc.)	Job structure	External equity
	Job grades	Individual equity
Ability to pay	Wage and salary survey	
Industry practices		
Organizational philosophy (e.g., train and develop skills vs. buy skills in labor market, etc.)		
Extent of unionization		
Tradition		
Discrimination		

their own needs; however, most are modifications or derivatives of the basic methods, and we need not review them here.

In 1976 the American Compensation Association surveyed its membership on the use of and satisfaction with the following job evaluation methods: (a) whole-job methods, (b) factor methods, and (c) combinations (or others not reported). The results of this survey appear in Table 11.4. As can be seen, factor methods were most commonly used for hourly jobs and nonexempt salaried jobs, while whole job methods were most commonly used for exempt salaried jobs at the time of the survey.

In our own survey of job evaluation approaches, we will examine both qualitative and quantitative methods. The former include market data pricing, ranking, classification, and slotting. The latter include factor comparison, point factors, and quantitative job analysis.

QUALITATIVE METHODS

The first part of this review focuses on the job evaluation methods that do not require an independent evaluation of jobs by component parts on compensable factors, in other words, qualitative approaches to job evaluation.

Market data approach. The "market data" (or market pricing) approach is a whole-job approach that simply compares an organization's job titles (and perhaps additional information) with the titles in a salary survey to obtain a market value of

TABLE 11.4. Use of Job Evaluation Methods

Method	Hourly	Nonexempt Salaried	Exempt Salaried
1. Whole-job methods	27.9%	30.7%	38.5
Ranking	21.1%	22.6%	24.1%
Benchmark comparison	6.7	5.3	10.1
Grade standards	.1	2.8	4.3
2. Factor methods	68.2	42.3	35.1
3. Combinations or type not reported	3.9	27.0	26.4

Opinion Rating of Plans	Good	Fair	Poor	Good	Fair	Poor	Good	Fair	Poor
1. Whole-job methods									
Ranking	60%	39%	1%	66%	33%	1%	73%	25%	2%
Benchmark comparison	70	30	0	66	33	1	46	54	0
Grade standards	24	76	0	77	23	0	50	50	0
2. Whole-job methods (weighted averages)	62	37	1	66	33	1	66	32	2
3. Factor methods	85	9	6	84	14	2	96	4	0

Source: American Compensation Association Survey (1976, p. 1).
Coverage: 275 larger U.S. corporations employing nearly 3 million employees in 35 different business fields, including manufacturing, finance, food, insurance, transportation, utilities, and health care.

a job or a group of critical jobs without describing the job's content. Other jobs within the organization are then compared to these jobs and prices are assigned (i.e., "slotted" as described below). Occasionally, job analysis may be conducted and job content compared to the labor market descriptions. In some instances, the information found through the job analysis is simply compared to the market price of similar jobs surveyed, and the job priced (i.e., assigned a dollar value) in relation to the survey if it is consistent with the organization's pay philosophy.

When using this "market data" approach, the organization should carefully scrutinize job content to be certain that the job content of the survey job is, in fact, equivalent to the internal position. It should also attempt to reconcile the value of the internal job as it is perceived by the compensation committee with external labor market prices. Reconciliation may be difficult since some jobs may be valued by the labor market far in excess of how a firm values the job internally, or vice versa.

In any case, job evaluation with this approach simply compares the position with the labor market, determines whether the labor market is "correct" with respect to other positions within the organization, and allows a price to be assigned. This is not really job evaluation, in that no internal standard or value of the job is determined, except through the use of labor market price. A hierarchy of jobs is thereby established by selecting certain jobs and finding survey data for those jobs; all other positions are paid ("slotted") with respect to these jobs. These jobs, often called "benchmark" or "key" jobs, have characteristics similar enough to those in other organizations that they can serve as market anchor points. These jobs should be important in the organization's internal hierarchy and contain many incumbents, should represent many organizational levels, be widely found in the labor market, and should generally be viewed as fairly priced with respect to the labor market (i.e., an abundance or scarcity of supply should not exist). Obviously, this is a relatively simple method of pricing and does not focus as much on job content as the other methods.

There are three other whole-job evaluation approaches: ranking, classification, and slotting. These methods determine the relative worth of jobs on the basis of an overall assessment of the job's content (not merely its title). This is in marked contrast to quantitative methods, which analyze segments or factors in job content on a factor-by-factor basis. The qualitative methods do not yield a numerical score for each job evaluated. However, they usually capture job content by some means of job analysis and sequence jobs to provide a job structure.

Ranking. The ranking method is probably the oldest, fastest, and easiest of the qualitative methods. Evaluators rank jobs by overall worth or value to the organization. The job believed to be worth the most is placed first and the one perceived to be worth the least is ranked last. This ranking produces a job hierarchy.

There are a number of variations of this method, some of which include instructing the evaluators to consider certain attributes in jobs (i.e., job content) in their rankings. One approach compares each position with all other positions one at a time. This paired comparison yields a score (i.e., an overall rank) based on the number of times a position is deemed more important than another position. An example of a factor-by-factor ranking of jobs is shown in Table 11.5. Without factor-by-factor ranking, the subjective judgments of evaluators may be problematic, and disagreement among those ranking the jobs is likely to be high.

Although the ranking method is quick and usually inexpensive, it is quite subjective and easily outmoded by changes in job content. Ranking is often done in small firms, and a job's "value" is usually not defined further. Basically, ranking systems constitute a comparison of jobs with respect to an ambiguous criterion of "worth"; they are not usually held in high repute as a method of job evaluation (International Labour Office, 1960; Lanham, 1955).

Classification. The classification system was originally developed by the federal government to establish its pay program (i.e., general schedule ratings)

TABLE 11.5. Example of Ranking Method (Forced Ranking)

	One Individual's Ranking of Jobs				
	1st	2nd	3rd	Average	Final
Job A	1	1	2	1.3	1
Job B	3	2	1	2.0	2
Job C	2	3	3	2.7	3
Job D	4	5	5	4.7	5
Job E	5	4	4	4.3	4

	Ranking among Three People in a Committee			
	#1	#2	#3	Final
Job A	1	2	1	1
Job B	2	1	2	2
Job C	3	3	3	3
Job D	5	4	5	5
Job E	4	5	4	4

by specifying a number of grades for which broad descriptions are written for types of jobs to be placed in each grade. Jobs are evaluated by comparison with the grade description, then each job is placed within the appropriate grade. For example, ten grades may be established, each being defined by the characteristics the jobs in it would have. Grade 3 might include those jobs in which people perform tasks without direct supervision; grade 1 might contain those jobs in which people perform tasks under constant supervision, and so on. Evaluators do not define each factor and then compare jobs on a factor-by-factor basis but compare whole jobs. The higher the grade, the more education or skill is required (Table 11.6). Expert judgment is heavily relied upon and the chances of bias or inconsistency are reasonably high, yet the system is relatively easy to implement.

Classification requires that an idealized hierarchical structure be predetermined, with categories based on factors such as skill or responsibility.[2] The general schedule (GS) classification of the U.S. Civil Service Commission is probably the best-known classification system. In this system, eighteen grades are defined by eight factors, and each job is assigned a GS level for pay purposes. One inherent problem with this system is that jobs high on one level but low on another (e.g., high educational qualifications but no supervisory responsibility)

2. Some of the criteria used for job groupings include (1) common skills, (2) common occupational qualifications, (3) common licensing, (4) common union jurisdictional demands, (5) common career paths, (6) common function, (7) common work place or unit, (8) common technology, and (9) tradition.

may not fit the grade well, and thus arbitrary decisions are made (International Labour Office, 1960).

Slotting. The final qualitative technique is a system that "slots" jobs. This is close to the classification system, where the evaluators compare descriptions of new jobs with jobs already in the structure and place them in the grade with those that are the most similar. Often some form of matrix is used, with grades on the vertical axis and departments or job families on the horizontal axis, to facilitate comparisons across organizational lines (see Table 11.7).

QUANTITATIVE METHODS

The quantitative approach to job content evaluation has three primary methods: factor comparison, point rating or point factor, and quantitative job analysis. Each method evaluates the content of jobs factor-by-factor and yields numerical scores for each job evaluated.

Factor comparison. The factor comparison approach entails a series of specific and somewhat complex steps. Ten to fifteen benchmark jobs that are assumed to be "fairly priced" are selected, usually based upon labor market data such as possessing a common widely held definition and adequate supply and demand. Benchmark jobs should show variation on traditional job worth factors such as skill, physical effort, responsibility, mental complexity, and working conditions. Usually four to seven factors are selected (Livy, 1975). Each benchmark job is then ranked on each factor, often in a comparison format. A judgment is then made for each job regarding the worth of each factor (see Table 11.8). Thus each job is evaluated by being assigned a factor dollar worth (see Table 11.9).

An example of this process may help. Assume that mail clerk and welder jobs have been selected as benchmarks. The mail clerk is paid $250 per week and the welder $600. Using the ranking for each job on each factor, dollar assignments are made concerning the dollar contribution each factor makes to each of the jobs. For example, judgments might be made that would assign $300 to the welder's skill, $50 to the welder's working conditions, $100 to mental complexity, and $150 to responsibility. For the mail clerk, $50 might be assigned to skill, $50 to mental complexity, and $75 each to responsibility and working conditions. A validity check is then made by comparing both sets of ranking to determine whether they are in agreement.

Discrepancies are resolved in the evaluations by discarding potential benchmark jobs that do not have congruent horizontal and vertical rankings (Table 11.10). Once all benchmark jobs are evaluated on each factor, other jobs are compared to them factor-by-factor. Thus each job is "best fitted" on each factor and a factor price is assigned. Then the dollar values on each factor are added to obtain a price for each job (see Table 11.11). Owing to its complexity, and because

TABLE 11.6. Example of Classification Method

Class	Production	Administration
1. Simple, routine work; no exercise of judgment; under supervisor	Laborer 1	Clerk 1
2. Difficult, routine work; no exercise of judgment; under supervisor	Semiskilled laborer	Secretary 1
3. Difficult routine work; exercise of judgment; under supervisor	Parts handler	Secretary 2

TABLE 11.7. Typical Composition of Job Families

Clerical	Production	Supervisory	Technical	Managerial
Administrative assistant	Maintenance technician	Plant superintendent	Project leader	Vice-president
Executive secretary	Quality controller			Manager
Secretary	Senior production worker	Shift supervisor	Senior engineer	Director
General clerk	Production worker	Group supervisor	Engineer	Analyst
Mail clerk	Labor pool	First-level supervisor	Engineer trainee	Staff assistant

TABLE 11.8. Factor Comparison Method Step 1: Vertical Ranking

Key Jobs/ Factors	Mental Requirements	Physical Requirements	Skill Requirements	Responsibility	Working Conditions
Job A	1	5	2	3	3
Job B	2	4	4	1	6
Job C	3	6	1	6	4
Job D	4	1	6	2	1
Job E	5	3	5	5	2

Source: Adapted from Beatty et al. (1981, p. 61).
Note: The rank of 6 is highest.

TABLE 11.9. Factor Comparison Method (Step 2: Allocation of Wage across Factors; Step 3: Ranking of Allocations across Jobs)

Key Jobs/ Factors	Mental Requirements	Physical Requirements	Skill Requirements	Respon- sibility	Working Conditions	Current Market Rate (Dollars/Hour)
Job A	.40 (1)	2.00 (5)	.40 (1)	.75 (3)	.30 (4)	3.85
Job B	1.75 (2)	1.50 (4)	1.95 (3)	.20 (1)	2.20 (6)	7.60
Job C	2.15 (3)	2.05 (6)	2.70 (5)	4.10 (6)	.35 (6)	11.35
Job D	3.00 (4)	.25 (1)	2.80 (6)	.40 (2)	.10 (1)	6.55
Job E	3.20 (5)	1.35 (3)	2.50 (4)	2.50 (5)	.25 (2)	9.80
Job F	4.10 (6)	.75 (2)	1.80 (2)	2.10 (4)	.70 (5)	9.45

Source: Adapted from Beatty et al. (1981, p. 56).
Note: The rank of 6 is highest.

TABLE 11.10. Reconciliation of Vertical Ranking and Allocation of Wages Ranking

Key Jobs/ Factors	Mental Requirements	Physical Requirements	Skill Requirements	Respon- sibility	Working Conditions
Job A	V-1	V-5	V-2	V-3	V-3
	A-1	A-5	A-1	A-3	A-4
Job B	V-2	V-4	V-4	V-1	V-6
	A-2	A-4	A-3	A-1	A-6
Job C	V-3	V-6	V-1	V-6	V-4
	A-3	A-6	A-5	A-6	A-3
Job D	V-4	V-1	V-6	V-2	V-1
	A-4	A-1	A-6	A-2	A-1
Job E	V-5	V-3	V-5	V-5	V-2
	A-5	A-3	A-5	A-5	A-2
Job F	V-6	V-2	V-3	V-4	V-5
	A-6	A-2	A-2	A-4	A-5

Source: Adapted from Beatty et al. (1981, p. 57).

it is time-consuming, highly subjective, and difficult to explain to employees, the factor comparison system is not widely used (Akalin, 1970; Livy, 1975).

Point factor approach. By far the most popular of the major methods of job evaluation in the private sector is the point method (Akalin, 1970). The point method requires the evaluator to rate each job on a series of factors (e.g., physical effort, complexity of tasks, education, risk) presumed to contribute to overall job worth. Points are assigned to the degree of the factor that each job possesses (see

TABLE 11.11. Example of Factor Comparison Method Using Horizontal Dollar Rankings

	Accountability Responsibility *Factor A*	Physical Effort *Factor B*	Working Conditions *Factor C*	Mental Complexity *Factor D*	Supervision Exercised *Factor E*	Dollar Rate
Job A	(5) 2.00	(1) .20	(1) .20	(5) 2.00	(5) 2.00	6.40
Job B	(2) .50	(4) 1.60	(2) .50	(2) .50	(4) 1.60	4.70
Job C	(3) 1.00	(2) .50	(3) 1.00	(3) 1.00	(3) 1.00	4.50
Job D	(1) .20	(3) 1.00	(4) 1.60	(4) 1.60	(2) .50	4.90
Job E	(4) 1.60	(5) 2.00	(5) 2.00	(1) .20	(1) .20	6.00
					Total	26.50

Table 11.12). Job descriptions are often used as the source data from which the job evaluation system measures the extent to which the factor is required in the job. Jobs are then compared on total points, which indicate relative worth, and are eventually assigned salary levels (see Table 11.13). The items used in the point factor system are defined in Figure 11.5. In contrast to factor comparison, the range of points is constant across jobs, which makes the system administratively simpler but creates excessive rigidity (Benge, 1948). This method probably has the best chance of attaining job-evaluation objectives because jobs can be differentiated reliably and because the system is simple enough to explain to employees. Job prices are assigned by grouping jobs into job families and within-job families by point totals. Key jobs are then selected within each group and pay data are drawn from salary surveys. The pay statistic selected by the organization (e. g., survey midpoint plus 10 percent for the key job) is then used to price all jobs within this job group.

Quantitative job analysis (QJA). In using quantitative job analysis (e.g., PAQ), job elements are identified and grouped in clusters for specific jobs (i. e., job structure). The dimension scores are then regressed against market prices as shown in Figure 11.6, which permits the construction of a wage structure (see Taylor, 1978; Taylor & Colbert, 1978). Although this method should afford consid-

TABLE 11.12. Example of One Factor in a Point Factor System (Complexity/Problem Solving)

The mental capacity required to perform the given job as expressed in resourcefulness in dealing with unfamiliar problems, interpretation of data, initiation of new ideas, complex data analysis, creative or developmental work.

Level	Point Value	Description of Characteristics and Measures
0	0	Seldom confronts problems not covered by job routine or organizational policy; analysis of data is negligible. *Benchmark:* General secretary, switchboard/receptionist.
1	40	Follows clearly prescribed standard practice and demonstrates straightforward application of readily understood rules and procedures. Analyzes noncomplicated data by established routine. *Benchmark:* Statistical clerk, billing clerk.
2	80	Frequently confronts problems not covered by job routine. Independent judgment exercised in making minor decisions where alternatives are limited and standard policies established. Analysis of standardized data for information of or use by others. *Benchmark:* Social worker, executive secretary.
3	120	Exercises independent judgment in making decisions involving nonroutine problems with general guidance only from higher supervision. Analyzes and evaluates data pertaining to nonroutine problems for solution in conjunction with others. *Benchmark:* Nurse, accountant, team leader.
4	160	Uses independent judgment in making decisions that are subject to review in the final stages only. Analyzes and solves nonroutine problems involving evaluation of a wide variety of data as a regular part of job duties. Makes decisions involving procedures. *Benchmark:* Associate director, business manager, park services director.
5	200	Uses independent judgment in making decisions that are not subject to review. Regularly exercises developmental or creative abilities in policy development. *Benchmark:* Executive director.

TABLE 11.13. Example of Point Method of Job Evaluation

	Degree		Points			Competitive Position Value (Benchmark)
	Skill	Effort	Skill	Effort	Points	
Typist	A	1	40	40	80	$13,500
Administrative	D	1	55	40	95	16,500
Salesperson	C	5	50	80	130	21,400
Controller	G	4	70	70	140	28,900
Vice-president, Personnel	H	6	75	90	165	36,000

FIGURE 11.5. Point method definitions

The points allotted to each factor are summed to arrive at one point total for each job.

Factor: A broad category of job content, qualifications, etc., that can be used to group jobs (e.g., education, training, physical demands). Each broad factor may have several subfactors.

Weight: The relative worth of factors to each other, usually on a scale of 1 to 100 (e.g., education, weight 35; physical demand, weight 55, etc.). The weights do not always sum to 100.

Degree: The relative amount of each factor a job possesses. For example, there may be four degrees of the factor "education." Degree 4 could be possession of a doctoral degree; degree 3, possession of a master's degree, and so on.

Points: The relative worth of each degree is designated in points, with the highest number of points given to the highest degree. For example, degree 4 of education may be worth 40 points, while degree 3 is only worth 20 points, as a doctoral degree is significantly more difficult to attain than a master's degree.

erable reliability, its validity can be questioned, as with other methods, because of its use of market prices for the determination of job worth. The QJA scores may also be regressed against the *Dictionary of Occupational Titles* (DOT) worker function ratings in terms of data, people, and things (refer back to Figure 1.2). The middle three digits of the DOT code represent more complex data management, broader responsibilities, or more complicated tasks. Thus jobs with lower numbers in the middle three digits are generally expected to be more highly valued in the labor market.

FIGURE 11.6. Example of regressing QJA scores against labor market prices

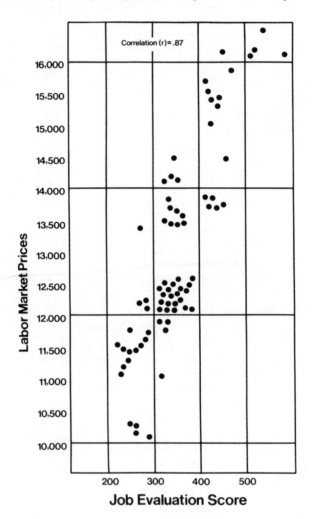

Before beginning a critical examination of problems with job evaluation as an approach to internal equity determination, we need to discuss a few issues with respect to job evaluation in general. These include the strengths and weaknesses of the job evaluation methods examined above, as well as specific problems with respect to technical issues and applications of job evaluation systems. The measurement problems relate mostly to reliability and validity issues, outlined in Figure 11.7.

FIGURE 11.7. Job evaluation processes and problems

Steps	Job analysis/ Job description →	Compensable factors →	Job evaluation →	Job structure → Determine hierarchical ranking of positions	Wage structure Assign wages and salaries to job structure

Potential Methods	• Functional language technique (and many variants)
	• Critical incidents technique
	• Job elements technique
	• Position analysis questionnaire
		• none
		• used with scaling/degrees (e.g., mental complexity, physical effort, working conditions, responsibility/ accountability, supervision exercised, education, experience)
			• Qualitative (whole job)
			  Market pricing
			  Ranking
			  Classification
			  Slotting
			• Quantitative
			  Point factor
			  Factor comparison
			  Quantitative job analysis		

Potential Measurement Problems	+ Reliability • Consistency of data collection + Validity • Accuracy of job content capture	+ Reliability • Consistency of selection for jobs studied + Validity • Accuracy in exhaustively capturing job content	+ Reliability • Consistency of job evaluation assignment + Validity • Accuracy of assignment relative to a standard	+ Reliability • Consistency of hierarchical rankings + Validity • Accuracy of assignment relative to a standard	+ Reliability • Consistency of prices assigned + Validity • Accuracy of pricing compared to a standard

Ranking. The simple ranking method without consideration of other information requires raters to provide a hierarchy of jobs without explicit standards for the ordering. It is difficult to determine why one job is valued more than another and to assess how much more one job is valued than another; thus ties (jobs with the same rank) are prohibited in most ranking systems. A change in the duties of one job may also necessitate a change in the job's rank, in the rankings of other jobs, and consequently, in the job evaluation system.

Classification and slotting. Classification systems and systems that "market slot" jobs also suffer from a lack of explicit criteria and reliability (although the judges may be consistent) because little detail is provided to guide decision makers. Furthermore, the decision makers may use different criteria for different classes. That is, the organizing principles for classifying may use one set of criteria for placing jobs in one class (e.g., nursing), while employing another set for other classes (e.g., managerial). The method also tends to force jobs into classes and prevents the legitimate movement of a job from one class to another.

Factor comparison. Quantitative approaches also have difficulties. The factor comparison method clearly increases the reliability of evaluation and addresses internal and external equity simultaneously, which is at least convenient, despite the preferences of some to separate these equity issues. Yet it requires considerable training of evaluators and cannot be changed rapidly with dollar changes in the labor market, and it is also very difficult to explain to employees.

Point factor approach. Point systems have advantages in that they are potentially more reliable, are immune to market fluctuations, are relatively easy to use, require little evaluator training, and measure the size of differences between jobs (although usually not with ratio scales). However, they are expensive, time consuming, and may have questionable validity (see Remick, 1981; Schwab, 1980).

Quantitative job analysis. Using quantitative job analysis has many of the advantages and disadvantages of point methods. However, because the procedure usually requires incumbents and supervisors to respond to questionnaires about their jobs, issues concerning the adequacy and uniformity of the job content captured may be minimized. The major contemporary issue seems to be regressing job content scores against prevailing labor rates to obtain job prices (or against the DOT codes as a surrogate for validity).

DESCRIPTION OF CURRENT PRACTICES

Current practices can be critiqued on the basis of observations of the applications of job evaluation systems in organizations. First, it should be remembered that organizations tend to use job evaluation systems to price jobs as a supplement to what the market indicates (i.e., to have the organization's internal value of the job specified) and as an aid in determining a price of a job for which inadequate (or unsatisfactory) market data exist.

Second, organizations often are not concerned about the measurement accuracy of job evaluation systems (i.e., reliability and validity), other than to make the wage determination process easier. In fact, issues regarding equity, reliability, and validity are usually not researched, since organizations generally believe labor market functioning resolves them. Many organizations never consider such issues but use job evaluation to price jobs when they feel "uncomfortable" with current practices. Or they simply use job evaluation as a post hoc rationalization of the prices paid. Thus it is easy to ascertain how sex bias may enter the wage determination process.

Third, the method of job evaluation chosen by organizations is generally selected according to ambiguous criteria, at best, and seems to remain rigid once adopted. The method selected is typically one of those described previously, which may have been recommended by a consultant or developed internally. Whether an explicit policy line is developed from a method or an implicit one is used in practice (where the wage and salary people feel "comfortable"), job prices appear fairly resistant to change once set by a "method," except when labor market changes are dramatically obvious.

Finally, the actual methods used to determine job structures and job families are seldom consistent or explicit. Job structures are influenced by job titles, technical specialties, points, the numbers of jobs in the system, line versus staff position, reporting relationships, career pathing, and so on. The choice of key jobs to price these structures suffers from the same problem. Indeed, the determination of job structures and key jobs should not be underemphasized because these subtle decisions greatly influence job pricing.

Up to this point, the methods of determining job prices in organizations have been reviewed. The numerous opportunities for human decision making (see Posner & McLeod, 1982) cause extreme differences in labor market prices, differences that may seem very "rational" to job evaluation decision makers. The remainder of the chapter is devoted to the specific technical problems of job evaluation in order to advise practitioners of the many, many difficulties of the job evaluation process.

TECHNICAL PROBLEMS

There are numerous technical problems in the job evaluation process, including difficulties with job analysis, compensable factor selection, the validity of job evaluation, and the administration of the process.[3] In fact, Tenopyr and Oeltjen's

---

3. Some of the following comments were included in Beatty and Beatty (1984).

review of industrial and organizational psychology emphasized that the measurement of the worth of a job skill cannot be accomplished with any scientific rigor and "involves so many value judgments that it probably can have no completely satisfactory answer" (1982, p. 586). This skepticism pervades the following examination of the job evaluation process. Figure 11.8 provides a guide for the discussion.

Selection of unit of analysis. Job analysis methods have measurement problems, beginning with the selection of the unit of analysis. Some methods take a "micro" focus by examining the job's tasks or elements within tasks, while some jobs are analyzed at the position level, job classification level, or occupational level (Milkovich, 1980). There is no theoretically defensible reason for the "molecular" approach to job content examination other than to permit a more finite differentiation of jobs, which enables more finite pricing policies. Certainly the precision of gradation is subject to question, but it can hardly be disputed that pricing decisions would be more complex if the level of analysis chosen were the position, job title, or occupational level.

Bias in data collection and analysis. Once the level of analysis is selected, the method of measuring job content must be designed. The methods previously described have obvious difficulties with reliability and validity. Further, a potential bias exists in selecting individuals to participate in the data collection and analysis. Some argue that for job evaluation purposes, incumbents should not participate because they attempt to enhance their job descriptions to obtain higher pay (Arvey et al., 1982). Thus, efforts are often undertaken to "field audit" all jobs by having trained job analysts visit incumbents and collect quantitative information that is in essence often qualitative. Such procedures are subject to reliability problems; they are often impossible to assess because auditors discuss the results and reach consensus before completing a job description. Thus some items may be omitted because the process does not require the capturing and reporting of independent job content. Obviously, in some instances, the auditors may over-influence the process and create the impression of consensus on a compensation committee when only compliance or conformity exists.

Rater bias in observing and documenting behavior is also possible (Bernardin & Cardy, 1982; Borman, 1979; Spool, 1978), inasmuch as people may be inaccurate observers or may attribute their evaluations to causes that are inconsistent with the purposes of the rating task (Cooper, 1981; Feldman, 1981; Kelley & Michela, 1980). Therefore, capturing job content using outside "expert" raters may give the appearance of validity, but can still be fraught with measurement error. Thus it may be helpful to use more than one method of job analysis and several sources of data input. An exhaustive search may not be foolproof, but it may at least help the organization to gain credibility in its efforts.

FIGURE 11.8. Sample jobs from the *Dictionary of Occupational Titles*

612.685.010 Lever tender (forging)
Tends power hammer or power press that forges metal stock. Moves levers, upon signal from HEAVY FORGER (forging), to control force and frequency of hammer blows, or ram pressure to shape forging. May be designated according to equipment tended as FORGING-PRESS-LEVER TENDER (forging). HAMMER DRIVER (forging).

612.685.014 Spring tester (spring)
Tends power press that tests resiliency of spiral springs and that compresses them to specified length. Positions spring over mandrel of press table and places metal plate over end of spring. Pulls lever that forces plunger of machine against plate to compress spring. Measures compressed length of spring, using micrometers, calipers, and gages. Releases press and measures uncompressed length of spring. Inserts metal wedge between spring coils and taps spring with mallet to adjust spring to specified length and pitch.

612.687.010 Heat reader (forging)
Compares glow inside forge shop furnace with color intensity chart to determine internal temperature of furnace, using pyrometer. Looks through pyrometer into furnace and compares intensity of light generated by furnace with chart depicting color at various temperatures to determine internal furnace temperature. Informs specified forging personnel of observed temperature to permit designated adjustment to furnace controls, maintenance work, and production rescheduling.

612.687.014 Heavy-forger helper (forging)
Assists HEAVY FORGER (forging) in shaping hot metal on power hammer or press equipped with open dies, working as member of crew. Pulls work piece from furnace with tongs and positions and turns it on hammer anvil. Removes scale from metal and anvil during forging using compressed air or broom. May assist in forging unheated metal. May be designated according to worker assisted as HAMMERSMITH HELPER (forging). PRESS-SMITH HELPER (forging). Performs other duties as described under HELPER (any ind.).

Job-position match. Once the problem of who provides the input and monitors the data is resolved, a new problem arises concerning the correct matching of the jobs with positions in the external labor market, especially if market pricing is used. Clearly, accurate job analysis is critical for comparison with labor market descriptions. Accurate data collection is also critical if job groupings are used (i.e., job classification), as in many public jurisdictions. The method of grouping jobs is often a mystery, and improper slotting can mean the loss of many dollars to employees. As previously mentioned, a job may be grouped by technical specialty and not by managerial class, which could mean the loss of several thousand dollars in annual salary. Thus accuracy in capturing content is essential for job pricing. In light of the many issues noted previously, the reliability of job analysis has often been questioned (Milkovich & Broderick, 1982; Schwab, 1980; Treiman, 1979) and is fertile ground for research as well as for critical examination by practitioners.

Specific job content. Aside from the inaccuracies inherent in whole-job analysis, the "micro" job content procedures are also open to serious error. First, if the compensable factors used in a plan are selected a priori, obvious bias may occur. A firm may intend to value its jobs with an internal equity system (for example, the Hay system, with its purported measure of "relative job difficulty and importance"), but most factors commonly used are highly correlated with labor market prices. Therefore, micro approaches or any approaches that use factors found in a job's content are most likely based on their association with prevailing labor rates. In fact, it would be economically imprudent not to allow prevailing labor rates to influence the price paid for human resources, just as market rates influence the price of other organizational resources.

Compensable factors. The use of compensable factors may further bias results (Doverspike & Barrett, 1984). For example, an interpersonal skills factor might include negotiating (e. g., conflict resolution in largely male jobs) and counseling (e. g., "helping" in women's jobs). Both are interpersonal skills but may earn points differently by being evaluated on traditional (male) cultural norms rather than on the contribution of the skill to the outcomes of the organization. The compensable factor bias is also maintained when factors are chosen by policy capturing, which employs the external market as the criterion (an allegedly biased criterion) that dictates an organization's internal values. However, it should be noted that no set of factors is bias-free with respect to sex. Even Jacques's 1961 "time span of discretion" studies are sex biased, either omitting "women's jobs" or correcting for bias by adding to salaries for "women's jobs." The latter strategy has been suggested by Treiman and Hartmann (1981) as a major remedy for sex-based pay discrimination.

Weights assigned to compensable factors. Job evaluations are obviously influenced by the weights assigned to compensable factors (Eyde, 1981; Remick, 1981; Treiman, 1979). Factors are often weighted a priori, and bias results if a popular method is perpetuated. The use of heavier weights for "women's" factors may not solve the problem. However, if there is little variation in the assignment of points for these factors, their effective weight obviously is substantially less. In fact, it should be noted that not only does the choice of compensable factors influence job evaluation outcomes, but also these outcomes can be used to remedy problems with job evaluation systems. This can be demonstrated through the choice of job evaluation systems, compensable factors, and their respective factor weights. Certainly when different job evaluation systems, with their respective strengths and weaknesses, are used, different results might be expected. This is clear in the following example.

Suppose the job of parking monitor (meter maid) is staffed largely by women alleging pay discrimination. Further assume that one of the jobs with which it is to be compared is animal control warden (dog catcher) and that the job evaluation systems chosen and properly applied are the American Association of Industrial Management plan (the old metal trades plan) and the relatively new factor evaluations system (FES) of the federal government.

Job descriptions from DOT are provided in Figure 11.9. Applications of the two job evaluation systems to the respective positions are shown in Figures 11.10 through 11.13. Their differences in the selection of compensable factors in number (11 vs. 9), nature (education and experience vs. knowledge required), factor weightings (the weight accounted for by education and experience in the AAIM plan is 36 percent of the total while knowledge is 41 percent of the FES plan), and total point values result in different evaluations of the positions. Notice that the parking monitor is rated more highly by the AAIM system (240 vs. 230),

FIGURE 11.9. Job descriptions from the *Dictionary of Occupational Titles* for positions of parking monitor and animal control warden

Parking Monitor
375.587.010 PARKING ENFORCEMENT OFFICER (gov. ser.) parking enforcement agent—Patrols assigned area, such as public parking lot or section of city, to issue tickets to overtime parking violators. Winds parking meter clocks. Surrenders ticket book at end of shift to supervisor to facilitate preparation of violations records. May report missing traffic signals or signs to superior at end of shift. May chalk tires of vehicles parked in unmetered spaces, record time, and return at specified intervals to ticket vehicles remaining in spaces illegally. May collect coins deposited in meters. When patrolling metered spaces, may be known as METER ATTENDANT (gov. ser.).

Animal Control Warden
379.673.010 DOG CATCHER (gov. ser.) dog warden—Captures and impounds unlicensed, stray, and uncontrolled animals: snares animal with net, rope, or device. Cages or secures animal in truck. Drives truck to shelter. Removes animal from truck to shelter cage of other enclosure. Supplies food, water, and personal care to retain animals. Investigates complaints of animal bite cases. Destroys rabid animals as directed. Examines dog licenses for validity and issues warnings or summonses to deliquent owners. May destroy unclaimed animals, using gun, or by gas or electrocution. May examine captured animals for injuries and deliver injured animals to VETERINARIAN (medical ser.) for medical treatment. May maintain file of number of animals impounded and disposition of each. May enforce regulations concerning treatment of domestic animals and be designated HUMANE OFFICER (gov. ser.).

FIGURE 11.10. AAIM job rating plan

Job Title: ___Parking Monitor___   Points: ___240___

Factor	Reason for Classification	Degree	Points
1. Education	Observe parking violations; write tickets; keep tally of tickets; answer questions and give directions; use two-way radio; mark tires to identify vehicles; requires writing, adding whole numbers, reading references for citation codes and voice communications.	1	14
2. Experience	Must be licensed to drive vehicles; know parking ordinances, tour routes, answers to inquiries for directions and job procedures; required to take vehicle safety training.	2	44
3. Initiative and ingenuity	Plans tour route in accordance with parking time limits; decides whether vehicles are to be towed; resourcefulness required in making parking violation decision.	3	42
4. Physical demand	Walks tour route; climbs in and out of and drives vehicle.	3	30
5. Mental or visual demand	Observes parking violations while operating vehicle.	3	15
6. Responsibility for equipment or process	Operation of vehicle may result in damage to vehicle; must check oil and service vehicle with gas and oil.	3	15
7. Responsibility for material or product	Little chance of loss.	1	5
8. Responsibility for safety of others	Operation of vehicle may result in lost-time injury of pedestrians or other drivers.	3	15
9. Responsibility for work of others	Responsible for own work; may direct work of tow truck operator.	1	5
10. Working conditions	Work year-round in all weather, sometimes very unpleasant.	3	30
11. Hazards	Alighting from double-parked vehicle or stepping out between parked vehicles may result in severe injury and possible death.	5	25

Total   240

FIGURE 11.11. AAIM job rating plan

Job Title: ___Animal Control Officer___   Points: ___230___

Factor	Reason for Classification	Degree	Points
1. Education	Observe infractions of city and state laws pertaining to animals; use two-way radio; write citations and reports; read references for citation codes; speak with various persons in making investigations and deciding actions to be taken.	1	14
2. Experience	Know how to handle animals best; have knowledge of job procedures, applicable city and state laws use of tranquilizer equipment; know how to relate to people in discharging duties; must be licensed driver; must maintain practice in use of gun.	2	44
3. Initiative and ingenuity	Must use judgment in handling animals, responding to calls, and taking follow-up action.	3	42
4. Physical demand	Climbs in and out of and drives vehicles; exerts effort to control and lift heavy animals.	3	30
5. Mental or visual demand	Observes violations; must be alert while tracking and controlling animals; continuous alertness required while driving vehicle.	3	15
6. Responsibility for equipment or process	Operation of vehicle may result in damage to vehicle.	3	15
7. Responsibility for material or product	Little chance of loss; responsible for contents of vehicle while parked.	1	5
8. Responsibility for safety of others	Operation of vehicle may result in lost-time injury of pedestrians or other drivers; must exercise care in use of gun.	3	15
9. Responsibility for work of others	Responsible for own work.	1	5
10. Working conditions	Works year-round in all weather.	3	30
11. Hazards	Danger of slippery conditions in winter; may be injured in lifting heavy animals or in controlling animals.	3	15
	Total		230

FIGURE 11.12. Factor evaluation system: Documentation form

Job Title: _____ Parking Monitor _____   Points: _____ 585 _____

Factor	Documentation	Degree	Points
1. Knowledge required	Must know parking ordinances and the city; how to drive a jeep with automatic transmission; operate a two-way radio; no written exam required.	2	200
2. Supervisory controls	Plans how route is to be covered; priorities are clearly defined (i.e., private property, time zones, abandonments); must obey dispatcher.	2	125
3. Guidelines	Must apply the city codes specifically; time allowances for violations, private property, obstruction, and abandonment are clearly stated.	1	25
4. Complexity	Transactions and entries are factual; must recognize differences in some applications such as when to tow vehicle.	2	75
5. Scope and effect	Responsible for own work; work may have impact on others such as tow truck operators or maintenance crews; work has impact on the public; work is of limited variety in enforcing parking ordinances; primary effect is as revenue source for parking utility.	2	75
6. Personal contacts	Operates two-way radio to communicate with others in agency; may meet face to face with public to give directions, answer questions, or resolve a dispute of a ticket.	2	25
7. Purpose of contacts	Contacts or is contacted to give factual information, such as directions or clarification of an ordinance.	1	20
8. Physical demands	Physical exertion is required by walking or getting in and out of a jeep; some stretching or bending is required.	2	20
9. Work environment	Subject to adverse weather, moving vehicles, potentially noxious fumes from exhausts.	2	20

Duties: Duties may vary somewhat depending on beats assigned, whether using a vehicle or not, etc.

Enforce parking regulations (by driving or walking) by observing
violations and writing tickets for various types of parking
violations   80%
Giving directions to public   2%
Responding to emergency towing calls   3%
Completing paperwork   15%

Skills required:
Basic mathematical calculations; operate jeep with automatic transmission;
endurance to walk routes; endurance for getting in and out of jeep; tolerance for adverse weather conditions; no test given, oral board only; public
relations; passing police check.

while the animal control warden is higher with the FES system (1,255 vs. 585).
Thus it is critical that the system selected be applicable to the jobs and the
organization. In this instance, the AAIM system was developed for metal trades
positions and would presumably be a very good choice for manufacturing jobs,
while the FES system would most likely be more applicable to government
positions.

Choice of key jobs. The choice of benchmark or key jobs is another major
problem. As noted earlier, key jobs are traditionally well-defined in the labor
market (in terms of tasks required, qualifications, etc.), relatively stable with
respect to salary, represent various hierarchical levels, and are thought to be
"fairly priced" by the labor market. Biases in the market thus affect job evaluation
results (Milkovich & Broderick, 1982). Policy-capturing techniques do not identify
the value of jobs to the organization or indicate that jobs that do not meet key-job
criteria produce job values in the same way as key jobs. In fact, sampling theory
suggests they would not. If key jobs are sex linked, their use will bias wage
structures.

Construct validity of job structure. Another major problem is the construct
validity of the job structure. Actually, there are two major problems. First, the
survey data are not representative; the data are not collected randomly, which
limits statistical inferences and the accuracy of an organization's prices. The
second problem is the incompleteness of the compensation data. Critical comparisons cannot actually be made because the data do not include information for
the effect of benefits, pay for overtime, training expenditures, and incentive pay
on the real costs of employee compensation. The U.S. Chamber of Commerce
survey data for 1980 suggested that benefits may equal 37 percent of payroll and
are increasing. Such practices with respect to supplemental pay and benefits differ
across industry, region, and job type and are not accounted for in wage data used

FIGURE 11.13. Factor evaluation system: Documentation form

Job Title: _____ Animal Control Officer _____   Points: _____ 1,255 _____

Factor	Documentation	Degree	Points
1. Knowledge required	Must know animals, animal diseases, drugs, and specific procedures for control and treatment; written examination given on job-related items relative to animal treatment, approach to animals, etc.	2	200
2. Supervisory controls	Duties and tasks vary; must adjust to changes within policy guidelines and legal status; little supervision received in action upon tasks assigned; may prioritize task assignment and coverage areas.	2	275
3. Guidelines	Considerable discretion must be exercised in judgment with respect to enforcement, approaches taken to animals and pet owners; many unique and potentially dangerous problems may occur.	3	275
4. Complexity	Analysis of difficult and potentially dangerous situations is required; many alternative approaches are available; must know how to catch or trail a snake or other dangerous animal; how to best protect the public; when to destroy vs. save a pet.	2	75
5. Scope and effect	Clear impact on the social, physical, and economic well-being of public; must exercise extreme caution in use of firearms.	3	150
6. Personal contacts	Most public contacts are new; officers must prescribe role for others such as the extent of involvement or help by public to control a specific situation.	3	60
7. Purpose of contacts	Specific purpose to control person's animals, issue warrants, interrogate/investigate; many contacts involve problem solving such as involving others in investigations, searches, administration of antidotes, etc.	3	120

8. Physical demands	Lifting and controlling animals; considerable physical strength, agility, quickness required.	3	50
9. Work environment	Always-present danger of bites, infection, and physical harm; use of firearms to tranquilize or destroy animals.	3	50

Duties:

Responding to calls to remove vicious/dangerous animals, convey injured animals	55%
Investigating animal bite cases	10%
Responding to complaints about animals	10%
Patrolling parks	5%
Completing reports	20%

Skills required:

Knowledge of animals and diseases; keep records; lift and control animals; public relations; extensive written examination; agility to trail and trap animals; knowledge of drugs (e.g., tranquilizer and antidotes); firearm accuracy/safety; passing police check.

in the job evaluation/wage-setting process. An employee's supplemental pay may therefore reduce or amplify the potential wage inequity within a job title.

Furthermore, even if these problems with surveys could be ignored, survey wage data reflect the market value of the job and not the value of the job to the organization.[4] The choice of any survey statistic as the market criterion (e.g., median, average, average maximum, weighted mean salary, average minimum) may change relative values of jobs in an organization depending on the salary distributions in the market and the choice of the market statistics for the key jobs in question. This indicates the potential subjectivity of job pricing within the bounds of the labor market.

Turnover and job vacancy. The influence of turnover and job vacancy in the market is also overlooked. If an organization has frequent turnover or long-term vacancies in a job, the value of the job should increase. If prices do not move

---

4. Wage determinants are also known to include a number of factors irrelevant to the job itself, especially industry and location. (For a review of economic determinants of job value see Wallace and Fay, 1982).

despite high vacancy rates, discrimination may occur because the supply and demand of jobs is not working.

Different job evaluation systems. The use in an organization of several job evaluation systems with different factors or factor weights is another source of error. The mere use of multiple systems with multiple measures makes it likely that jobs valued under one system may not be valued the same under another system. This is especially true if a quantitative point system is used for nonexempt jobs and a qualitative classification system is used for exempt jobs.

Assumptions of linear regression models. Finally, linear regression models are typically used to link job evaluation points to survey data. The assumptions required of those models (e.g., the independence of factors used to "predict" wages) are probably violated in that application. In fact, compensable factors used in many systems (such as Hay factors) have very high intercorrelations (i.e., $r \geq .9$) as do commonly used factors such as accountability, mental complexity, and supervision exercised. As expected, physical effort and working conditions are often intercorrelated with other factors and are often negatively weighted by market prices when correlated with all of an organization's key jobs. Even if linearity does not exist, it may be necessary to capture the relationships using nonlinear models (see Bloom & Killingsworth, 1982).

Future Directions and Needs

There are many reliability problems in the job evaluation process, including the selection of wage data used as criteria in the process. There are also fundamental problems in the administrative process of using multiple job evaluation systems for different sets of jobs and in adjusting to supply and demand fluctuations. However, even without reliability problems, job evaluation methods that rely on market data alone do not address the internal value of a job to an organization. Thus new methods of assessing internal equity must be investigated in terms of organizational contribution; for example, common contributions such as sales, production, profitability and less commonly measured assessments such as the long- and short-term financial impact on the organization if the job was not performed should be considered. Such values can then be assessed against prevailing rates to guide prudent purchases of job skills in the labor market.

The hope is that organizations that practice job evaluation can provide insight into compensation decision-making processes and will thereby stimulate (and perhaps fund) compensation research and eventually make restitution for pay discrimination. Organizations that are concerned about the issues addressed here and that wish to develop more equitable compensation systems should consider employing the following methods:

1. Exhaustive job analysis using several methods (e.g., interviews and questionnaires) and alternative sources of job content input.
2. Nonredundant compensable factors that represent the value of jobs to an organization and that demonstrate a correspondence with labor market prices for a majority of jobs.
3. Job evaluation systems with demonstrated and regularly monitored reliabilities in building job families through classification or hierarchies using quantitative job analysis.
4. Constant monitoring to ensure that survey methods and the statistics used are applied consistently across all jobs.
5. Assessment of all pricing practices (i.e., job analysis, compensable factor selection, job structure development and assignment, survey adequacy and comparability, key-job determination, and assignment of job prices) to ensure that discriminatory practices have been eliminated.

Attending to these concerns may require a considerable research effort and self-examination presently uncommon in organizational compensation units. Yet if pay equity and economic survival are objectives of organizations, the funds invested should not only be returned over time but should result in more efficient and equitable pay systems.

The future of job evaluation does not seem to lie in direct and total dependence upon market values or in developing market-based compensable factors. Organizations seem to be more concerned with capturing compensable factors that fit their internal values and human resource policies and with the strategic skills required to make their strategic plan operable. Thus, given new approaches to job evaluation and the use of psychometric tools for assessment of their compensation plans, organizations may have fewer questions or concerns over the "accuracy" and equity of job evaluation methods. Sadly, the current debate over job evaluation has not been brought about by the research of industrial psychologists; and even more regrettably, its demise will probably not be due to their efforts, but will be effected in the political and legal arenas.

References and Bibliography

Akalin, M. T. (1970). *Office job evaluation*. Des Plaines, IL: Industrial Management Society.

American Association of Industrial Management. (1980). *Job evaluation manual: Production maintenance and service occupations*. Willard Grove, PA: Author.

American Compensation Association. (1976). *Survey of job evaluation practices*. Scottsdale, AZ: Author.

American Society for Personnel Administration & American Compensation Association. (1981). *Elements of sound base pay administration*. Berea, OH: Author.

Arvey, R. D., Davis, G. A., McGovern S. L., & Dipboye R. L. (1982). Potential sources of bias in job analysis processes. *Academy of Management Journal, 25*, 618–629.

Arvey, R. D., & Mossholder, K. M. (1977). Proposed methodology for determining similarities and differences among jobs. *Personnel Psychology, 30*, 363–374.

Ash, P. (1968). The reliability of job evaluation rankings. *Journal of Applied Psychology, 32*, 313–320.

Ash, R. A. (1982). Job elements for task clusters: Arguements for using multi-methodological approaches to job analysis and a demonstration of their utility. *Public Personnel Management Journal, 11*, 80–90.

Ash, R. A., & Edgell, S. L. (1975). A note on the readability of the position analysis questionnaire (PAQ). *Journal of Applied Psychology, 60*, 765–766.

Beatty, R. W., & Beatty, J. R. (1982). Job evaluation and discrimination: Legal, economic, and measurement perspectives on comparable worth and women's pay. In H. J. Bernardin (Ed.), *Women in the work force* (pp. 205–234). New York: Praeger.

Beatty, R. W., & Beatty, J. R. (1984). Some problems with contemporary job evaluation systems. In H. Remick (Ed.), *Comparable worth and wage discrimination: Technical possibilities and political realities* (pp. 59–78). Philadelphia: Temple University Press.

Beatty, R. W., Crandall, N. F., Fay, C. H., Mathis, R., Milkovich, G. T., & Wallace, M. J., Jr. (1981). *How to administer wage-salary programs and perform job evaluation.* New York: Penton Learning Systems.

Benge, E. J. (1947). Statistical study of a job evaluation point system. *Modern Management, 7*, 17–23.

Benge, E. J. (1948). *Job evaluation and merit rating.* New York: National Foremen's Institute.

Bernardin, H. J., & Cardy, R. L. (1982). Appraisal accuracy: The ability and motivation to remember the past. *Public Personnel Management, 11*, 352–357.

Bloom, D. E., & Killingsworth, M. R. (1982). Pay discrimination research and litigation: The use of regression. *Industrial Relations, 21*, 318–339.

Borman, W. C. (1979). Format and training effects on rating accuracy and rater errors. *Journal of Applied Psychology, 64*, 410–421.

Bridgeport Guardians v. Police Department. (1977). 16 FEP 486.

Chalupsky, A. B. (1962). Comparative factor analyses of clerical jobs. *Journal of Applied Psychology, 46*, 62–67.

Chance v. Board of Examiners (Appeals). (1972). 4 FEP 596.

Commonwealth of Pennsylvania v. Flaherty. (1975). FEP 993.

Cooper, W. H. (1981). *Psychological Bulletin, 90*, 218–244.

Cornelius, E. T., Hakel, M. D., & Sackett, P. R. (1979). A methodological approach to job classification for performance appraisal purposes. *Personnel Psychology, 32*, 283–297.

Davis v. Washington, (1972). 5 FEP 293.

Doverspike, D., & Barrett, G. V. (1984). An internal bias analysis of a job evaluation instrument. *Journal of Applied Psychology, 69*, 648–662.

Doverspike, D., Carlisi, A. M., Barrett, G. V., & Alexander, R. A. (1983). Generalizability analysis of a point-method job evaluation instrument. *Journal of Applied Psychology, 68,* 476–483.

Eyde, L. D. (1981, Aug.). *Evaluating job evaluation: Emerging research issues for comparable analysis.* Paper presented at the annual meeting of the American Psychological Association, San Francisco.

Equal Pay Act. (1963). Pub. L. 88=38, 77 Stat. 56, 29 U.S.C. 206(d).

Feldman, J. M. (1981). Beyond attribution theory: Cognitive processes in performance appraisal. *Journal of Applied Psychology, 66,* 127–48.

Fleishmann, E. A. (1982). Systems for describing human tasks. *American Psychologist, 37,* 821–834.

Flanagan, J. C. (1954). The critical incident technique. *Psychological Bulletin, 51,* 327–358.

Fox, W. M. Purpose and validity in job evaluation. *Personnel Journal, 41,* 432–437.

Greenspan v. Automobile Club of Michigan. (1980). 22 FEP 195.

International Labour Office. (1960). *Job evaluation.* Geneva: Author.

Jacques, E. (1964). *Time-span handbook.* London: Heinemann.

Jenkins, G. D. (1975). Standardized observations: An approach to measuring the nature of jobs. *Journal of Applied Psychology, 60,* 53–83.

Jones, H. D. (1974). Union views on job evaluation: 1971 vs. 1978. *Personnel Journal, 58,* 80–89.

Jones v. New York Human Resources Administration. (1975). 12 FEP 265.

Kelley, H. H., & Michela. (1980). Attribution theory and research. *Annual Review of Psychology, 31,* 457–501.

Kirkland v. Department of Correctional Services. (1974). 7 FEP 694.

Krzystofiak, F. J., & Newman, J. M. (1979). A quantified approach to measurement of job content: Procedures and payoffs. *Personnel Psychology, 32,* 341–359.

Lanham, E. (1955). *Job evaluation.* New York: McGraw-Hill.

Levine, E. L., Bennett, N., & Ash, R. A. (1979). Evaluation and use of four job analysis methods for personnel selection. *Public Personnel Management, 8,* 146–157.

Livernash, E. R. (1957a). *Concepts in wage determination.* New York: McGraw-Hill.

Livernash, E. R. (1957b). The internal labor market. In G. W. Taylor & F. C. Pierson (Eds.), *New Concepts in wage determination* (pp. 141–172). New York: McGraw-Hill.

Livy, B. (1975). *Job evaluation: A critical review.* New York: Wiley.

Lytle, C. W. (1954). *Job evaluation methods.* New York: Ronald Press.

Madden, J. M. (1962). The effect of varying the degree of rater familiarity in job evaluation. *Personnel Administrator, 25,* 42–45.

Mahoney, T. A. (1982). Compensating for work. In K. Rowland & G. Ferris (Eds.), *Personnel Management* (pp. 227–263). Boston: Allyn and Bacon.

McCormick, E. J. (1974, October). *The application of structured job analysis information based on the position analysis questionnaire (PAQ).* West Lafayette, IN: Department of Psychological Science, Occupational Research Center, Purdue University.

McCormick, E. J. (1975). Job information: Its development and applications. In D.

Yoder & H. Heneman, Jr. (Eds.), *Staffing policies and strategies* (pp. 35–84). Washington, DC: Bureau of National Affairs.

McCormick, E. J. (1976). Job and task analysis. In M. D. Dunnette (Ed.), *Handbook of industrial and organizational psychology* (pp. 651–696). Chicago: Rand McNally.

McCormick, E. J., DeNisi, A. S., & Shaw, J. B. (1979). Use of the position analysis questionnaire for establishing the job component validity of tests. *Journal of Applied Psychology, 64,* 51–56.

McCormick, E. J., & Ilgen, D. (1971). *Industrial psychology,* Englewood Cliffs, NJ: Prentice-Hall.

McCormick, E. J., Jeanneret, P. R., & Mecham, R. D. (1972). A study of job characteristics and job dimensions as based on the position analysis questionnaire (PAQ). *Journal of Applied Psychology, 56,* 347–367.

Mecham, R. C., & McCormick, E. J. (1969, June). *The use in job evaluation of job elements and job dimensions based on the position analysis questionnaire.* Lafayette, IN: Department of Psychological Science, Occupational Research Center, Purdue University.

Milkovich, G. T. (1980). Wage differentials and comparable worth: The emerging debate. In E. R. Livernash (Ed.), *Comparable worth: Issues and alternatives* (pp. 79–106. Washington, DC: Equal Employment Advisory Council.

Milkovich, G. T., & Broderick, R. (1982). Pay discrimination: Legal issues and implications for research. *Industrial Relations, 21,* 309–317.

Otis, J. L., & Leukart, R. H. (1954). *Job evaluation: A basis for sound wage administration* (2nd ed.). Englewood Cliffs, NJ: Prentice-Hall.

Paterson, T. T. (1972a). *Job evaluation* (Vol. 1): *A new method.* London: Business Books.

Paterson, T. T. (1972b). *Job evaluation* (Vol. 2): *A manual for the Paterson method.* London: Business Books.

Pearlman, K. (1980). Job families: A review and discussion of their implications for personnel selection. *Psychological Bulletin, 87,* 1–28.

Posner, M. I., & McLeod, P. (1982). Information processing models—In search of elementary operations. In M. R. Rosenzwenz & L. W. Porter (Eds.), *Annual Review of Psychology.* Palo Alto: Annual Reviews.

Prien, E. P., & Ronan, W. W. (1971). Job analysis: A review of research findings. *Personnel Psychology, 74,* 371–396.

Primoff, E. S. (1957). The J-coefficient approach to jobs and tests. *Personnel Administration, 20,* 34–40.

Remick, H. (1979). Strategies for creating sound, bias free job evaluation systems. In *Job evaluation and EEO: The emerging issues* (pp. 85–112). New York: Industrial Relations Counselors.

Remick, H. (1981). The comparable worth controversy. *Public Personnel Management, 10,* 371–84.

Robinson, D. D., & Wahlstrom, O. W. (1974). Comparison of job evaluation methods: A policy-capturing approach using the position analysis questionnaire. *Journal of Applied Psychology, 59,* 633–637.

Schwab, D. P. (1980). Job evaluations and pay setting: Concepts' and practices' worth.

In E. R. Livernash (Ed.), *Comparable worth: Issues and alternatives* (pp. 49–77). Washington, DC: Equal Employment Advisory Council.

Shield Club v. City of Cleveland. (1974). 13 FEP 533.

Smith, L. (1978). The EEOC's bold foray into job evaluation. *Fortune, 78,* 58–60.

Sparks, C. P. (1982). Job analysis. In K. Rowland & G. Ferris (Eds.), *Personnel Management* (pp. 78–101). Boston: Allyn and Bacon.

Spool, M. D. (1978). Training programs for observers of behavior: A review. *Personnel Psychology, 31,* 853–888.

Strauss, G. (1982). Personnel management: Prospect for the eighties. In K. Rowland & G. Ferris (Eds.), *Personnel Management* (pp. 504–47).

Taylor, L. R. (1978). Empirically derived job families as a foundation for the study of validity generalization: Study 1, The constructions of job families based on the component and overall dimensions of the PAQ. *Personnel Psychology, 31,* 325–340.

Taylor, L. R., & Colbert, G. A. (1978). Empirically derived job families as a foundation for the study of validity generalization: Study 2, The construction of job families based on company-specific PAQ dimensions. *Personnel Psychology, 31,* 341–353.

Tenopyr, M. L., & Oeltjen, P. D. (1982). Personnel selection and classification. In M. R. Rosenzweig & E. W. Porter (Eds.), *Annual Review of Psychology* (pp. 581–618). Palo Alto: Annual Reviews.

Thomsen, D. J. (1978). Eliminating pay discrimination caused by job evaluation. *Personnel, 55,* 11–22.

Treiman, D. J. (1979). *Job evaluation: An analytical review* (Interim Report to the Equal Employment Opportunity Commission). Washington, DC: National Academy of Sciences.

Treiman, D. J., & Hartmann, H. I. (Eds.) (1981). *Women, work, and wages: Equal pay for jobs of equal value.* Washington, DC: National Academy Press.

U.S. v. City of St. Louis (Appeals). (1977). 14 FEP 1486.

U.S. Department of Labor. (1972). *Handbook on job analysis.* Washington, DC: Author.

U.S. Department of Labor. (1973). *Dictionary of occupational titles* (3rd ed.). Washington, DC: U.S. Government Printing Office.

U.S. Department of Labor, Bureau of Employment Security. (1977). *Dictionary of occupational titles.* (4th ed.). Washington, DC: U.S. Government Printing Office.

U.S. Equal Employment Opportunity Commission, U. S. Civil Service Commission, U.S. Department of Labor, & U.S. Department of Justice. (1978). Uniform guidelines on employee selection procedures. *Federal Register, 43*(166), 38290–38309.

U.S. War Manpower Commission. (1943). *Informational manual on industrial job evaluation systems.* Washington, DC: War Manpower Commission, Bureau of Manpower Utilization, Division of Occupational Analysis and Manning Tables.

Vulcan Society v. Civil Service Commission. (1973). 6 FEP 1045.

Wallace, M. J., Jr., & Fay, C. H. (1982). *Labor markets, job evaluation, and job worth: Towards a model of managerial judgments of job value* (Working Paper in Business Administration, No. BA 74). Lexington: University of Kentucky, College of Business and Economics.

Western Addition Community Organization v. Alioto. (1972). 4 FEP 772.
Western Addition Community Organization v. Alioto (Appeals). (1973). 6 FEP 85.
Zolitsch, H. G., & Langsner, A. (1970). *Wage and salary administration* (2nd ed.). Cincinnati, OH: South-Western.

12. PERSONNEL EVALUATION

Robert M. Guion

Introduction

In a work setting, at least, the idea of performance can be rather ambiguous, and it needs a tighter focus. In the title of their book, Campbell, Dunnette, Lawler, and Weick (1970) wrote of "behavior, performance, and effectiveness," in that order. "Behavior" at work might include such things as showing up on time, helping coworkers, greeting customers, or taking or foregoing rest periods. "Performance" implies a more restricted kind of behavior; it is what people do to carry out specifically assigned duties and responsibilities. "Effectiveness" refers to the evaluation of how well such duties have been performed or how well responsibilities have been met. For this chapter, "performance" will have this relatively restricted meaning, and "performance assessment" will refer to procedures for evaluating the effectiveness of performance of work. "Assessment" and "evaluation" will be used more or less interchangeably, and each of them implies measurement. The concern of this chapter, therefore, is the measurement of the effectiveness of job-related behavior.

PURPOSES OF PERFORMANCE ASSESSMENT

Evaluations of performance serve at least three different purposes in organizations where people work. First, performance assessments are used as criterion measures (or dependent variables) in research. Industrial and organizational psychologists are probably most often associated with performance measures for selection research, and they may devote more research energy on the measurement problems of criteria in selection research than in other kinds of behavioral research in organizations. Careful and systematic development of criterion measures is mandated by the *Uniform Guidelines on Employee Selection Procedures* (U.S. Equal Employment Opportunity Commission et al., 1978), and this may give the development of criterion measures somewhat more urgency in selection research than in, for example, research on motivation. Nevertheless, one should not lose sight of the fact that industrial and organizational psychology is largely concerned with the proposition that the effectiveness of performance at work is a function of any number of things. A psychologist who elects to do research on possible correlates of performance effectiveness must somehow measure that effectiveness if the ideas are to be investigated.

A second common use of performance assessment is as a basis for decisions

345

about people in the organization, for example, to decide which of two or more candidates to promote, which ones will be given special opportunities, or whether administrative actions (ranging from merit-pay increases to termination) will be taken. A good performance evaluation system would be invaluable to one organization I know. According to its contract with a union, promotions are to be based on merit when the choice is between two people of approximately equal seniority. Seniority is so broadly defined that people with the same number of years in the company, give or take a year or two, may all be considered essentially equal in seniority. Therefore, according to the contract, the company could use evaluations of past performance as a basis for determining merit and for deciding who, among those in this pool, should be promoted. Unfortunately, however, company officials feel so uncomfortable about defending their performance evaluation system that the literal number of days of seniority has been the de facto basis for promotion.

Personnel decisions often call for less pleasant choices than deciding who to promote. In times of reduction in force, in deciding whether to fire a tenured university professor, or in simply giving the pink slip to a local manager, the decision is often based on appraisal of that person's performance as inadequate. This decision can lead to litigation, particularly under civil rights laws. When performance assessments are used for such purposes, they may be subject to all of the issues of adverse impact, validity, and procedural uniformity that would attend the use of any other basis for decision making, such as standardized tests.

A third common purpose of performance evaluation, one that seems to be used systematically far less frequently than organizational theory would consider desirable, is its use in personnel development. Presumably, a measurement of the performance effectiveness of an individual will reveal the person's relative strengths and weaknesses so that, with appropriate feedback (Burke, Weitzel, & Weir, 1978), the employee can be guided to or can choose certain actions such as taking training courses, studying reading lists, seeking specialized training, or consulting with people within the organization who can provide help in overcoming the weaknesses and further developing the strengths.

Despite the variety of purposes, the essential problems of the measurement of performance remain pretty consistent. For each of these purposes, someone in the organization must decide what kinds of characteristics of people or of their performance are to be evaluated, the form and procedure in which the evaluation will be done, who will do the evaluating, and how well it must be done. There are relatively few special rules or special principles applicable only to the specific purposes.

We will start by identifying some methods of performance assessment. Examples of rating forms and rating procedures will be given, but they will be more or less disguised to protect both the guilty and the innocent. These will be followed with descriptions of some of the problems encountered in research on performance assessment and in developing an overall procedure or system for practical evaluation of performance. Finally, some needed new directions in both research and practice in performance appraisal at work will be suggested.

Applications to Performance at Work

The variety of methods used to evaluate performance at work is extensive indeed. There are many so-called objective procedures, procedures that involve counting something (e. g., quantity of production), measuring something (e. g., how closely work adheres to specifications), or otherwise evaluating either the process or the outcome of work performed. Each of these measures, despite the appearance of objectivity, is subject to its own special problems.

The most ubiquitous form of performance evaluation is the use of a procedure for obtaining subjective evaluations or ratings. This chapter will concentrate, therefore, on the use of ratings in the evaluation of performance. In no sense is this to be considered a comprehensive survey. Rather, it will attempt to show some reasonably sound rating procedures and the considerations that should temper one's enthusiasm for their soundness.

Ratings for administrative purposes are generally done periodically. At some specified time, such as the anniversary date of employment, a personnel officer notifes a rater (usually the supervisor) that it is time for the periodic review of performance. Forms are provided, calling perhaps for both narrative statements and for summary ratings of certain characteristics of the subordinate's performance (e. g., consistency or quality of work) and for overall evaluations. Specific characteristics of the form tend to dictate the kinds of evaluations to be made. Provision is usually made, at least once, for special training in the use of the appraisal procedure and, in particular, in the conduct of a feedback interview. Reviews of one's subordinates may be spread throughout the year.

Ratings for research purposes are more ad hoc in nature. That is, they are not periodic, so the supervisor may rate all employees under his or her supervision at about the same time. Feedback is not necessarily involved. A form is provided for recording judgments of performance effectiveness and, as with administrative appraisal, the form tends to dictate something about the nature of the judgments requested. There may or may not be formal training of the raters in its use.

In designing a rating procedure, plans should include procedures for observation or for recording observations on the rating forms themselves, and for evaluating the system. Psychometric evaluations are, of course, important. A great deal of attention has been given to the reliability of ratings. Similar emphasis has been placed on various kinds of rater bias: statistical bias (such as the classic psychometric errors of halo, leniency, or central tendency) and social biases (such as sex or ethnic discrimination). Relatively little attention has been given to evaluating the validity of the rating process until fairly recently, but Borman (1977) provided an impetus to validation and determining the accuracy of ratings in laboratory settings.

One frequently overlooked form of evaluation is determining rater and ratee acceptance. The story is told, and it seems not to be apocryphal, that the forced-choice methods that seemed so excellent in early military applications (Sisson, 1948) were abandoned by military organizations, not because they were ineffective, but because the raters did not like them. Performance appraisal systems for personnel development may be treated with disdain and be ineffective if the ratees do not perceive the raters as reasonably fair. A pair of studies (Landy, Barnes, & Murphy, 1978; Landy, Barnes-Farrell, & Cleveland, 1980) indicated that the perceived fairness of an evaluation system was based on such things as frequency of evaluation, the clarity of goal identification, and how well the supervisor knew the ratees; there was no biasing effect of prior ratings on the perceptions of fairness. Certainly, perceptions of fairness will be critically important if ratings are used for administrative actions that could, in turn, lead to litigation. Such perceptions depend on the perception of the total package that makes up the rating procedure.

RATING FORMS

It is not surprising that researchers and practitioners alike have given most of their attention to identifying preferred rating forms. As will become evident shortly, this may not be a particularly effective endeavor, but some system for guiding and recording evaluations is necessary. In this section, a few of the formats for ratings that seem, even without firm scientific demonstration, to have some merit are examined (see also Jacobs, chapter 2, and Borman, chapter 3).

Graphic rating scales. One of the oldest approaches to collecting subjective judgments about the effectiveness of performance is the use of graphic rating scales (Guion, 1965). Several decisions must be made in developing such scales. How many different scales will be used? What kinds of characteristics of people or of performance will be rated? Will there be a single overall rating scale? How will points on the scales be defined?

The number of dimensions should not be large. (I have personally seen rating forms with more than thirty scales; it is doubtful whether anyone can make that many distinct, independent judgments.) Kenneth Alvares and I developed graphic rating scales for evaluating police performance. We used four dimensions of performance, chosen and defined on the basis of many discussions with police personnel:

1. *Courtesy/sensitivity:* the ability to show concern and respect for people regardless of the situation. Police officers high on this ability could comfort victims of illnesses, calm hysterical parents of lost children, and generally be

sensitive to the problems that people are experiencing, regardless of the amount and nature of stress involved.

2. *Competence* (job effectiveness): the awareness and application of proper procedures in a wide variety of situations. One who is rated high on this dimension always seems to do the right thing at the right time. The productivity level of such officers is high, and they are generally evaluated positively by other police officers and the public.

3. *Awareness/curiosity:* the ability to notice what is going on and to check into out-of-the-ordinary things (e. g., a light out that is ordinarily on; a door ajar; a car staying in one place for an extended time), which might provide useful information. Patrol officers high on this dimension would notice such things that others might overlook completely.

4. *Work motivation:* the willingness to improve one's performance and capabilities. An officer high on this dimension would continue to produce the required quantity and quality of work when others do not and would generally display a willingness to do more than is required.

There was no indication that any of the raters were confused about the definitions of these dimensions or that they were unaware of the differences between them. It would have been desirable to have lower correlations than those obtained between the ratings on these dimensions, but they were not high enough to confuse with reliability coefficients. In contrast, administrative ratings on ten scales used by the police department had such high intercorrelations that, for all practical purposes, the same rating was given ten times. The fact that the ten dimensions were not neatly distinguishable in the understandings of the raters may have been due to poor definition; however, it is more likely due to the raters' inability to differentiate one dimension from another.

What kinds of dimensions should be rated? One should not be too dogmatic, but my strong preference is for rating scales to evaluate performance as it is defined in this chapter—task-relevant behavior—rather than to evaluate personal characteristics or traits so broadly defined that they describe relatively enduring behavior that is pervasive across a variety of job and nonjob situations. Landy and Farr (1980) dispensed with the topic of trait versus behavioral dimensions by pointing out that it is controversial. On the other hand, Feldman (1981) was unequivocal in pointing out that the theoretical foundation for behavioral ratings lies in cognitive control, while the foundation for trait ratings lies in unconscious categorization of ratees. The research reviewed by Landy and Farr may be contradictory, but the theoretical reasoning of Feldman seems convincing.

When the scales have been identified and defined, a decision must be made about the number of scale divisions to use. It sometimes seems as if the five-point scale has been decreed from heaven, but there are other options. Where distinctions are difficult to make, a three-point division of excellent, satisfactory, or inadequate performance may be optimal. In different settings, where one wants a five-point distribution and considers the tendency of raters to shun the lower levels of a rating scale, a seven-point scale might be chosen with the knowledge that the first two points will be used rarely if at all. Divisions of more than nine points, again, probably ask for finer distinctions than raters are able to make.

Finally, how should the scale points be defined? This question suggests several others: Will one use simple numbers ranging from 1 to 5 or more? Will the rating form use faces ranging from unhappy expressions to happy expressions (Kunin, 1955)? Will they use simple adjectives, and if so, will they have been scaled previously as recommended by Ghiselli and Brown (1955), or will they use more extensive phrases or even sentences or paragraphs to define the scale points (Taylor & Manson, 1951)? Even this list is not exhaustive; if numbers are to be the anchors, they might be integers as in the conventional rating scale or decimal notation as in those developed by Smith and Kendall (1963). It may make no difference, but it seems to be useful to use anchors that require some thought as opposed to those that fit well-established habits.

Behavioral scales. Behavioral scales are not mutually exclusive from graphic rating scales; the behaviorally anchored rating scales (BARS) first developed by Smith and Kendall (1963) were vertical graphic rating scales using behavioral anchors. Their method of obtaining ratings, however, involved something more than simply deciding on a format for a graphic rating scale and then writing some behavior descriptions to anchor the various scale points. It is that "something more" that characterizes behavioral scales as different from ordinary graphic rating scales and BARS from other kinds of behavioral scales.

The "something more" was clarified by Bernardin and Smith in a discussion starting with these words: "The procedure was designed to encourage raters to observe behavior more carefully, to infer the meaning of that behavior, and to record observed incidents on a continuum of effectiveness for specific dimensions" (1981, p. 458). Clearly, to Smith and Kendall (1963), behaviorally anchored rating scales implied much more than a new format for recording ratings.

Even if one concentrates only on the format itself, the use of behavioral anchors implies more than behavioral anchors on graphic scales. Virtually all efforts to develop behavioral scales (whether they are called BARS or behavioral expectation scales or behavioral observation scales) have involved a quantum change in the degree of precision required in identifying behavior descriptions to be scaled, whether scale developers seek critical or not-so-critical incidents leading to pleasant or unpleasant consequences, or have lists of descriptors developed by committees.

An unusual format consistent with the views of Bernardin and Smith (1981) was developed by Borman, Dunnette, and Johnson (1974) for evaluating performance of naval officers. In this format, the scale was not laid out linearly; rather, there were five discrete segments on a page, each page being devoted to a dimension of officer effectiveness. The upper left-hand segment of a scale for

FIGURE 12.1. Segment of a behaviorally based officer fitness report (from Borman, Dunnette, & Johnson, 1974)

```
                    VERY
                    HIGH
                   8 or 9

Officers Very High on this function can be
expected frequently to anticipate problems
and to coordinate resources for solving them
with such great efficiency as to result in
substantial savings of money, manpower, or
material resources.

              a.  An officer coordinated the complete
                  overhaul of a ship, including
                  consolidation and detailing of all
      P           schedules and developing full
      E           cooperation with shipyard personnel
      R E         to accomplish mission one month
      F X         ahead of schedule with a saving of
      O A         $500,000.
      R M
      M P    b.   An engineering officer, over a
      A L         period of three months, systematically
      N E         directed the overhaul and correction
      C S         of machinery and engineering
      E           deficiencies so that the entire
                  engineering plant performed as
                  designed, including ability to hold
                  fuel power rpm for the first time
                  within his ship's 15-year history.
```

"anticipating, planning, and executing" is shown in Figure 12.1. It identifies behavior illustrating the highest level of performance on this dimension, defining in general the expectations for officers rated at this level and giving two behavioral illustrations. Below this is a similar segment for high ratings. In a center segment of the page is a similar set of illustrative behaviors for "fully adequate" performance. Examples of low rated performance and very low rated performance are given in segments on the right-hand side of the page. No habitual position effect exists, no requirement is made that any illustrative behavior actually has described the performance of a specific officer, and the method requires the rater to have identified a typical example of the ratee's performance and to compare it with the illustrations provided.

Another distinction is that there is usually more thought in specifying the content of a behavioral scale than is given to the content of graphic rating scales. Long lists of behavioral statements might be factor analyzed to identify a basic dimensionality within them. Alternatively, panels of judges might allocate statements to different a priori categories, which had been developed and defined by an earlier independent panel. As a matter of fact, the specification of dimensions in the 1963 Smith and Kendall procedure was essentially a form of job analysis. People who knew the job well for which performance was to be rated were assembled. They decided among themselves the performance characteristics that would make a difference on a particular job, and it was from this kind of analysis of appropriate evaluation of performance on a job that the initial list of dimensions for writing behavioral examples was developed.

A common and major distinction between behavioral and graphic scales is that the behavioral descriptions are usually scaled by some independent group of judges. The scale values may or may not be known to the person who is doing the rating, but the description of performance and the evaluation of that description are to some extent independent processes.

Task-related analyses. One form of graphic rating scale that is not precisely behavioral, but is closely related, is the task-oriented scale. In these scales, a task analysis of a position provides a basis for and precedes performance evaluation. In a simple example of my own, twenty-two kinds of clerical activities were identified (excerpts are shown in Figure 12.2). No clerk actually had responsibility for all twenty-two categories, so a first pass through the ratings form required the rater to do a job or position analysis; that is, the rater indicated which statements described duties and responsibilities of the ratee and which did not. The second step, then, was to evaluate, on a seven-point scale, how well the ratee carried out each of the specific duties and responsibilities of his or her job. The overall rating on this form was simply the average of the ratings on the relevant job tasks. In litigation, the job-relatedness of this method of evaluation would seem obvious.

Scope of performance. For most purposes, overall job performance is evaluated, typically in relation to a specified period of time of six months or a year. For some purposes, however, the scope of the performance evaluated may be substantially reduced. For example, for many positions, it may be possible to obtain a work sample. When this is done, the dimensions, the appropriate behaviors or responsibilities, or perhaps the appropriate characteristics of a product become the variables or dimensions to be rated. A similar restriction exists when one is rating an assessment center exercise. The rating forms need to be developed explicitly to tap the dimensions appropriate to that exercise, and the assessment of performance may be assumed to generalize to a broader day-to-day performance, either in the past, if the assessment is for appraisal purposes, or in the future, if the assessment is for selection purposes, but the assumption is not commonly tested.

Futility of format discussions. A tremendous amount of research has gone into studying the relative merits of different formats. In the 1950s, a series of studies by Taylor and his associates (Barrett et al., 1958; Taylor et al., 1958; Taylor & Hastman, 1956; Taylor & Manson, 1951) tried a wide variety of formats

FIGURE 12.2. Portion of an activity-based rating scale for office workers

Performance Activities	Unsatisfactory	Well Below Average	Below Average	Average	Above Average	Well Above Average	Superior
____ 5. Develops letters based on thoughts expressed by supervisors.	1	2	3	4	5	6	7
____ 6. Summarizes or abstracts articles, agreements, documents, etc.	1	2	3	4	5	6	7
____ 7. Sorts, files, finds materials by any code or method.	1	2	3	4	5	6	7
____ 8. Codes and cross references materials for filing.	1	2	3	4	5	6	7
____ 9. Makes travel arrangements.	1	2	3	4	5	6	7
____ 10. Receives visitors in the office.	1	2	3	4	5	6	7

of graphic rating scales. In the final report of that series, the authors (Taylor, Parker, & Ford, 1959) expressed disillusionment with the rating process because, in the final application, the principles they thought they had derived did not work. In my own evaluation of that series of work, I reached a somewhat different conclusion (Guion, 1965): they had demonstrated that rater competence was more important than the details of format in obtaining predictable ratings.

More recently, other research has compared formats using such similar titles as "behaviorally anchored ratings scales," "behavioral expectation scales," and "behavioral observation scales"—as if these different titles really represented important differences. The inescapable conclusion seems to be that these different formats do not make important differences: "After more than 30 years of serious research, it seems that little progress has been made in developing an efficient and psychometrically sound alternative to the traditional graphic rating scale" (Landy & Farr, 1980, p. 89). In another review of the performance assessment problem, Feldman observed, "It should be realized that the search for a best evaluation form is foredoomed unless the processes generating responses to particular scale types are better understood. There seems to be no magic way of phrasing questions that will eliminate response biases, halo effects, leniency/stringency, and so on in the absence of changes in the raters themselves . . . or changes in the task" (1981, p. 142).

In the face of such expressions of futility, the practical problem for the practitioner is to try to choose the best of all forms in the most imaginative and effective way possible. An example of such care in the construction of a rating form is one developed by Arthur Young and Company in a project for the Edison Electric Institute. This project is an industrywide validation of some clerical tests, and the booklet for obtaining the ratings is an extensive combination of rater training, position analysis, and performance evaluation. The employee to be rated is identified on the cover of the form. Inside is identifying information for the rater, followed by general instructions. A section of the instructions is given to "rating errors to avoid"; these errors, of course, are the typical psychometric errors: halo, central tendency, or leniency. Part 1 draws upon earlier job analysis, listing and defining over two dozen broad activity areas of clerical work. The rater is required to identify for each of them (a) whether the ratee's position involves the activity and (b) if so, how important it is to the position. The second part of the booklet is the section for task performance evaluation. For each of the activity areas, a prior job analysis identified several component tasks associated with that activity. If an activity was described in part 1 as part of the position, the rater indicates on a seven-point scale his or her judgment of the level of performance for each task (except, of course, those that the ratee does not do). Part 3 is a generalized behavior list (e.g., "Finishes assignments before the established deadline"). A five-point scale is used to indicate how frequently the ratee performs, as described by the statement. The final page of the booklet consists of an overall rating on the seven-point performance scale.

This rating form seems to have more merit than simply a long form trying several approaches to rating. Although it is indeed long and complex, it guides the rater through a comprehensive thinking and evaluating process. It is more than a form for recording judgments. Unless it is assumed that the judgments are necessarily formed on the basis of general impressions long before the ratings are sought, such a form can be considered as a guide to the process of reaching judgments as well as to reporting them.

This, of course, is consistent with the Landy and Farr (1980) and Feldman (1981) positions. It is the process that must be understood before important improvements in performance assessments can be realized. Until there is a more substantial body of research leading to that understanding, practitioners must use their best judgment in attempting to make the process as thoughtful and as psychologically sound as possible. In the absence of better advice based on new research, my recommendation is that those who collect ratings use their imagination and ingenuity to develop novel forms requiring reporting of observed events, thus making it very difficult for raters to run through a batch of ratings like unthinking automatons.

RATER QUALIFICATIONS

An early list of rater qualifications included firsthand knowledge of the ratee's performance, a desire (or at least willingness) to rate, and skill. The latter requires training; "unfortunately, training must proceed along rather intuitive lines [because] there is little empirical knowledge about the subtle factors that influence ratings" (Guion, 1965, p. 112).

Other discussions of rater qualifications look to rater personality. Campbell and his associates noted that "observers differ considerably in their ability to do an effective, reliable, and valid job of observing and recording the job behavior of other persons" (1970, p. 115). Several rater characteristics have been proposed as describing the most qualified raters. A well-qualified rater is probably more intelligent, and has more self-insight and social skill than a less-qualified rater (Taft, 1955). Borman (1979b) referred to dependability, stability, maturity, patience, and verbal fluency along with intelligence and personal adjustment. More recently, there has been a substantial amount of discussion of cognitive complexity as an attribute of effective raters who can distinguish between different dimensions (Schneier, 1977). However, there appears to be a dead end in this research. Bernardin, Cardy, and Carlyle (1982) have concluded a series of studies on cognitive complexity and its influence on the rating process by suggesting that the researchers need to return to the drawing board.

One suspects that the search for the personal characteristics of the "good rater" will end very much as the search for the personal traits of effective leaders. Leadership research has pretty well abandoned the search for leadership traits, and the results of a study by Zedeck and Kafry (1977) suggest that it might as well be abandoned for rating research. They used a policy-capturing model to see how raters integrated information in reaching overall ratings of job performance. They included the same variables that Taft (1955) had found to be significantly related to the ability to make judgments, but they found that such variables had no significant relationships to rater judgment policies.

It does seem, however, that a minimum qualification is that a qualified rater should be able to make reliable judgments. One procedure I have used to identify unreliable raters is to incorporate two independent rating forms; ratings obtained on one form are regressed on ratings obtained using the other. Outlying data points tend to identify raters who are unreliable for some reason. This procedure does not tell us the reason. The outlier may have been unreliable because he or she is overly dependent on one form or the other, or because of carelessness in using one or both of the forms, or because of lack of necessary knowledge of the ratees' performance. Carelessness and opportunity to observe can be controlled in developing the complete rating process; individual rater idiosyncracies regarding particular formats are probably less easily controlled, and the procedure is probably justified for that reason.

Another approach to identifying the rater who is doing an inadequate job is through the use of a formal psychometric model, for example, the use of a latent trait model (cf. Guion & Ironson, 1983). Such techniques hold the promise of identifying raters whose set of ratings do not conform to the psychometric model. Again, the reason for the misfit is not identified, but data from misfitting raters can be excluded from a research study with a possible improvement in the predictability of the ratings.

Rater training. A workshop method of training raters was presented by Latham, Wexley, and Pursell (1975). Its effectiveness in reducing rater errors was experimentally demonstrated, and it can serve as a model for other rater training programs. The workshop was built around a set of videotapes of job candidates being appraised by a manager. After trainees had indicated on a nine-point scale their ratings and their guesses of the manager's ratings for the candidate, group discussions explored their reasons for their judgments. One exercise concentrated on the "similar-to-me" effect, the tendency to rate people seen as like oneself more favorably than those who seem different. Other tapes concentrated on halo errors, contrast effects, and first impressions.

Borman (1979a, p. 414) used this idea to develop a nine-step training program for performance rating:

1. A videotape of a job being performed was shown.
2. Trainees rated the performance on rating scales provided.
3. Each trainee's ratings were posted on a flip chart.
4. Differences and reasons for the differences in ratings were argued in group discussion.
5. Trainer gave the "correct" ratings that illustrate avoidance of the rating error being studied (whether similar-to-me, halo, or contrast error).
6. Trainer explained the "correct" ratings in terms of the ratee behavior that defined them.
7. Trainer discussed the general nature of the error being studied.
8. Trainees provided examples (in group discussion) of that kind of error in their own experiences.
9. Group discussed ways to overcome the error.

This procedure could be followed for each type of error thought to be a problem in a given rating situation. Although Borman (1979a) trained raters to avoid three of the errors corrected in the training by the Latham team (1975), a variety of different cognitive errors could be treated by a similar procedure.

These procedures can be distinguished from earlier rater training programs in that they emphasize observation and analysis more than "psychometric errors." It would seem that the key to effective rating must come from improving the psychological processes by which the rater becomes aware of performance, remembers that performance, and evaluates that performance on whatever form is provided. Training such as distinguishing between relevant observations and trivia and recalling, including the use of memory aids, seems to promise more immediate payoff in improved performance assessment.

Future Directions and Needs

Much of what has been said here so far may be perceived as pessimistic. A number of experiences and research reports have certainly contributed to such pessimism. An early example was the videotape analysis of checkout clerks and the failure to rate accurately on speed and quantity (Hamner et al., 1974). Arnold (1977), using videotapes of performance on an assessment center exercise, failed to find any consistency even in the errors people made across different episodes or different conditions. In contrast, however, Hunter (1983) demonstrated that there was some evidence across fourteen different studies that performance ratings are influenced in part by both the ability to perform as indicated by work sample and by job knowledge. This is admittedly scant cause for optimism, but it does provide some evidence, at least, that performance ratings are influenced by the kinds of things that they should be influenced by. Like death, taxes, and interviews, performance ratings are inevitable, and one should therefore grasp any available straws and start working toward more effective methods of rating.

The appropriate directions for new research and for practice can be taken economically from Feldman (1981). Feldman identified four aspects of the cognitive tasks of raters:

1. To recognize and to attend to relevant information. (I take this to imply much of what has been said earlier in this chapter about observation.)
2. Organize and store information. (This is not simply a matter of memory. It is a matter of categorizing observations as one makes them, integrating new information with old as it develops, etc.)
3. To recall salient information.
4. To integrate recalled information into a summary judgment.

Each of these steps contains booby traps. In the very first step, which involves attention to the degree to which the employee's behavior is consistent with expectations (which should not be confused with assignments), noting and storing that behavior tends to occur rather automatically. Conscious attention to and monitoring of the behavior requires either a departure from expectation or a job change. Perhaps some mechanical procedure requiring systematic, conscious observation might increase the attending to behavior consistent with expectations, but never completely.

The categorization required for organizing and storing information involves, for Feldman, a prototype of categories of people and events. Virtually every behavioral observation could potentially be classified under each of several different categories. The one that will be most salient for the observer who will later become a rater may depend on the context in which the behavior occurs, the categories that had been salient immediately before, particular prejudices or stereotypes that the observer may have, and a host of other influences. What will be remembered depends on the category from which the observation is to be recalled. The point is that it does not require prejudice, bias, or carelessness to produce inaccurate memories; it simply requires a chain of events that are more or less uncontrolled and that depend on individual differences in the personal constructs of the individual observer. Perhaps person perception can be systematized by establishing formal procedures for doing so, but the evidence that this can be done has not yet been shown. As a matter of fact, Feldman (1981) identified six different kinds of attributional biases that provide substantial roadblocks to attempts at improving recall of an observed event by procedural means.

The theory and the accumulated experience to which it speaks have several implications for practice. The most important of these is that one should separate the processes of observation and description from evaluation. With some methods, such as a behavioral checklist, this principle is already partially put into effect. For example, the people who identify the behavioral descriptions that fit a certain ratee are not necessarily the people who assigned scale values to the descriptions.

Earlier, I advocated the use of a diary system, although I did so without much hope that anyone would do it (Guion, 1965). I suggested that a supervisor should take some time at the end of each week to record for each employee the best thing and the worst thing that employee had done during that week. At the end of the year, there would then be a minimum of a hundred recorded behavioral observations, and the rater could then scale these behaviors at that time and use an average of the scale values as the rating.

I had occasion to try this on a daily basis with police training officers who were evaluating the performance of recruits. The attempt was rather traumatic; the training officers objected to "all that paper work" and provided some rather facetious examples. For example, the worst thing one recruit did all day was to kill an insect in the patrol car without asking permission, while the best thing he had done all day was to remove a dead insect from the patrol car on his own initiative! However, Bernardin and Walter (1977) tried the diary system in a study of student ratings of instructors and found substantial acceptance among student raters. Perhaps, among raters who are genuinely interested in benefits to be derived from honest and accurate ratings, keeping records of observations may not be such an onerous task, particularly if observers are given special training in observational skills (Boice, 1983).

The separation of observation from evaluation could go one step further if the diary system were to be used. That is, a supervisor or other person in a position to make observations could record at periodic intervals examples of behavior for each of the persons to be rated. These examples could be assembled after a designated time and submitted to a panel for scaling. The median of the resulting scale values could be taken as the evaluation of each ratee. The evaluation, in this case, would be conducted by a group of people independent of the description process, thereby improving reliability. While this procedure would not eliminate the problems of biased recording for such things as administrative decisions, it would make it possible to focus more clearly on training observers to recognize, with minimal attribution error, the kinds of behaviors to be recorded.

References

Arnold, J. D. (1977). *A study of the relationships among selected personal characteristics of raters and their rating behaviors.* Unpublished masters thesis, Bowling Green State University.

Barrett, R. S., Taylor, E. K., Parker, J. W., & Martens, L. (1958). Rating scale content: I. Scale information and supervisory ratings. *Personnel Psychology, 11,* 333–346.

Bernardin, H. J., Cardy, R. L., & Carlyle, J. J. (1982). Cognitive complexity and appraisal effectiveness: Back to the drawing board? *Journal of Applied Psychology, 67,* 151–160.

Bernardin, H. J., & Smith, P. C. (1981). A clarification of some issues regarding the development and use of behaviorally anchored rating scales (BARS). *Journal of Applied Psychology, 66,* 458–463.

Bernardin, H. J., & Walter, C. J. (1977). Effects of rater training and diary-keeping on psychometric error in ratings. *Journal of Applied Psychology, 62,* 64–69.

Boice, R. (1983). Observational skills. *Psychological Bulletin, 93,* 3–29.

Borman, W. C. (1977). Consistency of rating accuracy and rating errors in the judgment of human performance. *Organizational Behavior and Human Performance, 20,* 238–252.

Borman, W. C. (1979a). Format and training effects of rater accuracy and rater errors. *Journal of Applied Psychology, 64,* 410–421.

Borman, W. C. (1979b). Individual differences correlates of accuracy in evaluating others' performance effectiveness. *Applied Psychological Measurement, 3,* 103–115.

Borman, W. C., Dunnette, M. D., & Johnson, P. D. (1974). *The development and evaluation of a behavior based naval officer performance assessment package.* Minneapolis, MN: Personnel Decisions Research Institute.

Burke, R. J., Weitzel, W., & Weir, T. (1978). Characteristics of effective employee performance review and development interviews: Replications and extension. *Personnel Psychology, 31,* 903–919.

Campbell, J. P., Dunnette, M. D., Lawler, E. E., III, & Weick, K. E., Jr. (1970). *Managerial behavior, performance, and effectiveness.* New York: McGraw-Hill.

Feldman, J. M. (1981). Beyond attribution theory: Cognitive processes in performance appraisal. *Journal of Applied Psychology, 66,* 127–148.

Ghiselli, E. E., & Brown, C. W. (1955). *Personnel and industrial psychology* (2nd ed.). New York: McGraw-Hill.

Guion, R. M. (1965). *Personnel testing.* New York: McGraw-Hill.

Guion, R. M., & Ironson, G. H. (1983). Latent trait theory for organizational research. *Organizational Behavior and Human Performance, 31,* 54–87.

Hamner, W. C., Kim, J. S., Baird, L., & Bigoness, W. J. (1974). Race and sex as determinants of ratings by potential employers in a simulated work-sampling task. *Journal of Applied Psychology, 59,* 705–711.

Hunter, J. L. (1983). A path analytic study of rating validity. In F. J. Landy, S. Zedeck, & J. Cleveland (Eds.), *Performance measurement and theory* (pp. 257–266). Hillsdale, NJ: Erlbaum.

Kunin, T. (1955). The construction of a new type of attitude measure. *Personnel Psychology, 8*, 65–77.

Landy, F. J., Barnes, J. L., & Murphy, K. R. (1978). Correlates of perceived fairness and accuracy of performance evaluation. *Journal of Applied Psychology, 63*, 751–754.

Landy, F. J., Barnes-Farrell, J., & Cleveland, J. N. (1980). Perceived fairness and accuracy of performance evaluation: A follow-up. *Journal of Applied Psychology, 65*, 355–356.

Landy, F. J., & Farr, J. L. (1980). Performance rating. *Psychological Bulletin, 87*, 72–107.

Latham, G. P., Wexley, K. N., & Pursell, E. D. (1975). Training managers to minimize rating errors in the observation of behavior. *Journal of Applied Psychology, 60*, 550–555.

Schneier, C. E. (1977). Operational utility and psychometric characteristics of behavior expectation scales: A cognitive reinterpretation. *Journal of Applied Psychology, 62*, 541–548.

Sisson, D. E. (1948). Forced choice, the new army rating. *Personnel Psychology, 1*, 365–381.

Smith, P. C., & Kendall, L. M. (1963). Retranslation of expectations: An approach to the construction of unambiguous anchors for rating scales. *Journal of Applied Psychology, 47*, 149–155.

Taft, R. (1955). The ability to judge people. *Psychological Bulletin, 52*, 1–23.

Taylor, E. K., Barrett, R. S., Parker, J. W., & Martens, L. (1958). Rating scale content: II. Effect of rating on individual scales. *Personnel Psychology, 11*, 519–533.

Taylor, E. K., & Hastman, R. (1956). Relation of format and administration to the characteristics of graphic rating scales. *Personnel Psychology, 9*, 181–206.

Taylor, E. K., & Manson, G. E. (1951). Supervised ratings: Making graphic scales work. *Personnel, 27*, 504–514.

Taylor, E. K., Parker, J. W., & Ford, G. L. (1959). Rating scale content: IV. Predictability of structured and unstructured scales. *Personnel Psychology, 12*, 247–266.

U.S. Equal Employment Opportunity Commission, U.S. Civil Service Commission, U.S. Department of Labor, & U.S. Department of Justice. (1978). Uniform guidelines on employee selection procedures. *Federal Register, 43*(166), 38290–38309.

Zedeck, S., & Kafry, D. (1977). Capturing rater policies for processing evaluation data. *Organizational Behavior and Human Performance, 18*, 269–294.

13. TECHNICAL & MECHANICAL JOB PERFORMANCE APPRAISAL

Wayne F. Cascio

Introduction

At the outset it is important that certain terms be defined. First of all, what is performance appraisal? Performance appraisal is the systematic description of the job-relevant strengths and weaknesses within and between employees. But the title of this volume is *Performance Assessment: Methods and Applications*. What does performance assessment mean? In the context of this book, the domain to be assessed is perceived as a set of competencies or skills that can be defined operationally.

BEHAVIORAL BASIS FOR PERFORMANCE APPRAISAL OR ASSESSMENT SYSTEMS

A job analysis (either task oriented or behavior oriented) must be the foundation of any appraisal or assessment system. Job analysis identifies the work to be done, the skills needed, and the training required of the individual job holder (see also Fine, chapter 1). Job analysis enables us to make distinctions among jobs. Our goal in performance appraisal or assessment, however, is not to make distinctions among jobs, but rather to make distinctions among people, especially among people competing for or holding the same job. Performance standards provide the critical link in the process. Performance standards represent the levels of performance deemed acceptable or unacceptable for each of the job-relevant, critical areas of performance identified through job analysis. For some jobs (e.g., those involving the use of machines or instruments), performance standards can be set objectively on the basis of industrial engineering studies. For others, such as research, the process is considerably more subjective and is frequently a matter of manager-subordinate agreement. An example of one such set of standards is presented in Table 13.1.

To summarize, the sequence of the performance appraisal or assessment process is as follows: completion of job analysis, setting of performance standards, execution of performance appraisal or assessment.

TABLE 13.1. Performance Standards for Lung Examination by Respiratory Therapist

Task	Evaluate the functioning of a hospitalized patient's lungs.
Performance Standard	
Thorough	Observes patient's color; uses stethoscope on front, back, and both sides of patient's chest to check lung functioning; follows up each aspect of stethoscopic examination with tactile examination.
Acceptable	Observes patient's color; uses stethoscope on front and back of patient's chest to check lung functioning.
Unacceptable	Observes patient's color.

Survey of Applications

Perhaps the most popular approach to performance assessment for mechanical jobs is the work sample or performance test (see Siegel, chapter 4). Such work sample tests have been developed for a wide variety of mechanical and technical jobs, many of which are reviewed by Plumlee (1980). In one study, for example, an entire program of performance tests was evaluated (Cascio & Phillips, 1979). Data on twenty-one performance tests, entry level and promotional, motor and verbal, were evaluated for 263 applicants for city government jobs over a seventeen-month period. These jobs were water equipment mechanic, electrical helper, carpenter, parking meter technician, air conditioning mechanic, mason, electrician, utility worker, equipment attendant, plumber, plumber's helper, park maintenance supervisor, programmer/analyst, mechanical maintenance operations supervisor, library assistant, assistant chief accountant, parking meter checker 2, planner, central services supervisor, concession attendant, and recreation director. Use of the tests resulted in average interrater reliabilities of .93 (promotional), .87 (entry level), .91 (motor), and .89 (verbal) for the different types and levels of tests. There was no evidence of adverse impact, and turnover decreased from 40 percent to less than 3 percent in the nine to twenty-six months following the introduction of performance testing. In comparison to paper-and-pencil tests, performance tests were more cost effective, more face valid, and more acceptable to applicants in this situation.

HEAVY EQUIPMENT OPERATORS

In a somewhat different application of performance testing, functional job analysis (FJA) was used to develop job-related performance standards for heavy equipment operators (Olson et al., 1981). Two types of information are derived from functional job analysis: what gets done (the procedures, methods, and processes with which the worker is engaged as he or she performs a task), and how the worker does it (the physical, mental, and interpersonal involvement of the worker as he or she carries out procedures and processes). This information is then available to document and defend the procedure as well as the performance standards and measurement techniques derived from it (for details, see chapter 1). The Olson study involved bulldozers, backhoes, loaders, graders, and scrapers, the so-called blade equipment. Work sample tests were developed directly from the performance standards. Sample items (yes/no observations of performance and product) were based on the following questions:

1. Did the operator read grade stakes to determine slope, depth, height of cut and fill areas, and starting point for cut and fill?
2. Did the operator use caution when traveling up/down/parallel to rocky surfaces?
3. Did the operator load and unload downhill?

Additional items involved ratings of performance, product, and safety:

1. Did the operator use proper prestart check?
2. Did the operator obtain proper crown?
3. Did the operator maintain correct, uniform depth?

Clearly, the nature of heavy equipment operation lends itself to this approach, in that the work is readily observable and apparent, and thus no inferences are necessary about related variables or other underlying and unobservable determinants of behavior. Using the "known-group" technique for establishing criterion groups in a concurrent validity paradigm, results indicated that the tests showed adequate evidence of criterion-related validity. The tests significantly differentiated between skill levels among the operators, in which the most significant aspect of actual job performance is the degree of independence and autonomy the operator can be permitted in doing the work.

CITY BUS DRIVERS

In an unpublished study, Cascio (1978) evaluated a performance appraisal system for the Metropolitan Transit Authority (MTA) of Dade County, Florida. The system had been developed jointly by management and the union five years previously and it had been operating quite well since that time. It was a point system that worked as follows. At the beginning of each quarter, each driver (there were about 890 drivers at that time) received 100 points. During the quarter, points were deducted for violations of performance standards that the union and management had jointly developed. Violation of a standard that was of minor importance (e.g., failure to present a neat, well-groomed appearance) incurred a much smaller penalty than a violation of a very important standard (e.g., being charged with a preventable accident). Points were assessed in one of three ways: (1) by a supervisor if he or she directly observed the violation, (2) on the basis of a police report or ticket (e.g., for speeding), or (3) on the basis of an auditor's report. The county hired a large number of auditors who randomly rode bus routes, observing the performance of the drivers. Over a year's time, all drivers were observed approximately the same amount of time.

At the end of each quarter, the remaining points (out of 100) were tallied for each driver and the point total constituted his or her performance appraisal for that quarter. At the beginning of the next quarter each driver received another 100 points and the cycle repeated itself. At the end of the year, each driver's annual appraisal was the average of the four quarterly ratings. This total served as the basis for merit raises, promotions, and assignment to special projects like VIP charters.

While there were disadvantages to this type of system—for example, predominant emphasis on the negative (losing points for doing something bad) rather than on the positive (earning points for doing something good)—clearly there were a number of advantages as well. Since the average educational level of the drivers was slightly over nine years, the appraisal system had to be simple enough to be understood, yet fair enough to be used in practice. It was. The drivers knew exactly why they would lose points, and all penalties were directly job related. Beyond this, the fact that the system was acceptable to management as well as labor is a very positive feature. The system is still being used today, although drivers can now gain points (or earn them back) for exceptionally good performance.

SCIENTISTS

In 1961 an analysis of rating forms from sixty-nine research laboratories (Addison, Derr, & Yeagly, 1961) found that the vast majority applied a graphic rating scale, usually resulting in an overall point score. The graphic rating scales typically included items about job performance, personal characteristics, supervisory abilities, and promotional possibilities (see Jacobs, chapter 2). Only a few laboratories used other methods, such as a narrative response to general questions, rank-ordered ratings, or a performance standard and coaching method. Apparently most of the responding companies followed the rating procedure with an interview in which the results were communicated.

If this study were conducted today, there would probably be far less use of items pertaining to personal characteristics. With respect to the use of the ranking method, this approach may create a zero-sum kind of climate in which, by definition, half of all the engineers or scientists in a given unit are rated "below average." One way to avoid these difficulties is for managers to refrain from direct peer comparisons and to focus instead on the extent to which targets and goals are achieved and on collaborative problem solving. In this context, it may be more beneficial to compare scientists to standards rather than to compare them to each other. This is exactly what has been done.

Despite the emphasis on individual performance, recent evidence (Balkin & Gomez-Mejia, 1984) indicates that over half the variance in the salaries, benefits, and incentive pay of research and development employees in high tech firms can be accounted for by just four factors: sales volume, stage in the product life cycle, profitability, and turnover. Presumably, individual performance accounts for a large component of the remaining variance that was unexplained in this study.

With respect to communicating the results of the appraisal via a follow-up interview, a case study by an accountant who audited a research division of a large organization (Reeve, 1975) shed light on several relevant issues in performance assessment. When scientists were asked, "How do you judge the performance of your peers?" the answer received almost every time was, "By frequency of publication of papers." The auditor had readily available a means of evaluating this performance criterion—the library of the laboratory. The library produced an annual list of publications of all laboratory personnel. Surprisingly, about 20 percent of the scientists had not published in two years, while many others averaged twelve to fourteen published papers per year. Upon further investigation, the auditor found that a number of section leaders evaluated the performance of their personnel, but failed to communicate their results to the employees evaluated. The auditor discreetly pointed out that while doing the evaluations was commendable, company policy required that the evaluation be reviewed with the employee. These practices suggest that there may often be a large discrepancy between what company policy dictates and what supervisors actually do.

ENGINEERS

A study by South (1974) reported the development of a forced-choice appraisal system, the Engineer Performance Description Form (EPDF), that was applied to more than eighteen hundred young engineers employed by a nationally known company. The forced-choice approach requires a rater to describe (not evaluate) the performance of a ratee. As used by South, the rater must choose the statement in each set of two or more statements that is most descriptive of the engineer's performance. For example,

1.   _____A. Problems need not be stated in detail for him or her.
       _____B. Double checks work others do for him or her.
2.   _____A. Does more than his or her share of the work.
       _____B. Works to improve his or her main weaknesses.

Research is needed to (1) determine which statements indicate high performance, and (2) which statements have equal appeal value. Each pair of statements is constructed such that both statements have equal appeal value, but only one statement actually distinguishes effective from ineffective performance. In theory, therefore, the opportunity to bias overtly or to distort the ratings is reduced. A factor analysis of the 297 usable items obtained in the research yielded six basic components (factors) that seem to underly engineering performance. These combine to form two more general components—technical performance and overall performance. The six primary factors that describe early career success as an engineer are presented below:

1. *Communication:* oral and written transmission of information concerning work activities. Sample items: writes so anyone can understand it; reports seldom require extensive revision or rewriting; reports show careful thinking.
2. *Relating to others:* good personal adjustment and harmonious relations with coworkers; accepts rules, regulations, and supervisory directions. Sample items: does not offend coworkers; does not alienate others by his or her personal striving for recognition; can take advice.
3. *Administrative ability:* demonstrates interest in nontechnical problems such as scheduling and costs, as well as in the varied duties characteristic of administrative and supervisory positions. Sample items: wants to learn more about administrative duties; good at handling subordinates; is aware of the problems of management.
4. *Motivation:* puts forth effort, concentration, and a strong desire to complete an assigned task. Sample items: works long hours when the chips are down; has an earnest desire to get results; looks for work to do when he or she has some free time.
5. *Technical knowledge and ability:* demonstrates technical knowledge and ability in everyday work tasks. Sample items: keeps up with advances in the field; has technically sound ideas; spends time reading technical publications.
6. *Self-sufficiency:* displays resistance to work pressures and stresses, continued poise, flexibility, and the willingness to make decisions in work. Sample items: is not upset by sudden or unexpected changes in work; does not get upset by work pressures, time, work load, etc.; is not afraid to ask questions.

While all six factors relate to overall performance, only "relating to others" and "administrative ability" do not define the higher-order factor, technical ability. In its final form, the EPDF consists of thirty-five pairs of statements yielding an evaluative "overall performance score" and thirteen groups of six statements each providing the six scores (one per factor) that make up the "developmental profile." Spearman-Brown reliability estimates for each dimension ranged from .40 to .78 with a median of .65.

In a later study on the fakeability of the EPDF (South, 1980), it was shown that the evaluative overall performance score can be distorted, either higher or lower, approximately 18% of the range of the raw scores. The results also indicated that raters do not know and cannot accurately estimate the raw-score rating when they attempt to fake a low or high appraisal. A recurring problem, however, is that of rater resentment and resistance to the forced-choice approach. In no small measure this is due to the loss of control experienced by the rater. With the forced-choice approach, the rater simply does not know whether he or she is assigning a high or a low rating. Users of such instruments should be aware of these issues and be prepared with alternatives for handling such reactions (see Cozan, 1959; Huttner & Katzell, 1957; King, Hunter, & Schmidt, 1980).

Krausz and Fox (1981), working on an Israeli government project, attempted to identify performance criteria for engineers that could be used to evaluate their performance and that might also serve as a basis for awarding incentive pay. There are three major problems in trying to develop performance criteria across organizations. First, engineering is actually an umbrella term referring to a variety of subfields, each of which deals with very different materials. Second, even within a subfield, engineers operate in different functional areas such as research, development, supervision, or maintenance. Third, the engineers were employed in different branches of government and other segments of the private sector.

Krausz and Fox used semistructured interviews based on a critical incident approach with seventy engineers employed by the government. On the basis of a content analysis of the interview results, nine criteria of engineering excellence were identified: (1) creativity and originality; (2) ability to adapt and implement new ideas; (3) ability to cut costs or increase profits; (4) high work quality (defined in terms of a low error rate and fast detection of potential sources of problems); (5) leadership in a professional field (defined in terms of frequency of consultation by others in the field and of products designed or constructed that attracted professional visitors); (6) publication in scientific and professional journals; (7) number and complexity of projects for which responsible; (8) utilization of interdisciplinary knowledge; and (9) administrative and managerial ability. (Sprecher, in 1966, identified very similar dimensions using a critical incidents approach. The dimensions were loyalty, friendship, and teamwork; thoroughness and analytical ability; technical knowledge; problem-solving orientation; cost consciousness; and communication skills.)

The method of evaluation used in the Krausz and Fox study is unique in that the immediate supervisor plays almost no role in the process. Evaluation by a three-person committee is used. Two of the members are to be from the same subfield, with the third engineer committee member from a different field. Applications for review come from the engineers themselves or from their supervisors, but supervisors have no power to veto a subordinate's application.

Two advantages are proposed for the new system. First, it overcomes supervisors' resistance to doing appraisal, and second, it helps to ensure that decisions are based on professional criteria only, not on intraunit pressures to consider irrelevant criteria. The new system is intended to complement, not to replace, more common types of appraisal systems for engineers. Unfortunately there are no data available to buttress the proposed advantages of the system.

In a theoretical piece, Roberts and Fusfield (1981) identified and described five informal but critical behavioral functions that are needed for effective execution of technology-based innovative projects: (1) idea generating; (2) entrepreneuring or championing (recognizing, proposing, pushing, and demonstrating a new technical idea, approach, or procedure for formal management approval); (3) project leading; (4) gatekeeping (collecting and channeling information about important changes in the internal and external environments); and (5) sponsoring or coaching. The authors observed that some individuals are capable of performing concurrently more than one of these critical functions. They also found that a person's role in the innovation process may change over the course of his or her career. The managerial implications of these findings, particularly with respect to performance measurement and rewards, are that individuals should be rewarded specifically for the performance of a critical function. Doing so makes the function more manageable and open to discussion (e.g., in the goal-setting process). Some rewards that seem appropriate for each function are:

1. *Idea generating:* opportunities to publish; recognition from professional peers through symposia, etc.
2. *Entrepreneuring or championing:* visibility, publicity; further resources for project.
3. *Project leading:* bigger or more significant projects; material signs of organizational status.
4. *Gatekeeping:* travel budget; key "assists" acknowledged; increased autonomy and use for advice.
5. *Sponsoring or coaching:* increased autonomy; discretionary resources for support of others.

Salary and bonus compensation are not included in the list, not because they are unimportant to people, but because they do not seem to be linked explicitly to any one innovative function more than to another. Clearly, financial rewards should also be used as appropriate.

The emphasis on setting goals when managing scientists and engineers is almost a sine qua non in the current research literature on this topic. It is not found only in the behavioral science journals either. For example, Smith and Tuttle, writing in the *Journal of the Society for Research Administrators,* noted:

> The resolution to the problems of evaluating performance for research
> scientists is not an easy one; but there is a solution where managers
> have clearly established a hierarchy of goals and objectives. With the
> solicited participation of the scientists, managers must define a range of
> desired results. In other words, the determination of good performance

for a single research project, set of projects, or an entire organization's set of projects must be specified within a range of values *before* the projects are implemented. The definition of good performance prior to the initiation of a project essentially places the scientists at risk for achieving the objectives that they helped to formulate. (1982, pp. 35–36)

NURSES

The classic approach for developing behaviorally anchored rating scales (BARS) was described by Smith and Kendall (1963) (see Borman, chapter 3). The scales were developed for the purpose of assessing the job performance of nurses, and the steps used in the development process were as follows:

1. Several groups of head nurses participated in conferences devoted to discussing the use of performance appraisals for improving nursing performance.
2. Each group listed the major qualities involved in nursing, and critical incidents were gathered and classified to illustrate examples of behavior related to each quality. Throughout, the nurses' own terminology was retained.
3. The groups also formulated general statements defining high, low, and acceptable performance for each quality, and additional examples of actual performance incidents were suggested for each quality.
4. The head nurses then indicated independently what quality was illustrated by each incident. Incidents were eliminated if there was no clear agreement concerning the quality to which they belonged. Qualities were eliminated if the incidents were not consistently reassigned to the quality for which they were originally chosen as illustrative.
5. The incidents were then judged by another group of head nurses on a scale ranging from 0 to 2.0 according to the proper behavior for nursing. Incidents were eliminated if the judgments showed a large dispersion or if they fell into more than one distinct group. This procedure provided another safeguard, assuring absolute agreement and lack of ambiguity.

The outcome of this painstaking work was a job-behavior evaluation form including scales for judging six major qualities: knowledge and judgment, conscientiousness, skill in human relationships, organizational ability, objectivity, and observational ability. Each scale was firmly defined behaviorally, anchored at various points by incidents stated in the nurses' own language, and rigidly fixed according to scale location.

Despite the amount of effort involved in building BARS, and the large amount of empirical evidence that suggests that in terms of psychometric characteristics, the method is not superior to other appraisal methods (Jacobs, chapter 2; Jacobs, Kafry, & Zedeck, 1980; Schwab, Heneman, & DeCotiis, 1975), the approach continues to be chosen frequently as the method of choice for evaluating nurses (McAfee & Green, 1977).

In a more recent investigation, Sheridan and Vredenbergh (1978) used a sample of 216 nurses from a metropolitan hospital to investigate relationships of head nurses' leadership behavior and social power variables with staff nurses' job tension, performance, and terminations. The original Smith and Kendall BARS for nurses was used to evaluate nursing performance. A regression model explained a small, but statistically significant, amount of variance in the criterion variables. Leader consideration was inversely associated with tension and terminations, but also with job performance. Initiating structure was positively associated with terminations. Both reward and expert power were useful in predicting job tension.

A study by Klimoski and London (1974) is interesting because of the insight it provides into some of the characteristics of nurses that are rated in appraisal systems other than BARS. Measures of effectiveness were obtained from performance appraisal forms used by six different hospitals. Characteristics (both behaviors and traits) were selected that represented the range of effectiveness covered in the appraisal forms. The following dimensions were rated:

Technical competence	Skill in planning
Adaptability in emergencies	Dependability
Quality of work	Complete work schedule
Acceptability of completed work	Attendance and promptness
Amount of work	Communication skill
Effort applied	Willingness to perform
Impress visitors	Observe rules and regulations
Observance of rest and lunch periods	Personal appearance
Ability to organize and schedule work loads	Accepting responsibility for own behavior

Factor analysis of 153 self-, peer-, and supervisory ratings of registered nurses indicated that each rating source could be identified clearly and characterized. The data reaffirmed the notion that interrater disagreement may reflect systematic rater bias as well as meaningful differences in the ways that judgments are made.

A considerable number of trait dimensions were rated in the Klimoski and London study, and this is consistent with an argument made by Kavanagh (1972). His argument is that the appraisal of job performance in organizations is essentially a judgmental task. In terms of the kinds of information considered, ratings will vary along a continuum from subjective to objective information. Behavioral scientists often advise personnel departments to use primarily concrete, observable, objective characteristics to rate job performance. However, it is a rare supervisor who does not consider the subordinate's personality when he or she completes the appraisal form. The key is to rely on objective material as much as possible but to include personality traits as they appear relevant to job performance. Furthermore, if personality traits are demonstrably relevant to job performance, use them. If not, avoid them, for they can surely lead to legal challenge to the validity and fairness of the entire appraisal system (Cascio & Bernardin, 1981).

The final study to be reported for nurses used nurses as subjects but yielded insights for performance assessment and appraisal in general. Mitchell and Kalb (1981) suggested that supervisors' judgments about a poorly performing subordinate would be affected by knowledge of the outcome of the behavior and by the valence of the outcome. For example, if a nurse leaves a bed railing down, the supervisor's evaluation and treatment of the nurse may be influenced by the events that occur as a result of the action (e. g., the patient falls out of bed). Both the knowledge of the outcome and the valence of the outcome (whether positive or negative) are potentially important. In all, fifty-five nurses were provided with descriptions of two incidents of poor performance and were asked to take the role of the supervisor of the poorly performing subordinate. Half the nurses were provided with information about an outcome (either benign or negative) and half were not. Those with outcome knowledge, particularly in the case of a negative outcome, (a) rated the outcome as more probable, (b) saw the subordinate as more responsible for the behavior, and (c) made more internal attributions (i.e., attributed the cause of the behavior to the nurse's personal characteristics) than those with no outcome knowledge.

There is a practical message in these results. The message to be transmitted to supervisors is that poorly performing subordinates may be treated differently, depending on whether or not the supervisor knows the outcome of the performance and on the valence of that outcome. That is, the same behavior may have different outcomes and therefore results in different supervisory treatment. Such inequitable treatment may result in conflict and resentment. To avoid these problems, supervisors should focus on the behavior of their subordinates and attend less to the outcomes of their actions. Such an approach may well reduce attributional errors and the potential conflicts that always surround incidents of poor performance.

ATTORNEYS

Most attorneys want to be evaluated on the basis of their record, their prior accomplishments, and their achievements. The accomplishment record (AR) developed by Hough (1984) is a reliable method for doing this. There are five steps involved in developing the AR: (1) an analysis of job behaviors; (2) development of critical job dimensions to provide a structure for an AR inventory; (3) administration of the inventory to attorneys (who describe their major accomplishments on each job dimension); (4) development of rating scales and principles for scoring the accomplishments; and (5) scoring of the AR protocols. Protocols were reliably rated ($r = .82$ for the overall rating) for seven dimensions: researching/investigating, using knowledge, planning and organizing, writing, oral communication and assertive advocacy, working independently, and hard work/dedication. Perhaps the major advantage of the AR method when used for purposes of performance appraisal is that the standards and expectations of the organization or supervisor are specified clearly. In many other appraisal systems designed to rate professionals, this feature is noticeably absent.

MECHANICAL AND TECHNICAL JOBS

It is one thing to assess the performance of mechanical and technical job incumbents; it is quite another to assess the job performance of their supervisors (see Sokol & Oresick, chapter 14). The management research group at AT & T has developed one such approach, a one- to two-hour structured interview with the manager's immediate supervisor. The interview covers a series of questions that relate to eleven different areas plus two types of overall ratings ("A" and "B"). The eleven areas described in detail and then rated are (1) organizing and planning, (2) decisiveness, (3) quality of decisions, (4) oral presentation and communication, (5) written communication, (6) leadership, (7) interpersonal skills, (8) behavior flexibility, (9) fact-finding ability, (10) resistance to stress, and (11) energy. The instructions for overall rating "A" are

> Consider this person's length of service in the company and decide what is typical or average performance on the job. Now make your rating of this subordinate by comparing his or her behavior with the average or typical behavior of subordinates at his or her level doing comparable work.

Instructions for overall rating "B" are

> What do you think your rating would be if the manager were in a nonsupervisory position? What brings you to this position?

Here are some sample questions asked during the interview that relate to the quality of the subordinate's decisions:

1.   How appropriate are the decisions made?
2.   Does the individual consider the implications and consequences of acting one way or another?
3.   Is the reasoning behind the decision clear?
4.   Is the decision logical?
5.   Are the consequences of the decision favorable?

Currently this instrument is being used to assess managerial job performance for purposes of validating management selection tests. Unfortunately, it is so new that research results are not yet available for it.

Future Directions and Needs

Perhaps the most pressing need in this area is to develop and communicate job performance standards to all who may be affected by them. Whether one is talking about bus drivers, heavy equipment operators, engineers and scientists, nurses, attorneys, or any other mechanical or technical jobs, it is important that there be public communication of the "rules of the game." It is an all too common occurrence for supervisors to be assessing subordinates on one set of standards, while subordinates think that they are being judged according to a different set of standards. Such a state of affairs can only lead to demoralization, to resentment, and to defensiveness during appraisal interviews.

There are also broader issues to consider, for performance assessment and appraisal systems encompass measurement issues as well as attitudinal and behavioral issues. Traditionally there has been a tendency to focus attention on measurement issues per se; yet any measurement instrument or rating format probably has only a limited impact on performance appraisal scores (Borman & Dunnette, 1975; Schwab, Heneman, & DeCotiis, 1975).

Broader issues must be addressed, inasmuch as appraisal outcomes are likely to represent an interaction among organizational-contextual variables, rating formats, and rater motivation. Factors such as performance-pay contingencies, political and union pressures on raters, purpose of the rating, level of the rater, time constraints, and the need to justify ratings must all be considered (Landy & Farr, 1980; Warmke & Billings, 1979). For example, Ivancevich (1979) investigated the long-term impact of BARS in an organizational setting. At three measurement points over a twenty-month period, 121 BARS-rated engineers reported more favorable attitudes about the system (e. g., fair, accurate, comprehensive, provides meaningful feedback), less job-related tension, and improved scheduling performance than 128 of their counterparts who were rated on a trait-oriented scale. Unfortunately, since it was not possible to incorporate a true control group into the research design, there is no evidence that the BARS system caused the improvements. Nevertheless, the knowledge that such changes generated positive shifts in appraisal attitudes is no less important than the knowledge that a new appraisal format results in less halo, leniency, and central tendency biases. Both types of information are meaningful and useful; both must be considered in the wider context of performance appraisal.

References

Addison, A., Derr, T. B., & Yeagley, H. L. (1961). A method of performance evaluation for engineers and scientists. *IRE Transactions on Engineering Management, 8,* 179–181.

Balkin, D. B., & Gomez-Mejia, L. R. (1984). Determinants of R & D compensation strategies in the high tech industry. *Personnel Psychology, 37,* 635–650.

Borman, W. C., & Dunnette, M. D. (1975). Behavior-based versus trait-oriented performance ratings: An empirical study. *Journal of Applied Psychology, 60,* 561–565.

Cascio, W. F. (1978, August). *Analysis and update of employee selection criteria used by Metro Dade County, focusing on the job-relatedness and fairness of personnel procedures* (Third Quarter Report, IPA Grant G-45-36). Miami, FL: Metropolitan Transit Authority.

Cascio, W. F., & Bernardin, H. J. (1981). Implications of performance appraisal litigation for personnel decisions. *Personnel Psychology, 34,* 211–226.

Cascio, W. F., & Phillips, N. (1979). Performance testing: A rose among thorns? *Personnel Psychology, 32,* 751–766.

Cozan, L. W. (1959). Forced-choice: Better than other rating methods? *Personnel, 36,* 80–83.

Hough, L. M. (1984). Development and evaluation of the "accomplishment record" method of selecting and promoting professionals. *Journal of Applied Psychology, 69,* 135–146.

Huttner, L., & Katzell, R. (1957). Developing a yardstick of supervisory performance. *Personnel, 33,* 371–378.

Ivancevich, J. M. (1979). Longitudinal study of the effects of rater training on psychometric error in ratings. *Journal of Applied Psychology, 64,* 502–508.

Jacobs, R., Kafry, D., & Zedeck, S. (1980). Expectations of behaviorally anchored rating scales. *Personnel Psychology, 33,* 595–640.

Kavanagh, M. J. (1972). Put the person back in performance appraisal. *Supervisory Management, 17,* 9–14.

King, L. M., Hunter, J. E., & Schmidt, F. C. (1980). Halo in a multidimensional forced-choice performance evaluation scale. *Journal of Applied Psychology, 65,* 507–516.

Klimoski, R. J., & London, M. (1974). Role of the rater in performance appraisal. *Journal of Applied Psychology, 59,* 445–51.

Krausz, M., & Fox, S. (1981). Needed: Excellent engineers, not mediocre managers. *Personnel, 57,* 50–56.

Landy, F. J., & Farr, J. L. (1980). Performance rating. *Psychological Bulletin, 87,* 72–107.

McAfee, B., & Green, B. (1977). Selecting a performance appraisal method. *Personnel Administrator, 22,* 61–64.

Mitchell, T. R., & Kalb, L. S. (1981). Effects of outcome knowledge and outcome valence on supervisors' evaluations. *Journal of Applied Psychology, 66,* 604–612.

Olson, H. C., Fine, S. A., Myers, D. C., & Jennings, M. C. (1981). The use of functional job analysis in establishing performance standards for heavy equipment operators. *Personnel Psychology, 34,* 351–364.

Plumlee, L. B. (1980). *A short guide to the development of work sample and performance tests* (2nd ed.). Washington, DC: Personnel Research and Development Center, U.S. Office of Personnel Management.

Reeve, J. T. (1975). Auditing a research division. *Internal Auditor, 18,* 23–28.

Roberts, E. B., & Fusfield, A. R. (1981). Staffing the innovative technology-based organization. *Sloan Management Review, 19,* 19–34.

Schwab, D. P., Heneman, H. G., III, & DeCotiis, T. A. (1975). Behaviorally anchored rating scales: A review of the literature. *Personnel Psychology, 28,* 549–562.

Sheridan, J. E., & Vredenbergh, D. J. (1978). Usefulness of leadership behavior and social power variables in predicting job tension, performance, and turnover of nursing employees. *Journal of Applied Psychology, 63,* 89–95.

Smith, H. L., & Tuttle, W. C. (1982). Managing research scientists: Problems, solutions, and an agenda for research. *Journal of the Society of Research Administrators, 13,* 31–38.

Smith, P. C., & Kendall, L. M. (1963). Retranslation of expectations: An approach to the construction of unambiguous anchors for rating scales. *Journal of Applied Psychology, 47,* 149–155.

South, J. C. (1974). Early career performance of engineers—Its composition and measurement. *Personnel Psychology, 27,* 225–243.

South, J. C. (1980). Fakability and the Engineer Performance Description Form. *Personnel Psychology, 33,* 371–376.

Sprecher, T. B. (1966). Clarifying anchored rating scales based on performance incidents. Unpublished manuscript. Cited in M. D. Dunnette, *Personnel selection and placement.* Belmont, CA: Brooks/Cole.

Warmke, D. L., & Billings, R. S. (1979). Comparison of training methods for improving the psychometric quality of experimental and administrative performance ratings. *Journal of Applied Psychology, 64,* 124–131.

14. MANAGERIAL PERFORMANCE APPRAISAL

Michael Sokol & Robert Oresick

Introduction

Appraising the performance of managers is itself an important and challenging management activity. Its importance derives from the functions it serves. A systematic and equitable appraisal system provides information crucial for decisions about selecting managers and assigning them to appropriate jobs; for the allocation of rewards, both financial compensation and promotion; and for the development of managers (the information can indicate areas for feedback, further training, and planning a career path to include developmental assignments). Managerial performance appraisal is challenging because management is an inherently complex and various set of activities and because performance appraisal under the best of circumstances is problematic.

The problems posed by performance appraisal can be highlighted if one notices that appraisal is an evaluation of performance. That is, appraisal is the comparison of performance to some standards of adequacy or excellence. Logically, there are two distinct problems: how to determine what the performance actually was, that is, the measurement problem; and how to determine what the standards should be, that is, the criterion problem. Each of these will be considered in turn.

Techniques of Managerial Performance Appraisal

There is a spectrum of managerial performance appraisal techniques in use and a substantial literature corresponding to each. Fortunately, most of the prominent methods are discussed at length in other chapters in this volume, so when possible, the reader will be directed to them. Two other very helpful volumes are the contributions of Latham and Wexley (1981) and Meidan (1981). The purpose of this section is to describe the variety of appraisal methods and to highlight their respective criteria. Two surveys of managerial performance appraisal have been published recently. Eichel and Bender (1984) asked company representatives to rate the importance of appraisal methods; Lazer and Wikstrom (1977) surveyed the appraisal practices actually being used by corporations. Together these studies provide a picture of how several hundred American corporations appraise their managers.

Eichel and Bender (1984) group appraisal techniques into comparative, out-

376

come-oriented, and absolute methods. They define "comparative methods" as those systems that compare people with one another, including ranking, paired comparisons, and forced distributions (e.g., placing people into categories to approximate a statistically normal distribution). They note that only 25 percent of their sample judged these techniques to be important; Lazer and Wikstrom (1977) also found that only 10 to 15 percent of their sample used these methods.

The comparative methods are relatively simple and natural, but they lack sensitivity and behavioral specificity, as Eichel and Bender pointed out. These techniques might be adequate for compensation or promotion purposes (e.g., bonuses for the top 10 percent), but they are useless for giving precise feedback to improve performance. Notice that these techniques use people as the criteria of evaluation.

By "outcome-oriented" methods, Eichel and Bender mean techniques that measure the outcomes of performance. These may be direct indices such as profit for the unit, increased sales, or reduced turnover; or they may be standards of or goals for performance set by the supervisor, by the manager, or through negotiation and mutual agreement of both parties. In the case of management by objectives, for instance, the goals are set in advance and appraisal after six months or a year is in terms of those goals. These methods have in common their reliance on products as criteria of evaluation.

Eichel and Bender found outcome-oriented methods to be judged important by 78 percent of their sample; and Lazer and Wikstrom found between 40 and 63 percent of their sample used such techniques, with higher proportions reported for appraisal of higher management levels. Eichel and Bender suggest that the prevalence of these techniques is probably the result of their objectivity and specificity—qualities whose absence in performance appraisals had been noted by McGregor (1957) in an influential article. On the other hand, direct indices such as profitability or increased sales are not unequivocal signs of managerial performance; for example, changes in the economy or the business environment may confound these measures. Furthermore, managerial accomplishments that are not measured in terms of these specific outcomes may be overlooked, and since the emphasis is on the products of performance, not the behaviors used to achieve them, information for coaching feedback and for developmental training and career planning is missing.

Eichel and Bender's last grouping is "absolute methods," where the focus is on what the manager actually did, not on how he or she compared to others or what the products were. In this grouping, then, behaviors are the criteria of appraisal and the criterion problem becomes the isolation of a set of behaviors that are to be valued. This technique includes assessment by the supervisor on the basis of (usually day-to-day and informal) observation and is written in a narrative essay. Despite its typically unsystematic and subjective nature, 73 percent of Eichel and Bender's sample rated it as an important method and 36 to 37 percent of Lazer and Wikstrom's sample actually used it.

Another technique used to assess behavior without direct observation is the appraisal interview, which is also typically used to give feedback on the results of appraisal (Lazer & Wikstrom, 1977). (See Wexley, chapter 6, for a discussion of this method.)

In the "critical incidents" technique developed by Flanagan (1954), information about behavior is collected according to a structured format, usually written, which is designed to document behavioral detail about episodes of effective and ineffective performance. Behaviors abstracted from these reports are thought to be critical to performance. About 58 percent of the Eichel and Bender sample rated this an important method, and 11 to 15 percent of the Lazer and Wikstrom sample actually used the technique. A major disadvantage of this approach is the large time investment necessary.

Time is saved (and objectivity may be enhanced) by the various rating systems for behavior. A checklist of some sort was rated important by 38 percent of the Eichel and Bender companies while between 8 and 13 percent of the Lazer and Wikstrom sample actually used them. More popular, in fact, probably the most widely used behavior-based technique, is the graphic or numerical rating scale (see Jacobs, chapter 2). About 58 percent of the companies Eichel and Bender surveyed thought it was important and 10 to 17 percent of the companies surveyed by Lazer and Wikstrom used it. Smith and Kendall (1963) advocated anchoring the scales behaviorally (BARS), but in the surveys just mentioned, only 23 percent judged this an important technique, and only 8 to 9 percent used it. (See the discussion of behaviorally anchored rating scales in chapter 3.)

Probably the most comprehensive method for getting at behavior is the "assessment center" introduced by Bray (1976). (See Byham and Thornton's presentation of this method in chapter 5.)

These "absolute" methods are commonly used in combinations with each other and with techniques from the other categories as part of a multimethod assessment. This is illustrated, for example, in the 1977 survey by Lazer and Wikstrom, which shows that exemplary companies use mixed approaches (Lazer and Wikstrom's volume, incidentally, is especially useful because it contains several detailed case studies of companies' appraisal systems, including documents). Absolute methods emphasize behavior; in this respect they are helpful for giving feedback and assessing training needs or developmental assignments. However, these techniques, assuming their validity and reliability, and assuming a multimethod system, all rest on the presumption that relevant and valid behavioral criteria have been established.

CRITERIA FOR MANAGERIAL PERFORMANCE

From the preceding overview of managerial performance appraisal methods in use currently, it seems that they fall into three criterion categories, corresponding to Eichel and Bender's three methods of appraisal. Comparative methods are based on people, outcome-oriented methods rely on the products people produce, and absolute methods refer ultimately to criterion behaviors.

The criterion problem involves not only the types of criteria employed but also the processes used to establish and to define them. Although the determination of performance appraisal criteria is discussed by most authors, the discussion is typically only a passing prelude to a detailed exposition of the issues in the methods and techniques of assessment. An outstanding counterexample, though, is Blumenfeld's monograph (1976), one of the most comprehensive discussions of the criterion problem and a good source of references to the literature.

Performance appraisal criteria can be discussed and evaluated according to several dimensions: functional utility, validity, empirical base, sensitivity, systematic development, and legal appropriateness.

First, functional utility is crucial. Performance is used for selection, compensation, and development; the criteria for performance appraisal may be more or less useful for each of these functions. An important aspect of functional utility is the acceptance by the manager of the appraiser's evaluation and feedback: the manager must see it as valid, fair, and useful.

Second, the criteria must be valid. Ordinarily, validity is understood to be a property of a measurement instrument or method, but the criteria also must be true. By extension from the measurement case, criteria can be face valid, content valid, or criterion valid. For example, earning a profit for a quarter could be a "face-valid" criterion. Since managers must direct the activities of subordinates, being able to persuade others is a "content-valid" behavioral criterion for their job. "Criterion validity" also applies to criteria themselves; for example, using the comparative method, a company might establish a bonus for the top 10 percent of managers, as determined by a forced distribution. This criterion could be validated by showing that it was correlated to another important criterion, for example, profits (those top 10 percent of managers, say, headed units that showed the highest return on investment). This illustrates the important point that criteria ought not to be considered in isolation, a point forcefully argued by Ghiselli (1956).

Third, criteria may be empirical in the sense that the process employed to establish them utilizes empirical data to set thresholds and to revise and refine them.

Fourth, the sensitivity of criteria is also important. A criterion may be important to performance but may not differentiate levels, say, adequate from excellent performance.

Fifth, the determination of criteria may be more or less systematic. On the one hand, the criteria might be a rather haphazard conglomeration accrued over a particular historical period (characterized by a significant managerial and business change); on the other, they might be products of an explicit and systematic process, reevaluated periodically, and used in an integrated management process of selection, training and development, compensation, and promotion.

Finally, the criteria may be legally appropriate, where legality is broadly construed to include appropriate technical standards and social and organizational values (see Nathan & Cascio, Introduction).

These dimensions will be applied to the types of criteria to illustrate important considerations in the determination of appraisal criteria. Less is known about the current practices in determining criteria than about the methods used to appraise performance, so the following discussion can be taken as stimulus for thought and exploratory research by managerial appraisers.

People-based criteria. In general, people-based criteria have the most functional utility in selection and compensation, but they are sorely lacking in information for development. The validity of people-based criteria is typically face or content, but ideally, criterion validation would be important to establish. For example, should one hire the top ten nominations of paired comparisons unless those selected in this manner have been shown to be successful in the past or also have relevant abilities and skills? People-based criteria are, by definition, empirical, but empirical validation to other criteria would be desirable to refine and justify the thresholds, especially regarding sensitivity. People-based criteria can be adjusted to discriminate among various degrees of differences, but do those differences make a difference? And if one cannot demonstrate meaningful differences, what is the resulting legal or ethical position?

Product-based criteria. The functional utility of product-based criteria is considerably better than that of people-based criteria, primarily because in the case of performance standards or management by objectives, the goals set can be very close to explicit behavioral requirements and thus can direct behavior and serve as milestones for ongoing feedback. Often, however, the utility for feedback purposes is limited because the objective indices are a function of managerial performance and other factors such as the business cycle or performance of other units in the corporation. Some product-based criteria may have adequate face and content validity, particularly if they are expressions of company values or professional and legal requirements. For example, criteria such as low turnover, high profitability, and no lawsuits are compelling on the face of it. Other product criteria (especially those closely tied to behavioral expectations as part of a management by objectives program) raise selection issues very similar to ones encountered in the determination of behavior-based criteria, a topic addressed in the following section.

Behavior-based criteria. The family of behavior-based criteria is so large that they will be considered according to their sources.

One class of behavioral criteria is derived from legal, ethical, normative, and technical sources. They are less straightforward than might appear (see the Introduction for a fuller discussion). For instance, legal requirements, which may be the clearest case, are often difficult to interpret and to apply. Professional standards must be complied with, but standards vary in explicitness. What are the generally accepted practices in the diverse fields managers must direct? Adding to the complexity of the problem is the societal context that has an impact on these sorts of criteria. For instance, should an American company doing business in South Africa hire and promote according to the laws or norms of the United States? Should technical and safety standards in an Indian subsidiary conform to those of its parent organization in the United States? Legal and philosophical expertise may be required to determine such behavioral criteria.

The majority of behavioral criteria are probably set by the person who is most likely to be the appraiser, that is, the supervisor (Lazer & Wikstrom, 1977). The supervisor's determination of the criteria may be theoretical or observation based, or it may be intuitive, that is, a combination of both. In other words, the supervisors may have studied particular theories of management and decided to apply them. Or the supervisors may have performed the kinds of jobs the subordinates now do and extrapolated from their own experiences. Or they may observe and note what the successful (or well-liked) performers do. The major advantage of this type of criterion is its economy and the close control and participation it gives the appraisers/supervisors—they can transmit their expectations and develop, compensate, and promote accordingly. However, lack of systematic observation or empirical validation, political pressures, and other sources of bias hamper this approach.

To avoid the limitations of the immediate supervisor's perspective, outside experts can be consulted about the behavioral criteria. They may be peers or other supervisors in the company with similar responsibilities who can generate an inventory of desirable behaviors in a more systematic fashion and whose biases can be corrected to some extent by mutual discussion. But their knowledge may be limited and various forms of groupthink might influence the process.

The next possibility, then, is systematic research, either by in-house specialists or by outside consultants. The information base may include on-the-job observation, interviews with incumbents, off-the-job observation (e.g., assessment centers) and written reports (e.g., critical incidents). Both assessment centers and critical incidents are methods of assessment and methods of generating behavioral criteria, though they are probably used more frequently for the former purpose (see the discussion of assessment centers by Byham and Thornton in chapter 5). Such information can be analyzed to find criteria in the traits and abilities of people, in the behavioral requirements of the job, or in some combination of both. The personality assessment approach tries to identify the characteristics of good managers in general. There are clearly formidable psychometric problems here, but the most salient drawback is the recognition that managers actually perform, not in general, but in a particular job in a particular organization (see chapter 8).

Job analysis has now become a very sophisticated enterprise. Done well, it provides a systematic and empirically derived list of the behaviors required to accomplish the job. A comprehensive discussion of this type of analysis is given by Fine in chapter 1, so only two comments will be made here. First, the job of managing is so difficult to define across levels and industries and corporate climates that a job analysis probably has to be done on a case-by-case basis. Second, it is an open question whether the criteria resulting from the job analysis are capable of distinguishing adequacy versus excellence in the job.

Another important approach to the criterion problem, which combines a search for personality traits, skills, and so on, and the requirements of the particular job (though not a systematic job analysis), is through the identification of job competencies. Since this approach may be less familiar than the others mentioned thus far, a more detailed description will be given to illustrate it and the various desiderata expounded previously.

A COMPETENCY-BASED APPROACH TO THE CRITERION PROBLEM

Defining managerial competence. The first step in deciding what should be assessed is defining what a manager does. Defining the jobs of a structural engineer, a software designer, an accountant, or an English teacher is a formidable task; establishing competencies and measures of them is difficult but possible. But managerial jobs are among the most wide-ranging in their scope and variation and thus are much more difficult to categorize.

What does a manager do? A number of management experts have tried to answer this question (Appley, 1969; Drucker, 1973; Katz & Kahn, 1978). In general, their definitions comprise descriptions of the various functions that managers perform; managers are asked to set goals, plan, coordinate, make decisions, motivate others, and supervise the work of others. Katz and Kahn (1978) summarized the job of a manager as being concerned primarily with ensuring that the internal resources of an organization meet the external demands placed on that organization in such a way that everything runs smoothly. The actions that make one person better than another at carrying out this job are "managerial competencies."

A *managerial competency is a characteristic of an individual that underlies effective performance in a management position.* To make this definition clear, one must first understand what is meant by effective performance. Boyatzis (1982) argues that effective performance occurs when a job is carried out so that a specific, required outcome results from the performance of a specific action—an action that is carried out within the policies, procedures, and conditions of the organization environment. The key notion in this description is that specific actions lead to effective performance. In addition, what may be effective behavior leading to effective performance in one area will not necessarily work in another. For example, the same competencies that make one a good manager of a sales force in the computer industry are not the same as those that make one an effective manager of a manufacturing plant, though there may be some overlap.

Similarly, what may be effective managerial behavior leading to effective performance in a middle-level manager is likely to be quite different than the qualities for success in first-line supervision or in upper-level positions. (Boyatzis, 1982, identifies core competencies across a range of managerial jobs.)

Different mixes of competencies are needed in order for workers to function in different organizations; in a managerial position, specific actions that are carried out are governed by underlying competencies because the job demands them. Thus effective performance can be defined as occurring when an individual's underlying competencies lead to behaviors that meet the job demands within the parameters of the organizational environment and when a specific desired result occurs.

If managerial competencies make the difference between an effective manager and an ineffective manager, then the next question is, What is a managerial job competency? A job competency is defined by Klemp and Spencer (1980) as an underlying characteristic of a person that results in effective or superior performance in a job. They state that a competency can consist of a motive, trait, skill, aspect of self-image, social role, or body of knowledge that leads to effective performance.

A competency, then, can be any one of a set of notoriously elusive entities. Furthermore, a competency is generic in the sense that a single competency is manifested in several different behavioral indicators. For example, the competency "persuasion" might include persuading by appeals to the other's self-interest, the use of an influence network, and threats of sanctions.

Thus a more complete definition might be the following:

A managerial job competency is an underlying generic motive, trait, aspect of self-image, social role, or body of knowledge that is manifested in one or more particular behaviors that lead to effective managerial performance in a given job.

Determining competencies: A strategy. One method of establishing performance appraisal criteria for managers is based on the assumption that empirical research on a group of people who have been identified as superior performers in the organization under study will give the best information on what competencies are needed for effective performance. Thus these superior performers will define by their own behaviors the key competencies. This assumption directs us to the following tasks in the development of the performance appraisal criteria:

1. Selecting criterion groups
2. Collecting data on performance
3. Developing a competency model
4. Validating the model
5. Deploying the model for use in performance appraisal

Each will be discussed in turn.

Selecting criterion groups. The first step in the process of determining competency-based criteria is the selection of a sample of superior performers and a sample of merely average performers. The selection process is based upon three sources of information, whenever possible (i.e., as always, a multimethod approach is desirable): (1) a list of the managers who are considered to be outstanding performers by their supervisors; (2) ratings by incumbents themselves as to who are the best performers; and (3) measurable performance data on each incumbent from the organization's file. (Sources 1 and 2 employ comparative methods and people-based criteria, while source 3 reflects an outcome-oriented, product-based approach.) This process is intended to differentiate incumbents whose performance is characterized by excellence from those whose work is adequate or mediocre. The latter sample is selected to serve as a control group. The performance of this group provides baseline information for establishing the minimum, or threshold, competencies that people need to possess in order to carry out their jobs in an adequate manner. Thus the procedure seeks to build discriminative sensitivity into the criteria.

The selection process begins first by convening a panel of supervisors or, if there are too many supervisors, a specially chosen panel of experts. Once the purpose of the panel is explained, two experts are charged with indentifying the hard (data-based) outcomes that they would expect to observe in the performance of a superior performer. For example, a superior sales manager might be expected to have salespeople perform at a certain level of profit, do their paperwork in timely fashion, show a low rate of turnover, support the overall efforts of the marketing plan, and exhibit a high rate of promotion (indicating that the manager is developing them professionally).

Some of the expected outcomes will be readily available in corporate files, but some either will not be available because the data have not been collected or cannot be assessed in the eyes of top management. Sometimes, the information has been collected but, for political reasons, is not available. The purpose of having the panel identify what the criteria for outstanding performance should be is threefold: (1) it tells what to look for and where to find it; (2) it transforms the implicit theories used by the group to judge individuals into explicit theories, which in turn gives the group a set of common criteria by which to compile a list of superior and average incumbents; and (3) it begins to build acceptance of the process both by the people who will be using the criteria and by the people who are viewed as experts in the organization and who are therefore opinion leaders. The actual number of incumbents selected may vary between sixteen and forty depending on the nature of the job, the number of incumbents, and the funding and time available.

Parallel to the panel's efforts, a list of all the incumbents in the job is compiled and sent to all those incumbents, who are asked first to identify those people they know and then to identify those they think are performing their job in a superior fashion. These data are then analyzed. The people who are known by a sufficiently large number of their peers and who are judged to be superior by 80 percent of those who know them are assigned to the superior group. The average group is defined as those people who are known by a large number of people and are judged to be superior by no more than 20 percent of the people who know them.

The three sources of data—the panel nominations, the peer nominations, and the outcome data—are then examined. Based on this examination, clearly average and clearly superior people are selected. Disagreements on classification at this point must be resolved by discussion; later, when the competency model is developed, empirical data can clarify the marginal and borderline cases. That is one of the advantages of an empirical approach: it can sharpen our powers of discrimination and uncover the underlying bases of people-based comparisons.

Aside from the obvious advantages of examining from three different perspectives what it means to be a superior performer, all three groups—the people who will use the criteria to evaluate others, the people being evaluated, and corporate headquarters—benefit because each has had input into designating the criterion groups on which the model for outstanding performance is based. This approach also reduces some of the biases that have plagued the selection of criterion groups, such as halo effects and the fact that peers and superiors rate on the basis of different information or criteria. Armed with a final list of superior and average performers, data can now be collected.

Collecting data on performance. One approach to data collection is to go to the people who are actually on the job and observe or interview them. This approach facilitates the construction of a competency model by providing a foundation of sound empirical information. Alternatively, the performance criteria can be based on a job analysis checklist or the perspectives of an expert panel. Both of these approaches are based on a somewhat biased picture of what it takes to carry out a job effectively. The job analysis checklist constrains the information that can be gathered by forcing people to fit their perceptions of the job into a set list of characteristics. The expert panel is constrained by the group process, which generally leads to a job description laden with socially desirable criteria and burdened with current theories of management rather than to an accurate description of what superior managers actually do on the job, that is, their competencies.

For example, one company discovered that its top managers routinely inspected the desks of their subordinates to ensure that phone calls were promptly returned and customer needs were met in a timely fashion. It is hard to imagine a group of experts coming up with a managerial model that suggests going through subordinates' desks as a sign of effective management. Yet this was the case, and if this corporation is interested in an accurate description of excellent managerial performance, it needs to assess the degree of checking its managers do of their subordinates' work. To obtain information about behavior at this level of detail and specificity, contact with the incumbent managers is imperative.

One strategy for solving some of these problems is to obtain a clear, detailed picture of how superior and average performers do their jobs through a data-gathering technique called the "behavioral events interview" (BEI, when applied properly, eliminates many of the difficulties mentioned above through its probing, which requires incumbents to describe what they do on the job and does not require them to make judgments about what is right or wrong, relevant or irrelevant to successful performance of the job. Nor does the interviewer have to interpret or evaluate. The analytic function of this competency-finding process is separated from the data-gathering phase.

The BEI is based on the work of Flanagan (1954), who, while working for the Air Force, developed a methodology in which pilots were asked to write out what they did during a "critical incident," that is, a time when they were in some danger in the airplane. In this way he hoped to identify the key skills and abilities that helped pilots to survive. McClelland (1971) took up Flanagan's method of critical incidents and improved upon it in a number of ways. McClelland recommended that, rather than writing reports about their managerial critical incidents, the managers should be interviewed about high and low points of effectiveness so that an interviewer could probe beneath the surface for details of what actually happened during the incident; this retrieved more information than was usually obtained by writing, which is limited by people's motivation and expository writing ability.

The interviewer's primary job is to get interviewees to convey their critical incidents so the behaviors are described in sufficiently rich detail to form a data base for construction of a competency model. The interviewer's skill acts to focus those interviewees who philosophize about the theory of management on specific behaviors and (by building rapport) to elicit incidents from those individuals who have some resistance to giving information. The interviewer is able to inquire about thoughts and feelings as well as behavior, so important cognitive competencies can be identified.

The BEI differs from other types of interviews in two respects. The technique presses the interviewee for behavioral details, and the interviewer's job is to collect information, not to evaluate it. Other kinds of interviews either accept interviewees' vague generalities or require the interviewer to split attention between collecting and processing information (e.g., interpreting it or giving feedback). The only job of the individual conducting a BEI is to find out what the interviewee did, said, thought, and felt at the time of the incident. The interviewer makes no value judgment, offers no emotional support, asks no leading questions to test out his or her own hypotheses about what it takes to do an outstanding job, and gives no coaching or feedback. The BEI interviewer is like a newspaper reporter interested only in getting a factual and accurate record of what actually took place. Because of this definite purpose, special training for BEI interviewers is necessary.

The interview itself comprises three distinct parts. The first is an explanation of why the interviewee is being interviewed. This part not only informs the interviewee about the nature of the project but also develops a feeling of rapport or comfort.

The next part of the interview is a request for the major duties and responsibilities of the incumbent. This step is designed to get an interviewee talking about the job on a general level, that is, to determine what the individual understands the job to be. Since this step is relatively free of probing, it allows the interviewee to state general theories and ideas about the job. The interviewer makes no judgmental comments and in general agrees with whatever the interviewee is saying, with the goal of building rapport and facilitating conversation. Together the first two parts may last ten minutes.

The third phase in the interviewing process is eliciting the critical incidents. This is the core of the interview and takes forty-five to ninety minutes. The interviewer asks the interviewee to think of a time when he or she felt particularly effective in the job over the last two years; this time period is suggested to ensure the interviewee will probably be able to remember the incident in sufficient detail. That is, interviewees are asked to pick a time when they felt good about their job performance—not when the supervisor thought they were performing well, and not when they met a company goal, but when they personally felt effective in the job. This step virtually guarantees that the incident conveyed will have the interviewee in a central role at a time when a number of competencies were needed. People are also asked to tell about personal low points on the job. By acquiring information about what the interviewees did during these high and low points, one is able to observe how they met with adversity and challenge when the demands of the job were greatest. The analysis will not contrast behaviors in high and low points, but behaviors in both high and low points of superior managers will be compared to such behaviors in average managers.

This tactic of asking for high and low points of felt effectiveness avoids one problem typical of observational studies of jobs. Observers end up watching the day-to-day functioning of an individual but not the key situations and behaviors that indicate superior performance or lack of ability, especially if they are relatively infrequent. Observational studies may work well for jobs with a great deal of repetitiveness, where job demands are stable and the environment changes slowly, if at all; but they are not very useful in assessing what it takes to be a manager in a dynamic, ever-changing business environment, which is the most typical circumstance of managers. One basic assumption of this approach is a variation of Pareto's principle: 20 percent of the individual's behaviors make 80 percent of the difference. Competencies, even relatively rare ones, seem to emerge most clearly in challenging situations when people are either very successful or are finally overcome by adversity. It is these episodes that people remember, and the BEI exploits this property of memory.

The BEI also differs from other types of interviews in the level of detail that is extracted from the interviewees. Eliciting rich behavioral detail is accomplished by a number of techniques: (1) interviewees are asked to translate all forms of jargon, buzz words, or technical language into ordinary English; (2) all statements that convey a host of behaviors are probed until the interviewee either gives an adequate behavioral description or states that no more details can be remembered—for example, "I convinced him" is not left standing but is probed for exact dialogue and the thought process underlying the persuasion—and (3) the interviewer strives to get the complete story on a single incident; that is, the interviewer tries to keep the interviewee on track by getting the person to narrate what he or she did in chronological order. The interview should include what led up to the incident, what the interviewee did, said, felt, and thought during the course of the incident, and the outcome. Between four and six incidents are collected per interviewee, evenly split between high and low points.

Finally, the interviewees are asked what they would look for if they were to be hiring a person for their job and what type of training they feel would make them more effective in the job. This step gathers some final insights, cements the alliance with the manager, and allows a transition out of the interview.

Developing a competency model. Transcriptions of the tape-recorded interviews form the data base for developing the competency model. Half of the interviews are used to form the "derivation sample," while the other half are put aside for use in the validation phase. Each of the interviews in the derivation group is read by at least two members of the team who will build the model.

The model-building team is made up of at least four individuals who have been trained in the BEI technique and have also participated in several other model-building sessions. They read the derivation interviews and identify behaviors that result in the successful completion of a component of the job under study. Individual behaviors are recorded on index cards so that they can be easily sorted into different thematic groupings. The code number of each interviewee is also affixed to the card as well as the page number of the transcript where it was found. In this way, any one of the members of the model-building team can have easy access to the context in which the behaviors were exhibited. Each interview is read by at least two members of the team to ensure that behaviors are not missed and that each statement or interpretation of a behavior is accurate.

Next, the team members identify the overarching constructs that account for a number of behaviors they have seen across incidents and interviewees. As each theme is proposed, comments are solicited from all members of the team as to whether their experiences with interviewees can support or refine the theme. In this manner, all the behaviors that have been abstracted are clustered under thematic headings or they are discarded. A behavior is discarded when either no other behaviors like it have been found or it is recognized that it really isn't a behavior but only a hypothetical example or abstract concept espoused by the interviewee. Thus it is crucial to competency model building that the BEIs contain behaviorally rich information.

The next step in the process is refining and clustering the themes into competencies and their attendant behavioral indicators. This refinement is accomplished by crafting an accurate label that captures the essence of the motive, trait, skill, aspect of self-image, social role, or body of knowledge that has been displayed. Redundancies are eliminated and the behavioral indicators reworded to make them easily understood.

Validating the model. The competency model is then applied to the derivation sample of interviews. This is accomplished by having someone who was not involved in either the interviewing or the development of the competency model code each of the interviews. The coding involves recording any behavior that matches a behavioral indicator described in the competency model. The data from the coded interviews are then analyzed to test whether the superior performers differ statistically from the average performers on the coded provisional competencies. At this point, quantification is being introduced to obtain empirical feedback and to ensure discriminative sensitivity. Those indicators and provisional competencies that either have low frequencies of occurrence or do not statistically differentiate between the two sets of interviews (superior and average) are dropped.

The revised model is then applied to those interviews that were not used in the derivation sample, and the data collected are again tested statistically. Those indicators and the competencies that statistically differentiate the superior from the average performers are said to be cross-validated. Consequently, the model as a whole is refined and cross-validated.

Deploying the model. The validated competency model is the basis for a performance appraisal system, but it must be adapted, depending on the needs of the organization. These criteria can now be assessed by any of the measurement methods reviewed earlier. Appraisal interviews can be conducted by interviewers trained in the BEI format and evaluation can be based on the criteria defined in the model. The assessment center approach can be geared to elicit the competencies. The written form of the critical incidents report can be coded for the indicators. If ratings are preferred, a checklist of indicators or a BARS using the indicators is readily constructed.

Evaluation of the competency-based approach. The competency-based approach to the criterion problem has several advantages. Its functional utility is clear. The competencies are defined by behavioral indicators that are easily identifiable in performance records and so can be used for feedback and coaching. They are typically well-accepted by managers because the behaviors are clear and credibility is high, since many levels of the organization have had input into the process, including the superior performers.

The validity of the competency model is established. Face and content validity are obvious and criterion validity is documented when the competencies distinguish the criterion groups statistically.

The approach is clearly empirical—the whole model-building process is driven by the data; the indicators and competencies are derived from content analysis of the data and are refined by statistical analysis.

The sensitivity of the criteria is built-in, since the competencies are by definition those indicators that distinguish superior performers from merely adequate ones (who, by the way, in many organizations are quite good, just not excellent).

The process of establishing the criteria is very systematic, as shown above. It combines rational insight and analysis with empirical techniques. When possible, it uses multiple methods or criteria, and it enlists the efforts of many levels in the organization.

Legally, criteria generated in this fashion are probably as solid as one could get. They are clearly defined behaviors chosen precisely because of their relevance to the job; in fact, relevance to the job is documented statistically.

The major disadvantages are the expense and time required to execute a program like that just described and the blind spots inherent in the method. While the competency approach selects behaviors that distinguish superior from average performance, it neglects behaviors that are necessary for job performance but that do not happen to separate excellent performers. For example, the ability to understand a technical description for an engineering project may be essential for a manager of a chemical plant, but this ability may not be differentiating superior performers. Such threshold competencies need to be cataloged as well, which may require a more conventional job analysis. Legal and technical standards will also have to be addressed by another technique, with other expertise.

Despite these limitations, the competency-based approach incorporates many of the desiderata in the search for appraisal criteria. When complemented with the other approaches, it arguably represents the state of the art in managerial performance appraisal.

Future Directions and Needs

There are three major trends in the appraisal of managerial performance, extending from the current state of the art in rather direct ways: (1) there will be an increasing reliance on the use of observable and measurable behavior to evaluate a manager's performance; (2) performance appraisal for managers will be integrated into all decisions regarding their careers; and (3) technology in the form of computer-aided assessment techniques will make the performance appraisal of managers less labor intensive and less dependent on human judgment.

The performance appraisal of managers has been moving in two directions:

from a "gut" level judgment by supervisors to systematic assessment based on measurable data, and from a focus on task or job analysis to an emphasis on competencies of a particular manager in a particular job. These two trends are closely related to one another; as our ability to define abstract human characteristics in behaviorally specific terms increases, the "art" of assessing managers will become increasingly a "science." This trend from the intuitive to the rigorously data-based appraisal methods and criteria is driven by two factors: the increasing sophistication of the behavioral sciences and the press of social and legal challenges to the appraisal process. Neither factor shows any signs of diminishing.

As the recognition of the value of performance appraisal continues to grow, upper-level management will demand that more decisions be made using data generated by these techniques. Managers will be brought into organizations based on assessment interviews using criteria that also form the basic ongoing evaluation. Development, promotion or termination, job assignment, and compensation will all be part of an integrated, explicit, and relatively objective system.

Finally, like every other area of our society, performance appraisal will not escape computerization. The data base of appraisal will become more rich and yet more tractable. For example, with the advent of interactive video and computer systems, very sophisticated simulations can be designed and recorded in dramatic detail, and on-line feedback will be readily available. As the development of "expert systems" in the field of artificial intelligence extends into management, the best human judges and content analysts will be modeled in programs that will be available for use by the entire organization. The expertise will be spread around and costs in terms of time should decrease.

The future looks challenging, the future looks sophisticated, and the future for managerial performance appraisal looks assured.

References

Appley, L. A. (1969). *A management concept.* New York: American Management Association.

Blumenfeld, W. S. (1976). *Development and evaluation of job performance criteria: A procedural guide* (Research Monograph No. 64). Atlanta: Publishing Services Division, College of Business Administration, Georgia State University.

Boyatzis, R. E. (1982). *The competent manager: A model for effective performance.* New York: Wiley.

Bray, D. W. (1976). The assessment center method. In R. L. Craig (Ed.), *Training and development handbook* (2nd ed.) New York: McGraw-Hill.

Drucker, P. F. (1973). *Management: Tasks, responsibility, practice.* New York: Harper and Row.

Eichel, E., & Bender, H. E. (1984). *Performance appraisal: A study of current techniques.* New York: American Management Association.

Flanagan, J. C. (1954). The critical incidents technique. *Psychological Bulletin, 51,* 327–358.

Ghiselli, E. E. (1956). Dimensional problems of criteria. *Journal of Applied Psychology, 40,* 1–4.

Katz, D., & Kahn, R. (1978). *The social psychology of organizations* (2nd ed.). New York: Wiley.

Klemp, G. O., Jr., & Spencer, L. M., Jr. (1980). *Job competence assessment.* Boston: McBer and Co.

Latham, G. P., & Wexley, K. N. (1981). *Increasing productivity through performance appraisal.* Reading, MA: Addison-Wesley.

Lazer, R. I., & Wikstrom, W. S. (1977). *Appraising managerial performance: Current practices and future directions.* New York: Conference Board.

McClelland, D. C. (1971). *Assessing human motivation.* New York: General Learning Press.

McGregor, D. (1957). An uneasy look at performance appraisal. *Harvard Business Review, 35,* 89–94.

Meidan, A. (1981). *The appraisal of managerial performance* (AMA Management Briefing). New York: AMACOM.

Smith, P. C., & Kendall, L. M. (1963). Retranslations of expectations: An approach to the construction of unambiguous anchors for rating scales. *Journal of Applied Psychology, 47,* 149–155.

15. CLINICAL PERFORMANCE EVALUATION IN MEDICINE & LAW

Paula L. Stillman & Mina A. Gillers

Introduction

The past decade has witnessed a proliferation of attempts to develop valid and reliable methods of assessing clinical competence. Government and consumer interest groups are demanding more valid measurements of physicians' performance in order to improve the quality of health care. Medical school faculty and certification and licensing boards are assessing what is being taught and how it is being evaluated. Egan (1976) stressed the responsibility of a medical school faculty for evaluating the competence of candidates for the M.D. degree. However, it is questionable whether or not the usual parameters used by faculty to predict clinical performance are effective (Wingard & Williamson, 1973). Global rating scales are prone to "halo effect" (Cranton, Dauphinee, & McQueen, 1984). A summative subjective evaluation such as a dean's letter is based on a composite of grades and numerous faculty ratings, and its predictive validity is questionable at best (Leichner, Eusebio-Torres, & Harper, 1981; Stanton et al., 1979; Stimmel, 1975).

It is assumed that house staff, having graduated from medical school, are certified as clinically competent and possess the necessary diagnostic skills to care for patients. In 1976, Wiener and Nathanson seriously questioned that assumption when they reported that house staff demonstrated an unacceptably high level of errors in basic skills of physical diagnosis. Responding to this report, Engel (1976) underscored the need to reestablish the skills of clinical observation and reasoning as the cornerstones of clinical science. He noted that generally little time is devoted to supervised instruction in interviewing and physical examination in the average undergraduate curriculum. This deficiency is compounded by the observation that physician faculty members rarely check the accuracy of findings described by students and house staff. More recently, utilizing a clinical evaluation exercise, Woolliscroft, Stross, and Silva (1984) found recurrent inadequacies in history taking and physical examination skills of residents.

Law school curricula are undergoing similar critical reviews. Courses in research, writing, and trial and appellate advocacy have long been recognized as integral to the teaching of law. However, despite the importance of client interviewing and counseling to the practice of law, only recently has the teaching of these skills been incorporated in law school curricula (Galinson, 1975). In its

393

standards for approval of law schools, the American Bar Association encourages law faculty to be creative in developing programs of instruction in interviewing skills. As in medical education, various course formats and methodologies have been suggested (Galinson, 1975; Goodpaster, 1975; Sacks, 1959; Hunsacker, 1980). This area of legal education is in its infancy, and the emphasis is presently on the teaching rather than on the evaluation of these skills.

DEFINING CLINICAL COMPETENCE

Clearly, a workable definition of competence is necessary to redirect educational objectives and to improve evaluation methods at all levels of training. In 1961, the National Board of Medical Examiners (NBME) developed a definition of nine critical components of clinical competence (Hubbard et al., 1965). Since then, numerous other boards have redefined competence in an attempt to develop more valid evaluation strategies (American Board of Internal Medicine, 1979; American Medical Association Council on Medical Education, 1980; Burg et al., 1976; Burg, Lloyd, & Templeton, 1982; Newble, 1976). Yet even after the elements of competence are defined, establishing standards is made difficult by the demonstrated lack of agreement among physicians regarding interpretation of data, diagnosis, and management (Dunn & Conrath, 1977; Fisch et al., 1981; Koran, 1975).

TRADITIONAL EVALUATION TECHNIQUES

There is increasing evidence that traditional evaluation techniques such as written and oral examinations, subjective faculty and peer ratings, and chart reviews, even if found to be reliable, have little concurrent or predictive validity. Woo, Jen, Rosenthal, Bunn, and Goldman (1981) described an evaluation of the performance of first-year residents using explicit criteria-mapping techniques of chart audit. Performance as defined by the results of the chart audit did not correlate with grades, internship matching program rankings, or evaluations by residents or faculty. Many other researchers have found little or no correlation between medical school grades and clinical performance (Marienfeld & Reid, 1980; O'Donahue & Wergin, 1978). Margolis and Cook (1976) compared faculty ratings of pediatric house staff to their internship match rankings, NBME scores, and American Board of Pediatrics examination scores, and found no significant correlations. However, Veloski, Herman, Gonnella, Zeleznik, and Kellow (1979) did report significant correlations between medical school performance as judged by grades and NBME scores and ratings of house officers by faculty. The highest correlations were found for the best and worst house officers. Similarly, Kegel-Flom (1975) found that a combination of medical school grades and medical school faculty ratings of clinical performance were the best forecasters of supervisors' ratings of interns.

Since 1971, The American Board of Internal Medicine (ABIM) has required that residency program directors verify each resident's clinical skills in history taking, physical examination, record keeping, patient management, physician-patient relations, and overall clinical competence as a prerequisite for admission to the written certifying examination. The board has recommended the use of the "fully observed patient encounter" to document such an evaluation. Seventy-three percent of 166 internal medicine residency programs surveyed by the ABIM used some form of clinical exercise to evaluate the history taking and physical examination skills of house staff. However, only 21 percent could confirm the use of direct observation of the resident's performance by a faculty member. Other methods of assessment included subjective written evaluations by the program director, chief resident, or senior nurses, and chart audit. Thirty-four percent of programs provided the residents with formal feedback on their performance (Futcher, Sanderson, & Tusler, 1977).

In a 1978 national survey of psychiatric residency programs it was found that only 37 percent required that their residents participate in formal written or oral examinations. In most programs, emphasis was placed on subjective written evaluations (Procci et al., 1978). A panel discussion on the state of evaluation in surgical residencies (Anwar, Bosk, & Greenburg, 1981) likewise revealed that evaluation is based on subjective ratings, often by an attending physician who has little contact with the resident, and on written examinations.

Clinical competence is a multifaceted, complicated issue. It appears that each of the currently used evaluation methods provides relatively independent data relating to overall clinical competence and that there is no simple universal evaluation strategy. Consequently, medical schools and residency program directors often use a combination of numerous techniques that include written, oral, and clinical examinations, clinical ratings by faculty and peers, and chart audits (Anderson & Botticelli, 1981; Harden, 1979; Littlefield et al., 1981; O'Donohue & Wergin, 1978; Printen, Chappell, & Whitney, 1973; Siker, 1981).

Survey of Evaluation Techniques

SHORT ANSWER EXAMINATIONS

Written short-answer tests are the most extensively used form of evaluation. These examinations include multiple-choice items with single best answers that evaluate knowledge, and more complex items of branching logic that provide some evaluation of problem-solving skills. In an attempt to provide uniform standards, almost half of the medical schools in the country require successful completion of parts 1 and 2 of the NBME as a prerequisite for earning a medical degree (Holden & Levit, 1980). However, in a report by the Association of American Medical Colleges (1981), only twelve of fifty competencies identified by the NBME were found to be amenable to evaluations with a written examination. Written examinations cannot evaluate professional attitudes, interpersonal skills, or the motor and technical skills required of a clinician. Additionally, they do not fully measure the knowledge or problem-solving skills required in clinical practice.

Although some researchers have found that multiple-choice items provide a valid assessment of cognitive ability (Anderson, 1981) and can discriminate varying levels of clinical competence (Downing, 1980), there is no agreement on this issue. Other researchers (Gonella et al., 1970; Marienfeld & Reid, 1980; O'Donohue & Wergin, 1978) have found low correlations between scores on multiple-choice questions and other measures of physician competence including diagnostic accuracy, patient management, and subjective faculty ratings. In an internal medicine residency program, Wigton (1980) reported that scores obtained on written examinations by internal medicine residents did not discriminate between levels of training despite subjective evidence that knowledge had been gained during the years of training.

In an attempt to improve the validity of written examinations, Newble, Baxter, and Elmslie (1979) compared multiple-choice and free-response items in examinations of clinical competence and found that the results of multiple-choice testing consistently overestimated students' knowledge and did not detect serious deficiencies in knowledge that became apparent only in the free-response testing. They cited the various disadvantages of the multiple-choice test, including the cueing effect of options and encouragement of guessing, and concluded that the convenience in grading this type of examination does not compensate for the superficial measurement that it provides. Sarnacki (1981) has also demonstrated the susceptibility of the "type k, multiple true-false" question of the NBME to the "test-wiseness" of the examinee. A recent article, however, suggests that the same underlying abilities are assessed by both multiple-choice and free-response questions (Frederikson, 1984).

PATIENT MANAGEMENT PROBLEMS

Patient management problems (PMPs) attempt to provide a written simulation of the patient encounter to reflect clinical judgment and problem-solving skills more accurately. This technique has undergone many revisions and there have been numerous variations in format and scoring (Barro, 1973; Berner, Hamilton, & Best, 1974; Grace, et al., 1977; Helfer & Slater, 1971; Mazzuca & Cohen, 1982; McGuire & Babbott, 1967; Rimoldi, 1961; Tamblyn & Barrows, 1978; Vu, 1979).

Although early reports seemed to indicate that PMPs were fairly reliable (Barro, 1973), Elstein demonstrated a lack of consistency in individual performance across problems, with performance being case specific (Elstein, Shulman, & Sprafka, 1978); this inconsistency remains even when content is controlled (Norman et al., 1983). On the other hand, Juul, Noe, and Nerenberg (1979) demonstrated that given a sufficiently large sample of PMPs, individuals did exhibit a consistent pattern of performance, and it was possible to define two general skills that appeared to be evaluated by the PMPs: data gathering and management. Those two factors remained stable across time and across different groups. An investigation by Harasym and his colleagues (1980) also supported the theory that general problem-solving abilities do exist. In this study, seventy-one medical students took an examination consisting of three PMPs. It was observed that irrespective of the clinical problem, scores for data gathering and hypothesis generation correlated highly among themselves; scores on physical examination, laboratory investigation, and final diagnosis did not correlate highly and were felt to be case specific.

Research indicates that performance on PMPs does not correlate with actual clinical performance. In a study by Goran, Williamson, and Gonnella (1973), physicians' clinical performance in handling patients with urinary tract infections, for the most part, did not correlate with their scores on a PMP of the same clinical problem. Furthermore, those achieving high scores on the PMP were not those physicians whose clinical performance was judged best by chart review. In attempting to establish the criterion validity of PMPs, Page and Fielding (1980) compared students' performance on PMPs with their performance on patient simulators that had the same problem as the PMP patient. Major inconsistencies in performance were observed that were characterized by substantially greater errors of omission and commission in the practice setting. Norman's study (Norman & Feightner, 1981) corroborates these findings. Different as well as substantially more data were obtained from PMPs than from simulated patients. In addition, performance on PMPs does not correlate with performance on multiple-choice questions (McGuire & Babbott, 1967; Berner, Hamilton, & Best, 1974). These studies raise serious doubts about the criterion validity of PMPs.

In summary, PMPs have definite limitations as an evaluation tool. At best, they evaluate skills of data gathering, hypothesis generation, and management. They are low-fidelity simulations and are not comparable to performance in the real clinical setting. Their content, construct, and concurrent validities remain unconfirmed.

ORAL EXAMINATIONS

Oral examinations are the oldest form of clinical evaluation. In a comprehensive article on standard setting for examinations, Meskauskas and Norcini (1980) illustrated the various models currently used for oral interactive examinations. They clarified the difficulties inherent in this type of examination, which include variables of setting and design, personality of both examiner and examinee, range of examiner expertise, and nonuniformity of clinical material, all of which make it difficult to judge its reliability and validity. Nevertheless, sixteen of the twenty-three specialty boards still use oral examinations as part of the certification process. In the oral examinations described for certification in both emergency medicine (Maatsch, 1981) and family medicine (Van Wart, 1974), the examiner simulated the patient's problem while another examiner was also present as an observer. Maatsch reported a mean interrater reliability coefficient of .79, a moderate degree of case-specific variance in physician performance, and a high degree of discriminant validity for the examination between students and residents.

Another use for the oral examination is described by Vu, Johnson, and Mertz (1981). They reported faculty and student satisfaction using the oral format to assess medical students' cognitive knowledge. Students felt that the examination was fair and was a good learning experience, and faculty members felt more confident about their assessment of student knowledge using this technique.

Oral examinations provide a useful added dimension in evaluation and can assess many of the components of clinical competence. However, their reliability and validity are not well established and they require a large amount of physician time for implementation.

DIRECT FACULTY OBSERVATION

A variation of the oral interactive examination is direct observation and evaluation of the clinical encounter by faculty. This has been shown to be a useful educational tool (Engel, 1971; Hinz, 1966; Lagerkvist, Samuelsson, & Sjolin, 1976; Sternburg & Brockway, 1979; Wiener et al., 1976), and it is also used in certification examinations. As a method of evaluation, it suffers from a lack of clearly demonstrated reliability owing to problems of patient and examiner variability (Marshall & Ludbrook, 1972), although Andrew (1977) has demonstrated that with intensive rater training, a high degree of interrater reliability can be achieved.

An observed patient encounter is incorporated into the Canadian Certification Examination. A clinical skills assessment form, consisting of a twelve-point rating scale, is used to evaluate the candidates' skills in obtaining a history and performing a physical examination. Modest correlations are demonstrated between results of this evaluation and both the written examination and an evaluation report submitted by the candidates' supervisor (Skakun, 1981).

For the neurology certification examination, Bray (1979) compared the use of a face-to-face patient interview conducted by the candidate to a videotaped patient interview reviewed by the candidate as a means of assessing clinical competence and judgment. After each session, the resident discussed his or her evaluation of the patient with two or three examiners. The grades achieved with these two methods were compared for 816 candidates over a two-year period. Candidates achieved the same grade for both sessions 90 percent of the time. Based on factors of cost and efficiency, a recommendation was made to substitute the videotaped patient interview for the live patient encounter in the neurology certifying examination.

A similar study compared the use of videotaped interviews with live interviews for use in psychiatry examinations (Naftulin et al., 1977). The disadvantage of using actual patients was the inability to standardize the patient for all examinees. Although having the candidate observe a videotaped interview allowed for standardization of examination material, examiners had no way of evaluating the candidate's interpersonal skills or ability to obtain a history from a patient.

VIDEOTAPE

In an effort to improve reliability of evaluating clinical competence, some studies have focused on videotaping the actual clinical performance of the physician, followed by an evaluation conducted by several raters (Leake, Barnard, & Christophersen, 1978; Liu et al., 1980; Turner et al., 1972).

In the 1972 Turner study, four faculty members reviewed each tape and rated communication, interpersonal, and physical examination skills. Global judgments by raters were found to be unreliable. When the ratings were based on specific checklists, a high degree of interrater agreement was reported. Using specific checklists, Liu and his associates (1980) reported a similar degree of reliability for observed videotapes of residents' anesthesia skills. However, Liston, Yager, and Strauss (1981) reported very low interrater agreement when thirteen psychiatrists, using a detailed assessment form, rated the psychotherapy interviews of six residents.

The use of videotape permits the measurement of attitude and interpersonal, motor, and technical skills, including the history and physical examination. However, even in evaluating these competencies, there are limitations directly attributable to the single perspective of the video camera (Liu et al., 1980). The use of two cameras or a mobile camera introduces the confounding variable of having an observer present in the room.

RATING SCALES

In an effort to make individual assessments somewhat less subjective, there have been numerous attempts to codify the criteria that are used in rating scales (Graham, 1971; Littlefield et al., 1981; Oaks, Scheinok, & Husted, 1969; Wigton, 1980; Woodward & Dinham, 1982). Although attempts have been made to define the personal characteristics deemed important in clinical competence (Greganti, McGaghie, & Finn, 1982; Linn, 1979) and to determine the aspects of clinical performance that correlate with academic achievement (Willoughby, Gammon, & Jonas, 1979), the validity of rating scales cannot be established absolutely because of the absence of a "gold standard" with which they can be compared. In addition, ratings are often subjective and not based on actual observation of performance, and low interrater reliabilities are frequently obtained (Levine & McGuire, 1971). In a report by Orkin and Greenhow (1978), twenty-seven residents and thirty-four faculty members were asked to evaluate each resident according to performance criteria established by the American Board of Anesthesiology. No consensus could be achieved. In addition, it has been demonstrated that the relative importance of specific criteria is perceived differently by different faculty groups (Quarrick & Sloop, 1972; Wigton, 1980).

Supervisor evaluations. On the basis of Cowles's critical comments approach (1965), Dielman, Hull, and Davis (1980) developed an evaluation form that included fifteen behaviorally anchored scales. House staff and faculty completed nearly two thousand evaluations, which were analyzed over a 12-month period. Two main factors were identified: problem solving and interpersonal skills. Only moderate interrater agreement was reported. Interestingly, when house officers completed evaluations, they rated students higher than did faculty and achieved higher interrater reliabilities (Dielman, Hull, & Davis, 1980; Hull, 1982; Oaks, Scheinok, & Husted, 1969).

Peer evaluations. Peer evaluations can be an important adjunct to the assessment of students and house officers. Korman and Stubblefield (1971) studied intern performance, as predicted by grades, and ratings of faculty and peers during the senior year in medical school. Peer ratings were found to be the best predictor of internship performance. A rating scale developed by Linn, Arostegui, and Zeppa (1975) for peer evaluation showed a test-retest reliability of .90 over a one-week interval and correlation coefficients with final grades ranging from .24 to .50.

Arnold, Willoughby, Calkins, Gammon, and Eberhart (1981) described ex tensive use of peer evaluation as part of the formal promotion process at the University of Missouri–Kansas City School of Medicine. At least two peers assessed each student using a nine-point, eleven-dimension rating scale. Internal consistency was high, with an alpha coefficient of .94. However, interrater reliability was only .52. The high alpha coefficient suggests a possible halo effect. Peer ratings correlated significantly with the faculty's clinical performance evaluation, grades on internal examinations, and NBME part 2 scores. Peer evaluations were also significantly correlated with clinical performance scores given by supervisors during residency (coefficients were .34 and .37). This suggest that peer evaluations have moderate degrees of concurrent and predictive validity and can be an important addition to faculty evaluations of performance.

CHART AUDIT

Current methods used to assess the clinical skills of practitioners have focused on quality of care as documented in the medical record. The information in the record has been judged as a reasonable indicator of overall competence. Sanazaro (1980), Lyons and Payne (1974), and Payne (1979) have discussed both the limitations of record documentation as well as the value of record audit for measuring physician performance. Using chart audit as the criterion measure to predict clinical performance has serious flaws and limitations (Zuckerman et al., 1975). For example, chart audit cannot distinguish between errors of omission and lack of documentation, it may overlook errors of commission, and it does not consider interpersonal skills.

SIMULATED PATIENTS

The validity of the preceding evaluation techniques has been difficult to ascertain, primarily because there is no effective measure of clinical competence against which other measures or methods can be compared. Because substantial differences have been demonstrated among scores on written examinations, PMPs, and oral examinations, the evaluation of the physician's clinical competence might best be judged by his or her interaction with a patient in an actual clinical encounter.

Simulated, standardized, or programmed patients provide an exciting technique for evaluating clinical competence. The patients are either volunteers or paid workers and are trained to present any combination of medical or psychological problems in an unvarying manner for use in training and evaluation sessions. They can be real patients or can portray realistically an actual patient problem and replicate the clinical encounter with a high degree of fidelity (Barrows, 1971).

Barrows and Abrahamson (1964) were the first to use simulated patients to evaluate the clinical performance of medical students. Students elicited a history from and then performed a neurological examination on an actor who simulated a neurological problem. Following this encounter, the student and actor reported their findings to a faculty member who then reviewed the case with the student.

Simulated patients have since been used to measure practically all components of clinical competence at all levels of training. They have been used to evaluate the interpersonal, interviewing, and problem-solving skills of medical students (Coggan, Knight, & Davis, 1980; Helfer, Black, & Helfer, 1975) and the interactional skills of residents for certification in family medicine (Lamont & Hennen, 1972). In most instances, a faculty observer was present and functioned as the examiner, utilizing simulated patients to standardize the patient problem presented.

To evaluate the clinical competence of practitioners, simulators have been presented to physicians' offices as new patients. The simulators then reported their observations on the physician's data-gathering, interpersonal, and management skills directly to the project directors, thereby eliminating the need for physician observers (Burri, McCaughan, & Barrows, 1976; Renaud et al., 1980).

A study by Norman, Tugwell, and Feightner (1981) supported the validity of evaluating clinical competence through the use of simulated patients. They reported that no differences were found between residents examining real or simulated patients either in the amount of data-gathering activity, in specific diagnoses considered, or in the number of investigations planned by the residents. Furthermore, residents could not distinguish between the real and the simulated patient.

Helfer, Black, and Teitelbaum's work (1975) also supports the realism of this technique during the medical interview. A study was conducted to determine whether students used different approaches to interview simulated mothers as compared to real mothers. Thirty third-year medical students conducted two interviews each, one with a real mother and one with a simulated mother. Students were informed before each interview whether they would be interviewing a real or simulated mother. However, one-half of the time the real mothers were falsely presented as the simulators and the simulated mothers as real. Results indicated that no differences could be demonstrated between the students' interactions with real and simulated mothers.

Harden, Stevenson, Downie, and Wilson (1975) have incorporated the use of simulated patients in the development of an examination of clinical competence. The objective structured clinical exam (OSCE) consists of a series of five-minute stations that measure skills in history taking, physical examination, data interpretation, and specimen handling and interpretation, depending on the objectives of the particular examination (Harden & Gleeson, 1979). Numerous applications of this examination technique have been reported (Cuschieri et al., 1979; Harden & Cairncross, 1980; Newble & Elmslie, 1981; Waterston, Cater, & Mitchell, 1980).

Newble, Elmslie, and Baxter (1978) used the OSCE as part of a final examination for medical students that also included a written examination with multiple-choice questions and free-response short answers. Carefully constructed objectives determined items to be included on this problem-based criterion-referenced examination, and Newble demonstrated a high degree of content and construct validity. The concurrent and predictive validity of this examination could not be proven, owing to the inability to obtain reliable ratings of actual clinical performance on wards (Newble, Hoare, & Elmslie, 1981). On the other hand, Hart (1983) did find significant correlations between clinical ratings of performance in a senior clerkship with performance on an OSCE administered to medical students two years earlier.

PATIENT INSTRUCTORS

The patient instructor program was started at the University of Arizona College of Medicine in 1974. Patient instructors (PIs) are nonphysicians who are taught to simulate a patient encounter and to function in the multiple roles of patient, teacher, and evaluator, using their own medical histories and bodies as teaching materials. This program was developed to provide objective and reliable evaluation of interviewing and physical diagnosis skills of medical students, house officers, and practicing physicians. The uniqueness of this program is that after the PIs are trained, they function with minimal physician supervision, and there is no need for a physician observer to be present during the encounter.

Patient instructors as teachers and evaluators of interviewing skills. The first PIs to be recruited and trained were called "programmed mothers," a term used by Dr. Ray Helfer, who had initiated similar efforts at the University of Colorado and at Michigan State University (Helfer, 1970; Helfer & Ealy, 1972; Helfer & Hess, 1970). The University of Arizona program allowed for standardized teaching and objective evaluation of pediatric interviewing skills. A unique history content checklist was developed for each PI that contained the essential information that an interviewer should obtain relevant to a child's common medical problem. To facilitate training, the history contained as much true information as possible and was often a composite of data about several of the PIs' own children, with an incident from the past medical history changed to a current complaint.

Each PI was trained until the history provided was judged to be realistic and consistent. Physicians who were considered to be expert interviewers were videotaped and observed as they interviewed the programmed mothers. From those interviews, characteristics were identified that were believed to exemplify the criteria for an excellent medical interview. Each characteristic was weighted on a five-point scale with anchoring statements describing excellent (five points), average (three points), and poor (one point) performance for that trait. The resulting instrument for evaluating interviewing techniques was called the Arizona Clinical Interview Rating Scale (ACIR) (Appendix A). PIs were trained in the use of the scale until there was a high degree of reliability among the raters.

Several thousand interviews have occurred with these PIs since the inception of the program. The interviewers have been first-, second-, and third-year medical students, house officers, and practicing physicians. Patient instructors are trained to teach and to evaluate the pediatric, adult, geriatric, and psychiatric interview. An objective means of evaluating the mental status examination has been developed for the psychiatric interview, and the ACIR Scale has been modified continually as the program has progressed.

The PI is first interviewed and plays the role of a patient. At the completion of the interview, the PI switches roles and reviews the interaction. The PI assigns a *content score* that is based on the amount of historical information obtained compared to the total amount of information included in the history content checklist (Appendix B). The PI also assigns a *process score* based on the interviewer's rating on the ACIR Scale. The PI gives feedback on the interviewer's performance and suggests ways to improve interviewing skills.

Data collected on these encounters indicate that learning occurs during the feedback session at the end of the interview, and the interviewer-examinees demonstrate significant gains in both content and performance scores when they interview another PI at a later date.

A relatively high positive relationship has also been found between an interviewer's content score (the amount of historical information obtained) and process score (the score on the ACIR Scale). This finding has led to the conclusion that the content and process scores are not really independent, and the amount of information obtained in an interview seems to be dependent on the interviewing skills of the physician (Stillman, 1980; Stillman et al., 1977; Stillman & Burpeau-Di Gregorio, 1982; Stillman et al., 1983; Stillman & Sabers, 1978; Stillman, Sabers, & Redfield, 1976, 1977).

The interviewing program is now a required segment of the curriculum at the University of Arizona College of Medicine. Each student must achieve preset mastery criteria on the interview of a pediatric, geriatric, adult, and psychiatric patient instructor. If mastery is not achieved, the student simply reschedules with another PI in the same content area until the criteria are met.

Physical examination on asymptomatic adult patient instructors. In 1976 a grant from the National Fund for Medical Education (NFME) allowed the PI concept to be expanded to include teaching and evaluation of a student's ability to perform a complete physical examination on an asymptomatic adult. An objective performance checklist was developed that contained all the items deemed essential to the complete physical examination by consensus among faculty members from the Departments of Internal Medicine and Family Practice. Additional items to evaluate physician-patient interaction and examination techniques were included (Appendix C).

Several PIs were recruited to serve the multiple roles of the asymptomatic adult patient, teacher, and evaluator of a complete physical examination. After about twenty-five hours of training, the PI recognized the correct performance of each examination maneuver and was able to instruct the examiner on alternative acceptable techniques for performing many maneuvers. For example, the PI could determine whether the examiner actually observed the retinal vessels with the ophthalmoscope and traced them in four quadrants, whether the thyroid gland was palpated in the correct anatomical location, and whether adequate pressure was exerted on deep abdominal palpation.

In the program at Arizona, each examiner is scheduled for an individual session with the PI. After the examination is completed, the PI switches roles and reviews the examination with the examiner, correcting faulty technique and indicating omitted maneuvers. The PI assigns a performance score that compares the number of physical examination maneuvers performed correctly to the total included on the checklist.

This program has been used for second-year medical students for the past ten years. The students are given the performance checklist in advance and passing criteria are established. Students who fail to achieve a passing score are scheduled for a repeat session with a different PI at a later date. As was found with the interviewing program, significant learning appears to occur during the feedback session at the completion of the first examination. Scores on second examinations have been reported to be significantly higher than scores on first examinations (Stillman, Ruggill, & Sabers, 1978).

The asymptomatic PIs can be adapted for teaching and evaluating specialty examinations. Programs using asymptomatic adults to teach and to evaluate the neurological examination (Laguna & Stillman, 1978) and the female breast and pelvic examination have also been implemented at the College of Medicine.

Physical examination on symptomatic patient instructors. The asymptomatic PI program has been successful, but that evaluation is limited to a student's proficiency in examination technique and ability to go through a specified number of maneuvers rather than the ability to identify and to describe a patient's abnormal findings. In 1977, with initial grant support from the NFME and continuing support from the Department of Health, Education, and Welfare, and the National Institutes of Health, patients with relatively stable positive findings on physical examination were recruited to participate in the beginning of a symptomatic PI program. These symptomatic PIs are trained to evaluate examination techniques and the ability of the examiner to identify and describe abnormalities on physical examination.

For each specialty examination, it was necessary to develop performance checklists that included the essential physical examination maneuvers to be performed (Appendix D). All items are weighted equally and performance scores are reported as the percentage of the total items performed correctly. Corresponding content checklists that provide an opportunity for the examiner to record physical examination abnormalities have also been developed (Appendix E). Each item on the content checklist is assigned a point value that varies depending on its importance to the individual PI's diagnosis. For example, the description of the carotid upstroke would be weighted more heavily for a cardiac patient with aortic stenosis than for one with mitral insufficiency.

If specific findings of a PI are not stable, the PI is trained to perform a self-examination prior to, and again at the conclusion of, each encounter and to change the keyed response on the content checklist to represent present findings. Content scores are expressed as a percentage, and the number of points obtained by the examiner are compared to the total points available for the PI examined. Performance and content checklists have been developed for several separate systems-related specialty examinations. Symptomatic PIs have been recruited for the cardiovascular, pulmonary, musculoskeletal, orthopedic, and neurologic examinations.

The program that has been in effect at Arizona for nine years is used primarily for second-year medical students, but it has also been used for third-year students, house staff, and practicing physicians (Stillman & Kettel, 1979; Stillman, Ruggill, Rutala, Dinham, & Sabers, 1979; Stillman, Ruggill, Rutala, & Sabers, 1980). There have been more than three-thousand individual encounters between examiners and symptomatic PIs. Results to date indicate that within a given specialty examination, there is no correlation between an examiner's performance and content scores. Examiners who perform the most thorough examinations, as reflected by high performance scores, are not necessarily those who can describe the patient's findings most accurately, as reflected by high content scores.

Correlations have been computed on the scores obtained by students examining PIs in different specialties. The correlations between performance scores obtained by an examiner on any two specialty examinations approach zero; likewise, the correlation between an examiner's content scores on any two specialty examinations approaches zero. Across specialties, all scores appear to be independent, and each examination must be taught and evaluated separately. For a given examiner, neither a performance nor a content score on one specialty examination can be used to predict the corresponding score on another specialty examination (Stillman, Ruggill, Rutala, Dinham, & Sabers, 1979; Stillman, Ruggill, Rutala, & Sabers, 1980).

For the past six classes of medical students, passing criteria have been established. If these criteria are not achieved, the student is required to perform another examination on another PI in the same specialty area. The students have been given copies of the performance and content checklists in advance of any of their sessions.

The mean gain scores obtained by students who were required to examine two different PIs in the same specialty were analyzed to determine whether learning occurred during the feedback sessions. The gains in content scores were greater than one standard deviation and may be accounted for by learning. However, a ceiling effect due to relatively high performance scores on the first examination may have precluded significant gains in performance scores on the second examination (Stillman, Ruggill, Rutala, Dinham, & Sabers, 1979; Stillman, Ruggill, Rutala, & Sabers, 1980).

The relationship between examination scores and an examiner's level of medical training was also studied. For this purpose, the scores obtained on the cardiovascular examination by third-year medical students and by house officers in their first postgraduate year (PGY-1s) were compared. Although the PGY-1s obtained significantly higher content scores, there were no statistically significant differences in the performance scores of the two groups. These findings are essentially the same as those found with the pulmonary examination. These data suggest that as an examiner's level of medical training increases, the efficiency of the examination improves and more relevant data can be obtained.

In one pilot study, the PGY-1s at the University of Arizona hospital were asked to evaluate their peers. Peer evaluations correlated positively with content scores but were essentially independent of performance scores. These data indicate that the day-to-day interaction of peers in patient encounters may provide a prime opportunity to evaluate the diagnostic competence of a house officer.

When the house staff program directors ranked the PGY-1s, their rankings correlated with performance scores but not with content scores. Because the program directors primarily have contact with the PGY-1s during rounds and conferences, their evaluation may be based largely on the thoroughness of the house officer in an ordered setting rather than on the house officer's actual diagnostic ability (Rutala, Stillman, & Sabers, 1981a, 1981b).

Patient instructors as evaluators of the complete clinical encounter. Since 1981, the role of PIs in evaluating clinical competence of physicians has been expanded. This work has been supported by a grant from the Fund for the Improvement of Post Secondary Education (FIPSE). Rather than using PIs for interviewing skills or specialty examinations, the intent of the program is to simulate a complete clinical encounter. Several of the symptomatic PIs have been retrained and provided with a history that lends itself to a differential diagnosis compatible with the patient's actual findings on physical examination. For this new program, each PI presents a specific chief complaint, such as shortness of breath, that may be associated with pathology in one or more organ systems. The physician is asked to perform a relevant history and physical examination on the patient and then to record the findings, along with a differential diagnosis and management plan, on a special form that provides a minimum amount of prompting.

Instruments have been developed to measure the following: (1) interviewing style, (2) ability to obtain relevant historical data, (3) ability to select and perform appropriate and essential portions of the physical examination, (4) ability to detect and describe abnormalities on physical examination, and (5) formulation of a differential diagnosis and initial management plan. This system is intended to evaluate each physician's ability to collect accurate and complete information during a patient encounter and to synthesize these data to understand and to solve the patient's problem (Stillman, Rutala, Stillman, & Sabers, 1982).

There have been more than 250 encounters between these patient instructors and first- and second-year internal medicine and family practice residents in training at eight different sites. Preliminary data indicate that the PIs are a valuable asset in teaching and evaluating clinical skills and that they can be used to supplement current techniques. Once trained, they provide individualized instruction and sophisticated feedback to each examiner. They are able to discriminate among individuals and groups of students and residents as well as to document the strengths and weaknesses of a single examiner. If used early in a training program, they can provide objective data about each examiner's skills. They can also be used as part of a final evaluation to provide reliable and valid information about the clinical skills and competence of each examiner. The response to this program by the participating residents and program directors has been positive (Stillman, Rutala, Nicholson, Sabers, & Stillman, 1982).

APPLICATIONS TO LAW

Utilizing the patient instructor model, client instructors (CIs) have been trained to teach and to evaluate interviewing skills of law students (Stillman, Silverman, Burpeau, & Sabers, 1982). A two-hour interviewing and negotiating course had been given at the University of Arizona School of Law in which faculty critiqued and reviewed two videotaped student interviews following a twelve-hour course in interviewing. Although student response to the course was positive, and instructors noticed improvement in the interviewing skills of the students between first and second interviews, class enrollment had to be limited. The amount of time necessary to teach a limited number of students was disproportionately large. Additionally, the reliability of the method was hampered by the lack of a standardized method of evaluation.

A joint effort was therefore undertaken between the University of Arizona Colleges of Medicine and Law to determine whether the technique developed to teach medical interviewing skills could be adapted for law students and integrated into the law school's curriculum.

A rating scale (Arizona Clinical Interview Rating–Law, or ACIR–L) was developed that identified seventeen skills considered to be essential components of a good legal interview. These skills were categorized into six general areas: introduction of interview, questioning, data collection and interviewing sequence, feedback, rapport, and closure of interview. Each of the skills identified was defined on a five-point scale with three anchoring statements indicating the range of performance within that particular skill.

Two scenarios were then prepared for the CIs—one in family law and another in criminal law. These were then converted into history-content checklists. A content score could then be calculated based on the amount of information gathered by the interviewer compared to the total information available on the checklist. The recruiting and training of these client instructors was similar to that of the patient instructors, and a high degree of reliability was obtained.

After formal classroom instruction in interviewing, each law student was scheduled for a session with a family law CI and one with a criminal law CI. At the completion of each interview, the CI provided the student with immediate feedback on his or her interviewing skills, as well as assigning a process score (from the ACIR–L scale) and a content score (from the content checklist). The program was received with much enthusiasm, and after an initial pilot project in the 1981 spring semester, it was fully integrated into the curriculum during the following academic year. Results indicated that benefits and findings with law CIs are very similar to those reported previously for PIs trained for the teaching and evaluation of interviewing in medicine (Stillman, Silverman, Burpeau, & Sabers, 1982).

DISSEMINATION TO OTHER DISCIPLINES

The PI concept has also been disseminated to other disciplines. PIs are being used to teach and to evaluate clinical skills of nurse practitioners and pharmacy practitioner students. Client instructors have also been trained to teach and to evaluate the ability of educational psychology students to administer and score the Wechsler Adult Intelligence Scale. Students and professors from the University of Arizona and Arizona State University have been involved in the initial development of this project (Franklin et al., 1982).

Future Directions and Needs

In 1982, the senior author of this chapter accepted a position at the University of Massachusetts College of Medicine. A patient instructor program was implemented there within a year. Utilizing a consortial approach, the concept was expanded to provide a regional resource for the surrounding medical schools and residency training programs. Patient instructors are used throughout undergraduate and graduate training to teach and assess various aspects of clinical competence.

Clinical competence is multifaceted and difficult to assess. Traditional methods have demonstrated poor validity and have often been subjective and nonreproducible. Newer techniques employing standardized or simulated patients or patient instructors appear to provide objective evaluation of aspects of clinical competence that were previously considered to be nonmeasurable. Future research should emphasize measurement issues so that these techniques can be used to provide the "gold standard" of clinical performance evaluation.

APPENDIX A: ARIZONA CLINICAL INTERVIEW RATING SCALE

___ Total Obtained Score

_75_ Total Possible Score

Patient's Name _____

Examiner's Name _____

Date _____

ARIZONA CLINICAL INTERVIEW RATING SCALE

Standardized Patients
Evaluation of Medical Interviewing Skills

ITEM 1 - ORGANIZATION

[5]	[4]	[3]	[2]	[1]
The interviewer elicits detailed information about the patient's current problem [onset, duration, location, quality, intensity, setting, positives, significant negatives, aggravating and alleviating factors] and all additional data relevant to the problem under discussion [past medical history, family, and social history].		The interviewer elicits detailed information about the patient's current problem but fails to obtain all additional data relevant to the problem under discussion [past medical history, family, and social history].		The interviewer fails to elicit detailed information about the patient's current problem.

ITEM 2 - TIMELINE

[5]	[4]	[3]	[2]	[1]
The interviewer obtains information pertaining to the Chief Complaint and History of the Present Illness in a logical, systematic and orderly progression, gathering all necessary information, starting with the first signs and symptoms of current illness and following their progression to the present.		At times, the interviewer does not obtain information pertaining to Chief Complaint and History of Present Illness in a chronological order, but is still able to obtain most of the pertinent information.		The interviewer obtains information pertaining to the Chief Complaint and History of the Present Illness in a haphazard and unrelated fashion, resulting in the omission of pertinent data.

ITEM 3 - TRANSITIONAL STATEMENTS

[5]	[4]	[3]	[2]	[1]
The interviewer always progresses from one subsection to another, utilizing transitional statements which assure the patient that the information being sought is necessary and important, e.g., "Now I'm going to ask you some questions about your family, because we find that there are certain diseases that occur among blood relatives, and it will help us to know what health risks are in your family.		The interviewer sometimes introduces subsections with effective transitional statements, but fails to do so at other times. Some of the transitional statements used are lacking in quality, e.g., "Now I'm going to ask you some questions about your family."		The interviewer progresses from one subsection to another in such a manner that the patient is left with the feeling of uncertainty as to the purpose of the questions. (No transitions.)

ITEM 4 - QUESTIONING SKILLS - TYPE OF QUESTION

[5]
The interviewer starts information gathering with an open-ended question. For areas where the interviewer is required to deal with a large amount of potential information [e.g., History of Illness and Review of Systems], this is followed by direct and forced-choice questions which will allow him to narrow in on the pertinent positive and negative points that need further elaboration.

[4]

[3]
The interviewer often fails to begin a line of inquiry with open-ended questions but rather employs direct and forced-choice questions to obtain information.

[2]

[1]
The interviewer asks many leading questions, why questions and multiple questions, e.g., "Your child has never had diarrhea, has he?" "You want your child to have a tetanus shot, don't you?"

ITEM 5 - QUESTIONING SKILLS FACILITATIVE - SILENCE AND DELAYS IN DIALOGUE

[5]
The interviewer asks questions and/or takes notes in a manner which results in an interview that progresses smoothly with few unnecessary delays in the dialogue. If there are pauses, they are used deliberately as an effective interviewing technique.

[4]

[3]
At times the interview is marked with unnecessary delays which temporarily break the continuity of the interview and are not used as an interviewing technique.

[2]

[1]
The interview is conducted in such a manner that long delays occur which break the continuity of the interview.

ITEM 6 - QUESTIONING SKILLS DUPLICATION

[5]
The interviewer doesn't repeat questions, seeking duplication of information that has previously been provided, unless clarification or summarization of prior information is necessary.

[4]

[3]
The interviewer only rarely repeats questions seeking the duplication of information. Such information is sought not for the summarization or clarification of information, but as a result of the interviewer's failure to remember the data.

[2]

[1]
The interviewer frequently repeats questions seeking information previously provided because he fails to remember data already obtained.

ITEM 7 - QUESTIONING SKILLS - SUMMARIZING

[5]
At the end of each major line of inquiry or subsection [i.e., History of Present Illness, Past Medical History], the interviewer summarizes the data obtained in an effort to verify and/or clarify the information or as a precaution to assure that no important data omitted.

[4]

[3]
The interviewer sometimes summarizes the data at the end of some lines of inquiry but fails to do it consistently.

[2]

[1]
At the end of any specific line of inquiry, the interviewer fails to summarize the data obtained.

ITEM 8 - QUESTIONING SKILLS - JARGON

[5]
Questions asked, as well as information provided to the patient during the interview, are easily understandable; content is free of difficult medical terms and jargon. If jargon is used, the words are immediately defined for the patient.

[4]

[3]
The interviewer occasionally uses medical jargon during the interview, failing to define the medical terms for the patient unless specifically requested to do so by the patient.

[2]

[1]
Questions asked, as well as information provided to the patient during the interview, are confusing because of use of difficult medical terms and jargon.

ITEM 9 - QUESTIONING SKILLS - DOCUMENTATION

[5]
The interviewer always seeks specificity, documentation, and verification of the patient's responses, e.g.:
P: "I am allergic to penicillin."
I: "How do you know you are allergic? What kind of reaction have you had when you have had penicillin in the past?

[4]

[3]
The interviewer at times will seek specificity, documentation, and verification of the patient's responses, but not always.

[2]

[1]
The interviewer makes no attempt at documentation or verification of the patient's responses, accepting information at face value.

ITEM 10 - RAPPORT - EYE CONTACT - NON VERBAL FACILITATION - BODY LANGUAGE

[5]
The interviewer maintains good eye contact with the patient during the interview. There is good non verbal facilitation and positive body language and verbal facilitation.

[4]

[3]
The interviewer makes some eye contact; however, the frequency could be increased. Also, non verbal facilitative behavior and and body language could be better utilized to enhance the interview.

[2]

[1]
The interviewer makes no attempt to maintain eye contact with the patient. There is no attempt at positive non verbal or verbal facilitative behavior or facilitative body language.

ITEM 11 - RAPPORT - POSITIVE VERBAL REINFORCEMENT

[5]
The interviewer provides the patient with intermittent positive verbal reinforcement and feedback (e.g., Uh huh, go on, I see) and may verbally praise the patient for proper health care technique.

[4]

[3]
The interviewer is neither overly positive or negative is dispensing feedback and doesn't utilize verbal reinforcement frequently enough.

[2]

[1]
The interviewer provides the patient with little support or positive verbal reinforcement and is a detached data gatherer. The emphasis is on the negative rather than the positive attributes of the patient (e.g., "I can't believe you smoked for twenty years before you stopped.").

ITEM 12 - RAPPORT - INTERRUPTING THE PATIENT

[5]	[4]	[3]	[2]	[1]
The interviewer is attentive to the responses of the patient and allows him to complete statements without <u>undue</u> interruptions and allows patient sufficient time to complete statements and answer questions.		The interviewer is usually attentive but on a few occasions interrupts the patient unnecessarily [with no <u>apologies</u> given] and/or doesn't allow completion of thoughts. However, despite these interruptions, the interviewer's attentiveness is evident in that he is concerned with what the patient has to say even though he interrupts the patient occasionally.		The interviewer is nothing more than a detached data-gatherer, frequently interrupting the patient's statements without allowing him to complete his train of thought.

ITEM 13 - RAPPORT - POSSIBLE CONCERNS

[5]	[4]	[3]	[2]	[1]
The interviewer seems alert, sensitive and responsive to possible concerns expressed by the patient regardless of whether such concerns are immediately relevant to the patient's present physical problems; (e.g., marital problems, child discipline problems, depression, etc.), and is able to explore them in sufficient depth.		The interviewer <u>is able to detect</u> concerns expressed by the patient unrelated to the present physical problems, but <u>fails to explore</u> them in sufficient depth. This may be due to nervousness or being <u>unsure</u> as to how to broach the topic.		The interviewer seems unalert and/or insensitive to possible concerns expressed by the patient if such concerns are not directly related to the present physical problem. For whatever reasons the interviewer tends to avoid discussing possible problem areas which could have either immediate or future implications for the mental or physical health of his patient.

ITEM 14 - RAPPORT - ENCOURAGEMENT OF QUESTIONS AT END OF INTERVIEW

[5]	[4]	[3]	[2]	[1]
At the end of the complete interview, the interviewer encourages the patient to discuss any additional points or ask additional questions and provides him with an adequate opportunity to do so (e.g., "We've discussed many things. Are there <u>any questions you might like</u> to ask concerning your problem <u>and</u> is there <u>anything else at all</u> that you would like to bring up or discuss further?")		At the end of the complete interview, the interviewer provides the patient the opportunity to discuss any additional points <u>or</u> ask any additional questions <u>but neither</u> <u>encourages nor discourages him</u> (e.g., "Is there anything else--I don't have anything else so we are through.")		At the end of the complete interview, the interviewer <u>does</u> <u>not provide</u> the patient the opportunity to discuss any additional points <u>or</u> ask any additional questions.

ITEM 15 - CLOSURE OF THE INTERVIEW

[5]   [4]

At the end of the interview, the interviewer clearly specifies future plans (i.e., what the interviewer will do, what the patient should do, the time of the next communication).

[3]   [2]

At the end of the interview, the interviewer only partially details the plans for the future (e.g., "Some time you should bring in the name of the medicine you received", or "Call my secretary when you gather the information.").

[1]

At the end of the interview, the plans for the future are not specified and the patient leaves the interview without a sense of what to expect.

Paula L. Stillman, M.D., 1975
Revised May, 1984

APPENDIX B: HISTORY CONTENT CHECKLIST

Total # 80
Interviewer Score _____

Examiner's Name_____
Patient' Name_____
Date_____
Time Spent on Interview_____
Time Spent on Feedback_____

Timothy Harrity - History

I.   INTRODUCTION
_____   1.   Introduces self
_____   2.   Obtains and/or uses mother's name - Paula Harrity
_____   3.   Obtains and/or uses childs name - Timothy Harrity
_____   4.   Asks child age - 8 years

II.   CHIEF COMPLAINT & HISTORY OF PRESENT ILLNESS
_____   1.   Chief complaint: My child has headaches
_____   2.   Onset: First episode occurred at school one month ago
_____   3.   Called by school nurse to take him home
_____   4.   Frequency: total of three episodes in past month
_____   5.   Another episode 2 weeks ago. Came home from school with it.
_____   6.   The latest episode occurred yesterday as getting ready to go to school.
_____   7.   Kept him home from school
_____   8.   Duration: Last 3 hours
_____   9.   Location: both sides of forehead
_____   10.   Radiation: none
_____   11.   Description: Pain is constant, sharp ache
_____   12.   Meds: Each time treated with ASA put to bed with cold compress and he felt a little better
_____   13.   Document dose: one adult ASA
_____   14.   No associated symptoms: no elevated temperture, no nausea, no vomiting
_____   15.   Complained of blurred vision 1 month ago (significant positive)
_____   16.   Had normal eye screening at school last year
_____   17.   No convulsion, no weakness, no recent head trauma, no dizziness, no difficulty with speech or
             coordination (significant negative)
_____   18.   Might be related to stress in school
_____   19.   High expectations, high pressure
_____   20.   Excellent student
_____   21.   Headaches have never occurred on the weekends
_____   22.   Headaches don't appear to be related to position
_____   23.   No family history of headache
_____   24.   Other medications: Multi vitamins daily with flouride

III.   PAST MEDICAL HISTORY
    A.   Prenatal
_____   1.   G2 P2 Abo
_____   2.   Full term pregnancy - 2 weeks over due date
_____   3.   Exposed to CMV early in pregnancy
_____   4.   Went to doctor & had blood test, I was not infected
_____   5.   Meds: Vitamins with iron supplements 3x daily - anemic

    B.   Natal
_____   1.   Vaginal delivery
_____   2.   Total labor 14 hours
_____   3.   Baby cried right away
_____   4.   Birth weight: 8 lbs. 10 oz.

C. Postnatal
_____ 1. Hospitalized 4 days, went home with mother

D. Growth & Development
_____ 1. Small & thin
_____ 2. Walked at 8 months (or any major milestone)
_____ 3. Short sentences at 18 months (or any major language milestone)

E. Nutrition
_____ 1. Breast fed 12 months (only breast milk 10 months) and supplemented with similac 10-12 months
_____ 2. Whole milk at 12 months
_____ 3. Eats everything but picky eater

F. Immunizations
_____ 1. Up to date
_____ 2. 5 DPTs
_____ 3. 4 OPVs
_____ 4. MMR at 15 months
_____ 5. TB test and lead paint tests

G. Past Hospitalization
_____ 1. Out patient surgery - hernia repair, 7 months old

H. Past Injuries and Illnesses
_____ 1. Frequent colds & sore throats
_____ 2. Strep carrier
_____ 3. Documentation: confirmed by culture

I. Allergic History
_____ 1. Food, yes to strawberries
_____ 2. Documentation: got hives and brought to E.R. Treated with benadryl
_____ 3. Drugs, no
_____ 4. Environmental agents, no

J. Behavioral History
_____ 1. Quiet child
_____ 2. Gets along with siblings
_____ 3. Prefers to play alone, shy.

IV. FAMILY HISTORY
_____ 1. Mother: Paula 32 yrs. Good health
_____ 2. Father: David 33 yrs. Good health
_____ 3. Daughter: Jamie 18 months. Good health
_____ 4. Maternal Grandmother 56 yrs. Good health
_____ 5. Maternal Grandfather 60 yrs. High blood pressure
_____ 6. Paternal Grandmother 58 yrs. High blood pressure
_____ 7. Paternal Grandfather 56 yrs. Open heart surgery 2 times
_____ 8. Good health now
_____ 9. Several relatives on mother's side have high blood pressure (give if asked about other illnesses)
_____ 10. No early childhood deaths
_____ 11. No other significant illnesses that run in family

V.   SOCIAL HISTORY
_____   1.   Married 10 years - good relationship
_____   2.   Works 1 day per week in office
_____   3.   Husband production planner in large manufacturing company
_____   4.   Information about housing
_____   5.   Children covered by husband's health insurance

VI.   REVIEW OF SYSTEMS
_____   1.   Teeth: Sees dentist every 6 months, has protective sealent on teeth
_____   2.   Cardiovascular: told of heart murmur as infant - now almost gone
_____   3.   Bones and Joints: foot turned in when baby - better now

VII. OTHER CONCERNS
_____   1.   Friend's child has brain tumor, concerned that my child may have one.

APPENDIX C: PERFORMANCE CHECKLIST FOR ASYMPTOMATIC PATIENT INTERVIEW

THIS CHECKLIST IS TO BE BROUGHT WITH YOU TO YOUR APPOINTMENT WITH THE PATIENT!

PATIENT'S   NAME _____

EXAMINER'S NAME _____

OBSERVER'S NAME _____

DATE_____

PHYSICAL DIAGNOSIS II CHECKLIST FOR COMPLETE PHYSICAL EXAMINATION

A. GENERAL INSPECTION/VITAL SIGNS

____ 1. Wash hands before starting examination.
____ 2. Measure blood pressure in one arm.
____   a.   Place cuff snugly in correct anatomical location.
____ 3. Measure respiratory rate (for at least 30 seconds).
____ 4. Palpate radial (thumb side of wrist) pulse (for at least 15 seconds).
____ 5. Palpate radial (wrist) pulses simultaneously for symmetry.
____ 6. Check for postural changes in BP or pulse.
____   a.   Use correct technique in checking for postural changes (done within 1-2 minutes).

Total score (Part A) ____   Possible score: 8

B. HANDS AND ARMS
____   a.   Inspect both arms and forearms with clothing removed.
          HANDS
____ 1. Inspect both hands (dorsa and palms).

          PALPATE
____ 2. MCP (knuckles)
____ 3. PIP (proximal)
____ 4. DIP (distal)
          ROM
____ 5. Extension
____ 6. Claw
____ 7. Fist
____ 8. Thumb Opposition
          WRIST
          PALPATE
____ 9. Dorsal (top) surface
____ 10. Volar (palm side) surface
          ROM
____ 11. Flexion (bent in)
____ 12. Extension (bent back)
____ 13. Ulnar deviation (towards 5th finger)
____ 14. Radial deviation (towards thumb)
          ELBOW
          PALPATE
____ 15. Epicondyles
____ 16. Olecranon (& olecranon bursa)
          ROM
____ 17. Flexion
____ 18. Extension

____ 19. Pronation (palm down)
____   a. lock elbow at side
____ 20. Supination (palm up)
____   a. lock elbow at side
____ 21. Palpate epitrochlear nodes
____   a. located between biceps and triceps above elbow.
____ 22. Palpate axillary (underarm) nodes. (This may be done with breast exam.)
____   a. use thorough technique to palpate axillary nodes.
     SHOULDER
     PALPATE
____ 23. Sterno clavicular joint
____ 24. Acromioclavicular (A-C) joint
____ 25. Subdeltoid bursa
____ 26. Bicipital tendon
     ROM
____ 27. Forward flexion attempted
____   a. Full ROM achieved
____ 28. Extension (back) attempted
____   a. Full ROM achieved
____ 29. Abduction attempted
____   a. Full ROM achieved
____ 30. Adduction attempted
____   a. Full ROM achieved
____ 31. Internal Rotation (upper arm should be abducted) attempted
____   a. Full ROM achieved
____ 32. External Rotation attempted
____   a. Full ROM achieved

Total score (Part B) ____   Possible score: 43

C. HEAD AND NECK

____ 1. Palpate and observe scalp.
____   a. Palpate and observe thoroughly by parting hair.

     EYES

____ 2. Estimate visual acuity (near or far)
____   a. check each eye separately.
____ 3. Inspect external ocular structures (lids, cornea, conjunctiva [membrane inside eyelids]).
____   a. Gently move eyelids up and down to obtain better view.
____ 4. Evaluate extraocular muscle function in 4 (up, down, right, left) directions.
____ 5. Check for convergence and accommodation.
____ 6. Observe pupillary response to light (direct).
____ 7. Observe pupillary response to light (consensual).

Ophthalmoscopic Examination
____   a. Position patient at height comfortable for examiner.
____   b. Dim lights before ophthalmoscopic examination.
____   c. Hold ophthalmoscope properly and use index finger to switch lenses.
____   d. Hold ophthalmoscope at proper distance to visualize posterior (rear) structures in eye (i.e.,
              appropriately close to patient's eye).
____ 8. Hold ophthalmoscope with right hand when inspecting patient's right eye.
____ 9. Inspect anterior (frontal) structures with ophthalmoscope.
____ 10. Inspect optic nerve.
____ 11. Trace vessels in four quadrants.
____ 12. Observe macula (patient asked to look directly at light).
____ 13. Hold ophthalmoscope with left hand when inspecting patient's left eye.

____ 14. Inspect anterior structures with ophthalmoscope.
____ 15. Inspect optic nerve.
____ 16. Trace vessels in four quadrants.
____ 17. Observe macula (patient asked to look directly at light).
____ 18. Test visual fields by confrontation.

EARS

____ 19. Observe auricles (external ears) and postauricular (back of ears) regions bilaterally.
____ 20. Palpate auricles (external ears) bilaterally.
____ 21. Temporomandibular joint (PALPATE)
____   a. actually feel joint move
____ 22. Examine ears bilaterally with otoscope.
____   a. Insert speculum without causing pain to the patient.
____ 23. Test auditory acuity.
____   a. Use proper technique to test each ear separately.

NOSE

____ 24. Inspect nasal vaults with nasal speculum on otoscope.
____   a. Insert speculum without causing pain to the patient.
____ 25. Test for patency (openess) of both nasal passages.
____ 26. Palpate for frontal (above eye) sinus tenderness.
____ 27. Palpate for maxillary (below eye) sinus tenderness.

MOUTH

____ 28. Inspect lips, gums, tongue, teeth.
____ 29. Inspect floor of mouth and base of tongue
____   a. patient is asked to lift tip of tongue to roof of mouth.
____ 30. Inspect posterior pharynx (back of mouth and throat).
____   a. Examine patient without causing discomfort.
____ 31. Observe elevation of the palate (roof of mouth) by asking patient to say "ah".

NECK

Palpate lymph nodes:
____ 32. Preauricular (front of ears).
____ 33. Posterior auricular nodes (back of ears).
____ 34. Occipital nodes (base of skull).
____ 35. Tonsillar nodes (at angle of jaw).
____ 36. Submaxillary nodes (under jaw).
____ 37. Submental nodes (under chin).
____ 38. Superficial cervical nodes (in front of and on top of sternomastoid muscle).
____ 39. Posterior cervical nodes (behind and post to sternomastoid muscle).
____ 40. Supraclavicular nodes (above collarbone).
____ 41. Palpate thyroid with swallowing (isthmus and lobes).
____ 42. Palpate thyroid without swallowing (isthmus and lobes).
____   a. Palpate thyroid in correct anatomical location.
____ 43. Palpate carotids bilaterally.
____ 44. Auscultate carotids bilaterally.

Total score (Part C) ____   Possible score: 5

D. BACK

____ 1. Perform fist percussion of or palpate cervical(neck), thoracic, lumbar, sacral vertebrae
        and sacroiliac joints bilaterally.
____ 2. Perform fist percussion of CVA (kidneys for punch tenderness).

Total score (Part D) ____   Possible score: 2

THORAX

E. LUNGS

____ 1. Check thoracic (chest) expansion
____   a. fingers between ribs, loose skin pulled posteriorly.
____ 2. Percuss posterior lung fields.
____   a. Ask patient to cross arms to move scapulae and expose lung fields.
____   b. Percuss fields bilaterally and symmetrically, in all areas.
____ 3. Measure excursion of the diaphragm
____   a. check distance moved with maximum inspiration.
____ 4. Auscultate posterior lung fields.
____   a. Auscultate bilaterally and symmetrically.
____   b. Instruct patient to breathe through open mouth.

LATERAL

____ 5. Percuss lateral lung fields bilaterally.
____ 6. Auscultate lateral lung fields bilaterally.

ANTERIOR

____ 7. Percuss anterior lung fields.
____   a. Percuss fields bilaterally and symmetrically.
____ 8. Auscultate anterior lung fields.
____   a. Auscultate fields bilaterally and symmetrically.
____ 9. Auscultate apices in supraclavicular fossae (hollow above collarbone).

Total score (Part E) ____   Possible score: 17

F. BREASTS (Female)

      Inspect both breasts:
____ 1. Patient sitting, arms at sides.
____ 2. Patient sitting, arms above head.
____ 3. Patient leaning forward.
____ 4. Patient sitting, hands pressed to hips.

      Palpate breasts with patient in recumbent position:
____   a. Ask patient to put arm behind head to aid examination.
____   b. Examine all areas completely and systematically.
____ 5. 4 quadrants and tail.
____ 6. Nipple.
____ 7. Areola.
____ 8. Attempt to express material from the nipple.

Total score (Female)(Part F) ____   Possible score: 10

(Male)

____ 1. Palpate all 4 quadrants of each breast.
____ 2. Palpate nipples bilaterally.
____ 3. Palpate areolae.

Total score (Male)(Part F) ____   Possible score: 3

G. HEART

____ 1. Observe precordium
         PALPATE:
____ 2. Costochondral junctions
____ 3. Aortic area (2nd ICS(intercostal space)-right).
____ 4. Pulmonic area (2nd and 3rd ICS-left).
____ 5. Right ventricular area.
____ 6. Apical area (5th ICS-left).

     AUSCULTATE:
         Use diaphragm of stethoscope:
____ 7. Aortic area.
____ 8. Pulmonic area.
____ 9. Tricuspid area (4th and 5th ICS at left sternal edge).
____ 10. Mitral (apical) area.

         Use bell of stethoscope:
____ 11. Aortic area
____ 12. Pulmonic area
____ 13. Tricuspid area.
____ 14. Apical area.
____ 15. Observe neck veins and estimate jugular venous pressure.
____   a. Elevate trunk, head and neck so jugular venous pulses are visible.

Total score (Part G) ____   Possible score: 16

     For patient with suspected aortic valve disease: have patient sit up, lean forward and, using
     diaphragm of stethoscope, auscultate LSB 2-3rd ICS

     For patient with suspected mitral valve disease:
         --   Ask patient to roll to left lateral position.
         --   Relocate apex.
         --   Auscultate apex with bell.
         --   Auscultate apex with diaphragm.

     In patient with suspected heart disease: check effect of Valsalva, hard grip, squatting, etc.,
     on murmurs with stethoscope placed along LSB.

H.   ABDOMEN

____   a.   Teach patient to relax abdominal musculature.
____   b.   Watch patient's face as examine abdomen.
____   c.   Expose abdomen sufficiently so that all 4 quadrants and epigastrium are visible.
____   d.   Auscultate (before manipulation or palpation.)

____ 1. Left upper quadrant to include (L) renal artery.
____ 2. Right upper quadrant to include (R) renal artery.
____ 3. Right lower quadrant to include (R) iliac artery.
____ 4. Left lower quadrant to include (L) iliac artery.
____ 5. Aorta.

Palpate:
____ 6. Left upper quadrant.
____   a.   Use proper technique to palpate tip of spleen.
____ 7. Epigastrium to include aorta.
____   a.   Margins of aorta delineated
____ 8. Right upper quadrant.
____   a.   Use proper technique to palpate liver edge.
____ 9. Right lower quadrant.
____ 10. Left lower quadrant.
____ 11. Percuss liver span.

If suspect splenomegaly, roll patient to rt lateral decubitus position and check bimanually for spleen tip or percuss

Total score (Part H) ____   Possible score: 18

I. LOWER LIMBS

____ 1. Inspect bilaterally with outer clothes removed.
____   a.   Use proper draping to expose both legs.
____ 2. Inspect feet including toes. (Remove socks if present.)

Palpate pulses bilaterally:
____ 3. Femoral (groin).
____ 4. Palpate femoral and radial or carotid pulse simultaneously.
____ 5. Popliteal (back of knee).
____ 6. Posterior tibial (at ankle) behind medial malleolus.
____ 7. Dorsalis pedis (top of foot).
____ 8. Palpate inguinal lymph nodes.
____ 9. Auscultate for femoral bruit.
____ 10. Check for peripheral pitting edema.
____   a.   Use proper technique to check for pitting edema (at least 5 seconds, over soft tissue)

HIPS
    PALPATE
____ 11. Trochanteric bursa (teaching point--easiest to do with patient on side with knee bent.)
    ROM
____ 12. Flexion attempted
____   a.   Full ROM achieved
____ 13. Extension attempted
____   a.   Full ROM achieved
____ 14. Abduction attempted
____   a.   Full ROM achieved
____ 15. Adduction attempted
____   a.   Full ROM achieved
____ 16. Internal Rotation attempted
____   a.   Full ROM achieved
____ 17. External Rotation attempted
____   a.   Full ROM achieved

KNEE
    PALPATE (easiest to do with knee flexed)
____ 18. Joint line
____   a.   Examines full extent of joint line
____ 19. Patella
    ROM
____ 20. Flexion
____ 21. Extension
____ 22. Check for stability of collateral ligaments (medial, lateral)--(slight flexion, stabilize at thigh, push lower leg in opposite direction).
____ 23. Check for stability of cruciate ligaments (anterior, posterior)--(flex knee, sit on foot, hands in popliteal fossa, thumbs on joint line, move anterior and posterior).
____ 24. Perform bulge sign checking for fluid (milk fluid from inside of knee up, then displace patella medially).

ANKLE
    PALPATE
____ 25. Malleoli/tendon areas
____ 26. Achilles tendon/bursa
    ROM
____ 27. Dorsi flexion
____ 28. Plantar flexion
____ 29. Inversion
____ 30. Eversion

FOOT
    PALPATE
____ 31. MTP
____ 32. PIP
____ 33. DIP
    ROM
____ 34. Midfoot abduction/adduction
____   a.   stabilize ankle
____ 35. Toes extension
____ 36. Toes flexion

Total score (Part I) ____   Possible score: 46

J.   NEUROLOGICAL SCREENING EXAMINATION

PATIENT STANDING
____ 1. Observe gait.
____   a.   patient asked to swing arms fully.
____ 2. Have patient walk on toes.
____ 3. Have patient walk on heels.
____ 4. Have patient hop on each foot or climb stairs or do deep knee bend.
____ 5. Observe tandem gait (heel-to-toe).
____ 6. Perform Romberg test.
____   a.   eyes closed, feet together.

CERVICAL SPINE
    ROM
____ 7. Flex and extension
____ 8. Lateral flexion (ear to shoulder)
____ 9. Rotation (chin to shoulder)

LUMBAR SPINE
    ROM
____ 10. Perform screening test for scoliosis.
____   a.   uses proper technique--sights across back.
____ 11. Flexion
____ 12. Extension
____ 13. Lateral Bending
____ 14. Rotation

CRANIAL NERVES
____ 15. Test Nerve I: Sense of smell (not usually done)
           Ask patient if there has been any change in smell or taste.
      Test Nerve II: (May be done with EENT)
      a.   Visual acuity.
      b.   Visual fields.
      c.   Ophthalmoscopic (disc, blood vessels, retina)
      Test Nerves III, IV, VI:(May be done with EENT)
      a.   Pupillary reaction to light.
      b.   Extraocular movements.
      Test Nerve V:
           Sensory function:
____ 16. Briefly test all 3 divisions.

           Motor function:
____ 17. Test contraction of masseter (jaw) muscles or forced opening of
      mouth against resistance.

      Test Nerve VII:
           Motor function in mimetic musculature of the face:
____ 18. Raise eyebrows or forced eyelid closing (upper division).
____ 19. Show teeth, puff out cheeks, or smile (lower division).
      Test Nerve VIII:
           Hearing (may be done with EENT examination)
      Test Nerves IX and X:
           Observe elevation of palate vocalizing "ah". (may be done with EENT)
      Test Nerve XI:
____ 20. Test rotation of patient's head against resistance.
____ 21. Test shoulder shrug against resistance.
      Test Nerve XII:
____ 22. Observe midline protrusion of the tongue. (may be done with examination of the mouth.)

    MOTOR STATUS
           Examine functional groups of muscles for bulk, tone, consistency, and strength.
           This can be done while checking ROM
UPPER LIMB
____ 23. Proximal (close to trunk) muscles
____   a.   Test for drift of outstretched arms with eyes closed and palms up is most sensitive. (This can
        also be done while checking ROM around shoulder).
____ 24. Forearm (This can also be done while checking ROM around elbow and wrist.)
____ 25. Distal Muscles--Test for patient's grip or fine rapid movements of fingers or have patient form ring
      with thumb and index finger which examiner tries to break (This can also be done while checking ROM).

LOWER LIMB

    Proximal muscle: (Screening testing can be done with patient standing or else can test muscle strength around hip, knee and ankle joints while doing ROM)
    [Have patient hop on each foot or climb stairs or do deep knee bend].

____ 26. Distal (distant from trunk) muscles: Test fine rapid movements - feet or ask patient to push down on gas against resistance and then lift up feet against resistance. This can be done while testing ROM.

REFLEXES

    Deep tendon reflexes: (Test symmetrically)
____ 27. Test biceps reflex (inside elbow).
____   a. Elicits reflex.
____ 28. Test brachioradialis reflex (above wrist).
____   a. Elicits reflex.
____ 29. Test triceps reflex (back of elbow).
____   a. Elicits reflex.
____ 30. Test patellar reflex (knee).
____   a. Elicits reflex.
____ 31. Test achilles reflex (ankle).
____   a. Elicits reflex.

    Cutaneous reflexes:
____ 32. Test plantar reflex (sole of foot).

CEREBELLAR FUNCTION

____ 33. Test rapid alternating movements - hands.
____ 34. Test finger-to-nose bilaterally.
____   a. proper technique--upper arm abducted.
____ 35. Test heel-to-shin bilaterally
____   a. knee extended. Just allow patient to use heel.
    [Observe tandem gait - heel-to-toe (done with patient standing).]

SENSORY STATUS

____ 36. Test light touch or pin prick
____   a. demonstrate to patient difference between sharp and dull.
____   b. upper extremities.
____   c. lower extremities.
____   d. trunk.
____ 37. Test position sense at least in feet.
____   a. demonstrate to patient what is meant by up and down.
____   b. hold toes along side edges.
____ 38. Test vibration sense in at least both ankles.
____   a. first demonstrate what vibration feels like.
    (Romberg done with patient standing)

Total score (Part J) ____   Possible score: 56

Total Obtained _____   Possible Score: Female--274   Male--267

                                  Passing Score: Female--245   Male--240

INSTRUCTIONS TO EVALUATOR

For Question 1, Parts a and b, please circle yes or no for each item.

1. (a)   Did the examiner introduce himself/herself? Yes No
    (b)   Did the examiner demonstrate ability to
            develop rapport?   Yes No

For Questions 2 through 9, please circle the score which best describes the examiner's performance.

        5 = always
        4
        3 = about half the time
        2
        1 = very rarely

2. Did the examiner show concern for the patient's comfort and assure privacy during the
    examination?   5 4 3 2 1

3. Did the examiner present himself/herself in a professional manner (verbal and non-verbal
    behavior)?   5 4 3 2 1

4. Did the examiner explain procedures and prepare the patient for the use of instruments?
                                                                                     5 4 3 2 1

5. Did the examiner perform the complete PE in a logical sequence without repetition, progressing
    from one region to another?   5 4 3 2 1

6. Did the examiner examine and compare symmetrical parts of the body?   5 4 3 2 1

7. Did the examiner examine the patient with serial exposure appropriate to the steps of the
    examination?   5 4 3 2 1

8. Did the examiner examine the patient gently when there was patient contact?   5 4 3 2 1

9. Did the examiner demonstrate good percussion technique?   5 4 3 2 1

ADDITIONAL COMMENTS:

Possible Score (Evaluation)   40

APPENDIX D: PERFORMANCE CHECKLIST FOR SYMPTOMATIC PATIENT INTERVIEW

Examiner's Name: _____

Patient's Name: _____

Date: _____

CARDIOVASCULAR EXAMINATION PERFORMANCE CHECKLIST

A. GENERAL INSPECTION/VITAL SIGNS

_____ 1. Wash hands before starting examination.
_____ 2. Measure blood pressure in right upper limb, sitting or lying.
_____ 3. Measure blood pressure in left upper limb, sitting or lying.
_____ 4. Measure blood pressure in either upper limb standing.
_____ 5. Empty cuff completely before inflating it.
_____ 6. Measure respiratory rate for at least 60 seconds.
_____ 7. Palpate radial pulse for at least 15 seconds.
_____ 8. Palpate radial pulse simultaneously for symmetry.

B. HANDS AND ARMS

_____ 1. Inspect both hands.

C. HEAD AND NECK

_____ 1. Palpate carotids bilaterally.
_____ 2. Auscultate carotids bilaterally.

D. LUNGS

_____ 1. Ask patient to cross arms to move scapulae and expose lung fields.
_____ 2. Percuss posterior lung fields.
_____ 3.   Percuss fields bilaterally and symmetrically, in all areas.
_____ 4. Instruct patient to breathe through open mouth.
_____ 5. Auscultate posterior lung fields.
_____ 6.   Auscultate bilaterally and symmetrically, all areas with patient breathing through open mouth.

LATERAL LUNG FIELDS

_____ 7. Percuss lateral lung fields.
_____ 8. Auscultate lateral lung fields.

ANTERIOR LUNG FIELDS

_____ 9. Percuss anterior lung fields.
_____ 10. Percuss fields bilaterally and symmetrically.
_____ 11. Auscultate anterior lung fields
_____ 12. Auscultate anterior lung fields bilaterally and symmetrically.

Revised on 7/21/81

E. HEART

____1. Observe precordium.

Palpate with patient sitting:
____2. Aortic area (2nd ICS-right).
____3. Pulmonic area (2nd and 3rd ICS-left).
____4. Right ventricular area.
____5. Apical area (5th ICS-left).

Auscultate with patient sitting: (using diaphragm of stethoscope).
____6. Aortic area.
____7. Pulmonic area.
____8. Tricuspid area (4th and 5th ICS at left sternal edge).
____9. Mitral (apical) area.

Auscultate with patient sitting: (using bell of stethoscope).
____10. Aortic area.
____11. Pulmonic area.
____12. Tricuspid area.
____13. Apical area.

____14. Observe neck veins with patient in recumbent position.
Palpate with patient recumbent:
____15. Aortic area (2nd ICS-right).
____16. Pulmonic area (2nd and 3rd ICS-left).
____17. Right ventricular area.
____18. Apical area (5th ICS-left).
____19. Ectopic area (between right ventricular and apical areas).

Auscultate with patient recumbent: (using diaphragm of stethoscope).
____20. Aortic area.
____21. Pulmonic area.
____22. Tricuspid area.
____23. Mitral (apical) area.

Auscultate with patient recumbent (using bell of stethoscope).
____24. Aortic area.
____25. Pulmonic area.
____26. Tricuspid area.
____27. Mitral(apical) area.
____28. Ask patient to roll to left lateral position.
____29. Relocate apex.
____30. Auscultate apex with bell.
____31. Auscultate apex with diaphragm.

F. ABDOMEN

____1. Patient is taught to relax abdominal musculature.
____2. Watch patient's face as you examine abdomen.
____3. Auscultate before manipulation or palpation.

Auscultate:
____ 4. Aorta.
____ 5. Renal arteries.
____ 6. Iliac arteries.

____ 7. Palpate epigastrium superficially.
____ 8. Palpate epigastrium deeply.
____ 9. Palpate right upper quadrant.
____ 10. Use proper technique to palpate liver edge.
____ 11. Percuss liver span.

LOWER LIMBS

____ 1. Inspect bilaterally with outer clothes removed.
____ 2. Inspect feet including toes.

Palpate pulses bilaterally:
____ 3. Femoral
____ 4. Popliteal
____ 5. Posterior tibial
____ 6. Dorsalis pedis
____ 7. Auscultate for femoral bruits.
____ 8. Check for peripheral pitting edema.
____ 9. Use proper technique to check for pitting edema.

TOTAL OBTAINED SCORE ____

TOTAL SCORE POSSIBLE 74

FOR THE EVALUATOR

KEY: 5 = Always
      4 = Most of the time
      3 = Half of the time
      2 = Rarely
      1 = Never

1. Did the student show concern for the patient's comfort   5   4   3   2   1
    and assure privacy during the examination?

2. Did the student present himself/herself in a professional
    manner?   5   4   3   2   1
    a. Did the student generate a sense of confidence?   5   4   3   2   1
    b. Did the student put the patient at ease?   5   4   3   2   1
    c. Did the student demonstrate proficiency in exam-
        ination techniques?   5   4   3   2   1
    d. Was the student pleasant but in command of the
        examination?   5   4   3   2   1

3. Did the student explain procedures and prepare patient for
    what was being done/   5   4   3   2   1

4. Did the student perform the examination in a logical sequence pro-
    gressing from one region to another without repetition?   5   4   3   2   1

5. Did the student examine and compare symmetric parts of the
    body?   5   4   3   2   1

6. Did the student use jargon not understood by patient?   5   4   3   2   1

7. Was the examination too rough?   5   4   3   2   1

Paula L. Stillman, M.D.

Paul J. Rutala, M.D.

APPENDIX E: CONTENT CHECKLIST FOR SYMPTOMATIC PATIENT INTERVIEW

Examiner's Name: _____

Patient's Name: _____

Date:. _____

CARDIOVASCULAR EXAMINATION CONTENT CHECKLIST

By having performed the 78 maneuvers of the cardiovascular examination checklist, you will now be able to answer the following questions:

VITAL SIGNS/INSPECTION

1. Blood pressure:
    (a) Right arm (sitting or lying): _____/_____
    (b) Left arm (sitting or lying): _____/_____
    (c) Either arm (standing): _____/_____

2. Respiratory rate: _____/min.

3. Radial pulse:
    (a) Rate: _____/min.
    (b) Rhythm: regular_____ ; irregular_____
    (c) Symmetrical in both forearms: yes_____ no_____ .
         If asymmetrical in timing: is right pulse delayed? yes____ no____
                                     is left pulse delayed? yes____ no____
                                     estimate length of delay: ____ sec.

        If asymmetrical in strength, estimate (on a scale of 0-4+):

        Right   Left
        0 1 2 3 4   0 1 2 3 4

4. Fingernail beds:
    (a) evidence of cyanosis: present_____ absent_____
    (b) evidence of clubbing: present_____ absent_____

CAROTID PULSE

5. (a) Carotid pulse upstroke: normal_____ abnormal_____ .

    If abnormal: rapid_____ slow_____ .

   (b) Carotid pulse contour: normal_____ bisferiens_____ .

6. Strength of carotid pulse (estimate on a scale of 0-4+):

        Right   Left
        0 1 2 3 4   0 1 2 3 4

7. Carotid bruits: present_____ absent_____ .
    If present, were bruits heard: (a) on right side_____ .
                                    (b) on left side_____ .
    If present, grade bruit (on a scale of 0-4+):

        Right   Left
        0 1 2 3 4   0 1 2 3 4

THORAX AND LUNGS

8. Pattern of percussion: normal_____abnormal_____.
    If abnormal, is it dull_____ or hyperresonant_____?

    On the accompanying diagram, shade all areas of dullness and/or
    hyperresonance:

    Posterior   Right Lateral   Left Lateral   Anterior

9. Rales (crackles): present_____absent_____.
    If present, the quality can be described as: fine_____coarse_____

    On the accompanying diagram, shade all areas in which rales are heard:

    Posterior   Right Lateral   Left Lateral   Anterior

10. Wheezes with quiet breathing:
        (a) present on inspiration? yes_____no_____.
        (b) present on expiration? yes_____no_____.

    If present, shade all areas on the accompanying diagram, in which
    wheezes are heard:

    Posterior   Right Lateral   Left Lateral   Anterior

HEART

11. Visible precordial motions: present_____absent_____.
     If present, locate with a dark dot on the accompanying diagram:

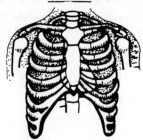

12. Palpable precordial impulses:
     (a) Aortic area (2nd RICS): normal ____hyperactive____sustained____.
     (b) Pulmonic area (2nd LICS): normal____hyperactive____sustained____.
     (c) Tricuspid area (4th LICS): normal____hyperactive____sustained____.
     (d) Apical area: normal____hyperactive____sustained____.
     (e) Point of maximal impulse: localized____diffuse____. Please mark
          with an x on the above diagram.
     (f) Palpable S4 at the apex: present____absent____.
     (g) Ectopic area of precordial impulse: present____absent____.
     (h) Left ventricular heave: present____absent____.
     (i) Right ventricular lift: present____absent____.

13. Auscultation:
     (a) S1: single____split____.
     (b) Intensity of S1: normal____loud____soft____.
     (c) S2: single____split____.
          If split, is splitting: physiologic____paradoxical____wide____
                                   fixed____.
     (d) Intensity of S2: normal____loud____soft____.
     (e) Intensity of pulmonic component of S2: normal____loud____soft____.
     (f) Ejection sound heard in 2nd LICS (pulmonic area): yes____no____.
     (g) S3 present at the apex: yes____no____.
     (h) S4 present at the apex: yes____no____.
     (i) Midsystolic clicks: present____absent____.
          If present: single____multiple____.
     (j) Opening snap mitral valve: present____absent____.

14.   (a) Systolic murmur(s): present_____absent_____.
       If present, indicate on the accompanying diagram with a dark dot where
       they are best heard and:

       (b) Grade the murmur(s) on a 1-6+ scale. Grade_____. (If there is more
than one murmur, indicate the grade of each near the dot on the diagram above)
       (c) Does murmur(s) vary with inspiration: yes_____no_____.
       If yes, does it increase_____or decrease_____.

15.   (a) Diastolic murmur(s): present_____absent_____.
       If present, indicate on the accompanying diagram with a dark dot
       where murmur(s) are best heard and:

       (b) Grade the murmur(s) on a 1-6+ scale. Grade_____. (If there is more
than one murmur, indicate the grade of each near the dot on the diagram above)
       (c) Does murmur(s) vary with inspiration: yes_____no_____.
       If yes, does it increase_____or decrease_____.

16. Diagram all sounds heard during the cardiac cycle.

| S1 | S2 | S1 | S2 | S1 | S2 | S1 |

17. Venous pressure (observed in neck veins): normal_____; abnormal_____.
     If abnormal, is venous pulse pressure decreased_____or elevated_____.
     If elevated, estimate height in cms: _____cm.

18. Abdominal bruits heard: yes_____ no_____.
    If yes, grade on a scale of 1-4+ in each area where they occur.

	Right	Left
(a) Aorta	1 2 3 4	1 2 3 4
(b) Renal arteries	1 2 3 4	1 2 3 4
(c) Iliac arteries	1 2 3 4	1 2 3 4

19. Aorta: palpable_____not palpable_____.
    If palpable, estimate diameter in cms: _____cms.

20. (a) Overall span of liver to percussion: _____cms.
    (b) Liver edge: palpable_____not palpable_____.
         If palpable:
         How far below the right costal margin (RCM):_____cms.
         tender_____non-tender_____.
         pulsatile____Non-pulsatile____.

21. Toe nail beds:
    (a) evidence of cyanosis: present_____absent_____.
    (b) evidence of clubbing: present_____absent_____.

22. Femoral pulse:
    (a) Symmetrical strength in both groins: yes_____no_____.
         Grade pulse from 0-4+ in each groin:

Right	Left
0 1 2 3 4	0 1 2 3 4

23. Femoral bruits: present_____absent_____.
    If present, bruits are heard on: (a) right yes_____no_____.
                                     (b) left yes_____no_____

24. Grade peripheral pulse strengths (0-4+) for the following:

	Right	Left
(a) popliteal pulse	0 1 2 3 4	0 1 2 3 4
(b) posterior tibial pulse	0 1 2 3 4	0 1 2 3 4
(c) dorsalis pedis pulse	0 1 2 3 4	0 1 2 3 4

25. Peripheral edema: present____absent____.
      If present, grade (0-4+)

           Right Limb   Left Limb
           0 1 2 3 4   0 1 2 3 4

If present, how far up the limb does it ascend (i.e., ankle, pretibial):

right limb_____

left limb_____

26. Please list any additional findings not specifically listed on this form
    that you feel are pertinent to the patient's condition:

27. Briefly explain the patient's underlying disease process based on the
    abnormalities found on physical examination

Paula L. Stillman, M.D.
Paul J. Rutala, M.D.

References

American Board of Internal Medicine. (1979). Clinical competence in internal medicine. *Annals of Internal Medicine, 90,* 402–411.

American Medical Association Council on Medical Education. (1980). Physician competence. *Connecticut Medicine, 44,* 593–595.

Anderson, A. S., & Botticelli, M. G. (1981). Evaluating M.D.-level competence in internal medicine. *Journal of Medical Education, 56,* 587–592.

Anderson, J. (1981). The MCQ controversy—A review. *Medical Teacher, 3,* 150–156.

Andrew, B. J. (1977). The use of behavioral checklists to assess physical examination skills. *Journal of Medical Education, 52,* 589–591.

Anwar, R. A. H., Bosk, C., & Greenburg, A. G. (1981). Resident evaluation: Is it, can it, should it be objective? *Journal of Surgical Research, 30,* 27–41.

Arnold, L., Willoughby, L., Calkins, V., Gammon, L., & Eberhart, G. (1981). Use of peer evaluation in the assessment of medical students. *Journal of Medical Education, 56,* 35–42.

Association of American Medical Colleges. (1981). External examinations for the evaluation of medical education achievement and for licensure. *Journal of Medical Education, 56,* 933–962.

Barro, A. R. (1973). Survey and evaluation of approaches to physician performance measurement. *Journal of Medical Education, 48,* 1051–1093.

Barrows, H. S. (1971). *Simulated patients (programmed patients): The development and use of a new technique in medical education.* Springfield, IL: Charles C Thomas.

Barrows, H. S., & Abrahamson, S. (1964). The programmed patient: A technique for appraising student performance in clinical neurology. *Journal of Medical Education, 39,* 802–805.

Berner, E. S., Hamilton, L. A., Jr., & Best, W. R. (1974). A new approach to evaluating problem-solving in medical students. *Journal of Medical Education, 49,* 666–672.

Bray, P. F. (1979). Reliability of the oral certifying examination for neurologists: Comparison of test results using live patient interviews and audiovisual techniques. *Annals of Neurology, 6,* 91–93.

Burg, F. D., Brownlee, R. C., Wright, F. H., Levine, H., Daeschner, C. W., Vaughan, V. C., III, & Anderson, J. A. (1976). A method for defining competency in pediatrics. *Journal of Medical Education, 51,* 824–828.

Burg, F. D., Lloyd, J. S., & Templeton, B. (1982). Competence in medicine. *Medical Teacher, 4,* 60–64.

Burri, A., McCaughan, K., & Barrows, H. (1976). The feasibility of using the simulated patient as a means to evaluate clinical competence of practicing physicians in a community (a pilot project). *Research in Medical Education: Proceedings of the Fifteenth Annual Conference,* 295–300.

Coggan, P. G., Knight, P., & Davis, P. (1980). Evaluating students in family medicine using simulated patients. *Journal of Family Practice, 10,* 259–265.

Cowles, J. T. (1965). A critical-comments approach to the rating of medical students' clinical performance. *Journal of Medical Education, 40,* 188–198.

Cranton, P. A., Dauphiree, W. D., McQueen, M. M., & Smith, L. P. (1984). The reliability and validity of in-training evaluation reports in obstetrics and gynecology. *Research in Medical Education: Proceedings of the Twenty-third Annual Conference,* 59–64.

Cuschieri, A., Gleeson, F. A., Harden, R. M., & Wood, R. A. B. (1979). A new approach to a final examination in surgery. *Annals of the Royal College of Surgeons of England, 61,* 400–405.

Dielman, T. E., Hull, A. L., & Davis, W. K. (1980). Psychometric properties of clinical performance ratings. *Evaluation and the Health Professions, 3,* 103–117.

Downing, S. M. (1980). The assessment of clinical competence on the emergency medicine specialty certification examination: The validity of clinically relevant multiple-choice items. *Annals of Emergency Medicine, 9,* 554–556.

Dunn, E. V., & Conrath, D. W. (1977). Primary care: Clinical judgment and reliability. *New York State Journal of Medicine, 77,* 748–754.

Egan, R. L. (1976). Faculty responsibility for the competence of new physicians. *Journal of the American Medical Association, 236,* 3043–3044.

Elstein, A. S., Shulman, L. S., & Sprafka, S. A. (1978). *Medical problem solving: An analysis of clinical reasoning.* Cambridge, MA: Harvard University Press.

Engel, G. L. (1971). The deficiencies of the case presentation as a method of clinical teaching. *New England Journal of Medicine, 284,* 20–24.

Engel, G. L. (1976). Are medical schools neglecting clinical skills? *Journal of the American Medical Association, 236,* 861–863.

Fisch, H. U., Hammond, K. R., Joyce, C. R. B., & O'Reilly, M. (1981). An experimental study of the clinical judgment of general physicians in evaluating and prescribing for depression. *British Journal of Psychiatry, 138,* 100–109.

Franklin, M. R., Stillman, P. L., Burpeau, M. Y., & Sabers, D. L. (1982). Examiner error in intelligence testing: Are you a source? *Psychology in the Schools, 19,* 563–569.

Frederikson, N. (1984). The real test bias. *American Psychologist, 39,* 193–202.

Futcher, P. H., Sanderson, E. V., & Tusler, P. A. (1977). Evaluation of clinical skills for a specialty board during residency training. *Journal of Medical Education, 52,* 567–577.

Galinson, M. L. (1975). Interviewing, negotiating, and counseling. *Journal of Legal Education, 27,* 352.

Gonnella, J. S., Goran, M. J., Williamson, J. W., & Cotsonas, N. J., Jr. (1970). Evaluation of patient care—An approach. *Journal of the American Medical Association, 214,* 2040–2043.

Goodpaster, G. S. (1975). The human arts of lawyering: Interviewing and counseling. *Journal of Legal Education, 27,* 5.

Goran, M. J., Williamson, J. W., & Gonnella, J. S. (1973). The validity of patient management problems. *Journal of Medical Education, 48,* 171–177.

Grace, M., Hanson, J., Fincham, S. M., Skakun, E. N., & Taylor, W. C. (1977). A scoring technique for computerized patient management problems. *Medical Education, 11,* 335–340.

Graham, J. R. (1971). Systematic evaluation of clinical competence. *Journal of Medical Education, 46,* 625–629.

Greganti, M. A., McGaghie, W. C., & Finn, W. F. (1982). Personal characteristics of house staff candidates: A quantitative analysis of relative weights. *Annals of Internal Medicine, 97,* 108–111.

Harasym, P., Baumber, J., Bryant, H., Fundytus, D., Preshaw, R., Watanabe, M., & Wyse, G. (1980). An evaluation of the clinical problem-solving process using a simulation technique. *Medical Education, 14,* 381–386.

Harden, R. M. (1979). How to assess clinical competence—An overview. *Medical Teacher, 1,* 289–296.

Harden, R. M., & Cairncross, R. G. (1980). Assessment of practical skills: The objective structured practical examination (OSPE). *Studies in Higher Education, 5,* 187–195.

Harden, R. M., & Gleeson, F. A. (1979). Assessment of clinical competence using an objective structured clinical examination (OSCE). *Medical Education, 13,* 41–54.

Harden, R. M., Stevenson, M., Downie, W. W., & Wilson, G. M. (1975). Assessment of clinical competence using objective structured examination. *British Medical Journal, 1,* 447–451.

Hart, I. (1983). Correlation of performance in the OSCE with later clinical performance. *Annals of the Royal College of Physical Surgeons (Canada), 16,* 356.

Helfer, R. E. (1970). An objective comparison of the pediatric interviewing skills of freshman and senior medical students. *Pediatrics, 54,* 623–627.

Helfer, R. E., Black, M. A., & Helfer, M. E. (1975). Pediatric interviewing skills taught by nonphysicians. *American Journal of Diseases of Children, 129,* 1053–1057.

Helfer, R. E., Black, M. A., & Teitelbaum, H. (1975). A comparing of pediatric interviewing skills using real and simulated mothers. *Pediatrics, 55,* 397–400.

Helfer, R. E., & Ealy, K. F. (1972). Observations of pediatric interviewing skills. *American Journal of Diseases of Children, 123,* 556–560.

Helfer, R. E., & Hess, J. (1970). An experimental model for making objective measurements of interviewing skills. *Journal of Clinical Psychology, 26,* 327–331.

Helfer, R. E., & Slater, C. H. (1971). Measuring the process of solving clinical diagnostic problems. *British Journal of Medical Education, 5,* 48–52.

Hinz, C. F. (1966). Direct observation as a means of teaching and evaluating clinical skills. *Journal of Medical Education, 41,* 150–161.

Holden, W. D., & Levit, E. J. (1980). Medical education, licensure, and the National Board of Medical Examiners. *New England Journal of Medicine, 303,* 1357–1360.

Hubbard, J. P., Levit, E., Schumacher, C. F., & Schnabel, T. G. (1965). An objective evaluation of clinical competence. *New England Journal of Medicine, 272,* 1321–1328.

Hull, A. L. (1982). Medical student performance: A comparison of house officers and attending staff as evaluators. *Evaluation and the Health Professions, 5,* 87–94.

Hunsacker, D. M., (1980). Law humanism and communication: Suggestions for limited curricular reform. *Journal of Legal Education, 30,* 417, 433.

Juul, D. H., Noe, M. J., & Nerenberg, R. L. (1979). A factor analytic study of branching patient management problems. *Medical Education, 13,* 199–203.

Kegel-Flom, P. (1975). Predicting supervisor, peer, and self-ratings of intern performance. *Journal of Medical Education, 50,* 812–815.

Koran, L. M. (1975). The reliability of clinical methods, data, and judgments. *New England Journal of Medicine, 293,* 642–646 (part 1), 695–701 (part 2).

Korman, M., & Stubblefield, R. L. (1971). Communications: Medical school evaluation and internship performance. *Journal of Medical Education, 46,* 670–673.

Lagerkvist, B., Samuelsson, B., & Sjolin, S. (1976). Evaluation of the clinical performance and skill in pediatrics of medical students. *Medical Education, 10,* 176–178.

Laguna, J., & Stillman, P. L. (1978). Teaching undergraduate medical students the neurological examination. *Journal of Medical Education, 53,* 990–992.

Lamont, C. T., & Hennen, B. K. E. (1972). The use of simulated patients in a certification examination in family medicine. *Journal of Medical Education, 47,* 789–795.

Leake, H. C., III, Barnard, J. D., & Christophersen, E. R. (1978). Evaluation of pediatric resident performance during the well-child visit. *Journal of Medical Education, 53,* 361–363.

Leichner, P., Eusebio-Torres, E., & Harper, D. (1981). The validity of reference letters in predicting resident performance. *Journal of Medical Education, 56,* 1019–1021.

Levine, H. G., & McGuire, C. H. (1971). Rating habitual performance in graduate medical education. *Journal of Medical Education, 46,* 306–311.

Linn, B. S., Arostegui, M., & Zeppa, R. (1975). Performance rating scale for peer and self assessment. *British Journal of Medical Education, 9,* 98–101.

Linn, L. S. (1979). Interns' attitudes and values as antecedents of clinical performance. *Journal of Medical Education, 54,* 238–240.

Liston, E. H., Yager, J., & Strauss, G. D. (1981). Assessment of psychotherapy skills: The problem of interrater agreement. *American Journal of Psychiatry, 138,* 1069–1074.

Littlefield, J. H., Harrington, J. T., Anthracite, N. E., & Garman, R. E. (1981). A description and four-year analysis of a clinical clerkship evaluation system. *Journal of Medical Education, 56,* 334–340.

Liu, P., Miller, E., Herr, G., Hardy, C., Sivarajan, M., & Willenkin, R. (1980). Videotape reliability: A method of evaluation of a clinical performance examination. *Journal of Medical Education, 55,* 713–715.

Lyons, T. F., & Payne, B. C. (1974). The relationship of physicians' medical recording performance to their medical care performance. *Medical Care, 12,* 463–469.

Maatsch, J. L. (1981). Assessment of clinical competence on the emergency medicine specialty certification examination: The validity of examiner ratings of simulated clinical encounters. *Annals of Emergency Medicine, 10,* 504–507.

Margolis, C. Z., & Cook, C. D. (1976). Rating pediatric house officer performance. *Connecticut Medicine, 40,* 539–543.

Marienfeld, R. D., & Reid, J. C. (1980). Subjective vs. objective evaluation of clinical clerks. *New England Journal of Medicine, 302,* 1036–1037.

Marshall, V. R., & Ludbrook, J. (1972). The relative importance of patient and examiner variability in a test of clinical skills. *British Journal of Medical Education, 6,* 212–217.

Mazzuca, S. A., & Cohen, S. J. (1982). Scoring patient management problems: External validation of expert consensus. *Evaluation and the Health Professions, 5,* 210–217.

McGuire, C. H., & Babbott, D. (1967). Simulation technique in the measurement of problem-solving skills. *Journal of Educational Measurement, 4,* 1–10.

Meskauskas, J. A., & Norcini, J. J. (1980). Standard-setting in written and interactive (oral) specialty certification examinations: Issues, models, methods, challenges. *Evaluation and the Health Professions, 3,* 321–360.

Naftulin, D. H., Wolkon, G. H., Donnelly, F. A., Burgoyne, R. W., Kline, F. M., & Hansen, H. E. (1977). A comparison of videotaped and live patient interview examinations and written examinations in psychiatry. *American Journal of Psychiatry, 134,* 1093–1097.

Newble, D. I. (1976). The evaluation of clinical competence. *Medical Journal of Australia, 2,* 180–183.

Newble, D. I., Baxter, A., & Elmslie, R. G. (1979). A comparison of multiple-choice tests and free-response tests in examinations of clinical competence. *Medical Education, 13,* 263–268.

Newble, D. I., & Elmslie, R. G. (1981). A new approach to the final examinations in medicine and surgery. *Lancet, 2,* 517–518.

Newble, D. I., Elmslie, R. G., & Baxter, A. (1978). A problem-based criterion-referenced examination of clinical competence. *Journal of Medical Education, 53,* 720–726.

Newble, D. I., Hoare, J., & Elmslie, R. G. (1981). The validity and reliability of a new examination of the clinical competence of medical students. *Medical Education, 15,* 46–52.

Norman, G. R., & Feightner, J. W. (1981). A comparison of behaviour on simulated patients and patient management problems. *Medical Education, 15,* 26–32.

Norman, G. R., Tugwell, P., & Feightner, J. W. (1981). The validity of simulated patients. *Research in Medical Education: Proceedings of the Twentieth Annual Conference,* 215–220.

Norman, G. R., Tugwell, P., Jacoby, L. L., & Muzzin, L. J. (1983). The generalizability of measures of clinical problem solving. *Research in Medical Education: Proceedings of the Twenty-second Annual Conference,* 110–114.

Oaks, W. W., Scheinok, P. A., & Husted, F. L. (1969). Objective evaluation of a method of assessing student performance in a clinical clerkship. *Journal of Medical Education, 44,* 207–213.

O'Donohue, W. J., & Wergin, J. F. (1978). Evaluation of medical students during a clinical clerkship in internal medicine. *Journal of Medical Education, 53,* 55–58.

Orkin, F. K., & Greenhow, D. E. (1978). A study of decision making: How faculty define competence. *Anesthesiology, 48,* 267–271.

Page, G. G., & Fielding, D. W. (1980). Performance on PMPs and performance in practice: Are they related? *Journal of Medical Education, 55,* 529–537.

Payne, B. C. (1979). The medical record as a basis for assessing physician competence. *Annals of Internal Medicine, 91,* 623–629.

Printen, K. J., Chappell, W., & Whitney, D. R. (1973). Clinical performance evaluation of junior medical students. *Journal of Medical Education, 48,* 343–348.

Procci, W., Friedman, C., Prizant, G., & Woods, S. M. (1978). A national survey of resident assessment methods. *American Journal of Psychiatry, 135*, 845–847.

Quarrick, E. A., & Sloop, E. W. (1972). A method for identifying the criteria of good performance in a medical clerkship program. *Journal of Medical Education, 47*, 188–197.

Renaud, M., Beauchemin, J., Lalonde, C., Poirier, H., & Berthiaume, S. (1980). Practice settings and prescribing profiles: The simulation of tension headaches to general practitioners working in different practice settings in the Montreal area. *American Journal of Public Health, 70*, 1068–1073 (reprint).

Rimoldi, H. J. A. (1961). The test of diagnostic skills. *Journal of Medical Education, 36*, 73–79.

Rutala, P. J., Stillman, P. L., & Sabers, D. L. (1981a). Housestaff evaluation using patient instructors: A brief report. *Arizona Medicine, 38*, 531–532.

Rutala, P. J., Stillman, P. L., & Sabers, D. L. (1981b). Housestaff evaluation using patient instructors: A report of clinical competence. *Evaluation and the Health Professions, 4*, 419–432.

Sacks, H. R. (1959). Human relations training for law students and lawyers. *Journal of Legal Education, 11*, 316.

Sanazaro, P. J. (1980). Measurement of physicians' performance using existing techniques. *Western Journal of Medicine, 133*, 81–88.

Sarnacki, R. E. (1981). The effects of test-wiseness in medical education. *Evaluation and the Health Professions, 4*, 207–221.

Siker, E. S. (1981). A measure of competence. *Anaesthesia, 31*, 732–742.

Skakun, E. N. (1981). The clinical skills assessment form: A preliminary examination in pediatric clinical examinations. *Evaluation and the Health Professions, 4*, 330–337.

Stanton, B. C., Burstein, A. G., Kabos, J. C., & Loucks, S. (1979). The Dean's letter of recommendation and resident performance. *Journal of Medical Education, 54*, 812–813.

Sternburg, J. K., & Brockway, B. S. (1979). Evaluation of clinical skills: An asset-oriented approach. *Journal of Family Practice, 8*, 1243–1245.

Stillman, P. L. (1980). Arizona clinical interview medical rating scale. *Medical Teacher, 2*, 248–251.

Stillman, P. L., Brown, D. R., Redfield, D. L., & Sabers, D. L. (1977). Construct validation of the Arizona clinical interview rating scale. *Educational and Psychological Measurement, 37*, 1031–1038.

Stillman, P. L., & Burpeau-Di Gregorio, M. Y. (1982). Teaching and evaluating interviewing skills. *Advances in Behavioral Pediatrics, 5*, 109–145.

Stillman, P. L., Burpeau-DiGregorio, M. Y., Nicholson, G. I., Sabers, D. L., & Stillman, A. E. (1983). Six years of experience using patient instructors to teach interviewing skills. *Journal of Medical Education, 58*, 941–946.

Stillman, P. L., & Kettel, L. J. (1979). Non-physician patient instructors. *Arizona Medicine, 36*, 297–298.

Stillman, P. L., Ruggill, J. S., Rutala, P. J., Dinham, S. M., & Sabers, D. L. (1979). Students transferring into an American medical school: Remediating their deficiencies. *Journal of the American Medical Association, 243*, 129–133.

Stillman, P. L., Ruggill, J. S., Rutala, P. J., & Sabers, D. L. (1980). Patient instructors as teachers and evaluators. *Journal of Medical Education, 55,* 186–193.

Stillman, P. L., Ruggill, J. S., & Sabers, D. L. (1978). The use of practical instructors to teach and evaluate a complete physical examination. *Evaluation and the Health Professions, 1,* 49–54.

Stillman, P. L., Rutala, P. J., Nicholson, G. I., Sabers, D. L., & Stillman, A. E. (1982). Measurement of clinical competence of residents using patient instructors. *Research in Medical Education: Proceedings of the Twenty-first Annual Conference,* 111–116.

Stillman, P. L., Rutala, P. J., Stillman, A. E., & Sabers, D. L. (1982). Use of patient instructors to evaluate the clinical competence of physicians. *Proceedings of American Board of Medical Specialties Conference on Evaluation of Noncognitive Skills and Clinical Performance,* 127–138.

Stillman, P. L., & Sabers, D. L. Using a competency-based program to assess interviewing skills of pediatric house staff. *Journal of Medical Education, 53,* 493–496.

Stillman, P. L., Sabers, D. L., & Redfield, D. L. (1976). The use of paraprofessionals to teach and evaluate interviewing skills. *Pediatrics, 57,* 769–774.

Stillman, P. L., Sabers, D. L., & Redfield, D. L. (1977). Use of trained mothers to teach interviewing skills to first-year medical students: A follow-up study. *Pediatrics, 60,* 165–169.

Stillman, P. L., Silverman, A., Burpeau, M. Y., & Sabers, D. L. (1982). Use of client instructors to teach interviewing skills to law students. *Journal of Legal Education, 32,* 395–402.

Stimmel, B. (1975). The use of pass/fail grades to assess academic achievement and house staff performance. *Journal of Medical Education, 50,* 657–661.

Tamblyn, R., & Barrows, H. (1978). *Evaluation trial of the P4 system* (Problem-based learning system) (Monograph 4). Ontario. McMaster University.

Turner, E. V., Helper, M., Kriska, S. D., Singer, S. A., & Ruma, S. J. (1972). Evaluating clinical skills of students in pediatrics. *Journal of Medical Education, 47,* 959–965.

Van Wart, A. D. (1974). A problem-solving oral examination for family medicine. *Journal of Medical Education, 49,* 673–680.

Veloski, J., Herman, M. W., Gonnella, J. S., Zeleznik, C., & Kellow, W. F. (1979). Relationships between performance in medical school and first postgraduate year. *Journal of Medical Education, 54,* 909–916.

Vu, N. V. (1979). Medical problem-solving assessment: A review of methods and instruments. *Evaluation and the Health Professions, 2,* 281–307.

Vu, N. V., Johnson, R., & Mertz, S. A. (1981). Oral examination: A model for its use within a clinical clerkship. *Journal of Medical Education, 56,* 665–667.

Waterston, T., Cater, J. I., & Mitchell, R. G. (1980). An objective undergraduate clinical examination in child health. *Archives of Disease in Childhood, 55,* 917–922.

Wiener, S. L., Koran, L., Mitchell, P., Schattner, G., Fierstein, J., & Hotchkiss, E. (1976). Clinical skills quantitative measurement. *New York State Journal of Medicine, 76,* 610–612.

Wiener, S. L., & Nathanson, M. (1976). Physical examination frequently observed errors. *Journal of American Medical Association, 236,* 852–855.

Wigton, R. S. (1980). Factors important in the evaluation of clinical performance of internal medicine residents. *Journal of Medical Education, 55,* 206–208.

Willoughby, T. L., Gammon, L. C., & Jonas, H. S. (1979). Correlates of clinical performance during medical school. *Journal of Medical Education, 54,* 453–460.

Wingard, J. R., & Williamson, J. W. (1973). Grades as predictors of physicians' career performance: An evaluative literature review. *Journal of Medical Education, 48,* 311–322.

Woo, B., Jen, P., Rosenthal, P. E., Bunn, H. F., & Goldman, L. (1981). Anemic inpatients. *Archives of Internal Medicine, 141,* 1199–1202.

Woodward, C. A., & Dinham, S. M. (1982). Methodological factors in studying medical graduates: A review of six internship performance studies. *Evaluation and the Health Professions, 4,* 95–111.

Woolliscroft, J. O., Stross, J. L., & Silva, J., Jr. (1984). Clinical competence certification: A critical appraisal. *Journal of Medical Education, 59,* 799–805.

Zuckerman, A. E., Starfield, B., Hochreiter, C., & Kovasznay, B. (1975). Validating the content of pediatric outpatient medical records by means of tape-recording doctor-patient encounters. *Pediatrics, 56,* 407–411.

16. TEACHER EVALUATION

James Sweeney & Richard P. Manatt

Introduction

If education is the cornerstone upon which a great nation builds, then teaching is our most important human activity. Evaluating the competence or proficiency of the more than two million public elementary and secondary teachers who shoulder the responsibility for educating America's youth has become a hot issue, triggering a proliferation of journal articles and books replete with schemes and tips on how to evaluate teachers. The concern is hardly surprising. A 1978 study by Educational Research Services (Kowalski, 1978) found that 98 percent of the districts surveyed have some type of formal evaluation system. Many question the efficacy of those systems. Scriven (1981), of the Institute of Evaluation at the University of San Francisco, described teacher evaluation as a disaster, characterized by shoddy practices and unclear principles. He maintained that despite recent efforts to clarify issues and make procedures equitable and reasonably valid, there was not a single exemplary system in which practice matches the knowledge base. Soar, Medley, and Coker (1983) charged that practices are subjective, unreliable, biased, and based on irrelevancies. We must desist from feverishly building better mousetraps and examine the state of the art: where we have been, where we are, and where we wish to go.

As this chapter was being developed, we were reminded of our youthful experiences with erector sets. What were thought to be the finishing touches on a windmill sometimes turned out to be the first steps in dismantling, accompanied by the joy (and sorrow) of reexamining dozens of odd-shaped components. As we confidently set out to describe the major teacher evaluation models or systems, we ran into one small problem, and ended with a basketful of thingamabobs. While an optimist might describe teacher evaluation as chaotic, we are less charitable; teacher evaluation is a mess! Our goal in this chapter, however, is not to debunk but to explain and to suggest.

Teacher evaluation has an etiology and a context. We briefly address both in the first section. In the second section, we highlight the major philosophical and theoretical issues. The heart of the chapter is a description and critique of two models, the Redfern and the teacher performance evaluation models. We highlight the latter since it shows the direction we feel teacher evaluation systems should be heading. In the final section, we suggest directions for future research and development. While this chapter is an examination of current practices, our analysis is not value free. It reflects biases imposed by years of experience and study in the area.

446

The assessment of teacher performance, like many activities, is influenced by past practices; by movements in government, industry, and research; and by sociological factors influencing the values, sentiments, and preferences of American society. While the evolution of past practices is not completely discernible, the scrutiny of teachers appears to have been given its initial thrust in the English grammar school of the seventeenth century, where teacher competency was operationally defined as the teacher's proficiency in classroom and student management. A series of pamphlets published by Hoole (1659, reproduced in 1668 and 1907) captured the prevailing view of the era—the burden for learning was placed on the pupil, not on the teacher. If the classroom was correctly managed, then the pupil had ample opportunity for learning. A deficiency of learning was a sign of pupil irresponsibility. Providing the proper learning environment was the teacher's primary task. Thus it became the primary criterion by which to assess competency. Early American educators followed the lead of their colleagues across the sea. Horace Mann, upon visiting common schools in Massachusetts, observed that teachers were largely responsible for managing work and spent little time with individual students. Educators assumed that all children were equally capable of learning. Ergo, differences in student achievement were attributable to the extent to which students applied themselves.

The first "evaluators" on the American educational scene appeared in the early part of the eighteenth century in the form of committees of citizens whose primary tasks were to inspect the plant and check on pupil achievement. Since the citizens had no special professional expertise, they simply acted as checkers, making no effort to improve teaching or teachers (Wiles & Lovell, 1975).

The teacher's role and function, however, changed dramatically in the nineteenth century. While a number of factors contributed to this change, the demise of the one room school and the introduction of the Prussian system of dividing children into grades by age groups were most salient. Since teachers had smaller classes and also more uniformity in their assignments, it was presumed that they could improve learning through knowledge of subject matter and their ability to impart learning.

Early 1900s. Dovetailing with changes on the educational scene were dramatic events in American society in the early 1900s. The transition from an agricultural and craft society to an industrial society was part of a revolution marked by scientific management and a seemingly unquenchable thirst for efficiency. Frederick Winslow Taylor blazed the trail to efficiency and effectiveness. By virtue of his success with the Bethlehem Steel Company and other industries and the appeal of his classic work, *The Principles of Scientific Management* (1911), Taylor convinced leadership personnel across the nation that specialization, standardization, and other principles of industrial engineering unlocked the gates to organizational success. Educators jumped on the bandwagon. The work of

Charles Bobbitt (1912) and Elwood Cubberly (1916) was particularly noteworthy; both urged school administrators to work toward turning out a standard product with scientific measurement of the product. Children were *tabula rasa,* raw material to be shaped according to the specifications of society.

Measurement, particularly as it related to efficiency, was a major concern of leaders in the private sector. Not surprisingly, it spilled over into public schools. Two major studies reported by Davis in *Contemporary Research on Teacher Effectiveness* (1964) are illuminating. Boyce (1915) surveyed 350 cities of over ten thousand inhabitants, requesting a statement of their methods of determining and recording teacher efficiency. About 60 percent of the 242 cities that returned questionnaires reported using some type of rating or formal evaluation of teachers. Although the number of items on which teaching efficiency was judged ranged from as few as two to as many as eighty, four types of analysis prevailed: (1) descriptive reports dealing with specific points; (2) lists of questions answered by yes or no; (3) lists of items to be evaluated by a statistical classification, for example, excellent, good, medium, unsatisfactory; and (4) lists of items to each of which was assigned a numerical value representing the maximum score that might be given. Boyce's analysis of the instruments revealed that "discipline" was the quality most frequently assessed (98 percent), followed by "instructional skill" and "cooperation and loyalty" (60 percent each).

King (1925), in a report to the National Education Association, reported that at least 75 percent of the large city school systems were using some type of efficiency rating. His analysis of the instruments used in these schools revealed that "technique of instruction," "personality," and "classroom management" appeared most frequently (in the order presented), along with criteria such as "professional attitude," "cooperation," "health or vitality," and others. It should be noted that "discipline" and "classroom management" were separate categories in the analysis. When aggregated, they occupied the most frequently used category. King found that single words or descriptive phrases were by far the most popular response mode, followed by rankings, letters, and weighted point scales.

1930s and 1940s. A singular event, the success of the Hawthorne studies, pushed scientific management into the background and stimulated what has been labeled the "human relations era." The work of Mayo (1933) and of Roethlisberger and Dixon (1939) at the Hawthorne Plant of Western Electric convinced public and private sector managers that human relations was more influential in producing results than was rigid adherence to scientific principles. The informal organization and interpersonal relations were more important than specialization and standardization. Teacher evaluation reflected that theme. Reavis and Cooper (1945) found that the three items most frequently used for rating teachers were social relations, personal characteristics, and noninstructional school service. The researchers also noted that a five-point scale was most prevalent in rating teachers and that the same weaknesses that appeared in early evaluation systems were still present, namely, ambiguous terms, lack of definition of items, and items that linked two independent elements to form a single judgment.

1960s to the present. The 1960s and early 1970s were punctuated by social upheaval, a search for relevance in the classroom, and a thirst for individuality and human dignity in all activities. It is not surprising that the emotional content of lessons, measured by an instrument such as the Flanders Interaction Analysis (Flanders, 1960), was an object of scrutiny. Self-evaluation became popular; evaluation by an administrator was often a ceremonial rite, an opportunity for the supervisor to bestow general thanks and hand out other platitudes.

While relevancy and humanism are still alive, they may be breathing their last gasps, suffocated by a reincarnation of scientific management, this time in the guise of "accountability." Life in America is characterized by affluence, a glorification of individuality, and a belief that every American is entitled to a better and richer life. But the 1980s find America facing the menaces of inflation, unemployment, and scarce resources. Schools are threatened by declining enrollment, declining test scores, and by parents concerned about the alleged illiteracy of high school graduates. In a nervous economy, the public is demanding "a bang for their buck." Teacher evaluation appears to be here to stay; more than half of the states have enacted legislation mandating teacher evaluation (see Appendix).

PHILOSOPHICAL AND THEORETICAL ISSUES

Effective teacher evaluation is linked to the soundness of its underlying philosophical assumptions as well as to the elegance of its theoretical foundation. Unfortunately, both are bounded by an abundance of opinion, a dearth of facts, and a handful of dilemmas emanating from the basic questions that have plagued evaluators for decades: why, who, what, and how? A cursory review of the issues and their current standing is illuminating, for they are inextricably woven into the fabric of teacher evaluation, present and future.

Why evaluate teachers? Teacher evaluation has multiple, conflicting purposes. The purposes of evaluation are normally lumped under two complementary but dichotomous concepts: formative and summative evaluation. Formative evaluation is a continuous, year-long process in which the supervisor, usually the school principal, observes a teacher in the classroom and provides the teacher with specific, descriptive feedback about the lesson. They discuss the lesson (and teaching) and how to improve performance.

Summative evaluation has a different thrust. The supervisor utilizes a broad sample of information about a teacher's overall year-long performance to provide feedback and to make administrative decisions. It is primarily designed to identify the level at which the teacher performed during the evaluation period, to identify strengths, and to set goals for the following year. Therein lies the rub, and the classic dilemma plaguing evaluators—they are expected to do something *for* teachers while, implicitly, they may have to do something *to* them. Teachers have developed a strategy for dealing with this problem: game playing. Evaluation charades are enacted daily in school principals' offices across the nation. Teachers role play their way through conferences thinking, "No! No! No!" but saying, "Yes! Yes! Yes!"

Blumberg, a noted expert in supervision, presented the game-playing scenario as follows:

> Each side is aware of the game and it frequently gets played out to the end with each party feeling that he won. In supervision, it seems, games also get played. The teacher knows he is going to be observed and evaluated. He tells the students. If they like the teacher, they "take care of him" and the supervisor, who probably went through the same process as a beginning teacher, observes a good lesson. The teacher gets what he wants, and the supervisor gets what he wants. (1980, pp. 24–25)

Blumberg further maintained that as long as supervisors are saddled with the responsibility of rating teachers, they are incapable of establishing a collegial relationship with them and therefore are unable to provide help.

Who conducts the evaluation? At first blush, the question seems moot. In more than 90 percent of our schools, the principal has primary responsibility for formally evaluating teachers (Kowalski, 1978). Yet research on the efficiency of supervision does little to support the efficacy of present practice. Findings by Blumberg (1970) and others indicated that the evaluator is a source of anxiety and, therefore, is ineffective as a supervisor or helper.

Other approaches are being championed. A 1974 National School Public Relations Association report showed a trend toward *peer evaluation,* emanating from the apparent ability of peers to reduce threat and open communication levels between the evaluator and the evaluatee. But lack of training, time, and the reluctance of some teachers may hinder the movement. *Self-evaluation* has both supporters and critics. The former contend that the teacher is the best source of information regarding competency, while critics maintain self-evaluation is distorted by egocentrism or by professional or personal defensiveness. In practice, its use is limited. One-third of the school districts surveyed by Educational Research Services (Kowalski, 1978) required teachers to evaluate themselves, while other districts suggested it as an option and encouraged teachers to share the results with the principal.

There is also the matter of *student input* into evaluation. Although only a small percentage of schools use student evaluations (Kowalski, 1978), there are many who advocate more extensive usage. Aleamoni (1981) has written persuasively on the subject. He concluded that fifty years of extensive research at the college level indicates that student ratings are highly stable and represent a sound choice for evaluating higher education faculty. What little research exists at the elementary and secondary levels supports Aleamoni's position. Student ratings appear to be reliable (Bryan, 1963), and are reasonably good indicators of teacher influence on learning. In a well-designed study, McCall and Krause (1959) found the relationship between student ratings and student achievement gains to be higher than between supervisor's ratings and achievement.

In summary, while student ratings may be a valid measure of teacher performance, the political climate has limited their use. As teachers struggle for recognition as professionals, they vigorously reject evaluation by students. We foresee no change in their position. There has been little use of or research into the effectiveness of peer evaluation. Given the emergence of peer coaching and the utilization of peers as part of the team selecting teachers for career ladders and merit pay, this is a fertile area for future action and research.

What is evaluated? Research on teaching designed to produce factors related to quality of performance has been conducted for many years and has generated thousands of studies. Early studies were fruitless inasmuch as they focused on teacher characteristics rather than on the actual process of teaching in the classroom. Recent studies and meta-analyses of research on teaching have been more productive. A relatively new criterion (or set of criteria) has been eagerly embraced by educators. Researchers have identified effective teaching behaviors through *in situ* observation involving the systematic recording of a variety of specific, discrete teacher behaviors that are assumed, according to a theoretical framework, to be related to pupil growth. After these behaviors are observed and recorded, they are correlated with indices of pupil change to validate their importance. The correlational data are used to identify "more effective" and "less effective" teachers and teacher behaviors. Predictably, educators have concluded that the search for the Holy Grail has ended. In workshops across the country, evaluators are boning up on how to identify and rate effective teaching behaviors despite the fact that the researchers who uncovered the behaviors have issued strong caveats related to context. Content, grade level, and student characteristics are but a few of the factors that make generalization a risky business. The researchers' pleas, for the most part, have fallen on deaf ears. Evaluators are eager to use the recipe for good teaching. It is our guess that the behaviors uncovered by effective teaching research will continue to be the primary criterion used by the majority of school organizations. While in most school organizations, evaluative criteria include items that fall under "professional responsibility," most supervisors provide teachers with commendations for professionalism unless they are confronted with what they perceive as deviant behavior.

How should teachers be evaluated? "How?" is, of course, the major question. While there are a number of ways to skin the proverbial cat, with divergent views accompanying each, perhaps the issue that is most important and least agreed upon is how to gather and record the evidence. Bolton (1973) summarized the pertinent factors for ascertaining the quality of a teacher's performance as follows: (1) in-class behavior of the teacher as perceived by administrators and others; (2) out-of-classroom behavior as perceived by the administrators and others; and (3) student accomplishments as measured by standardized tests, teacher-made tests, student projects, and observation of student behavior. The debate rages as to which factors are most valid. Given the ambiguity and complexity inherent in teaching and learning, this is hardly surprising. If there is one area in which the parties to teacher assessment agree, it is on what might be labeled "data imperative"—the necessity for basing the evaluation on reliable and valid data. Common practice has changed dramatically. Evaluators once relied heavily on what they saw as they roamed the building, as well as on unannounced visits and how they felt about the teachers. Contractual agreements have rendered those practices obsolete, while advances in the technology have spawned an array of systematic evidence-gathering techniques designed to minimize the influence of observer bias and maximize the reliability of the data-gathering methods.

Principals and supervisors are being trained to gather descriptive, nonjudgmental data, to reproduce a "mirror of the classroom" for teachers. Acheson and Gall (1980) provided a comprehensive, clear description of the data-gathering process that includes anecdotal record keeping, time-on-task charting, and student-teacher interaction analysis. The rationale for gathering descriptive data is simple and intuitively appealing; not only is the teacher provided a descriptive account of the significant teacher and learner behaviors that occurred during a lesson, but both teacher and supervisor are afforded the opportunity to examine the lesson and discuss ways to improve teaching.

The majority of teacher evaluation systems also provide a cumulative rating of the teacher. The appraisal should be made after, not in conjunction with, classroom observation and other data collection, in order to summarize the frequency and quality of teacher behaviors associated with student achievement as well as assess their "professionalism." Since the level of teacher proficiency is a major concern, most instruments utilize some type of rating scale or a checklist that has the characteristics of a rating scale. The semantic differential scale, the Guttman scale, and various other types of scales enjoy some popularity, but summated ratings or Likert scales are used most frequently (Borich, 1977). Unfortunately, the use of rating scales provides further evidence that the science of measurement lags behind the art of evaluation. Since the distances between response alternatives on ordinal scales are unequal, and since the lower end denotes unacceptable performance or incompetence, the raters have a tendency to make judgments toward the upper end of the scale. This imbalance is even further exacerbated by a tendency to use other teachers' ratings as an anchoring point.

There is also what might be called "grade inflation." Most teachers (and administrators) have become conditioned to receiving high grades through their public and postsecondary educations. Most received an "A" in student teaching with accompanying plaudits. They tend to equate the rating scale with letter grades. As a result, a rating in the middle of the scale is viewed as a "C," even though the response may be "meets district standards." Many administrators, well aware of this and anxious to please the teachers, award the teacher a rating toward the upper end of the scale. Some evaluators still use a checklist for evaluating teachers. While the checklist does direct the evaluator's attention and lends a degree of objectivity, Griffith (1973) contended that it makes the evaluation a mechanical, routine procedure, neglects the relative weight of the items, highlights superficial items, and influences evaluators to make judgments without reflection and careful analysis. Rater bias, which has received considerable attention in the private sector, has been virtually ignored in teacher evaluation. We suspect that the clamor for merit pay will bring added scrutiny to rater bias.

Finally, there are still a number of school districts utilizing the open-ended approach. Typically, the principal is required to provide the teacher with feedback in selected areas. This is usually accomplished through a "comments" section in a written report where the supervisor points out strengths or areas for improvement. There is virtually no research as to the efficacy of this approach, but it is supposedly less threatening and more collegial and therefore more helpful. This method suffers from a lack of specificity, particularly with respect to the level or quality of performance.

What, then, do we have? We have an important activity beset by conflicting purposes and political infighting on the verge of open warfare. We have uncertainty as to who should gather evidence on elusive criteria on which there has been more disagreement than agreement, plus a tangled web of measurement devices. We also have some significant trends. The school principal has been accorded the responsibility for evaluation. It appears that effective teaching behaviors will be the criteria for evaluating teacher performance. While principals struggle with the summative versus formative dilemma, it appears that they will use narrative reporting for formative data gathering and rating scales to record the summative judgments. How evaluations will be conducted remains to be seen.

Survey of Teacher Evaluation Models

School organizations employ virtually hundreds of approaches to assessing teacher competency. Most are very similar; some are remarkably different. Consider the following. As we examined the various methods, we found a school district that had a formal evaluation system with no summative component. Evaluation was designed solely to help teachers improve; therefore a judgment on the level of proficiency was studiously avoided. In another rather large district, a much different approach was noted. The evaluation process was specifically designed to weed out unsatisfactory teachers. Any member of the school community—parent, employee, student—can request, in writing, a "review of service." If the teacher is deemed in need of remediation, a team provides intensive assistance and performance is monitored. If the teacher has not improved after five months, he or she is terminated with thirty days notice.

To uncover the significant models used by school organizations, we decided to forsake the product-process approaches and apply five criteria. These five criteria were suggested by Strike and Bull (1981), who contended that for a school organization to make evaluations legal and morally acceptable, the evaluation system must (1) make clear the formal administrative policies of the school board and provide a reasonably precise explanation of the criteria for effective teaching of uniform procedures for making personnel decisions; (2) guarantee that the evaluation will focus only on those aspects of a teacher's performance behavior and activities that are directly or indirectly relevant to the teacher's ability to execute the legitimate responsibilities of the job; (3) allow teachers legal due process; (4) be nonalienating, produce cooperative working relationships, and aim at increasing the professional skills of the teaching staff; and (5) share the evaluation data with teachers and provide them with assistance. A number of evaluation schemes exhibited salient characteristics, but only two, the Redfern model and teacher performance evaluation (TPE), appeared to have sound philosophical and theoretical bases and to incorporate the criteria into a coherent system.

REDFERN MODEL

The use of behavior patterns in setting goals became popular in the private sector in the 1950s and 1960s, spread to government, and then emerged in schools. The Redfern model is anchored in two assumptions: (1) teachers have inherent competencies that can be identified and described, and (2) these competencies can be expressed in terms of techniques that are instrumental in carrying out the teaching/learning process and in attaining measurable learner outcomes (Redfern, 1980). Therefore appraisal procedures can be designed to ascertain the extent to which an individual demonstrates such competencies. The evaluator and evaluatee work together as partners to reach these objectives. While the model centers on setting and assessing performance objectives, it has six components that are sequenced to produce the cyclical process shown in Figure 16.1.

Definition of responsibility criteria. The first step in the evaluation process is to define the content and scope of the job responsibility criteria. These criteria

FIGURE 16.1. The Redfern model

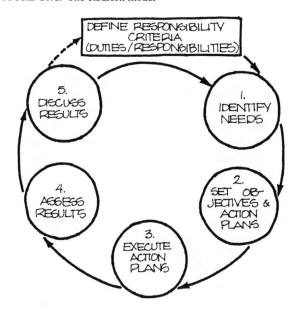

are expressed as broad statements with descriptors of teacher behaviors that define each criterion more explicitly. For example, "motivates students" serves as a criterion for assessing all teachers. A typical descriptor for the criterion might be "utilize positive feedback, praise, and rewards." Criteria and descriptors are linked by a numbering system that subsequently facilitates the identification of needs.

Identification of needs. Implementing this component requires a mutual effort by the evaluator and evaluatee. Needs are defined by gaps between ideal and actual performance. A useful way to identify needs is to regard them as areas to emphasize in order to attain the maximum degree of improvement in performance.

Setting of objectives and action plans. Objective setting helps to ameliorate deficiencies and to meet the needs of teachers who desire improvement. While Redfern leaves the door open for those who wish to write performance objectives in general terms, the valence of specific objectives written in behavioral terms is emphasized. Objectives, whether general or behavioral, should be accompanied by an action plan—a description of how the evaluator and evaluatee will work together to reach objectives. It typically includes, but is not limited to, (1) the kinds and amount of assistance the evaluator will provide, (2) the extent of observations or other contacts that the evaluator will make with the evaluatee, (3) the frequency of follow-up and feedback conferences, and (4) an explanation of the type of data that will be collected and used in making the assessments.

Execution of action plans. During this phase, the evaluator monitors the evaluatee's performance and gathers a substantial volume of appropriate data related to teacher performance. While collecting data, the evaluator must be sure (1) to collect relevant information, (2) to obtain representative data (i.e., samples of the full range of performance behavior), and (3) to use a variety of techniques throughout the process. The evaluator works hard to assure the person being evaluated that data are being collected for analysis and that subsequently the evaluatee will play an active role in the data analysis and assessment.

Assessment of results. Although the assessment of results focuses primarily on the extent to which performance objectives have been achieved, it does not preclude assessments of overall accomplishment. Whatever the intent, it should be clearly understood by participants prior to the process and reinforced throughout. While data may be collected by surveying students, from electronic devices (audio and video recordings), and from other sources, Redfern advocates self-evaluation and supervisor evaluation as the major interacting components in the process. Self-evaluation is a guide for planning further self-improvement; supervisor evaluation provides the evaluatee with objective evidence of his or her performance in the responsibility criteria. Assessment and data gathering are not a one-shot activity; they are continuous and ongoing. To communicate the achievement of performance objectives and overall performance, it is necessary to record the assessment on a summative evaluation report. The report provides the evaluator with an opportunity to furnish the evaluatee with comments explaining ratings of performance. Less than satisfactory ratings must be accompanied by anecdotal comments; there is typically a space for the evaluatee to respond.

Discussion of results. According to Redfern, the evaluation conference is perhaps the most important component of the process, for it provides both parties with an opportunity to discuss progress and to increase their understanding of goals and problems. Emphasis in evaluation conferences should not be solely on discussing problems. Redfern recommends that the conference discussion include (1) discussion of long- and short-range goals and objectives, (2) recognition of good work, (3) exchange of suggestions for improvement, (4) selection of top-priority job tasks or job targets, (5) clarification of the responsibilities of both parties, (6) correction of misinformation and misunderstanding, and (7) attention to whatever other topics may seem important to either party at that particular time.

The final activity provides the impetus for recycling the process. The evaluator and evaluatee once again identify needs from an assessment of performance based on the data and the perceptions that both bring to the evaluation conference. These needs are translated into performance objectives as the cycle continues to flow. Follow-up planning by the evaluator plays an important role; it helps to outline the activities that he or she should carry out to promote the development of the individual.

Advantages and disadvantages of the model. The Redfern model is a systematic approach to assessing teacher competency. It has several advantages:

1. It provides clear perceptions of performance expectations plus evaluation based on predetermined criteria related to teacher duties and responsibilities.
2. It provides opportunity for mutual discussion of teacher strengths and weaknesses plus feedback to refine performance.
3. It provides for specific, concise, and measurable objectives for performance improvement.
4. It provides documentation of the extent of competency through early identification of deficiencies and help in overcoming them.
5. It places the responsibility for improvement with the teacher, thus raising the level of concern and the desire to improve.

The Redfern model, like any approach, is open to questions related to its underlying assumptions and application of technical concepts. It seems relevant here to concentrate on the major propositions that anchor the system. We raise three questions: the first is related to what Redfern has labeled "a partnership in evaluation," the second deals with the type of written objectives used, and the third addresses the use of student achievement scores as an evaluative criterion.

Question 1: Is performance evaluation a partnership? This is a most important question, for mutuality is the cornerstone upon which the model is built. Redfern maintained that evaluation and supervision are compatible, that mutual goal setting removes the hesitancy that supervisors generally exhibit toward rating, and that the approach encourages a partnership between the evaluator and evaluatee. This has not been our experience. Given the unpredictability of today's labor market, the frailties of human nature, and the fragile relationship between principals and teachers, we wonder if mutual goal setting is possible within the context of evaluation.

The difficulties inherent in the self-formulation of realistic job targets has been well documented in times of less stress and strain (National School Public Relations Association, 1974). One wonders about the equality of the partnership between evaluator and evaluatee. In *Evaluating Teachers and Administrators: A Performance Objective Approval* (1980), Redfern referred to "partners in the duet" in his description of responsibilities in carrying out the plan. The term has the ring of clinical supervision. Performance evaluation and clinical supervision should not be confused. Evaluation of teachers must assess their competence, despite its other lofty goals. Clinical supervision has as its goal professional growth, not inspection. There may be no inherent danger in packaging an evaluation model as a partnership; indeed, it is less threatening to teachers and supervisors to do so. Both parties, however, will be rudely awakened when problems surface.

Question 2: Can expected outcomes be effectively translated into behavioral terms? This question has been raised before. Cardellichio (1974) explored the issue a decade ago. Written performance objectives are a vital component of the model. Redfern noted that there is a place for general goals, but they are difficult to measure and do not lend themselves to documentation. He lauds the elegance of precise behavioral objectives. But by his own admission, they are of little use in formulating targets in the affective domain. While Redfern advised prospective users to ponder the merits and demerits of both general goals and behavioral objectives, he provided little guidance, claiming time and circumstances will determine the best approach. What circumstances should be considered and how much time is required for the formulation of appropriate objectives remain unanswered.

Question 3: Are student achievement scores a valid and reliable method of assessing teacher efficacy? The answer to this question would appear to be a resounding "No!" While Redfern recommended that student achievement data be included in the evaluation data, the research evidence strongly suggests that the use of student achievement scores for evaluating the productivity of teachers is not only unproductive but probably counterproductive. Soar, Medley, and Coker (1983) pointed out three major problems: (1) student variability (individual differences in intelligence, previous knowledge, home background, peer groups, learning styles, and other factors, over which teachers have little or no control, strongly influence student achievement); (2) regression effect (gain scores of students are biased such that teachers of high-achieving students will consistently show less annual gain than those of low-ability students); and (3) limitations of achievement tests (standardized tests measure important but more limited, simpler objectives of education). It is doubtful whether multiple-choice tests alone measure what we want students to extract from learning experiences.

Berk (1984) recently scrutinized the issue in the context of merit pay—is a direct measure of productivity (test scores) a feasible approach to measuring and rewarding teacher productivity? His extensive review of research supported the conclusions of Soar, Medley, and Coker (1983). He came to the following conclusions:

1. The pretest-posttest gain score model is afflicted with numerous sources of invalidity and measurement error.
2. Between-class, between-grade, and between-subject variability of objectives, instruction, resources, and student characteristics pre-

clude (a) the trouble-free selection of an appropriate achievement test, (b) the precise estimation of gain, (c) the setting of a meaningful criterion for superior teacher productivity, and (d) the inference that estimated gain is attributable solely to teacher effort.

3. Although there does not seem to be any single source of invalidity or error (systematic or random) that is large enough to invalidate the model, the combination of multiple sources analyzed cumulatively does prove fatal and warrants rejection of the model.

4. Gain score evidence can be so misleading that it should not even be used to corroborate other evidence of teacher effectiveness or performance (e.g., administrator ratings). (1984, p. 25)

Berk therefore argues that "it is premature to use achievement gain scores to infer superior teacher productivity as criteria for awarding merit pay. . . . Such a practice [is] indefensible" (1984, p. 25).

Inclusion of student achievement data in the Redfern model appears to be neither theoretically sound nor consistent with the model's philosophical base.

TEACHER PERFORMANCE EVALUATION MODEL

The teacher performance evaluation model (TPE) developed by Manatt is a product of many years of research, investigation, and practical experience in teacher evaluation. It flows from two basic assumptions: (1) participatory planning offers maximum opportunity to incorporate organizational members' preferences and needs into the system, and (2) formative and summative evaluations are necessary components of a successful evaluation system.

Planning. Planning is a prerequisite for important organizational endeavors. TPE enables the school organization to involve the school community in planning a system that is congruent with the school's goals and philosophy while providing an opportunity to test and try the system. The planning process includes development of three major components: (1) evaluation instruments and procedures, (2) evaluator training, and (3) ongoing staff development to improve instructional leadership. Figure 16.2 shows the time frame of the system development, as well as the system components.

The steering committee is the fulcrum of the process. Ten to twenty people are chosen according to the contribution each can make to the total effort. Typically, the committee includes teachers from a variety of curriculum areas and grade levels, administrators, parents, board of education members, and secondary school students. The committee's major tasks are (1) to create and manage the timeline, (2) to serve as a link to the board and superintendent, (3) to determine the use of consultants, (4) to guide system development, and (5) to inform and consult with the staff.

Usually, five subcommittees are designated, each with a specific charge. As they meet and confer, they generate ideas that are discussed with the total group

FIGURE 16.2. Time frame for developing a performance evaluation system

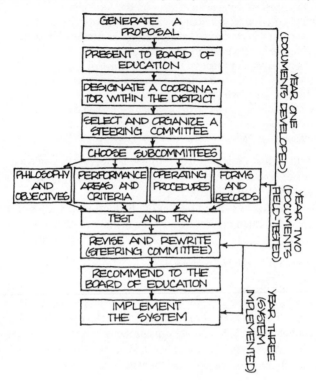

and used to develop prototypic instruments and procedures. The philosophy and objectives subcommittee has an important role: it must clearly define the purpose of the evaluation system and communicate it across all levels of the school organization. Productive teaching behavior is defined by the performance areas and criteria subcommittee. The operational procedures subcommittee determines procedures and establishes the TPE cycle. The forms and records subcommittee determines the most efficient way to record data and prepares the appropriate documents. The test-and-try subcommittee, in addition to planning the orientation and determining the extent of training needed by the evaluators, designs the field test that precedes system implementation. While TPE is a stand-alone system, many school organizations tie administrator performance evaluation (APE) to it, implementing TPE in the first year and APE in the second.

TPE cycle. The TPE cycle is an integral part of the model. Figure 16.3 depicts the flow of activities that make up a cycle that provides both formative and summative evaluation. The preobservation conference begins the formative pro-

FIGURE 16.3. Flow chart of TPE cycle

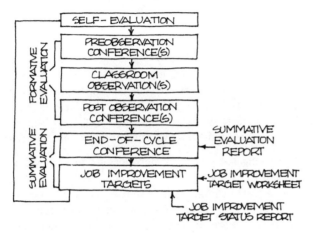

cess. The teacher and evaluator meet briefly and discuss the lesson to be observed. The evaluator then observes the lesson, using whatever data-gathering techniques are appropriate, considering the objectives of the lesson as well as other factors. Since the data collected in the lesson are for formative purposes, they are usually recorded in a narrative form, although they may be reflected in frequencies of teacher or learner behaviors. These data are used in the postobservation conferences as the basis for discussion of the teacher's performance in the lesson. This process may be repeated several times, depending on contractual agreements and need.

The end-of-cycle conference is a summative assessment of the teacher's performance. The assessment is recorded on the summative evaluation instrument that was developed by the forms and records subcommittee. During the end-of-cycle conference, job improvement targets are discussed and formalized in writing. The summative evaluation report and job improvement targets are used to initiate reentry into the cycle the following year.

Advantages and disadvantages of TPE. There are two sources of evidence for the analysis of this model: (1) the application of the criteria, and (2) a data base generated by the track record of the model in a number of school systems. TPE has the following advantages:

1. It provides an opportunity for the participants to tailor the system to meet their needs.
2. It provides a timeline and methods for field-testing procedures and prototypic instruments as well as for refining both.

3. The steering committee and subcommittees provide optimum opportunity for teacher and administrator interaction, involvement, and consultation.
4. The TPE cycle provides for both formative and summative evaluation. It guarantees teachers the opportunity to receive assistance throughout the year while providing the board of education and community assurance that a systematic process for assessing and improving performance is in place.
5. Job improvement targets define the professional development goals of teachers, the timeline for reaching these goals, and the role of the supervisor in assisting teachers to achieve their goals.
6. It provides for professional growth activities for teachers and supervisors.

In summary, TPE contains the essential ingredients of an effective evaluation: (a) a logical and workable system, clearly defined procedures, and instrumentation that fits the school organization; (b) a vehicle to enhance consultation and information giving; (c) the opportunity for continuous performance improvement; and (d) components that are conceptually sound and congruent with the organization's philosophy and objectives.

TPE is not a panacea, nor has it achieved perfection. Although one of its obvious strengths is participatory planning, certain aspects are open to question. Incorporating a clinical supervision cycle into a process that culminates in summative evaluation is no easy task. Finally, there is the matter of job improvement targets. Three questions address these issues.

Question 1: Should the planning process be revised? The TPE planning process explicitly provides for representative participation in decisions regarding system development and implementation. Yet because of its extensive usage, TPE has been refined to a point where many of its instruments and processes appear to be relatively efficient and effective. While there are a number of important decisions for the steering committee and subcommittees to make, the leadership is often more intent on gaining acceptance of the system. For example, the philosophy and objectives subcommittee has the very real task of developing and articulating the purpose of the system, while other (test-and-try) subcommittees act more like "checkers," making small revisions in documents or adjusting time periods. There is some danger in a system that offers a democratic approach in areas where personnel are involved in decisions. As teacher organizations become more concerned and involved in the evaluation process, perhaps it would be wise to delimit the discretion of the subcommittees.

Question 2: Should job improvement targets be included in the formative cycle? In a number of school organizations, the busy principal observes the teacher once and holds a postobservation conference, which is also the end-of-cycle conference. This short-circuits the cycle and is of little assistance in helping the teacher to improve. It seems likely that if the supervisor conducts a classroom observation early in the year, then assists the teacher in developing job improvement targets, and later observes the teacher and conducts a second conference, it would enhance growth and make the end-of-cycle conference and end-of-year job improvement target more effective. While it is presently recommended that supervisors hold two or more conferences with teachers, many principals, claiming a lack of time, revert to the minimum contractual stipulation. Building goal setting into the system might help to enhance the system.

Question 3: Can TPE improve on the use of job improvement targets? Despite the fact that principals and supervisors receive vigorous training in writing job improvement targets, the targets set tend to be in unimportant areas and are poorly written. Targets are often vague, and supervisors fail to specify what behaviors the teacher must exhibit to meet them. A bank of important job targets, written so as to make them effective vehicles for improvement, might alleviate this weakness. Obviously, the principals must modify the target by specifying target dates, the assistance to be provided, and the assessment.

Future Directions and Needs

Teacher assessment is here, and it is here to stay. One is reminded of the fable of the grasshopper and the owl:

> It seemed that the grasshopper suffered severe pains in the winter because of the savage cold. In distress, he sought the advice of the wise old owl, who gave him this counsel, "Simply turn yourself into a cricket and hibernate during the winter." Having received this wonderful advice, the grasshopper was overjoyed. Joy turned to sorrow, however, when he discovered this knowledge could not be transformed into action. Upon confronting the owl, he was admonished: "Look," said the owl, "I gave you the principle. It's up to you to work out the details."

The story has value to those who assess teacher competence. We must stop tilting at windmills, build our knowledge base, and work out the details.

There is a desperate need to develop teacher evaluation centers at selected sites across the nation. This development effort should be a cooperative venture between school organizations and centers, as well as between centers. In addition to conducting research and developing the system, centers should provide assistance to school organizations and disseminate important findings and advancements to them.

The next question to be addressed seems obvious: In what specific areas should we concentrate the research and development effort? Our extensive literature review and experience with TPE suggest that we focus on the following goals.

1. *Continue and broaden the effort to identify effective teaching criteria.* Despite the tremendous value of recent research findings, we must go further by investigating the relationship between situational elements and effective training. We also need to identify criteria for effectiveness in special areas (e.g., music, practical arts, physical education).

2. *Perform task analysis on each of the evaluation components.* Classroom observation and supervisory conferences should be high on that list, for data gathering and feedback constitute the heart of evaluation.

3. *Develop training packages for teaching evaluators the necessary skills.* No model is effective unless it provides training for evaluators. Classroom observation and supervisory conferences, the most essential activities, are complex technical and human activities requiring a minimum of fifty hours of training.

4. *Develop a subsystem for assisting the marginal or unsatisfactory teacher.* There is little substantive information on how to help these individuals. It is a subject of great concern to supervisors.

5. *Develop efficient ways to instruct teacher evaluators in the elements of effective teaching.* Approaches that take hundreds of hours are admirable but consume too much time and money, resources that are in short supply. It seems likely that concepts and methods could be condensed and implemented more efficiently.

We have omitted a dimension that has tremendous potential—the use of the computer in evaluation research and development. The potential uses of data banks are unlimited. One would hope that the power of the computer in research and development will not be overlooked.

FINAL THOUGHTS

The most striking aspect of teacher evaluation is its inevitability. Describing the state of the art is bittersweet; the lack of uniformity is disturbing but progress made in the last half decade is encouraging. Earlier in the chapter, it was pointed out that teacher evaluation does not occur in a vacuum; it has a context, tethered to social action and thought. To date, three states (Florida, California, and North Carolina) have enacted legislation mandating some form of merit pay. It remains an open question as to whether teacher evaluation, which is such a highly individual activity, can experience great success in today's social milieu. It is a practical imperative that we give to this effort every possible resource that we can muster. We are extremely optimistic. We have recently completed a major project that indicates that training, self-analysis, and peer coaching using videotapes significantly improves the conferencing skills of supervisors.

At Iowa State University, we have research and development activities aimed at improving classroom observation and data-gathering skills. A data bank of job improvement targets and instructional videotapes or videodiscs to help teachers improve is being developed. Supervision remains, as it always will, an art. But as we enhance the technical dimension, we narrow its ambiguity and increase its utility. The future of teacher evaluation rests on our ability (1) to maintain an environment that stimulates professional growth, (2) to improve processes and systems that provide fundamental fairness to all involved, (3) to enhance the interpersonal skills of our supervisors, and (4) to perfect technical skills. It will require a tremendous commitment on the part of teachers, supervisors, and researchers. The key, in our view, is systematic research and development, driven by debate within the academic community and between community members and practitioners.

It will be difficult, not simple. It will take great commitment and diligence. However, to the extent that we are slipshod, unfair, or shirk our responsibility, we are harming teachers and students.

APPENDIX. STATES REQUIRING TEACHER EVALUATION

States	Statute/ Regulation	Year(s) Established	Dismissal	Purpose Improve- ment	Account- ability
Arizona	Statute	1981		x	
Arkansas	Statute	1979	x		
California	Statute	1972/1976		x	
Connecticut	Statute	1974		x	
Florida	Statute	1961		x	
Georgia*					
Hawaii	Statute	1965	x	x	
Iowa	Statute	1976	x		
Kansas	Statute	1973		x	
Kentucky	Regulation	1981		x	
Louisiana	Statute	1977/1980		x	
Nevada	Statute	1973/1979	x	x	
New Jersey	Both	1973/1977/ 1979		x	
New Mexico	Regulation	1974/1981		x	
North Carolina	Statute	1982		x	x
Ohio	Both	1968/1980		x	
Oklahoma	Statute	1977	x	x	
Oregon	Statute	1971/1979	x	x	
Pennsylvania	Both	1949 (as amended)	x	x	
South Carolina	Statute	1979	x	x	
South Dakota		1969/1975	x	x	

(continued)

APPENDIX *(cont.)*

States	Statute/ Regulation	Year(s) Established	Purpose		
			Dismissal	Improve-ment	Account-ability
Tennessee	Statute	1979		x	
Texas	Statute	1975	x	x	
Vermont	Regulation	1981			x
Virginia	Statute	1972		x	
Washington	Statute	1975	x	x	
West Virginia	Statute	Unknown	x	x	

*Georgia requires teacher performance appraisal for probationary teachers only (three years).

References

Acheson, K., & Gall, M. (1980). *Techniques in the clinical supervision of teachers.* New York: Longmans.

Aleamoni, L. M. (1981). Student ratings of instruction. In J. Millman (Ed.), *Handbook of teacher evaluation* (pp. 110–145). Beverly Hills, CA: Sage.

Berk, R. A. (1984, March). *The use of student achievement test scores as criteria for allocation of teacher merit pay.* Paper presented at the National Conference on Merit Pay for Teachers, Sarasota, FL.

Blumberg, A. (1970). *Supervision and teachers: A private cold war.* Berkeley, CA: McCutchan.

Bobbitt, J. F. (1912). The elimination of waste in education. *Elementary School Teacher, 12,* 260.

Bolton, D. (1973). *Selection and evaluation of teachers.* Berkeley, CA: McCutchan.

Borich, G. D. (1977). *The appraisal of teaching: Concepts and process.* Reading, MA: Addison-Wesley.

Boyce, A. C. (1915). Methods of measuring teachers' efficiency. In *The fourteenth yearbook of the National Society for the Study of Education* (Part 2). Chicago: University of Chicago Press.

Bridges, E. M. (1974). Faculty evaluation—A critique and a proposal. *Administrator's Notebook, 22,* 1–4.

Bryan, R. C. (1963). *Reactions to teachers by students, parents, and administrators* (United States Office of Education, Cooperative Research Project No. 668). Kalamazoo: Western Michigan University.

Cardellichio, T. L. (1974). Evaluating teachers' methods. *NASSP Bulletin, 58,* 8–12.

Cubberly, E. (1916). *Public school administration.* Boston, MA: Houghton Mifflin.

Davis, H. (1964). Evolution of current practices in evaluating teacher competence. In B. J. Biddle & W. J. Ellena (Eds.), *Contemporary research on teacher effectiveness* (pp. 641–679). New York: Holt, Rinehart and Winston.

Flanders, N. A. (1960). *Interaction analysis in the classroom: A manual for observers.* Unpublished manuscript, University of Michigan.

Galloway, C. M. (1973). The nonverbal realities of classroom life. In C. Beegle & R. Brandt (Eds.), *Observational methods in the classroom* (pp. 44–45). Washington, DC: Association for Supervision and Curriculum Development.

Glass, G. V. (1974). A review of three methods of determining teacher effectiveness. In H. J. Walberg (Ed.), *Evaluating educational performance* (pp. 11–32). Berkeley, CA: McCutchan.

Griffith, F. (1973). *A handbook for the observation of teaching and learning.* Midland, MI: Pendell.

Hoole, C. (1907). Scholastic discipline. *American Journal of Education, 17,* 293–324.

King, L. A. (1925). The present status of teacher rating. *American School Board Journal, 70,* 44–46.

Kowalski, J. P. S. (1978). Evaluating teacher performance (ERS Report No. 219-21618). Arlington, VA: Educational Research Services.

Lewis, A. C. (1982). *Evaluating educational personnel.* Arlington, VA: American Association of School Administrators.

Mayo, E. (1933). *The social problems of an industrial civilization.* Cambridge, MA: Harvard University Press.

McCall, W., & Krause, G. (1959). Measurement of teacher merit. *Journal of Educational Research, 53,* 73–75.

Medley, D. M. (1973). Measuring the complex classroom of today. In C. W. Beegle & R. M. Brandt (Eds.), *Observational methods in the classroom.* Washington, DC: Association for Supervision and Curriculum Development.

Millman, J. (Ed.) (1981). *Handbook of teacher evaluation.* Beverly Hills, CA: Sage.

National School Public Relations Association. (1974). *Evaluating teachers for professional growth: Current trends in school policies and programs.* Arlington, VA: Authors.

Pine, G. J., & Boy, A. V. (1975). Necessary conditions for evaluating teachers. *NASSP Bulletin, 59,* 18–23.

Popham, W. J., & McNeil, J. D. (1973). The assessment of teacher competence. In R. M. Travers (Ed.), *Second handbook of research on teaching* (pp. 230–236). Chicago: Rand McNally.

Reavis, W. C., & Cooper, D. H. (1945). *Evaluation of teacher merit in city school systems* (Supplementary Educational Monographs No. 59). Chicago: University of Chicago Press.

Redfern, G. B. (1980). *Evaluating teachers and administrators: A performance objectives approach.* Boulder, CO: Westview Press.

Roethlisberger, F. J., & Dixon, W. J. (1939). *Management and the worker.* Cambridge, MA: Harvard University Press.

Scriven, M. (1981). Summative teacher evaluation. In J. Millman (Ed.), *Handbook of teacher evaluation* (pp. 244–271). Beverly Hills, CA: Sage.

Soar, R. S., Medley, D. M., & Coker, H. (1983). Teacher evaluation: A critique of currently used methods. *Phi Delta Kappan, 65,* 239–246.

Stow, S., & Sweeney, J. (1981). Developing a teacher performance evaluation system. *Educational Leadership, 38,* 538–542.

Strike, K., & Bull, B. (1981). Fairness and the legal context of teacher evaluation. In J. Millman (Ed.), *Handbook of teacher evaluation* (pp. 303–341). Beverly Hills, CA: Sage.

Sweeney, J., & Stow, S. (1981). Performance improvement—A people program. *Education, 101,* 267–269.

Taylor, F. W. (1911). *The principles of scientific management.* New York: Harper and Row.

Wiles, W., & Lovell, J. T. (1975). *Supervision for better schools.* Englewood Cliffs, NJ: Prentice-Hall.

Wuhs, S. (1982). *State mandates for evaluation.* Unpublished manuscript, Iowa State University.

17. STUDENT EVALUATION

Richard J. Stiggins & Nancy J. Bridgeford

Introduction

Teachers use many assessment methods to track student growth and development. They devise many of those assessments themselves. Some are paper-and-pencil measures; others are based on behavioral observations. This chapter explores teachers' observation and rating of student behavior and products as these measures relate to the larger context of day-to-day classroom assessment. Specifically, the discussion addresses (a) teachers' skills, attitudes, perceptions, and concerns about day-to-day classroom assessment; (b) the extent to which performance tests (behavioral observations and ratings) versus other forms of assessment are used in classrooms; (c) the nature of classroom performance tests (uses, exercises, responses, and performance rating procedures); and (d) whether (or how) teachers check and attempt to improve the quality of their classroom performance assessments.

The measurement community has tended to limit its study of testing in the schools to the role of large-scale standardized testing programs. Far less attention has been given to the nature or quality of teacher-developed classroom assessments. And almost no attention has been given to the nature or quality of observational assessment methods like performance assessment. For example, nearly all major recent studies of teachers' testing practices and attitudes have focused on the role of standardized tests in the education process (Airasian et al., 1977; Goslin, 1967; Kellaghan, Madaus, & Airasian, 1982; Lortie, 1975; Rudman et al., 1980; Salmon-Cox, 1981; Sproull & Zubrow, 1981; Stetz & Beck, 1979). A recent special issue of the *Journal of Educational Measurement* on the state of the art in linking testing and instruction is introduced as follows:

> Linking testing and instruction is a fundamental and enduring concern in educational practice. . . . Fundamental questions about how well achievement test items reflect both student knowledge and the content of instruction are clearly at the heart of the matter. . . . Yet the

The material presented in this chapter represents an adaptation of a paper entitled "The Ecology of Classroom Assessment" published in the *Journal of Educational Measurement, 22*, 271–286, copyright 1985, National Council on Measurement in Education, Washington, D.C. The research was conducted under Contract No. 400-83-005 with the National Institute of Education (NIE). Opinions expressed do not necessarily reflect the position of NIE, and no official endorsement should be inferred.

contributors to this special issue were asked to limit their conception of achievement testing to include standardized achievement tests, curriculum embedded or locally developed domain-referenced and proficiency tests, and state assessments. *Thus, teacher made tests . . . were systematically excluded.* (Burstein, 1983, p. 99; italics added)

Thus this "state of the art" review linking testing and instruction was limited by the kind of test information obtained from instruments developed outside of the classroom—measures providing only a portion of the data teachers use to integrate testing and instruction.

This emphasis by measurement researchers on large-scale and standardized tests may result from the strong tradition of scientific inquiry in educational research and psychometric models in educational measurement (Calfee & Drum, 1976; Coffman, 1983). These emphases lead to admonitions in our measurement testbooks that teachers should strive to gather "hard data" on student achievement by relying on objective tests. Yet several researchers conclude from their studies of testing in the schools that teachers purposefully go beyond test scores and are intent on using observation-based modes of assessment to acquire information for decision making. For example, in a national study of classroom assessment, Herman and Dorr-Bremme (1982) report that almost all survey respondents reported that their own observations and students' class work were crucial sources of information. In another study, Salmon-Cox (1981) found that teachers, when talking of how they assess their students, most frequently mention "observation," not standardized tests. And Kellaghan, Madaus, and Airasian (1982) pointed out that standardized test information was clearly a secondary criterion in teacher judgment. Nearly all teachers reported that the most common grouping criteria were the teachers' own observations and tests.

In fact, the Herman and Dorr-Bremme study, along with that of Yeh (1978), are among the few investigations of testing in the schools to go beyond the role of standardized tests and focus on teacher-developed tests. Their national survey results suggest that, depending on grade level, a third to three-quarters of tests used in the classroom are teacher developed.

If measurement researchers continue to emphasize only those tests that serve large-scale assessment purposes, we may fail to serve teachers' primary measurement needs. Measurement training that relies on traditional objective tests does not meet the day-to-day assessment needs of teachers. It disregards the full range of measurement options available to teachers and, more important, it fails to help teachers obtain the types of data needed to address the day-to-day decisions they face. The discussion presented here is designed to broaden our understanding of teachers' day-to-day assessment needs.

One goal of the performance assessment research program being conducted by the Center for Performance Assessment of the Northwest Regional Educational Laboratory is to determine the role and relative importance of several types of measurement in the classroom: the teachers' own objective tests, published tests, structured performance assessments, and spontaneous performance assessments.

The teachers' own objective tests are defined to include those multiple-choice, true-false, matching, and short-answer tests teachers design for use on a day-to-day basis in their classrooms. Published tests are defined to include both standardized objective achievement tests and objective tests supplied as part of published text materials.

Performance assessment, as defined for the purpose of this research, is testing to be sure, but not in the traditional sense of objective tests. Rather, performance assessment calls for the observation and rating of student behavior and requires that students actually demonstrate proficiency (Stiggins, 1984).

Performance tests have several important characteristics. First, students are called upon to apply the skills and knowledge they have learned. Second, performance assessment involves completion of a specified task (or tasks) in the context of real or simulated assessment exercises. Third, the assessment task or product completed by the examinee is observed and rated with respect to specified criteria, in accordance with specified procedures.

In this chapter, we make an important distinction with respect to performance assessments by distinguishing between *structured* and *spontaneous* performance assessment. The former is planned and systematically designed to include prespecified purposes, exercises, observations, and scoring procedures. The latter arises spontaneously from the classroom environment and leads the teacher to a judgment about an individual student's level of development.

The presentation that follows is a summary of results of a large-scale survey of teachers' uses of these various testing methods, their concerns about assessment, and the specific characteristics of their performance assessments.

RESEARCH METHODOLOGY

Teachers surveyed. The study was designed to probe assessment practices in a stratified sample of teachers selected from eight varied districts across the country. Five districts were urban, three suburban; three were in the East, two in the Northwest, and three in the West. Each district was to recruit forty-eight volunteer teachers to complete a comprehensive questionnaire on classroom assessment. Twelve teachers were to be recruited from each of four grades (2, 5, 8 and 11). Of those twelve teachers at each grade level, three were to describe their assessment methods in writing, three in speaking, three in science, and three in math. Thus each respondent described assessment methods in only one subject and at only one grade level.

All districts responded with completed surveys; however, the number of completed forms differed substantially across districts. A total of 228 completed questionnaires were received. The respondents were distributed almost equally across districts, grades, and subjects.

Although 228 responses represented less than our desired sample of 384, the group was sufficiently large to proceed with the analysis. In analyzing the data and in their subsequent interpretation, however, we proceeded with caution for two reasons. First, the sample size precluded an analysis of teachers by subject area within each grade level (e. g., eighth-grade science teachers). Analyses of the responses were limited to grade, subject, and district totals. Second, generalizations beyond the volunteer sample were not attempted.

Questionnaire design. The questionnaire was designed in several steps. First, questions were devised to tap various levels of concern about the use of basic types of classroom assessment. The initial version of the questionnaire served as the basis for structured interviews with teachers, during which the questionnaire underwent extensive revision (Stiggins & Bridgeford, 1982). It was then reviewed and critiqued by numerous teachers, educational researchers, and editors in a long series of revisions and refinements. As a final step, the questionnaire was field tested with thirty teachers from several grades and subjects.

To ensure that teachers understood the meaning of each type of assessment covered in the questionnaire, they were provided with concise definitions of teacher-made objective tests, published tests, structured performance tests, and spontaneous assessments at the beginning of the questionnaire. In each case, the teacher was asked to supply an example of each kind of test from his or her experience. If the example revealed that the teacher did not understand the definitions of and distinctions between assessment types, that teacher's responses were not included in the analysis. A small number of booklets from each district (usually two or three) were eliminated for this reason.

One major set of questions probed teachers' use of four specific assessment options. Teachers were asked to describe the importance of different test options as a function of their specific reasons for testing; that is, for diagnosis, grouping, grading, evaluating instruction, and reporting achievement results. Respondents were given these instructions:

> Describe the relative importance of each type of assessment by indicating the weight you give to each in achieving your various classroom assessment purposes. Each question below identifies a specific instructional purpose. If a certain type of assessment carries no weight in achieving a given purpose, you should enter 0% next to it. On the other hand, if you rely completely on one type of assessment for a specific purpose, you should enter 100% next to that type. As another

example, a response of 25% to each of the four indicates equal weight to each in achieving that purpose. Percentages for each purpose should total 100.

Second, to determine the extent to which each assessment option was used, we used an adaptation of a system developed by the University of Texas Research and Development Center in Teacher Education (Hall & Loucks, 1978) to pinpoint teachers' levels of use of the four alternative assessment methods, as indicated in the following scale:

Nonuse: no action is being currently taken or anticipated with respect to this type of assessment.

Anticipated use: the user has decided to start using this type of assessment but has not yet acted upon that decision.

Preparation to use: the user is preparing to use (studying, taking action to begin using) this type of assessment but is not yet doing so.

Effortful use: the user is using that test type, but that use is labored, requiring much effort.

Comfortable use: the user is using this type of assessment with ease.

Refining use: the user is making changes in assessment procedures to increase outcomes and is working alone on this.

Collaboration in using: the user is making deliberate efforts to coordinate with others in developing and using this type of assessment.

Scaling on the teachers' level of use was accomplished by having the respondent answer a branching series of questions about their use of each test type.

We also investigated teachers' concerns about each individual type of test by adapting the "levels of concern model" developed at the University of Texas Research and Development Center (Hall, George, & Rutherford, 1977). This model helps uncover teachers' perceptions of their own assessment needs by asking teachers to identify their primary concern (e.g., lack of information, management issues) about each type of classroom assessment. Possible concerns about teacher-made objective tests, published tests, and performance assessment (structured and spontaneous) are listed below. Teachers were asked to identify their primary concerns by selecting the statement that most closely defined their situation.

Teachers' concerns	*Selected statements*
Lack of information	I am concerned about my lack of information about developing and using [my own objective paper-and-pencil tests].
Competence	I am concerned about my level of training, skill, and experience in developing and using [my own objective paper-and-pencil tests].

Time management issues	I am concerned about the amount of time required to manage the development and use of tests.
Consequences of use	I am concerned about how my students react when I administer [my own objective tests].
Collaboration in using	I am concerned about establishing working relationships with other teachers to develop and use [objective tests].
Test improvement	I am concerned about making such tests better and using them more effectively.

Teachers who had no primary concern were asked to leave the item blank.

Teachers' concerns indicate the type of information about testing that is likely to be of greatest interest and use to them at any given point in time. For example, if a teacher is concerned about the adequacy of his or her training and skill in assessment, that teacher is unlikely to be interested in strategies for working with other teachers to improve testing. The competence concern must be satisfactorily addressed first. To assist us in interpreting concerns more accurately, teachers were also requested to cite the specific reason(s) why the response they selected was primary for them.

Performance assessment. The remaining questionnaire items focused specifically on structured performance assessment. These questions were asked in two forms. First, teachers were asked to give an example of a structured performance test they had used previously. They were then asked a series of questions about its development, administration, scoring, use, and quality. These initial sample questions were designed to ensure that teachers understood the characteristics of performance tests as distinct from other teacher-developed tests. After describing the example, teachers were asked to answer a parallel set of questions about their general use of structured performance tests. These latter questions provided the specific information that was analyzed in order to understand teachers' use of performance assessments in each subject area and grade level.

Survey of Classroom Assessment Practices

Results are summarized in several parts. First, teachers' patterns of test use are reported in terms of the levels-of-test-use scale and the relative weight teachers assigned to different test types for different purposes. The analysis then turns to teachers' concerns about assessment. Concerns of respondents are summarized in the following manner: (1) the types of concern, and (2) teachers' stated reasons for those concerns. The third part of the analysis addresses teachers' use of structured performance assessments, describing test characteristics and quality control procedures. In all three cases, data are explored across test type (teacher-made objective, published, and structured performance assessment, and spontaneous performance assessment), grade level (2, 5, 8, and 11), and subject area (writing, speaking, science, and math).

The overall goal of the analysis is to describe the classroom assessment practices—use, preferences, attitudes, and role of performance assessment—of these 228 volunteer teachers. Since these teachers may not be representative of the general teacher population and since the practices described reflect what teachers say they do, not necessarily what they actually do, inferences about the testing practices of all teachers are not justified.

To explore the significance of differences in proportions across grade levels and school subjects, contingency analyses were conducted. Each analysis focused on a component of Tables 17.1, 17.2, and 17.3 crossing a set of response categories (e.g., nonuses, anticipated use, etc., of teacher-made objective tests in Table 17.1) with grade or subject. Discussion of differences focuses on those components yielding a significant chi-square, noting those rows showing greatest differences.

PATTERNS OF TEST USE

Levels of use. Table 17.1 reports the percentage of respondents in each category on the level-of-use scale.

Looking first at *teacher-made objective tests,* about half of the responding teachers report comfortable use. This proportion holds across grades and subjects. The other half of the teachers vary in level of use. For instance, use of teacher-made objective tests tends to increase steadily as grade increases (i.e., nonuse percentage declines); but teachers may have to work at increasing use of this type of test, as indicated by the increase in the effortful use category. Further, math and science teachers tend to use their own objective tests slightly more than those who teach writing and speaking.

Note also that (a) about 20% of respondents claim they do not use their own objective tests, (b) few teachers anticipate use of this test type, (c) few are preparing for future use, and (d) collaboration in use of teacher-developed objective tests is very low. Points b, c, and d remain constant for all test types, grades, and subjects.

Regarding *published tests,* again, nearly half report that they use these tests with relative ease, with most of the others reporting that they do not use them at all. There appears to be slightly more use in early grades and appreciably more use in math relative to other subjects. Here again there is no preparation for change and no collaboration.

The levels of use for *performance assessment*—structured and spontaneous—differ from the objective tests. Eighty-five percent of these teachers report some use of structured performance tests. Forty-eight percent report

TABLE 17.1. Level of Use by Test Type, Grade, and Subject (in percentage of respondents)

Level	N	Grade				Subject*				Total Sample
		2	5	8	11	WR	SP	SC	MA	
		57	58	58	55	58	61	50	59	228

Teacher-made Objective Tests

Level		2	5	8	11	WR	SP	SC	MA	Total
Nonuse		32%	26	15	9	26	29	12	14	21
Anticipated use		—	—	2	—	2	—	—	—	.4
Preparation to use		2	—	—	2	—	2	2	—	1
Effortful use		5	10	15	25	11	21	8	14	14
Comfortable use		53	45	53	47	47	40	61	51	49
Refinement		9	19	15	15	14	9	14	20	14
Collaboration		—	—	2	2	—	—	2	2	1
χ^2_6			22.52 p<.01				17.07 p<.01			

Published Tests

Level		2	5	8	11	WR	SP	SC	MA	Total
Nonuse		30	25	40	44	34	54	34	15	35
Anticipated use		—	4	2	2	2	—	6	—	2
Preparation to use		4	—	3	7	5	3	4	2	4
Effortful use		9	7	7	4	4	3	4	15	7
Comfortable use		49	56	38	35	41	38	38	61	45
Refinement		9	9	9	6	14	2	10	7	8
Collaboration		—	—	2	2	—	—	4	—	1
χ^2_6			16.65 p<.01				52.20 p<.01			

Structured Performance Assessment

Level		2	5	8	11	WR	SP	SC	MA	Total
Nonuse		17	4	14	8	4	13	11	14	10
Anticipated use		—	2	2	—	—	2	—	2	1
Preparation to use		—	4	—	—	2	2	—	—	1
Effortful use		11	14	16	17	18	10	23	9	15
Comfortable use		57	51	46	40	52	52	36	52	48
Refinement		13	26	21	26	25	17	23	22	22
Collaboration		2	—	2	10	—	—	6	2	3
χ^2_6			14.47 N.S.				10.23 N.S.			

Spontaneous Performance Assessment

Level		2	5	8	11	WR	SP	SC	MA	Total
Nonuse		2	2	—	9	2	3	4	4	3
Anticipated use		—	—	—	—	—	—	—	—	—
Preparation to use		—	—	—	2	—	—	2	—	1
Effortful use		2	5	2	4	7	3	2	—	3
Comfortable use		84	83	82	66	77	85	72	79	79
Refinement		11	9	17	17	14	8	17	14	13
Collaboration		2	2	—	2	—	—	2	4	1
χ^2_6			17.79 p<.01				10.71 N.S.			

*WR stands for writing, SP for speaking, SC for science, MA for mathematics comfortable use, with another quarter refining their use of these assessments, and 15% of the teachers also report effortful use. Nearly 95% of respondents report use of spontaneous performance assessments, with nearly 80% reporting comfortable use. All of these patterns seem relatively constant across grades and subjects.

Role of test type as a function of purpose. Patterns of reliance on test types vary slightly as testing purpose changes. Table 17.2 summarizes the relative importance that teachers assigned to the various test types for diagnosing the strengths and weaknesses of individual students, grouping for instruction, assigning grades, evaluating the effectiveness of an instructional treatment, and reporting results to parents. Since teachers assigned higher percentages to the methods that contribute most to each decision, these data are hereafter called "reliance percentages" in describing and interpreting the results. The higher the reliance percentage, the more weight given to a type of test for a particular purpose.

For diagnosis, teacher-developed objective tests are reported to be given most weight, with both types of performance assessment close behind. Published tests play a secondary role. Patterns vary across grades. Teacher-made objective tests appear somewhat more important in later grades, while published tests seem somewhat less so. Structured performance assessment is given more importance in diagnosing in grade 11 than in lower grades, while spontaneous performance assessment is reported to be least important at grade 11. Across school subjects, teacher-made objective tests appear most important for diagnosing in science and math, while structured performance assessment is most important in writing assessment, and spontaneous performance assessment is given most weight in diagnosing speaking.

On the average, when forming instructional groups, these teachers give approximately equal weight to all four types of tests. However, examination of grade and subject differences reveals some notable variations. For instance, as grade increases, the importance of published tests and spontaneous performance assessment decreases, while weight given to structured performance assessment and teacher-made objective tests increases. Also, for grouping (as for diagnosing), math and science teachers tend to rely on their own objective tests, while writing teachers give most weight to structured performance assessment and speech teachers rely most heavily on spontaneous performance assessment.

When assigning grades, teacher-made objective tests stand out as most important, followed by structured performance assessment. Published tests and spontaneous performance assessment play lesser roles. Within this pattern, however, there are clear trends across grades. As grade level increases, the weight given to objective tests and structured performance assessment goes up, while that given to published tests and spontaneous performance assessment goes down. Across school subjects, once again, math and science teachers give most

TABLE 17.2. Role of Test Type as a Function of Purpose for Assessment, Reported by Grade and Subject (in reliance percentages)

Purpose		N	Grade				Subject				Total Sample
			2	5	8	11	WR	SP	SC	MA	
			57	58	58	55	58	61	50	59	228
Diagnosing	OBJ*		25%	27	33	37	24	24	41	34	31
	PUB		20	25	12	13	19	14	15	21	17
	ST PA		24	23	27	35	37	26	23	22	27
	SP PA		32	26	28	15	20	35	21	24	25
	χ_9^2		20.70 N.S.				19.53 N.S.				
Grouping	OBJ		26	27	32	32	20	24	36	38	29
	PUB		29	32	21	19	28	21	20	30	25
	ST PA		18	22	23	32	34	21	20	19	24
	SP PA		28	19	24	14	18	33	24	12	22
	χ_9^2		15.22 N.S.				28.34 p<.01				
Grading	OBJ		29	36	43	48	34	33	46	44	39
	PUB		19	22	8	9	14	11	12	20	15
	ST PA		23	22	28	34	36	27	24	20	27
	SP PA		28	20	17	10	16	24	18	16	19
	χ_9^2		27.41 p<.01				14.17 N.S.				
Evaluating	OBJ		30	35	36	39	31	33	44	35	35
	PUB		19	24	12	14	18	11	15	25	17
	ST PA		21	22	32	29	36	28	19	20	26
	SP PA		30	20	19	18	15	29	22	20	22
	χ_9^2		13.82 N.S.				20.93 N.S.				
Reporting	OBJ		29	30	38	44	29	30	45	38	35
	PUB		22	29	14	10	20	14	17	26	19
	ST PA		25	23	30	31	35	28	22	23	27
	SP PA		26	18	18	14	17	28	18	13	19
	χ_9^2		19.89 N.S.				19.32 N.S.				

*OBJ stands for teacher-made objective tests, PUB for published tests, ST PA for structured performance assessment, and SP PA for spontaneous performance assessment.

credence to their own objective tests, while teachers of writing rely most on structured performance tests.

In order to evaluate the effectiveness of an instructional treatment, these teachers tend to use their own objective tests, followed by structured and spontaneous performance assessments. Published tests are secondary. Reliance on objective tests increases with grade, as does reliance on structured performance assessment. Reliance on published tests fluctuates with grade, while the weight given to spontaneous performance assessment drops after grade 2. Across subjects, science and math teachers evaluate most heavily based on their own objective tests, while structured performance assessment is more important in writing and speaking.

Finally, when the purpose of the assessment is to report achievement results to parents, teachers rely most heavily on their own objective tests and structured performance assessment. Many of the same grade and subject patterns referenced above appear here also. Objective and structured performance tests increase in importance as grade increases, while published and spontaneous performance assessment decrease in importance. Thus math and science teachers weight their own objective tests most heavily, while teachers of writing and speaking tend to use performance assessment.

CONCERNS ABOUT ASSESSMENT

Type of concern. Table 17.3 reports teachers' types of concern about different kinds of tests. The percentage of teachers selecting each category as her or his primary concern is reported.

Note that 28% of the total sample of teachers registered no concern about teacher-made objective tests. Thus nearly three-quarters expressed some primary concern. By far the most common concern about teacher-made objective tests focused on test improvement, reflecting teachers' desire to improve their use of this kind of test. The other common concern is management, reflecting uneasiness with the amount of time required to manage this mode of assessment in the classroom. The teachers do not tend to be concerned about a lack of information about these tests, their competence in using them, the student reactions to their use, or collaborating with others in using them. These patterns of concern vary with grade and vary slightly with subject. For example, about half of the second-grade respondents expressed some concern, while 85% of the eleventh-grade teachers did so. There is an increasing concern about quality and management of teacher-made objective tests as grade increases, and for math and science teachers in contrast to those teaching writing and speaking.

Fewer teachers expressed specific concerns about published tests. About 40% of the total sample expressed no concern. Of those expressing some concern, most were uneasy about (1) student reactions and (2) test improvement. More eleventh-grade teachers seem concerned about consequences than teachers at other grades. Beyond this, response patterns were generally stable across grades and subjects.

Expressions of concern about structured performance assessments were similar to those for teacher-made objective tests—improving quality and time management were most crucial. Some grade-level trends appear, with indications that concern for improving such assessments and using them more effectively increases with grade level.

TABLE 17.3. Summary of Concerns about Assessment by Test Type, Grade, and Subject (in percentage of respondents)

Concern	N	Grade 2	5	8	11	Subject WR	SP	SC	MA	Total Sample
		57	58	58	55	58	61	59	59	228

Teacher-made Objective Tests

No concern		46%	22	30	15	31	35	20	25	28
Lack of information		5	—	—	—	3	2	—	—	1
Competence		2	2	2	—	—	2	2	2	1
Time management		14	22	18	22	24	15	22	15	19
Consequence		—	7	5	7	9	7	2	2	5
Collaboration		4	3	—	7	3	2	2	7	4
Improvement		30	43	45	49	29	38	51	49	42
χ^2_6		26.18 p<.01				15.65 N.S.				

Published Tests

No concern		41	31	42	38	38	37	32	45	38
Lack of information		5	9	5	9	10	8	10	—	7
Competence		—	3	—	—	2	—	—	2	1
Time management		13	12	5	6	7	5	10	14	9
Consequence		20	17	14	33	19	15	28	22	21
Collaboration		2	3	4	4	3	2	2	5	3
Improvement		20	24	30	11	21	33	18	12	21
χ^2_6		26.61 p<.01				22.81 p<.01				

Structured Performance Assessment

No concern		50	33	35	24	29	44	25	42	35
Lack of information		4	—	4	—	3	2	2	—	2
Competence		4	4	7	2	3	—	10	4	4
Time management		20	21	16	26	21	12	27	25	21
Consequence		2	11	9	6	7	10	10	—	7
Collaboration		—	4	7	6	5	3	2	5	4
Improvement		20	28	23	38	31	29	25	25	27
χ^2_6		19.35 p<.01				14.97 N.S.				

Spontaneous Performance Assessment

No concern		59	48	39	39	41	58	39	46	46
Lack of information		2	2	2	6	3	2	2	4	3
Competence		2	5	7	6	5	3	10	2	5
Time management		9	10	2	4	10	3	6	5	6
Consequence		2	7	5	9	5	5	6	7	6
Collaboration		2	—	2	7	2	2	4	4	3
Improvement		24	28	44	30	33	27	33	33	31
χ^2_6		13.25 p<.01				5.65 N.S.				

Spontaneous performance assessments elicit the fewest expressions of concern, with only half of the respondents reporting some concern. Most of these related to the improvement of the assessments. Again, the frequency of this concern seemed to increase gradually with grade level.

Reasons for concern. After teachers indicated their primary concern, they were also asked to specify why that concern was primary for them.

The two most common types of concerns mentioned about teacher-made objective tests were improving test quality and time management. The reason for the teachers' concern about the time required to develop and to use their own tests is that it interferes with instructional time. Teachers who indicated uneasiness about the objective tests they developed and used posed such questions as, Are my tests effective? How can I make them better? Do they focus on students' real skills? Are they challenging enough? Do they aid in learning?

The two most frequent concerns about published tests related to students' reactions and to improving the quality of test use. Those concerned about student reactions to published tests tended to view the tests as invalid, undependable, too long, and so on, and thus anticipated that the tests were not helpful to students. Those concerned about improving test use see published tests as time-consuming, not matching their instruction, failing to reflect true student characteristics, and as generally not meeting important instructional needs, such as identifying material to teach or reteach. For these reasons, they would like the tests revised and improved or would like to learn to use them more effectively. Published tests generated the most negative comments in respondents' expressions of concerns. Many teachers see them as interfering with instruction.

Concerns about performance assessment—structured and spontaneous—dealt primarily with the desire to improve both the assessment and its use. Teachers' concerns focused on accuracy of assessment, difficulty in defining levels of performance, and the need to be objective. Test-use issues reflected a desire to measure growth, to challenge (but not intimidate) students, and to provide diagnostic information. Some teachers were also concerned about the time demands of performance assessments.

CLASSROOM PERFORMANCE ASSESSMENTS

Seventy-eight percent of the teachers completing the questionnaire reported using structured performance assessments in their classrooms. Those 177 teachers responded to a series of questions that described their assessments. Results are presented by grade and subject in Table 17.4.

Responses to item 1 in Table 17.4 describe teachers' quality control procedures. Teachers were asked to indicate the percentage of their performance assessments in which they include various procedures. On the average, teachers do the following in the majority of their assessments:

TABLE 17.4. Description of Performance Assessment by Grade and Subject

---

Question

---

1. In what percentage of all your *structured performance assessments* do you
   A. Specify the reason for assessment in your own mind prior to conducting that assessment?
   B. Write down scoring criteria before assessment?
   C. Inform students of scoring criteria before assessment?
   D. Plan actual scoring or rating procedures before assessment?
   E. Clearly define levels of performance from adequate to inadequate before rating performance?
   F. Conduct "blind" ratings of student products (i.e., rate performance without knowledge of who the respondent is)?
   G. Observe and rate performance more than once before making a judgment?
   H. Check your judgments against objective or published test scores before making a final decision?
2. What percentage of all of your *structured performance tests* involve the evaluation of
   Students doing things (behavior)?
   Products created by students?
3. As you observe and rate performance, with what percentage of your assessments do you use the following procedures to record your judgments?
   A. Checklists (list of skills present or absent)
   B. Rating scales (continuum from good to poor quality performance)
   C. Anecdotal records (written descriptions of performance)
   D. A grade (in a record book)
   E. Mental notes (accumulated in memory over time)
4. What proportion of all of your *structured performance assessments* do you score
   Holistically—scoring overall proficiency?
   Analytically—scoring specific subskills?
   Both holistically and analytically?
5. What proportion of your *structured performance assessments* are conducted without students being aware that you are assessing them?
6. When rating students, do you always do the rating or do colleagues or the students themselves play a role? Indicate the appropriate percentage of ratings conducted by each potential rater listed below.
   A. I (the teacher) do the rating
   B. Colleague rates student performance
   C. Students rate each other's performance
   D. Students rate their own performance
7. What proportion of your *structured performance assessment* results is interpreted primarily by comparing student performance to
   That of other students (norm-referenced interpretation)?
   Specific preset standards of criteria of minimum acceptable performance (criterion-referenced interpretation)?

	Grade				Subject			Total Sample
2	5	8	11	WR	SP	SC	MA	
N 38	51	41	47	46	46	38	47	177
79	82	88	85	87	86	76	84	83
28	41	63	58	48	61	34	46	48
35	62	73	78	66	73	57	55	63
57	61	76	75	70	73	57	68	67
48	58	76	69	66	69	56	60	63
8	14	28	23	10	12	32	23	18
51	42	47	41	44	43	42	50	45
21	21	22	18	12	13	19	38	21
52	49	55	55	32	67	56	57	53
48	51	43	47	68	32	46	42	47
31	30	35	35	35	40	24	21	33
28	33	45	42	34	41	35	39	37
23	23	35	33	26	41	20	25	28
38	63	85	86	71	65	66	70	68
46	37	50	28	39	40	48	33	40
26	28	29	22	27	15	32	31	26
18	21	15	20	20	12	19	23	19
54	51	55	60	50	75	49	44	55
40	25	13	13	17	22	26	23	22
90	84	82	90	86	87	88	85	87
6	2	2	4	1	6	2	4	4
5	11	19	14	14	19	7	9	12
13	19	16	10	15	18	12	13	15
38	34	25	32	27	27	40	35	32
62	64	75	69	71	72	60	64	67

Specify a reason in their mind for assessment prior to testing (part A)
Inform students of their scoring criteria (part C)
Plan scoring procedures in advance (part D)
Define levels of performance assessment (part E)

On the other hand, less than half of the assessments include written performance assessment criteria (part B) or multiple performance observations (part G) before making a judgment. And finally, teachers seldom rated performance without knowledge of the students' identity (part F), or cross-checked judgments about performance with other test scores (part H).

There are some differences in responses across grades. For instance, as grade increases, so does the tendency to write down criteria and inform students of them, plan scoring procedures, define levels of performance, and conduct blind ratings. Differences across subjects are less pronounced, but quality control activities do appear to vary somewhat on this dimension also. For instance, teachers dealing with speaking assessment appear more likely to write down scoring criteria than others and are more likely to inform students of them than are math and science teachers. Further, it appears that science teachers are somewhat less likely to plan scoring procedures in advance of the assessment than are the others. Math and science teachers use blind scoring more frequently than do their colleagues who teach writing and speaking. And finally, teachers appear more likely to check their judgments against test scores when dealing with math in contrast to other subjects.

In the remaining items in Table 17.4, teachers further described characteristics of their structured performance assessments. Teachers reported that these assessments tended to be equally divided between evaluations of process and product (item 2); recorded most frequently as a grade in the record book and less frequently as mental notes, rating scales, checklists, and anecdotal records (item 3); scored both holistically and analytically (item 4); conducted with the awareness of the student (item 5); based on teachers' judgments, with students rarely playing a role in peer or self-assessment (item 6); and criterion-referenced or based on preestablished standards of acceptable performance (item 7).

The data reported in Table 17.4 reveal some notable differences in test characteristics across grades and subjects. For instance, as grade increases, so does reliance on rating scales and grades. However, the use of unobtrusive assessment (item 5) decreases as grade increases. Comparing subjects, writing assessment is most frequently based on product evaluation (presumably writing samples), while others are more process oriented. Speaking assessments use slightly more checklists and rating scales than others, while science assessors rely heavily on mental record keeping. Speaking assessments tend to be scored more completely (holistically and analytically) than others. All other characteristics are quite constant across subjects.

Future Directions and Needs

From these results, we have selected five major issues for further analysis and discussion. These issues capture what we feel are the most important insights about student assessment to be derived from the data. In this section, we draw conclusions about (1) the use and importance of performance assessment in the classroom; (2) the stability of results across grades, subjects, and contexts; (3) teachers' concerns about assessment, particularly with respect to improving test quality and use; (4) specific issues of assessment quality, including potential difficulties in classroom performance assessment procedures; and (5) actions needed to overcome some of the assessment problems.

THE NATURE AND ROLE OF PERFORMANCE ASSESSMENT IN THE CLASSROOM

Our previous studies (Stiggins & Bridgeford, 1982) led to the conclusion that performance assessment—the observation and rating of student behavior and products—plays a key role in the day-to-day measurement of student achievement in the classroom. This study reinforces that conclusion. A large majority of the teachers in this study (177 of 228) report using structured performance assessment in the classroom. More important, the weights assigned to structured and spontaneous performance assessments show them to be heavily used modes of assessment in all five decision contexts explored. This appears to be true across the grades and school subjects examined. Our data indicate that performance assessment and teacher-made objective tests form the basis of most classroom assessment. Published tests play a secondary role. Teachers, moreover, have considerable confidence in their ability to make accurate observations and professional judgments; they express comfort with performance assessment and rely on it as a key method of judging students' learning. But the data also indicate that this confidence should not be confused with complacency. As we have seen, many teachers are sensitive to the fact that there may be problems in their assessments, and they are interested in improving test quality.

What are classroom performance assessments like? In one sense, they vary greatly across teachers and subject areas and in another sense they remain quite similar. Exercises, performance criteria, and student responses obviously vary as a function of school subject. However, the form of the assessment remains constant. Teachers evaluate both behaviors and products in approximately equal proportions. They tend to use prespecified standards (rather than student comparisons) to record assessment results with a grade in a record book, and they usually do not involve students in performance ratings. Though most teachers know in advance why they are assessing—a key to quality assessment—some may fail to apply other quality control procedures to their performance assessments. We will explore this point in greater detail shortly.

Examining common characteristics of these assessments leads to the conclusion that performance assessment may not be used as effectively as is possible. For instance, students represent an untapped reservoir of performance raters, especially when teacher time is at a premium. Students can successfully rate their own and one another's performance and can learn a great deal from doing so (Spandel, 1981). For another example, recording systems other than grades often provide valuable and rich feedback to students. Checklists, rating scales, and anecdotal records, for example, offer the detail often needed to describe performance and make careful assessments. The heavy reliance on grades seen in the data suggests that these alternatives are not being used to the greatest advantage.

Thus results from this study confirm that performance assessment is an important assessment tool for teachers in the classroom. Results also indicate that the use of this assessment method could be enhanced and expanded.

STABILITY AND CHANGE IN ASSESSMENT PROCEDURES

Within the pattern of relatively constant assessment methods, however, there are a few variations worthy of note. In this section, we explore the implications of those variations across grade, subject, and test type.

We found three interesting changes in assessment procedures as grade increases: (1) the higher the grade level, the greater the tendency for teachers to report using their own assessments rather than published tests; (2) teachers' concern about assessment increases with grade level; and (3) teachers' attention to quality control issues with performance assessments increases slightly with grade level. Levels of use of performance assessment as well as specific attributes of those assessments vary somewhat across grades. Thus grade level appears to be an important variable in understanding classroom assessment. Elementary, junior high, and high school environments differ in fundamental ways. The increased use of teacher-developed tests at higher grade levels might reflect the teacher's need to tailor tests to cover unique classroom objectives at higher levels. The reason for increased concern about assessment across grade levels may relate to the increased importance placed on grades as a measure of student progress and success as grade increases. And increased attention to quality control may reflect the increased concern with accurately judging and grading students. Clearly, grades take on more importance as students advance in the school system, and grades can and do influence future decisions about students. These and other speculations deserve further consideration in future research.

Assessment procedures also differ as a function of school subject. Such differences are to be expected and our data support this notion. Math and science teachers tend to rely more heavily on paper-and-pencil tests than do those who teach writing and speaking. Speaking and writing teachers tend to use more performance assessments, and the performance assessments they use tend to differ somewhat from those used by math and science teachers. In spite of those findings, concerns about improving test quality and use tend to remain quite constant across subject.

Conclusions can also be drawn about variations in assessment approach among teachers and for a given teacher. For instance, there is evidence that the teachers we surveyed are relatively consistent in the assessment methods they use. They do not vary their testing methods very much as the purpose for assessment varies. This finding calls into question our conclusion in earlier studies that performance tests are instructional tools, while objective tests are grading tools (Stiggins & Bridgeford, 1982). Both tests appear to play a role in both purposes. As our teachers described their levels of use, only a handful of the 228 reported that they anticipated using or were preparing to use a new type of assessment in the future. These teachers are not exploring new assessment approaches. This conclusion has implications for the action plans outlined next.

TEACHERS' CONCERNS ABOUT ASSESSMENT

At least three-quarters of the 228 teachers queried in this study expressed some concern about the assessments they used. Further, over half of the respondents indicated concern about each of the four assessment methods. Even when teachers reported relatively comfortable use of a given form of assessment, they were not reluctant to express a desire to improve their tests and the manner in which those tests are used. Their most frequently expressed concern involved improving the quality and use of assessments. Added to that, teachers frequently reported concern about their ability to integrate assessment effectively given the time constraints imposed by the classroom. Overall, teachers' responses in this study indicated concern about assessment quality and frustration at the lack of time available to deal more adequately with the problem.

But even more paradoxical and potentially troubling is the fact that although teachers are obviously concerned about and want to improve their own performance, at the same time they do not appear to be in the process of changing or improving their assessment methods. Clearly, many teachers lack the opportunity, time, means, or motivation to revise their assessment approaches. This dilemma is considered further in our discussion of needed action programs.

THE EXTENT OF THE PROBLEM

Obviously, many teachers wonder about the effectiveness of the assessments they are using. But is there really reason to be concerned? Information on this issue from our data is limited but provides some insight. From the self-report data on quality control efforts in structured performance assessments, teachers' uneasiness may be justified. For example, in at least a third of the structured performance assessments conducted by these teachers, important assessment procedures do not appear to be followed; that is, students are not informed of performance criteria, scoring procedures are not planned in advance, and levels of performance (adequate to inadequate) are not defined before rating performance. On average, in over half of these assessments, scoring criteria are not written down, judgments are based on a single observation, and performance ratings are not checked against other indicators, such as test scores. Finally, in an average of 40 percent of the structured performance assessments, teachers rely on mental record keeping. Since these practices can contribute significantly to the invalidity or unreliability of structured performance assessment results, there seems to be reason for concern.

Thus the data suggest real problems. But caution is needed in interpreting these problems. The statistics presented previously can be interpreted from a "glass half empty" or "glass half full" perspective. Pessimists say we have much to do. Optimists say much is already being done. Both are right. Many teachers do an excellent job of assessing, adhering to key aspects of quality control in important assessments. In our discussions, interviews, and questionnaire responses, we found many very creative applications of performance assessment in the classroom, and there appears to be a strong foundation of good assessment present in many classrooms. We can build from that foundation. Many teachers are not complacent. We can count on that. So how do we proceed?

MOVING TOWARD A SOLUTION

Though the extent and depth of the assessment problem is only suggested by our data, the problem is obviously significant. To deal with it, we propose a solution including four parts: (1) greater sensitivity to teachers' needs on the part of the measurement community, (2) more qualitative research on classroom assessment practices, (3) collaboration among teachers, and (4) in-service training designed to meet teachers' needs. We have two key factors in our favor as we consider changes. First, our data on concerns suggest that many teachers are aware of the need to use assessment more effectively; they want to improve. Second, many teachers are strong assessors.

How can we use these factors to advantage? First and foremost, the measurement community must give greater attention to classroom assessment. With a few notable exceptions, as a community of educators, we have only a limited understanding of the classroom assessment environment and teachers' most pressing assessment concerns in evaluating students. Evidence to support these observations is presented in Table 17.5. Teachers rely on both observational assessment and teacher-made objective tests; published tests have considerably less influence on teachers. Yet textbooks used in teacher training provide almost no instruction in the assessment methods most relevant for classroom use. Even more important, measurement research (as reported in professional journals) concentrates on assessment methods that have the least utility for teachers'

TABLE 17.5. Relative Importance of Test Type in the Professional Literature and in Terms of Teachers' Needs

Emphasis on	In Texts[1]	In Research[2]	For teachers[3]
Teacher-made objective tests	47%	29%	34%
Published tests	47%	62%	19%
Performance assessment	6%	9%	47%

[1]Approximate percentage of text pages on test construction and use in six introductory measurement textbooks: Ahmann and Glock (1981); Brown (1983); Ebel (1979); Gronlund (1981); Mehrens and Lehmann (1983); Noll, Scannell, and Craig (1979).

[2]Approximate percentage of articles dealing with those tests and test development in volumes 17, 18, 19, and 20 of the *Journal of Educational Measurement* (1980–83).

[3]Reliance percentages summarized from Table 17.2, averaged across purposes and combined structure and spontaneous performance assessments.

decision making. As researchers, our focus must be redirected to include assessment methods and quality control issues in the classroom environment that affect student learning and instruction.

Second, more research on classroom performance assessment should be conducted. Extensive research on the role and use of standardized test scores in the classroom has certainly played an important role in helping us deal with some key assessment problems. But the time has now come to move to a new emphasis, namely, understanding the role of strategies such as teacher observation in classroom assessment. The research reported here represents a small but potentially useful step in that direction. We might also follow the lead of Good and Brophy (1978), who have provided teachers with systematic strategies for observing in the classroom.

Third, teachers who are competent assessors are a vital training resource that must be tapped. Results of this study suggest that teachers who rely most heavily on performance assessments tend to use such tests somewhat more carefully than those who use them less. Teachers with assessment skill can assist their colleagues. Our previous research revealed that teachers regard colleagues as one of the two most important sources of assessment ideas (Stiggins & Bridgeford, 1982). Yet this study revealed little or no collaboration among teachers in test use. These two findings identify a valuable source of ideas that is not being explored. Why? Because there is no time, encouragement, or plan to do so. Test quality may be readily improved by encouraging and promoting collaboration in assessment.

Greater awareness of the classroom assessment environment and its demands can form the basis for another important element in our plan of action: namely, relevant training for teachers. Based on the textbooks examined in Table 17.5, current and past training is out of balance. Further, a large proportion of teachers have had no measurement training at all (Coffman, 1983; Stiggins & Bridgeford, 1982). Many teacher preparation programs (graduate and under-graduate) do not require measurement training, and given a choice, teachers often avoid it. One reason for this avoidance is that our training fails by reputation to meet important teacher needs.

As we design and develop more relevant training, all available resources must be investigated. For instance, graduate and undergraduate teacher prepara-tion courses, including the student teaching experience, should be structured to deal directly with classroom assessment issues. In-service training also provides a significant opportunity for us to put our knowledge to use. But the key to success in each setting will not be to present more "strategies to interpret standardized test scores." These, as Kellaghan, Madaus, and Airasian (1982) have shown, have minimal impact on teachers' testing practices. Instead, training must focus on teachers' need to use their most important resource—teacher-made tests—to evaluate students effectively and accurately.

References

Ahmann, J. S., & Glock, M. D. (1981). *Evaluating student progress* (6th ed.). Boston: Allyn and Bacon.

Airasian, P. W., Kellaghan, T., Madaus, G. F., & Pedulla, J. (1977). Proportion and direction of teacher rating changes of pupil progress attributable to standardized test information. *Journal of Educational Psychology, 69,* 702–709.

Brown, F. G. (1983). *Principles of educational and psychological testing* (3rd ed.). New York: Holt, Rinehart and Winston.

Burstein, L. (1983). A word about this issue. *Journal of Educational Measurement, 20,* 99–101.

Calfee, R. C., & Drum, P. A. (1976). *How the researcher can help the reading teacher with classroom assessment.* Unpublished manuscript, Stanford University.

Coffman, W. E. (1983). *Testing in the schools: A historical perspective.* Paper presented at the Center for the Study of Evaluation annual invitational conference, Univer-sity of California, Los Angeles.

Ebel, R. L. (1979). *Essentials of educational measurement* (3rd ed.). Englewood Cliffs, NJ: Prentice-Hall.

Good, T. L., & Brophy, J. E. (1978). *Looking in classrooms* (2nd ed.). New York: Harper and Row.

Goslin, D. A. (1967). *Teachers and testing* (2nd ed.). New York: Russell Sage Foundation.

Gronlund, N. E. (1981). *Measurement and evaluation in teaching* (4th ed.). New York: Macmillan.

Hall, G. E., & Loucks, S. (1978). Teachers' concerns as a basis for facilitating and personalizing staff development. *Teachers' College Record, 80,* 36–53.

Hall, G. E., George, A. A., & Rutherford, W. L. (1977). *Measuring stages of concern about the innovation: A manual for use of the SoC questionnaire.* Austin, TX: Research and Development Center for Teacher Education, University of Texas.

Herman, J., & Dorr-Bremme, D. W. (1982, March). *Assessing students: Teachers' routine practices and reasoning.* Paper presented at the annual meeting of the American Educational Research Association, New York.

Kellaghan, T., Madaus, G. F., & Airasian, P. W. (1982). *The effects of standardized testing.* Hingham, MA: Kluwer-Nijhoff.

Lortie, D. (1975). *School teacher.* Chicago: University of Chicago Press.

Mehrens, W. A., & Lehmann, I. J. (1983). *Measurement and evaluation in education and psychology* (3rd ed.). New York: Holt, Rinehart and Winston.

Noll, V. H., Scannell, D. P., & Craig, R. C. (1979). *Introduction to educational measurement* (4th ed.). Boston: Houghton Mifflin.

Rudman, H. E., Kelly, J. L., Wanous, D. S., Mehrens, W. A., Clark, C. M., & Porter, A. C. (1980). *Integrating assessment with instruction: A review (1922–1980)* (Research Series No. 75). East Lansing, MI: College of Education, Michigan State University.

Salmon-Cox, L. (1981). Teachers and standardized achievement tests: What's really happening? *Phi Delta Kappan, 63,* 631–634.

Spandel, V. (1981). *Classroom applications of writing assessment.* Portland, OR: Northwest Regional Educational Laboratory.

Sproull, L., & Zubrow, D. (1981). Standardized testing from the administrative perspective. *Phi Delta Kappan, 63,* 628–631.

Stetz, F., & Beck, M. (1979, April). *Comments from the classroom: Teachers' and students' opinions of achievement tests.* Paper presented at the annual meeting of the American Educational Research Association, San Francisco.

Stiggins, R. J. (1984). *Evaluating students through classroom observation: Watching students grow.* Washington, DC: National Education Association.

Stiggins, R. J., & Bridgeford, N. J. (1982). *Final research report on the nature, role, and quality of classroom performance assessment.* Portland, OR: Northwest Regional Educational Laboratory.

Yeh, J. (1978). *Test use in the schools.* Los Angeles: Center for the Study of Evaluation, University of California.

18. WRITING SKILLS ASSESSMENT

Edys S. Quellmalz

Introduction

Writing skills assessment shares the methodological problems inherent in the assessment of any constructed response test format. Procedures used to specify the domain, establish criteria, assure reliable rating, and establish the validity of the assessment vary considerably. Writing assessment methodology is also particularly complicated, however, by writing's status as a basic communication skill.

In many other skill domains, particularly in work settings, the range of application of the measured skill is more narrowly bounded, performance is observable (e.g., repairing a pump, defusing a bomb), and the acceptability of the end product is apparent (the pump works, the bomb does not explode). The writing domain, however, seems to defy limitation. Furthermore, the writing process is covert, and there is little agreement on criteria for evaluating the highly variable writing samples produced. Since schools are required to teach writing as a basic skill and to offer curricula that will prepare students to "write well" in any academic, work, or personal environment, the aims of writing instruction and assessment can become very broad or very fractionated. Therefore, the conflict regarding the nature of writing as a construct is a source of many problems in the assessment of writing competence. These diverse views of writing have in turn produced a multitude of writing assessment methods.

The first section of this chapter summarizes issues relating to methods currently used to assess writing skills and draws upon some recent research in the areas of test design and language development to suggest methods that might improve the design and interpretation of writing tests. The second section describes representative applications of varying methods in large-scale writing assessments. The final section discusses trends and needs.

Issues in Writing Assessment Methodology

Issues in writing methodology range from specifying the domain to documenting technical quality. Within each component of the assessment, literary and practical views of writing may often produce quite different, even conflicting tasks, criteria, and performance descriptions.

492

SPECIFYING THE DOMAIN

Because schools are trying to prepare students to write for a range of purposes and in a range of contexts, the goals of instruction and assessment have been very broad. There has been little consensus on what students at various age levels should write or how well they should write it. Moreover, different purposes of the assessment (e.g., selection, certification, or diagnosis) further complicate decisions about the level and breadth of goals.

One source of definitions in the writing domain derives from rhetorical or literary theories of discourse that analyze great works and classify them according to their purposes and generic discourse structures. An example of this conceptualization of writing is the familiar Aristotelian division of discourse into four modes: narration, exposition, persuasion, and description. Another is James Kinneavy's scheme based on the intentions or aims of discourse. His differentiations of expressive, persuasive, referential, and literary purposes were used in the Third National Assessment of Educational Progress (Kinneavy, 1971). From an extensive analysis of students' school writing, James Britton (1978) proposed three types: expressive, transactional, and poetic.

A second, more pragmatic view of the domain narrows types of writing to be assessed to functional writing tasks, that is, to the types of writing that adults are likely to need to survive in their personal and work environments. This view grew in response to demands for competency tests to certify minimum levels of performance. In public schools, however, functional goals are often based on assumptions about survival skills rather than on empirically documented task analyses of an identified body of job or personal writing activities. Some universities offer composition courses that instruct students on the discourse structures, formats, and styles prevalent in the publications of academic disciplines, but critics of these courses point out that the structures and styles of writing in some fields are not necessarily models of good writing. In the same vein, studies are beginning to describe types of writing required in various work settings (Gentry, 1982).

A third, more recent approach views writing as a process of making meaning. This school of thought arises from recent research by sociolinguists and cognitive psychologists on the composing process and asserts that writing competence is not well represented by just the written product (Hayes & Flower, 1979). These researchers propose that any writing evaluation must allow for and consider the entire writing process, especially competency tests that attempt to provide instructionally useful, diagnostic information. The influence of this view can be seen in assessments that provide extended time, cues, or even separate tasks for components of the writing process such as planning, drafting, revising, and copyediting.

Goals. Within each of these approaches to specifying even broad components of writing, the levels of expectation vary considerably. Differences in standards are reflected both by the complexity of the assessment tasks (e.g., discourse aim, method of development, topic familiarity, level of interpretation, length) as well as by the level of quality expected in the various essay features (e.g., specificity of focus, type and amount of support or elaboration, sophistication of discourse structures and signaling devices).

The influence of rhetorical and literary views may be seen in tests at the secondary and postsecondary levels. These writing tests ask for lengthy compositions, often for narrative or persuasive aims. Evaluative criteria frequently reference originality, quality of ideas, organization, adherence to conventions, and style. Most minimum competency tests, on the other hand, reflect the functional view. These tests tend to ask for paragraph-length compositions, usually on expository topics, and stress basic, less aesthetic criteria such as clarity, coherence, and correctness. The process view is represented less in large-scale, formal assessments than in instructional programs developed for the college or elementary levels (Graves, 1978; Perl, 1979). Evaluation of writing in this paradigm is usually for expressive or persuasive writing and ample time is given for prewriting, drafting, and revising. Peer, instructor, and self-evaluations of multiple drafts are not uncommon. Criteria may include effectiveness, coherence, sensitivity to audience, and authenticity of voice.

Recently, in reaction to the limitations of the multiple-choice format, attention has begun to turn to essay exams. In these assessments, writing is viewed as a vehicle for students to explain their understanding, interpretation, and evaluation of subject matter in, for example, social science, science, and literature. These assessments focus on quality of content rather than discourse structure and conventions. At present, then, the writing domain does not have a unified theory of skill development that can provide a framework for coordinating a system of broad task types, standard goals, operational objectives, and instructional and assessment tasks. Consequently, the differing views of the writing domain can result in quite different approaches to the design, interpretation, and validation of writing assessments.

OBJECTIVES

The diversity of objectives specified for writing tests reflects the diversity of conceptualizations of the writing domain itself. For both measurement and instructional purposes, it is critical that objectives describe the class of content and performance being assessed. Unlike other academic subject matter domains or job specializations, it is unclear just what information should be specified as the content and response dimensions of a writing skill. Like reading, writing is essentially a set of strategies students use to express their reactions, understandings, and interpretations of experience and academic subjects. Objectives such as "The student will write a composition" could refer to a wide range of discourse structures and lengths. Similarly, the objective "The student will write a letter" is deceptive since it seems to specify *what* but in fact specifies only a format, not the rhetorical requirements such as discourse structure and method of development. A more appropriate level of specification for a writing test might be "The student will write a letter to the editor giving at least three reasons to persuade readers why an action should be taken." This objective describes more precisely what is expected to the designers, teachers, parents, and students.

Fortunately, research on reading and writing processes and on the design of writing assessments is beginning to identify features of writing assignments that reveal differences in writing skill. The research paradigm studies the relationship between dimensions of writing tasks and the strategies and performance they elicit in students with different levels of writing expertise. Some of the research can now provide an empirical basis for designing writing tasks and evaluative criteria, structuring rating scales, and reporting results. In general, it seems that the *what*, or the content, of the writing domain is knowledge of discourse frameworks and conventions. The process dimension appears to involve strategies for applying these frameworks and conventions to particular topics and rhetorical situations.

STRUCTURING WRITING TASKS

The methodology for designing test tasks has changed substantially from the times when test makers dashed off "fix-this-comma-error" multiple-choice items and familiar and interesting essay topics. The debate about the relative merits of direct and indirect measures is being resolved by research that investigates how closely the requirements and conditions of the writing-test assignment relate to the rhetorical requirements of occasions for writing that students encounter in academic and personal situations. A body of literature now provides considerable direction to the problem of how to construct items to appraise written performance.

Direct versus indirect measures of writing. Publishers of large-scale tests of writing and researchers studying language development continually debate the suitability of multiple-choice test items as indicators of writing skill. Since this chapter focuses on methodological issues in direct assessment, the status of the debate will be summarized briefly.

The central issue has been one of construct validity. Critics of multiple-choice formats have argued that those formats tend to emphasize copyediting and reading comprehension; they do not tap the same psychological processes required by production tasks (Bourne, 1966; Cooper, 1979; Quellmalz, 1981; Simon, 1981). The psychometric argument has been that multiple-choice scores correlated highly with essay scores. However, recent studies comparing students' scores on the two kinds of measures report considerably lower correlations between direct and indirect measures of writing skill component scores (Moss, Cole, & Khampalikit, 1982; Quellmalz, Capell, & Chou, 1982). Furthermore, Quellmalz, Capell, and Chou (1982) used confirmatory factor analyses and found that multiple-choice test scores provided less distinctive information about underlying writing skill constructs or traits than did essay ratings. In sum, evidence challenging the construct validity of selected response tasks is sufficient to require the evaluation of samples of students' actual writing.

Discourse aim. The feature of the writing assignment that has been shown to affect students' writing performance significantly is the writing purpose or discourse aim. Although the particular labels used to identify forms of writing vary, classification of the different genres directs attention to their implications for designing tests and instruction. Different forms of discourse present different challenges to students, and the resulting performance can present conflicting pictures of writing competence. Research on the effect of background knowledge on reading comprehension, for example, has documented that the recurring structural features of the generic discourse structures are extracted by readers and stored as schemata or frameworks that readers use to help them comprehend similar texts (Meyer, 1975; Stein & Glenn, 1980). Writing research also demonstrates the need to include discourse structure as a factor in the design of writing assignments. Studies have shown that writers use different linguistic structures when writing for different purposes, and that they represent information on a topic quite differently (Crowhurst & Piche, 1980; San Jose, 1972). Several studies have shown that when the prompts in writing tests reflect differing discourse aims, the performance of both elementary and high school students vary (Baker & Quellmalz, 1980; Praeter & Padia, 1980; Quellmalz, Capell, & Chou, 1982; Veal & Tillman, 1971). The implication of these studies is that when writing tests present assignments calling for different discourse aims, different profiles of writing competence may result. Clearly, interpretations of a student's writing competence should not generalize beyond the particular discourse structures tested.

Topic. Another critical dimension of the writing assignment is the subject matter or content the examinee is expected to use. In order to focus on students' writing strategies, writing tests seek to minimize the role of the topic by selecting subject matters that are familiar and interesting. While classroom assessments can tailor writing topics to students' background knowledge (content schema) or provide time to gather relevant content information, large-scale assessments have great difficulty identifying subjects that will not disadvantage some students. One means of overcoming this problem has been to provide short background reading passages. This procedure has been criticized, however, for confounding reading skill with writing skill. Another promising technique has been to present pictures that convey the minimum information students might need to formulate a composition. In one study investigating the influence of pictures on student test performance, it was found that students who were given pictures used more of the pictured information in their essays (Quellmalz, Baker, & Enright, 1980). In another study, students who received tests with pictures wrote essays comparable in quality to responses written by students with higher reading scores (Baker & Quellmalz, 1980). Far more research is needed to identify techniques for equating the difficulty level and information load of writing topics at the design stage of test development.

Rhetorical contexts. A major criticism of large-scale, formal writing tests is that such tests do not present full rhetorical contexts (Britton, 1978; Scribner & Cole, 1978). Researchers argue that a test should not only set the writing purpose and topic but should also specify the intended audience, the writer's role, and the expected criteria. Moreover, they urge that tests be designed to provide sufficient time for students to engage in the full writing process. To date, there is little empirical evidence about the magnitude of these effects on writing test performance. Polin (1981) found that when writers were given extended time and cues to attend to the rhetorical demands of the task during planning or revision, some were able to improve features of their test performance.

SPECIFYING SCORING CRITERIA

Comparisons of the criteria used to evaluate writing samples accentuate the problem of defining just what a writing test measures. Criteria may be qualitative or quantitative, global or specific, comprehensive or limited. A qualitative criterion might be "effectiveness" or "quality of ideas," while a quantitative criterion might be number of reasons or number of T-units. A global criterion might be "coherence"; a specific criterion might be number of cohesive ties. Comprehensive criteria might reference a range of essay features, such as focus, organization, support, content, and mechanics; while limited criteria might focus only on a primary trait (usually support) or sentence-level error counts.

At the qualitative end of the continuum are general impression scoring schemes where readers apply their own criteria to give a global score. Some teachers' A–F grades represent this type of scheme. Global quality ratings are also given in holistic rating schemes, but they are based on slightly more specific and recognized criteria. The most specific scales tend to be analytic rating schemes that provide separate scores for component features of the composition.

Since the type and mixture of criteria appearing in rating scales vary so widely, it is helpful to understand where the criteria come from, the inferences about writing skill they are intended to support, and the actions they inform. In addition to the standards of literary theory, good writing has been judged on features cited by "knowledgeable" readers as components of high-quality papers (Diederich, 1974; Freedman, 1979). In past studies, criteria from these two standards have been derived as readers were asked to rank papers to select students who were good, or at least acceptable, writers. Often, however, criteria used for these purposes were not sufficiently specific to permit consistent application by raters within or across rating sessions (Mullis, 1979). In empirical studies comparing the scores given to essays rated according to different scoring schemes, the score variations found have often been attributable to differences in essay features and quality expectations of the scales. For example, Winters (1978) found that various scoring rubrics, including a general impression guide, two analytic guides, and a T-unit analysis, placed students quite differently into remedial or freshman writing classes. During rater training sessions, Winters observed that raters spent considerable time refining and interpreting ambiguous criteria; she predicted that the same criteria might be specified quite differently by another group of raters. Quellmalz, Smith, Winters, and Baker (1980) also found that three separate holistic rubrics and an analytic rubric yielded conflicting classifications of entering freshmen. Similarly, Polin (1981) found very low correlations between primary trait and analytic ratings of the same essays. The problems in each of these studies seemed to be that the scoring rubric referenced nominally similar criteria, but, in application, the criteria cued variable characterizations of the same essays.

Now that many testing programs are relied upon to diagnose and place students, they are seeking criteria that will discriminate among papers written by students who are at identifiably different levels of writing competence. The development of various detailed discourse analysis techniques has been a particularly useful contribution of cognitive oriented writing research. Meyer (1975), for example, developed procedures for diagramming discourse structures. Halliday and Hasan (1976) have detailed ways to count cohesive ties, i.e., techniques for signaling logical connections. The more detailed language units used in discourse analyses can be used to describe features of compositions written by students at different levels of competence and, more important, to inform instructional decisions. As writing research continues to identify aspects of compositions that distinguish among levels of judged quality, these features will replace or refine more ambiguous, global criteria.

SELECTING A RATING GUIDE FORMAT

The criteria used to evaluate compositions can be combined into two major rating guide formats: a single score or several scores. The single score may represent a summary judgment of the overall quality of the paper, or it may represent a particular feature. General impression and holistic scores are summary judgments; a primary trait score references a distinctive feature. Multiple, analytic scores may represent component features or a combination of a summary evaluation and components. The holistic scoring method has been widely used both because it is economical and because it is supported by the aesthetic view of some literary theorists that the effectiveness of the whole is greater than the sum of its parts.

Teachers complain that a holistic score does not credit the strengths of a paper or identify weaknesses. Furthermore, research in psychology and pedagogy suggests that learners advance when they are taught how to combine components into competent performance (e.g., Anderson, 1977; Resnick & Ford, 1981; Skinner, 1963). Consequently, many school systems are becoming dissatisfied with evaluations of writing samples that simply label the student's writing with a single number.

In order to provide individual diagnosis and instructional direction, some large-scale testing programs are turning to combined holistic and analytic rating guides that report both a summary judgment and separate scores for components such as focus, support, organization, and mechanics. Other systems use a diagnostic checklist for papers that receive holistic scores below the mastery level.

In one study (Quellmalz, 1981), I attempted to isolate the effects of rating scale format by training two groups of readers to use the same criteria. One group gave a holistic, general competence score and diagnostic checks for component features of papers falling below mastery; the other group gave a holistic, general competence score and separate scores for each component feature. Each format yielded agreement levels of over 90 percent on the general competence scale. Agreement levels of the numerical scores for component features given by the raters using the combined holistic/analytic approach were much higher, however, than the agreement between diagnostic checks given by the holistic raters. It appears that the requirement to give separate scores resulted in more focused, careful rating.

A major problem for large-scale writing assessment and classroom essay evaluation is, to be sure, the additional time and expense of providing detailed ratings. Currently available data on scoring costs indicate that training time for holistic and primary trait scores averages 2 to 4 hours (Mullis, 1979; Powills, Bowers, & Conlan, 1979), and for combined holistic analytic scores, 4 to 8 hours (Quellmalz, 1981, 1985; Quellmalz, Capell, & Chou, 1982; Smith, 1978). Trained raters can assign a holistic or primary trait score to a student's paper reliably in 30 seconds to 1.5 minutes. The time it took to give five to eight separate scores for the holistic/analytic guide ranged from 4 minutes for multiparagraph essays and from 1 to 3 minutes for single paragraphs. In my study comparing the two rating scale formats (Quellmalz, 1981), it was found that training times were 6 hours for the combined holistic/analytic guide and 3.5 hours for the holistic guide. Scoring time per paper averaged 3.4 minutes for the combined format and 2.7 minutes per paper for the holistic scoring. The teachers in the survey received some test scores reported in each format and preferred the analytic format as "most useful." More recently, in a pilot test of direct writing assessment for the California Assessment Program, sixty raters scored 17,000 essays on a combined holistic/analytic guide in approximately 2 minutes per paper. Raters estimated that eliminating a conventions score (requiring attention to sentence formation, usage, etc.) would reduce rating times to 1–1.5 minutes per paper (Quellmalz, 1985). Rating time per paper is therefore becoming less of an issue in the selection of a score format.

Specification of rating criteria and score formats are two of the central decisions affecting the utility of either classroom or large-scale assessments. In an ideal assessment system, large-scale assessment criteria would reflect criteria used to evaluate classroom assignments. Currently the criteria in many large-scale assessments are being used to create or supplant classroom criteria. Specifications of clear, valued, basic criteria could provide a more coherent framework for focusing instruction and feedback.

ESTABLISHING AND MAINTAINING JUDGES' RATINGS

Many performance appraisal systems do not routinely amass raters to judge thousands of performances. Formal assessments of school writing, however, usually test large numbers of students. Much of the methodology for training judges has been developed by assessments needing to document that readers apply criteria uniformly within and between rating occasions. Generally, raters are trained on practice papers before independent rating begins.

Current rating procedures (e.g., Conlan, 1979; Quellmalz, Capell, & Chou, 1982; Meredith & Williams, 1984) have built upon methods recommended by Braddock, Lloyd-Jones, and Shoer (1963) and Coffman (1971). Following an introduction to the rating scale by one or more trainers, raters read prescored anchor papers representing the various scale points, then practice applying the rubric to a sample set of papers. The amount of training time varies according to the nature and specificity of the scale criteria and scoring formats. When large numbers of raters are involved, they may be divided into smaller groups and instructed by different trainers. Often there is group discussion of training papers and considerable shaping of interpretations. Of course, the clarity of the written criteria simplifies the training problem. One method of training raters in analytic scoring techniques has been to have several experts prescore a set of check papers. A feedback sheet for each paper is prepared that presents the consensus score for the global score and separate essay features. Scores are accompanied by citations from the rating guide and the essay to explain the rating (Quellmalz, 1981).

Training sessions continue until trainers decide that agreement levels are sufficiently high. Sometimes consensus is checked statistically on a pilot or qualifying set before independent rating begins; sometimes it is indicated by a show of hands. A problem with the "show of hands" technique is that although raters may seem to conform in a situation of social pressure, they may continue to be confused or to use idiosyncratic rules when rating independently. Without a qualifying check of independent rating, such aberrations may go undetected.

Some test programs may dismiss raters who have difficulty during training; however, school districts using staff teachers may have political problems with such a procedure. In these situations, they may continue to train erratic readers, but more often the test program relies on some form of correction procedure. Norm-referenced test programs sometimes simply sum the scores given by the two raters. Competency testing programs often require a third reading when discrepancies, particularly pass/fail discrepancies, occur. Other testing programs may use monitoring procedures to maintain uniform scoring decisions. These may be some kind of a periodic check procedure where raters score common, pre-scored check papers independently or as a group and check their agreement with other raters or with scores previously established by a panel of experts. These interspersed reliability checks can be very effective in controlling rater drift; they could also be useful as spot checks of on-the-job performance ratings. Procedures for training raters and for monitoring their consistent application of established criteria have improved considerably in the last few years. Carefully structured training procedures, along with more precise rating criteria, can now eliminate most sources of scoring unreliability.

DOCUMENTING THE TECHNICAL QUALITY OF THE ASSESSMENT SYSTEM

Assessment programs must document that the information they provide about an examinee's performance is dependable and meaningful. Traditionally, these technical qualities have been reported by statistical indices of reliability and validity. Contemporary studies of the psychological and measurement problems in understanding constructed responses suggest that some of the techniques for documenting the reliability and validity of a multiple-choice test must be greatly modified for performance assessment.

Reliability. A useful point of departure for considering ways to document the reliability and validity of writing assessments is to reference the four sources of error identified by Braddock, Lloyd-Jones, and Shoer (1963): (1) the writer, (2) the assignment, (3) the rater, and (4) between raters. In multiple-choice testing, the repeated sampling of particular behaviors has been used to minimize fluctuations due to the idiosyncracies of individuals and assignments; that is, the test presents several items on each skill. In performance assessment systems, however, it has been logistically and economically difficult to observe many different performances. In the area of writing assessment, often only one composition is collected, yet there is quite a bit of research indicating that an individual's performance varies from one time, topic, and discourse structure to the next. In many instances, the fluctuation is often also confounded with differences in the discourse structures, methods of development, and topics of the different assignments (Godshalk, Swineford, & Coffman, 1966).

One way writing assessments attempt to deal with performance variability irrelevant to the underlying competence is to collect more than one essay. When multiple essays are gathered, it is important to consider the structural features of writing tasks. Specification of such features as discourse aim and topic should guide the organization of homogeneous writing tasks and limit generalizations about resulting written performance. For example, an assessment program should be particularly sensitive to potentially low correlations among scores on tasks calling for different discourse structures. Organization subscale scores are likely to differ most; ratings of sentence-level skills are likely to differ least (Quellmalz, Capell, & Chou, 1982).

Advances in rating methodology discussed in the previous section have also managed to reduce sources of error in the rating process. More precise rating criteria, structured training sessions, and agreement checks have decreased the magnitude of scoring fluctuations within a rating session.

Another form of score consistency has not been well documented in writing assessments. Few assessments have tracked the stability of the rating guide and process to new rating sessions and groups of raters. Using anchor papers from previous assessments to train new groups is a technique used in norm-referenced writing assessments. However, the instructions given to raters in norm-referenced training sessions may not result in application of criteria that will be comparable to the decision rules used in previous scoring sessions. The norm-referenced procedure directs raters to rank papers within a sample. If the quality range between two groups of examinees differs, then a sliding scale results. For example, a paper might be ranked a "2" in a fall testing that included papers from students of all writing skill levels; that same paper might be ranked a passing "3" in a spring scoring where the pool of papers is from the more restricted range of students who failed in the fall. Researchers for the National Assessment of Educational Progress (NAEP) found that scores on a set of papers rescored using a holistic guide and rating procedures differed significantly from the original scores (Mullis, 1979). As a result, NAEP reseachers devised the primary trait scoring system to provide assignment-specific, stable criteria (Lloyd-Jones, 1977).

Since competency testing programs need to document that scoring criteria are uniformly applied by different groups of raters across multiple scoring sessions, they, too, need guides with specific, stable criteria. As part of the field test of its scoring system, North Carolina checked the stability of dispersed regional scorings by having several state-appointed judges rescore a sample of papers (Freijo & Freijo, 1981). Yet another method for documenting guide stability involves rescoring sets of papers from previous assessments.

A set of reasonable procedures is currently available for large-scale writing assessment programs to use for documenting rater and score reliability. Most systems report rater reliabilities; fewer report stability of ratings across assessments or consistency of student performance within and between types of writing assignments. Other performance assessments must deal with similar threats to their reliability. Some of the procedures developed for writing assessment could be used to develop and monitor reliability of performance tests and scoring in classroom writing activities or in other performance domains.

Validity. Methods for documenting the validity of writing assessments are also changing. Predictive validity has frequently been reported as correlations of a holistic writing essay score with criterion variables such as course grades or admission to or completion of a program. A problem with this method is that there has often not been a careful match of the skills measured on the writing test with the skills of the criterion. For example, grades in an English class may well reflect far more of students' grasp of literary criticism than of their writing skills. Similarly, when writing tests are "validated" against other "related verbal measures," such as reading tests, the match of the skills in the two measures may be remote, at best.

Another method used to validate competency tests is *content validity*, where judges rate how well writing prompts match objectives. One limitation of such content validation procedures for writing tests is that judges are seldom asked to relate writing objectives to prompts and to rating guide criteria. They may also not be asked to rate objectives and tasks for their comprehensive representation of writing skills. Again, the diversity of writing skills complicates attempts to limit and validate assessment objectives and procedures.

As a consequence of the increase in competency testing and the study of language development in natural contexts, the term *ecological validity* has become common. Formal large-scale tests of writing are often criticized for not measuring writing skills that students or adults use in school, home, and work settings. Basic skills assessments are trying to answer these criticisms by more carefully specifying and tracing the match between writing skills targeted in curricula and skills required in out-of-school settings. The methodology evolving for documenting ecological validity includes both logical analyses of writing skills required in other settings and empirical studies of how students who master identified skills survive in the other environments.

A more refined version of this methodology is used in the most central type of validity, *construct validity.* Cognitive studies of writing attempt to distinguish among the kinds of writing tasks and degrees of skills that novice versus expert writers can accomplish. The analyses provide a basis for rating essays on specific features. The analyses can also guide specification of component writing traits that can be used in causal modeling studies to test statistically the factor structure underlying multiple measures of writing skills.

Survey of Applications

In school systems, writing is being assessed directly at all levels. Unfortunately, information about teachers' evaluation procedures is not at all comprehensive or encouraging. Writing is not an integral activity in most school subjects, including English classes. Furthermore, grading practices tend to yield only a global grade or numerous red marks. Perhaps the greatest influence on classroom assessment has been the use of district, state, and national writing assessments for accountability purposes. As a consequence of such test programs, there have been substantial curricular and instructional initiatives. Frequently, at least one of the evaluation approaches used by teachers is that of the district or state assessment board.

To date, approximately twenty-five states collect student essays; several others are planning to do so. Fourteen of the states test all students in targeted grades; nine states test a representative sample. Seven of the states require the writing exam for graduation. Approximately fifteen of the states use holistic scoring; six of these support the holistic score with analytic scores. Six states use analytic guides and three use the primary trait system. In the spring 1984 special issue of *Educational Measurement: Issues and Practice,* which focuses on writing assessment methods, five states' writing assessments are described. Three of the states—South Carolina, Texas, and Maryland—administer competency tests, Illinois conducts status testing on a sample of students, and Connecticut conducts both a competency assessment and a status assessment.

The states test a range of discourse aims. South Carolina and Texas vary aims at different grades; Maryland tests narrative and expository aims. Illinois tests persuasive writing and is field testing expository and narrative prompts; Connecticut administers narrative prompts for the competency test and narrative and persuasive prompts for its status assessment.

To identify students needing remediation, South Carolina, Maryland, Texas, and Connecticut use focused holistic guides. South Carolina, Maryland, and Texas provide further analytic ratings. Analytic guides are used for all essays scored in Illinois and in Connecticut's status assessments in order to track improvement as well as to identify weakness.

Despite their variations, the states have banded together to form a consortium for the study of writing. The purpose of the consortium is to coordinate systematic, empirical studies of many methodological issues confronting large-scale writing assessments.

In addition to district and state programs, the National Assessment of Educational Progress has also conducted direct assessments of writing. Since 1969, NAEP has tested the writing of nine, thirteen, and seventeen year olds on a range of writing tasks. NAEP began using a holistic scoring method, then developed the primary trait scoring system to get a more stable, assignment-specific description of content required for particular prompts.

For the first time, the International Evaluation of Educational Achievement is conducting a writing assessment. Students from fifteen countries have written on nine assignments representing a range of discourse structures. The international scoring system combines a general impression judgment with analytic ratings of content, organization, and style. In addition, there are national options to score conventions and orthography.

Future Directions and Needs

Advances in the assessment of writing skills are likely to come from three fronts: (1) continued empirical studies of large-scale assessment methods; (2) the study of effective writing instruction; and (3) research on text analysis schemes that describe features of compositions distinguishing among levels of expertise. The most important targets of investigation will be, not surprisingly, specification of the portion of the writing domain to be assessed, development of prompts, formulation of rating guides, and instructional validity.

The development of methods to assess writing directly on a large scale highlights the need to identify a tractable set of clearly delineated writing tasks and concomitant writing skills that are both representative of important writing tasks and can be developed by instruction. These core writing tasks will form the writing domain to be assessed, but they will be, by necessity, only a subset of the full domain of potential writing assignments. For example, poetry and journal entries are significant writing forms, although they may not be selected as the discourse structures most important to test.

Systematic procedures for developing writing prompts are also receiving considerable attention. Although there is theoretical support for the uniqueness of each rhetorical problem ("no two snowflakes are alike"), there is also the practical need to build prompt banks of homogeneous, parallel classes of assignments. Ideally, such item/prompt pools could be used for testing and instructional purposes. A highly significant product of these banks will be assignment production guidelines for the preparation of compatible classroom writing assignments.

Assessment programs will also explore a broader range of prompts. Writing tasks will go beyond the reiteration of experience or knowledge. Higher-order thinking skills will be tapped by assignments asking for analyses, comparisons, interpretations, and evaluations of experience and knowledge. New types of writing assignments will also use alternative formats for cueing topic-relevant information. Visual formats will present pictures, graphs, and diagrams. Written formats may present more extensive background information.

Writing assignments may allow extended time for planning, revising, and editing. New kinds of writing tasks may also test these planning, revising, and editing skills. Rating guides will continue to present more specific criteria that reference observable features of compositions. Criteria such as "control" will be replaced by criteria such as "thesis statement summarizes key points developed."

Finally, studies of instructional validity will examine how the quality of compositions written under formal testing conditions relates to the quality of a portfolio of classroom compositions. Studies will, and must, begin to identify the kind and form of information that is useful for instruction.

There have been substantial conceptual and technical advances in writing assessment methodology. Although many problems remain, the progress toward valid, useful writing assessment is unmistakable.

References

Anderson, R. C. (1977). The notion of schemata and the educational enterprise. In R. C. Anderson, R. J. Spiro, & W. E. Montague (Eds.), *Schooling and the acquisition of knowledge.* Hillsdale, NJ: Erlbaum.

Baker, E. L., & Quellmalz, E. S. (1980, April). *Issues in eliciting writing performance: Problems in alternative prompting strategies.* Paper presented at the annual meeting of the National Council on Measurement in Education, Boston.

Bourne, L. J. (1966). *Human conceptual behavior.* Boston: Allyn and Bacon.

Braddock, R., Lloyd-Jones, R., & Schoer, L. (1963). *Research in written composition.* Champaign, IL: National Council of Teachers of English.

Britton, J. (1978). The composing process and the functions of writing. In C. R. Cooper & L. Odell (Eds.), *Research on composing: Points of departure.* Urbana, IL: National Council of Teachers of English.

Coffman, W. E. (1971). Essay exams. In R. L. Thorndike (Ed.), *Educational Measurement* (2nd ed., pp. 271–302). Washington, DC: American Council on Education.

Conlan, G. (1979). *Comparison of analytic and holistic scoring techniques.* Princeton, NJ: Educational Testing Service.

Cooper, C. R. (1979, April). *Current studies of writing achievement and writing competence.* Paper presented at the annual meeting of the American Educational Research Association, San Francisco.

Crowhurst, M., & Piche, G. L. (1980). Audience and mode of discourse effects on syntactic complexity in writing at two grade levels. *Research in the Teaching of English, 13,* 101–109.

Diederich, P. B. (1974). *Measuring growth in English.* Urbana, IL: National Council of Teachers of English.

Freedman, S. (1979). How characteristics of student essays influence teachers' evaluation. *Journal of Educational Psychology, 71,* 328–338.

Freijo, T. D., & Freijo, K. K. (1981). *North Carolina fall 1980–1981 writing field test: Final report.* Raleigh, NC: Department of Public Instruction.

Gentry, L. (Ed.). (1982). *Research and instruction in practical writing.* Los Angeles: SWRL Educational Research and Development.

Godshalk, F. I., Swineford, F., & Coffman, W. E. (1966). *The measurement of writing ability.* New York: College Entrance Examination Board.

Graves, D. (1978). *Balance the basic: Let them write.* New York: Ford Foundation.

Halliday, M. A., & Hasan, R. (1976). *Cohesion in English.* London: Longmans.

Hayes, J. R., & Flower, L. (1979, April). *Writing as problem solving.* Paper presented at the annual meeting of the American Educational Research Association, San Francisco.

Kinneavy, J. L. (1971). *A theory of discourse: The aims of discourse*. Englewood Cliffs, NJ: Prentice-Hall.

Lloyd-Jones, R. (1977). Primary trait scoring. In C. R. Cooper & L. Odell (Eds.), *Evaluating writing: Describing, measuring, judging* (pp. 33–68). Urbana, IL: National Council of Teachers of English.

Meredith, V. H., & Williams, P. L. (1984). Issues in direct assessment: Problem identification and control. *Educational Measurement: Issues and Practice, 3*, 11–15, 35.

Meyer, B. F. (1975). *The organization of prose and its effects on memory. North Holland studies in theoretical poetics* (Vol. 1). Amsterdam: North Holland.

Moss, P., Cole, N., & Khampalikit, C. (1982). A comparison of direct and indirect writing assessment methods. *Journal of Educational Measurement, 19*, 37–48.

Mullis, I. A. (1979). *Using the primary trait system for evaluating writing*. Boulder, CO: National Assessment of Educational Progress.

Perl, S. (1979). The composing process of unskilled college writers. *Research in the Teaching of Writing, 13*, 317–336.

Polin, L. (1981, March). *Effects of time and strategy use on writing performance*. Paper presented at the annual meeting of the American Educational Research Association, New York.

Powills, J. A., Bowers, R., & Conlan, G. (1979, April). *Holistic essay scoring: An application of the model for the evaluation of writing ability and the measurement of growth in writing ability over time*. Paper presented at the annual meeting of the American Educational Research Association, San Francisco.

Praeter, D., & Padia, W. (1980, April). *Effects of modes of discourse in writing performance in grades four and six*. Paper presented at the annual meeting of the American Educational Research Association, Boston.

Quellmalz, E. S. (1981). *Report on Conejo Valley's fourth-grade writing assessment*. Los Angeles: Center for the Study of Evaluation, University of California.

Quellmalz, E. S. (1985). *An investigation of prompt and scoring variations*. Paper presented at the annual meeting of the American Educational Research Association, Chicago.

Quellmalz, E. S., Baker, E., & Enright, G. (1980, November). *Studies in test design: A comparison of modalities of writing prompts*. Los Angeles: Center for the Study of Evaluation, University of California.

Quellmalz, E. S., Capell, F., & Chou, C-P. (1982). Defining writing domains: Effects of discourse and response mode. *Journal of Educational Measurement, 19*, 241–258.

Quellmalz, E. S., Smith, L. S., Winters, L. S., & Baker, E. (1980). *Characteristics of student writing competence: An investigation of alternative scoring systems* (Report to the National Institute of Education). Los Angeles, CA: Center for the Study of Evaluation, University of California.

Resnick, L. B., & Ford, W. W. (1981). *The psychology of mathematics for instruction*. Hillsdale, NJ: Erlbaum.

San Jose, C. P. M. (1973). Grammatical structures in four modes of writing at the fourth grade level (Doctoral dissertation, Syracuse University, 1972). *Dissertation Abstracts International, 33,* 5411–A.

Scribner, S., & Cole, M. (1978). Unpackaging literacy. *Social Science Information, 17,* 19–40.

Simon, H. A. (1981). *The sciences of the artificial* (2nd ed.). Cambridge, MA: MIT Press.

Skinner, B. F. (1963). *Teaching machines and programmed learning.* New York: Appleton-Century-Crofts.

Smith, L. S. (1978, November). *Investigation of writing assessment strategies* (Report to the National Institute of Education). Los Angeles: Center for the Study of Evaluation, University of California.

Stein, N., & Glenn, J. (1980). An analysis of story comprehension in elementary school children. In R. Freedle (Ed.), *New directions in discourse processing.* New York: Holt, Reinhart and Winston.

Veal, R. L., & Tillman, M. (1971). Mode of discourse variation in the evaluation of children's writing. *Research in the Teaching of English, 5,* 37–45.

Winters, L. S. (1978). *The effects of differing response criteria on the assessment of writing competence* (Report to the National institute of Education). Los Angeles, CA: Center for the Study of Evaluation, University of California.

19. LISTENING & SPEAKING SKILLS ASSESSMENT

Nancy A. Mead

Introduction

Historically, oral communication skills have been assessed using performance measures. Students typically have been asked to present a speech or listen to material read aloud. Generally, they have not been asked to answer knowledge questions about speaking and listening, although multiple-choice tests about good speaking or listening skills do exist. The methods used for assessing speaking and listening performance have been limited in the range of skills and applications that they assess. These limitations are grounded, in many cases, in the nature of oral communication and in the unique measurement problems that it poses.

Oral communication is an interactive process. As we communicate with individuals, we must take into account the characteristics of our listeners, we must listen to and evaluate their responses to what we say, and we must modify and create new messages based on the input we receive. In a typical oral communication situation, we are both a speaker and a listener interacting with other speaker-listeners in a dynamic process.

Furthermore, the information transmitted in a typical oral communication situation is both verbal and nonverbal. Meaning is exchanged through the words that are spoken, but also through the tone of the voice, the accompanying gestures, the facial expressions, and so forth. Beyond some universal expressions of basic emotions, nonverbal signals tend to be idiosyncratic.

The evaluation of a communicator also depends upon criteria that are culturally and situationally based. In some social groups, aggressive verbal behavior is extremely effective, whereas in other groups, it is offensive. Talking is appropriate social behavior at a cocktail party but very bothersome in a library reading room. Thus the criteria of effective communication are tied to the culture of the communicators and the specific situation in which the communication takes place.

The unique aspects of oral communication translate into a variety of assessment problems. These measurement issues may be grouped into the areas of validity, reliability, and feasibility. In order to assess oral communication performance, it is necessary to define both the verbal and nonverbal aspects of communication and to identify criteria of competence that take into account cultural and situational differences.

Because communication is shaped by culture, and culture is embedded in the

509

designers and administrators of communication measures, the issue of bias is substantial (Stiggins, 1981). In fact, problems of bias might limit assessment to certain populations with a similar cultural background or to certain types of communication functions that are performed fairly consistently across different cultural groups.

For any given definition of communication competence, it is necessary to develop methods for assessing performance consistently and accurately. These methods must not only work with an almost infinite variety of communication responses, they also must work for a variety of raters, who have their own attitudes toward communication competence.

The methods needed to address problems of validity and reliability often pose major obstacles to implementing an assessment. Feasibility may be inhibited by use of expensive equipment, extensive training of raters, lengthy assessments, and so forth.

The sections that follow address the issues of validity, reliability, and feasibility as they relate to various methods of assessing oral communication performance. Current assessment methods are described and strengths and weaknesses identified (for similar reviews of assessment methods and available instruments, see Powers, 1984; Rubin & Mead, 1984; Brown et al., 1979; and Larson et al., 1978). The presentation focuses primarily on assessment in school settings, but inasmuch as concern with speaking and listening skills on the job is gaining prominence, the issues discussed are equally applicable to assessment in work settings.

Survey of Speaking and Listening Assessment Methods

ASSESSMENT OF SPEAKING PERFORMANCE

Definition of speaking skills. Traditionally, instruction in speaking focused on skills rather than knowledge, and assessment required demonstration of speaking performance. Generally, instruction was limited to public speaking situations, and students were evaluated on the content and organization of their speech and their oral delivery technique. While in theory speaking involves interactive, nonverbal, cultural, and situational factors, in practice, speaking instruction and assessment have focused on a very narrow range of skills.

Recently, descriptions of speaking skills have been expanded. One trend has been to focus on *communication activities* that are typical for large group, small group, interpersonal, and mass media situations (Brown, 1981). Large group situations encompass the traditional public speaking skills. Small group situations focus on various group discussion and group leadership skills. Interpersonal situations concentrate primarily on affective components of personal interactions, such as sharing feelings and conflict. Mass media situations focus on particular communication methods used in radio, television, and film as well as on understanding the powerful and pervasive nature of mass media in American society.

Another approach has been to focus on the *functional uses of communication.* Allen and Brown (1976) described four basic purposes for communicating: informing, controlling, sharing feelings, and ritualizing. An effective communicator has a repertoire of strategies for each of these functions and selects from them appropriate methods, depending upon the nature of the situation.

Another way of defining speaking skills is the *basic competencies approach,* which was adopted in response to the broader movement in education to identify the most basic skills that students need to function in everyday life. For example, students should be able to ask for information, give directions, provide basic information in emergency situations, and so forth. Partly as a result of the basic skills movement, about 60 percent of the states have adopted oral communication objectives for instruction or assessment (Backlund, 1981), and the Speech Communication Association has developed guidelines that identify basic speaking skills for graduating high school students (Bassett, Whittington, & Staton-Spicer, 1978).

Expansion of the definition of speaking skills has led to new assessment approaches. Issues related to these approaches include methods for eliciting speaking performance, types of rating systems, rater objectivity, and test administration. These issues and examples of specific assessment techniques are described next. (See Rubin, 1981, for a similar discussion of speaking assessment issues.)

Observational versus structured methods. Two distinct approaches to measuring speaking skills are an observational method and a structured method. An *observational approach* uses unobtrusive measures of a student's spontaneous communication with other people in a natural setting. A *structured approach* uses contrived speaking activities, which may or may not require the student to interact with other people.

The observational approach provides the most accurate measure of a student's normal communication performance in realistic settings. It generally taps a broad range of communication behaviors and usually takes the form of a checklist of communication behaviors that will be observed. The observer then keeps track of instances of these behaviors, usually following predetermined schedules that indicate how frequently and for how long a student will be observed. In some cases, observations are made from audiotapes or videotapes. One example of a typical observation system is Bales's Process Interaction Analysis system (1951). This method counts instances of various communication behaviors, such as asking questions, answering questions, showing friendliness, and showing hostility.

The observational approach poses a variety of administration problems. There is no assurance that the behaviors of interest will occur during a given period of time. The observer must deal with a large amount of activity, only some of which is relevant for the assessment. Further, the observer can focus on only one or, at most, a few students at a time.

The observational approach is also subject to problems related to reliability and validity. The communication behavior of the student being observed may be influenced by other people in the classroom. For example, the student may dislike the teacher or may be dominated by a particularly vocal classmate. It is also possible that the observer's ratings may be influenced by factors other than the student's communication ability, for example, sociability or overall achievement. Since criteria regarding appropriate amounts of various types of communication behaviors are difficult to determine, the observational approach tends to be used as a descriptive measure of communication rather than as an evaluative measure.

The structured approach provides a more accurate measure of a student's optimal communication performance, but this approach suffers from artificiality and generally assesses only a narrow range of communication behaviors. There are several ways to organize a structured approach and each method has associated advantages and disadvantages.

One structured approach is to set up a situation in which a group of students are asked to interact with one another on a particular task, for example, a problem-solving task. The evaluator may rate the students on the spot or rate them later from audiotapes or videotapes. This type of situation simulates the interactive nature of communication, but all students may not have the opportunity to participate equally. Also, students may be affected by the racial or ethnic, sex, or friendship characteristics of the group.

Another structured approach is to set up a situation in which students are asked to perform the same or parallel communication tasks in front of the class, and the evaluator rates each student's performance. The classic example of this approach is the prepared classroom speech. Numerous examples of assessments of this type are given by Bock and Bock (1981). In a more innovative and engaging adaptation of this developed by Rubin and Bazzle (1981), students are asked to present various issues to a mock school board made up of other students. These situations give the student a sense of audience and purpose. However, as in the previous structured approach, the makeup of the group might affect a student's response. Also, it gives some students more rehearsal time or the possibility of modeling other students.

A third structured situation is one in which the test administrator gives a single student a specific task and rates the student's performance on the spot or later, from videotapes or audiotapes. An example of this approach is the Massachusetts Department of Education's assessment of basic speaking competencies (1980). In this assessment, a test administrator gives each student four different speaking tasks—a description, a sequence, an emergency, and a persuasion task—and rates the response to each task on the spot.

The one-on-one assessment method is limited to a student-adult communication framework. This limitation may be ameliorated by creating hypothetical situations. For example, it is possible to give a task to a student and to ask the student to respond as if he or she were talking with another student. It is also possible to increase the plausibility of the situation by having the test administrator introduce systematic probes or contingencies into the situation (for example, simulation of an employment interview). Both approaches require role playing. In the one-on-one approach, each student has a chance to do his or her best without being influenced by other students. However, for some students the student-adult situation may evoke more anxiety than a student-student situation.

The nature of the situation and the tasks are critical for any of the structured approaches. The student must feel comfortable and free to talk, and the task must stimulate talk. If a series of probes are used, they must be consistently applied. If a simulation task is used, it is necessary to get the student to respond as though he or she were actually in the situation, rather than describing what he or she would say and do in the situation.

The task must be based on topics that all students can talk about. For example, describing a favorite class is more generic than describing a vacation, because not all students take vacations. The tasks must be equally difficult for all students. A task that requires students to give directions from home to school creates problems when one student lives across the street from the school and another lives across town. If parallel tasks are used, they must be equivalent in difficulty.

Some tasks produce fairly standard responses (for example, describing a picture of four geometric figures), whereas others produce quite varied responses (for example, persuading the principal to make a change in school procedures). All tasks must stimulate responses that can be scored in a standard way.

Holistic versus focused rating systems. Irrespective of the type of assessment approach selected, the scoring system must describe acceptable and unacceptable levels of speaking performance. Two distinctive types of scoring systems are *holistic ratings* and *focused ratings*.

A holistic rating provides a global rating of speaking performance. An example of this system is the Purdue Basic Oral Communication Evaluation Form (Pace & Simons, 1963). This scale utilizes an interview situation, and the rater makes several impressionistic ratings, including one "overall impression" rating.

A focused rating assesses specific speaking skills. An example of this system is the Massachusetts Department of Education's assessment of basic speaking skills (1980). This assessment uses four scales: content, organization, language, and delivery. The rater rates a student's performance on four speaking tasks, each time rating the student according to the four skill areas.

The decision about which rating system is to be used depends in part upon one's view of the nature of communication competence. One who sees communication competence as a unitary trait that is demonstrated in all communication situations would favor a holistic approach. One who sees communication competence as a set of subskills would favor a focused approach.

Another factor contributing to a decision about the type of rating is the reliability of the approach. A focused approach uses rating scales that measure very specific definable behaviors, for example, the student can or cannot be heard. Although it is relatively easy to establish interrater reliability with these types of scales, there is a danger that the rating scales can be trivial and fail to represent the complexity of communication tasks. At the other extreme, a holistic approach employs rating scales that focus on behaviors that are so general (for example, effective communication) that they are difficult to define objectively. Holistic ratings can be used reliably by raters, but it is difficult to know exactly what criteria the raters are using to make their ratings; indeed, different raters can use different criteria but still be consistent with one another.

Rater objectivity. An overriding concern, without regard to the specific assessment approach or rating system, is the objectivity of the rater. The best way of dealing with this problem is to prepare rating scales and scoring guides with directions so explicit that interpretations by the raters are minimized. However, completely objective scales are difficult to develop, and it would be short-sighted to design easy-to-score but trivial rating schemes.

A critical aspect of rater objectivity is the relationship between the rater and the student. One aspect of this issue is whether or not the rater knows the student. A person who knows the student brings a particular sensitivity and understanding to the testing situation. It is also possible that such a person might also bring preconceived notions about the student to the testing situation. Using a stranger eliminates this possibility. It is not certain whether students would be more at ease with a familiar person or a stranger; some might be more comfortable with their teachers, others more comfortable with a stranger.

Another aspect of the relationship between the rater and the student that may affect rater objectivity is the respective sex, racial or ethnic, and other background characteristics of the rater and the student. Some raters tend to rate students with characteristics similar to their own differently from those with dissimilar characteristics. Nevertheless, it is impossible to match rater and student on all possible confounding factors.

A third concern related to rater objectivity is the halo effect. In any rating approach (whether the rating is done on the spot or later) there is a danger that the rater's experience with previous students may affect the rating of subsequent students. For example, a mediocre response after a poor response might be rated higher than a mediocre response after an exemplary response.

The related problems of fatigue and boredom are more readily dealt with in a situation in which ratings are done later and regular breaks and consistency and calibration checks can be scheduled. When ratings are done on the spot, the best solution involves random ordering of test takers, reasonable time schedules, and regular reviews of training material.

Test administration. A final set of issues related to structured approaches to speaking assessment deals with various aspects of test administration—testing site, length of test, and when student responses will be rated. From a management standpoint, it is desirable to test students within their own classroom. However, this poses problems of disruptions by students not involved in the testing and of lack of privacy.

The length of testing is also a major management issue. All structured assessment approaches require setting aside time for the test. Even with a very short test, this represents a major time commitment. Fortunately, even a relatively short assessment (for example, five minutes) yields considerable information about speaking ability.

The final concern is with the rating approach. Student responses may be rated on the spot or they may be audiotaped or videotaped for later scoring. The advantages of on-the-spot ratings are mostly practical ones. If test administrators can be trained to be reliable scorers, having them do the ratings at the same time they adminster the tests is more efficient. Videotaping provides a good record of communication responses, but it is quite expensive. One successful implementation of videotaping has been Rubin's 1981 assessment of basic communication skills of college students. Although audiotaping provides a less complete record of communication responses and does not provide visual information, it is much cheaper and easier to use.

ASSESSMENT OF LISTENING PERFORMANCE

It is more difficult to identify the characteristics of a performance measure of listening skills than of speaking skills. Certainly a performance assessment would require the students to listen to something. Historically, virtually all listening tests have included actual listening activity, although some have also included questions about effective listening strategies, but the mode of response in listening tests varies. The most common method requires the student to complete multiple-choice questions about what he or she heard. A second method requires a written or verbal response to questions about what the student has heard. A third method requires the student to perform a task based on what he or she has heard, for example, tracing a route given in the stimulus on a map.

Some people would describe only the third technique as a true performance measure, but this method is really only useful in assessing one aspect of listening: the ability to follow directions. It seems that the other methods, even though they may rely on paper-and-pencil responses, are legitimate and necessary approaches for measuring other aspects of listening, such as comprehension of details, grasp of main idea, and so forth. In this chapter, assessment of listening performance is considered broadly, and methods that rely on traditional paper-and-pencil responses as well as other types of responses are discussed.

Definition of listening skills. Like speaking, assessment of listening performance is hampered by an inadequate definition of the construct. The degree to which listening is an isolated skill is still an open question. Research has substantiated relatively high positive correlations between listening and intelligence and verbal aptitude. The relationship between listening and reading has also been well established. Although there is evidence that tests of listening correlate as well with tests of verbal aptitude and reading skills as they do with one another (Kelly, 1965), Spearitt (1962), in a factor analysis of thirty-four tests given to 300 sixth-grade pupils, was able to identify a separate "listening comprehension" factor.

Even if one accepts that there is an identifiable listening competence, there still is no agreed-upon model that describes the components of listening. Most definitions of listening are derived from the work of curriculum or test developers. Many follow typical definitions of reading comprehension. Only tentative attempts have been made to distinguish a hierarchy of listening skills (see Lundsteen, 1979, for one proposal).

Two areas within listening seem to be particularly difficult to define and to measure: critical listening and nonverbal listening. Critical listening focuses on higher-level inferential skills such as analyzing, interpreting, and evaluating information. This aspect of listening clearly requires going beyond what is said and is highly dependent on background knowledge and general higher-order thinking skills. Nonverbal listening focuses on tone of voice, facial expressions, gestures, and other nonverbal cues. These signals communicate a great deal of information about the feelings of the speaker, his or her attitudes, and even his or her status and social and cultural background.

The different approaches to describing listening skills have led to a variety of assessment approaches. Issues related to these approaches include the stimulus material, response formats, and test administration procedures. These issues and examples of specific assessment techniques are described in the sections that follow.

Listening stimuli. The listening stimulus must reflect natural spoken language. The characteristics of oral communication are significantly different from those of written communication. Spoken language tends to be nonlinear, incomplete, and redundant. It is ephemeral, accompanied by nonverbal communication (vocal, facial, and gestural), and frequently occurs in an interactive situation. Therefore it seems essential to utilize natural spoken language for listening stimuli. The mere reworking of reading tests into listening tests is inappropriate.

How to deal with the nonverbal and interactive nature of listening in an assessment situation is less obvious. In order to assess nonverbal listening, it is possible to use audiotapes or videotapes as stimuli, but nonverbal signals tend to be subtle and individualistic. It is therefore difficult to develop a measure of recognition of these factors that is reliable and valid.

One attempt to measure recognition of feelings is the Jones-Mohr listening test (1976). This instrument is primarily used for training individuals, not evaluating them. Another interesting attempt to measure listening in a way that includes a nonverbal aspect was made by Wilkinson, Stratta, and Dudley (1974). They developed a test that measures comprehension of many aspects of spoken messages: (1) the content of what is said; (2) the additional meaning conveyed by the stress or emphasis of words; (3) the contextual constraints of grammar, word meanings, topic, and so forth; (4) the appropriateness of language for a given situation; and (5) the roles and relationships of speakers based on the language they use.

In order to assess listening in interactive situations, it is possible to assess students in live, face-to-face situations. However, in this type of assessment, it is difficult to sort out failures of the listener from failures in the speaker. Dickson, Patterson, and Tracy (1981) have developed a number of interactive referential communication tasks that may be used for instruction or assessment.

Another important aspect of the listening stimulus is any factor that might contribute to bias. Although it is impossible to eliminate from listening material all references to culture, sex, or setting, it is important that the content not give an unfair advantage to students from a particular group. It is also important that the material not be presented in a stereotypic way that might offend a particular group of students. Finally, stimulus material should be free of unusual accents or patterns of speech.

Motivation and attention play important roles in listening and must be kept in mind in order to facilitate optimal listening performance. Not all material we listen to in our daily lives is interesting, but to aid comprehension it seems important to include fairly interesting or at least familiar material in listening stimuli. Furthermore, to assure that any assessment measures listening rather than memory, it is important for stimuli to be kept relatively short.

Assessment of listening is correlated with general verbal ability. This problem can be mitigated to some extent by selecting listening stimuli that are fairly easy in vocabulary and syntax. Particularly in basic listening competency tests, students should be asked to demonstrate their listening ability without having to deal with highly complex concepts or language.

Responses to listening stimuli. The most important issue related to developing listening items is content validity, the adequate sampling of the domain. Another aspect of validity relates to focusing the assessment on listening skills. Students should be required to demonstrate only their listening ability and should not be penalized for lack of skills in reading instructions or questions or writing answers.

Issues related to developing listening comprehension items are similar to those related to developing reading comprehension items. First, it is necessary to define the various levels of skills that will be assessed. Comprehension usually is discussed as a continuum of literal, inferential, and critical skills. As the level of comprehension increases, it becomes more difficult to differentiate between the specific reading or listening skills and general reasoning or verbal skills. It is also more difficult to distinguish between responses that are considered to be correct inferences and those that are considered to be faulty. The Brown-Carlsen listening comprehension test (1955) represents one attempt to measure higher-order listening skills.

A relevant concern is with the degree to which the items are directly related to the text. Some questions are highly dependent upon the written or spoken text; others require the student to bring outside knowledge or experience to the text in order to answer the questions. One must consider whether such knowledge or experience is commonly shared by all students.

Another assessment issue is the format of the items. One approach allows for free responses to questions where students are asked to respond orally or to write out their answers to questions. This approach provides the most direct measure of students' comprehension of the material, but the scoring is cumbersome and, as suggested previously, listening achievement might be confounded with writing ability.

A second, and the most commonly used approach, is the multiple-choice format. The student is asked to select the best answer from several response options. This approach is problematic, in that the options might not reflect the student's own response to a question. It also gives the student a chance to guess. Countervailing these concerns is the fact that multiple-choice items can provide response options that represent common misconceptions and mistakes students make and can thus be diagnostic in nature. In addition, multiple-choice items are easy to score.

A third type of format, used to assess ability to follow directions, presents graphic material, such as a map, and asks the student to complete a task, such as drawing a route on the map. Educational Testing Service incorporated items of this type in its recent revision of the Sequential Tests of Educational Progress test (STEP) of listening skills. A variation of this format presents a description of an object and asks the student to draw the object or to select the appropriate object from a set of pictures.

Items must meet appropriate psychometric standards. Items in a norm-referenced achievement test should discriminate clearly between good and poor students and should be moderately difficult. These criteria do not apply in the same way to a criterion-referenced test. However, in all types of tests, the discrimination power and difficulty level of items provide useful information for detecting items that are confusing or extremely difficult or extremely easy. For multiple-choice formats, it is important to attend to numerous measurement standards, such as phrasing items positively, making options parallel, and assuring a single correct answer.

Test administration. Finally, there are concerns that relate to test administration. Probably the most important requirement is providing clear, distinct listening stimuli in an environment that is free from distractions. Although in everyday life we do not always hear material clearly with no extraneous noise, in order to measure optimal listening ability, distractions should be minimized. It would be appropriate to introduce distractions deliberately only if the goal is to measure a student's ability to recognize and overcome these problems.

The actual production of stimulus material may take two forms. The material may be written in script form so that it can be read aloud by the test administrator. Alternatively, it may be recorded on audiotape or videotape. The advantage of taped materials is that they guarantee standard administration and allow for variety in stimulus material, such as different voices, conversations, or sound effects.

Future Directions and Needs

The preceding review of the various methods available for assessing speaking and listening performance indicates a broad range of alternatives. Recently, instruments have been developed that incorporate some of the more complex properties of communication—interactive, nonverbal, cultural, and situational aspects. However, certain problems remain—problems that are perhaps insurmountable, given the nature of communication and the requirements for testing.

Several validity issues are unsettled. Definitions of speaking and listening have been developed based upon logical analysis of the constructs or upon curriculum priorities. These definitions have not been tested empirically. Moreover, these definitions are not consistent. Thus one assessment approach does not necessarily yield the same information that another would. Until the theoretical issues related to the nature of oral communication are settled, assessment instruments will lack construct and concurrent validity.

Another unresolved validity issue concerns the degree to which oral communication skills should be segmented. The interactive nature of communication suggests that speaking and listening are best assessed as a single skill. However, from a testing perspective, it is desirable to disentangle the various factors that contribute to a construct. Indeed, most existing instruments separate speaking and listening competencies and eliminate other confounding factors such as content knowledge, reading ability, and writing ability. An interesting alternative would be a composite measure that integrates speaking and listening skills with other higher-order inferential skills and social skills, because all these factors are critical for effective communication. One assessment approach that follows along these lines is the American College Testing Program's 1980 College Outcomes

Measures Project test (COMP). This instrument assesses both listening and speaking skills of college students in a way that also requires some general content knowledge and skills in analysis, problem solving, reading, writing, and viewing.

Issues of reliability and bias in assessing speaking and listening skills are problematic but are being resolved. However, the solution requires some constraints on the comprehensiveness of the measure. Communication competence is judged to some extent by criteria that are culturally determined. To assure that ratings are made reliably and without bias, it is often necessary to focus the assessment on areas that are not sensitive to cultural differences. In many cases, this means limiting the assessment to formal or functional situations, in which case reliability and bias concerns are addressed at the expense of generalizability and other types of validity.

Even if issues of validity and reliability are resolved, feasibility of assessing speaking and listening skills remains a problem. Performance measures are usually expensive and difficult to implement, particularly performance measures of speaking and listening.

Assessing speaking and listening performance is challenging and important. Clearly, effective communication is a critical skill in all areas of our lives—educational, occupational, functional, and social. Developing and implementing assessment measures in this area can contribute significantly to understanding the nature of human interactions and human effectiveness.

References

Allen, R. R., & Brown, K. L. (Eds.). (1976). *Developing communication competence in children*. Skokie, IL: National Textbook Company.

American College Testing Program (1980). *The college outcomes measures project*. Iowa City.

Backlund, P. (1981). A national survey of state practices in speaking and listening assessment. In R. J. Stiggins (Ed.), *Perspectives on oral communication assessment in the 1980s* (pp. 3–24). Portland, OR: Clearinghouse for Applied Performance Testing, Northwest Regional Educational Laboratory.

Bales, R. (1951). *Process interaction analysis*. Cambridge, MA: Addison-Wesley.

Bassett, R. E., Whittington, N., & Staton-Spicer, A. (1978). The basics in speaking for high school graduates: What should be assessed? *Communication Education, 27*, 293–303.

Bock, D. G., & Bock, E. H. (1981). *Evaluating classroom speaking*. Urbana, IL: ERIC Clearinghouse on Reading and Communication.

Brown, J., & Carlsen, G. (1955). *Brown-Carlsen Listening Comprehension Test*. New York: Harcourt, Brace and World.

Brown, K. L. (1981). *Teaching speaking and listening skills in the elementary and secondary school*. Boston: Massachusetts Department of Education.

Brown, K. L., Backlund, P., Gurry, J., & Jandt, F. (1979). *Assessment of basic speaking and listening skills: State of the art and recommendations for instrument development* (2 vols.). Boston: Massachusetts Department of Education.

Dickson, W. P., Patterson, J. H., & Tracy, K. (1981, April). *Referential communication activities: A tool for assessing speaking and listening in the classroom.* Paper presented at the annual meeting of the American Education Research Association, Los Angeles.

Educational Testing Service. (1979). *Sequential Tests of Educational Progress.* Princeton, NJ: Author.

Jones, J. E., & Mohr, L. (1976). *Jones-Mohr Listening Test.* La Jolla, CA: University Associates.

Kelly, C. M. (1965). An investigation of the construct validity of two commercially published listening tests. *Speech Monographs, 32,* 139–143.

Larson, C., Backlund, P., Redmond, M., & Barbour, A. (1978). *Assessing functional communication.* Urbana, IL: ERIC Clearinghouse on Reading and Communication Skills.

Lundsteen, S. W. (1979). *Listening: Its impact on reading and the other language arts.* Urbana, IL: National Council of Teachers of English.

Massachusetts Department of Education (1980). *Massachusetts assessment of basic skills 1979–80: Summary report.* Boston: Author.

Pace, R. W., & Simons, H. W. (1963). Preliminary validation report on the Purdue Basic Oral Communication Evaluation Form. *Personnel Journal, 42,* 191–193.

Powers, D. E. (1984). *Considerations for developing measures of speaking and listening.* New York: College Entrance Examination Board.

Rubin, D. L. (1981). Using performance rating scales in large-scale assessments of oral communication proficiency. In R. J. Stiggins (Ed.), *Perspectives on oral communication assessment in the 1980s* (pp. 51–67). Portland, OR: Clearinghouse for Applied Performance Testing, Northwest Regional Educational Laboratory.

Rubin, D. L., & Bazzle, R. E. (1981). *Development of an oral communication assessment program: The Glynn County speech proficiency examination for high school students.* Brunswick, GA: Glynn County Board of Education.

Rubin, D. L., & Mead, N. A. (1984). *Large scale assessment of oral communication skills.* Urbana, IL: ERIC Clearinghouse on Reading and Communication Skills.

Rubin, R. B. (1981). Assessment of college-level speaking and listening skills. In R. J. Stiggins (Ed.), *Perspectives on oral communication assessment in the 1980s* (pp. 25–41. Portland, OR: Clearinghouse for Applied Performance Testing, Northwest Regional Educational Laboratory.

Spearitt, D. (1962). *Listening comprehension: A factorial analysis* (Series No. 76). Melbourne: Australian Council for Educational Research.

Stiggins, R.J. (1981). Potential sources of bias in speaking and listening assessment. In R. J. Stiggins (Ed.), *Perspectives on oral communication assessment in the 1980s* (pp. 43–49). Portland, OR: Clearinghouse for Applied Performance Testing, Northwest Regional Educational Laboratory.

Wilkinson, A., Stratta, L., & Dudley, P. (1974). *The quality of listening.* Basingstoke, England: Macmillan Education.

CONTRIBUTORS

James R. Beatty, Professor, Department of Management, San Diego State University, San Diego, California

Richard W. Beatty, Professor, Institute of Management and Labor Relations, Rutgers University, Management Development Center, Cook Campus, New Brunswick, New Jersey

Ronald A. Berk, Professor, Division of Education, Johns Hopkins University, Baltimore, Maryland

H. John Bernardin, Director of Research and Professor of Management, College of Business and Public Administration, Florida Atlantic University, Boca Raton, Florida

Walter C. Borman, President, Personnel Decisions Research Institute, Minneapolis, Minnesota

Nancy J. Bridgeford, Research Specialist, Center for Performance Assessment, Northwest Regional Educational Laboratory, Portland, Oregon

Michael J. Burke, Assistant Professor, Department of Management, New York University, New York, New York

William C. Byham, President, Development Dimensions International, Pittsburgh, Pennsylvania

Wayne F. Cascio, Professor, Graduate School of Business Administration, University of Colorado, Denver, Colorado

Stephen B. Dunbar, Assistant Professor, College of Education, University of Iowa, Iowa City, Iowa

Sidney A. Fine, Consulting Research Scientist, Advanced Research Resources Organization, Washington, D.C.

Mina A. Gillers, Consultant, Patient Instructor Program, University of Massachusetts Medical School, Worcester, Massachusetts

Robert M. Guion, University Professor, Department of Psychology, Bowling Green State University, Bowling Green, Ohio

Rick R. Jacobs, Associate Professor, Department of Psychology, Pennsylvania State University, University Park, Pennsylvania

Jeffrey S. Kane, Associate Professor, Department of Management, University of Massachusetts, Amherst, Massachusetts

Robert L. Linn, Professor, Department of Educational Psychology, University of Illinois, Champaign, Illinois

Richard P. Manatt, Director, School Improvement Model, College of Education, Iowa State University, Ames, Iowa

Nancy A. Mead, Program Administrator, Listening and Speaking Skills Assessment, Educational Testing Service, Princeton, New Jersey

Barry R. Nathan, Assistant Professor, School of Business Administration, University of Southern California, Los Angeles, California

Robert Oresick, Assistant Professor, College of Basic Studies, Boston University, Boston, Massachusetts

Edys S. Quellmalz, Acting Associate Professor, School of Education, Stanford University, Stanford, California

Nambury S. Raju, Associate Professor and Director, I/O Program, Department of Psychology, Illinois Institute of Technology, Chicago, Illinois

Arthur I. Siegel, Deceased

Michael Sokol, Manager, Management and Organizational Development, Data General, Milford, Massachusetts

Richard J. Stiggins, Director, Center for Performance Assessment, Northwest Regional Educational Laboratory, Portland, Oregon

Paula L. Stillman, Associate Dean for Curriculum and Professor of Pediatrics, University of Massachusetts Medical School, Worcester, Massachusetts

James Sweeney, Professor, Professional Studies Department, Iowa State University, Ames, Iowa

George C. Thornton III, Professor, Department of Psychology, Colorado State University, Ft. Collins, Colorado

Kenneth N. Wexley, Professor, Department of Management, Michigan State University, East Lansing, Michigan

INDEX